Fourth Edition

"The multiprocessor is here and it can _____. As we bid farewell to single-core processors and move into _____ processing age, it is great timing for a new edition of Hennessy and Patterson's classic. Few books have had as significant an impact on the way their discipline is taught, and the current edition will ensure its place at the top for some time to come."

—Luiz André Barroso, Google Inc.

"What do the following have in common: Beatles' tunes, HP calculators, chocolate chip cookies, and *Computer Architecture*? They are all classics that have stood the test of time."

—Robert P. Colwell, Intel lead architect

"Not only does the book provide an authoritative reference on the concepts that all computer architects should be familiar with, but it is also a good starting point for investigations into emerging areas in the field."

—Krisztián Flautner, ARM Ltd.

"The best keeps getting better! This new edition is updated and very relevant to the key issues in computer architecture today. Plus, its new exercise paradigm is much more useful for both students and instructors."

—Norman P. Jouppi, HP Labs

"*Computer Architecture* builds on fundamentals that yielded the RISC revolution, including the enablers for CISC translation. Now, in this new edition, it clearly explains and gives insight into the latest microarchitecture techniques needed for the new generation of multithreaded multicore processors."

—Marc Tremblay, Fellow & VP, Chief Architect, Sun Microsystems

"This is a great textbook on all key accounts: pedagogically superb in exposing the ideas and techniques that define the art of computer organization and design, stimulating to read, and comprehensive in its coverage of topics. The first edition set a standard of excellence and relevance; this latest edition does it again."

—Miloš Ercegovac, UCLA

"They've done it again. Hennessy and Patterson emphatically demonstrate why they are the doyens of this deep and shifting field. Fallacy: Computer architecture isn't an essential subject in the information age. Pitfall: You don't need the 4th edition of *Computer Architecture*."

—Michael D. Smith, Harvard University

"Hennessy and Patterson have done it again! The 4th edition is a classic encore that has been adapted beautifully to meet the rapidly changing constraints of 'late-CMOS-era' technology. The detailed case studies of real processor products are especially educational, and the text reads so smoothly that it is difficult to put down. This book is a must-read for students and professionals alike!"

—Pradip Bose, IBM

"This latest edition of *Computer Architecture* is sure to provide students with the architectural framework and foundation they need to become influential architects of the future."

— Ravishankar Iyer, Intel Corp.

"As technology has advanced, and design opportunities and constraints have changed, so has this book. The 4th edition continues the tradition of presenting the latest in innovations with commercial impact, alongside the foundational concepts: advanced processor and memory system design techniques, multithreading and chip multiprocessors, storage systems, virtual machines, and other concepts. This book is an excellent resource for anybody interested in learning the architectural concepts underlying real commercial products."

—Gurindar Sohi, University of Wisconsin–Madison

"I am very happy to have my students study computer architecture using this fantastic book and am a little jealous for not having written it myself."

—Mateo Valero, UPC, Barcelona

"Hennessy and Patterson continue to evolve their teaching methods with the changing landscape of computer system design. Students gain unique insight into the factors influencing the shape of computer architecture design and the potential research directions in the computer systems field."

—Dan Connors, University of Colorado at Boulder

"With this revision, *Computer Architecture* will remain a must-read for all computer architecture students in the coming decade."

—Wen-mei Hwu, University of Illinois at Urbana–Champaign

"The 4th edition of *Computer Architecture* continues in the tradition of providing a relevant and cutting edge approach that appeals to students, researchers, and designers of computer systems. The lessons that this new edition teaches will continue to be as relevant as ever for its readers."

—David Brooks, Harvard University

"With the 4th edition, Hennessy and Patterson have shaped *Computer Architecture* back to the lean focus that made the 1st edition an instant classic."

—Mark D. Hill, University of Wisconsin–Madison

Computer Architecture
A Quantitative Approach

Fourth Edition

John L. Hennessy is the president of Stanford University, where he has been a member of the faculty since 1977 in the departments of electrical engineering and computer science. Hennessy is a Fellow of the IEEE and ACM, a member of the National Academy of Engineering and the National Academy of Science, and a Fellow of the American Academy of Arts and Sciences. Among his many awards are the 2001 Eckert-Mauchly Award for his contributions to RISC technology, the 2001 Seymour Cray Computer Engineering Award, and the 2000 John von Neumann Award, which he shared with David Patterson. He has also received seven honorary doctorates.

In 1981, he started the MIPS project at Stanford with a handful of graduate students. After completing the project in 1984, he took a one-year leave from the university to cofound MIPS Computer Systems, which developed one of the first commercial RISC microprocessors. After being acquired by Silicon Graphics in 1991, MIPS Technologies became an independent company in 1998, focusing on microprocessors for the embedded marketplace. As of 2006, over 500 million MIPS microprocessors have been shipped in devices ranging from video games and palmtop computers to laser printers and network switches.

David A. Patterson has been teaching computer architecture at the University of California, Berkeley, since joining the faculty in 1977, where he holds the Pardee Chair of Computer Science. His teaching has been honored by the Abacus Award from Upsilon Pi Epsilon, the Distinguished Teaching Award from the University of California, the Karlstrom Award from ACM, and the Mulligan Education Medal and Undergraduate Teaching Award from IEEE. Patterson received the IEEE Technical Achievement Award for contributions to RISC and shared the IEEE Johnson Information Storage Award for contributions to RAID. He then shared the IEEE John von Neumann Medal and the C & C Prize with John Hennessy. Like his co-author, Patterson is a Fellow of the American Academy of Arts and Sciences, ACM, and IEEE, and he was elected to the National Academy of Engineering, the National Academy of Sciences, and the Silicon Valley Engineering Hall of Fame. He served on the Information Technology Advisory Committee to the U.S. President, as chair of the CS division in the Berkeley EECS department, as chair of the Computing Research Association, and as President of ACM. This record led to a Distinguished Service Award from CRA.

At Berkeley, Patterson led the design and implementation of RISC I, likely the first VLSI reduced instruction set computer. This research became the foundation of the SPARC architecture, currently used by Sun Microsystems, Fujitsu, and others. He was a leader of the Redundant Arrays of Inexpensive Disks (RAID) project, which led to dependable storage systems from many companies. He was also involved in the Network of Workstations (NOW) project, which led to cluster technology used by Internet companies. These projects earned three dissertation awards from the ACM. His current research projects are the RAD Lab, which is inventing technology for reliable, adaptive, distributed Internet services, and the Research Accelerator for Multiple Processors (RAMP) project, which is developing and distributing low-cost, highly scalable, parallel computers based on FPGAs and open-source hardware and software.

Computer Architecture
A Quantitative Approach

Fourth Edition

John L. Hennessy
Stanford University

David A. Patterson
University of California at Berkeley

With Contributions by

Andrea C. Arpaci-Dusseau
University of Wisconsin–Madison

Remzi H. Arpaci-Dusseau
University of Wisconsin–Madison

Krste Asanovic
Massachusetts Institute of Technology

Robert P. Colwell
R&E Colwell & Associates, Inc.

Thomas M. Conte
North Carolina State University

José Duato
Universitat Politècnica de València and *Simula*

Diana Franklin
California Polytechnic State University, San Luis Obispo

David Goldberg
Xerox Palo Alto Research Center

Wen-mei W. Hwu
University of Illinois at Urbana–Champaign

Norman P. Jouppi
HP Labs

Timothy M. Pinkston
University of Southern California

John W. Sias
University of Illinois at Urbana–Champaign

David A. Wood
University of Wisconsin–Madison

ELSEVIER

Amsterdam • Boston • Heidelberg • London
New York • Oxford • Paris • San Diego
San Francisco • Singapore • Sydney • Tokyo

MORGAN KAUFMANN PUBLISHERS

Publisher Denise E. M. Penrose
Project Manager Dusty Friedman, The Book Company
In-house Senior Project Manager Brandy Lilly
Developmental Editor Nate McFadden
Editorial Assistant Kimberlee Honjo
Cover Design Elisabeth Beller and Ross Carron Design
Cover Image Richard I'Anson's Collection: Lonely Planet Images
Composition Nancy Logan
Text Design: Rebecca Evans & Associates
Technical Illustration David Ruppe, Impact Publications
Copyeditor Ken Della Penta
Proofreader Jamie Thaman
Indexer Nancy Ball
Printer Maple-Vail Book Manufacturing Group

Morgan Kaufmann Publishers is an Imprint of Elsevier
500 Sansome Street, Suite 400, San Francisco, CA 94111

This book is printed on acid-free paper.

Published 1990. Fourth edition 2007

Designations used by companies to distinguish their products are often claimed as trademarks or registered trademarks. In all instances in which Morgan Kaufmann Publishers is aware of a claim, the product names appear in initial capital or all capital letters. Readers, however, should contact the appropriate companies for more complete information regarding trademarks and registration.

Permissions may be sought directly from Elsevier's Science & Technology Rights Department in Oxford, UK: phone: (+44) 1865 843830, fax: (+44) 1865 853333, e-mail: permissions@elsevier.com. You may also complete your request on-line via the Elsevier Science homepage (*http://elsevier.com*), by selecting "Customer Support" and then "Obtaining Permissions."

Library of Congress Cataloging-in-Publication Data

Hennessy, John L.
  Computer architecture : a quantitative approach / John L. Hennessy, David A. Patterson ; with contributions by Andrea C. Arpaci-Dusseau . . . [et al.]. —4th ed.
      p.cm.
  Includes bibliographical references and index.
  ISBN 13: 978-0-12-370490-0 (pbk. : alk. paper)
  ISBN 10: 0-12-370490-1 (pbk. : alk. paper) 1. Computer architecture. I. Patterson, David A. II. Arpaci-Dusseau, Andrea C. III. Title.

QA76.9.A73P377 2006
004.2'2—dc22

2006024358

For all information on all Morgan Kaufmann publications,
visit our website at *www.mkp.com* or *www.books.elsevier.com*

Printed in the United States of America
06 07 08 09 10   5 4 3 2 1

To Andrea, Linda, and our four sons

Foreword

by Fred Weber, President and CEO of MetaRAM, Inc.

I am honored and privileged to write the foreword for the fourth edition of this most important book in computer architecture. In the first edition, Gordon Bell, my first industry mentor, predicted the book's central position as the definitive text for computer architecture and design. He was right. I clearly remember the excitement generated by the introduction of this work. Rereading it now, with significant extensions added in the three new editions, has been a pleasure all over again. No other work in computer architecture—frankly, no other work I have read in any field—so quickly and effortlessly takes the reader from ignorance to a breadth and depth of knowledge.

This book is dense in facts and figures, in rules of thumb and theories, in examples and descriptions. It is stuffed with acronyms, technologies, trends, formulas, illustrations, and tables. And, this is thoroughly appropriate for a work on architecture. The architect's role is not that of a scientist or inventor who will deeply study a particular phenomenon and create new basic materials or techniques. Nor is the architect the craftsman who masters the handling of tools to craft the finest details. The architect's role is to combine a thorough understanding of the state of the art of what is possible, a thorough understanding of the historical and current styles of what is desirable, a sense of design to conceive a harmonious total system, and the confidence and energy to marshal this knowledge and available resources to go out and get something built. To accomplish this, the architect needs a tremendous density of information with an in-depth understanding of the fundamentals and a quantitative approach to ground his thinking. That is exactly what this book delivers.

As computer architecture has evolved—from a world of mainframes, minicomputers, and microprocessors, to a world dominated by microprocessors, and now into a world where microprocessors themselves are encompassing all the complexity of mainframe computers—Hennessy and Patterson have updated their book appropriately. The first edition showcased the IBM 360, DEC VAX, and Intel 80x86, each the pinnacle of its class of computer, and helped introduce the world to RISC architecture. The later editions focused on the details of the 80x86 and RISC processors, which had come to dominate the landscape. This latest edition expands the coverage of threading and multiprocessing, virtualization and memory hierarchy, and storage systems, giving the reader context appropriate to today's most important directions and setting the stage for the next decade of design. It highlights the AMD Opteron and SUN Niagara as the best examples of the x86 and SPARC (RISC) architectures brought into the new world of multiprocessing and system-on-a-chip architecture, thus grounding the art and science in real-world commercial examples.

The first chapter, in less than 60 pages, introduces the reader to the taxonomies of computer design and the basic concerns of computer architecture, gives an overview of the technology trends that drive the industry, and lays out a quantitative approach to using all this information in the art of computer design. The next two chapters focus on traditional CPU design and give a strong grounding in the possibilities and limits in this core area. The final three chapters build out an understanding of system issues with multiprocessing, memory hierarchy, and storage. Knowledge of these areas has always been of critical importance to the computer architect. In this era of system-on-a-chip designs, it is essential for every CPU architect. Finally the appendices provide a great depth of understanding by working through specific examples in great detail.

In design it is important to look at both the forest and the trees and to move easily between these views. As you work through this book you will find plenty of both. The result of great architecture, whether in computer design, building design or textbook design, is to take the customer's requirements and desires and return a design that causes that customer to say, "Wow, I didn't know that was possible." This book succeeds on that measure and will, I hope, give you as much pleasure and value as it has me.

Contents

Foreword		**ix**
Preface		**xv**
Acknowledgments		**xxiii**

Chapter 1	**Fundamentals of Computer Design**	
	1.1 Introduction	2
	1.2 Classes of Computers	4
	1.3 Defining Computer Architecture	8
	1.4 Trends in Technology	14
	1.5 Trends in Power in Integrated Circuits	17
	1.6 Trends in Cost	19
	1.7 Dependability	25
	1.8 Measuring, Reporting, and Summarizing Performance	28
	1.9 Quantitative Principles of Computer Design	37
	1.10 Putting It All Together: Performance and Price-Performance	44
	1.11 Fallacies and Pitfalls	48
	1.12 Concluding Remarks	52
	1.13 Historical Perspectives and References	54
	Case Studies with Exercises by Diana Franklin	55

Chapter 2	**Instruction-Level Parallelism and Its Exploitation**	
	2.1 Instruction-Level Parallelism: Concepts and Challenges	66
	2.2 Basic Compiler Techniques for Exposing ILP	74
	2.3 Reducing Branch Costs with Prediction	80
	2.4 Overcoming Data Hazards with Dynamic Scheduling	89
	2.5 Dynamic Scheduling: Examples and the Algorithm	97
	2.6 Hardware-Based Speculation	104
	2.7 Exploiting ILP Using Multiple Issue and Static Scheduling	114

2.8 Exploiting ILP Using Dynamic Scheduling, Multiple Issue,
and Speculation   118
2.9 Advanced Techniques for Instruction Delivery and Speculation   121
2.10 Putting It All Together: The Intel Pentium 4   131
2.11 Fallacies and Pitfalls   138
2.12 Concluding Remarks   140
2.13 Historical Perspective and References   141
Case Studies with Exercises by Robert P. Colwell   142

Chapter 3   **Limits on Instruction-Level Parallelism**

3.1 Introduction   154
3.2 Studies of the Limitations of ILP   154
3.3 Limitations on ILP for Realizable Processors   165
3.4 Crosscutting Issues: Hardware versus Software Speculation   170
3.5 Multithreading: Using ILP Support to Exploit
Thread-Level Parallelism   172
3.6 Putting It All Together: Performance and Efficiency in Advanced
Multiple-Issue Processors   179
3.7 Fallacies and Pitfalls   183
3.8 Concluding Remarks   184
3.9 Historical Perspective and References   185
Case Study with Exercises by Wen-mei W. Hwu and
John W. Sias   185

Chapter 4   **Multiprocessors and Thread-Level Parallelism**

4.1 Introduction   196
4.2 Symmetric Shared-Memory Architectures   205
4.3 Performance of Symmetric Shared-Memory Multiprocessors   218
4.4 Distributed Shared Memory and Directory-Based Coherence   230
4.5 Synchronization: The Basics   237
4.6 Models of Memory Consistency: An Introduction   243
4.7 Crosscutting Issues   246
4.8 Putting It All Together: The Sun T1 Multiprocessor   249
4.9 Fallacies and Pitfalls   257
4.10 Concluding Remarks   262
4.11 Historical Perspective and References   264
Case Studies with Exercises by David A. Wood   264

Chapter 5   **Memory Hierarchy Design**

5.1 Introduction   288
5.2 Eleven Advanced Optimizations of Cache Performance   293
5.3 Memory Technology and Optimizations   310

5.4	Protection: Virtual Memory and Virtual Machines	315
5.5	Crosscutting Issues: The Design of Memory Hierarchies	324
5.6	Putting It All Together: AMD Opteron Memory Hierarchy	326
5.7	Fallacies and Pitfalls	335
5.8	Concluding Remarks	341
5.9	Historical Perspective and References	342
	Case Studies with Exercises by Norman P. Jouppi	342

Chapter 6   **Storage Systems**

6.1	Introduction	358
6.2	Advanced Topics in Disk Storage	358
6.3	Definition and Examples of Real Faults and Failures	366
6.4	I/O Performance, Reliability Measures, and Benchmarks	371
6.5	A Little Queuing Theory	379
6.6	Crosscutting Issues	390
6.7	Designing and Evaluating an I/O System—The Internet Archive Cluster	392
6.8	Putting It All Together: NetApp FAS6000 Filer	397
6.9	Fallacies and Pitfalls	399
6.10	Concluding Remarks	403
6.11	Historical Perspective and References	404
	Case Studies with Exercises by Andrea C. Arpaci-Dusseau and Remzi H. Arpaci-Dusseau	404

Appendix A   **Pipelining: Basic and Intermediate Concepts**

A.1	Introduction	A-2
A.2	The Major Hurdle of Pipelining—Pipeline Hazards	A-11
A.3	How Is Pipelining Implemented?	A-26
A.4	What Makes Pipelining Hard to Implement?	A-37
A.5	Extending the MIPS Pipeline to Handle Multicycle Operations	A-47
A.6	Putting It All Together: The MIPS R4000 Pipeline	A-56
A.7	Crosscutting Issues	A-65
A.8	Fallacies and Pitfalls	A-75
A.9	Concluding Remarks	A-76
A.10	Historical Perspective and References	A-77

Appendix B   **Instruction Set Principles and Examples**

B.1	Introduction	B-2
B.2	Classifying Instruction Set Architectures	B-3
B.3	Memory Addressing	B-7
B.4	Type and Size of Operands	B-13
B.5	Operations in the Instruction Set	B-14

B.6	Instructions for Control Flow	B-16
B.7	Encoding an Instruction Set	B-21
B.8	Crosscutting Issues: The Role of Compilers	B-24
B.9	Putting It All Together: The MIPS Architecture	B-32
B.10	Fallacies and Pitfalls	B-39
B.11	Concluding Remarks	B-45
B.12	Historical Perspective and References	B-47

Appendix C   **Review of Memory Hierarchy**

C.1	Introduction	C-2
C.2	Cache Performance	C-15
C.3	Six Basic Cache Optimizations	C-22
C.4	Virtual Memory	C-38
C.5	Protection and Examples of Virtual Memory	C-47
C.6	Fallacies and Pitfalls	C-56
C.7	Concluding Remarks	C-57
C.8	Historical Perspective and References	C-58

Companion CD Appendices

Appendix D   **Embedded Systems**
Updated by Thomas M. Conte

Appendix E   **Interconnection Networks**
Revised by Timothy M. Pinkston and José Duato

Appendix F   **Vector Processors**
Revised by Krste Asanovic

Appendix G   **Hardware and Software for VLIW and EPIC**

Appendix H   **Large-Scale Multiprocessors and Scientific Applications**

Appendix I   **Computer Arithmetic**
by David Goldberg

Appendix J   **Survey of Instruction Set Architectures**

Appendix K   **Historical Perspectives and References**

Online Appendix (textbooks.elsevier.com/0123704901)

Appendix L   **Solutions to Case Study Exercises**

References	R-1
Index	I-1

Preface

Why We Wrote This Book

Through four editions of this book, our goal has been to describe the basic principles underlying what will be tomorrow's technological developments. Our excitement about the opportunities in computer architecture has not abated, and we echo what we said about the field in the first edition: "It is not a dreary science of paper machines that will never work. No! It's a discipline of keen intellectual interest, requiring the balance of marketplace forces to cost-performance-power, leading to glorious failures and some notable successes."

Our primary objective in writing our first book was to change the way people learn and think about computer architecture. We feel this goal is still valid and important. The field is changing daily and must be studied with real examples and measurements on real computers, rather than simply as a collection of definitions and designs that will never need to be realized. We offer an enthusiastic welcome to anyone who came along with us in the past, as well as to those who are joining us now. Either way, we can promise the same quantitative approach to, and analysis of, real systems.

As with earlier versions, we have strived to produce a new edition that will continue to be as relevant for professional engineers and architects as it is for those involved in advanced computer architecture and design courses. As much as its predecessors, this edition aims to demystify computer architecture through an emphasis on cost-performance-power trade-offs and good engineering design. We believe that the field has continued to mature and move toward the rigorous quantitative foundation of long-established scientific and engineering disciplines.

This Edition

The fourth edition of *Computer Architecture: A Quantitative Approach* may be the most significant since the first edition. Shortly before we started this revision, Intel announced that it was joining IBM and Sun in relying on multiple processors or cores per chip for high-performance designs. As the first figure in the book documents, after 16 years of doubling performance every 18 months, single-processor performance improvement has dropped to modest annual improvements. This fork in the computer architecture road means that for the first time in history, no one is building a much faster sequential processor. If you want your program to run significantly faster, say, to justify the addition of new features, you're going to have to parallelize your program.

Hence, after three editions focused primarily on higher performance by exploiting instruction-level parallelism (ILP), an equal focus of this edition is thread-level parallelism (TLP) and data-level parallelism (DLP). While earlier editions had material on TLP and DLP in big multiprocessor servers, now TLP and DLP are relevant for single-chip multicores. This historic shift led us to change the order of the chapters: the chapter on multiple processors was the sixth chapter in the last edition, but is now the fourth chapter of this edition.

The changing technology has also motivated us to move some of the content from later chapters into the first chapter. Because technologists predict much higher hard and soft error rates as the industry moves to semiconductor processes with feature sizes 65 nm or smaller, we decided to move the basics of dependability from Chapter 7 in the third edition into Chapter 1. As power has become the dominant factor in determining how much you can place on a chip, we also beefed up the coverage of power in Chapter 1. Of course, the content and examples in all chapters were updated, as we discuss below.

In addition to technological sea changes that have shifted the contents of this edition, we have taken a new approach to the exercises in this edition. It is surprisingly difficult and time-consuming to create interesting, accurate, and unambiguous exercises that evenly test the material throughout a chapter. Alas, the Web has reduced the half-life of exercises to a few months. Rather than working out an assignment, a student can search the Web to find answers not long after a book is published. Hence, a tremendous amount of hard work quickly becomes unusable, and instructors are denied the opportunity to test what students have learned.

To help mitigate this problem, in this edition we are trying two new ideas. First, we recruited experts from academia and industry on each topic to write the exercises. This means some of the best people in each field are helping us to create interesting ways to explore the key concepts in each chapter and test the reader's understanding of that material. Second, each group of exercises is organized around a set of case studies. Our hope is that the quantitative example in each case study will remain interesting over the years, robust and detailed enough to allow instructors the opportunity to easily create their own new exercises, should they choose to do so. Key, however, is that each year we will continue to release new exercise sets for each of the case studies. These new exercises will have critical changes in some parameters so that answers to old exercises will no longer apply.

Another significant change is that we followed the lead of the third edition of *Computer Organization and Design (COD)* by slimming the text to include the material that almost all readers will want to see and moving the appendices that some will see as optional or as reference material onto a companion CD. There were many reasons for this change:

1. Students complained about the size of the book, which had expanded from 594 pages in the chapters plus 160 pages of appendices in the first edition to 760 chapter pages plus 223 appendix pages in the second edition and then to 883 chapter pages plus 209 pages in the paper appendices and 245 pages in online appendices. At this rate, the fourth edition would have exceeded 1500 pages (both on paper and online)!

2. Similarly, instructors were concerned about having too much material to cover in a single course.

3. As was the case for *COD,* by including a CD with material moved out of the text, readers could have quick access to all the material, regardless of their ability to access Elsevier's Web site. Hence, the current edition's appendices will always be available to the reader even after future editions appear.

4. This flexibility allowed us to move review material on pipelining, instruction sets, and memory hierarchy from the chapters and into Appendices A, B, and C. The advantage to instructors and readers is that they can go over the review material much more quickly and then spend more time on the advanced topics in Chapters 2, 3, and 5. It also allowed us to move the discussion of some topics that are important but are not core course topics into appendices on the CD. Result: the material is available, but the printed book is shorter. In this edition we have 6 chapters, none of which is longer than 80 pages, while in the last edition we had 8 chapters, with the longest chapter weighing in at 127 pages.

5. This package of a slimmer core print text plus a CD is far less expensive to manufacture than the previous editions, allowing our publisher to significantly lower the list price of the book. With this pricing scheme, there is no need for a separate international student edition for European readers.

Yet another major change from the last edition is that we have moved the embedded material introduced in the third edition into its own appendix, Appendix D. We felt that the embedded material didn't always fit with the quantitative evaluation of the rest of the material, plus it extended the length of many chapters that were already running long. We believe there are also pedagogic advantages in having all the embedded information in a single appendix.

This edition continues the tradition of using real-world examples to demonstrate the ideas, and the "Putting It All Together" sections are brand new; in fact, some were announced after our book was sent to the printer. The "Putting It All Together" sections of this edition include the pipeline organizations and memory hierarchies of the Intel Pentium 4 and AMD Opteron; the Sun T1 ("Niagara") 8-processor, 32-thread microprocessor; the latest NetApp Filer; the Internet Archive cluster; and the IBM Blue Gene/L massively parallel processor.

Topic Selection and Organization

As before, we have taken a conservative approach to topic selection, for there are many more interesting ideas in the field than can reasonably be covered in a treatment of basic principles. We have steered away from a comprehensive survey of every architecture a reader might encounter. Instead, our presentation focuses on core concepts likely to be found in any new machine. The key criterion remains that of selecting ideas that have been examined and utilized successfully enough to permit their discussion in quantitative terms.

Our intent has always been to focus on material that is not available in equivalent form from other sources, so we continue to emphasize advanced content wherever possible. Indeed, there are several systems here whose descriptions cannot be found in the literature. (Readers interested strictly in a more basic introduction to computer architecture should read *Computer Organization and Design: The Hardware/Software Interface,* third edition.)

An Overview of the Content

Chapter 1 has been beefed up in this edition. It includes formulas for static power, dynamic power, integrated circuit costs, reliability, and availability. We go into more depth than prior editions on the use of the geometric mean and the geometric standard deviation to capture the variability of the mean. Our hope is that these topics can be used through the rest of the book. In addition to the classic quantitative principles of computer design and performance measurement, the benchmark section has been upgraded to use the new SPEC2006 suite.

Our view is that the instruction set architecture is playing less of a role today than in 1990, so we moved this material to Appendix B. It still uses the MIPS64 architecture. For fans of ISAs, Appendix J covers 10 RISC architectures, the 80x86, the DEC VAX, and the IBM 360/370.

Chapters 2 and 3 cover the exploitation of instruction-level parallelism in high-performance processors, including superscalar execution, branch prediction, speculation, dynamic scheduling, and the relevant compiler technology. As mentioned earlier, Appendix A is a review of pipelining in case you need it. Chapter 3 surveys the limits of ILP. New to this edition is a quantitative evaluation of multithreading. Chapter 3 also includes a head-to-head comparison of the AMD Athlon, Intel Pentium 4, Intel Itanium 2, and IBM Power5, each of which has made separate bets on exploiting ILP and TLP. While the last edition contained a great deal on Itanium, we moved much of this material to Appendix G, indicating our view that this architecture has not lived up to the early claims.

Given the switch in the field from exploiting only ILP to an equal focus on thread- and data-level parallelism, we moved multiprocessor systems up to Chapter 4, which focuses on shared-memory architectures. The chapter begins with the performance of such an architecture. It then explores symmetric and distributed–memory architectures, examining both organizational principles and performance. Topics in synchronization and memory consistency models are next. The example is the Sun T1 ("Niagara"), a radical design for a commercial product. It reverted to a single-instruction issue, 6-stage pipeline microarchitecture. It put 8 of these on a single chip, and each supports 4 threads. Hence, software sees 32 threads on this single, low-power chip.

As mentioned earlier, Appendix C contains an introductory review of cache principles, which is available in case you need it. This shift allows Chapter 5 to start with 11 advanced optimizations of caches. The chapter includes a new section on virtual machines, which offers advantages in protection, software management, and hardware management. The example is the AMD Opteron, giving both its cache hierarchy and the virtual memory scheme for its recently expanded 64-bit addresses.

Chapter 6, "Storage Systems," has an expanded discussion of reliability and availability, a tutorial on RAID with a description of RAID 6 schemes, and rarely found failure statistics of real systems. It continues to provide an introduction to queuing theory and I/O performance benchmarks. Rather than go through a series of steps to build a hypothetical cluster as in the last edition, we evaluate the cost, performance, and reliability of a real cluster: the Internet Archive. The "Putting It All Together" example is the NetApp FAS6000 filer, which is based on the AMD Opteron microprocessor.

This brings us to Appendices A through L. As mentioned earlier, Appendices A and C are tutorials on basic pipelining and caching concepts. Readers relatively new to pipelining should read Appendix A before Chapters 2 and 3, and those new to caching should read Appendix C before Chapter 5.

Appendix B covers principles of ISAs, including MIPS64, and Appendix J describes 64-bit versions of Alpha, MIPS, PowerPC, and SPARC and their multimedia extensions. It also includes some classic architectures (80x86, VAX, and IBM 360/370) and popular embedded instruction sets (ARM, Thumb, SuperH, MIPS16, and Mitsubishi M32R). Appendix G is related, in that it covers architectures and compilers for VLIW ISAs.

Appendix D, updated by Thomas M. Conte, consolidates the embedded material in one place.

Appendix E, on networks, has been extensively revised by Timothy M. Pinkston and José Duato. Appendix F, updated by Krste Asanovic, includes a description of vector processors. We think these two appendices are some of the best material we know of on each topic.

Appendix H describes parallel processing applications and coherence protocols for larger-scale, shared-memory multiprocessing. Appendix I, by David Goldberg, describes computer arithmetic.

Appendix K collects the "Historical Perspective and References" from each chapter of the third edition into a single appendix. It attempts to give proper credit for the ideas in each chapter and a sense of the history surrounding the inventions. We like to think of this as presenting the human drama of computer design. It also supplies references that the student of architecture may want to pursue. If you have time, we recommend reading some of the classic papers in the field that are mentioned in these sections. It is both enjoyable and educational to hear the ideas directly from the creators. "Historical Perspective" was one of the most popular sections of prior editions.

Appendix L (available at *textbooks.elsevier.com/0123704901*) contains solutions to the case study exercises in the book.

Navigating the Text

There is no single best order in which to approach these chapters and appendices, except that all readers should start with Chapter 1. If you don't want to read everything, here are some suggested sequences:

- *ILP:* Appendix A, Chapters 2 and 3, and Appendices F and G
- *Memory Hierarchy:* Appendix C and Chapters 5 and 6
- *Thread-and Data-Level Parallelism:* Chapter 4, Appendix H, and Appendix E
- *ISA:* Appendices B and J

Appendix D can be read at any time, but it might work best if read after the ISA and cache sequences. Appendix I can be read whenever arithmetic moves you.

Chapter Structure

The material we have selected has been stretched upon a consistent framework that is followed in each chapter. We start by explaining the ideas of a chapter. These ideas are followed by a "Crosscutting Issues" section, a feature that shows how the ideas covered in one chapter interact with those given in other chapters. This is followed by a "Putting It All Together" section that ties these ideas together by showing how they are used in a real machine.

Next in the sequence is "Fallacies and Pitfalls," which lets readers learn from the mistakes of others. We show examples of common misunderstandings and architectural traps that are difficult to avoid even when you know they are lying in wait for you. The "Fallacies and Pitfalls" sections is one of the most popular sections of the book. Each chapter ends with a "Concluding Remarks" section.

Case Studies with Exercises

Each chapter ends with case studies and accompanying exercises. Authored by experts in industry and academia, the case studies explore key chapter concepts and verify understanding through increasingly challenging exercises. Instructors should find the case studies sufficiently detailed and robust to allow them to create their own additional exercises.

Brackets for each exercise (<chapter.section>) indicate the text sections of primary relevance to completing the exercise. We hope this helps readers to avoid exercises for which they haven't read the corresponding section, in addition to providing the source for review. Note that we provide solutions to the case study exercises in Appendix L. Exercises are rated, to give the reader a sense of the amount of time required to complete an exercise:

[10] Less than 5 minutes (to read and understand)

[15] 5–15 minutes for a full answer

[20] 15–20 minutes for a full answer

[25] 1 hour for a full written answer

[30] Short programming project: less than 1 full day of programming

[40] Significant programming project: 2 weeks of elapsed time

[Discussion] Topic for discussion with others

A second set of alternative case study exercises are available for instructors who register at *textbooks.elsevier.com/0123704901*. This second set will be revised every summer, so that early every fall, instructors can download a new set of exercises and solutions to accompany the case studies in the book.

Supplemental Materials

The accompanying CD contains a variety of resources, including the following:

■ Reference appendices—some guest authored by subject experts—covering a range of advanced topics

■ Historical Perspectives material that explores the development of the key ideas presented in each of the chapters in the text

■ Search engine for both the main text and the CD-only content

Additional resources are available at *textbooks.elsevier.com/0123704901*. The instructor site (accessible to adopters who register at *textbooks.elsevier.com*) includes:

■ Alternative case study exercises with solutions (updated yearly)

■ Instructor slides in PowerPoint

■ Figures from the book in JPEG and PPT formats

The companion site (accessible to all readers) includes:

■ Solutions to the case study exercises in the text

■ Links to related material on the Web

■ List of errata

New materials and links to other resources available on the Web will be added on a regular basis.

Helping Improve This Book

Finally, it is possible to make money while reading this book. (Talk about cost-performance!) If you read the Acknowledgments that follow, you will see that we went to great lengths to correct mistakes. Since a book goes through many printings, we have the opportunity to make even more corrections. If you uncover any remaining resilient bugs, please contact the publisher by electronic mail (*ca4bugs@mkp.com*). The first reader to report an error with a fix that we incorporate in a future printing will be rewarded with a $1.00 bounty. Please check the errata sheet on the home page (*textbooks.elsevier.com/0123704901*) to see if the bug has already been reported. We process the bugs and send the checks about once a year or so, so please be patient.

We welcome general comments to the text and invite you to send them to a separate email address at *ca4comments@mkp.com*.

Concluding Remarks

Once again this book is a true co-authorship, with each of us writing half the chapters and an equal share of the appendices. We can't imagine how long it would have taken without someone else doing half the work, offering inspiration when the task seemed hopeless, providing the key insight to explain a difficult concept, supplying reviews over the weekend of chapters, and commiserating when the weight of our other obligations made it hard to pick up the pen. (These obligations have escalated exponentially with the number of editions, as one of us was President of Stanford and the other was President of the Association for Computing Machinery.) Thus, once again we share equally the blame for what you are about to read.

John Hennessy ■ *David Patterson*

Acknowledgments

Although this is only the fourth edition of this book, we have actually created nine different versions of the text: three versions of the first edition (alpha, beta, and final) and two versions of the second, third, and fourth editions (beta and final). Along the way, we have received help from hundreds of reviewers and users. Each of these people has helped make this book better. Thus, we have chosen to list all of the people who have made contributions to some version of this book.

Contributors to the Fourth Edition

Like prior editions, this is a community effort that involves scores of volunteers. Without their help, this edition would not be nearly as polished.

Reviewers

Krste Asanovic, Massachusetts Institute of Technology; Mark Brehob, University of Michigan; Sudhanva Gurumurthi, University of Virginia; Mark D. Hill, University of Wisconsin–Madison; Wen-mei Hwu, University of Illinois at Urbana–Champaign; David Kaeli, Northeastern University; Ramadass Nagarajan, University of Texas at Austin; Karthikeyan Sankaralingam, Univeristy of Texas at Austin; Mark Smotherman, Clemson University; Gurindar Sohi, University of Wisconsin–Madison; Shyamkumar Thoziyoor, University of Notre Dame, Indiana; Dan Upton, University of Virginia; Sotirios G. Ziavras, New Jersey Institute of Technology

Focus Group

Krste Asanovic, Massachusetts Institute of Technology; José Duato, Universitat Politècnica de València and Simula; Antonio González, Intel and Universitat Politècnica de Catalunya; Mark D. Hill, University of Wisconsin–Madison; Lev G. Kirischian, Ryerson University; Timothy M. Pinkston, University of Southern California

Appendices

Krste Asanovic, Massachusetts Institute of Technology (Appendix F); Thomas M. Conte, North Carolina State University (Appendix D); José Duato, Universitat Politècnica de València and Simula (Appendix E); David Goldberg, Xerox PARC (Appendix I); Timothy M. Pinkston, University of Southern California (Appendix E)

Case Studies with Exercises

Andrea C. Arpaci-Dusseau, University of Wisconsin–Madison (Chapter 6); Remzi H. Arpaci-Dusseau, University of Wisconsin–Madison (Chapter 6); Robert P. Colwell, R&E Colwell & Assoc., Inc. (Chapter 2); Diana Franklin, California Polytechnic State University, San Luis Obispo (Chapter 1); Wen-mei W. Hwu, University of Illinois at Urbana–Champaign (Chapter 3); Norman P. Jouppi, HP Labs (Chapter 5); John W. Sias, University of Illinois at Urbana–Champaign (Chapter 3); David A. Wood, University of Wisconsin–Madison (Chapter 4)

Additional Material

John Mashey (geometric means and standard deviations in Chapter 1); Chenming Hu, University of California, Berkeley (wafer costs and yield parameters in Chapter 1); Bill Brantley and Dan Mudgett, AMD (Opteron memory hierarchy evaluation in Chapter 5); Mendel Rosenblum, Stanford and VMware (virtual machines in Chapter 5); Aravind Menon, EPFL Switzerland (Xen measurements in Chapter 5); Bruce Baumgart and Brewster Kahle, Internet Archive (IA cluster in Chapter 6); David Ford, Steve Kleiman, and Steve Miller, Network Appliances (FX6000 information in Chapter 6); Alexander Thomasian, Rutgers (queueing theory in Chapter 6)

Finally, a special thanks once again to Mark Smotherman of Clemson University, who gave a final technical reading of our manuscript. Mark found numerous bugs and ambiguities, and the book is much cleaner as a result.

This book could not have been published without a publisher, of course. We wish to thank all the Morgan Kaufmann/Elsevier staff for their efforts and support. For this fourth edition, we particularly want to thank Kimberlee Honjo who coordinated surveys, focus groups, manuscript reviews and appendices, and Nate McFadden, who coordinated the development and review of the case studies. Our warmest thanks to our editor, Denise Penrose, for her leadership in our continuing writing saga.

We must also thank our university staff, Margaret Rowland and Cecilia Pracher, for countless express mailings, as well as for holding down the fort at Stanford and Berkeley while we worked on the book.

Our final thanks go to our wives for their suffering through increasingly early mornings of reading, thinking, and writing.

Contributors to Previous Editions

Reviewers

George Adams, Purdue University; Sarita Adve, University of Illinois at Urbana–Champaign; Jim Archibald, Brigham Young University; Krste Asanovic, Massachusetts Institute of Technology; Jean-Loup Baer, University of Washington; Paul Barr, Northeastern University; Rajendra V. Boppana, University of Texas, San Antonio; Doug Burger, University of Texas, Austin; John Burger, SGI; Michael Butler; Thomas Casavant; Rohit Chandra; Peter Chen, University of Michigan; the classes at SUNY Stony Brook, Carnegie Mellon, Stanford, Clemson, and Wisconsin; Tim Coe, Vitesse Semiconductor; Bob Colwell, Intel; David Cummings; Bill Dally; David Douglas; Anthony Duben, Southeast Missouri State University; Susan Eggers, University of Washington; Joel Emer; Barry Fagin, Dartmouth; Joel Ferguson, University of California, Santa Cruz; Carl Feynman; David Filo; Josh Fisher, Hewlett-Packard Laboratories; Rob Fowler, DIKU; Mark Franklin, Washington University (St. Louis); Kourosh Gharachorloo; Nikolas Gloy, Harvard University; David Goldberg, Xerox Palo Alto Research Center; James Goodman, University of Wisconsin–Madison; David Harris, Harvey Mudd College; John Heinlein; Mark Heinrich, Stanford; Daniel Helman, University of California, Santa Cruz; Mark Hill, University of Wisconsin–Madison; Martin Hopkins, IBM; Jerry Huck, Hewlett-Packard Laboratories; Mary Jane Irwin, Pennsylvania State University; Truman Joe; Norm Jouppi; David Kaeli, Northeastern University; Roger Kieckhafer, University of Nebraska; Earl Killian; Allan Knies, Purdue University; Don Knuth; Jeff Kuskin, Stanford; James R. Larus, Microsoft Research; Corinna Lee, University of Toronto; Hank Levy; Kai Li, Princeton University; Lori Liebrock, University of Alaska, Fairbanks; Mikko Lipasti, University of Wisconsin–Madison; Gyula A. Mago, University of North Carolina, Chapel Hill; Bryan Martin; Norman Matloff; David Meyer; William Michalson, Worcester Polytechnic Institute; James Mooney; Trevor Mudge, University of Michigan; David Nagle, Carnegie Mellon University; Todd Narter; Victor Nelson; Vojin Oklobdzija, University of California, Berkeley; Kunle Olukotun, Stanford University; Bob Owens, Pennsylvania State University; Greg Papadapoulous, Sun; Joseph Pfeiffer; Keshav Pingali, Cornell University; Bruno Preiss, University of Waterloo; Steven Przybylski; Jim Quinlan; Andras Radics; Kishore Ramachandran, Georgia Institute of Technology; Joseph Rameh, University of Texas, Austin; Anthony Reeves, Cornell University; Richard Reid, Michigan State University; Steve Reinhardt, University of Michigan; David Rennels, University of California, Los Angeles; Arnold L. Rosenberg, University of Massachusetts, Amherst; Kaushik Roy, Purdue University; Emilio Salgueiro, Unysis; Peter Schnorf; Margo Seltzer; Behrooz Shirazi, Southern Methodist University; Daniel Siewiorek, Carnegie Mellon University; J. P. Singh, Princeton; Ashok Singhal; Jim Smith, University of Wisconsin–Madison; Mike Smith, Harvard University; Mark Smotherman, Clemson University; Guri Sohi, University of Wisconsin–Madison; Arun Somani, University of

Washington; Gene Tagliarin, Clemson University; Evan Tick, University of Oregon; Akhilesh Tyagi, University of North Carolina, Chapel Hill; Mateo Valero, Universidad Politécnica de Cataluña, Barcelona; Anujan Varma, University of California, Santa Cruz; Thorsten von Eicken, Cornell University; Hank Walker, Texas A&M; Roy Want, Xerox Palo Alto Research Center; David Weaver, Sun; Shlomo Weiss, Tel Aviv University; David Wells; Mike Westall, Clemson University; Maurice Wilkes; Eric Williams; Thomas Willis, Purdue University; Malcolm Wing; Larry Wittie, SUNY Stony Brook; Ellen Witte Zegura, Georgia Institute of Technology

Appendices

The vector appendix was revised by Krste Asanovic of the Massachusetts Institute of Technology. The floating-point appendix was written originally by David Goldberg of Xerox PARC.

Exercises

George Adams, Purdue University; Todd M. Bezenek, University of Wisconsin–Madison (in remembrance of his grandmother Ethel Eshom); Susan Eggers; Anoop Gupta; David Hayes; Mark Hill; Allan Knies; Ethan L. Miller, University of California, Santa Cruz; Parthasarathy Ranganathan, Compaq Western Research Laboratory; Brandon Schwartz, University of Wisconsin–Madison; Michael Scott; Dan Siewiorek; Mike Smith; Mark Smotherman; Evan Tick; Thomas Willis.

Special Thanks

Duane Adams, Defense Advanced Research Projects Agency; Tom Adams; Sarita Adve, University of Illinois at Urbana–Champaign; Anant Agarwal; Dave Albonesi, University of Rochester; Mitch Alsup; Howard Alt; Dave Anderson; Peter Ashenden; David Bailey; Bill Bandy, Defense Advanced Research Projects Agency; L. Barroso, Compaq's Western Research Lab; Andy Bechtolsheim; C. Gordon Bell; Fred Berkowitz; John Best, IBM; Dileep Bhandarkar; Jeff Bier, BDTI; Mark Birman; David Black; David Boggs; Jim Brady; Forrest Brewer; Aaron Brown, University of California, Berkeley; E. Bugnion, Compaq's Western Research Lab; Alper Buyuktosunoglu, University of Rochester; Mark Callaghan; Jason F. Cantin; Paul Carrick; Chen-Chung Chang; Lei Chen, University of Rochester; Pete Chen; Nhan Chu; Doug Clark, Princeton University; Bob Cmelik; John Crawford; Zarka Cvetanovic; Mike Dahlin, University of Texas, Austin; Merrick Darley; the staff of the DEC Western Research Laboratory; John DeRosa; Lloyd Dickman; J. Ding; Susan Eggers, University of Washington; Wael El-Essawy, University of Rochester; Patty Enriquez, Mills; Milos Ercegovac; Robert Garner; K. Gharachorloo, Compaq's Western Research Lab; Garth Gibson; Ronald Greenberg; Ben Hao; John Henning, Compaq; Mark Hill, University of Wisconsin–Madison; Danny Hillis; David Hodges; Urs Hoelzle, Google; David Hough; Ed Hudson; Chris Hughes, University of Illinois at Urbana–Champaign; Mark Johnson; Lewis Jordan; Norm Jouppi; William Kahan; Randy Katz; Ed Kelly; Richard Kessler; Les Kohn; John Kowaleski, Compaq Computer Corp; Dan Lambright; Gary Lauterbach, Sun Microsystems; Corinna Lee; Ruby Lee; Don Lewine; Chao-Huang Lin; Paul Losleben, Defense Advanced Research Projects Agency; Yung-Hsiang Lu; Bob Lucas, Defense Advanced Research Projects Agency; Ken Lutz; Alan Mainwaring, Intel Berkeley Research Labs; Al Marston; Rich Martin, Rutgers; John Mashey; Luke McDowell; Sebastian Mirolo, Trimedia Corporation; Ravi Murthy; Biswadeep Nag; Lisa Noordergraaf, Sun Microsystems; Bob Parker, Defense Advanced Research Projects Agency; Vern Paxson, Center for Internet Research; Lawrence Prince; Steven Przybylski; Mark Pullen, Defense Advanced Research Projects Agency; Chris Rowen; Margaret Rowland; Greg Semeraro, University of Rochester; Bill Shannon; Behrooz Shirazi; Robert Shomler; Jim Slager; Mark Smotherman, Clemson University; the SMT research group at the University of Washington; Steve Squires, Defense Advanced Research Projects Agency; Ajay Sreekanth; Darren Staples; Charles Stapper; Jorge Stolfi; Peter Stoll; the students at Stanford and Berkeley who endured our first attempts at creating this book; Bob Supnik; Steve Swanson; Paul Taysom; Shreekant Thakkar; Alexander Thomasian, New Jersey Institute of Technology; John Toole, Defense Advanced Research Projects Agency; Kees A. Vissers, Trimedia Corporation; Willa Walker; David Weaver; Ric Wheeler, EMC; Maurice Wilkes; Richard Zimmerman.

John Hennessy ▪ *David Patterson*

1.1	Introduction	2
1.2	Classes of Computers	4
1.3	Defining Computer Architecture	8
1.4	Trends in Technology	14
1.5	Trends in Power in Integrated Circuits	17
1.6	Trends in Cost	19
1.7	Dependability	25
1.8	Measuring, Reporting, and Summarizing Performance	28
1.9	Quantitative Principles of Computer Design	37
1.10	Putting It All Together: Performance and Price-Performance	44
1.11	Fallacies and Pitfalls	48
1.12	Concluding Remarks	52
1.13	Historical Perspectives and References	54
	Case Studies with Exercises by Diana Franklin	55

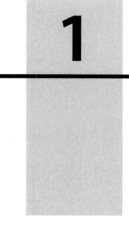

1

Fundamentals of
Computer Design

And now for something completely different.

Monty Python's Flying Circus

1.1 Introduction

Computer technology has made incredible progress in the roughly 60 years since the first general-purpose electronic computer was created. Today, less than $500 will purchase a personal computer that has more performance, more main memory, and more disk storage than a computer bought in 1985 for 1 million dollars. This rapid improvement has come both from advances in the technology used to build computers and from innovation in computer design.

Although technological improvements have been fairly steady, progress arising from better computer architectures has been much less consistent. During the first 25 years of electronic computers, both forces made a major contribution, delivering performance improvement of about 25% per year. The late 1970s saw the emergence of the microprocessor. The ability of the microprocessor to ride the improvements in integrated circuit technology led to a higher rate of improvement—roughly 35% growth per year in performance.

This growth rate, combined with the cost advantages of a mass-produced microprocessor, led to an increasing fraction of the computer business being based on microprocessors. In addition, two significant changes in the computer marketplace made it easier than ever before to be commercially successful with a new architecture. First, the virtual elimination of assembly language programming reduced the need for object-code compatibility. Second, the creation of standardized, vendor-independent operating systems, such as UNIX and its clone, Linux, lowered the cost and risk of bringing out a new architecture.

These changes made it possible to develop successfully a new set of architectures with simpler instructions, called RISC (Reduced Instruction Set Computer) architectures, in the early 1980s. The RISC-based machines focused the attention of designers on two critical performance techniques, the exploitation of *instruction-level parallelism* (initially through pipelining and later through multiple instruction issue) and the use of caches (initially in simple forms and later using more sophisticated organizations and optimizations).

The RISC-based computers raised the performance bar, forcing prior architectures to keep up or disappear. The Digital Equipment Vax could not, and so it was replaced by a RISC architecture. Intel rose to the challenge, primarily by translating x86 (or IA-32) instructions into RISC-like instructions internally, allowing it to adopt many of the innovations first pioneered in the RISC designs. As transistor counts soared in the late 1990s, the hardware overhead of translating the more complex x86 architecture became negligible.

Figure 1.1 shows that the combination of architectural and organizational enhancements led to 16 years of sustained growth in performance at an annual rate of over 50%—a rate that is unprecedented in the computer industry.

The effect of this dramatic growth rate in the 20th century has been twofold. First, it has significantly enhanced the capability available to computer users. For many applications, the highest-performance microprocessors of today outperform the supercomputer of less than 10 years ago.

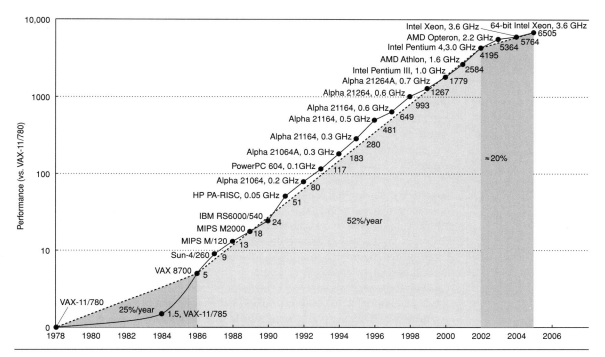

Figure 1.1 Growth in processor performance since the mid-1980s. This chart plots performance relative to the VAX 11/780 as measured by the SPECint benchmarks (see Section 1.8). Prior to the mid-1980s, processor performance growth was largely technology driven and averaged about 25% per year. The increase in growth to about 52% since then is attributable to more advanced architectural and organizational ideas. By 2002, this growth led to a difference in performance of about a factor of seven. Performance for floating-point-oriented calculations has increased even faster. Since 2002, the limits of power, available instruction-level parallelism, and long memory latency have slowed uniprocessor performance recently, to about 20% per year. Since SPEC has changed over the years, performance of newer machines is estimated by a scaling factor that relates the performance for two different versions of SPEC (e.g., SPEC92, SPEC95, and SPEC2000).

Second, this dramatic rate of improvement has led to the dominance of microprocessor-based computers across the entire range of the computer design. PCs and Workstations have emerged as major products in the computer industry. Minicomputers, which were traditionally made from off-the-shelf logic or from gate arrays, have been replaced by servers made using microprocessors. Mainframes have been almost replaced with multiprocessors consisting of small numbers of off-the-shelf microprocessors. Even high-end supercomputers are being built with collections of microprocessors.

These innovations led to a renaissance in computer design, which emphasized both architectural innovation and efficient use of technology improvements. This rate of growth has compounded so that by 2002, high-performance microprocessors are about seven times faster than what would have been obtained by relying solely on technology, including improved circuit design.

However, Figure 1.1 also shows that this 16-year renaissance is over. Since 2002, processor performance improvement has dropped to about 20% per year due to the triple hurdles of maximum power dissipation of air-cooled chips, little instruction-level parallelism left to exploit efficiently, and almost unchanged memory latency. Indeed, in 2004 Intel canceled its high-performance uniprocessor projects and joined IBM and Sun in declaring that the road to higher performance would be via multiple processors per chip rather than via faster uniprocessors. This signals a historic switch from relying solely on instruction-level parallelism (ILP), the primary focus of the first three editions of this book, to *thread-level parallelism* (TLP) and *data-level parallelism* (DLP), which are featured in this edition. Whereas the compiler and hardware conspire to exploit ILP implicitly without the programmer's attention, TLP and DLP are explicitly parallel, requiring the programmer to write parallel code to gain performance.

This text is about the architectural ideas and accompanying compiler improvements that made the incredible growth rate possible in the last century, the reasons for the dramatic change, and the challenges and initial promising approaches to architectural ideas and compilers for the 21st century. At the core is a quantitative approach to computer design and analysis that uses empirical observations of programs, experimentation, and simulation as its tools. It is this style and approach to computer design that is reflected in this text. This book was written not only to explain this design style, but also to stimulate you to contribute to this progress. We believe the approach will work for explicitly parallel computers of the future just as it worked for the implicitly parallel computers of the past.

1.2 Classes of Computers

In the 1960s, the dominant form of computing was on large mainframes—computers costing millions of dollars and stored in computer rooms with multiple operators overseeing their support. Typical applications included business data processing and large-scale scientific computing. The 1970s saw the birth of the minicomputer, a smaller-sized computer initially focused on applications in scientific laboratories, but rapidly branching out with the popularity of time-sharing—multiple users sharing a computer interactively through independent terminals. That decade also saw the emergence of supercomputers, which were high-performance computers for scientific computing. Although few in number, they were important historically because they pioneered innovations that later trickled down to less expensive computer classes. The 1980s saw the rise of the desktop computer based on microprocessors, in the form of both personal computers and workstations. The individually owned desktop computer replaced time-sharing and led to the rise of servers—computers that provided larger-scale services such as reliable, long-term file storage and access, larger memory, and more computing power. The 1990s saw the emergence of the Internet and the World Wide Web, the first successful handheld computing devices (personal digi-

Feature	Desktop	Server	Embedded
Price of system	$500–$5000	$5000–$5,000,000	$10–$100,000 (including network routers at the high end)
Price of microprocessor module	$50–$500 (per processor)	$200–$10,000 (per processor)	$0.01–$100 (per processor)
Critical system design issues	Price-performance, graphics performance	Throughput, availability, scalability	Price, power consumption, application-specific performance

Figure 1.2 A summary of the three mainstream computing classes and their system characteristics. Note the wide range in system price for servers and embedded systems. For servers, this range arises from the need for very large-scale multiprocessor systems for high-end transaction processing and Web server applications. The total number of embedded processors sold in 2005 is estimated to exceed 3 billion if you include 8-bit and 16-bit microprocessors. Perhaps 200 million desktop computers and 10 million servers were sold in 2005.

tal assistants or PDAs), and the emergence of high-performance digital consumer electronics, from video games to set-top boxes. The extraordinary popularity of cell phones has been obvious since 2000, with rapid improvements in functions and sales that far exceed those of the PC. These more recent applications use *embedded computers*, where computers are lodged in other devices and their presence is not immediately obvious.

These changes have set the stage for a dramatic change in how we view computing, computing applications, and the computer markets in this new century. Not since the creation of the personal computer more than 20 years ago have we seen such dramatic changes in the way computers appear and in how they are used. These changes in computer use have led to three different computing markets, each characterized by different applications, requirements, and computing technologies. Figure 1.2 summarizes these mainstream classes of computing environments and their important characteristics.

Desktop Computing

The first, and still the largest market in dollar terms, is desktop computing. Desktop computing spans from low-end systems that sell for under $500 to high-end, heavily configured workstations that may sell for $5000. Throughout this range in price and capability, the desktop market tends to be driven to optimize *price-performance*. This combination of performance (measured primarily in terms of compute performance and graphics performance) and price of a system is what matters most to customers in this market, and hence to computer designers. As a result, the newest, highest-performance microprocessors and cost-reduced microprocessors often appear first in desktop systems (see Section 1.6 for a discussion of the issues affecting the cost of computers).

Desktop computing also tends to be reasonably well characterized in terms of applications and benchmarking, though the increasing use of Web-centric, interactive applications poses new challenges in performance evaluation.

Servers

As the shift to desktop computing occurred, the role of servers grew to provide larger-scale and more reliable file and computing services. The World Wide Web accelerated this trend because of the tremendous growth in the demand and sophistication of Web-based services. Such servers have become the backbone of large-scale enterprise computing, replacing the traditional mainframe.

For servers, different characteristics are important. First, dependability is critical. (We discuss dependability in Section 1.7.) Consider the servers running Google, taking orders for Cisco, or running auctions on eBay. Failure of such server systems is far more catastrophic than failure of a single desktop, since these servers must operate seven days a week, 24 hours a day. Figure 1.3 estimates revenue costs of downtime as of 2000. To bring costs up-to-date, Amazon.com had $2.98 billion in sales in the fall quarter of 2005. As there were about 2200 hours in that quarter, the average revenue per hour was $1.35 million. During a peak hour for Christmas shopping, the potential loss would be many times higher.

Hence, the estimated costs of an unavailable system are high, yet Figure 1.3 and the Amazon numbers are purely lost revenue and do not account for lost employee productivity or the cost of unhappy customers.

A second key feature of server systems is scalability. Server systems often grow in response to an increasing demand for the services they support or an increase in functional requirements. Thus, the ability to scale up the computing capacity, the memory, the storage, and the I/O bandwidth of a server is crucial.

Lastly, servers are designed for efficient throughput. That is, the overall performance of the server—in terms of transactions per minute or Web pages served

		Annual losses (millions of $) with downtime of		
Application	Cost of downtime per hour (thousands of $)	1% (87.6 hrs/yr)	0.5% (43.8 hrs/yr)	0.1% (8.8 hrs/yr)
Brokerage operations	$6450	$565	$283	$56.5
Credit card authorization	$2600	$228	$114	$22.8
Package shipping services	$150	$13	$6.6	$1.3
Home shopping channel	$113	$9.9	$4.9	$1.0
Catalog sales center	$90	$7.9	$3.9	$0.8
Airline reservation center	$89	$7.9	$3.9	$0.8
Cellular service activation	$41	$3.6	$1.8	$0.4
Online network fees	$25	$2.2	$1.1	$0.2
ATM service fees	$14	$1.2	$0.6	$0.1

Figure 1.3 The cost of an unavailable system is shown by analyzing the cost of downtime (in terms of immediately lost revenue), assuming three different levels of availability, and that downtime is distributed uniformly. These data are from Kembel [2000] and were collected and analyzed by Contingency Planning Research.

per second—is what is crucial. Responsiveness to an individual request remains important, but overall efficiency and cost-effectiveness, as determined by how many requests can be handled in a unit time, are the key metrics for most servers. We return to the issue of assessing performance for different types of computing environments in Section 1.8.

A related category is *supercomputers*. They are the most expensive computers, costing tens of millions of dollars, and they emphasize floating-point performance. Clusters of desktop computers, which are discussed in Appendix H, have largely overtaken this class of computer. As clusters grow in popularity, the number of conventional supercomputers is shrinking, as are the number of companies who make them.

Embedded Computers

Embedded computers are the fastest growing portion of the computer market. These devices range from everyday machines—most microwaves, most washing machines, most printers, most networking switches, and all cars contain simple embedded microprocessors—to handheld digital devices, such as cell phones and smart cards, to video games and digital set-top boxes.

Embedded computers have the widest spread of processing power and cost. They include 8-bit and 16-bit processors that may cost less than a dime, 32-bit microprocessors that execute 100 million instructions per second and cost under $5, and high-end processors for the newest video games or network switches that cost $100 and can execute a billion instructions per second. Although the range of computing power in the embedded computing market is very large, price is a key factor in the design of computers for this space. Performance requirements do exist, of course, but the primary goal is often meeting the performance need at a minimum price, rather than achieving higher performance at a higher price.

Often, the performance requirement in an embedded application is real-time execution. A *real-time performance* requirement is when a segment of the application has an absolute maximum execution time. For example, in a digital set-top box, the time to process each video frame is limited, since the processor must accept and process the next frame shortly. In some applications, a more nuanced requirement exists: the average time for a particular task is constrained as well as the number of instances when some maximum time is exceeded. Such approaches—sometimes called *soft real-time*—arise when it is possible to occasionally miss the time constraint on an event, as long as not too many are missed. Real-time performance tends to be highly application dependent.

Two other key characteristics exist in many embedded applications: the need to minimize memory and the need to minimize power. In many embedded applications, the memory can be a substantial portion of the system cost, and it is important to optimize memory size in such cases. Sometimes the application is expected to fit totally in the memory on the processor chip; other times the application needs to fit totally in a small off-chip memory. In any event, the importance of memory size translates to an emphasis on code size, since data size is dictated by the application.

Larger memories also mean more power, and optimizing power is often critical in embedded applications. Although the emphasis on low power is frequently driven by the use of batteries, the need to use less expensive packaging—plastic versus ceramic—and the absence of a fan for cooling also limit total power consumption. We examine the issue of power in more detail in Section 1.5.

Most of this book applies to the design, use, and performance of embedded processors, whether they are off-the-shelf microprocessors or microprocessor cores, which will be assembled with other special-purpose hardware.

Indeed, the third edition of this book included examples from embedded computing to illustrate the ideas in every chapter. Alas, most readers found these examples unsatisfactory, as the data that drives the quantitative design and evaluation of desktop and server computers has not yet been extended well to embedded computing (see the challenges with EEMBC, for example, in Section 1.8). Hence, we are left for now with qualitative descriptions, which do not fit well with the rest of the book. As a result, in this edition we consolidated the embedded material into a single appendix. We believe this new appendix (Appendix D) improves the flow of ideas in the text while still allowing readers to see how the differing requirements affect embedded computing.

1.3 Defining Computer Architecture

The task the computer designer faces is a complex one: Determine what attributes are important for a new computer, then design a computer to maximize performance while staying within cost, power, and availability constraints. This task has many aspects, including instruction set design, functional organization, logic design, and implementation. The implementation may encompass integrated circuit design, packaging, power, and cooling. Optimizing the design requires familiarity with a very wide range of technologies, from compilers and operating systems to logic design and packaging.

In the past, the term *computer architecture* often referred only to instruction set design. Other aspects of computer design were called *implementation,* often insinuating that implementation is uninteresting or less challenging.

We believe this view is incorrect. The architect's or designer's job is much more than instruction set design, and the technical hurdles in the other aspects of the project are likely more challenging than those encountered in instruction set design. We'll quickly review instruction set architecture before describing the larger challenges for the computer architect.

Instruction Set Architecture

We use the term *instruction set architecture* (ISA) to refer to the actual programmer-visible instruction set in this book. The ISA serves as the boundary between the software and hardware. This quick review of ISA will use examples from MIPS and 80x86 to illustrate the seven dimensions of an ISA. Appendices B and J give more details on MIPS and the 80x86 ISAs.

1. *Class of ISA*—Nearly all ISAs today are classified as general-purpose register architectures, where the operands are either registers or memory locations. The 80x86 has 16 general-purpose registers and 16 that can hold floating-point data, while MIPS has 32 general-purpose and 32 floating-point registers (see Figure 1.4). The two popular versions of this class are *register-memory* ISAs such as the 80x86, which can access memory as part of many instructions, and *load-store* ISAs such as MIPS, which can access memory only with load or store instructions. All recent ISAs are load-store.

2. *Memory addressing*—Virtually all desktop and server computers, including the 80x86 and MIPS, use byte addressing to access memory operands. Some architectures, like MIPS, require that objects must be *aligned*. An access to an object of size s bytes at byte address A is aligned if A mod $s = 0$. (See Figure B.5 on page B-9.) The 80x86 does not require alignment, but accesses are generally faster if operands are aligned.

3. *Addressing modes*—In addition to specifying registers and constant operands, addressing modes specify the address of a memory object. MIPS addressing modes are Register, Immediate (for constants), and Displacement, where a constant offset is added to a register to form the memory address. The 80x86 supports those three plus three variations of displacement: no register (absolute), two registers (based indexed with displacement), two registers where

Name	Number	Use	Preserved across a call?
$zero	0	The constant value 0	N.A.
$at	1	Assembler temporary	No
$v0–$v1	2–3	Values for function results and expression evaluation	No
$a0–$a3	4–7	Arguments	No
$t0–$t7	8–15	Temporaries	No
$s0–$s7	16–23	Saved temporaries	Yes
$t8–$t9	24–25	Temporaries	No
$k0–$k1	26–27	Reserved for OS kernel	No
$gp	28	Global pointer	Yes
$sp	29	Stack pointer	Yes
$fp	30	Frame pointer	Yes
$ra	31	Return address	Yes

Figure 1.4 MIPS registers and usage conventions. In addition to the 32 general-purpose registers (R0–R31), MIPS has 32 floating-point registers (F0–F31) that can hold either a 32-bit single-precision number or a 64-bit double-precision number.

one register is multiplied by the size of the operand in bytes (based with scaled index and displacement). It has more like the last three, minus the displacement field: register indirect, indexed, and based with scaled index.

4. *Types and sizes of operands*—Like most ISAs, MIPS and 80x86 support operand sizes of 8-bit (ASCII character), 16-bit (Unicode character or half word), 32-bit (integer or word), 64-bit (double word or long integer), and IEEE 754 floating point in 32-bit (single precision) and 64-bit (double precision). The 80x86 also supports 80-bit floating point (extended double precision).

5. *Operations*—The general categories of operations are data transfer, arithmetic logical, control (discussed next), and floating point. MIPS is a simple and easy-to-pipeline instruction set architecture, and it is representative of the RISC architectures being used in 2006. Figure 1.5 summarizes the MIPS ISA. The 80x86 has a much richer and larger set of operations (see Appendix J).

6. *Control flow instructions*—Virtually all ISAs, including 80x86 and MIPS, support conditional branches, unconditional jumps, procedure calls, and returns. Both use PC-relative addressing, where the branch address is specified by an address field that is added to the PC. There are some small differences. MIPS conditional branches (BE, BNE, etc.) test the contents of registers, while the 80x86 branches (JE, JNE, etc.) test condition code bits set as side effects of arithmetic/logic operations. MIPS procedure call (JAL) places the return address in a register, while the 80x86 call (CALLF) places the return address on a stack in memory.

7. *Encoding an ISA*—There are two basic choices on encoding: *fixed length* and *variable length*. All MIPS instructions are 32 bits long, which simplifies instruction decoding. Figure 1.6 shows the MIPS instruction formats. The 80x86 encoding is variable length, ranging from 1 to 18 bytes. Variable-length instructions can take less space than fixed-length instructions, so a program compiled for the 80x86 is usually smaller than the same program compiled for MIPS. Note that choices mentioned above will affect how the instructions are encoded into a binary representation. For example, the number of registers and the number of addressing modes both have a significant impact on the size of instructions, as the register field and addressing mode field can appear many times in a single instruction.

The other challenges facing the computer architect beyond ISA design are particularly acute at the present, when the differences among instruction sets are small and when there are distinct application areas. Therefore, starting with this edition, the bulk of instruction set material beyond this quick review is found in the appendices (see Appendices B and J).

We use a subset of MIPS64 as the example ISA in this book.

Instruction type/opcode	Instruction meaning
Data transfers	*Move data between registers and memory, or between the integer and FP or special registers; only memory address mode is 16-bit displacement + contents of a GPR*
LB, LBU, SB	Load byte, load byte unsigned, store byte (to/from integer registers)
LH, LHU, SH	Load half word, load half word unsigned, store half word (to/from integer registers)
LW, LWU, SW	Load word, load word unsigned, store word (to/from integer registers)
LD, SD	Load double word, store double word (to/from integer registers)
L.S, L.D, S.S, S.D	Load SP float, load DP float, store SP float, store DP float
MFC0, MTC0	Copy from/to GPR to/from a special register
MOV.S, MOV.D	Copy one SP or DP FP register to another FP register
MFC1, MTC1	Copy 32 bits to/from FP registers from/to integer registers
Arithmetic/logical	*Operations on integer or logical data in GPRs; signed arithmetic trap on overflow*
DADD, DADDI, DADDU, DADDIU	Add, add immediate (all immediates are 16 bits); signed and unsigned
DSUB, DSUBU	Subtract; signed and unsigned
DMUL, DMULU, DDIV, DDIVU, MADD	Multiply and divide, signed and unsigned; multiply-add; all operations take and yield 64-bit values
AND, ANDI	And, and immediate
OR, ORI, XOR, XORI	Or, or immediate, exclusive or, exclusive or immediate
LUI	Load upper immediate; loads bits 32 to 47 of register with immediate, then sign-extends
DSLL, DSRL, DSRA, DSLLV, DSRLV, DSRAV	Shifts: both immediate (DS__) and variable form (DS__V); shifts are shift left logical, right logical, right arithmetic
SLT, SLTI, SLTU, SLTIU	Set less than, set less than immediate; signed and unsigned
Control	*Conditional branches and jumps; PC-relative or through register*
BEQZ, BNEZ	Branch GPRs equal/not equal to zero; 16-bit offset from PC + 4
BEQ, BNE	Branch GPR equal/not equal; 16-bit offset from PC + 4
BC1T, BC1F	Test comparison bit in the FP status register and branch; 16-bit offset from PC + 4
MOVN, MOVZ	Copy GPR to another GPR if third GPR is negative, zero
J, JR	Jumps: 26-bit offset from PC + 4 (J) or target in register (JR)
JAL, JALR	Jump and link: save PC + 4 in R31, target is PC-relative (JAL) or a register (JALR)
TRAP	Transfer to operating system at a vectored address
ERET	Return to user code from an exception; restore user mode
Floating point	*FP operations on DP and SP formats*
ADD.D, ADD.S, ADD.PS	Add DP, SP numbers, and pairs of SP numbers
SUB.D, SUB.S, SUB.PS	Subtract DP, SP numbers, and pairs of SP numbers
MUL.D, MUL.S, MUL.PS	Multiply DP, SP floating point, and pairs of SP numbers
MADD.D, MADD.S, MADD.PS	Multiply-add DP, SP numbers, and pairs of SP numbers
DIV.D, DIV.S, DIV.PS	Divide DP, SP floating point, and pairs of SP numbers
CVT._._	Convert instructions: CVT.x.y converts from type x to type y, where x and y are L (64-bit integer), W (32-bit integer), D (DP), or S (SP). Both operands are FPRs.
C.__.D, C.__.S	DP and SP compares: "__" = LT,GT,LE,GE,EQ,NE; sets bit in FP status register

Figure 1.5 Subset of the instructions in MIPS64. SP = single precision; DP = double precision. Appendix B gives much more detail on MIPS64. For data, the most significant bit number is 0; least is 63.

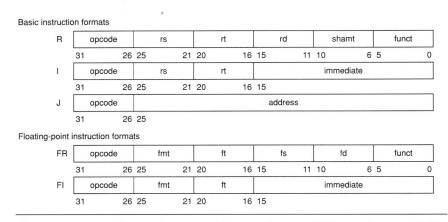

Figure 1.6 MIPS64 instruction set architecture formats. All instructions are 32 bits long. The R format is for integer register-to-register operations, such as DADDU, DSUBU, and so on. The I format is for data transfers, branches, and immediate instructions, such as LD, SD, BEQZ, and DADDIs. The J format is for jumps, the FR format for floating point operations, and the FI format for floating point branches.

The Rest of Computer Architecture: Designing the Organization and Hardware to Meet Goals and Functional Requirements

The implementation of a computer has two components: organization and hardware. The term *organization* includes the high-level aspects of a computer's design, such as the memory system, the memory interconnect, and the design of the internal processor or CPU (central processing unit—where arithmetic, logic, branching, and data transfer are implemented). For example, two processors with the same instruction set architectures but very different organizations are the AMD Opteron 64 and the Intel Pentium 4. Both processors implement the x86 instruction set, but they have very different pipeline and cache organizations.

Hardware refers to the specifics of a computer, including the detailed logic design and the packaging technology of the computer. Often a line of computers contains computers with identical instruction set architectures and nearly identical organizations, but they differ in the detailed hardware implementation. For example, the Pentium 4 and the Mobile Pentium 4 are nearly identical, but offer different clock rates and different memory systems, making the Mobile Pentium 4 more effective for low-end computers.

In this book, the word *architecture* covers all three aspects of computer design—instruction set architecture, organization, and hardware.

Computer architects must design a computer to meet functional requirements as well as price, power, performance, and availability goals. Figure 1.7 summarizes requirements to consider in designing a new computer. Often, architects

Functional requirements	Typical features required or supported
Application area	*Target of computer*
General-purpose desktop	Balanced performance for a range of tasks, including interactive performance for graphics, video, and audio (Ch. 2, 3, 5, App. B)
Scientific desktops and servers	High-performance floating point and graphics (App. I)
Commercial servers	Support for databases and transaction processing; enhancements for reliability and availability; support for scalability (Ch. 4, App. B, E)
Embedded computing	Often requires special support for graphics or video (or other application-specific extension); power limitations and power control may be required (Ch. 2, 3, 5, App. B)
Level of software compatibility	*Determines amount of existing software for computer*
At programming language	Most flexible for designer; need new compiler (Ch. 4, App. B)
Object code or binary compatible	Instruction set architecture is completely defined—little flexibility—but no investment needed in software or porting programs
Operating system requirements	*Necessary features to support chosen OS (Ch. 5, App. E)*
Size of address space	Very important feature (Ch. 5); may limit applications
Memory management	Required for modern OS; may be paged or segmented (Ch. 5)
Protection	Different OS and application needs: page vs. segment; virtual machines (Ch. 5)
Standards	*Certain standards may be required by marketplace*
Floating point	Format and arithmetic: IEEE 754 standard (App. I), special arithmetic for graphics or signal processing
I/O interfaces	For I/O devices: Serial ATA, Serial Attach SCSI, PCI Express (Ch. 6, App. E)
Operating systems	UNIX, Windows, Linux, CISCO IOS
Networks	Support required for different networks: Ethernet, Infiniband (App. E)
Programming languages	Languages (ANSI C, C++, Java, FORTRAN) affect instruction set (App. B)

Figure 1.7 Summary of some of the most important functional requirements an architect faces. The left-hand column describes the class of requirement, while the right-hand column gives specific examples. The right-hand column also contains references to chapters and appendices that deal with the specific issues.

also must determine what the functional requirements are, which can be a major task. The requirements may be specific features inspired by the market. Application software often drives the choice of certain functional requirements by determining how the computer will be used. If a large body of software exists for a certain instruction set architecture, the architect may decide that a new computer should implement an existing instruction set. The presence of a large market for a particular class of applications might encourage the designers to incorporate requirements that would make the computer competitive in that market. Many of these requirements and features are examined in depth in later chapters.

Architects must also be aware of important trends in both the technology and the use of computers, as such trends not only affect future cost, but also the longevity of an architecture.

Trends in Technology

If an instruction set architecture is to be successful, it must be designed to survive rapid changes in computer technology. After all, a successful new instruction set architecture may last decades—for example, the core of the IBM mainframe has been in use for more than 40 years. An architect must plan for technology changes that can increase the lifetime of a successful computer.

To plan for the evolution of a computer, the designer must be aware of rapid changes in implementation technology. Four implementation technologies, which change at a dramatic pace, are critical to modern implementations:

■ *Integrated circuit logic technology*—Transistor density increases by about 35% per year, quadrupling in somewhat over four years. Increases in die size are less predictable and slower, ranging from 10% to 20% per year. The combined effect is a growth rate in transistor count on a chip of about 40% to 55% per year. Device speed scales more slowly, as we discuss below.

■ *Semiconductor DRAM* (dynamic random-access memory)—Capacity increases by about 40% per year, doubling roughly every two years.

■ *Magnetic disk technology*—Prior to 1990, density increased by about 30% per year, doubling in three years. It rose to 60% per year thereafter, and increased to 100% per year in 1996. Since 2004, it has dropped back to 30% per year. Despite this roller coaster of rates of improvement, disks are still 50–100 times cheaper per bit than DRAM. This technology is central to Chapter 6, and we discuss the trends in detail there.

■ *Network technology*—Network performance depends both on the performance of switches and on the performance of the transmission system. We discuss the trends in networking in Appendix E.

These rapidly changing technologies shape the design of a computer that, with speed and technology enhancements, may have a lifetime of five or more years. Even within the span of a single product cycle for a computing system (two years of design and two to three years of production), key technologies such as DRAM change sufficiently that the designer must plan for these changes. Indeed, designers often design for the next technology, knowing that when a product begins shipping in volume that next technology may be the most cost-effective or may have performance advantages. Traditionally, cost has decreased at about the rate at which density increases.

Although technology improves continuously, the impact of these improvements can be in discrete leaps, as a threshold that allows a new capability is reached. For example, when MOS technology reached a point in the early 1980s where between 25,000 and 50,000 transistors could fit on a single chip, it became possible to build a single-chip, 32-bit microprocessor. By the late 1980s, first-level caches could go on chip. By eliminating chip crossings within the processor and between the processor and the cache, a dramatic improvement in cost-performance and power-performance was possible. This design was simply infeasible until the technology reached a certain point. Such technology thresholds are not rare and have a significant impact on a wide variety of design decisions.

Performance Trends: Bandwidth over Latency

As we shall see in Section 1.8, *bandwidth* or *throughput* is the total amount of work done in a given time, such as megabytes per second for a disk transfer. In contrast, *latency* or *response time* is the time between the start and the completion of an event, such as milliseconds for a disk access. Figure 1.8 plots the relative improvement in bandwidth and latency for technology milestones for microprocessors, memory, networks, and disks. Figure 1.9 describes the examples and milestones in more detail. Clearly, bandwidth improves much more rapidly than latency.

Performance is the primary differentiator for microprocessors and networks, so they have seen the greatest gains: 1000–2000X in bandwidth and 20–40X in latency. Capacity is generally more important than performance for memory and disks, so capacity has improved most, yet their bandwidth advances of 120–140X are still much greater than their gains in latency of 4–8X. Clearly, bandwidth has outpaced latency across these technologies and will likely continue to do so.

A simple rule of thumb is that bandwidth grows by at least the square of the improvement in latency. Computer designers should make plans accordingly.

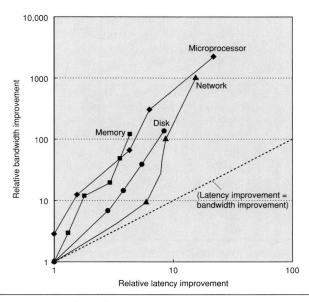

Figure 1.8 Log-log plot of bandwidth and latency milestones from Figure 1.9 relative to the first milestone. Note that latency improved about 10X while bandwidth improved about 100X to 1000X. From Patterson [2004].

Microprocessor	16-bit address/bus, microcoded	32-bit address.bus, microcoded	5-stage pipeline, on-chip I & D caches, FPU	2-way superscalar, 64-bit bus	Out-of-order 3-way superscalar	Out-of-order superpipelined, on-chip 1.2 cache
Product	Intel 80286	Intel 80386	Intel 80486	Intel Pentium	Intel Pentium Pro	Intel Pentium 4
Year	1982	1985	1989	1993	1997	2001
Die size (mm^2)	47	43	81	90	308	217
Transistors	134,000	275,000	1,200,000	3,100,000	5,500,000	42,000,000
Pins	68	132	168	273	387	423
Latency (clocks)	6	5	5	5	10	22
Bus width (bits)	16	32	32	64	64	64
Clock rate (MHz)	12.5	16	25	66	200	1500
Bandwidth (MIPS)	2	6	25	132	600	4500
Latency (ns)	320	313	200	76	50	15
Memory module	DRAM	Page mode DRAM	Fast page mode DRAM	Fast page mode DRAM	Synchronous DRAM	Double data rate SDRAM
Module width (bits)	16	16	32	64	64	64
Year	1980	1983	1986	1993	1997	2000
Mbits/DRAM chip	0.06	0.25	1	16	64	256
Die size (mm^2)	35	45	70	130	170	204
Pins/DRAM chip	16	16	18	20	54	66
Bandwidth (MBit/sec)	13	40	160	267	640	1600
Latency (ns)	225	170	125	75	62	52
Local area network	Ethernet	Fast Ethernet	Gigabit Ethernet	10 Gigabit Ethernet		
IEEE standard	802.3	803.3u	802.3ab	802.3ac		
Year	1978	1995	1999	2003		
Bandwidth (MBit/sec)	10	100	1000	10000		
Latency (μsec)	3000	500	340	190		
Hard disk	3600 RPM	5400 RPM	7200 RPM	10,000 RPM	15,000 RPM	
Product	CDC WrenI 94145-36	Seagate ST41600	Seagate ST15150	Seagate ST39102	Seagate ST373453	
Year	1983	1990	1994	1998	2003	
Capacity (GB)	0.03	1.4	4.3	9.1	73.4	
Disk form factor	5.25 inch	5.25 inch	3.5 inch	3.5 inch	3.5 inch	
Media diameter	5.25 inch	5.25 inch	3.5 inch	3.0 inch	2.5 inch	
Interface	ST-412	SCSI	SCSI	SCSI	SCSI	
Bandwidth (MBit/sec)	0.6	4	9	24	86	
Latency (ms)	48.3	17.1	12.7	8.8	5.7	

Figure 1.9 Performance milestones over 20 to 25 years for microprocessors, memory, networks, and disks. The microprocessor milestones are six generations of IA-32 processors, going from a 16-bit bus, microcoded 80286 to a 64-bit bus, superscalar, out-of-order execution, superpipelined Pentium 4. Memory module milestones go from 16-bit-wide, plain DRAM to 64-bit-wide double data rate synchronous DRAM. Ethernet advanced from 10 Mb/sec to 10 Gb/sec. Disk milestones are based on rotation speed, improving from 3600 RPM to 15,000 RPM. Each case is best-case bandwidth, and latency is the time for a simple operation assuming no contention. From Patterson [2004].

Scaling of Transistor Performance and Wires

Integrated circuit processes are characterized by the *feature size,* which is the minimum size of a transistor or a wire in either the x or y dimension. Feature sizes have decreased from 10 microns in 1971 to 0.09 microns in 2006; in fact, we have switched units, so production in 2006 is now referred to as "90 nanometers," and 65 nanometer chips are underway. Since the transistor count per square millimeter of silicon is determined by the surface area of a transistor, the density of transistors increases quadratically with a linear decrease in feature size.

The increase in transistor performance, however, is more complex. As feature sizes shrink, devices shrink quadratically in the horizontal dimension and also shrink in the vertical dimension. The shrink in the vertical dimension requires a reduction in operating voltage to maintain correct operation and reliability of the transistors. This combination of scaling factors leads to a complex interrelationship between transistor performance and process feature size. To a first approximation, transistor performance improves linearly with decreasing feature size.

The fact that transistor count improves quadratically with a linear improvement in transistor performance is both the challenge and the opportunity for which computer architects were created! In the early days of microprocessors, the higher rate of improvement in density was used to move quickly from 4-bit, to 8-bit, to 16-bit, to 32-bit microprocessors. More recently, density improvements have supported the introduction of 64-bit microprocessors as well as many of the innovations in pipelining and caches found in Chapters 2, 3, and 5.

Although transistors generally improve in performance with decreased feature size, wires in an integrated circuit do not. In particular, the signal delay for a wire increases in proportion to the product of its resistance and capacitance. Of course, as feature size shrinks, wires get shorter, but the resistance and capacitance per unit length get worse. This relationship is complex, since both resistance and capacitance depend on detailed aspects of the process, the geometry of a wire, the loading on a wire, and even the adjacency to other structures. There are occasional process enhancements, such as the introduction of copper, which provide one-time improvements in wire delay.

In general, however, wire delay scales poorly compared to transistor performance, creating additional challenges for the designer. In the past few years, wire delay has become a major design limitation for large integrated circuits and is often more critical than transistor switching delay. Larger and larger fractions of the clock cycle have been consumed by the propagation delay of signals on wires. In 2001, the Pentium 4 broke new ground by allocating 2 stages of its 20+-stage pipeline just for propagating signals across the chip.

1.5   Trends in Power in Integrated Circuits

Power also provides challenges as devices are scaled. First, power must be brought in and distributed around the chip, and modern microprocessors use hundreds of pins and multiple interconnect layers for just power and ground. Second, power is dissipated as heat and must be removed.

For CMOS chips, the traditional dominant energy consumption has been in switching transistors, also called *dynamic power*. The power required per transistor is proportional to the product of the load capacitance of the transistor, the square of the voltage, and the frequency of switching, with watts being the unit:

$$\text{Power}_{\text{dynamic}} = 1/2 \times \text{Capacitive load} \times \text{Voltage}^2 \times \text{Frequency switched}$$

Mobile devices care about battery life more than power, so energy is the proper metric, measured in joules:

$$\text{Energy}_{\text{dynamic}} = \text{Capacitive load} \times \text{Voltage}^2$$

Hence, dynamic power and energy are greatly reduced by lowering the voltage, and so voltages have dropped from 5V to just over 1V in 20 years. The capacitive load is a function of the number of transistors connected to an output and the technology, which determines the capacitance of the wires and the transistors. For a fixed task, slowing clock rate reduces power, but not energy.

Example   Some microprocessors today are designed to have adjustable voltage, so that a 15% reduction in voltage may result in a 15% reduction in frequency. What would be the impact on dynamic power?

Answer   Since the capacitance is unchanged, the answer is the ratios of the voltages and frequencies:

$$\frac{\text{Power}_{\text{new}}}{\text{Power}_{\text{old}}} = \frac{(\text{Voltage} \times 0.85)^2 \times (\text{Frequency switched} \times 0.85)}{\text{Voltage}^2 \times \text{Frequency switched}} = 0.85^3 = 0.61$$

thereby reducing power to about 60% of the original.

As we move from one process to the next, the increase in the number of transistors switching, and the frequency with which they switch, dominates the decrease in load capacitance and voltage, leading to an overall growth in power consumption and energy. The first microprocessors consumed tenths of a watt, while a 3.2 GHz Pentium 4 Extreme Edition consumes 135 watts. Given that this heat must be dissipated from a chip that is about 1 cm on a side, we are reaching the limits of what can be cooled by air. Several Intel microprocessors have temperature diodes to reduce activity automatically if the chip gets too hot. For example, they may reduce voltage and clock frequency or the instruction issue rate.

Distributing the power, removing the heat, and preventing hot spots have become increasingly difficult challenges. Power is now the major limitation to using transistors; in the past it was raw silicon area. As a result of this limitation, most microprocessors today turn off the clock of inactive modules to save energy and dynamic power. For example, if no floating-point instructions are executing, the clock of the floating-point unit is disabled.

Although dynamic power is the primary source of power dissipation in CMOS, static power is becoming an important issue because leakage current flows even when a transistor is off:

$$\text{Power}_{\text{static}} = \text{Current}_{\text{static}} \times \text{Voltage}$$

Thus, increasing the number of transistors increases power even if they are turned off, and leakage current increases in processors with smaller transistor sizes. As a result, very low power systems are even gating the voltage to inactive modules to control loss due to leakage. In 2006, the goal for leakage is 25% of the total power consumption, with leakage in high-performance designs sometimes far exceeding that goal. As mentioned before, the limits of air cooling have led to exploration of multiple processors on a chip running at lower voltages and clock rates.

1.6   Trends in Cost

Although there are computer designs where costs tend to be less important—specifically supercomputers—cost-sensitive designs are of growing significance. Indeed, in the past 20 years, the use of technology improvements to lower cost, as well as increase performance, has been a major theme in the computer industry.

Textbooks often ignore the cost half of cost-performance because costs change, thereby dating books, and because the issues are subtle and differ across industry segments. Yet an understanding of cost and its factors is essential for designers to make intelligent decisions about whether or not a new feature should be included in designs where cost is an issue. (Imagine architects designing skyscrapers without any information on costs of steel beams and concrete!)

This section discusses the major factors that influence the cost of a computer and how these factors are changing over time.

The Impact of Time, Volume, and Commodification

The cost of a manufactured computer component decreases over time even without major improvements in the basic implementation technology. The underlying principle that drives costs down is the *learning curve*—manufacturing costs decrease over time. The learning curve itself is best measured by change in *yield*—the percentage of manufactured devices that survives the testing procedure. Whether it is a chip, a board, or a system, designs that have twice the yield will have half the cost.

Understanding how the learning curve improves yield is critical to projecting costs over a product's life. One example is that the price per megabyte of DRAM has dropped over the long term by 40% per year. Since DRAMs tend to be priced in close relationship to cost—with the exception of periods when there is a shortage or an oversupply—price and cost of DRAM track closely.

Microprocessor prices also drop over time, but because they are less standardized than DRAMs, the relationship between price and cost is more complex. In a period of significant competition, price tends to track cost closely, although microprocessor vendors probably rarely sell at a loss. Figure 1.10 shows processor price trends for Intel microprocessors.

Volume is a second key factor in determining cost. Increasing volumes affect cost in several ways. First, they decrease the time needed to get down the learning curve, which is partly proportional to the number of systems (or chips) manufactured. Second, volume decreases cost, since it increases purchasing and manufacturing efficiency. As a rule of thumb, some designers have estimated that cost decreases about 10% for each doubling of volume. Moreover, volume decreases the amount of development cost that must be amortized by each computer, thus allowing cost and selling price to be closer.

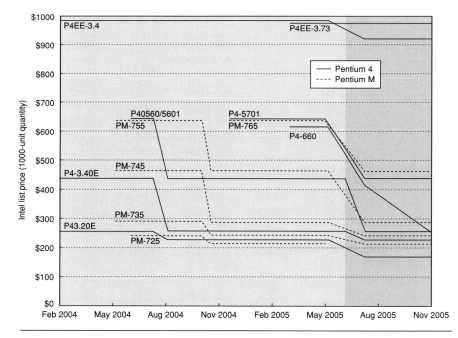

Figure 1.10 The price of an Intel Pentium 4 and Pentium M at a given frequency decreases over time as yield enhancements decrease the cost of a good die and competition forces price reductions. The most recent introductions will continue to decrease until they reach similar prices to the lowest-cost parts available today ($200). Such price decreases assume a competitive environment where price decreases track cost decreases closely. Data courtesy of *Microprocessor Report,* May 2005.

Commodities are products that are sold by multiple vendors in large volumes and are essentially identical. Virtually all the products sold on the shelves of grocery stores are commodities, as are standard DRAMs, disks, monitors, and keyboards. In the past 15 years, much of the low end of the computer business has become a commodity business focused on building desktop and laptop computers running Microsoft Windows.

Because many vendors ship virtually identical products, it is highly competitive. Of course, this competition decreases the gap between cost and selling price, but it also decreases cost. Reductions occur because a commodity market has both volume and a clear product definition, which allows multiple suppliers to compete in building components for the commodity product. As a result, the overall product cost is lower because of the competition among the suppliers of the components and the volume efficiencies the suppliers can achieve. This has led to the low end of the computer business being able to achieve better price-performance than other sectors and yielded greater growth at the low end, although with very limited profits (as is typical in any commodity business).

Cost of an Integrated Circuit

Why would a computer architecture book have a section on integrated circuit costs? In an increasingly competitive computer marketplace where standard parts—disks, DRAMs, and so on—are becoming a significant portion of any system's cost, integrated circuit costs are becoming a greater portion of the cost that varies between computers, especially in the high-volume, cost-sensitive portion of the market. Thus, computer designers must understand the costs of chips to understand the costs of current computers.

Although the costs of integrated circuits have dropped exponentially, the basic process of silicon manufacture is unchanged: A *wafer* is still tested and chopped into *dies* that are packaged (see Figures 1.11 and 1.12). Thus the cost of a packaged integrated circuit is

$$\text{Cost of integrated circuit} = \frac{\text{Cost of die} + \text{Cost of testing die} + \text{Cost of packaging and final test}}{\text{Final test yield}}$$

In this section, we focus on the cost of dies, summarizing the key issues in testing and packaging at the end.

Learning how to predict the number of good chips per wafer requires first learning how many dies fit on a wafer and then learning how to predict the percentage of those that will work. From there it is simple to predict cost:

$$\text{Cost of die} = \frac{\text{Cost of wafer}}{\text{Dies per wafer} \times \text{Die yield}}$$

The most interesting feature of this first term of the chip cost equation is its sensitivity to die size, shown below.

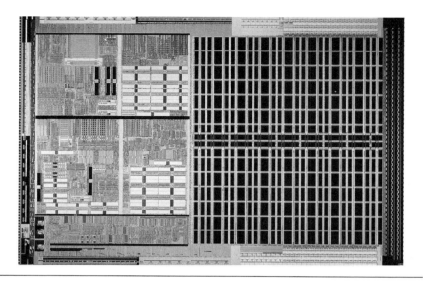

Figure 1.11 Photograph of an AMD Opteron microprocessor die. (Courtesy AMD.)

The number of dies per wafer is approximately the area of the wafer divided by the area of the die. It can be more accurately estimated by

$$\text{Dies per wafer} = \frac{\pi \times (\text{Wafer diameter}/2)^2}{\text{Die area}} - \frac{\pi \times \text{Wafer diameter}}{\sqrt{2} \times \text{Die area}}$$

The first term is the ratio of wafer area (πr^2) to die area. The second compensates for the "square peg in a round hole" problem—rectangular dies near the periphery of round wafers. Dividing the circumference (πd) by the diagonal of a square die is approximately the number of dies along the edge.

Example   Find the number of dies per 300 mm (30 cm) wafer for a die that is 1.5 cm on a side.

Answer   The die area is 2.25 cm². Thus

$$\text{Dies per wafer} = \frac{\pi \times (30/2)^2}{2.25} - \frac{\pi \times 30}{\sqrt{2 \times 2.25}} = \frac{706.9}{2.25} - \frac{94.2}{2.12} = 270$$

However, this only gives the maximum number of dies per wafer. The critical question is: What is the fraction of good dies on a wafer number, or the *die yield*? A simple model of integrated circuit yield, which assumes that defects are randomly distributed over the wafer and that yield is inversely proportional to the complexity of the fabrication process, leads to the following:

$$\text{Die yield} = \text{Wafer yield} \times \left(1 + \frac{\text{Defects per unit area} \times \text{Die area}}{\alpha}\right)^{-\alpha}$$

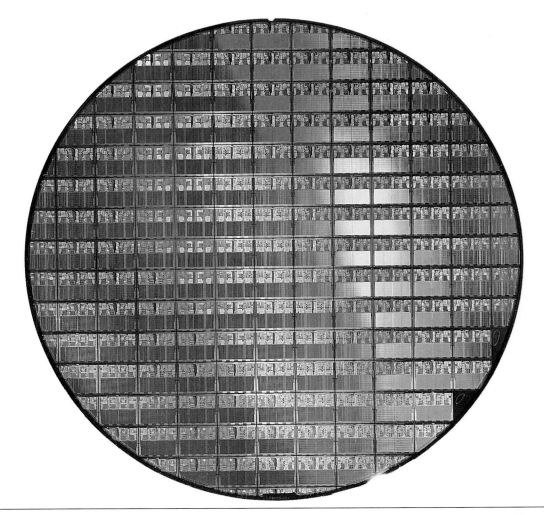

Figure 1.12 This 300mm wafer contains 117 AMD Opteron chips implemented in a 90 nm process. (Courtesy AMD.)

The formula is an empirical model developed by looking at the yield of many manufacturing lines. *Wafer yield* accounts for wafers that are completely bad and so need not be tested. For simplicity, we'll just assume the wafer yield is 100%. Defects per unit area is a measure of the random manufacturing defects that occur. In 2006, these value is typically 0.4 defects per square centimeter for 90 nm, as it depends on the maturity of the process (recall the learning curve, mentioned earlier). Lastly, α is a parameter that corresponds roughly to the number of critical masking levels, a measure of manufacturing complexity. For multilevel metal CMOS processes in 2006, a good estimate is $\alpha = 4.0$.

Example   Find the die yield for dies that are 1.5 cm on a side and 1.0 cm on a side, assuming a defect density of 0.4 per cm^2 and α is 4.

Answer   The total die areas are 2.25 cm^2 and 1.00 cm^2. For the larger die, the yield is

$$\text{Die yield} = \left(1 + \frac{0.4 \times 2.25}{4.0}\right)^{-4} = 0.44$$

For the smaller die, it is $\text{Die yield} = \left(1 + \frac{0.4 \times 1.00}{4.0}\right)^{-4} = 0.68$

That is, less than half of all the large die are good but more than two-thirds of the small die are good.

The bottom line is the number of good dies per wafer, which comes from multiplying dies per wafer by die yield to incorporate the effects of defects. The examples above predict about 120 good 2.25 cm^2 dies from the 300 mm wafer and 435 good 1.00 cm^2 dies. Many 32-bit and 64-bit microprocessors in a modern 90 nm technology fall between these two sizes. Low-end embedded 32-bit processors are sometimes as small as 0.25 cm^2, and processors used for embedded control (in printers, automobiles, etc.) are often less than 0.1 cm^2.

Given the tremendous price pressures on commodity products such as DRAM and SRAM, designers have included redundancy as a way to raise yield. For a number of years, DRAMs have regularly included some redundant memory cells, so that a certain number of flaws can be accommodated. Designers have used similar techniques in both standard SRAMs and in large SRAM arrays used for caches within microprocessors. Obviously, the presence of redundant entries can be used to boost the yield significantly.

Processing of a 300 mm (12-inch) diameter wafer in a leading-edge technology costs between $5000 and $6000 in 2006. Assuming a processed wafer cost of $5500, the cost of the 1.00 cm^2 die would be around $13, but the cost per die of the 2.25 cm^2 die would be about $46, or almost four times the cost for a die that is a little over twice as large.

What should a computer designer remember about chip costs? The manufacturing process dictates the wafer cost, wafer yield, and defects per unit area, so the sole control of the designer is die area. In practice, because the number of defects per unit area is small, the number of good dies per wafer, and hence the cost per die, grows roughly as the square of the die area. The computer designer affects die size, and hence cost, both by what functions are included on or excluded from the die and by the number of I/O pins.

Before we have a part that is ready for use in a computer, the die must be tested (to separate the good dies from the bad), packaged, and tested again after packaging. These steps all add significant costs.

The above analysis has focused on the variable costs of producing a functional die, which is appropriate for high-volume integrated circuits. There is, however, one very important part of the fixed cost that can significantly affect the cost of an integrated circuit for low volumes (less than 1 million parts), namely, the cost of a mask set. Each step in the integrated circuit process requires a separate mask. Thus, for modern high-density fabrication processes with four to six metal layers, mask costs exceed $1 million. Obviously, this large fixed cost affects the cost of prototyping and debugging runs and, for small-volume production, can be a significant part of the production cost. Since mask costs are likely to continue to increase, designers may incorporate reconfigurable logic to enhance the flexibility of a part, or choose to use gate arrays (which have fewer custom mask levels) and thus reduce the cost implications of masks.

Cost versus Price

With the commoditization of the computers, the margin between the cost to the manufacture a product and the price the product sells for has been shrinking. Those margins pay for a company's research and development (R&D), marketing, sales, manufacturing equipment maintenance, building rental, cost of financing, pretax profits, and taxes. Many engineers are surprised to find that most companies spend only 4% (in the commodity PC business) to 12% (in the high-end server business) of their income on R&D, which includes all engineering.

1.7   Dependability

Historically, integrated circuits were one of the most reliable components of a computer. Although their pins may be vulnerable, and faults may occur over communication channels, the error rate inside the chip was very low. That conventional wisdom is changing as we head to feature sizes of 65 nm and smaller, as both transient faults and permanent faults will become more commonplace, so architects must design systems to cope with these challenges. This section gives an quick overview of the issues in dependability, leaving the official definition of the terms and approaches to Section 6.3.

Computers are designed and constructed at different layers of abstraction. We can descend recursively down through a computer seeing components enlarge themselves to full subsystems until we run into individual transistors. Although some faults are widespread, like the loss of power, many can be limited to a single component in a module. Thus, utter failure of a module at one level may be considered merely a component error in a higher-level module. This distinction is helpful in trying to find ways to build dependable computers.

One difficult question is deciding when a system is operating properly. This philosophical point became concrete with the popularity of Internet services. Infrastructure providers started offering *Service Level Agreements* (SLA) or *Service Level Objectives* (SLO) to guarantee that their networking or power service would be dependable. For example, they would pay the customer a penalty if they did not meet an agreement more than some hours per month. Thus, an SLA could be used to decide whether the system was up or down.

Systems alternate between two states of service with respect to an SLA:

1. *Service accomplishment,* where the service is delivered as specified
2. *Service interruption,* where the delivered service is different from the SLA

Transitions between these two states are caused by *failures* (from state 1 to state 2) or *restorations* (2 to 1). Quantifying these transitions leads to the two main measures of dependability:

▪ *Module reliability* is a measure of the continuous service accomplishment (or, equivalently, of the time to failure) from a reference initial instant. Hence, the *mean time to failure* (MTTF) is a reliability measure. The reciprocal of MTTF is a rate of failures, generally reported as failures per billion hours of operation, or *FIT* (for *failures in time*).Thus, an MTTF of 1,000,000 hours equals $10^9/10^6$ or 1000 FIT. Service interruption is measured as *mean time to repair* (MTTR). *Mean time between failures* (MTBF) is simply the sum of MTTF + MTTR. Although MTBF is widely used, MTTF is often the more appropriate term. If a collection of modules have exponentially distributed lifetimes—meaning that the age of a module is not important in probability of failure—the overall failure rate of the collection is the sum of the failure rates of the modules.

▪ *Module availability* is a measure of the service accomplishment with respect to the alternation between the two states of accomplishment and interruption. For nonredundant systems with repair, module availability is

$$\text{Module availability} = \frac{\text{MTTF}}{(\text{MTTF} + \text{MTTR})}$$

Note that reliability and availability are now quantifiable metrics, rather than synonyms for dependability. From these definitions, we can estimate reliability of a system quantitatively if we make some assumptions about the reliability of components and that failures are independent.

Example   Assume a disk subsystem with the following components and MTTF:

▪ 10 disks, each rated at 1,000,000-hour MTTF
▪ 1 SCSI controller, 500,000-hour MTTF
▪ 1 power supply, 200,000-hour MTTF
▪ 1 fan, 200,000-hour MTTF
▪ 1 SCSI cable, 1,000,000-hour MTTF

Using the simplifying assumptions that the lifetimes are exponentially distributed and that failures are independent, compute the MTTF of the system as a whole.

Answer   The sum of the failure rates is

$$\text{Failure rate}_{\text{system}} = 10 \times \frac{1}{1,000,000} + \frac{1}{500,000} + \frac{1}{200,000} + \frac{1}{200,000} + \frac{1}{1,000,000}$$

$$= \frac{10 + 2 + 5 + 5 + 1}{1,000,000 \text{ hours}} = \frac{23}{1,000,000} = \frac{23,000}{1,000,000,000 \text{ hours}}$$

or 23,000 FIT. The MTTF for the system is just the inverse of the failure rate:

$$\text{MTTF}_{\text{system}} = \frac{1}{\text{Failure rate}_{\text{system}}} = \frac{1,000,000,000 \text{ hours}}{23,000} = 43,500 \text{ hours}$$

or just under 5 years.

The primary way to cope with failure is redundancy, either in time (repeat the operation to see if it still is erroneous) or in resources (have other components to take over from the one that failed). Once the component is replaced and the system fully repaired, the dependability of the system is assumed to be as good as new. Let's quantify the benefits of redundancy with an example.

Example   Disk subsystems often have redundant power supplies to improve dependability. Using the components and MTTFs from above, calculate the reliability of a redundant power supply. Assume one power supply is sufficient to run the disk subsystem and that we are adding one redundant power supply.

Answer   We need a formula to show what to expect when we can tolerate a failure and still provide service. To simplify the calculations, we assume that the lifetimes of the components are exponentially distributed and that there is no dependency between the component failures. MTTF for our redundant power supplies is the mean time until one power supply fails divided by the chance that the other will fail before the first one is replaced. Thus, if the chance of a second failure before repair is small, then MTTF of the pair is large.

Since we have two power supplies and independent failures, the mean time until one disk fails is $\text{MTTF}_{\text{power supply}} / 2$. A good approximation of the probability of a second failure is MTTR over the mean time until the other power supply fails. Hence, a reasonable approximation for a redundant pair of power supplies is

$$\text{MTTF}_{\text{power supply pair}} = \frac{\text{MTTF}_{\text{power supply}}/2}{\dfrac{\text{MTTR}_{\text{power supply}}}{\text{MTTF}_{\text{power supply}}}} = \frac{\text{MTTF}^2_{\text{power supply}}/2}{\text{MTTR}_{\text{power supply}}} = \frac{\text{MTTF}^2_{\text{power supply}}}{2 \times \text{MTTR}_{\text{power supply}}}$$

Using the MTTF numbers above, if we assume it takes on average 24 hours for a human operator to notice that a power supply has failed and replace it, the reliability of the fault tolerant pair of power supplies is

$$\text{MTTF}_{\text{power supply pair}} = \frac{\text{MTTF}^2_{\text{power supply}}}{2 \times \text{MTTR}_{\text{power supply}}} = \frac{200,000^2}{2 \times 24} \cong 830,000,000$$

making the pair about 4150 times more reliable than a single power supply.

Having quantified the cost, power, and dependability of computer technology, we are ready to quantify performance.

Measuring, Reporting, and Summarizing Performance

When we say one computer is faster than another is, what do we mean? The user of a desktop computer may say a computer is faster when a program runs in less time, while an Amazon.com administrator may say a computer is faster when it completes more transactions per hour. The computer user is interested in reducing *response time*—the time between the start and the completion of an event— also referred to as *execution time*. The administrator of a large data processing center may be interested in increasing *throughput*—the total amount of work done in a given time.

In comparing design alternatives, we often want to relate the performance of two different computers, say, X and Y. The phrase "X is faster than Y" is used here to mean that the response time or execution time is lower on X than on Y for the given task. In particular, "X is *n* times faster than Y" will mean

$$\frac{\text{Execution time}_Y}{\text{Execution time}_X} = n$$

Since execution time is the reciprocal of performance, the following relationship holds:

$$n = \frac{\text{Execution time}_Y}{\text{Execution time}_X} = \frac{\dfrac{1}{\text{Performance}_Y}}{\dfrac{1}{\text{Performance}_X}} = \frac{\text{Performance}_X}{\text{Performance}_Y}$$

The phrase "the throughput of X is 1.3 times higher than Y" signifies here that the number of tasks completed per unit time on computer X is 1.3 times the number completed on Y.

Unfortunately, time is not always the metric quoted in comparing the performance of computers. Our position is that the only consistent and reliable measure of performance is the execution time of real programs, and that all proposed alternatives to time as the metric or to real programs as the items measured have eventually led to misleading claims or even mistakes in computer design.

Even execution time can be defined in different ways depending on what we count. The most straightforward definition of time is called *wall-clock time, response time,* or *elapsed time,* which is the latency to complete a task, including disk accesses, memory accesses, input/output activities, operating system over-head—everything. With multiprogramming, the processor works on another program while waiting for I/O and may not necessarily minimize the elapsed time of one program. Hence, we need a term to consider this activity. *CPU time* recognizes this distinction and means the time the processor is computing, *not* including the time waiting for I/O or running other programs. (Clearly, the response time seen by the user is the elapsed time of the program, not the CPU time.)

Computer users who routinely run the same programs would be the perfect candidates to evaluate a new computer. To evaluate a new system the users would simply compare the execution time of their *workloads*—the mixture of programs and operating system commands that users run on a computer. Few are in this happy situation, however. Most must rely on other methods to evaluate computers, and often other evaluators, hoping that these methods will predict performance for their usage of the new computer.

Benchmarks

The best choice of benchmarks to measure performance are real applications, such as a compiler. Attempts at running programs that are much simpler than a real application have led to performance pitfalls. Examples include

- *kernels*, which are small, key pieces of real applications;
- *toy programs*, which are 100-line programs from beginning programming assignments, such as quicksort; and
- *synthetic benchmarks*, which are fake programs invented to try to match the profile and behavior of real applications, such as Dhrystone.

All three are discredited today, usually because the compiler writer and architect can conspire to make the computer appear faster on these stand-in programs than on real applications.

Another issue is the conditions under which the benchmarks are run. One way to improve the performance of a benchmark has been with benchmark-specific flags; these flags often caused transformations that would be illegal on many programs or would slow down performance on others. To restrict this process and increase the significance of the results, benchmark developers often require the vendor to use one compiler and one set of flags for all the programs in the same language (C or FORTRAN). In addition to the question of compiler flags, another question is whether source code modifications are allowed. There are three different approaches to addressing this question:

1. No source code modifications are allowed.
2. Source code modifications are allowed, but are essentially impossible. For example, database benchmarks rely on standard database programs that are tens of millions of lines of code. The database companies are highly unlikely to make changes to enhance the performance for one particular computer.
3. Source modifications are allowed, as long as the modified version produces the same output.

The key issue that benchmark designers face in deciding to allow modification of the source is whether such modifications will reflect real practice and provide useful insight to users, or whether such modifications simply reduce the accuracy of the benchmarks as predictors of real performance.

To overcome the danger of placing too many eggs in one basket, collections of benchmark applications, called *benchmark suites*, are a popular measure of performance of processors with a variety of applications. Of course, such suites are only as good as the constituent individual benchmarks. Nonetheless, a key advantage of such suites is that the weakness of any one benchmark is lessened by the presence of the other benchmarks. The goal of a benchmark suite is that it will characterize the relative performance of two computers, particularly for programs not in the suite that customers are likely to run.

As a cautionary example, the EDN Embedded Microprocessor Benchmark Consortium (or EEMBC, pronounced "embassy") is a set of 41 kernels used to predict performance of different embedded applications: automotive/industrial, consumer, networking, office automation, and telecommunications. EEMBC reports unmodified performance and "full fury" performance, where almost anything goes. Because they use kernels, and because of the reporting options, EEMBC does not have the reputation of being a good predictor of relative performance of different embedded computers in the field. The synthetic program Dhrystone, which EEMBC was trying to replace, is still reported in some embedded circles.

One of the most successful attempts to create standardized benchmark application suites has been the SPEC (Standard Performance Evaluation Corporation), which had its roots in the late 1980s efforts to deliver better benchmarks for workstations. Just as the computer industry has evolved over time, so has the need for different benchmark suites, and there are now SPEC benchmarks to cover different application classes. All the SPEC benchmark suites and their reported results are found at *www.spec.org*.

Although we focus our discussion on the SPEC benchmarks in many of the following sections, there are also many benchmarks developed for PCs running the Windows operating system.

Desktop Benchmarks

Desktop benchmarks divide into two broad classes: processor-intensive benchmarks and graphics-intensive benchmarks, although many graphics benchmarks include intensive processor activity. SPEC originally created a benchmark set focusing on processor performance (initially called SPEC89), which has evolved into its fifth generation: SPEC CPU2006, which follows SPEC2000, SPEC95 SPEC92, and SPEC89. SPEC CPU2006 consists of a set of 12 integer benchmarks (CINT2006) and 17 floating-point benchmarks (CFP2006). Figure 1.13 describes the current SPEC benchmarks and their ancestry.

SPEC benchmarks are real programs modified to be portable and to minimize the effect of I/O on performance. The integer benchmarks vary from part of a C compiler to a chess program to a quantum computer simulation. The floating-point benchmarks include structured grid codes for finite element modeling, par-

SPEC2006 benchmark description	SPEC2006	Benchmark name by SPEC generation			
		SPEC2000	SPEC95	SPEC92	SPEC89
GNU C compiler	←				gcc
Interpreted string processing	←		perl		espresso
Combinatorial optimization	←	mcf			li
Block-sorting compression	←	bzip2		compress	eqntott
Go game (AI)	go	vortex	go	sc	
Video compression	h264avc	gzip	ijpeg		
Games/path finding	astar	eon	m88ksim		
Search gene sequence	hmmer	twolf			
Quantum computer simulation	libquantum	vortex			
Discrete event simulation library	omnetpp	vpr			
Chess game (AI)	sjeng	crafty			
XML parsing	xalancbmk	parser			
CFD/blast waves	bwaves				fpppp
Numerical relativity	cactusADM				tomcatv
Finite element code	calculix				doduc
Differential equation solver framework	dealll				nasa7
Quantum chemistry	gamess				spice
EM solver (freq/time domain)	GemsFDTD			swim	matrix300
Scalable molecular dynamics (~NAMD)	gromacs		apsi	hydro2d	
Lattice Boltzman method (fluid/air flow)	lbm		mgrid	su2cor	
Large eddie simulation/turbulent CFD	LESlie3d	wupwise	applu	wave5	
Lattice quantum chromodynamics	milc	apply	turb3d		
Molecular dynamics	namd	galgel			
Image ray tracing	povray	mesa			
Spare linear algebra	soplex	art			
Speech recognition	sphinx3	equake			
Quantum chemistry/object oriented	tonto	facerec			
Weather research and forecasting	wrf	ammp			
Magneto hydrodynamics (astrophysics)	zeusmp	lucas			
		fma3d			
		sixtrack			

Figure 1.13   SPEC2006 programs and the evolution of the SPEC benchmarks over time, with integer programs above the line and floating-point programs below the line. Of the 12 SPEC2006 integer programs, 9 are written in C, and the rest in C++. For the floating-point programs the split is 6 in FORTRAN, 4 in C++, 3 in C, and 4 in mixed C and Fortran. The figure shows all 70 of the programs in the 1989, 1992, 1995, 2000, and 2006 releases. The benchmark descriptions on the left are for SPEC2006 only and do not apply to earlier ones. Programs in the same row from different generations of SPEC are generally not related; for example, fpppp is not a CFD code like bwaves. Gcc is the senior citizen of the group. Only 3 integer programs and 3 floating-point programs survived three or more generations. Note that all the floating-point programs are new for SPEC2006. Although a few are carried over from generation to generation, the version of the program changes and either the input or the size of the benchmark is often changed to increase its running time and to avoid perturbation in measurement or domination of the execution time by some factor other than CPU time.

ticle method codes for molecular dynamics, and sparse linear algebra codes for fluid dynamics. The SPEC CPU suite is useful for processor benchmarking for both desktop systems and single-processor servers. We will see data on many of these programs throughout this text.

In Section 1.11, we describe pitfalls that have occurred in developing the SPEC benchmark suite, as well as the challenges in maintaining a useful and predictive benchmark suite. Although SPEC CPU2006 is aimed at processor performance, SPEC also has benchmarks for graphics and Java.

Server Benchmarks

Just as servers have multiple functions, so there are multiple types of benchmarks. The simplest benchmark is perhaps a processor throughput-oriented benchmark. SPEC CPU2000 uses the SPEC CPU benchmarks to construct a simple throughput benchmark where the processing rate of a multiprocessor can be measured by running multiple copies (usually as many as there are processors) of each SPEC CPU benchmark and converting the CPU time into a rate. This leads to a measurement called the SPECrate.

Other than SPECrate, most server applications and benchmarks have significant I/O activity arising from either disk or network traffic, including benchmarks for file server systems, for Web servers, and for database and transaction-processing systems. SPEC offers both a file server benchmark (SPECSFS) and a Web server benchmark (SPECWeb). SPECSFS is a benchmark for measuring NFS (Network File System) performance using a script of file server requests; it tests the performance of the I/O system (both disk and network I/O) as well as the processor. SPECSFS is a throughput-oriented benchmark but with important response time requirements. (Chapter 6 discusses some file and I/O system benchmarks in detail.) SPECWeb is a Web server benchmark that simulates multiple clients requesting both static and dynamic pages from a server, as well as clients posting data to the server.

Transaction-processing (TP) benchmarks measure the ability of a system to handle transactions, which consist of database accesses and updates. Airline reservation systems and bank ATM systems are typical simple examples of TP; more sophisticated TP systems involve complex databases and decision-making. In the mid-1980s, a group of concerned engineers formed the vendor-independent Transaction Processing Council (TPC) to try to create realistic and fair benchmarks for TP. The TPC benchmarks are described at *www.tpc.org*.

The first TPC benchmark, TPC-A, was published in 1985 and has since been replaced and enhanced by several different benchmarks. TPC-C, initially created in 1992, simulates a complex query environment. TPC-H models ad hoc decision support—the queries are unrelated and knowledge of past queries cannot be used to optimize future queries. TPC-W is a transactional Web benchmark. The workload is performed in a controlled Internet commerce environment that simulates the activities of a business-oriented transactional Web server. The most recent is TPC-App, an application server and Web services benchmark. The workload simulates the activities of a business-to-business transactional application server operating in a 24x7 environment.

All the TPC benchmarks measure performance in transactions per second. In addition, they include a response time requirement, so that throughput performance is measured only when the response time limit is met. To model real-world systems, higher transaction rates are also associated with larger systems, in terms of both users and the database to which the transactions are applied. Finally, the system cost for a benchmark system must also be included, allowing accurate comparisons of cost-performance.

Reporting Performance Results

The guiding principle of reporting performance measurements should be *reproducibility*—list everything another experimenter would need to duplicate the results. A SPEC benchmark report requires an extensive description of the computer and the compiler flags, as well as the publication of both the baseline and optimized results. In addition to hardware, software, and baseline tuning parameter descriptions, a SPEC report contains the actual performance times, shown both in tabular form and as a graph. A TPC benchmark report is even more complete, since it must include results of a benchmarking audit and cost information. These reports are excellent sources for finding the real cost of computing systems, since manufacturers compete on high performance and cost-performance.

Summarizing Performance Results

In practical computer design, you must evaluate myriads of design choices for their relative quantitative benefits across a suite of benchmarks believed to be relevant. Likewise, consumers trying to choose a computer will rely on performance measurements from benchmarks, which hopefully are similar to the user's applications. In both cases, it is useful to have measurements for a suite of benchmarks so that the performance of important applications is similar to that of one or more benchmarks in the suite and that variability in performance can be understood. In the ideal case, the suite resembles a statistically valid sample of the application space, but such a sample requires more benchmarks than are typically found in most suites and requires a randomized sampling, which essentially no benchmark suite uses.

Once we have chosen to measure performance with a benchmark suite, we would like to be able to summarize the performance results of the suite in a single number. A straightforward approach to computing a summary result would be to compare the arithmetic means of the execution times of the programs in the suite. Alas, some SPEC programs take four times longer than others, so those programs would be much more important if the arithmetic mean were the single number used to summarize performance. An alternative would be to add a weighting factor to each benchmark and use the weighted arithmetic mean as the single number to summarize performance. The problem would be then how to pick weights; since SPEC is a consortium of competing companies, each company might have their own favorite set of weights, which would make it hard to reach consensus. One approach is to use weights that make all programs execute an equal time on some reference computer, but this biases the results to the performance characteristics of the reference computer.

Rather than pick weights, we could normalize execution times to a reference computer by dividing the time on the reference computer by the time on the computer being rated, yielding a ratio proportional to performance. SPEC uses this approach, calling the ratio the SPECRatio. It has a particularly useful property that it matches the way we compare computer performance throughout this text—namely, comparing performance ratios. For example, suppose that the SPECRatio of computer A on a benchmark was 1.25 times higher than computer B; then you would know

$$1.25 = \frac{\text{SPECRatio}_A}{\text{SPECRatio}_B} = \frac{\dfrac{\text{Execution time}_{\text{reference}}}{\text{Execution time}_A}}{\dfrac{\text{Execution time}_{\text{reference}}}{\text{Execution time}_B}} = \frac{\text{Execution time}_B}{\text{Execution time}_A} = \frac{\text{Performance}_A}{\text{Performance}_B}$$

Notice that the execution times on the reference computer drop out and the choice of the reference computer is irrelevant when the comparisons are made as a ratio, which is the approach we consistently use. Figure 1.14 gives an example.

Because a SPECRatio is a ratio rather than an absolute execution time, the mean must be computed using the *geometric* mean. (Since SPECRatios have no units, comparing SPECRatios arithmetically is meaningless.) The formula is

$$\text{Geometric mean} = \sqrt[n]{\prod_{i=1}^{n} sample_i}$$

In the case of SPEC, $sample_i$ is the SPECRatio for program i. Using the geometric mean ensures two important properties:

1. The geometric mean of the ratios is the same as the ratio of the geometric means.

2. The ratio of the geometric means is equal to the geometric mean of the performance ratios, which implies that the choice of the reference computer is irrelevant.

Hence, the motivations to use the geometric mean are substantial, especially when we use performance ratios to make comparisons.

Example   Show that the ratio of the geometric means is equal to the geometric mean of the performance ratios, and that the reference computer of SPECRatio matters not.

Benchmarks	Ultra 5 Time (sec)	Opteron Time (sec)	SPECRatio	Itanium 2 Time (sec)	SPECRatio	Opteron/Itanium Times (sec)	Itanium/Opteron SPECRatios
wupwise	1600	51.5	31.06	56.1	28.53	0.92	0.92
swim	3100	125.0	24.73	70.7	43.85	1.77	1.77
mgrid	1800	98.0	18.37	65.8	27.36	1.49	1.49
applu	2100	94.0	22.34	50.9	41.25	1.85	1.85
mesa	1400	64.6	21.69	108.0	12.99	0.60	0.60
galgel	2900	86.4	33.57	40.0	72.47	2.16	2.16
art	2600	92.4	28.13	21.0	123.67	4.40	4.40
equake	1300	72.6	17.92	36.3	35.78	2.00	2.00
facerec	1900	73.6	25.80	86.9	21.86	0.85	0.85
ammp	2200	136.0	16.14	132.0	16.63	1.03	1.03
lucas	2000	88.8	22.52	107.0	18.76	0.83	0.83
fma3d	2100	120.0	17.48	131.0	16.09	0.92	0.92
sixtrack	1100	123.0	8.95	68.8	15.99	1.79	1.79
apsi	2600	150.0	17.36	231.0	11.27	0.65	0.65
Geometric mean			20.86		27.12	1.30	1.30

Figure 1.14 SPECfp2000 execution times (in seconds) for the Sun Ultra 5—the reference computer of SPEC2000—and execution times and SPECRatios for the AMD Opteron and Intel Itanium 2. (SPEC2000 multiplies the ratio of execution times by 100 to remove the decimal point from the result, so 20.86 is reported as 2086.) The final two columns show the ratios of execution times and SPECratios. This figure demonstrates the irrelevance of the reference computer in relative performance. The ratio of the execution times is identical to the ratio of the SPECRatios, and the ratio of the geometric means (27.12/20.86 = 1.30) is identical to the geometric mean of the ratios (1.30).

Answer   Assume two computers A and B and a set of SPECRatios for each.

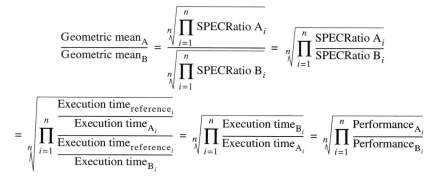

That is, the ratio of the geometric means of the SPECRatios of A and B is the geometric mean of the performance ratios of A to B of all the benchmarks in the suite. Figure 1.14 demonstrates the validity using examples from SPEC.

A key question is whether a single mean summarizes the performance of the programs in the benchmark suite well. If we characterize the variability of the distribution, using the standard deviation, we can decide whether the mean is likely to be a good predictor. The standard deviation is more informative if we know the distribution has one of several standard forms.

One useful possibility is the well-known bell-shaped *normal distribution*, whose sample data are, of course, symmetric around the mean. Another is the *lognormal distribution*, where the logarithms of the data—not the data itself—are normally distributed on a logarithmic scale, and thus symmetric on that scale. (On a linear scale, a lognormal is not symmetric, but has a long tail to the right.)

For example, if each of two systems is 10X faster than the other on two different benchmarks, the relative performance is the set of ratios {.1, 10}. However, the performance summary should be equal performance. That is, the average should be 1.0, which in fact is true on a logarithmic scale.

To characterize variability about the arithmetic mean, we use the arithmetic standard deviation (stdev), often called σ. It is defined as:

$$ \text{stdev} = \sqrt{\sum_{i=1}^{n}(sample_i - \text{Mean})^2} $$

Like the geometric mean, the geometric standard deviation is multiplicative rather than additive. For working with the geometric mean and the geometric standard deviation, we can simply take the natural logarithm of the samples, compute the standard mean and standard deviation, and then take the exponent to convert back. This insight allows us to describe the multiplicative versions of mean and standard deviation (gstdev), also often called σ, as

$$ \text{Geometric mean} = \exp\left(\frac{1}{n} \times \sum_{i=1}^{n} \ln(sample_i)\right) $$

$$ \text{gstdev} = \exp\left(\sqrt{\frac{\sum_{i=1}^{n}(\ln(sample_i) - \ln(\text{Geometric mean}))^2}{n}}\right) $$

Note that functions provided in a modern spreadsheet program, like EXP( ) and LN( ), make it easy to calculate the geometric mean and the geometric standard deviation.

For a lognormal distribution, we expect that 68% of the samples fall in the range [Mean / gstdev, Mean × gstdev], 95% within [Mean / gstdev^2, Mean × gstdev^2], and so on.

Example Using the data in Figure 1.14, calculate the geometric standard deviation and the percentage of the results that fall within a single standard deviation of the geometric mean. Are the results compatible with a lognormal distribution?

Answer The geometric means are 20.86 for Opteron and 27.12 for Itanium 2. As you might guess from the SPECRatios, the standard deviation for the Itanium 2 is much higher—1.93 versus 1.38—indicating that the results will differ more widely from the mean, and therefore are likely less predictable. The single standard deviation range is [27.12 / 1.93, 27.12 × 1.93] or [14.06, 52.30] for Itanium 2 and [20.86 / 1.38, 20.86 × 1.38] or [15.12, 28.76] for Opteron. For Itanium 2, 10 of 14 benchmarks (71%) fall within one standard deviation; for Opteron, it is 11 of 14 (78%). Thus, both results are quite compatible with a lognormal distribution.

1.9 Quantitative Principles of Computer Design

Now that we have seen how to define, measure, and summarize performance, cost, dependability, and power, we can explore guidelines and principles that are useful in the design and analysis of computers. This section introduces important observations about design, as well as two equations to evaluate alternatives.

Take Advantage of Parallelism

Taking advantage of parallelism is one of the most important methods for improving performance. Every chapter in this book has an example of how performance is enhanced through the exploitation of parallelism. We give three brief examples, which are expounded on in later chapters.

Our first example is the use of parallelism at the system level. To improve the throughput performance on a typical server benchmark, such as SPECWeb or TPC-C, multiple processors and multiple disks can be used. The workload of handling requests can then be spread among the processors and disks, resulting in improved throughput. Being able to expand memory and the number of processors and disks is called *scalability*, and it is a valuable asset for servers.

At the level of an individual processor, taking advantage of parallelism among instructions is critical to achieving high performance. One of the simplest ways to do this is through pipelining. The basic idea behind pipelining, which is explained in more detail in Appendix A and is a major focus of Chapter 2, is to overlap instruction execution to reduce the total time to complete an instruction sequence. A key insight that allows pipelining to work is that not every instruction depends on its immediate predecessor, and thus, executing the instructions completely or partially in parallel may be possible.

Parallelism can also be exploited at the level of detailed digital design. For example, set-associative caches use multiple banks of memory that are typically searched in parallel to find a desired item. Modern ALUs use carry-lookahead, which uses parallelism to speed the process of computing sums from linear to logarithmic in the number of bits per operand.

Principle of Locality

Important fundamental observations have come from properties of programs. The most important program property that we regularly exploit is the *principle of locality:* Programs tend to reuse data and instructions they have used recently. A widely held rule of thumb is that a program spends 90% of its execution time in only 10% of the code. An implication of locality is that we can predict with reasonable accuracy what instructions and data a program will use in the near future based on its accesses in the recent past. The principle of locality also applies to data accesses, though not as strongly as to code accesses.

Two different types of locality have been observed. *Temporal locality* states that recently accessed items are likely to be accessed in the near future. *Spatial locality* says that items whose addresses are near one another tend to be referenced close together in time. We will see these principles applied in Chapter 5.

Focus on the Common Case

Perhaps the most important and pervasive principle of computer design is to focus on the common case: In making a design trade-off, favor the frequent case over the infrequent case. This principle applies when determining how to spend resources, since the impact of the improvement is higher if the occurrence is frequent.

Focusing on the common case works for power as well as for resource allocation and performance. The instruction fetch and decode unit of a processor may be used much more frequently than a multiplier, so optimize it first. It works on dependability as well. If a database server has 50 disks for every processor, as in the next section, storage dependability will dominate system dependability.

In addition, the frequent case is often simpler and can be done faster than the infrequent case. For example, when adding two numbers in the processor, we can expect overflow to be a rare circumstance and can therefore improve performance by optimizing the more common case of no overflow. This may slow down the case when overflow occurs, but if that is rare, then overall performance will be improved by optimizing for the normal case.

We will see many cases of this principle throughout this text. In applying this simple principle, we have to decide what the frequent case is and how much performance can be improved by making that case faster. A fundamental law, called *Amdahl's Law,* can be used to quantify this principle.

Amdahl's Law

The performance gain that can be obtained by improving some portion of a computer can be calculated using Amdahl's Law. Amdahl's Law states that the performance improvement to be gained from using some faster mode of execution is limited by the fraction of the time the faster mode can be used.

Amdahl's Law defines the *speedup* that can be gained by using a particular feature. What is speedup? Suppose that we can make an enhancement to a computer that will improve performance when it is used. Speedup is the ratio

$$\text{Speedup} = \frac{\text{Performance for entire task using the enhancement when possible}}{\text{Performance for entire task without using the enhancement}}$$

Alternatively,

$$\text{Speedup} = \frac{\text{Execution time for entire task without using the enhancement}}{\text{Execution time for entire task using the enhancement when possible}}$$

Speedup tells us how much faster a task will run using the computer with the enhancement as opposed to the original computer.

Amdahl's Law gives us a quick way to find the speedup from some enhancement, which depends on two factors:

1. *The fraction of the computation time in the original computer that can be converted to take advantage of the enhancement*—For example, if 20 seconds of the execution time of a program that takes 60 seconds in total can use an enhancement, the fraction is 20/60. This value, which we will call $\text{Fraction}_{\text{enhanced}}$, is always less than or equal to 1.

2. *The improvement gained by the enhanced execution mode; that is, how much faster the task would run if the enhanced mode were used for the entire program*—This value is the time of the original mode over the time of the enhanced mode. If the enhanced mode takes, say, 2 seconds for a portion of the program, while it is 5 seconds in the original mode, the improvement is 5/2. We will call this value, which is always greater than 1, $\text{Speedup}_{\text{enhanced}}$.

The execution time using the original computer with the enhanced mode will be the time spent using the unenhanced portion of the computer plus the time spent using the enhancement:

$$\text{Execution time}_{\text{new}} = \text{Execution time}_{\text{old}} \times \left((1 - \text{Fraction}_{\text{enhanced}}) + \frac{\text{Fraction}_{\text{enhanced}}}{\text{Speedup}_{\text{enhanced}}} \right)$$

The overall speedup is the ratio of the execution times:

$$\text{Speedup}_{\text{overall}} = \frac{\text{Execution time}_{\text{old}}}{\text{Execution time}_{\text{new}}} = \frac{1}{(1 - \text{Fraction}_{\text{enhanced}}) + \frac{\text{Fraction}_{\text{enhanced}}}{\text{Speedup}_{\text{enhanced}}}}$$

Example   Suppose that we want to enhance the processor used for Web serving. The new processor is 10 times faster on computation in the Web serving application than the original processor. Assuming that the original processor is busy with computation 40% of the time and is waiting for I/O 60% of the time, what is the overall speedup gained by incorporating the enhancement?

Answer $\text{Fraction}_{\text{enhanced}} = 0.4$, $\text{Speedup}_{\text{enhanced}} = 10$, $\text{Speedup}_{\text{overall}} = \dfrac{1}{0.6 + \dfrac{0.4}{10}} = \dfrac{1}{0.64} \approx 1.56$

Amdahl's Law expresses the law of diminishing returns: The incremental improvement in speedup gained by an improvement of just a portion of the computation diminishes as improvements are added. An important corollary of Amdahl's Law is that if an enhancement is only usable for a fraction of a task, we can't speed up the task by more than the reciprocal of 1 minus that fraction.

A common mistake in applying Amdahl's Law is to confuse "fraction of time converted to use an enhancement" and "fraction of time after enhancement is in use." If, instead of measuring the time that we *could use* the enhancement in a computation, we measure the time *after* the enhancement is in use, the results will be incorrect!

Amdahl's Law can serve as a guide to how much an enhancement will improve performance and how to distribute resources to improve cost-performance. The goal, clearly, is to spend resources proportional to where time is spent. Amdahl's Law is particularly useful for comparing the overall system performance of two alternatives, but it can also be applied to compare two processor design alternatives, as the following example shows.

Example   A common transformation required in graphics processors is square root. Implementations of floating-point (FP) square root vary significantly in performance, especially among processors designed for graphics. Suppose FP square root (FPSQR) is responsible for 20% of the execution time of a critical graphics benchmark. One proposal is to enhance the FPSQR hardware and speed up this operation by a factor of 10. The other alternative is just to try to make all FP instructions in the graphics processor run faster by a factor of 1.6; FP instructions are responsible for half of the execution time for the application. The design team believes that they can make all FP instructions run 1.6 times faster with the same effort as required for the fast square root. Compare these two design alternatives.

Answer   We can compare these two alternatives by comparing the speedups:

$$\text{Speedup}_{\text{FPSQR}} = \frac{1}{(1 - 0.2) + \dfrac{0.2}{10}} = \frac{1}{0.82} = 1.22$$

$$\text{Speedup}_{\text{FP}} = \frac{1}{(1 - 0.5) + \dfrac{0.5}{1.6}} = \frac{1}{0.8125} = 1.23$$

Improving the performance of the FP operations overall is slightly better because of the higher frequency.

Amdahl's Law is applicable beyond performance. Let's redo the reliability example from page 27 after improving the reliability of the power supply via redundancy from 200,000-hour to 830,000,000-hour MTTF, or 4150X better.

Example   The calculation of the failure rates of the disk subsystem was

$$\text{Failure rate}_{system} = 10 \times \frac{1}{1,000,000} + \frac{1}{500,000} + \frac{1}{200,000} + \frac{1}{200,000} + \frac{1}{1,000,000}$$

$$= \frac{10 + 2 + 5 + 5 + 1}{1,000,000 \text{ hours}} = \frac{23}{1,000,000 \text{ hours}}$$

Therefore, the fraction of the failure rate that could be improved is 5 per million hours out of 23 for the whole system, or 0.22.

Answer   The reliability improvement would be

$$\text{Improvement}_{power\ supply\ pair} = \frac{1}{(1 - 0.22) + \dfrac{0.22}{4150}} = \frac{1}{0.78} = 1.28$$

Despite an impressive 4150X improvement in reliability of one module, from the system's perspective, the change has a measurable but small benefit.

In the examples above we needed the fraction consumed by the new and improved version; often it is difficult to measure these times directly. In the next section, we will see another way of doing such comparisons based on the use of an equation that decomposes the CPU execution time into three separate components. If we know how an alternative affects these three components, we can determine its overall performance. Furthermore, it is often possible to build simulators that measure these components before the hardware is actually designed.

The Processor Performance Equation

Essentially all computers are constructed using a clock running at a constant rate. These discrete time events are called *ticks, clock ticks, clock periods, clocks, cycles,* or *clock cycles.* Computer designers refer to the time of a clock period by its duration (e.g., 1 ns) or by its rate (e.g., 1 GHz). CPU time for a program can then be expressed two ways:

$$\text{CPU time} = \text{CPU clock cycles for a program} \times \text{Clock cycle time}$$

or

$$\text{CPU time} = \frac{\text{CPU clock cycles for a program}}{\text{Clock rate}}$$

In addition to the number of clock cycles needed to execute a program, we can also count the number of instructions executed—the *instruction path length* or *instruction count* (IC). If we know the number of clock cycles and the instruction count, we can calculate the average number of *clock cycles per instruction* (CPI). Because it is easier to work with, and because we will deal with simple processors in this chapter, we use CPI. Designers sometimes also use *instructions per clock* (IPC), which is the inverse of CPI.

CPI is computed as

$$CPI = \frac{CPU \text{ clock cycles for a program}}{\text{Instruction count}}$$

This processor figure of merit provides insight into different styles of instruction sets and implementations, and we will use it extensively in the next four chapters.

By transposing instruction count in the above formula, clock cycles can be defined as $IC \times CPI$. This allows us to use CPI in the execution time formula:

$$CPU \text{ time } = \text{Instruction count} \times \text{Cycles per instruction} \times \text{Clock cycle time}$$

Expanding the first formula into the units of measurement shows how the pieces fit together:

$$\frac{\text{Instructions}}{\text{Program}} \times \frac{\text{Clock cycles}}{\text{Instruction}} \times \frac{\text{Seconds}}{\text{Clock cycle}} = \frac{\text{Seconds}}{\text{Program}} = CPU \text{ time}$$

As this formula demonstrates, processor performance is dependent upon three characteristics: clock cycle (or rate), clock cycles per instruction, and instruction count. Furthermore, CPU time is *equally* dependent on these three characteristics: A 10% improvement in any one of them leads to a 10% improvement in CPU time.

Unfortunately, it is difficult to change one parameter in complete isolation from others because the basic technologies involved in changing each characteristic are interdependent:

■ *Clock cycle time*—Hardware technology and organization

■ *CPI*—Organization and instruction set architecture

■ *Instruction count*—Instruction set architecture and compiler technology

Luckily, many potential performance improvement techniques primarily improve one component of processor performance with small or predictable impacts on the other two.

Sometimes it is useful in designing the processor to calculate the number of total processor clock cycles as

$$CPU \text{ clock cycles} = \sum_{i=1}^{n} IC_i \times CPI_i$$

where IC_i represents number of times instruction i is executed in a program and CPI_i represents the average number of clocks per instruction for instruction i. This form can be used to express CPU time as

$$CPU\ time = \left(\sum_{i=1}^{n} IC_i \times CPI_i \right) \times Clock\ cycle\ time$$

and overall CPI as

$$CPI = \frac{\sum_{i=1}^{n} IC_i \times CPI_i}{Instruction\ count} = \sum_{i=1}^{n} \frac{IC_i}{Instruction\ count} \times CPI_i$$

The latter form of the CPI calculation uses each individual CPI_i and the fraction of occurrences of that instruction in a program (i.e., $IC_i \div$ Instruction count). CPI_i should be measured and not just calculated from a table in the back of a reference manual since it must include pipeline effects, cache misses, and any other memory system inefficiencies.

Consider our performance example on page 40, here modified to use measurements of the frequency of the instructions and of the instruction CPI values, which, in practice, are obtained by simulation or by hardware instrumentation.

Example   Suppose we have made the following measurements:

Frequency of FP operations = 25%

Average CPI of FP operations = 4.0

Average CPI of other instructions = 1.33

Frequency of FPSQR= 2%

CPI of FPSQR = 20

Assume that the two design alternatives are to decrease the CPI of FPSQR to 2 or to decrease the average CPI of all FP operations to 2.5. Compare these two design alternatives using the processor performance equation.

Answer   First, observe that only the CPI changes; the clock rate and instruction count remain identical. We start by finding the original CPI with neither enhancement:

$$CPI_{original} = \sum_{i=1}^{n} CPI_i \times \left(\frac{IC_i}{Instruction\ count} \right)$$
$$= (4 \times 25\%) + (1.33 \times 75\%) = 2.0$$

We can compute the CPI for the enhanced FPSQR by subtracting the cycles saved from the original CPI:

$$CPI_{\text{with new FPSQR}} = CPI_{\text{original}} - 2\% \times (CPI_{\text{old FPSQR}} - CPI_{\text{of new FPSQR only}})$$
$$= 2.0 - 2\% \times (20 - 2) = 1.64$$

We can compute the CPI for the enhancement of all FP instructions the same way or by summing the FP and non-FP CPIs. Using the latter gives us

$$CPI_{\text{new FP}} = (75\% \times 1.33) + (25\% \times 2.5) = 1.62$$

Since the CPI of the overall FP enhancement is slightly lower, its performance will be marginally better. Specifically, the speedup for the overall FP enhancement is

$$Speedup_{\text{new FP}} = \frac{CPU\ time_{\text{original}}}{CPU\ time_{\text{new FP}}} = \frac{IC \times Clock\ cycle \times CPI_{\text{original}}}{IC \times Clock\ cycle \times CPI_{\text{new FP}}}$$

$$= \frac{CPI_{\text{original}}}{CPI_{\text{new FP}}} = \frac{2.00}{1.625} = 1.23$$

Happily, we obtained this same speedup using Amdahl's Law on page 40.

It is often possible to measure the constituent parts of the processor performance equation. This is a key advantage of using the processor performance equation versus Amdahl's Law in the previous example. In particular, it may be difficult to measure things such as the fraction of execution time for which a set of instructions is responsible. In practice, this would probably be computed by summing the product of the instruction count and the CPI for each of the instructions in the set. Since the starting point is often individual instruction count and CPI measurements, the processor performance equation is incredibly useful.

To use the processor performance equation as a design tool, we need to be able to measure the various factors. For an existing processor, it is easy to obtain the execution time by measurement, and the clock speed is known. The challenge lies in discovering the instruction count or the CPI. Most new processors include counters for both instructions executed and for clock cycles. By periodically monitoring these counters, it is also possible to attach execution time and instruction count to segments of the code, which can be helpful to programmers trying to understand and tune the performance of an application. Often, a designer or programmer will want to understand performance at a more fine-grained level than what is available from the hardware counters. For example, they may want to know why the CPI is what it is. In such cases, simulation techniques like those used for processors that are being designed are used.

1.10 Putting It All Together: Performance and Price-Performance

In the "Putting It All Together" sections that appear near the end of every chapter, we show real examples that use the principles in that chapter. In this section, we look at measures of performance and price-performance, in desktop systems using the SPEC benchmark and then in servers using the TPC-C benchmark.

Performance and Price-Performance for Desktop and Rack-Mountable Systems

Although there are many benchmark suites for desktop systems, a majority of them are OS or architecture specific. In this section we examine the processor performance and price-performance of a variety of desktop systems using the SPEC CPU2000 integer and floating-point suites. As mentioned in Figure 1.14, SPEC CPU2000 summarizes processor performance using a geometric mean normalized to a Sun Ultra 5, with larger numbers indicating higher performance.

Figure 1.15 shows the five systems including the processors and price. Each system was configured with one processor, 1 GB of DDR DRAM (with ECC if available), approximately 80 GB of disk, and an Ethernet connection. The desktop systems come with a fast graphics card and a monitor, while the rack-mountable systems do not. The wide variation in price is driven by a number of factors, including the cost of the processor, software differences (Linux or a Microsoft OS versus a vendor-specific OS), system expandability, and the commoditization effect, which we discussed in Section 1.6.

Figure 1.16 shows the performance and the price-performance of these five systems using SPEC CINT2000base and CFP2000base as the metrics. The figure also plots price-performance on the right axis, showing CINT or CFP per $1000 of price. Note that in every case, floating-point performance exceeds integer performance relative to the base computer.

Vendor/model	Processor	Clock rate	L2 cache	Type	Price
Dell Precision Workstation 380	Intel Pentium 4 Xeon	3.8 GHz	2 MB	Desk	$3346
HP ProLiant BL25p	AMD Opteron 252	2.6 GHz	1 MB	Rack	$3099
HP ProLiant ML350 G4	Intel Pentium 4 Xeon	3.4 GHz	1 MB	Desk	$2907
HP Integrity rx2620-2	Itanium 2	1.6 GHz	3 MB	Rack	$5201
Sun Java Workstation W1100z	AMD Opteron 150	2.4 GHz	1 MB	Desk	$2145

Figure 1.15 Five different desktop and rack-mountable systems from three vendors using three different microprocessors showing the processor, its clock rate, L2 cache size, and the selling price. Figure 1.16 plots absolute performance and price performance. All these systems are configured with 1 GB of ECC SDRAM and approximately 80 GB of disk. (If software costs were not included, we added them.) Many factors are responsible for the wide variation in price despite these common elements. First, the systems offer different levels of expandability (with the Sun Java Workstation being the least expandable, the Dell systems being moderately expandable, and the HP BL25p blade server being the most expandable). Second, the cost of the processor varies by at least a factor of 2, with much of the reason for the higher costs being the size of the L2 cache and the larger die. In 2005, the Opteron sold for about $500 to $800 and Pentium 4 Xeon sold for about $400 to $700, depending on clock rates and cache size. The Itanium 2 die size is much larger than the others, so it's probably at least twice the cost. Third, software differences (Linux or a Microsoft OS versus a vendor-specific OS) probably affect the final price. These prices were as of August 2005.

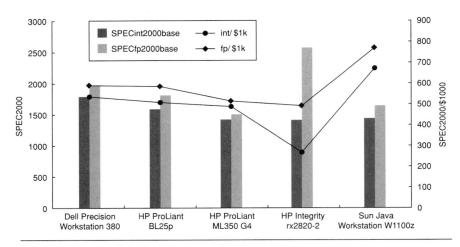

Figure 1.16 Performance and price-performance for five systems in Figure 1.15 measured using SPEC CINT2000 and CFP2000 as the benchmark. Price-performance is plotted as CINT2000 and CFP2000 performance per $1000 in system cost. These performance numbers were collected in January 2006 and prices were as of August 2005. The measurements are available online at *www.spec.org*.

The Itanium 2–based design has the highest floating-point performance but also the highest cost, and hence has the lowest performance per thousand dollars, being off a factor of 1.1–1.6 in floating-point and 1.8–2.5 in integer performance. While the Dell based on the 3.8 GHz Intel Xeon with a 2 MB L2 cache has the high performance for CINT and second highest for CFP, it also has a much higher cost than the Sun product based on the 2.4 GHz AMD Opteron with a 1 MB L2 cache, making the latter the price-performance leader for CINT and CFP.

Performance and Price-Performance for Transaction-Processing Servers

One of the largest server markets is online transaction processing (OLTP). The standard industry benchmark for OLTP is TPC-C, which relies on a database system to perform queries and updates. Five factors make the performance of TPC-C particularly interesting. First, TPC-C is a reasonable approximation to a real OLTP application. Although this is complex and time-consuming, it makes the results reasonably indicative of real performance for OLTP. Second, TPC-C measures total system performance, including the hardware, the operating system, the I/O system, and the database system, making the benchmark more predictive of real performance. Third, the rules for running the benchmark and reporting execution time are very complete, resulting in numbers that are more comparable. Fourth, because of the importance of the benchmark, computer system vendors devote significant effort to making TPC-C run well. Fifth, vendors are required to report both performance and price-performance, enabling us to examine both. For TPC-C, performance is measured in transactions per minute (TPM), while price-performance is measured in dollars per TPM.

Figure 1.17 shows the characteristics of 10 systems whose performance or price-performance is near the top in one measure or the other. Figure 1.18 plots absolute performance on a log scale and price-performance on a linear scale. The number of disks is determined by the number of I/Os per second to match the performance target rather than the storage capacity need to run the benchmark.

The highest-performing system is a 64-node shared-memory multiprocessor from IBM, costing a whopping $17 million. It is about twice as expensive and twice as fast as the same model half its size, and almost three times faster than the third-place cluster from HP. These five computers average 35–50 disks per processor and 16–20 GB of DRAM per processor. Chapter 4 discusses the design of multiprocessor systems, and Chapter 6 and Appendix E describe clusters.

The computers with the best price-performance are all uniprocessors based on Pentium 4 Xeon processors, although the L2 cache size varies. Notice that these systems have about three to four times better price-performance than the

Vendor and system	Processors	Memory	Storage	Database/OS	Price
IBM eServer p5 595	64 IBM POWER 5 @1.9 GHz, 36 MB L3	64 cards, 2048 GB	6548 disks 243,236 GB	IBM DB2 UDB 8.2/ IBM AIX 5L V5.3	$16,669,230
IBM eServer p5 595	32 IBM POWER 5 @1.9 GHz, 36 MB L3	32 cards, 1024 GB	3298 disks 112,885 GB	Orcale 10g EE/ IBM AIX 5L V5.3	$8,428,470
HP Integrity rx5670 Cluster	64 Intel Itanium 2 @ 1.5 GHz, 6 MB L3	768 dimms, 768 GB	2195 disks, 93,184 GB	Orcale 10g EE/ Red Hat E Linux AS 3	$6,541,770
HP Integrity Superdome	64 Intel Itanium 2 @ 1.6 GHz, 9 MB L3	512 dimms, 1024 GB	1740 disks, 53,743 GB	MS SQL Server 2005 EE/MS Windows DE 64b	$5,820,285
IBM eServer pSeries 690	32 IBM POWER4+ @ 1.9 GHz, 128 MB L3	4 cards, 1024 GB	1995 disks, 74,098 GB	IBM DB2 UDB 8.1/ IBM AIX 5L V5.2	$5,571,349
Dell PowerEdge 2800	1 Intel Xeon @ 3.4 GHz, 2MB L2	2 dimms, 2.5 GB	76 disks, 2585 GB	MS SQL Server 2000 WE/ MS Windows 2003	$39,340
Dell PowerEdge 2850	1 Intel Xeon @ 3.4 GHz, 1MB L2	2 dimms, 2.5 GB	76 disks, 1400 GB	MS SQL Server 2000 SE/ MS Windows 2003	$40,170
HP ProLiant ML350	1 Intel Xeon @ 3.1 GHz, 0.5MB L2	3 dimms, 2.5 GB	34 disks, 696 GB	MS SQL Server 2000 SE/ MS Windows 2003 SE	$27,827
HP ProLiant ML350	1 Intel Xeon @ 3.1 GHz, 0.5MB L2	4 dimms, 4 GB	35 disks, 692 GB	IBM DB2 UDB EE V8.1/ SUSE Linux ES 9	$29,990
HP ProLiant ML350	1 Intel Xeon @ 2.8 GHz, 0.5MB L2	4 dimms, 3.25 GB	35 disks, 692 GB	IBM DB2 UDB EE V8.1/ MS Windows 2003 SE	$30,600

Figure 1.17 **The characteristics of 10 OLTP systems, using TPC-C as the benchmark, with either high total performance (top half of the table, measured in transactions per minute) or superior price-performance (bottom half of the table, measured in U.S. dollars per transactions per minute).** Figure 1.18 plots absolute performance and price performance, and Figure 1.19 splits the price between processors, memory, storage, and software.

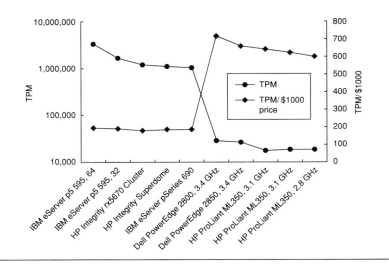

Figure 1.18 Performance and price-performance for the 10 systems in Figure 1.17 using TPC-C as the benchmark. Price-performance is plotted as TPM per $1000 in system cost, although the conventional TPC-C measure is $/TPM (715 TPM/$1000 = $1.40 $/TPM). These performance numbers and prices were as of July 2005. The measurements are available online at *www.tpc.org*.

high-performance systems. Although these five computers also average 35–50 disks per processor, they only use 2.5–3 GB of DRAM per processor. It is hard to tell whether this is the best choice or whether it simply reflects the 32-bit address space of these less expensive PC servers. Since doubling memory would only add about 4% to their price, it is likely the latter reason.

1.11   Fallacies and Pitfalls

The purpose of this section, which will be found in every chapter, is to explain some commonly held misbeliefs or misconceptions that you should avoid. We call such misbeliefs *fallacies*. When discussing a fallacy, we try to give a counterexample. We also discuss *pitfalls*—easily made mistakes. Often pitfalls are generalizations of principles that are true in a limited context. The purpose of these sections is to help you avoid making these errors in computers that you design.

Pitfall   *Falling prey to Amdahl's Law.*

Virtually every practicing computer architect knows Amdahl's Law. Despite this, we almost all occasionally expend tremendous effort optimizing some feature before we measure its usage. Only when the overall speedup is disappointing do we recall that we should have measured first before we spent so much effort enhancing it!

Pitfall   *A single point of failure.*

The calculations of reliability improvement using Amdahl's Law on page 41 show that dependability is no stronger than the weakest link in a chain. No matter how much more dependable we make the power supplies, as we did in our example, the single fan will limit the reliability of the disk subsystem. This Amdahl's Law observation led to a rule of thumb for fault-tolerant systems to make sure that every component was redundant so that no single component failure could bring down the whole system.

Fallacy   *The cost of the processor dominates the cost of the system.*

Computer science is processor centric, perhaps because processors seem more intellectually interesting than memories or disks and perhaps because algorithms are traditionally measured in number of processor operations. This fascination leads us to think that processor utilization is the most important figure of merit. Indeed, the high-performance computing community often evaluates algorithms and architectures by what fraction of peak processor performance is achieved. This would make sense if most of the cost were in the processors.

Figure 1.19 shows the breakdown of costs for the computers in Figure 1.17 into the processor (including the cabinets, power supplies, and so on), DRAM

	Processor + cabinetry	Memory	Storage	Software
IBM eServer p5 595	28%	16%	51%	6%
IBM eServer p5 595	13%	31%	52%	4%
HP Integrity rx5670 Cluster	11%	22%	35%	33%
HP Integrity Superdome	33%	32%	15%	20%
IBM eServer pSeries 690	21%	24%	48%	7%
Median of high-performance computers	21%	24%	48%	7%
Dell PowerEdge 2800	6%	3%	80%	11%
Dell PowerEdge 2850	7%	3%	76%	14%
HP ProLiant ML350	5%	4%	70%	21%
HP ProLiant ML350	9%	8%	65%	19%
HP ProLiant ML350	8%	6%	65%	21%
Median of price-performance computers	7%	4%	70%	19%

Figure 1.19 Cost of purchase split between processor, memory, storage, and software for the top computers running the TPC-C benchmark in Figure 1.17. Memory is just the cost of the DRAM modules, so all the power and cooling for the computer is credited to the processor. TPC-C includes the cost of the clients to drive the TPC-C benchmark and the three-year cost of maintenance, which are not included here. Maintenance would add about 10% to the numbers here, with differences in software maintenance costs making the range be 5% to 22%. Including client hardware would add about 2% to the price of the high-performance servers and 7% to the PC servers.

memory, disk storage, and software. Even giving the processor category the credit for the sheet metal, power supplies, and cooling, it's only about 20% of the costs for the large-scale servers and less than 10% of the costs for the PC servers.

Fallacy   *Benchmarks remain valid indefinitely.*

Several factors influence the usefulness of a benchmark as a predictor of real performance, and some change over time. A big factor influencing the usefulness of a benchmark is its ability to resist "cracking," also known as "benchmark engineering" or "benchmarksmanship." Once a benchmark becomes standardized and popular, there is tremendous pressure to improve performance by targeted optimizations or by aggressive interpretation of the rules for running the benchmark. Small kernels or programs that spend their time in a very small number of lines of code are particularly vulnerable.

For example, despite the best intentions, the initial SPEC89 benchmark suite included a small kernel, called matrix300, which consisted of eight different 300 × 300 matrix multiplications. In this kernel, 99% of the execution time was in a single line (see SPEC [1989]). When an IBM compiler optimized this inner loop (using an idea called blocking, discussed in Chapter 5), performance improved by a factor of 9 over a prior version of the compiler! This benchmark tested compiler tuning and was not, of course, a good indication of overall performance, nor of the typical value of this particular optimization.

Even after the elimination of this benchmark, vendors found methods to tune the performance of others by the use of different compilers or preprocessors, as well as benchmark-specific flags. Although the baseline performance measurements require the use of one set of flags for all benchmarks, the tuned or optimized performance does not. In fact, benchmark-specific flags are allowed, even if they are illegal in general and could lead to incorrect compilation!

Over a long period, these changes may make even a well-chosen benchmark obsolete; Gcc is the lone survivor from SPEC89. Figure 1.13 on page 31 lists the status of all 70 benchmarks from the various SPEC releases. Amazingly, almost 70% of all programs from SPEC2000 or earlier were dropped from the next release.

Fallacy   *The rated mean time to failure of disks is 1,200,000 hours or almost 140 years, so disks practically never fail.*

The current marketing practices of disk manufacturers can mislead users. How is such an MTTF calculated? Early in the process, manufacturers will put thousands of disks in a room, run them for a few months, and count the number that fail. They compute MTTF as the total number of hours that the disks worked cumulatively divided by the number that failed.

One problem is that this number far exceeds the lifetime of a disk, which is commonly assumed to be 5 years or 43,800 hours. For this large MTTF to make some sense, disk manufacturers argue that the model corresponds to a user who buys a disk, and then keeps replacing the disk every 5 years—the planned lifetime of the disk. The claim is that if many customers (and their great-grandchildren) did this for the next century, on average they would replace a disk 27 times before a failure, or about 140 years.

A more useful measure would be percentage of disks that fail. Assume 1000 disks with a 1,000,000-hour MTTF and that the disks are used 24 hours a day. If you replaced failed disks with a new one having the same reliability characteristics, the number that would fail in a year (8760 hours) is

$$\text{Failed disks} = \frac{\text{Number of disks} \times \text{Time period}}{\text{MTTF}} = \frac{1000 \text{ disks} \times 8760 \text{ hours/drive}}{1,000,000 \text{ hours/failure}} = 9$$

Stated alternatively, 0.9% would fail per year, or 4.4% over a 5-year lifetime.

Moreover, those high numbers are quoted assuming limited ranges of temperature and vibration; if they are exceeded, then all bets are off. A recent survey of disk drives in real environments [Gray and van Ingen 2005] claims about 3–6% of SCSI drives fail per year, or an MTTF of about 150,000–300,000 hours, and about 3–7% of ATA drives fail per year, or an MTTF of about 125,000–300,000 hours. The quoted MTTF of ATA disks is usually 500,000–600,000 hours. Hence, according to this report, real-world MTTF is about 2–4 times worse than manufacturer's MTTF for ATA disks and 4–8 times worse for SCSI disks.

Fallacy   *Peak performance tracks observed performance.*

The only universally true definition of peak performance is "the performance level a computer is guaranteed not to exceed." Figure 1.20 shows the percentage of peak performance for four programs on four multiprocessors. It varies from 5% to 58%. Since the gap is so large and can vary significantly by benchmark, peak performance is not generally useful in predicting observed performance.

Pitfall   *Fault detection can lower availability.*

This apparently ironic pitfall is because computer hardware has a fair amount of state that may not always be critical to proper operation. For example, it is not fatal if an error occurs in a branch predictor, as only performance may suffer.

In processors that try to aggressively exploit instruction-level parallelism, not all the operations are needed for correct execution of the program. Mukherjee et al. [2003] found that less than 30% of the operations were potentially on the critical path for the SPEC2000 benchmarks running on an Itanium 2.

The same observation is true about programs. If a register is "dead" in a program—that is, the program will write it before it is read again—then errors do not matter. If you were to crash the program upon detection of a transient fault in a dead register, it would lower availability unnecessarily.

Sun Microsystems lived this pitfall in 2000 with an L2 cache that included parity, but not error correction, in its Sun E3000 to Sun E10000 systems. The SRAMs they used to build the caches had intermittent faults, which parity detected. If the data in the cache was not modified, the processor simply reread the data from the cache. Since the designers did not protect the cache with ECC, the operating system had no choice but report an error to dirty data and crash the

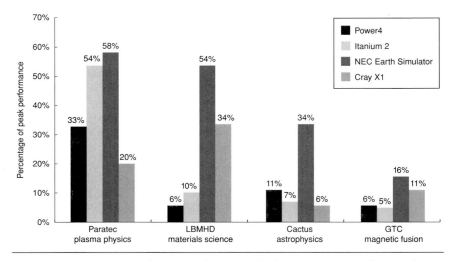

Figure 1.20 Percentage of peak performance for four programs on four multiprocessors scaled to 64 processors. The Earth Simulator and X1 are vector processors. (See Appendix F.) Not only did they deliver a higher fraction of peak performance, they had the highest peak performance and the lowest clock rates. Except for the Paratec program, the Power 4 and Itanium 2 systems deliver between 5% and 10% of their peak. From Oliker et al. [2004].

program. Field engineers found no problems on inspection in more than 90% of the cases.

To reduce the frequency of such errors, Sun modified the Solaris operating system to "scrub" the cache by having a process that proactively writes dirty data to memory. Since the processor chips did not have enough pins to add ECC, the only hardware option for dirty data was to duplicate the external cache, using the copy without the parity error to correct the error.

The pitfall is in detecting faults without providing a mechanism to correct them. Sun is unlikely to ship another computer without ECC on external caches.

1.12 Concluding Remarks

This chapter has introduced a number of concepts that we will expand upon as we go through this book.

In Chapters 2 and 3, we look at instruction-level parallelism (ILP), of which pipelining is the simplest and most common form. Exploiting ILP is one of the most important techniques for building high-speed uniprocessors. The presence of two chapters reflects the fact that there are several approaches to exploiting ILP and that it is an important and mature technology. Chapter 2 begins with an extensive discussion of basic concepts that will prepare you for the wide range of ideas examined in both chapters. Chapter 2 uses examples that span about 35 years, drawing from one of the first supercomputers (IBM 360/91) to the fastest processors in the market in 2006. It emphasizes what is called the dynamic or run time approach to exploiting ILP. Chapter 3 focuses on limits and extensions to the ILP ideas presented in Chapter 2, including multithreading to get more from an out-of-order organization. Appendix A is introductory material on pipelining for readers without much experience and background in pipelining. (We expect it to be review for many readers, including those of our introductory text, *Computer Organization and Design: The Hardware/Software Interface.*)

Chapter 4 focuses on the issue of achieving higher performance using multiple processors, or multiprocessors. Instead of using parallelism to overlap individual instructions, multiprocessing uses parallelism to allow multiple instruction streams to be executed simultaneously on different processors. Our focus is on the dominant form of multiprocessors, shared-memory multiprocessors, though we introduce other types as well and discuss the broad issues that arise in any multiprocessor. Here again, we explore a variety of techniques, focusing on the important ideas first introduced in the 1980s and 1990s.

In Chapter 5, we turn to the all-important area of memory system design. We will examine a wide range of techniques that conspire to make memory look infinitely large while still being as fast as possible. As in Chapters 2 through 4, we will see that hardware-software cooperation has become a key to high-performance memory systems, just as it has to high-performance pipelines. This chapter also covers virtual machines. Appendix C is introductory material on caches for readers without much experience and background in them.

In Chapter 6, we move away from a processor-centric view and discuss issues in storage systems. We apply a similar quantitative approach, but one based on observations of system behavior and using an end-to-end approach to performance analysis. It addresses the important issue of how to efficiently store and retrieve data using primarily lower-cost magnetic storage technologies. Such technologies offer better cost per bit by a factor of 50–100 over DRAM. In Chapter 6, our focus is on examining the performance of disk storage systems for typical I/O-intensive workloads, like the OLTP benchmarks we saw in this chapter. We extensively explore advanced topics in RAID-based systems, which use redundant disks to achieve both high performance and high availability. Finally, the chapter introduces queing theory, which gives a basis for trading off utilization and latency.

This book comes with a plethora of material on the companion CD, both to lower cost and to introduce readers to a variety of advanced topics. Figure 1.21 shows them all. Appendices A, B, and C, which appear in the book, will be review for many readers. Appendix D takes the embedded computing perspective on the ideas of each of the chapters and early appendices. Appendix E explores the topic of system interconnect broadly, including wide area and system area networks used to allow computers to communicate. It also describes clusters, which are growing in importance due to their suitability and efficiency for database and Web server applications.

Appendix	Title
A	Pipelining: Basic and Intermediate Concepts
B	Instruction Set Principles and Examples
C	Review of Memory Hierarchies
D	Embedded Systems (CD)
E	Interconnection Networks (CD)
F	Vector Processors (CD)
G	Hardware and Software for VLIW and EPIC (CD)
H	Large-Scale Multiprocessors and Scientific Applications (CD)
I	Computer Arithmetic (CD)
J	Survey of Instruction Set Architectures (CD)
K	Historical Perspectives and References (CD)
L	Solutions to Case Study Exercises (Online)

Figure 1.21 List of appendices.

Appendix F explores vector processors, which have become more popular since the last edition due in part to the NEC Global Climate Simulator being the world's fastest computer for several years. Appendix G reviews VLIW hardware and software, which in contrast, are less popular than when EPIC appeared on the scene just before the last edition. Appendix H describes large-scale multiprocessors for use in high performance computing. Appendix I is the only appendix that remains from the first edition, and it covers computer arithmetic. Appendix J is a survey of instruction architectures, including the 80x86, the IBM 360, the VAX, and many RISC architectures, including ARM, MIPS, Power, and SPARC. We describe Appendix K below. Appendix L has solutions to Case Study exercises.

1.13 Historical Perspectives and References

Appendix K on the companion CD includes historical perspectives on the key ideas presented in each of the chapters in this text. These historical perspective sections allow us to trace the development of an idea through a series of machines or describe significant projects. If you're interested in examining the initial development of an idea or machine or interested in further reading, references are provided at the end of each history. For this chapter, see Section K.2, The Early Development of Computers, for a discussion on the early development of digital computers and performance measurement methodologies.

As you read the historical material, you'll soon come to realize that one of the important benefits of the youth of computing, compared to many other engineering fields, is that many of the pioneers are still alive—we can learn the history by simply asking them!

Case Studies with Exercises by Diana Franklin

Case Study 1: Chip Fabrication Cost

Concepts illustrated by this case study

■ Fabrication Cost

■ Fabrication Yield

■ Defect Tolerance through Redundancy

There are many factors involved in the price of a computer chip. New, smaller technology gives a boost in performance and a drop in required chip area. In the smaller technology, one can either keep the small area or place more hardware on the chip in order to get more functionality. In this case study, we explore how different design decisions involving fabrication technology, area, and redundancy affect the cost of chips.

1.1 [10/10/Discussion] <1.5, 1.5> Figure 1.22 gives the relevant chip statistics that influence the cost of several current chips. In the next few exercises, you will be exploring the trade-offs involved between the AMD Opteron, a single-chip processor, and the Sun Niagara, an 8-core chip.

    a. [10] <1.5> What is the yield for the AMD Opteron?

    b. [10] <1.5> What is the yield for an 8-core Sun Niagara processor?

    c. [Discussion] <1.4, 1.6> Why does the Sun Niagara have a worse yield than the AMD Opteron, even though they have the same defect rate?

1.2 [20/20/20/20/20] <1.7> You are trying to figure out whether to build a new fabrication facility for your IBM Power5 chips. It costs $1 billion to build a new fabrication facility. The benefit of the new fabrication is that you predict that you will be able to sell 3 times as many chips at 2 times the price of the old chips. The new chip will have an area of 186 mm^2, with a defect rate of .7 defects per cm^2. Assume the wafer has a diameter of 300 mm. Assume it costs $500 to fabricate a wafer in either technology. You were previously selling the chips for 40% more than their cost.

Chip	Die size (mm^2)	Estimated defect rate (per cm^2)	Manufacturing size (nm)	Transistors (millions)
IBM Power5	389	.30	130	276
Sun Niagara	380	.75	90	279
AMD Opteron	199	.75	90	233

Figure 1.22 Manufacturing cost factors for several modern processors. $\alpha = 4$.

    a. [20] <1.5> What is the cost of the old Power5 chip?

    b. [20] <1.5> What is the cost of the new Power5 chip?

    c. [20] <1.5> What was the profit on each old Power5 chip?

    d. [20] <1.5> What is the profit on each new Power5 chip?

    e. [20] <1.5> If you sold 500,000 old Power5 chips per month, how long will it take to recoup the costs of the new fabrication facility?

1.3   [20/20/10/10/20] <1.7> Your colleague at Sun suggests that, since the yield is so poor, it might make sense to sell two sets of chips, one with 8 working processors and one with 6 working processors. We will solve this exercise by viewing the yield as a probability of no defects occurring in a certain area given the defect rate. For the Niagara, calculate probabilities based on each Niagara core separately (this may not be entirely accurate, since the yield equation is based on empirical evidence rather than a mathematical calculation relating the probabilities of finding errors in different portions of the chip).

    a. [20] <1.7> Using the yield equation for the defect rate above, what is the probability that a defect will occur on a single Niagara core (assuming the chip is divided evenly between the cores) in an 8-core chip?

    b. [20] <1.7> What is the probability that a defect will occur on one or two cores (but not more than that)?

    c. [10] <1.7> What is the probability that a defect will occur on none of the cores?

    d. [10] <1.7> Given your answers to parts (b) and (c), what is the number of 6-core chips you will sell for every 8-core chip?

    e. [20] <1.7> If you sell your 8-core chips for $150 each, the 6-core chips for $100 each, the cost per die sold is $80, your research and development budget was $200 million, and testing itself costs $1.50 per chip, how many processors would you need to sell in order to recoup costs?

Case Study 2: Power Consumption in Computer Systems

Concepts illustrated by this case study

■ Amdahl's Law

■ Redundancy

■ MTTF

■ Power Consumption

Power consumption in modern systems is dependent on a variety of factors, including the chip clock frequency, efficiency, the disk drive speed, disk drive utilization, and DRAM. The following exercises explore the impact on power that different design decisions and/or use scenarios have.

Component type	Product	Performance	Power
Processor	Sun Niagara 8-core	1.2 GHz	72-79W peak
	Intel Pentium 4	2 GHz	48.9-66W
DRAM	Kingston X64C3AD2 1 GB	184-pin	3.7W
	Kingston D2N3 1 GB	240-pin	2.3W
Hard drive	DiamondMax 16	5400 rpm	7.0W read/seek, 2.9 W idle
	DiamondMax Plus 9	7200 rpm	7.9W read/seek, 4.0 W idle

Figure 1.23 **Power consumption of several computer components.**

1.4 [20/10/20] <1.6> Figure 1.23 presents the power consumption of several computer system components. In this exercise, we will explore how the hard drive affects power consumption for the system.

a. [20] <1.6> Assuming the maximum load for each component, and a power supply efficiency of 70%, what wattage must the server's power supply deliver to a system with a Sun Niagara 8-core chip, 2 GB 184-pin Kingston DRAM, and two 7200 rpm hard drives?

b. [10] <1.6> How much power will the 7200 rpm disk drive consume if it is idle roughly 40% of the time?

c. [20] <1.6> Assume that rpm is the only factor in how long a disk is not idle (which is an oversimplification of disk performance). In other words, assume that for the same set of requests, a 5400 rpm disk will require twice as much time to read data as a 10,800 rpm disk. What percentage of the time would the 5400 rpm disk drive be idle to perform the same transactions as in part (b)?

1.5 [10/10/20] <1.6, 1.7> One critical factor in powering a server farm is cooling. If heat is not removed from the computer efficiently, the fans will blow hot air back onto the computer, not cold air. We will look at how different design decisions affect the necessary cooling, and thus the price, of a system. Use Figure 1.23 for your power calculations.

a. [10] <1.6> A cooling door for a rack costs $4000 and dissipates 14 KW (into the room; additional cost is required to get it out of the room). How many servers with a Sun Niagara 8-core processor, 1 GB 240-pin DRAM, and a single 5400 rpm hard drive can you cool with one cooling door?

b. [10] <1.6, 1.8> You are considering providing fault tolerance for your hard drive. RAID 1 doubles the number of disks (see Chapter 6). Now how many systems can you place on a single rack with a single cooler?

c. [20] <1.8> In a single rack, the MTTF of each processor is 4500 hours, of the hard drive is 9 million hours, and of the power supply is 30K hours. For a rack with 8 processors, what is the MTTF for the rack?

	Sun Fire T2000	IBM x346
Power (watts)	298	438
SPECjbb (op/s)	63,378	39,985
Power (watts)	330	438
SPECWeb (composite)	14,001	4,348

Figure 1.24 **Sun power / performance comparison as selectively reported by Sun.**

1.6   [10/10/Discussion] <1.2, 1.9> Figure 1.24 gives a comparison of power and performance for several benchmarks comparing two servers: Sun Fire T2000 (which uses Niagara) and IBM x346 (using Intel Xeon processors).

   a. [10] <1.9> Calculate the performance/power ratio for each processor on each benchmark.

   b. [10] <1.9> If power is your main concern, which would you choose?

   c. [Discussion] <1.2> For the database benchmarks, the cheaper the system, the lower cost *per database operation* the system is. This is counterintuitive: larger systems have more throughput, so one might think that buying a larger system would be a larger absolute cost, but lower per operation cost. Since this is true, why do any larger server farms buy expensive servers? (*Hint:* Look at exercise 1.4 for some reasons.)

1.7   [10/20/20/20] <1.7, 1.10> Your company's internal studies show that a single-core system is sufficient for the demand on your processing power. You are exploring, however, whether you could save power by using two cores.

   a. [10] <1.10> Assume your application is 100% parallelizable. By how much could you decrease the frequency and get the same performance?

   b. [20] <1.7> Assume that the voltage may be decreased linearly with the frequency. Using the equation in Section 1.5, how much dynamic power would the dual-core system require as compared to the single-core system?

   c. [20] <1.7, 1.10> Now assume the voltage may not decrease below 30% of the original voltage. This voltage is referred to as the "voltage floor," and any voltage lower than that will lose the state. What percent of parallelization gives you a voltage at the voltage floor?

   d. [20] <1.7, 1.10> Using the equation in Section 1.5, how much dynamic power would the dual-core system require from part (a) compared to the single-core system when taking into account the voltage floor?

Case Study 3: The Cost of Reliability (and Failure) in Web Servers

Concepts illustrated by this case study

- TPCC
- Reliability of Web Servers
- MTTF

This set of exercises deals with the cost of not having reliable Web servers. The data is in two sets: one gives various statistics for Gap.com, which was down for maintenance for two weeks in 2005 [AP 2005]. The other is for Amazon.com, which was not down, but has better statistics on high-load sales days. The exercises combine the two data sets and require estimating the economic cost to the shutdown.

1.8   [10/10/20/20] <1.2, 1.9> On August 24, 2005, three Web sites managed by the Gap—Gap.com, OldNavy.com, and BananaRepublic.com—were taken down for improvements [AP 2005]. These sites were virtually inaccessible for the next two weeks. Using the statistics in Figure 1.25, answer the following questions, which are based in part on hypothetical assumptions.

    a.   [10] <1.2> In the third quarter of 2005, the Gap's revenue was $3.9 billion [Gap 2005]. The Web site returned live on September 7, 2005 [Internet Retailer 2005]. Assume that online sales total $1.4 million per day, and that everything else remains constant. What would the Gap's estimated revenue be third quarter 2005?

    b.   [10] <1.2> If this downtime occurred in the fourth quarter, what would you estimate the cost of the downtime to be?

Company	Time period	Amount	Type
Gap	3rd qtr 2004	$4 billion	Sales
	4th qtr 2004	$4.9 billion	Sales
	3rd qtr 2005	$3.9 billion	Sales
	4th qtr 2005	$4.8 billion	Sales
	3rd qtr 2004	$107 million	Online sales
	3rd qtr 2005	$106 million	Online sales
Amazon	3rd qtr 2005	$1.86 billion	Sales
	4th qtr 2005	$2.98 billion	Sales
	4th qtr 2005	108 million	Items sold
	Dec 12, 2005	3.6 million	Items sold

Figure 1.25 Statistics on sales for Gap and Amazon. Data compiled from AP [2005], Internet Retailer [2005], Gamasutra [2005], Seattle PI [2005], MSN Money [2005], Gap [2005], and Gap [2006].

   c. [20] <1.2> When the site returned, the number of users allowed to visit the site at one time was limited. Imagine that it was limited to 50% of the customers who wanted to access the site. Assume that each server costs $7500 to purchase and set up. How many servers, per day, could they purchase and install with the money they are losing in sales?

   d. [20] <1.2, 1.9> Gap.com had 2.6 million visitors in July 2004 [AP 2005]. On average, a user views 8.4 pages per day on Gap.com. Assume that the high-end servers at Gap.com are running SQLServer software, with a TPCC benchmark estimated cost of $5.38 per transaction. How much would it cost for them to support their online traffic at Gap.com.?

1.9   [10/10] <1.8> The main reliability measure is MTTF. We will now look at different systems and how design decisions affect their reliability. Refer to Figure 1.25 for company statistics.

   a. [10] <1.8> We have a single processor with an FIT of 100. What is the MTTF for this system?

   b. [10] <1.8> If it takes 1 day to get the system running again, what is the availability of the system?

1.10   [20] <1.8> Imagine that the government, to cut costs, is going to build a super-computer out of the cheap processor system in Exercise 1.9 rather than a special-purpose reliable system. What is the MTTF for a system with 1000 processors? Assume that if one fails, they all fail.

1.11   [20/20] <1.2, 1.8> In a server farm such as that used by Amazon or the Gap, a single failure does not cause the whole system to crash. Instead, it will reduce the number of requests that can be satisfied at any one time.

   a. [20] <1.8> If a company has 10,000 computers, and it experiences catastrophic failure only if 1/3 of the computers fail, what is the MTTF for the system?

   b. [20] <1.2, 1.8> If it costs an extra $1000, per computer, to double the MTTF, would this be a good business decision? Show your work.

Case Study 4: Performance

Concepts illustrated by this case study

■ Arithmetic Mean

■ Geometric Mean

■ Parallelism

■ Amdahl's Law

■ Weighted Averages

In this set of exercises, you are to make sense of Figure 1.26, which presents the performance of selected processors and a fictional one (Processor X), as reported by *www.tomshardware.com*. For each system, two benchmarks were run. One benchmark exercised the memory hierarchy, giving an indication of the speed of the memory for that system. The other benchmark, Dhrystone, is a CPU-intensive benchmark that does not exercise the memory system. Both benchmarks are displayed in order to distill the effects that different design decisions have on memory and CPU performance.

1.12   [10/10/Discussion/10/20/Discussion] <1.7> Make the following calculations on the raw data in order to explore how different measures color the conclusions one can make. (Doing these exercises will be much easier using a spreadsheet.)

   a.   [10] <1.8> Create a table similar to that shown in Figure 1.26, except express the results as normalized to the Pentium D for each benchmark.

   b.   [10] <1.9> Calculate the arithmetic mean of the performance of each processor. Use both the original performance and your normalized performance calculated in part (a).

   c.   [Discussion] <1.9> Given your answer from part (b), can you draw any conflicting conclusions about the relative performance of the different processors?

   d.   [10] <1.9> Calculate the geometric mean of the normalized performance of the dual processors and the geometric mean of the normalized performance of the single processors for the Dhrystone benchmark.

   e.   [20] <1.9> Plot a 2D scatter plot with the *x*-axis being Dhrystone and the *y*-axis being the memory benchmark.

   f.   [Discussion] <1.9> Given your plot in part (e), in what area does a dual-processor gain in performance? Explain, given your knowledge of parallel processing and architecture, why these results are as they are.

Chip	# of cores	Clock frequency (MHz)	Memory performance	Dhrystone performance
Athlon 64 X2 4800+	2	2,400	3,423	20,718
Pentium EE 840	2	2,200	3,228	18,893
Pentium D 820	2	3,000	3,000	15,220
Athlon 64 X2 3800+	2	3,200	2,941	17,129
Pentium 4	1	2,800	2,731	7,621
Athlon 64 3000+	1	1,800	2,953	7,628
Pentium 4 570	1	2,800	3,501	11,210
Processor X	1	3,000	7,000	5,000

Figure 1.26 Performance of several processors on two benchmarks.

1.13 [10/10/20] <1.9> Imagine that your company is trying to decide between a single-processor system and a dual-processor system. Figure 1.26 gives the performance on two sets of benchmarks—a memory benchmark and a processor benchmark. You know that your application will spend 40% of its time on memory-centric computations, and 60% of its time on processor-centric computations.

a. [10] <1.9> Calculate the weighted execution time of the benchmarks.

b. [10] <1.9> How much speedup do you anticipate getting if you move from using a Pentium 4 570 to an Athlon 64 X2 4800+ on a CPU-intensive application suite?

c. [20] <1.9> At what ratio of memory to processor computation would the performance of the Pentium 4 570 be equal to the Pentium D 820?

1.14 [10/10/20/20] <1.10> Your company has just bought a new dual Pentium processor, and you have been tasked with optimizing your software for this processor. You will run two applications on this dual Pentium, but the resource requirements are not equal. The first application needs 80% of the resources, and the other only 20% of the resources.

a. [10] <1.10> Given that 40% of the first application is parallelizable, how much speedup would you achieve with that application if run in isolation?

b. [10] <1.10> Given that 99% of the second application is parallelizable, how much speedup would this application observe if run in isolation?

c. [20] <1.10> Given that 40% of the first application is parallelizable, how much *overall system speedup* would you observe if you parallelized it?

d. [20] <1.10> Given that 99% of the second application is parallelizable, how much overall system speedup would you get?

2.1	Instruction-Level Parallelism: Concepts and Challenges	66
2.2	Basic Compiler Techniques for Exposing ILP	74
2.3	Reducing Branch Costs with Prediction	80
2.4	Overcoming Data Hazards with Dynamic Scheduling	89
2.5	Dynamic Scheduling: Examples and the Algorithm	97
2.6	Hardware-Based Speculation	104
2.7	Exploiting ILP Using Multiple Issue and Static Scheduling	114
2.8	Exploiting ILP Using Dynamic Scheduling, Multiple Issue, and Speculation	118
2.9	Advanced Techniques for Instruction Delivery and Speculation	121
2.10	Putting It All Together: The Intel Pentium 4	131
2.11	Fallacies and Pitfalls	138
2.12	Concluding Remarks	140
2.13	Historical Perspective and References	141
	Case Studies with Exercises by Robert P. Colwell	142

2

Instruction-Level Parallelism and Its Exploitation

"Who's first?"

"America."

"Who's second?"

"Sir, there is no second."

Dialog between two observers of the sailing race later named "The America's Cup" and run every few years—the inspiration for John Cocke's naming of the IBM research processor as "America." This processor was the precursor to the RS/6000 series and the first superscalar microprocessor.

2.1 Instruction-Level Parallelism: Concepts and Challenges

All processors since about 1985 use pipelining to overlap the execution of instructions and improve performance. This potential overlap among instructions is called *instruction-level parallelism* (ILP), since the instructions can be evaluated in parallel. In this chapter and Appendix G, we look at a wide range of techniques for extending the basic pipelining concepts by increasing the amount of parallelism exploited among instructions.

This chapter is at a considerably more advanced level than the material on basic pipelining in Appendix A. If you are not familiar with the ideas in Appendix A, you should review that appendix before venturing into this chapter.

We start this chapter by looking at the limitation imposed by data and control hazards and then turn to the topic of increasing the ability of the compiler and the processor to exploit parallelism. These sections introduce a large number of concepts, which we build on throughout this chapter and the next. While some of the more basic material in this chapter could be understood without all of the ideas in the first two sections, this basic material is important to later sections of this chapter as well as to Chapter 3.

There are two largely separable approaches to exploiting ILP: an approach that relies on hardware to help discover and exploit the parallelism dynamically, and an approach that relies on software technology to find parallelism, statically at compile time. Processors using the dynamic, hardware-based approach, including the Intel Pentium series, dominate in the market; those using the static approach, including the Intel Itanium, have more limited uses in scientific or application-specific environments.

In the past few years, many of the techniques developed for one approach have been exploited within a design relying primarily on the other. This chapter introduces the basic concepts and both approaches. The next chapter focuses on the critical issue of limitations on exploiting ILP.

In this section, we discuss features of both programs and processors that limit the amount of parallelism that can be exploited among instructions, as well as the critical mapping between program structure and hardware structure, which is key to understanding whether a program property will actually limit performance and under what circumstances.

The value of the CPI (cycles per instruction) for a pipelined processor is the sum of the base CPI and all contributions from stalls:

Pipeline CPI = Ideal pipeline CPI + Structural stalls + Data hazard stalls + Control stalls

The *ideal pipeline CPI* is a measure of the maximum performance attainable by the implementation. By reducing each of the terms of the right-hand side, we minimize the overall pipeline CPI or, alternatively, increase the IPC (instructions per clock). The equation above allows us to characterize various techniques by what component of the overall CPI a technique reduces. Figure 2.1 shows the

Technique	Reduces	Section
Forwarding and bypassing	Potential data hazard stalls	A.2
Delayed branches and simple branch scheduling	Control hazard stalls	A.2
Basic dynamic scheduling (scoreboarding)	Data hazard stalls from true dependences	A.7
Dynamic scheduling with renaming	Data hazard stalls and stalls from antidependences and output dependences	2.4
Branch prediction	Control stalls	2.3
Issuing multiple instructions per cycle	Ideal CPI	2.7, 2.8
Hardware speculation	Data hazard and control hazard stalls	2.6
Dynamic memory disambiguation	Data hazard stalls with memory	2.4, 2.6
Loop unrolling	Control hazard stalls	2.2
Basic compiler pipeline scheduling	Data hazard stalls	A.2, 2.2
Compiler dependence analysis, software pipelining, trace scheduling	Ideal CPI, data hazard stalls	G.2, G.3
Hardware support for compiler speculation	Ideal CPI, data hazard stalls, branch hazard stalls	G.4, G.5

Figure 2.1   The major techniques examined in Appendix A, Chapter 2, or Appendix G are shown together with the component of the CPI equation that the technique affects.

techniques we examine in this chapter and in Appendix G, as well as the topics covered in the introductory material in Appendix A. In this chapter we will see that the techniques we introduce to decrease the ideal pipeline CPI can increase the importance of dealing with hazards.

What Is Instruction-Level Parallelism?

All the techniques in this chapter exploit parallelism among instructions. The amount of parallelism available within a *basic block*—a straight-line code sequence with no branches in except to the entry and no branches out except at the exit—is quite small. For typical MIPS programs, the average dynamic branch frequency is often between 15% and 25%, meaning that between three and six instructions execute between a pair of branches. Since these instructions are likely to depend upon one another, the amount of overlap we can exploit within a basic block is likely to be less than the average basic block size. To obtain substantial performance enhancements, we must exploit ILP across multiple basic blocks.

The simplest and most common way to increase the ILP is to exploit parallelism among iterations of a loop. This type of parallelism is often called *loop-level parallelism*. Here is a simple example of a loop, which adds two 1000-element arrays, that is completely parallel:

```
for (i=1; i<=1000; i=i+1)
        x[i] = x[i] + y[i];
```

Every iteration of the loop can overlap with any other iteration, although within each loop iteration there is little or no opportunity for overlap.

There are a number of techniques we will examine for converting such loop-level parallelism into instruction-level parallelism. Basically, such techniques work by unrolling the loop either statically by the compiler (as in the next section) or dynamically by the hardware (as in Sections 2.5 and 2.6).

An important alternative method for exploiting loop-level parallelism is the use of vector instructions (see Appendix F). A vector instruction exploits data-level parallelism by operating on data items in parallel. For example, the above code sequence could execute in four instructions on some vector processors: two instructions to load the vectors x and y from memory, one instruction to add the two vectors, and an instruction to store back the result vector. Of course, these instructions would be pipelined and have relatively long latencies, but these latencies may be overlapped.

Although the development of the vector ideas preceded many of the techniques for exploiting ILP, processors that exploit ILP have almost completely replaced vector-based processors in the general-purpose processor market. Vector instruction sets, however, have seen a renaissance, at least for use in graphics, digital signal processing, and multimedia applications.

Data Dependences and Hazards

Determining how one instruction depends on another is critical to determining how much parallelism exists in a program and how that parallelism can be exploited. In particular, to exploit instruction-level parallelism we must determine which instructions can be executed in parallel. If two instructions are *parallel*, they can execute simultaneously in a pipeline of arbitrary depth without causing any stalls, assuming the pipeline has sufficient resources (and hence no structural hazards exist). If two instructions are dependent, they are not parallel and must be executed in order, although they may often be partially overlapped. The key in both cases is to determine whether an instruction is dependent on another instruction.

Data Dependences

There are three different types of dependences: *data dependences* (also called true data dependences), *name dependences*, and *control dependences*. An instruction *j* is *data dependent* on instruction *i* if either of the following holds:

■ instruction *i* produces a result that may be used by instruction *j*, or

■ instruction *j* is data dependent on instruction *k*, and instruction *k* is data dependent on instruction *i*.

The second condition simply states that one instruction is dependent on another if there exists a chain of dependences of the first type between the two instructions. This dependence chain can be as long as the entire program. Note that a dependence within a single instruction (such as ADDD R1,R1,R1) is not considered a dependence.

For example, consider the following MIPS code sequence that increments a vector of values in memory (starting at 0(R1), and with the last element at 8(R2)), by a scalar in register F2. (For simplicity, throughout this chapter, our examples ignore the effects of delayed branches.)

```
Loop:      L.D      F0,0(R1)       ;F0=array element
           ADD.D    F4,F0,F2       ;add scalar in F2
           S.D      F4,0(R1)       ;store result
           DADDUI   R1,R1,#-8      ;decrement pointer 8 bytes
           BNE      R1,R2,LOOP     ;branch R1!=R2
```

The data dependences in this code sequence involve both floating-point data:

```
Loop:      L.D      F0,0(R1)       ;F0=array element
           ADD.D    F4,F0,F2       ;add scalar in F2
           S.D      F4,0(R1)       ;store result
```

and integer data:

```
           DADDIU   R1,R1,-8       ;decrement pointer
                                   ;8 bytes (per DW)
           BNE      R1,R2,Loop     ;branch R1!=R2
```

Both of the above dependent sequences, as shown by the arrows, have each instruction depending on the previous one. The arrows here and in following examples show the order that must be preserved for correct execution. The arrow points from an instruction that must precede the instruction that the arrowhead points to.

If two instructions are data dependent, they cannot execute simultaneously or be completely overlapped. The dependence implies that there would be a chain of one or more data hazards between the two instructions. (See Appendix A for a brief description of data hazards, which we will define precisely in a few pages.) Executing the instructions simultaneously will cause a processor with pipeline interlocks (and a pipeline depth longer than the distance between the instructions in cycles) to detect a hazard and stall, thereby reducing or eliminating the overlap. In a processor without interlocks that relies on compiler scheduling, the compiler cannot schedule dependent instructions in such a way that they completely overlap, since the program will not execute correctly. The presence of a data dependence in an instruction sequence reflects a data dependence in the source code from which the instruction sequence was generated. The effect of the original data dependence must be preserved.

Dependences are a property of *programs*. Whether a given dependence results in an actual hazard being detected and whether that hazard actually causes a stall are properties of the *pipeline organization*. This difference is critical to understanding how instruction-level parallelism can be exploited.

A data dependence conveys three things: (1) the possibility of a hazard, (2) the order in which results must be calculated, and (3) an upper bound on how much parallelism can possibly be exploited. Such limits are explored in Chapter 3.

Since a data dependence can limit the amount of instruction-level parallelism we can exploit, a major focus of this chapter is overcoming these limitations. A dependence can be overcome in two different ways: maintaining the dependence but avoiding a hazard, and eliminating a dependence by transforming the code. Scheduling the code is the primary method used to avoid a hazard without altering a dependence, and such scheduling can be done both by the compiler and by the hardware.

A data value may flow between instructions either through registers or through memory locations. When the data flow occurs in a register, detecting the dependence is straightforward since the register names are fixed in the instructions, although it gets more complicated when branches intervene and correctness concerns force a compiler or hardware to be conservative.

Dependences that flow through memory locations are more difficult to detect, since two addresses may refer to the same location but look different: For example, 100(R4) and 20(R6) may be identical memory addresses. In addition, the effective address of a load or store may change from one execution of the instruction to another (so that 20(R4) and 20(R4) may be different), further complicating the detection of a dependence.

In this chapter, we examine hardware for detecting data dependences that involve memory locations, but we will see that these techniques also have limitations. The compiler techniques for detecting such dependences are critical in uncovering loop-level parallelism, as we will see in Appendix G.

Name Dependences

The second type of dependence is a *name dependence*. A name dependence occurs when two instructions use the same register or memory location, called a *name*, but there is no flow of data between the instructions associated with that name. There are two types of name dependences between an instruction *i* that *precedes* instruction *j* in program order:

1. An *antidependence* between instruction *i* and instruction *j* occurs when instruction *j* writes a register or memory location that instruction *i* reads. The original ordering must be preserved to ensure that *i* reads the correct value. In the example on page 69, there is an antidependence between S.D and DADDIU on register R1.

2. An *output dependence* occurs when instruction *i* and instruction *j* write the same register or memory location. The ordering between the instructions must be preserved to ensure that the value finally written corresponds to instruction *j*.

Both antidependences and output dependences are name dependences, as opposed to true data dependences, since there is no value being transmitted between the instructions. Since a name dependence is not a true dependence, instructions involved in a name dependence can execute simultaneously or be reordered, if the name (register number or memory location) used in the instructions is changed so the instructions do not conflict.

This renaming can be more easily done for register operands, where it is called *register renaming*. Register renaming can be done either statically by a compiler or dynamically by the hardware. Before describing dependences arising from branches, let's examine the relationship between dependences and pipeline data hazards.

Data Hazards

A hazard is created whenever there is a dependence between instructions, and they are close enough that the overlap during execution would change the order of access to the operand involved in the dependence. Because of the dependence, we must preserve what is called *program order,* that is, the order that the instructions would execute in if executed sequentially one at a time as determined by the original source program. The goal of both our software and hardware techniques is to exploit parallelism by preserving program order *only where it affects the outcome of the program.* Detecting and avoiding hazards ensures that necessary program order is preserved.

Data hazards, which are informally described in Appendix A, may be classified as one of three types, depending on the order of read and write accesses in the instructions. By convention, the hazards are named by the ordering in the program that must be preserved by the pipeline. Consider two instructions *i* and *j*, with *i* preceding *j* in program order. The possible data hazards are

- RAW *(read after write)*—*j* tries to read a source before *i* writes it, so *j* incorrectly gets the *old* value. This hazard is the most common type and corresponds to a true data dependence. Program order must be preserved to ensure that *j* receives the value from *i*.

- WAW *(write after write)*—*j* tries to write an operand before it is written by *i*. The writes end up being performed in the wrong order, leaving the value written by *i* rather than the value written by *j* in the destination. This hazard corresponds to an output dependence. WAW hazards are present only in pipelines that write in more than one pipe stage or allow an instruction to proceed even when a previous instruction is stalled.

■ WAR *(write after read)*—*j* tries to write a destination before it is read by *i,* so *i* incorrectly gets the *new* value. This hazard arises from an antidependence. WAR hazards cannot occur in most static issue pipelines—even deeper pipelines or floating-point pipelines—because all reads are early (in ID) and all writes are late (in WB). (See Appendix A to convince yourself.) A WAR hazard occurs either when there are some instructions that write results early in the instruction pipeline *and* other instructions that read a source late in the pipeline, or when instructions are reordered, as we will see in this chapter.

Note that the RAR *(read after read)* case is not a hazard.

Control Dependences

The last type of dependence is a *control dependence.* A control dependence determines the ordering of an instruction, *i,* with respect to a branch instruction so that the instruction *i* is executed in correct program order and only when it should be. Every instruction, except for those in the first basic block of the program, is control dependent on some set of branches, and, in general, these control dependences must be preserved to preserve program order. One of the simplest examples of a control dependence is the dependence of the statements in the "then" part of an if statement on the branch. For example, in the code segment

```
if p1 {
      S1;
};
if p2 {
      S2;
}
```

S1 is control dependent on p1, and S2 is control dependent on p2 but not on p1. In general, there are two constraints imposed by control dependences:

1. An instruction that is control dependent on a branch cannot be moved *before* the branch so that its execution *is no longer controlled* by the branch. For example, we cannot take an instruction from the then portion of an if statement and move it before the if statement.

2. An instruction that is not control dependent on a branch cannot be moved *after* the branch so that its execution *is controlled* by the branch. For example, we cannot take a statement before the if statement and move it into the then portion.

When processors preserve strict program order, they ensure that control dependences are also preserved. We may be willing to execute instructions that should not have been executed, however, thereby violating the control dependences, *if* we can do so without affecting the correctness of the program. Control dependence is not the critical property that must be preserved. Instead, the two properties critical to program correctness—and normally preserved by maintaining both data and control dependence—are the *exception behavior* and the *data flow*.

Preserving the exception behavior means that any changes in the ordering of instruction execution must not change how exceptions are raised in the program. Often this is relaxed to mean that the reordering of instruction execution must not cause any new exceptions in the program. A simple example shows how maintaining the control and data dependences can prevent such situations. Consider this code sequence:

```
        DADDU     R2,R3,R4
        BEQZ      R2,L1
        LW        R1,0(R2)
L1:
```

In this case, it is easy to see that if we do not maintain the data dependence involving R2, we can change the result of the program. Less obvious is the fact that if we ignore the control dependence and move the load instruction before the branch, the load instruction may cause a memory protection exception. Notice that *no data dependence* prevents us from interchanging the BEQZ and the LW; it is only the control dependence. To allow us to reorder these instructions (and still preserve the data dependence), we would like to just ignore the exception when the branch is taken. In Section 2.6, we will look at a hardware technique, *speculation*, which allows us to overcome this exception problem. Appendix G looks at software techniques for supporting speculation.

The second property preserved by maintenance of data dependences and control dependences is the data flow. The *data flow* is the actual flow of data values among instructions that produce results and those that consume them. Branches make the data flow dynamic, since they allow the source of data for a given instruction to come from many points. Put another way, it is insufficient to just maintain data dependences because an instruction may be data dependent on more than one predecessor. Program order is what determines which predecessor will actually deliver a data value to an instruction. Program order is ensured by maintaining the control dependences.

For example, consider the following code fragment:

```
        DADDU     R1,R2,R3
        BEQZ      R4,L
        DSUBU     R1,R5,R6
L:      . . .

        OR        R7,R1,R8
```

In this example, the value of R1 used by the OR instruction depends on whether the branch is taken or not. Data dependence alone is not sufficient to preserve correctness. The OR instruction is data dependent on both the DADDU and DSUBU instructions, but preserving that order alone is insufficient for correct execution.

Instead, when the instructions execute, the data flow must be preserved: If the branch is not taken, then the value of R1 computed by the DSUBU should be used by the OR, and if the branch is taken, the value of R1 computed by the DADDU should be used by the OR. By preserving the control dependence of the OR on the branch, we prevent an illegal change to the data flow. For similar reasons, the DSUBU instruction cannot be moved above the branch. Speculation, which helps with the exception problem, will also allow us to lessen the impact of the control dependence while still maintaining the data flow, as we will see in Section 2.6.

Sometimes we can determine that violating the control dependence cannot affect either the exception behavior or the data flow. Consider the following code sequence:

```
          DADDU     R1,R2,R3
          BEQZ      R12,skip
          DSUBU     R4,R5,R6
          DADDU     R5,R4,R9
skip:     OR        R7,R8,R9
```

Suppose we knew that the register destination of the DSUBU instruction (R4) was unused after the instruction labeled skip. (The property of whether a value will be used by an upcoming instruction is called *liveness.*) If R4 were unused, then changing the value of R4 just before the branch would not affect the data flow since R4 would be *dead* (rather than live) in the code region after skip. Thus, if R4 were dead and the existing DSUBU instruction could not generate an exception (other than those from which the processor resumes the same process), we could move the DSUBU instruction before the branch, since the data flow cannot be affected by this change.

If the branch is taken, the DSUBU instruction will execute and will be useless, but it will not affect the program results. This type of code scheduling is also a form of speculation, often called software speculation, since the compiler is betting on the branch outcome; in this case, the bet is that the branch is usually not taken. More ambitious compiler speculation mechanisms are discussed in Appendix G. Normally, it will be clear when we say speculation or speculative whether the mechanism is a hardware or software mechanism; when it is not clear, it is best to say "hardware speculation" or "software speculation."

Control dependence is preserved by implementing control hazard detection that causes control stalls. Control stalls can be eliminated or reduced by a variety of hardware and software techniques, which we examine in Section 2.3.

2.2   Basic Compiler Techniques for Exposing ILP

This section examines the use of simple compiler technology to enhance a processor's ability to exploit ILP. These techniques are crucial for processors that use static issue or static scheduling. Armed with this compiler technology, we will shortly examine the design and performance of processors using static issuing. Appendix G will investigate more sophisticated compiler and associated hardware schemes designed to enable a processor to exploit more instruction-level parallelism.

Basic Pipeline Scheduling and Loop Unrolling

To keep a pipeline full, parallelism among instructions must be exploited by finding sequences of unrelated instructions that can be overlapped in the pipeline. To avoid a pipeline stall, a dependent instruction must be separated from the source instruction by a distance in clock cycles equal to the pipeline latency of that source instruction. A compiler's ability to perform this scheduling depends both on the amount of ILP available in the program and on the latencies of the functional units in the pipeline. Figure 2.2 shows the FP unit latencies we assume in this chapter, unless different latencies are explicitly stated. We assume the standard five-stage integer pipeline, so that branches have a delay of 1 clock cycle. We assume that the functional units are fully pipelined or replicated (as many times as the pipeline depth), so that an operation of any type can be issued on every clock cycle and there are no structural hazards.

In this subsection, we look at how the compiler can increase the amount of available ILP by transforming loops. This example serves both to illustrate an important technique as well as to motivate the more powerful program transformations described in Appendix G. We will rely on the following code segment, which adds a scalar to a vector:

```
for (i=1000; i>0; i=i−1)
        x[i] = x[i] + s;
```

We can see that this loop is parallel by noticing that the body of each iteration is independent. We will formalize this notion in Appendix G and describe how we can test whether loop iterations are independent at compile time. First, let's look at the performance of this loop, showing how we can use the parallelism to improve its performance for a MIPS pipeline with the latencies shown above.

Instruction producing result	Instruction using result	Latency in clock cycles
FP ALU op	Another FP ALU op	3
FP ALU op	Store double	2
Load double	FP ALU op	1
Load double	Store double	0

Figure 2.2 Latencies of FP operations used in this chapter. The last column is the number of intervening clock cycles needed to avoid a stall. These numbers are similar to the average latencies we would see on an FP unit. The latency of a floating-point load to a store is 0, since the result of the load can be bypassed without stalling the store. We will continue to assume an integer load latency of 1 and an integer ALU operation latency of 0.

The first step is to translate the above segment to MIPS assembly language. In the following code segment, R1 is initially the address of the element in the array with the highest address, and F2 contains the scalar value *s*. Register R2 is precomputed, so that 8(R2) is the address of the last element to operate on.

The straightforward MIPS code, not scheduled for the pipeline, looks like this:

```
Loop:   L.D     F0,0(R1)      ;F0=array element
        ADD.D   F4,F0,F2      ;add scalar in F2
        S.D     F4,0(R1)      ;store result
        DADDUI  R1,R1,#-8     ;decrement pointer
                              ;8 bytes (per DW)
        BNE     R1,R2,Loop    ;branch R1!=R2
```

Let's start by seeing how well this loop will run when it is scheduled on a simple pipeline for MIPS with the latencies from Figure 2.2.

Example   Show how the loop would look on MIPS, both scheduled and unscheduled, including any stalls or idle clock cycles. Schedule for delays from floating-point operations, but remember that we are ignoring delayed branches.

Answer   Without any scheduling, the loop will execute as follows, taking 9 cycles:

Clock cycle issued

```
Loop:   L.D     F0,0(R1)           1
        stall                      2
        ADD.D   F4,F0,F2           3
        stall                      4
        stall                      5
        S.D     F4,0(R1)           6
        DADDUI  R1,R1,#-8          7
        stall                      8
        BNE     R1,R2,Loop         9
```

We can schedule the loop to obtain only two stalls and reduce the time to 7 cycles:

```
Loop:   L.D     F0,0(R1)
        DADDUI  R1,R1,#-8
        ADD.D   F4,F0,F2
        stall
        stall
        S.D     F4,8(R1)
        BNE     R1,R2,Loop
```

The stalls after ADD.D are for use by the S.D.

In the previous example, we complete one loop iteration and store back one array element every 7 clock cycles, but the actual work of operating on the array element takes just 3 (the load, add, and store) of those 7 clock cycles. The remaining 4 clock cycles consist of loop overhead—the DADDUI and BNE—and two stalls. To eliminate these 4 clock cycles we need to get more operations relative to the number of overhead instructions.

A simple scheme for increasing the number of instructions relative to the branch and overhead instructions is *loop unrolling*. Unrolling simply replicates the loop body multiple times, adjusting the loop termination code.

Loop unrolling can also be used to improve scheduling. Because it eliminates the branch, it allows instructions from different iterations to be scheduled together. In this case, we can eliminate the data use stalls by creating additional independent instructions within the loop body. If we simply replicated the instructions when we unrolled the loop, the resulting use of the same registers could prevent us from effectively scheduling the loop. Thus, we will want to use different registers for each iteration, increasing the required number of registers.

Example   Show our loop unrolled so that there are four copies of the loop body, assuming R1 − R2 (that is, the size of the array) is initially a multiple of 32, which means that the number of loop iterations is a multiple of 4. Eliminate any obviously redundant computations and do not reuse any of the registers.

Answer   Here is the result after merging the DADDUI instructions and dropping the unnecessary BNE operations that are duplicated during unrolling. Note that R2 must now be set so that 32(R2) is the starting address of the last four elements.

```
Loop:   L.D       F0,0(R1)
        ADD.D     F4,F0,F2
        S.D       F4,0(R1)      ;drop DADDUI & BNE
        L.D       F6,-8(R1)
        ADD.D     F8,F6,F2
        S.D       F8,-8(R1)     ;drop DADDUI & BNE
        L.D       F10,-16(R1)
        ADD.D     F12,F10,F2
        S.D       F12,-16(R1)   ;drop DADDUI & BNE
        L.D       F14,-24(R1)
        ADD.D     F16,F14,F2
        S.D       F16,-24(R1)
        DADDUI    R1,R1,#-32
        BNE       R1,R2,Loop
```

We have eliminated three branches and three decrements of R1. The addresses on the loads and stores have been compensated to allow the DADDUI instructions on R1 to be merged. This optimization may seem trivial, but it is not; it requires symbolic substitution and simplification. Symbolic substitution and simplification will rearrange expressions so as to allow constants to be collapsed, allowing an expression such as "$((i + 1) + 1)$" to be rewritten as "$(i +(1 + 1))$" and then simplified to "$(i + 2)$." We will see more general forms of these optimizations that eliminate dependent computations in Appendix G.

Without scheduling, every operation in the unrolled loop is followed by a dependent operation and thus will cause a stall. This loop will run in 27 clock cycles—each LD has 1 stall, each ADDD 2, the DADDUI 1, plus 14 instruction issue cycles—or 6.75 clock cycles for each of the four elements, but it can be scheduled to improve performance significantly. Loop unrolling is normally done early in the compilation process, so that redundant computations can be exposed and eliminated by the optimizer.

In real programs we do not usually know the upper bound on the loop. Suppose it is *n,* and we would like to unroll the loop to make *k* copies of the body. Instead of a single unrolled loop, we generate a pair of consecutive loops. The first executes (*n* mod *k*) times and has a body that is the original loop. The second is the unrolled body surrounded by an outer loop that iterates (*n/k*) times. For large values of *n,* most of the execution time will be spent in the unrolled loop body.

In the previous example, unrolling improves the performance of this loop by eliminating overhead instructions, although it increases code size substantially. How will the unrolled loop perform when it is scheduled for the pipeline described earlier?

Example Show the unrolled loop in the previous example after it has been scheduled for the pipeline with the latencies shown in Figure 2.2.

Answer
```
Loop:    L.D       F0,0(R1)
         L.D       F6,-8(R1)
         L.D       F10,-16(R1)
         L.D       F14,-24(R1)
         ADD.D     F4,F0,F2
         ADD.D     F8,F6,F2
         ADD.D     F12,F10,F2
         ADD.D     F16,F14,F2
         S.D       F4,0(R1)
         S.D       F8,-8(R1)
         DADDUI    R1,R1,#-32
         S.D       F12,16(R1)
         S.D       F16,8(R1)
         BNE       R1,R2,Loop
```

The execution time of the unrolled loop has dropped to a total of 14 clock cycles, or 3.5 clock cycles per element, compared with 9 cycles per element before any unrolling or scheduling and 7 cycles when scheduled but not unrolled.

The gain from scheduling on the unrolled loop is even larger than on the original loop. This increase arises because unrolling the loop exposes more computation that can be scheduled to minimize the stalls; the code above has no stalls. Scheduling the loop in this fashion necessitates realizing that the loads and stores are independent and can be interchanged.

Summary of the Loop Unrolling and Scheduling

Throughout this chapter and Appendix G, we will look at a variety of hardware and software techniques that allow us to take advantage of instruction-level parallelism to fully utilize the potential of the functional units in a processor. The key to most of these techniques is to know when and how the ordering among instructions may be changed. In our example we made many such changes, which to us, as human beings, were obviously allowable. In practice, this process must be performed in a methodical fashion either by a compiler or by hardware. To obtain the final unrolled code we had to make the following decisions and transformations:

- Determine that unrolling the loop would be useful by finding that the loop iterations were independent, except for the loop maintenance code.

- Use different registers to avoid unnecessary constraints that would be forced by using the same registers for different computations.

- Eliminate the extra test and branch instructions and adjust the loop termination and iteration code.

- Determine that the loads and stores in the unrolled loop can be interchanged by observing that the loads and stores from different iterations are independent. This transformation requires analyzing the memory addresses and finding that they do not refer to the same address.

- Schedule the code, preserving any dependences needed to yield the same result as the original code.

The key requirement underlying all of these transformations is an understanding of how one instruction depends on another and how the instructions can be changed or reordered given the dependences.

There are three different types of limits to the gains that can be achieved by loop unrolling: a decrease in the amount of overhead amortized with each unroll, code size limitations, and compiler limitations. Let's consider the question of loop overhead first. When we unrolled the loop four times, it generated sufficient parallelism among the instructions that the loop could be scheduled with no stall cycles. In fact, in 14 clock cycles, only 2 cycles were loop overhead: the DADDUI, which maintains the index value, and the BNE, which terminates the loop. If the loop is unrolled eight times, the overhead is reduced from 1/2 cycle per original iteration to 1/4.

A second limit to unrolling is the growth in code size that results. For larger loops, the code size growth may be a concern particularly if it causes an increase in the instruction cache miss rate.

Another factor often more important than code size is the potential shortfall in registers that is created by aggressive unrolling and scheduling. This secondary effect that results from instruction scheduling in large code segments is called *register pressure*. It arises because scheduling code to increase ILP causes the number of live values to increase. After aggressive instruction scheduling, it may not be possible to allocate all the live values to registers. The transformed code, while theoretically faster, may lose some or all of its advantage because it generates a shortage of registers. Without unrolling, aggressive scheduling is sufficiently limited by branches so that register pressure is rarely a problem. The combination of unrolling and aggressive scheduling can, however, cause this problem. The problem becomes especially challenging in multiple-issue processors that require the exposure of more independent instruction sequences whose execution can be overlapped. In general, the use of sophisticated high-level transformations, whose potential improvements are hard to measure before detailed code generation, has led to significant increases in the complexity of modern compilers.

Loop unrolling is a simple but useful method for increasing the size of straight-line code fragments that can be scheduled effectively. This transformation is useful in a variety of processors, from simple pipelines like those we have examined so far to the multiple-issue superscalars and VLIWs explored later in this chapter.

2.3   Reducing Branch Costs with Prediction

Because of the need to enforce control dependences through branch hazards and stalls, branches will hurt pipeline performance. Loop unrolling is one way to reduce the number of branch hazards; we can also reduce the performance losses of branches by predicting how they will behave.

The behavior of branches can be predicted both statically at compile time and dynamically by the hardware at execution time. Static branch predictors are sometimes used in processors where the expectation is that branch behavior is highly predictable at compile time; static prediction can also be used to assist dynamic predictors.

Static Branch Prediction

In Appendix A, we discuss an architectural feature that supports static branch prediction, namely, delayed branches. Being able to accurately predict a branch at compile time is also helpful for scheduling data hazards. Loop unrolling is another example of a technique for improving code scheduling that depends on predicting branches.

To reorder code around branches so that it runs faster, we need to predict the branch statically when we compile the program. There are several different methods to statically predict branch behavior. The simplest scheme is to predict a branch as taken. This scheme has an average misprediction rate that is equal to the untaken branch frequency, which for the SPEC programs is 34%. Unfortunately, the misprediction rate for the SPEC programs ranges from not very accurate (59%) to highly accurate (9%).

A more accurate technique is to predict branches on the basis of profile information collected from earlier runs. The key observation that makes this worthwhile is that the behavior of branches is often bimodally distributed; that is, an individual branch is often highly biased toward taken or untaken. Figure 2.3 shows the success of branch prediction using this strategy. The same input data were used for runs and for collecting the profile; other studies have shown that changing the input so that the profile is for a different run leads to only a small change in the accuracy of profile-based prediction.

The effectiveness of any branch prediction scheme depends both on the accuracy of the scheme and the frequency of conditional branches, which vary in SPEC from 3% to 24%. The fact that the misprediction rate for the integer programs is higher and that such programs typically have a higher branch frequency is a major limitation for static branch prediction. In the next section, we consider dynamic branch predictors, which most recent processors have employed.

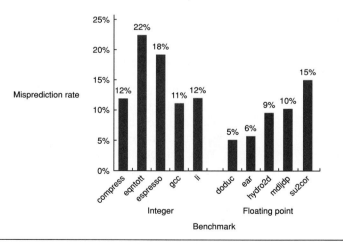

Figure 2.3 Misprediction rate on SPEC92 for a profile-based predictor varies widely but is generally better for the FP programs, which have an average misprediction rate of 9% with a standard deviation of 4%, than for the integer programs, which have an average misprediction rate of 15% with a standard deviation of 5%. The actual performance depends on both the prediction accuracy and the branch frequency, which vary from 3% to 24%.

Dynamic Branch Prediction and Branch-Prediction Buffers

The simplest dynamic branch-prediction scheme is a *branch-prediction buffer* or *branch history table*. A branch-prediction buffer is a small memory indexed by the lower portion of the address of the branch instruction. The memory contains a bit that says whether the branch was recently taken or not. This scheme is the simplest sort of buffer; it has no tags and is useful only to reduce the branch delay when it is longer than the time to compute the possible target PCs.

With such a buffer, we don't know, in fact, if the prediction is correct—it may have been put there by another branch that has the same low-order address bits. But this doesn't matter. The prediction is a hint that is assumed to be correct, and fetching begins in the predicted direction. If the hint turns out to be wrong, the prediction bit is inverted and stored back.

This buffer is effectively a cache where every access is a hit, and, as we will see, the performance of the buffer depends on both how often the prediction is for the branch of interest and how accurate the prediction is when it matches. Before we analyze the performance, it is useful to make a small, but important, improvement in the accuracy of the branch-prediction scheme.

This simple 1-bit prediction scheme has a performance shortcoming: Even if a branch is almost always taken, we will likely predict incorrectly twice, rather than once, when it is not taken, since the misprediction causes the prediction bit to be flipped.

To remedy this weakness, 2-bit prediction schemes are often used. In a 2-bit scheme, a prediction must miss twice before it is changed. Figure 2.4 shows the finite-state processor for a 2-bit prediction scheme.

A branch-prediction buffer can be implemented as a small, special "cache" accessed with the instruction address during the IF pipe stage, or as a pair of bits attached to each block in the instruction cache and fetched with the instruction. If the instruction is decoded as a branch and if the branch is predicted as taken, fetching begins from the target as soon as the PC is known. Otherwise, sequential fetching and executing continue. As Figure 2.4 shows, if the prediction turns out to be wrong, the prediction bits are changed.

What kind of accuracy can be expected from a branch-prediction buffer using 2 bits per entry on real applications? Figure 2.5 shows that for the SPEC89 benchmarks a branch-prediction buffer with 4096 entries results in a prediction accuracy ranging from over 99% to 82%, or a *misprediction rate* of 1% to 18%. A 4K entry buffer, like that used for these results, is considered small by 2005 standards, and a larger buffer could produce somewhat better results.

As we try to exploit more ILP, the accuracy of our branch prediction becomes critical. As we can see in Figure 2.5, the accuracy of the predictors for integer programs, which typically also have higher branch frequencies, is lower than for the loop-intensive scientific programs. We can attack this problem in two ways: by increasing the size of the buffer and by increasing the accuracy of the scheme we use for each prediction. A buffer with 4K entries, however, as Figure 2.6 shows, performs quite comparably to an infinite buffer, at least for benchmarks like those in SPEC. The data in Figure 2.6 make it clear that the hit rate of the

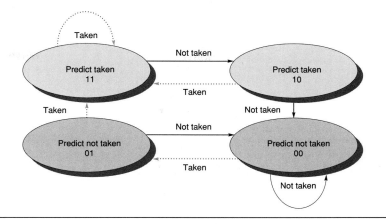

Figure 2.4 The states in a 2-bit prediction scheme. By using 2 bits rather than 1, a branch that strongly favors taken or not taken—as many branches do—will be mispredicted less often than with a 1-bit predictor. The 2 bits are used to encode the four states in the system. The 2-bit scheme is actually a specialization of a more general scheme that has an n-bit saturating counter for each entry in the prediction buffer. With an n-bit counter, the counter can take on values between 0 and $2^n - 1$: When the counter is greater than or equal to one-half of its maximum value ($2^n - 1$), the branch is predicted as taken; otherwise, it is predicted untaken. Studies of n-bit predictors have shown that the 2-bit predictors do almost as well, and thus most systems rely on 2-bit branch predictors rather than the more general n-bit predictors.

buffer is not the major limiting factor. As we mentioned above, simply increasing the number of bits per predictor without changing the predictor structure also has little impact. Instead, we need to look at how we might increase the accuracy of each predictor.

Correlating Branch Predictors

The 2-bit predictor schemes use only the recent behavior of a single branch to predict the future behavior of that branch. It may be possible to improve the prediction accuracy if we also look at the recent behavior of *other* branches rather than just the branch we are trying to predict. Consider a small code fragment from the eqntott benchmark, a member of early SPEC benchmark suites that displayed particularly bad branch prediction behavior:

```
if (aa==2)
        aa=0;
if (bb==2)
        bb=0;
if (aa!=bb) {
```

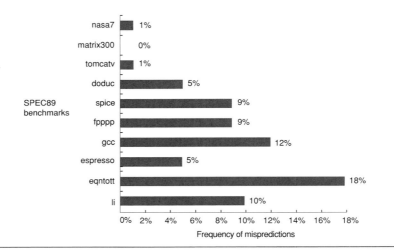

Figure 2.5 Prediction accuracy of a 4096-entry 2-bit prediction buffer for the SPEC89 benchmarks. The misprediction rate for the integer benchmarks (gcc, espresso, eqntott, and li) is substantially higher (average of 11%) than that for the FP programs (average of 4%). Omitting the FP kernels (nasa7, matrix300, and tomcatv) still yields a higher accuracy for the FP benchmarks than for the integer benchmarks. These data, as well as the rest of the data in this section, are taken from a branch-prediction study done using the IBM Power architecture and optimized code for that system. See Pan, So, and Rameh [1992]. Although this data is for an older version of a subset of the SPEC benchmarks, the newer benchmarks are larger and would show slightly worse behavior, especially for the integer benchmarks.

Here is the MIPS code that we would typically generate for this code fragment assuming that aa and bb are assigned to registers R1 and R2:

```
        DADDIU    R3,R1,#-2
        BNEZ      R3,L1         ;branch b1   (aa!=2)
        DADD      R1,R0,R0      ;aa=0
L1:     DADDIU    R3,R2,#-2
        BNEZ      R3,L2         ;branch b2   (bb!=2)
        DADD      R2,R0,R0      ;bb=0
L2:     DSUBU     R3,R1,R2      ;R3=aa-bb
        BEQZ      R3,L3         ;branch b3   (aa==bb)
```

Let's label these branches b1, b2, and b3. The key observation is that the behavior of branch b3 is correlated with the behavior of branches b1 and b2. Clearly, if branches b1 and b2 are both not taken (i.e., if the conditions both evaluate to true and aa and bb are both assigned 0), then b3 will be taken, since aa and bb are clearly equal. A predictor that uses only the behavior of a single branch to predict the outcome of that branch can never capture this behavior.

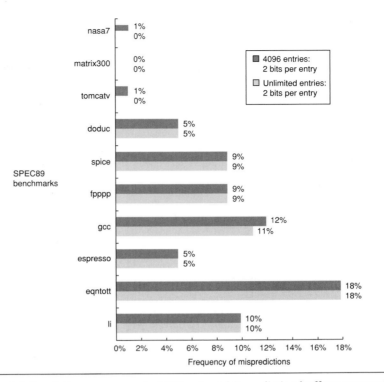

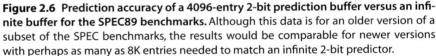

Figure 2.6 Prediction accuracy of a 4096-entry 2-bit prediction buffer versus an infinite buffer for the SPEC89 benchmarks. Although this data is for an older version of a subset of the SPEC benchmarks, the results would be comparable for newer versions with perhaps as many as 8K entries needed to match an infinite 2-bit predictor.

Branch predictors that use the behavior of other branches to make a prediction are called *correlating predictors* or *two-level predictors*. Existing correlating predictors add information about the behavior of the most recent branches to decide how to predict a given branch. For example, a (1,2) predictor uses the behavior of the last branch to choose from among a pair of 2-bit branch predictors in predicting a particular branch. In the general case an (*m*,*n*) predictor uses the behavior of the last *m* branches to choose from 2^m branch predictors, each of which is an *n*-bit predictor for a single branch. The attraction of this type of correlating branch predictor is that it can yield higher prediction rates than the 2-bit scheme and requires only a trivial amount of additional hardware.

The simplicity of the hardware comes from a simple observation: The global history of the most recent *m* branches can be recorded in an *m*-bit shift register, where each bit records whether the branch was taken or not taken. The branch-prediction buffer can then be indexed using a concatenation of the low-order bits from the branch address with the *m*-bit global history. For example, in a (2,2) buffer with 64 total entries, the 4 low-order address bits of the branch (word address) and the 2 global bits representing the behavior of the two most recently executed branches form a 6-bit index that can be used to index the 64 counters.

How much better do the correlating branch predictors work when compared with the standard 2-bit scheme? To compare them fairly, we must compare predictors that use the same number of state bits. The number of bits in an (m,n) predictor is

$$2^m \times n \times \text{Number of prediction entries selected by the branch address}$$

A 2-bit predictor with no global history is simply a $(0,2)$ predictor.

Example How many bits are in the $(0,2)$ branch predictor with 4K entries? How many entries are in a $(2,2)$ predictor with the same number of bits?

Answer The predictor with 4K entries has

$$2^0 \times 2 \times 4K = 8K \text{ bits}$$

How many branch-selected entries are in a $(2,2)$ predictor that has a total of 8K bits in the prediction buffer? We know that

$$2^2 \times 2 \times \text{Number of prediction entries selected by the branch} = 8K$$

Hence, the number of prediction entries selected by the branch = 1K.

Figure 2.7 compares the misprediction rates of the earlier $(0,2)$ predictor with 4K entries and a $(2,2)$ predictor with 1K entries. As you can see, this correlating predictor not only outperforms a simple 2-bit predictor with the same total number of state bits, it often outperforms a 2-bit predictor with an unlimited number of entries.

Tournament Predictors: Adaptively Combining Local and Global Predictors

The primary motivation for correlating branch predictors came from the observation that the standard 2-bit predictor using only local information failed on some important branches and that, by adding global information, the performance could be improved. *Tournament predictors* take this insight to the next level, by using multiple predictors, usually one based on global information and one based on local information, and combining them with a selector. Tournament predictors can achieve both better accuracy at medium sizes (8K–32K bits) and also make use of very large numbers of prediction bits effectively. Existing tournament predictors use a 2-bit saturating counter per branch to choose among two different predictors based on which predictor (local, global, or even some mix) was most

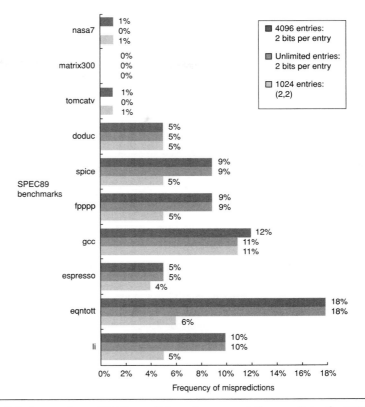

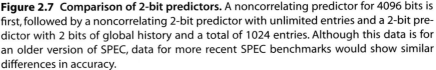

Figure 2.7 Comparison of 2-bit predictors. A noncorrelating predictor for 4096 bits is first, followed by a noncorrelating 2-bit predictor with unlimited entries and a 2-bit predictor with 2 bits of global history and a total of 1024 entries. Although this data is for an older version of SPEC, data for more recent SPEC benchmarks would show similar differences in accuracy.

effective in recent predictions. As in a simple 2-bit predictor, the saturating counter requires two mispredictions before changing the identity of the preferred predictor.

The advantage of a tournament predictor is its ability to select the right predictor for a particular branch, which is particularly crucial for the integer benchmarks. A typical tournament predictor will select the global predictor almost 40% of the time for the SPEC integer benchmarks and less than 15% of the time for the SPEC FP benchmarks.

Figure 2.8 looks at the performance of three different predictors (a local 2-bit predictor, a correlating predictor, and a tournament predictor) for different numbers of bits using SPEC89 as the benchmark. As we saw earlier, the prediction

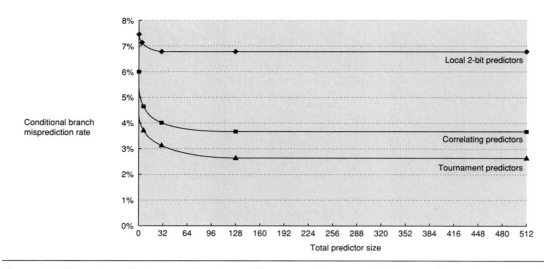

Figure 2.8 The misprediction rate for three different predictors on SPEC89 as the total number of bits is increased. The predictors are a local 2-bit predictor, a correlating predictor, which is optimally structured in its use of global and local information at each point in the graph, and a tournament predictor. Although this data is for an older version of SPEC, data for more recent SPEC benchmarks would show similar behavior, perhaps converging to the asymptotic limit at slightly larger predictor sizes.

capability of the local predictor does not improve beyond a certain size. The correlating predictor shows a significant improvement, and the tournament predictor generates slightly better performance. For more recent versions of the SPEC, the results would be similar, but the asymptotic behavior would not be reached until slightly larger-sized predictors.

In 2005, tournament predictors using about 30K bits are the standard in processors like the Power5 and Pentium 4. The most advanced of these predictors has been on the Alpha 21264, although both the Pentium 4 and Power5 predictors are similar. The 21264's tournament predictor uses 4K 2-bit counters indexed by the local branch address to choose from among a global predictor and a local predictor. The global predictor also has 4K entries and is indexed by the history of the last 12 branches; each entry in the global predictor is a standard 2-bit predictor.

The local predictor consists of a two-level predictor. The top level is a local history table consisting of 1024 10-bit entries; each 10-bit entry corresponds to the most recent 10 branch outcomes for the entry. That is, if the branch was taken 10 or more times in a row, the entry in the local history table will be all 1s. If the branch is alternately taken and untaken, the history entry consists of alternating 0s and 1s. This 10-bit history allows patterns of up to 10 branches to be discovered and predicted. The selected entry from the local history table is used to index a table of 1K entries consisting of 3-bit saturating counters, which provide the local prediction. This combination, which uses a total of 29K bits, leads to high accuracy in branch prediction.

To examine the effect on performance, we need to know the prediction accuracy as well as the branch frequency, since the importance of accurate prediction is larger in programs with higher branch frequency. For example, the integer programs in the SPEC suite have higher branch frequencies than those of the more easily predicted FP programs. For the 21264's predictor, the SPECfp95 benchmarks have less than 1 misprediction per 1000 completed instructions, and for SPECint95, there are about 11.5 mispredictions per 1000 completed instructions. This corresponds to misprediction rates of less than 0.5% for the floating-point programs and about 14% for the integer programs.

Later versions of SPEC contain programs with larger data sets and larger code, resulting in higher miss rates. Thus, the importance of branch prediction has increased. In Section 2.11, we will look at the performance of the Pentium 4 branch predictor on programs in the SPEC2000 suite and see that, despite more aggressive branch prediction, the branch-prediction miss rates for the integer programs remain significant.

2.4   Overcoming Data Hazards with Dynamic Scheduling

A simple statically scheduled pipeline fetches an instruction and issues it, unless there was a data dependence between an instruction already in the pipeline and the fetched instruction that cannot be hidden with bypassing or forwarding. (Forwarding logic reduces the effective pipeline latency so that the certain dependences do not result in hazards.) If there is a data dependence that cannot be hidden, then the hazard detection hardware stalls the pipeline starting with the instruction that uses the result. No new instructions are fetched or issued until the dependence is cleared.

In this section, we explore *dynamic scheduling,* in which the hardware rearranges the instruction execution to reduce the stalls while maintaining data flow and exception behavior. Dynamic scheduling offers several advantages: It enables handling some cases when dependences are unknown at compile time (for example, because they may involve a memory reference), and it simplifies the compiler. Perhaps most importantly, it allows the processor to tolerate unpredictable delays such as cache misses, by executing other code while waiting for the miss to resolve. Almost as importantly, dynamic scheduling allows code that was compiled with one pipeline in mind to run efficiently on a different pipeline. In Section 2.6, we explore hardware speculation, a technique with significant performance advantages, which builds on dynamic scheduling. As we will see, the advantages of dynamic scheduling are gained at a cost of a significant increase in hardware complexity.

Although a dynamically scheduled processor cannot change the data flow, it tries to avoid stalling when dependences are present. In contrast, static pipeline scheduling by the compiler (covered in Section 2.2) tries to minimize stalls by separating dependent instructions so that they will not lead to hazards. Of course, compiler pipeline scheduling can also be used on code destined to run on a processor with a dynamically scheduled pipeline.

Dynamic Scheduling: The Idea

A major limitation of simple pipelining techniques is that they use in-order instruction issue and execution: Instructions are issued in program order, and if an instruction is stalled in the pipeline, no later instructions can proceed. Thus, if there is a dependence between two closely spaced instructions in the pipeline, this will lead to a hazard and a stall will result. If there are multiple functional units, these units could lie idle. If instruction j depends on a long-running instruction i, currently in execution in the pipeline, then all instructions after j must be stalled until i is finished and j can execute. For example, consider this code:

```
DIV.D    F0,F2,F4
ADD.D    F10,F0,F8
SUB.D    F12,F8,F14
```

The SUB.D instruction cannot execute because the dependence of ADD.D on DIV.D causes the pipeline to stall; yet SUB.D is not data dependent on anything in the pipeline. This hazard creates a performance limitation that can be eliminated by not requiring instructions to execute in program order.

In the classic five-stage pipeline, both structural and data hazards could be checked during instruction decode (ID): When an instruction could execute without hazards, it was issued from ID knowing that all data hazards had been resolved.

To allow us to begin executing the SUB.D in the above example, we must separate the issue process into two parts: checking for any structural hazards and waiting for the absence of a data hazard. Thus, we still use in-order instruction issue (i.e., instructions issued in program order), but we want an instruction to begin execution as soon as its data operands are available. Such a pipeline does *out-of-order execution,* which implies *out-of-order completion.*

Out-of-order execution introduces the possibility of WAR and WAW hazards, which do not exist in the five-stage integer pipeline and its logical extension to an in-order floating-point pipeline. Consider the following MIPS floating-point code sequence:

```
DIV.D    F0,F2,F4
ADD.D    F6,F0,F8
SUB.D    F8,F10,F14
MUL.D    F6,F10,F8
```

There is an antidependence between the ADD.D and the SUB.D, and if the pipeline executes the SUB.D before the ADD.D (which is waiting for the DIV.D), it will violate the antidependence, yielding a WAR hazard. Likewise, to avoid violating output dependences, such as the write of F6 by MUL.D, WAW hazards must be handled. As we will see, both these hazards are avoided by the use of register renaming.

Out-of-order completion also creates major complications in handling exceptions. Dynamic scheduling with out-of-order completion must preserve exception behavior in the sense that *exactly* those exceptions that would arise if the program were executed in strict program order *actually* do arise. Dynamically scheduled processors preserve exception behavior by ensuring that no instruction can generate an exception until the processor knows that the instruction raising the exception will be executed; we will see shortly how this property can be guaranteed.

Although exception behavior must be preserved, dynamically scheduled processors may generate *imprecise* exceptions. An exception is *imprecise* if the processor state when an exception is raised does not look exactly as if the instructions were executed sequentially in strict program order. Imprecise exceptions can occur because of two possibilities:

1. The pipeline may have *already completed* instructions that are *later* in program order than the instruction causing the exception.

2. The pipeline may have *not yet completed* some instructions that are *earlier* in program order than the instruction causing the exception.

Imprecise exceptions make it difficult to restart execution after an exception. Rather than address these problems in this section, we will discuss a solution that provides precise exceptions in the context of a processor with speculation in Section 2.6. For floating-point exceptions, other solutions have been used, as discussed in Appendix J.

To allow out-of-order execution, we essentially split the ID pipe stage of our simple five-stage pipeline into two stages:

1. *Issue*—Decode instructions, check for structural hazards.

2. *Read operands*—Wait until no data hazards, then read operands.

An instruction fetch stage precedes the issue stage and may fetch either into an instruction register or into a queue of pending instructions; instructions are then issued from the register or queue. The EX stage follows the read operands stage, just as in the five-stage pipeline. Execution may take multiple cycles, depending on the operation.

We distinguish when an instruction *begins execution* and when it *completes execution;* between the two times, the instruction is *in execution.* Our pipeline allows multiple instructions to be in execution at the same time, and without this capability, a major advantage of dynamic scheduling is lost. Having multiple instructions in execution at once requires multiple functional units, pipelined functional units, or both. Since these two capabilities—pipelined functional units and multiple functional units—are essentially equivalent for the purposes of pipeline control, we will assume the processor has multiple functional units.

In a dynamically scheduled pipeline, all instructions pass through the issue stage in order (in-order issue); however, they can be stalled or bypass each other in the second stage (read operands) and thus enter execution out of order. *Scoreboarding* is a technique for allowing instructions to execute out of order when there are sufficient resources and no data dependences; it is named after the CDC 6600 scoreboard, which developed this capability, and we discuss it in Appendix

A. Here, we focus on a more sophisticated technique, called *Tomasulo's algorithm,* that has several major enhancements over scoreboarding.

Dynamic Scheduling Using Tomasulo's Approach

The IBM 360/91 floating-point unit used a sophisticated scheme to allow out-of-order execution. This scheme, invented by Robert Tomasulo, tracks when operands for instructions are available, to minimize RAW hazards, and introduces register renaming, to minimize WAW and WAR hazards. There are many variations on this scheme in modern processors, although the key concepts of tracking instruction dependences to allow execution as soon as operands are available and renaming registers to avoid WAR and WAW hazards are common characteristics.

IBM's goal was to achieve high floating-point performance from an instruction set and from compilers designed for the entire 360 computer family, rather than from specialized compilers for the high-end processors. The 360 architecture had only four double-precision floating-point registers, which limits the effectiveness of compiler scheduling; this fact was another motivation for the Tomasulo approach. In addition, the IBM 360/91 had long memory accesses and long floating-point delays, which Tomasulo's algorithm was designed to overcome. At the end of the section, we will see that Tomasulo's algorithm can also support the overlapped execution of multiple iterations of a loop.

We explain the algorithm, which focuses on the floating-point unit and load-store unit, in the context of the MIPS instruction set. The primary difference between MIPS and the 360 is the presence of register-memory instructions in the latter architecture. Because Tomasulo's algorithm uses a load functional unit, no significant changes are needed to add register-memory addressing modes. The IBM 360/91 also had pipelined functional units, rather than multiple functional units, but we describe the algorithm as if there were multiple functional units. It is a simple conceptual extension to also pipeline those functional units.

As we will see, RAW hazards are avoided by executing an instruction only when its operands are available. WAR and WAW hazards, which arise from name dependences, are eliminated by register renaming. *Register renaming* eliminates these hazards by renaming all destination registers, including those with a pending read or write for an earlier instruction, so that the out-of-order write does not affect any instructions that depend on an earlier value of an operand.

To better understand how register renaming eliminates WAR and WAW hazards, consider the following example code sequence that includes both a potential WAR and WAW hazard:

```
DIV.D    F0,F2,F4
ADD.D    F6,F0,F8
S.D      F6,0(R1)
SUB.D    F8,F10,F14
MUL.D    F6,F10,F8
```

There is an antidependence between the ADD.D and the SUB.D and an output dependence between the ADD.D and the MUL.D, leading to two possible hazards: a WAR hazard on the use of F8 by ADD.D and a WAW hazard since the ADD.D may finish later than the MUL.D. There are also three true data dependences: between the DIV.D and the ADD.D, between the SUB.D and the MUL.D, and between the ADD.D and the S.D.

These two name dependences can both be eliminated by register renaming. For simplicity, assume the existence of two temporary registers, S and T. Using S and T, the sequence can be rewritten without any dependences as

```
DIV.D    F0,F2,F4
ADD.D    S,F0,F8
S.D      S,0(R1)
SUB.D    T,F10,F14
MUL.D    F6,F10,T
```

In addition, any subsequent uses of F8 must be replaced by the register T. In this code segment, the renaming process can be done statically by the compiler. Finding any uses of F8 that are later in the code requires either sophisticated compiler analysis or hardware support, since there may be intervening branches between the above code segment and a later use of F8. As we will see, Tomasulo's algorithm can handle renaming across branches.

In Tomasulo's scheme, register renaming is provided by *reservation stations,* which buffer the operands of instructions waiting to issue. The basic idea is that a reservation station fetches and buffers an operand as soon as it is available, eliminating the need to get the operand from a register. In addition, pending instructions designate the reservation station that will provide their input. Finally, when successive writes to a register overlap in execution, only the last one is actually used to update the register. As instructions are issued, the register specifiers for pending operands are renamed to the names of the reservation station, which provides register renaming.

Since there can be more reservation stations than real registers, the technique can even eliminate hazards arising from name dependences that could not be eliminated by a compiler. As we explore the components of Tomasulo's scheme, we will return to the topic of register renaming and see exactly how the renaming occurs and how it eliminates WAR and WAW hazards.

The use of reservation stations, rather than a centralized register file, leads to two other important properties. First, hazard detection and execution control are distributed: The information held in the reservation stations at each functional unit determine when an instruction can begin execution at that unit. Second, results are passed directly to functional units from the reservation stations where they are buffered, rather than going through the registers. This bypassing is done with a common result bus that allows all units waiting for an operand to be loaded simultaneously (on the 360/91 this is called the *common data bus,* or CDB). In pipelines with multiple execution units and issuing multiple instructions per clock, more than one result bus will be needed.

Figure 2.9 shows the basic structure of a Tomasulo-based processor, including both the floating-point unit and the load-store unit; none of the execution control tables are shown. Each reservation station holds an instruction that has been issued and is awaiting execution at a functional unit, and either the operand values for that instruction, if they have already been computed, or else the names of the reservation stations that will provide the operand values.

The load buffers and store buffers hold data or addresses coming from and going to memory and behave almost exactly like reservation stations, so we distinguish them only when necessary. The floating-point registers are connected by a pair of buses to the functional units and by a single bus to the store buffers. All

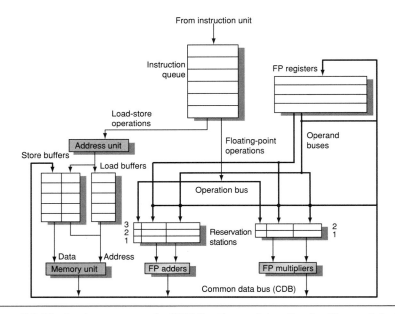

Figure 2.9 The basic structure of a MIPS floating-point unit using Tomasulo's algorithm. Instructions are sent from the instruction unit into the instruction queue from which they are issued in FIFO order. The reservation stations include the operation and the actual operands, as well as information used for detecting and resolving hazards. Load buffers have three functions: hold the components of the effective address until it is computed, track outstanding loads that are waiting on the memory, and hold the results of completed loads that are waiting for the CDB. Similarly, store buffers have three functions: hold the components of the effective address until it is computed, hold the destination memory addresses of outstanding stores that are waiting for the data value to store, and hold the address and value to store until the memory unit is available. All results from either the FP units or the load unit are put on the CDB, which goes to the FP register file as well as to the reservation stations and store buffers. The FP adders implement addition and subtraction, and the FP multipliers do multiplication and division.

results from the functional units and from memory are sent on the common data bus, which goes everywhere except to the load buffer. All reservation stations have tag fields, employed by the pipeline control.

Before we describe the details of the reservation stations and the algorithm, let's look at the steps an instruction goes through. There are only three steps, although each one can now take an arbitrary number of clock cycles:

1. *Issue*—Get the next instruction from the head of the instruction queue, which is maintained in FIFO order to ensure the maintenance of correct data flow. If there is a matching reservation station that is empty, issue the instruction to the station with the operand values, if they are currently in the registers. If there is not an empty reservation station, then there is a structural hazard and the instruction stalls until a station or buffer is freed. If the operands are not in the registers, keep track of the functional units that will produce the operands. This step renames registers, eliminating WAR and WAW hazards. (This stage is sometimes called *dispatch* in a dynamically scheduled processor.)

2. *Execute*—If one or more of the operands is not yet available, monitor the common data bus while waiting for it to be computed. When an operand becomes available, it is placed into any reservation station awaiting it. When all the operands are available, the operation can be executed at the corresponding functional unit. By delaying instruction execution until the operands are available, RAW hazards are avoided. (Some dynamically scheduled processors call this step "issue," but we use the name "execute," which was used in the first dynamically scheduled processor, the CDC 6600.)

    Notice that several instructions could become ready in the same clock cycle for the same functional unit. Although independent functional units could begin execution in the same clock cycle for different instructions, if more than one instruction is ready for a single functional unit, the unit will have to choose among them. For the floating-point reservation stations, this choice may be made arbitrarily; loads and stores, however, present an additional complication.

    Loads and stores require a two-step execution process. The first step computes the effective address when the base register is available, and the effective address is then placed in the load or store buffer. Loads in the load buffer execute as soon as the memory unit is available. Stores in the store buffer wait for the value to be stored before being sent to the memory unit. Loads and stores are maintained in program order through the effective address calculation, which will help to prevent hazards through memory, as we will see shortly.

    To preserve exception behavior, no instruction is allowed to initiate execution until all branches that precede the instruction in program order have completed. This restriction guarantees that an instruction that causes an exception during execution really would have been executed. In a processor using branch prediction (as all dynamically scheduled processors do), this means that the processor must know that the branch prediction was correct before allowing an instruction after the branch to begin execution. If the processor records the occurrence of the exception, but does not actually raise it, an instruction can start execution but not stall until it enters Write Result.

As we will see, speculation provides a more flexible and more complete method to handle exceptions, so we will delay making this enhancement and show how speculation handles this problem later.

3. *Write result*—When the result is available, write it on the CDB and from there into the registers and into any reservation stations (including store buffers) waiting for this result. Stores are buffered in the store buffer until both the value to be stored and the store address are available, then the result is written as soon as the memory unit is free.

The data structures that detect and eliminate hazards are attached to the reservation stations, to the register file, and to the load and store buffers with slightly different information attached to different objects. These tags are essentially names for an extended set of virtual registers used for renaming. In our example, the tag field is a 4-bit quantity that denotes one of the five reservation stations or one of the five load buffers. As we will see, this produces the equivalent of 10 registers that can be designated as result registers (as opposed to the 4 double-precision registers that the 360 architecture contains). In a processor with more real registers, we would want renaming to provide an even larger set of virtual registers. The tag field describes which reservation station contains the instruction that will produce a result needed as a source operand.

Once an instruction has issued and is waiting for a source operand, it refers to the operand by the reservation station number where the instruction that will write the register has been assigned. Unused values, such as zero, indicate that the operand is already available in the registers. Because there are more reservation stations than actual register numbers, WAW and WAR hazards are eliminated by renaming results using reservation station numbers. Although in Tomasulo's scheme the reservation stations are used as the extended virtual registers, other approaches could use a register set with additional registers or a structure like the reorder buffer, which we will see in Section 2.6.

In Tomasulo's scheme, as well as the subsequent methods we look at for supporting speculation, results are broadcasted on a bus (the CDB), which is monitored by the reservation stations. The combination of the common result bus and the retrieval of results from the bus by the reservation stations implements the forwarding and bypassing mechanisms used in a statically scheduled pipeline. In doing so, however, a dynamically scheduled scheme introduces one cycle of latency between source and result, since the matching of a result and its use cannot be done until the Write Result stage. Thus, in a dynamically scheduled pipeline, the effective latency between a producing instruction and a consuming instruction is at least one cycle longer than the latency of the functional unit producing the result.

In describing the operation of this scheme, we use a terminology taken from the CDC scoreboard scheme (see Appendix A) rather than introduce new terminology, showing the terminology used by the IBM 360/91 for historical reference. It is important to remember that the tags in the Tomasulo scheme refer to the buffer or unit that will produce a result; the register names are discarded when an instruction issues to a reservation station.

Each reservation station has seven fields:

■   Op—The operation to perform on source operands S1 and S2.

■   Qj, Qk—The reservation stations that will produce the corresponding source operand; a value of zero indicates that the source operand is already available in Vj or Vk, or is unnecessary. (The IBM 360/91 calls these SINKunit and SOURCEunit.)

■   Vj, Vk—The value of the source operands. Note that only one of the V field or the Q field is valid for each operand. For loads, the Vk field is used to hold the offset field. (These fields are called SINK and SOURCE on the IBM 360/91.)

■   A—Used to hold information for the memory address calculation for a load or store. Initially, the immediate field of the instruction is stored here; after the address calculation, the effective address is stored here.

■   Busy—Indicates that this reservation station and its accompanying functional unit are occupied.

The register file has a field, Qi:

■   Qi—The number of the reservation station that contains the operation whose result should be stored into this register. If the value of Qi is blank (or 0), no currently active instruction is computing a result destined for this register, meaning that the value is simply the register contents.

The load and store buffers each have a field, A, which holds the result of the effective address once the first step of execution has been completed.

In the next section, we will first consider some examples that show how these mechanisms work and then examine the detailed algorithm.

2.5   Dynamic Scheduling: Examples and the Algorithm

Before we examine Tomasulo's algorithm in detail, let's consider a few examples, which will help illustrate how the algorithm works.

Example   Show what the information tables look like for the following code sequence when only the first load has completed and written its result:

```
1.    L.D      F6,32(R2)
2.    L.D      F2,44(R3)
3.    MUL.D    F0,F2,F4
4.    SUB.D    F8,F2,F6
5.    DIV.D    F10,F0,F6
6.    ADD.D    F6,F8,F2
```

Answer Figure 2.10 shows the result in three tables. The numbers appended to the names add, mult, and load stand for the tag for that reservation station—Add1 is the tag for the result from the first add unit. In addition we have included an instruction status table. This table is included only to help you understand the algorithm; it is *not* actually a part of the hardware. Instead, the reservation station keeps the state of each operation that has issued.

Tomasulo's scheme offers two major advantages over earlier and simpler schemes: (1) the distribution of the hazard detection logic and (2) the elimination of stalls for WAW and WAR hazards.

The first advantage arises from the distributed reservation stations and the use of the Common Data Bus (CDB). If multiple instructions are waiting on a single result, and each instruction already has its other operand, then the instructions can be released simultaneously by the broadcast of the result on the CDB. If a centralized register file were used, the units would have to read their results from the registers when register buses are available.

The second advantage, the elimination of WAW and WAR hazards, is accomplished by renaming registers using the reservation stations, and by the process of storing operands into the reservation station as soon as they are available.

For example, the code sequence in Figure 2.10 issues both the DIV.D and the ADD.D, even though there is a WAR hazard involving F6. The hazard is eliminated in one of two ways. First, if the instruction providing the value for the DIV.D has completed, then Vk will store the result, allowing DIV.D to execute independent of the ADD.D (this is the case shown). On the other hand, if the L.D had not completed, then Qk would point to the Load1 reservation station, and the DIV.D instruction would be independent of the ADD.D. Thus, in either case, the ADD.D can issue and begin executing. Any uses of the result of the DIV.D would point to the reservation station, allowing the ADD.D to complete and store its value into the registers without affecting the DIV.D.

We'll see an example of the elimination of a WAW hazard shortly. But let's first look at how our earlier example continues execution. In this example, and the ones that follow in this chapter, assume the following latencies: load is 1 clock cycle, add is 2 clock cycles, multiply is 6 clock cycles, and divide is 12 clock cycles.

Instruction		Instruction status		
Instruction		Issue	Execute	Write Result
L.D	F6,32(R2)	√	√	√
L.D	F2,44(R3)	√	√	
MUL.D	F0,F2,F4	√		
SUB.D	F8,F2,F6	√		
DIV.D	F10,F0,F6	√		
ADD.D	F6,F8,F2	√		

				Reservation stations				
Name	Busy	Op	Vj	Vk	Qj	Qk	A	
Load1	no							
Load2	yes	Load					45 + Regs[R3]	
Add1	yes	SUB		Mem[34 + Regs[R2]]	Load2			
Add2	yes	ADD			Add1	Load2		
Add3	no							
Mult1	yes	MUL		Regs[F4]	Load2			
Mult2	yes	DIV		Mem[34 + Regs[R2]]	Mult1			

				Register status					
Field	F0	F2	F4	F6	F8	F10	F12	...	F30
Qi	Mult1	Load2		Add2	Add1	Mult2			

Figure 2.10 **Reservation stations and register tags shown when all of the instructions have issued, but only the first load instruction has completed and written its result to the CDB.** The second load has completed effective address calculation, but is waiting on the memory unit. We use the array Regs[ ] to refer to the register file and the array Mem[ ] to refer to the memory. Remember that an operand is specified by either a Q field or a V field at any time. Notice that the ADD.D instruction, which has a WAR hazard at the WB stage, has issued and could complete before the DIV.D initiates.

Example   Using the same code segment as in the previous example (page 97), show what the status tables look like when the MUL.D is ready to write its result.

Answer   The result is shown in the three tables in Figure 2.11. Notice that ADD.D has completed since the operands of DIV.D were copied, thereby overcoming the WAR hazard. Notice that even if the load of F6 was delayed, the add into F6 could be executed without triggering a WAW hazard.

	Instruction status		
Instruction	**Issue**	**Execute**	**Write Result**
L.D F6,32(R2)	√	√	√
L.D F2,44(R3)	√	√	√
MUL.D F0,F2,F4	√	√	
SUB.D F8,F2,F6	√	√	√
DIV.D F10,F0,F6	√		
ADD.D F6,F8,F2	√	√	√

			Reservation stations				
Name	**Busy**	**Op**	**Vj**	**Vk**	**Qj**	**Qk**	**A**
Load1	no						
Load2	no						
Add1	no						
Add2	no						
Add3	no						
Mult1	yes	MUL	Mem[45 + Regs[R3]]	Regs[F4]			
Mult2	yes	DIV		Mem[34 + Regs[R2]]	Mult1		

				Register status				
Field	**F0**	**F2**	**F4**	**F6**	**F8**	**F10**	**F12**	**...**	**F30**
Qi	Mult1					Mult2			

Figure 2.11 Multiply and divide are the only instructions not finished.

Tomasulo's Algorithm: The Details

Figure 2.12 specifies the checks and steps that each instruction must go through. As mentioned earlier, loads and stores go through a functional unit for effective address computation before proceeding to independent load or store buffers. Loads take a second execution step to access memory and then go to Write Result to send the value from memory to the register file and/or any waiting reservation stations. Stores complete their execution in the Write Result stage, which writes the result to memory. Notice that all writes occur in Write Result, whether the destination is a register or memory. This restriction simplifies Tomasulo's algorithm and is critical to its extension with speculation in Section 2.6.

Instruction state	Wait until	Action or bookkeeping

Issue
FP operation
	Station r empty	`if (RegisterStat[rs].Qi≠0)`
		`    {RS[r].Qj ← RegisterStat[rs].Qi}`
		`else {RS[r].Vj ← Regs[rs]; RS[r].Qj ← 0};`
		`if (RegisterStat[rt].Qi≠0)`
		`    {RS[r].Qk ← RegisterStat[rt].Qi`
		`else {RS[r].Vk ← Regs[rt]; RS[r].Qk ← 0};`
		`RS[r].Busy ← yes; RegisterStat[rd].Q ← r;`

Load or store	Buffer r empty	`if (RegisterStat[rs].Qi≠0)`
		`    {RS[r].Qj ← RegisterStat[rs].Qi}`
		`else {RS[r].Vj ← Regs[rs]; RS[r].Qj ← 0};`
		`RS[r].A ← imm; RS[r].Busy ← yes;`

Load only		`RegisterStat[rt].Qi ← r;`

Store only		`if (RegisterStat[rt].Qi≠0)`
		`    {RS[r].Qk ← RegisterStat[rs].Qi}`
		`    else {RS[r].Vk ← Regs[rt]; RS[r].Qk ← 0};`

Execute FP operation	(RS[r].Qj = 0) and (RS[r].Qk = 0)	Compute result: operands are in Vj and Vk
Load-store step 1	RS[r].Qj = 0 & r is head of load-store queue	`RS[r].A ← RS[r].Vj + RS[r].A;`
Load step 2	Load step 1 complete	Read from Mem[RS[r].A]

Write Result
FP operation
or
load
	Execution complete at r &
	CDB available
		`∀x(if (RegisterStat[x].Qi=r) {Regs[x] ← result;`
		`    RegisterStat[x].Qi ← 0});`
		`∀x(if (RS[x].Qj=r) {RS[x].Vj ← result;RS[x].Qj ←`
		`    0});`
		`∀x(if (RS[x].Qk=r) {RS[x].Vk ← result;RS[x].Qk ←`
		`    0});`
		`RS[r].Busy ← no;`

Store	Execution complete at r & RS[r].Qk = 0	`Mem[RS[r].A] ← RS[r].Vk;` `RS[r].Busy ← no;`

Figure 2.12 Steps in the algorithm and what is required for each step. For the issuing instruction, rd is the destination, rs and rt are the source register numbers, imm is the sign-extended immediate field, and r is the reservation station or buffer that the instruction is assigned to. RS is the reservation station data structure. The value returned by an FP unit or by the load unit is called result. RegisterStat is the register status data structure (not the register file, which is Regs[]). When an instruction is issued, the destination register has its Qi field set to the number of the buffer or reservation station to which the instruction is issued. If the operands are available in the registers, they are stored in the V fields. Otherwise, the Q fields are set to indicate the reservation station that will produce the values needed as source operands. The instruction waits at the reservation station until both its operands are available, indicated by zero in the Q fields. The Q fields are set to zero either when this instruction is issued, or when an instruction on which this instruction depends completes and does its write back. When an instruction has finished execution and the CDB is available, it can do its write back. All the buffers, registers, and reservation stations whose value of Qj or Qk is the same as the completing reservation station update their values from the CDB and mark the Q fields to indicate that values have been received. Thus, the CDB can broadcast its result to many destinations in a single clock cycle, and if the waiting instructions have their operands, they can all begin execution on the next clock cycle. Loads go through two steps in Execute, and stores perform slightly differently during Write Result, where they may have to wait for the value to store. Remember that to preserve exception behavior, instructions should not be allowed to execute if a branch that is earlier in program order has not yet completed. Because any concept of program order is not maintained after the Issue stage, this restriction is usually implemented by preventing any instruction from leaving the Issue step, if there is a pending branch already in the pipeline. In Section 2.6, we will see how speculation support removes this restriction.

Tomasulo's Algorithm: A Loop-Based Example

To understand the full power of eliminating WAW and WAR hazards through dynamic renaming of registers, we must look at a loop. Consider the following simple sequence for multiplying the elements of an array by a scalar in F2:

```
Loop:    L.D        F0,0(R1)
         MUL.D      F4,F0,F2
         S.D        F4,0(R1)
         DADDIU     R1,R1,-8
         BNE        R1,R2,Loop; branches if R1≠R2
```

If we predict that branches are taken, using reservation stations will allow multiple executions of this loop to proceed at once. This advantage is gained without changing the code—in effect, the loop is unrolled dynamically by the hardware, using the reservation stations obtained by renaming to act as additional registers.

Let's assume we have issued all the instructions in two successive iterations of the loop, but none of the floating-point load-stores or operations has completed. Figure 2.13 shows reservation stations, register status tables, and load and store buffers at this point. (The integer ALU operation is ignored, and it is assumed the branch was predicted as taken.) Once the system reaches this state, two copies of the loop could be sustained with a CPI close to 1.0, provided the multiplies could complete in 4 clock cycles. With a latency of 6 cycles, additional iterations will need to be processed before the steady state can be reached. This requires more reservation stations to hold instructions that are in execution. As we will see later in this chapter, when extended with multiple instruction issue, Tomasulo's approach can sustain more than one instruction per clock.

A load and a store can safely be done out of order, provided they access different addresses. If a load and a store access the same address, then either

■ the load is before the store in program order and interchanging them results in a WAR hazard, or

■ the store is before the load in program order and interchanging them results in a RAW hazard.

Similarly, interchanging two stores to the same address results in a WAW hazard.

Hence, to determine if a load can be executed at a given time, the processor can check whether any uncompleted store that precedes the load in program order shares the same data memory address as the load. Similarly, a store must wait until there are no unexecuted loads or stores that are earlier in program order and share the same data memory address. We consider a method to eliminate this restriction in Section 2.9.

To detect such hazards, the processor must have computed the data memory address associated with any earlier memory operation. A simple, but not necessarily optimal, way to guarantee that the processor has all such addresses is to perform the effective address calculations in program order. (We really only need

	Instruction status			
Instruction	From iteration	Issue	Execute	Write Result
L.D F0,0(R1)	1	√	√	
MUL.D F4,F0,F2	1	√		
S.D F4,0(R1)	1	√		
L.D F0,0(R1)	2	√	√	
MUL.D F4,F0,F2	2	√		
S.D F4,0(R1)	2	√		

	Reservation stations						
Name	Busy	Op	Vj	Vk	Qj	Qk	A
Load1	yes	Load					Regs[R1] + 0
Load2	yes	Load					Regs[R1] − 8
Add1	no						
Add2	no						
Add3	no						
Mult1	yes	MUL		Regs[F2]	Load1		
Mult2	yes	MUL		Regs[F2]	Load2		
Store1	yes	Store	Regs[R1]			Mult1	
Store2	yes	Store	Regs[R1] − 8			Mult2	

	Register status								
Field	F0	F2	F4	F6	F8	F10	F12	...	F30
Qi	Load2		Mult2						

Figure 2.13 Two active iterations of the loop with no instruction yet completed. Entries in the multiplier reservation stations indicate that the outstanding loads are the sources. The store reservation stations indicate that the multiply destination is the source of the value to store.

to keep the relative order between stores and other memory references; that is, loads can be reordered freely.)

Let's consider the situation of a load first. If we perform effective address calculation in program order, then when a load has completed effective address calculation, we can check whether there is an address conflict by examining the A field of all active store buffers. If the load address matches the address of any active entries in the store buffer, that load instruction is not sent to the load buffer until the conflicting store completes. (Some implementations bypass the value directly to the load from a pending store, reducing the delay for this RAW hazard.)

Stores operate similarly, except that the processor must check for conflicts in both the load buffers and the store buffers, since conflicting stores cannot be reordered with respect to either a load or a store.

A dynamically scheduled pipeline can yield very high performance, provided branches are predicted accurately—an issue we addressed in the last section. The major drawback of this approach is the complexity of the Tomasulo scheme, which requires a large amount of hardware. In particular, each reservation station must contain an associative buffer, which must run at high speed, as well as complex control logic. The performance can also be limited by the single CDB. Although additional CDBs can be added, each CDB must interact with each reservation station, and the associative tag-matching hardware would need to be duplicated at each station for each CDB.

In Tomasulo's scheme two different techniques are combined: the renaming of the architectural registers to a larger set of registers and the buffering of source operands from the register file. Source operand buffering resolves WAR hazards that arise when the operand is available in the registers. As we will see later, it is also possible to eliminate WAR hazards by the renaming of a register together with the buffering of a result until no outstanding references to the earlier version of the register remain. This approach will be used when we discuss hardware speculation.

Tomasulo's scheme was unused for many years after the 360/91, but was widely adopted in multiple-issue processors starting in the 1990s for several reasons:

1. It can achieve high performance without requiring the compiler to target code to a specific pipeline structure, a valuable property in the era of shrink-wrapped mass market software.

2. Although Tomasulo's algorithm was designed before caches, the presence of caches, with the inherently unpredictable delays, has become one of the major motivations for dynamic scheduling. Out-of-order execution allows the processors to continue executing instructions while awaiting the completion of a cache miss, thus hiding all or part of the cache miss penalty.

3. As processors became more aggressive in their issue capability and designers are concerned with the performance of difficult-to-schedule code (such as most nonnumeric code), techniques such as register renaming and dynamic scheduling become more important.

4. Because dynamic scheduling is a key component of speculation, it was adopted along with hardware speculation in the mid-1990s.

2.6 Hardware-Based Speculation

As we try to exploit more instruction-level parallelism, maintaining control dependences becomes an increasing burden. Branch prediction reduces the direct stalls attributable to branches, but for a processor executing multiple instructions per clock, just predicting branches accurately may not be sufficient to generate the desired amount of instruction-level parallelism. A wide issue processor may need to execute a branch every clock cycle to maintain maximum performance. Hence, exploiting more parallelism requires that we overcome the limitation of control dependence.

Overcoming control dependence is done by speculating on the outcome of branches and executing the program as if our guesses were correct. This mechanism represents a subtle, but important, extension over branch prediction with dynamic scheduling. In particular, with speculation, we fetch, issue, and *execute* instructions, as if our branch predictions were always correct; dynamic scheduling only fetches and issues such instructions. Of course, we need mechanisms to handle the situation where the speculation is incorrect. Appendix G discusses a variety of mechanisms for supporting speculation by the compiler. In this section, we explore *hardware speculation,* which extends the ideas of dynamic scheduling.

Hardware-based speculation combines three key ideas: dynamic branch prediction to choose which instructions to execute, speculation to allow the execution of instructions before the control dependences are resolved (with the ability to undo the effects of an incorrectly speculated sequence), and dynamic scheduling to deal with the scheduling of different combinations of basic blocks. (In comparison, dynamic scheduling without speculation only partially overlaps basic blocks because it requires that a branch be resolved before actually executing any instructions in the successor basic block.)

Hardware-based speculation follows the predicted flow of data values to choose when to execute instructions. This method of executing programs is essentially a *data flow execution:* Operations execute as soon as their operands are available.

To extend Tomasulo's algorithm to support speculation, we must separate the bypassing of results among instructions, which is needed to execute an instruction speculatively, from the actual completion of an instruction. By making this separation, we can allow an instruction to execute and to bypass its results to other instructions, without allowing the instruction to perform any updates that cannot be undone, until we know that the instruction is no longer speculative.

Using the bypassed value is like performing a speculative register read, since we do not know whether the instruction providing the source register value is providing the correct result until the instruction is no longer speculative. When an instruction is no longer speculative, we allow it to update the register file or memory; we call this additional step in the instruction execution sequence *instruction commit.*

The key idea behind implementing speculation is to allow instructions to execute out of order but to force them to commit *in order* and to prevent any irrevocable action (such as updating state or taking an exception) until an instruction commits. Hence, when we add speculation, we need to separate the process of completing execution from instruction commit, since instructions may finish execution considerably before they are ready to commit. Adding this commit phase to the instruction execution sequence requires an additional set of hardware buffers that hold the results of instructions that have finished execution but have not committed. This hardware buffer, which we call the *reorder buffer,* is also used to pass results among instructions that may be speculated.

The reorder buffer (ROB) provides additional registers in the same way as the reservation stations in Tomasulo's algorithm extend the register set. The ROB holds the result of an instruction between the time the operation associated with the instruction completes and the time the instruction commits. Hence, the ROB is a source of operands for instructions, just as the reservation stations provide operands in Tomasulo's algorithm. The key difference is that in Tomasulo's algorithm, once an instruction writes its result, any subsequently issued instructions will find the result in the register file. With speculation, the register file is not updated until the instruction commits (and we know definitively that the instruction should execute); thus, the ROB supplies operands in the interval between completion of instruction execution and instruction commit. The ROB is similar to the store buffer in Tomasulo's algorithm, and we integrate the function of the store buffer into the ROB for simplicity.

Each entry in the ROB contains four fields: the instruction type, the destination field, the value field, and the ready field. The instruction type field indicates whether the instruction is a branch (and has no destination result), a store (which has a memory address destination), or a register operation (ALU operation or load, which has register destinations). The destination field supplies the register number (for loads and ALU operations) or the memory address (for stores) where the instruction result should be written. The value field is used to hold the value of the instruction result until the instruction commits. We will see an example of ROB entries shortly. Finally, the ready field indicates that the instruction has completed execution, and the value is ready.

Figure 2.14 shows the hardware structure of the processor including the ROB. The ROB subsumes the store buffers. Stores still execute in two steps, but the second step is performed by instruction commit. Although the renaming function of the reservation stations is replaced by the ROB, we still need a place to buffer operations (and operands) between the time they issue and the time they begin execution. This function is still provided by the reservation stations. Since every instruction has a position in the ROB until it commits, we tag a result using the ROB entry number rather than using the reservation station number. This tagging requires that the ROB assigned for an instruction must be tracked in the reservation station. Later in this section, we will explore an alternative implementation that uses extra registers for renaming and the ROB only to track when instructions can commit.

Here are the four steps involved in instruction execution:

1. *Issue*—Get an instruction from the instruction queue. Issue the instruction if there is an empty reservation station and an empty slot in the ROB; send the operands to the reservation station if they are available in either the registers

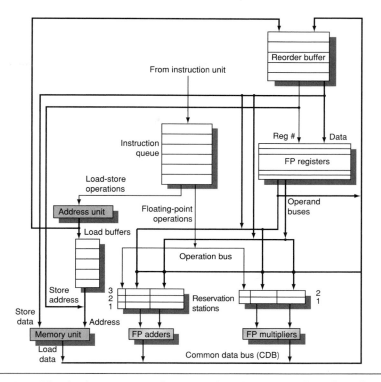

Figure 2.14 The basic structure of a FP unit using Tomasulo's algorithm and extended to handle speculation. Comparing this to Figure 2.9 on page 94, which implemented Tomasulo's algorithm, the major change is the addition of the ROB and the elimination of the store buffer, whose function is integrated into the ROB. This mechanism can be extended to multiple issue by making the CDB wider to allow for multiple completions per clock.

or the ROB. Update the control entries to indicate the buffers are in use. The number of the ROB entry allocated for the result is also sent to the reservation station, so that the number can be used to tag the result when it is placed on the CDB. If either all reservations are full or the ROB is full, then instruction issue is stalled until both have available entries.

2. *Execute*—If one or more of the operands is not yet available, monitor the CDB while waiting for the register to be computed. This step checks for RAW hazards. When both operands are available at a reservation station, execute the operation. Instructions may take multiple clock cycles in this stage, and loads still require two steps in this stage. Stores need only have the base register available at this step, since execution for a store at this point is only effective address calculation.

3. *Write result*—When the result is available, write it on the CDB (with the ROB tag sent when the instruction issued) and from the CDB into the ROB, as well as to any reservation stations waiting for this result. Mark the reservation station as available. Special actions are required for store instructions. If the value to be stored is available, it is written into the Value field of the ROB entry for the store. If the value to be stored is not available yet, the CDB must be monitored until that value is broadcast, at which time the Value field of the ROB entry of the store is updated. For simplicity we assume that this occurs during the Write Results stage of a store; we discuss relaxing this requirement later.

4. *Commit*—This is the final stage of completing an instruction, after which only its result remains. (Some processors call this commit phase "completion" or "graduation.") There are three different sequences of actions at commit depending on whether the committing instruction is a branch with an incorrect prediction, a store, or any other instruction (normal commit). The normal commit case occurs when an instruction reaches the head of the ROB and its result is present in the buffer; at this point, the processor updates the register with the result and removes the instruction from the ROB. Committing a store is similar except that memory is updated rather than a result register. When a branch with incorrect prediction reaches the head of the ROB, it indicates that the speculation was wrong. The ROB is flushed and execution is restarted at the correct successor of the branch. If the branch was correctly predicted, the branch is finished.

Once an instruction commits, its entry in the ROB is reclaimed and the register or memory destination is updated, eliminating the need for the ROB entry. If the ROB fills, we simply stop issuing instructions until an entry is made free. Now, let's examine how this scheme would work with the same example we used for Tomasulo's algorithm.

Example   Assume the same latencies for the floating-point functional units as in earlier examples: add is 2 clock cycles, multiply is 6 clock cycles, and divide is 12 clock cycles. Using the code segment below, the same one we used to generate Figure 2.11, show what the status tables look like when the MUL.D is ready to go to commit.

```
L.D      F6,32(R2)
L.D      F2,44(R3)
MUL.D    F0,F2,F4
SUB.D    F8,F6,F2
DIV.D    F10,F0,F6
ADD.D    F6,F8,F2
```

Answer   Figure 2.15 shows the result in the three tables. Notice that although the SUB.D instruction has completed execution, it does not commit until the MUL.D commits. The reservation stations and register status field contain the same basic information that they did for Tomasulo's algorithm (see page 97 for a description of those fields). The differences are that reservation station numbers are replaced with ROB entry numbers in the Qj and Qk fields, as well as in the register status fields, and we have added the Dest field to the reservation stations. The Dest field designates the ROB entry that is the destination for the result produced by this reservation station entry.

The above example illustrates the key important difference between a processor with speculation and a processor with dynamic scheduling. Compare the content of Figure 2.15 with that of Figure 2.11 on page 100, which shows the same code sequence in operation on a processor with Tomasulo's algorithm. The key difference is that, in the example above, no instruction after the earliest uncompleted instruction (MUL.D above) is allowed to complete. In contrast, in Figure 2.11 the SUB.D and ADD.D instructions have also completed.

One implication of this difference is that the processor with the ROB can dynamically execute code while maintaining a precise interrupt model. For example, if the MUL.D instruction caused an interrupt, we could simply wait until it reached the head of the ROB and take the interrupt, flushing any other pending instructions from the ROB. Because instruction commit happens in order, this yields a precise exception.

By contrast, in the example using Tomasulo's algorithm, the SUB.D and ADD.D instructions could both complete before the MUL.D raised the exception. The result is that the registers F8 and F6 (destinations of the SUB.D and ADD.D instructions) could be overwritten, and the interrupt would be imprecise.

Some users and architects have decided that imprecise floating-point exceptions are acceptable in high-performance processors, since the program will likely terminate; see Appendix G for further discussion of this topic. Other types of exceptions, such as page faults, are much more difficult to accommodate if they are imprecise, since the program must transparently resume execution after handling such an exception.

The use of a ROB with in-order instruction commit provides precise exceptions, in addition to supporting speculative execution, as the next example shows.

Example   Consider the code example used earlier for Tomasulo's algorithm and shown in Figure 2.13 in execution:

```
Loop:    L.D       F0,0(R1)
         MUL.D     F4,F0,F2
         S.D       F4,0(R1)
         DADDIU    R1,R1,#-8
         BNE       R1,R2,Loop    ;branches if R1≠R2
```

Assume that we have issued all the instructions in the loop twice. Let's also assume that the L.D and MUL.D from the first iteration have committed and all other instructions have completed execution. Normally, the store would wait in

Reorder buffer

Entry	Busy	Instruction		State	Destination	Value
1	no	L.D	F6,32(R2)	Commit	F6	Mem[34 + Regs[R2]]
2	no	L.D	F2,44(R3)	Commit	F2	Mem[45 + Regs[R3]]
3	yes	MUL.D	F0,F2,F4	Write result	F0	#2 × Regs[F4]
4	yes	SUB.D	F8,F2,F6	Write result	F8	#2 – #1
5	yes	DIV.D	F10,F0,F6	Execute	F10	
6	yes	ADD.D	F6,F8,F2	Write result	F6	#4 + #2

Reservation stations

Name	Busy	Op	Vj	Vk	Qj	Qk	Dest	A
Load1	no							
Load2	no							
Add1	no							
Add2	no							
Add3	no							
Mult1	no	MUL.D	Mem[45 + Regs[R3]]	Regs[F4]			#3	
Mult2	yes	DIV.D		Mem[34 + Regs[R2]]	#3		#5	

FP register status

Field	F0	F1	F2	F3	F4	F5	F6	F7	F8	F10
Reorder #	3						6		4	5
Busy	yes	no	no	no	no	no	yes	. . .	yes	yes

Figure 2.15 At the time the MUL.D is ready to commit, only the two L.D instructions have committed, although several others have completed execution. The MUL.D is at the head of the ROB, and the two L.D instructions are there only to ease understanding. The SUB.D and ADD.D instructions will not commit until the MUL.D instruction commits, although the results of the instructions are available and can be used as sources for other instructions. The DIV.D is in execution, but has not completed solely due to its longer latency than MUL.D. The Value column indicates the value being held; the format #X is used to refer to a value field of ROB entry X. Reorder buffers 1 and 2 are actually completed, but are shown for informational purposes. We do not show the entries for the load-store queue, but these entries are kept in order.

the ROB for both the effective address operand (R1 in this example) and the value (F4 in this example). Since we are only considering the floating-point pipeline, assume the effective address for the store is computed by the time the instruction is issued.

Answer Figure 2.16 shows the result in two tables.

Reorder buffer					
Entry	Busy	Instruction	State	Destination	Value
1	no	L.D F0,0(R1)	Commit	F0	Mem[0 + Regs[R1]]
2	no	MUL.D F4,F0,F2	Commit	F4	#1 × Regs[F2]
3	yes	S.D F4,0(R1)	Write result	0 + Regs[R1]	#2
4	yes	DADDIU R1,R1,#-8	Write result	R1	Regs[R1] − 8
5	yes	BNE R1,R2,Loop	Write result		
6	yes	L.D F0,0(R1)	Write result	F0	Mem[#4]
7	yes	MUL.D F4,F0,F2	Write result	F4	#6 × Regs[F2]
8	yes	S.D F4,0(R1)	Write result	0 + #4	#7
9	yes	DADDIU R1,R1,#-8	Write result	R1	#4 − 8
10	yes	BNE R1,R2,Loop	Write result		

FP register status									
Field	F0	F1	F2	F3	F4	F5	F6	F7	F8
Reorder #	6				7				
Busy	yes	no	no	no	yes	no	no	...	no

Figure 2.16 Only the **L.D** and **MUL.D** instructions have committed, although all the others have completed execution. Hence, no reservation stations are busy and none are shown. The remaining instructions will be committed as fast as possible. The first two reorder buffers are empty, but are shown for completeness.

Because neither the register values nor any memory values are actually written until an instruction commits, the processor can easily undo its speculative actions when a branch is found to be mispredicted. Suppose that the branch BNE is not taken the first time in Figure 2.16. The instructions prior to the branch will simply commit when each reaches the head of the ROB; when the branch reaches the head of that buffer, the buffer is simply cleared and the processor begins fetching instructions from the other path.

In practice, processors that speculate try to recover as early as possible after a branch is mispredicted. This recovery can be done by clearing the ROB for all entries that appear after the mispredicted branch, allowing those that are before the branch in the ROB to continue, and restarting the fetch at the correct branch successor. In speculative processors, performance is more sensitive to the branch prediction, since the impact of a misprediction will be higher. Thus, all the aspects of handling branches—prediction accuracy, latency of misprediction detection, and misprediction recovery time—increase in importance.

Exceptions are handled by not recognizing the exception until it is ready to commit. If a speculated instruction raises an exception, the exception is recorded in the ROB. If a branch misprediction arises and the instruction should not have been executed, the exception is flushed along with the instruction when the ROB is cleared. If the instruction reaches the head of the ROB, then we know it is no longer speculative and the exception should really be taken. We can also try to handle exceptions as soon as they arise and all earlier branches are resolved, but this is more challenging in the case of exceptions than for branch mispredict and, because it occurs less frequently, not as critical.

Figure 2.17 shows the steps of execution for an instruction, as well as the conditions that must be satisfied to proceed to the step and the actions taken. We show the case where mispredicted branches are not resolved until commit. Although speculation seems like a simple addition to dynamic scheduling, a comparison of Figure 2.17 with the comparable figure for Tomasulo's algorithm in Figure 2.12 shows that speculation adds significant complications to the control. In addition, remember that branch mispredictions are somewhat more complex as well.

There is an important difference in how stores are handled in a speculative processor versus in Tomasulo's algorithm. In Tomasulo's algorithm, a store can update memory when it reaches Write Result (which ensures that the effective address has been calculated) and the data value to store is available. In a speculative processor, a store updates memory only when it reaches the head of the ROB. This difference ensures that memory is not updated until an instruction is no longer speculative.

Figure 2.17 has one significant simplification for stores, which is unneeded in practice. Figure 2.17 requires stores to wait in the Write Result stage for the register source operand whose value is to be stored; the value is then moved from the Vk field of the store's reservation station to the Value field of the store's ROB entry. In reality, however, the value to be stored need not arrive until *just before* the store commits and can be placed directly into the store's ROB entry by the sourcing instruction. This is accomplished by having the hardware track when the source value to be stored is available in the store's ROB entry and searching the ROB on every instruction completion to look for dependent stores.

This addition is not complicated, but adding it has two effects: We would need to add a field to the ROB, and Figure 2.17, which is already in a small font, would be even longer! Although Figure 2.17 makes this simplification, in our examples, we will allow the store to pass through the Write Result stage and simply wait for the value to be ready when it commits.

Like Tomasulo's algorithm, we must avoid hazards through memory. WAW and WAR hazards through memory are eliminated with speculation because the actual updating of memory occurs in order, when a store is at the head of the ROB, and hence, no earlier loads or stores can still be pending. RAW hazards through memory are maintained by two restrictions:

1. not allowing a load to initiate the second step of its execution if any active ROB entry occupied by a store has a Destination field that matches the value of the A field of the load, and

Status	Wait until	Action or bookkeeping

Issue
all
instructions
	Reservation
	station (r)
	and
	ROB (b)
	both available
		`if (RegisterStat[rs].Busy)/*in-flight instr. writes rs*/`
		`    {h ← RegisterStat[rs].Reorder;`
		`     if (ROB[h].Ready)/* Instr completed already */`
		`         {RS[r].Vj ← ROB[h].Value; RS[r].Qj ← 0;}`
		`     else {RS[r].Qj ← h;} /* wait for instruction */`
		`} else {RS[r].Vj ← Regs[rs]; RS[r].Qj ← 0;};`
		`RS[r].Busy ← yes; RS[r].Dest ← b;`
		`ROB[b].Instruction ← opcode; ROB[b].Dest ← rd;ROB[b].Ready ← no;`

FP
operations
and stores
		`if (RegisterStat[rt].Busy) /*in-flight instr writes rt*/`
		`    {h ← RegisterStat[rt].Reorder;`
		`     if (ROB[h].Ready)/* Instr completed already */`
		`         {RS[r].Vk ← ROB[h].Value; RS[r].Qk ← 0;}`
		`     else {RS[r].Qk ← h;} /* wait for instruction */`
		`} else {RS[r].Vk ← Regs[rt]; RS[r].Qk ← 0;};`

FP operations		`RegisterStat[rd].Reorder ← b; RegisterStat[rd].Busy ← yes;` `ROB[b].Dest ← rd;`
Loads		`RS[r].A ← imm; RegisterStat[rt].Reorder ← b;` `RegisterStat[rt].Busy ← yes; ROB[b].Dest ← rt;`
Stores		`RS[r].A ← imm;`
Execute FP op	(RS[r].Qj == 0) and (RS[r].Qk == 0)	Compute results—operands are in Vj and Vk
Load step 1	(RS[r].Qj == 0) and there are no stores earlier in the queue	`RS[r].A ← RS[r].Vj + RS[r].A;`
Load step 2	Load step 1 done and all stores earlier in ROB have different address	Read from Mem[RS[r].A]
Store	(RS[r].Qj == 0) and store at queue head	`ROB[h].Address ← RS[r].Vj + RS[r].A;`

Write result
all but store
	Execution done at r
	and CDB available
		`b ← RS[r].Dest; RS[r].Busy ← no;`
		`∀x(if (RS[x].Qj==b) {RS[x].Vj ← result; RS[x].Qj ← 0});`
		`∀x(if (RS[x].Qk==b) {RS[x].Vk ← result; RS[x].Qk ← 0});`
		`ROB[b].Value ← result; ROB[b].Ready ← yes;`

Store	Execution done at r and (RS[r].Qk == 0)	`ROB[h].Value ← RS[r].Vk;`

Commit	Instruction is at the
	head of the ROB
	(entry h) and
	ROB[h].ready ==
	yes
		`d ← ROB[h].Dest; /* register dest, if exists */`
		`if (ROB[h].Instruction==Branch)`
		`    {if (branch is mispredicted)`
		`        {clear ROB[h], RegisterStat; fetch branch dest;};}`
		`else if (ROB[h].Instruction==Store)`
		`        {Mem[ROB[h].Destination] ← ROB[h].Value;}`
		`else /* put the result in the register destination */`
		`        {Regs[d] ← ROB[h].Value;};`
		`ROB[h].Busy ← no; /* free up ROB entry */`
		`/* free up dest register if no one else writing it */`
		`if (RegisterStat[d].Reorder==h) {RegisterStat[d].Busy ← no;};`

Figure 2.17 Steps in the algorithm and what is required for each step. For the issuing instruction, rd is the destination, rs and rt are the sources, r is the reservation station allocated, b is the assigned ROB entry, and h is the head entry of the ROB. RS is the reservation station data structure. The value returned by a reservation station is called the result. RegisterStat is the register data structure, Regs represents the actual registers, and ROB is the reorder buffer data structure.

2. maintaining the program order for the computation of an effective address of a load with respect to all earlier stores.

Together, these two restrictions ensure that any load that accesses a memory location written to by an earlier store cannot perform the memory access until the store has written the data. Some speculative processors will actually bypass the value from the store to the load directly, when such a RAW hazard occurs. Another approach is to predict potential collisions using a form of value prediction; we consider this in Section 2.9.

Although this explanation of speculative execution has focused on floating point, the techniques easily extend to the integer registers and functional units, as we will see in the "Putting It All Together" section. Indeed, speculation may be more useful in integer programs, since such programs tend to have code where the branch behavior is less predictable. Additionally, these techniques can be extended to work in a multiple-issue processor by allowing multiple instructions to issue and commit every clock. In fact, speculation is probably most interesting in such processors, since less ambitious techniques can probably exploit sufficient ILP within basic blocks when assisted by a compiler.

2.7 Exploiting ILP Using Multiple Issue and Static Scheduling

The techniques of the preceding sections can be used to eliminate data and control stalls and achieve an ideal CPI of one. To improve performance further we would like to decrease the CPI to less than one. But the CPI cannot be reduced below one if we issue only one instruction every clock cycle.

The goal of the *multiple-issue processors,* discussed in the next few sections, is to allow multiple instructions to issue in a clock cycle. Multiple-issue processors come in three major flavors:

1. statically scheduled superscalar processors,

2. VLIW (very long instruction word) processors, and

3. dynamically scheduled superscalar processors.

The two types of superscalar processors issue varying numbers of instructions per clock and use in-order execution if they are statically scheduled or out-of-order execution if they are dynamically scheduled.

VLIW processors, in contrast, issue a fixed number of instructions formatted either as one large instruction or as a fixed instruction packet with the parallelism among instructions explicitly indicated by the instruction. VLIW processors are inherently statically scheduled by the compiler. When Intel and HP created the IA-64 architecture, described in Appendix G, they also introduced the name EPIC—explicitly parallel instruction computer—for this architectural style.

Common name	Issue structure	Hazard detection	Scheduling	Distinguishing characteristic	Examples
Superscalar (static)	dynamic	hardware	static	in-order execution	mostly in the embedded space: MIPS and ARM
Superscalar (dynamic)	dynamic	hardware	dynamic	some out-of-order execution, but no speculation	none at the present
Superscalar (speculative)	dynamic	hardware	dynamic with speculation	out-of-order execution with speculation	Pentium 4, MIPS R12K, IBM Power5
VLIW/LIW	static	primarily software	static	all hazards determined and indicated by compiler (often implicitly)	most examples are in the embedded space, such as the TI C6x
EPIC	primarily static	primarily software	mostly static	all hazards determined and indicated explicitly by the compiler	Itanium

Figure 2.18 The five primary approaches in use for multiple-issue processors and the primary characteristics that distinguish them. This chapter has focused on the hardware-intensive techniques, which are all some form of superscalar. Appendix G focuses on compiler-based approaches. The EPIC approach, as embodied in the IA-64 architecture, extends many of the concepts of the early VLIW approaches, providing a blend of static and dynamic approaches.

Although statically scheduled superscalars issue a varying rather than a fixed number of instructions per clock, they are actually closer in concept to VLIWs, since both approaches rely on the compiler to schedule code for the processor. Because of the diminishing advantages of a statically scheduled superscalar as the issue width grows, statically scheduled superscalars are used primarily for narrow issue widths, normally just two instructions. Beyond that width, most designers choose to implement either a VLIW or a dynamically scheduled superscalar. Because of the similarities in hardware and required compiler technology, we focus on VLIWs in this section. The insights of this section are easily extrapolated to a statically scheduled superscalar.

Figure 2.18 summarizes the basic approaches to multiple issue and their distinguishing characteristics and shows processors that use each approach.

The Basic VLIW Approach

VLIWs use multiple, independent functional units. Rather than attempting to issue multiple, independent instructions to the units, a VLIW packages the multiple operations into one very long instruction, or requires that the instructions in the issue packet satisfy the same constraints. Since there is no fundamental difference in the two approaches, we will just assume that multiple operations are placed in one instruction, as in the original VLIW approach.

Since this advantage of a VLIW increases as the maximum issue rate grows, we focus on a wider-issue processor. Indeed, for simple two-issue processors, the overhead of a superscalar is probably minimal. Many designers would probably argue that a four-issue processor has manageable overhead, but as we will see in the next chapter, the growth in overhead is a major factor limiting wider-issue processors.

Let's consider a VLIW processor with instructions that contain five operations, including one integer operation (which could also be a branch), two floating-point operations, and two memory references. The instruction would have a set of fields for each functional unit—perhaps 16–24 bits per unit, yielding an instruction length of between 80 and 120 bits. By comparison, the Intel Itanium 1 and 2 contain 6 operations per instruction packet.

To keep the functional units busy, there must be enough parallelism in a code sequence to fill the available operation slots. This parallelism is uncovered by unrolling loops and scheduling the code within the single larger loop body. If the unrolling generates straight-line code, then *local scheduling* techniques, which operate on a single basic block, can be used. If finding and exploiting the parallelism requires scheduling code across branches, a substantially more complex *global scheduling* algorithm must be used. Global scheduling algorithms are not only more complex in structure, but they also must deal with significantly more complicated trade-offs in optimization, since moving code across branches is expensive.

In Appendix G, we will discuss *trace scheduling,* one of these global scheduling techniques developed specifically for VLIWs; we will also explore special hardware support that allows some conditional branches to be eliminated, extending the usefulness of local scheduling and enhancing the performance of global scheduling.

For now, we will rely on loop unrolling to generate long, straight-line code sequences, so that we can use local scheduling to build up VLIW instructions and focus on how well these processors operate.

Example   Suppose we have a VLIW that could issue two memory references, two FP operations, and one integer operation or branch in every clock cycle. Show an unrolled version of the loop x[i] = x[i] + s (see page 76 for the MIPS code) for such a processor. Unroll as many times as necessary to eliminate any stalls. Ignore delayed branches.

Answer   Figure 2.19 shows the code. The loop has been unrolled to make seven copies of the body, which eliminates all stalls (i.e., completely empty issue cycles), and runs in 9 cycles. This code yields a running rate of seven results in 9 cycles, or 1.29 cycles per result, nearly twice as fast as the two-issue superscalar of Section 2.2 that used unrolled and scheduled code.

Memory reference 1	Memory reference 2	FP operation 1	FP operation 2	Integer operation/branch
L.D F0,0(R1)	L.D F6,-8(R1)			
L.D F10,-16(R1)	L.D F14,-24(R1)			
L.D F18,-32(R1)	L.D F22,-40(R1)	ADD.D F4,F0,F2	ADD.D F8,F6,F2	
L.D F26,-48(R1)		ADD.D F12,F10,F2	ADD.D F16,F14,F2	
		ADD.D F20,F18,F2	ADD.D F24,F22,F2	
S.D F4,0(R1)	S.D F8,-8(R1)	ADD.D F28,F26,F2		
S.D F12,-16(R1)	S.D F16,-24(R1)			DADDUI R1,R1,#-56
S.D F20,24(R1)	S.D F24,16(R1)			
S.D F28,8(R1)				BNE R1,R2,Loop

Figure 2.19   VLIW instructions that occupy the inner loop and replace the unrolled sequence. This code takes 9 cycles assuming no branch delay; normally the branch delay would also need to be scheduled. The issue rate is 23 operations in 9 clock cycles, or 2.5 operations per cycle. The efficiency, the percentage of available slots that contained an operation, is about 60%. To achieve this issue rate requires a larger number of registers than MIPS would normally use in this loop. The VLIW code sequence above requires at least eight FP registers, while the same code sequence for the base MIPS processor can use as few as two FP registers or as many as five when unrolled and scheduled.

For the original VLIW model, there were both technical and logistical problems that make the approach less efficient. The technical problems are the increase in code size and the limitations of lockstep operation. Two different elements combine to increase code size substantially for a VLIW. First, generating enough operations in a straight-line code fragment requires ambitiously unrolling loops (as in earlier examples), thereby increasing code size. Second, whenever instructions are not full, the unused functional units translate to wasted bits in the instruction encoding. In Appendix G, we examine software scheduling approaches, such as software pipelining, that can achieve the benefits of unrolling without as much code expansion.

To combat this code size increase, clever encodings are sometimes used. For example, there may be only one large immediate field for use by any functional unit. Another technique is to compress the instructions in main memory and expand them when they are read into the cache or are decoded. In Appendix G, we show other techniques, as well as document the significant code expansion seen on IA-64.

Early VLIWs operated in lockstep; there was no hazard detection hardware at all. This structure dictated that a stall in any functional unit pipeline must cause the entire processor to stall, since all the functional units must be kept synchronized. Although a compiler may be able to schedule the deterministic functional units to prevent stalls, predicting which data accesses will encounter a cache stall and scheduling them is very difficult. Hence, caches needed to be blocking and to cause *all* the functional units to stall. As the issue rate and number of memory references becomes large, this synchronization restriction becomes unacceptable.

In more recent processors, the functional units operate more independently, and the compiler is used to avoid hazards at issue time, while hardware checks allow for unsynchronized execution once instructions are issued.

Binary code compatibility has also been a major logistical problem for VLIWs. In a strict VLIW approach, the code sequence makes use of both the instruction set definition and the detailed pipeline structure, including both functional units and their latencies. Thus, different numbers of functional units and unit latencies require different versions of the code. This requirement makes migrating between successive implementations, or between implementations with different issue widths, more difficult than it is for a superscalar design. Of course, obtaining improved performance from a new superscalar design may require recompilation. Nonetheless, the ability to run old binary files is a practical advantage for the superscalar approach.

The EPIC approach, of which the IA-64 architecture is the primary example, provides solutions to many of the problems encountered in early VLIW designs, including extensions for more aggressive software speculation and methods to overcome the limitation of hardware dependence while preserving binary compatibility.

The major challenge for all multiple-issue processors is to try to exploit large amounts of ILP. When the parallelism comes from unrolling simple loops in FP programs, the original loop probably could have been run efficiently on a vector processor (described in Appendix F). It is not clear that a multiple-issue processor is preferred over a vector processor for such applications; the costs are similar, and the vector processor is typically the same speed or faster. The potential advantages of a multiple-issue processor versus a vector processor are their ability to extract some parallelism from less structured code and their ability to easily cache all forms of data. For these reasons multiple-issue approaches have become the primary method for taking advantage of instruction-level parallelism, and vectors have become primarily an extension to these processors.

2.8 Exploiting ILP Using Dynamic Scheduling, Multiple Issue, and Speculation

So far, we have seen how the individual mechanisms of dynamic scheduling, multiple issue, and speculation work. In this section, we put all three together, which yields a microarchitecture quite similar to those in modern microprocessors. For simplicity, we consider only an issue rate of two instructions per clock, but the concepts are no different from modern processors that issue three or more instructions per clock.

Let's assume we want to extend Tomasulo's algorithm to support a two-issue superscalar pipeline with a separate integer and floating-point unit, each of which can initiate an operation on every clock. We do not want to issue instructions to the reservation stations out of order, since this could lead to a violation of the program semantics. To gain the full advantage of dynamic scheduling we will allow the pipeline to issue any combination of two instructions in a clock, using the scheduling hardware to actually assign operations to the integer and floating-point unit. Because the interaction of the integer and floating-point instructions is crucial, we also extend Tomasulo's scheme to deal with both the integer and floating-point functional units and registers, as well as incorporating speculative execution.

Two different approaches have been used to issue multiple instructions per clock in a dynamically scheduled processor, and both rely on the observation that the key is assigning a reservation station and updating the pipeline control tables. One approach is to run this step in half a clock cycle, so that two instructions can be processed in one clock cycle. A second alternative is to build the logic necessary to handle two instructions at once, including any possible dependences between the instructions. Modern superscalar processors that issue four or more instructions per clock often include both approaches: They both pipeline and widen the issue logic.

Putting together speculative dynamic scheduling with multiple issue requires overcoming one additional challenge at the back end of the pipeline: we must be able to complete and commit multiple instructions per clock. Like the challenge of issuing multiple instructions, the concepts are simple, although the implementation may be challenging in the same manner as the issue and register renaming process. We can show how the concepts fit together with an example.

Example   Consider the execution of the following loop, which increments each element of an integer array, on a two-issue processor, once without speculation and once with speculation:

```
Loop:   LD       R2,0(R1)        ;R2=array element
        DADDIU   R2,R2,#1        ;increment R2
        SD       R2,0(R1)        ;store result
        DADDIU   R1,R1,#8        ;increment pointer
        BNE      R2,R3,LOOP      ;branch if not last element
```

Assume that there are separate integer functional units for effective address calculation, for ALU operations, and for branch condition evaluation. Create a table for the first three iterations of this loop for both processors. Assume that up to two instructions of any type can commit per clock.

Answer   Figures 2.20 and 2.21 show the performance for a two-issue dynamically scheduled processor, without and with speculation. In this case, where a branch can be a critical performance limiter, speculation helps significantly. The third branch in

Iteration number	Instructions		Issues at clock cycle number	Executes at clock cycle number	Memory access at clock cycle number	Write CDB at clock cycle number	Comment
1	LD	R2,0(R1)	1	2	3	4	First issue
1	DADDIU	R2,R2,#1	1	5		6	Wait for LW
1	SD	R2,0(R1)	2	3	7		Wait for DADDIU
1	DADDIU	R1,R1,#8	2	3		4	Execute directly
1	BNE	R2,R3,LOOP	3	7			Wait for DADDIU
2	LD	R2,0(R1)	4	8	9	10	Wait for BNE
2	DADDIU	R2,R2,#1	4	11		12	Wait for LW
2	SD	R2,0(R1)	5	9	13		Wait for DADDIU
2	DADDIU	R1,R1,#8	5	8		9	Wait for BNE
2	BNE	R2,R3,LOOP	6	13			Wait for DADDIU
3	LD	R2,0(R1)	7	14	15	16	Wait for BNE
3	DADDIU	R2,R2,#1	7	17		18	Wait for LW
3	SD	R2,0(R1)	8	15	19		Wait for DADDIU
3	DADDIU	R1,R1,#8	8	14		15	Wait for BNE
3	BNE	R2,R3,LOOP	9	19			Wait for DADDIU

Figure 2.20 The time of issue, execution, and writing result for a dual-issue version of our pipeline *without* speculation. Note that the LD following the BNE cannot start execution earlier because it must wait until the branch outcome is determined. This type of program, with data-dependent branches that cannot be resolved earlier, shows the strength of speculation. Separate functional units for address calculation, ALU operations, and branch-condition evaluation allow multiple instructions to execute in the same cycle. Figure 2.21 shows this example with speculation,

the speculative processor executes in clock cycle 13, while it executes in clock cycle 19 on the nonspeculative pipeline. Because the completion rate on the non-speculative pipeline is falling behind the issue rate rapidly, the nonspeculative pipeline will stall when a few more iterations are issued. The performance of the nonspeculative processor could be improved by allowing load instructions to complete effective address calculation before a branch is decided, but unless speculative memory accesses are allowed, this improvement will gain only 1 clock per iteration.

This example clearly shows how speculation can be advantageous when there are data-dependent branches, which otherwise would limit performance. This advantage depends, however, on accurate branch prediction. Incorrect speculation will not improve performance, but will, in fact, typically harm performance.

Iteration number	Instructions	Issues at clock number	Executes at clock number	Read access at clock number	Write CDB at clock number	Commits at clock number	Comment
1	LD R2,0(R1)	1	2	3	4	5	First issue
1	DADDIU R2,R2,#1	1	5		6	7	Wait for LW
1	SD R2,0(R1)	2	3			7	Wait for DADDIU
1	DADDIU R1,R1,#8	2	3		4	8	Commit in order
1	BNE R2,R3,LOOP	3	7			8	Wait for DADDIU
2	LD R2,0(R1)	4	5	6	7	9	No execute delay
2	DADDIU R2,R2,#1	4	8		9	10	Wait for LW
2	SD R2,0(R1)	5	6			10	Wait for DADDIU
2	DADDIU R1,R1,#8	5	6		7	11	Commit in order
2	BNE R2,R3,LOOP	6	10			11	Wait for DADDIU
3	LD R2,0(R1)	7	8	9	10	12	Earliest possible
3	DADDIU R2,R2,#1	7	11		12	13	Wait for LW
3	SD R2,0(R1)	8	9			13	Wait for DADDIU
3	DADDIU R1,R1,#8	8	9		10	14	Executes earlier
3	BNE R2,R3,LOOP	9	13			14	Wait for DADDIU

Figure 2.21 The time of issue, execution, and writing result for a dual-issue version of our pipeline *with* speculation. Note that the LD following the BNE can start execution early because it is speculative.

<hr/>

2.9   Advanced Techniques for Instruction Delivery and Speculation

In a high-performance pipeline, especially one with multiple issue, predicting branches well is not enough; we actually have to be able to deliver a high-bandwidth instruction stream. In recent multiple-issue processors, this has meant delivering 4–8 instructions every clock cycle. We look at methods for increasing instruction delivery bandwidth first. We then turn to a set of key issues in implementing advanced speculation techniques, including the use of register renaming versus reorder buffers, the aggressiveness of speculation, and a technique called value prediction, which could further enhance ILP.

Increasing Instruction Fetch Bandwidth

A multiple issue processor will require that the average number of instructions fetched every clock cycle be at least as large as the average throughput. Of course, fetching these instructions requires wide enough paths to the instruction cache, but the most difficult aspect is handling branches. In this section we look at two methods for dealing with branches and then discuss how modern processors integrate the instruction prediction and prefetch functions.

Branch-Target Buffers

To reduce the branch penalty for our simple five-stage pipeline, as well as for deeper pipelines, we must know whether the as-yet-undecoded instruction is a branch and, if so, what the next PC should be. If the instruction is a branch and we know what the next PC should be, we can have a branch penalty of zero. A branch-prediction cache that stores the predicted address for the next instruction after a branch is called a *branch-target buffer* or *branch-target cache*. Figure 2.22 shows a branch-target buffer.

Because a branch-target buffer predicts the next instruction address and will send it out *before* decoding the instruction, we *must* know whether the fetched instruction is predicted as a taken branch. If the PC of the fetched instruction matches a PC in the prediction buffer, then the corresponding predicted PC is used as the next PC. The hardware for this branch-target buffer is essentially identical to the hardware for a cache.

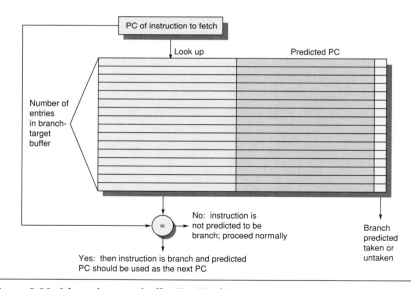

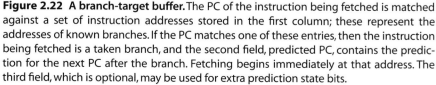

Figure 2.22 A branch-target buffer. The PC of the instruction being fetched is matched against a set of instruction addresses stored in the first column; these represent the addresses of known branches. If the PC matches one of these entries, then the instruction being fetched is a taken branch, and the second field, predicted PC, contains the prediction for the next PC after the branch. Fetching begins immediately at that address. The third field, which is optional, may be used for extra prediction state bits.

If a matching entry is found in the branch-target buffer, fetching begins immediately at the predicted PC. Note that unlike a branch-prediction buffer, the predictive entry must be matched to this instruction because the predicted PC will be sent out before it is known whether this instruction is even a branch. If the processor did not check whether the entry matched this PC, then the wrong PC would be sent out for instructions that were not branches, resulting in a slower processor. We only need to store the predicted-taken branches in the branch-target buffer, since an untaken branch should simply fetch the next sequential instruction, as if it were not a branch.

Figure 2.23 shows the detailed steps when using a branch-target buffer for a simple five-stage pipeline. From this we can see that there will be no branch delay if a branch-prediction entry is found in the buffer and the prediction is correct. Otherwise, there will be a penalty of at least 2 clock cycles. Dealing with the mispredictions and misses is a significant challenge, since we typically will have to halt instruction fetch while we rewrite the buffer entry. Thus, we would like to make this process fast to minimize the penalty.

To evaluate how well a branch-target buffer works, we first must determine the penalties in all possible cases. Figure 2.24 contains this information for the simple five-stage pipeline.

Example   Determine the total branch penalty for a branch-target buffer assuming the penalty cycles for individual mispredictions from Figure 2.24. Make the following assumptions about the prediction accuracy and hit rate:

- Prediction accuracy is 90% (for instructions in the buffer).
- Hit rate in the buffer is 90% (for branches predicted taken).

Answer   We compute the penalty by looking at the probability of two events: the branch is predicted taken but ends up being not taken, and the branch is taken but is not found in the buffer. Both carry a penalty of 2 cycles.

Probability (branch in buffer, but actually not taken) = Percent buffer hit rate × Percent incorrect predictions

$$= 90\% \times 10\% = 0.09$$

Probability (branch not in buffer, but actually taken) = 10%

$$\text{Branch penalty} = (0.09 + 0.10) \times 2$$

$$\text{Branch penalty} = 0.38$$

This penalty compares with a branch penalty for delayed branches, which we evaluate in Appendix A, of about 0.5 clock cycles per branch. Remember, though, that the improvement from dynamic branch prediction will grow as the pipeline length and, hence, the branch delay grows; in addition, better predictors will yield a larger performance advantage.

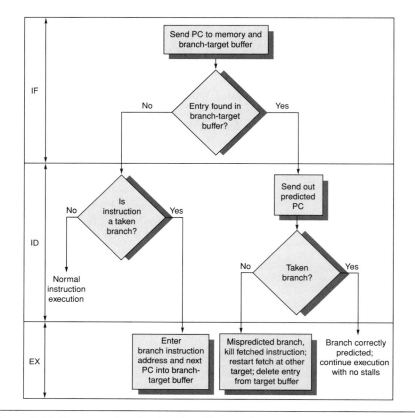

Figure 2.23 The steps involved in handling an instruction with a branch-target buffer.

Instruction in buffer	Prediction	Actual branch	Penalty cycles
yes	taken	taken	0
yes	taken	not taken	2
no		taken	2
no		not taken	0

Figure 2.24 Penalties for all possible combinations of whether the branch is in the buffer and what it actually does, assuming we store only taken branches in the buffer. There is no branch penalty if everything is correctly predicted and the branch is found in the target buffer. If the branch is not correctly predicted, the penalty is equal to 1 clock cycle to update the buffer with the correct information (during which an instruction cannot be fetched) and 1 clock cycle, if needed, to restart fetching the next correct instruction for the branch. If the branch is not found and taken, a 2-cycle penalty is encountered, during which time the buffer is updated.

One variation on the branch-target buffer is to store one or more *target instructions* instead of, or in addition to, the predicted *target address*. This variation has two potential advantages. First, it allows the branch-target buffer access to take longer than the time between successive instruction fetches, possibly allowing a larger branch-target buffer. Second, buffering the actual target instructions allows us to perform an optimization called *branch folding*. Branch folding can be used to obtain 0-cycle unconditional branches, and sometimes 0-cycle conditional branches. Consider a branch-target buffer that buffers instructions from the predicted path and is being accessed with the address of an unconditional branch. The only function of the unconditional branch is to change the PC. Thus, when the branch-target buffer signals a hit and indicates that the branch is unconditional, the pipeline can simply substitute the instruction from the branch-target buffer in place of the instruction that is returned from the cache (which is the unconditional branch). If the processor is issuing multiple instructions per cycle, then the buffer will need to supply multiple instructions to obtain the maximum benefit. In some cases, it may be possible to eliminate the cost of a conditional branch when the condition codes are preset.

Return Address Predictors

As we try to increase the opportunity and accuracy of speculation we face the challenge of predicting indirect jumps, that is, jumps whose destination address varies at run time. Although high-level language programs will generate such jumps for indirect procedure calls, select or case statements, and FORTRAN-computed gotos, the vast majority of the indirect jumps come from procedure returns. For example, for the SPEC95 benchmarks, procedure returns account for more than 15% of the branches and the vast majority of the indirect jumps on average. For object-oriented languages like C++ and Java, procedure returns are even more frequent. Thus, focusing on procedure returns seems appropriate.

Though procedure returns can be predicted with a branch-target buffer, the accuracy of such a prediction technique can be low if the procedure is called from multiple sites and the calls from one site are not clustered in time. For example, in SPEC CPU95, an aggressive branch predictor achieves an accuracy of less than 60% for such return branches. To overcome this problem, some designs use a small buffer of return addresses operating as a stack. This structure caches the most recent return addresses: pushing a return address on the stack at a call and popping one off at a return. If the cache is sufficiently large (i.e., as large as the maximum call depth), it will predict the returns perfectly. Figure 2.25 shows the performance of such a return buffer with 0–16 elements for a number of the SPEC CPU95 benchmarks. We will use a similar return predictor when we examine the studies of ILP in Section 3.2.

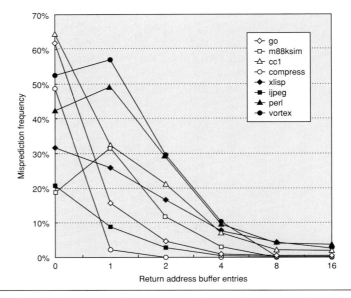

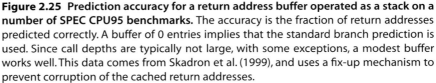

Figure 2.25 Prediction accuracy for a return address buffer operated as a stack on a number of SPEC CPU95 benchmarks. The accuracy is the fraction of return addresses predicted correctly. A buffer of 0 entries implies that the standard branch prediction is used. Since call depths are typically not large, with some exceptions, a modest buffer works well. This data comes from Skadron et al. (1999), and uses a fix-up mechanism to prevent corruption of the cached return addresses.

Integrated Instruction Fetch Units

To meet the demands of multiple-issue processors, many recent designers have chosen to implement an integrated instruction fetch unit, as a separate autonomous unit that feeds instructions to the rest of the pipeline. Essentially, this amounts to recognizing that characterizing instruction fetch as a simple single pipe stage given the complexities of multiple issue is no longer valid.

Instead, recent designs have used an integrated instruction fetch unit that integrates several functions:

1. *Integrated branch prediction*—The branch predictor becomes part of the instruction fetch unit and is constantly predicting branches, so as to drive the fetch pipeline.

2. *Instruction prefetch*—To deliver multiple instructions per clock, the instruction fetch unit will likely need to fetch ahead. The unit autonomously manages the prefetching of instructions (see Chapter 5 for a discussion of techniques for doing this), integrating it with branch prediction.

3. *Instruction memory access and buffering*—When fetching multiple instructions per cycle a variety of complexities are encountered, including the difficulty that fetching multiple instructions may require accessing multiple cache lines. The instruction fetch unit encapsulates this complexity, using prefetch to try to hide the cost of crossing cache blocks. The instruction fetch unit also provides buffering, essentially acting as an on-demand unit to provide instructions to the issue stage as needed and in the quantity needed.

As designers try to increase the number of instructions executed per clock, instruction fetch will become an ever more significant bottleneck, and clever new ideas will be needed to deliver instructions at the necessary rate. One of the newer ideas, called *trace caches* and used in the Pentium 4, is discussed in Appendix C.

Speculation: Implementation Issues and Extensions

In this section we explore three issues that involve the implementation of speculation, starting with the use of register renaming, the approach that has almost totally replaced the use of a reorder buffer. We then discuss one important possible extension to speculation on control flow: an idea called value prediction.

Speculation Support: Register Renaming versus Reorder Buffers

One alternative to the use of a reorder buffer (ROB) is the explicit use of a larger physical set of registers combined with register renaming. This approach builds on the concept of renaming used in Tomasulo's algorithm and extends it. In Tomasulo's algorithm, the values of the *architecturally visible registers* (R0, . . . , R31 and F0, . . . , F31) are contained, at any point in execution, in some combination of the register set and the reservation stations. With the addition of speculation, register values may also temporarily reside in the ROB. In either case, if the processor does not issue new instructions for a period of time, all existing instructions will commit, and the register values will appear in the register file, which directly corresponds to the architecturally visible registers.

In the register-renaming approach, an extended set of physical registers is used to hold both the architecturally visible registers as well as temporary values. Thus, the extended registers replace the function of both the ROB and the reservation stations. During instruction issue, a renaming process maps the names of architectural registers to physical register numbers in the extended register set, allocating a new unused register for the destination. WAW and WAR hazards are avoided by renaming of the destination register, and speculation recovery is handled because a physical register holding an instruction destination does not become the architectural register until the instruction commits. The renaming map is a simple data structure that supplies the physical register number of the register that currently corresponds to the specified architectural register. This structure is similar in structure and function to the register status table in Tomasulo's algorithm. When an instruction commits, the renaming table is permanently updated to indicate that a physical register corresponds to the actual architectural register, thus effectively finalizing the update to the processor state.

An advantage of the renaming approach versus the ROB approach is that instruction commit is simplified, since it requires only two simple actions: record that the mapping between an architectural register number and physical register number is no longer speculative, and free up any physical registers being used to hold the "older" value of the architectural register. In a design with reservation stations, a station is freed up when the instruction using it completes execution, and a ROB entry is freed up when the corresponding instruction commits.

With register renaming, deallocating registers is more complex, since before we free up a physical register, we must know that it no longer corresponds to an architectural register, and that no further uses of the physical register are outstanding. A physical register corresponds to an architectural register until the architectural register is rewritten, causing the renaming table to point elsewhere. That is, if no renaming entry points to a particular physical register, then it no longer corresponds to an architectural register. There may, however, still be uses of the physical register outstanding. The processor can determine whether this is the case by examining the source register specifiers of all instructions in the functional unit queues. If a given physical register does not appear as a source and it is not designated as an architectural register, it may be reclaimed and reallocated.

Alternatively, the processor can simply wait until another instruction that writes the same architectural register commits. At that point, there can be no further uses of the older value outstanding. Although this method may tie up a physical register slightly longer than necessary, it is easy to implement and hence is used in several recent superscalars.

One question you may be asking is, How do we ever know which registers are the architectural registers if they are constantly changing? Most of the time when the program is executing it does not matter. There are clearly cases, however, where another process, such as the operating system, must be able to know exactly where the contents of a certain architectural register reside. To understand how this capability is provided, assume the processor does not issue instructions for some period of time. Eventually all instructions in the pipeline will commit, and the mapping between the architecturally visible registers and physical registers will become stable. At that point, a subset of the physical registers contains the architecturally visible registers, and the value of any physical register not associated with an architectural register is unneeded. It is then easy to move the architectural registers to a fixed subset of physical registers so that the values can be communicated to another process.

Within the past few years most high-end superscalar processors, including the Pentium series, the MIPS R12000, and the Power and PowerPC processors, have chosen to use register renaming, adding from 20 to 80 extra registers. Since all results are allocated a new virtual register until they commit, these extra registers replace a primary function of the ROB and largely determine how many instructions may be in execution (between issue and commit) at one time.

How Much to Speculate

One of the significant advantages of speculation is its ability to uncover events that would otherwise stall the pipeline early, such as cache misses. This potential advantage, however, comes with a significant potential disadvantage. Speculation is not free: it takes time and energy, and the recovery of incorrect speculation further reduces performance. In addition, to support the higher instruction execution rate needed to benefit from speculation, the processor must have additional resources, which take silicon area and power. Finally, if speculation causes an exceptional event to occur, such as a cache or TLB miss, the potential for significant performance loss increases, if that event would not have occurred without speculation.

To maintain most of the advantage, while minimizing the disadvantages, most pipelines with speculation will allow only low-cost exceptional events (such as a first-level cache miss) to be handled in speculative mode. If an expensive exceptional event occurs, such as a second-level cache miss or a translation lookaside buffer (TLB) miss, the processor will wait until the instruction causing the event is no longer speculative before handling the event. Although this may slightly degrade the performance of some programs, it avoids significant performance losses in others, especially those that suffer from a high frequency of such events coupled with less-than-excellent branch prediction.

In the 1990s, the potential downsides of speculation were less obvious. As processors have evolved, the real costs of speculation have become more apparent, and the limitations of wider issue and speculation have been obvious. We return to this issue in the next chapter.

Speculating through Multiple Branches

In the examples we have considered in this chapter, it has been possible to resolve a branch before having to speculate on another. Three different situations can benefit from speculating on multiple branches simultaneously: a very high branch frequency, significant clustering of branches, and long delays in functional units. In the first two cases, achieving high performance may mean that multiple branches are speculated, and it may even mean handling more than one branch per clock. Database programs, and other less structured integer computations, often exhibit these properties, making speculation on multiple branches important. Likewise, long delays in functional units can raise the importance of speculating on multiple branches as a way to avoid stalls from the longer pipeline delays.

Speculating on multiple branches slightly complicates the process of speculation recovery, but is straightforward otherwise. A more complex technique is predicting and speculating on more than one branch per cycle. The IBM Power2 could resolve two branches per cycle but did not speculate on any other instructions. As of 2005, no processor has yet combined full speculation with resolving multiple branches per cycle.

Value Prediction

One technique for increasing the amount of ILP available in a program is value prediction. *Value prediction* attempts to predict the value that will be produced by an instruction. Obviously, since most instructions produce a different value every time they are executed (or at least a different value from a set of values), value prediction can have only limited success. There are, however, certain instructions for which it is easier to predict the resulting value—for example, loads that load from a constant pool, or that load a value that changes infrequently. In addition, when an instruction produces a value chosen from a small set of potential values, it may be possible to predict the resulting value by correlating it without an instance.

Value prediction is useful if it significantly increases the amount of available ILP. This possibility is most likely when a value is used as the source of a chain of dependent computations, such as a load. Because value prediction is used to enhance speculations and incorrect speculation has detrimental performance impact, the accuracy of the prediction is critical.

Much of the focus of research on value prediction has been on loads. We can estimate the maximum accuracy of a load value predictor by examining how often a load returns a value that matches a value returned in a recent execution of the load. The simplest case to examine is when the load returns a value that matches the value on the last execution of the load. For a range of SPEC CPU2000 benchmarks, this redundancy occurs from less than 5% of the time to almost 80% of the time. If we allow the load to match any of the most recent 16 values returned, the frequency of a potential match increases, and many benchmarks show a 80% match rate. Of course, matching 1 of 16 recent values does not tell you what value to predict, but it does mean that even with additional information it is impossible for prediction accuracy to exceed 80%.

Because of the high costs of misprediction and the likely case that misprediction rates will be significant (20% to 50%), researchers have focused on assessing which loads are more predictable and only attempting to predict those. This leads to a lower misprediction rate, but also fewer candidates for accelerating through prediction. In the limit, if we attempt to predict only those loads that always return the same value, it is likely that only 10% to 15% of the loads can be predicted. Research on value prediction continues. The results to date, however, have not been sufficiently compelling that any commercial processor has included the capability.

One simple idea that has been adopted and is related to value prediction is address aliasing prediction. *Address aliasing prediction* is a simple technique that predicts whether two stores or a load and a store refer to the same memory address. If two such references do not refer to the same address, then they may be safely interchanged. Otherwise, we must wait until the memory addresses accessed by the instructions are known. Because we need not actually predict the address values, only whether such values conflict, the prediction is both more stable and simpler. Hence, this limited form of address value speculation has been used by a few processors.

2.10   Putting It All Together: The Intel Pentium 4

The Pentium 4 is a processor with a deep pipeline supporting multiple issue with speculation. In this section, we describe the highlights of the Pentium 4 microarchitecture and examine its performance for the SPEC CPU benchmarks. The Pentium 4 also supports multithreading, a topic we discuss in the next chapter.

The Pentium 4 uses an aggressive out-of-order speculative microarchitecture, called Netburst, that is deeply pipelined with the goal of achieving high instruction throughput by combining multiple issue and high clock rates. Like the microarchitecture used in the Pentium III, a front-end decoder translates each IA-32 instruction to a series of micro-operations (uops), which are similar to typical RISC instructions. The uops are than executed by a dynamically scheduled speculative pipeline.

The Pentium 4 uses a novel *execution trace cache* to generate the uop instruction stream, as opposed to a conventional instruction cache that would hold IA-32 instructions. A *trace cache* is a type of instruction cache that holds sequences of instructions to be executed including nonadjacent instructions separated by branches; a trace cache tries to exploit the temporal sequencing of instruction execution rather than the spatial locality exploited in a normal cache; trace caches are explained in detail in Appendix C.

The Pentium 4's execution trace cache is a trace cache of uops, corresponding to the decoded IA-32 instruction stream. By filling the pipeline from the execution trace cache, the Pentium 4 avoids the need to redecode IA-32 instructions whenever the trace cache hits. Only on trace cache misses are IA-32 instructions fetched from the L2 cache and decoded to refill the execution trace cache. Up to three IA-32 instructions may be decoded and translated every cycle, generating up to six uops; when a single IA-32 instruction requires more than three uops, the uop sequence is generated from the microcode ROM.

The execution trace cache has its own branch target buffer, which predicts the outcome of uop branches. The high hit rate in the execution trace cache (for example, the trace cache miss rate for the SPEC CPUINT2000 benchmarks is less than 0.15%), means that the IA-32 instruction fetch and decode is rarely needed.

After fetching from the execution trace cache, the uops are executed by an out-of-order speculative pipeline, similar to that in Section 2.6, but using register renaming rather than a reorder buffer. Up to three uops per clock can be renamed and dispatched to the functional unit queues, and three uops can be committed each clock cycle. There are four dispatch ports, which allow a total of six uops to be dispatched to the functional units every clock cycle. The load and store units each have their own dispatch port, another port covers basic ALU operations, and a fourth handles FP and integer operations. Figure 2.26 shows a diagram of the microarchitecture.

Since the Pentium 4 microarchitecture is dynamically scheduled, uops do not follow a simple static set of pipeline stages during their execution. Instead various stages of execution (instruction fetch, decode, uop issue, rename, schedule, execute, and retire) can take varying numbers of clock cycles. In the Pentium III,

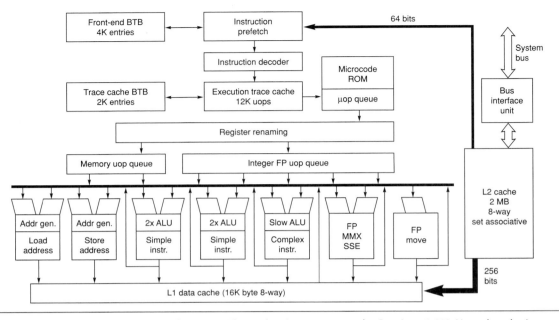

Figure 2.26 The Pentium 4 microarchitecture. The cache sizes represent the Pentium 4 640. Note that the instructions are usually coming from the trace cache; only when the trace cache misses is the front-end instruction prefetch unit consulted. This figure was adapted from Boggs et al. [2004].

the minimum time for an instruction to go from fetch to retire was 11 clock cycles, with instructions requiring multiple clock cycles in the execution stage taking longer. As in any dynamically scheduled pipeline, instructions could take much longer if they had to wait for operands. As stated earlier, the Pentium 4 introduced a much deeper pipeline, partitioning stages of the Pentium III pipeline so as to achieve a higher clock rate. In the initial Pentium 4 introduced in 1990, the minimum number of cycles to transit the pipeline was increased to 21, allowing for a 1.5 GHz clock rate. In 2004, Intel introduced a version of the Pentium 4 with a 3.2 GHz clock rate. To achieve this high clock rate, further pipelining was added so that a simple instruction takes 31 clock cycles to go from fetch to retire. This additional pipelining, together with improvements in transistor speed, allowed the clock rate to more than double over the first Pentium 4.

Obviously, with such deep pipelines and aggressive clock rates the cost of cache misses and branch mispredictions are both very high A two-level cache is used to minimize the frequency of DRAM accesses. Branch prediction is done with a branch-target buffer using a two-level predictor with both local and global branch histories; in the most recent Pentium 4, the size of the branch-target buffer was increased, and the static predictor, used when the branch-target buffer misses, was improved. Figure 2.27 summarizes key features of the microarchitecture, and the caption notes some of the changes since the first version of the Pentium 4 in 2000.

Feature	Size	Comments
Front-end branch-target buffer	4K entries	Predicts the next IA-32 instruction to fetch; used only when the execution trace cache misses.
Execution trace cache	12K uops	Trace cache used for uops.
Trace cache branch-target buffer	2K entries	Predicts the next uop.
Registers for renaming	128 total	128 uops can be in execution with up to 48 loads and 32 stores.
Functional units	7 total: 2 simple ALU, complex ALU, load, store, FP move, FP arithmetic	The simple ALU units run at twice the clock rate, accepting up to two simple ALU uops every clock cycle. This allows execution of two dependent ALU operations in a single clock cycle.
L1 data cache	16 KB; 8-way associative; 64-byte blocks write through	Integer load to use latency is 4 cycles; FP load to use latency is 12 cycles; up to 8 outstanding load misses.
L2 cache	2 MB; 8-way associative; 128-byte blocks write back	256 bits to L1, providing 108 GB/sec; 18-cycle access time; 64 bits to memory capable of 6.4 GB/sec. A miss in L2 does not cause an automatic update of L1.

Figure 2.27 Important characteristics of the recent Pentium 4 640 implementation in 90 nm technology (code named Prescott). The newer Pentium 4 uses larger caches and branch-prediction buffers, allows more loads and stores outstanding, and has higher bandwidth between levels in the memory system. Note the novel use of double-speed ALUs, which allow the execution of back-to-back dependent ALU operations in a single clock cycle; having twice as many ALUs, an alternative design point, would not allow this capability. The original Pentium 4 used a trace cache BTB with 512 entries, an L1 cache of 8 KB, and an L2 cache of 256 KB.

An Analysis of the Performance of the Pentium 4

The deep pipeline of the Pentium 4 makes the use of speculation, and its dependence on branch prediction, critical to achieving high performance. Likewise, performance is very dependent on the memory system. Although dynamic scheduling and the large number of outstanding loads and stores supports hiding the latency of cache misses, the aggressive 3.2 GHz clock rate means that L2 misses are likely to cause a stall as the queues fill up while awaiting the completion of the miss.

Because of the importance of branch prediction and cache misses, we focus our attention on these two areas. The charts in this section use five of the integer SPEC CPU2000 benchmarks and five of the FP benchmarks, and the data is captured using counters within the Pentium 4 designed for performance monitoring. The processor is a Pentium 4 640 running at 3.2 GHz with an 800 MHz system bus and 667 MHz DDR2 DRAMs for main memory.

Figure 2.28 shows the branch-misprediction rate in terms of mispredictions per 1000 instructions. Remember that in terms of pipeline performance, what matters is the number of mispredictions per instruction; the FP benchmarks generally have fewer branches per instruction (48 branches per 1000 instructions) versus the integer benchmarks (186 branches per 1000 instructions), as well as

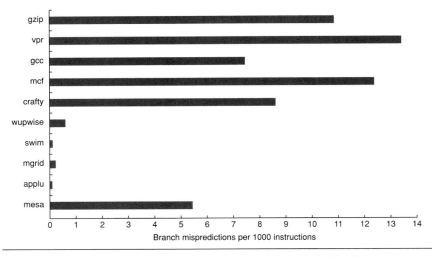

Figure 2.28 Branch misprediction rate per 1000 instructions for five integer and five floating-point benchmarks from the SPEC CPU2000 benchmark suite. This data and the rest of the data in this section were acquired by John Holm and Dileep Bhandarkar of Intel.

better prediction rates (98% versus 94%). The result, as Figure 2.28 shows, is that the misprediction rate per instruction for the integer benchmarks is more than 8 times higher than the rate for the FP benchmarks.

Branch-prediction accuracy is crucial in speculative processors, since incorrect speculation requires recovery time and wastes energy pursuing the wrong path. Figure 2.29 shows the fraction of executed uops that are the result of misspeculation. As we would suspect, the misspeculation rate results look almost identical to the misprediction rates.

How do the cache miss rates contribute to possible performance losses? The trace cache miss rate is almost negligible for this set of the SPEC benchmarks, with only one benchmark (186.craft) showing any significant misses (0.6%). The L1 and L2 miss rates are more significant. Figure 2.30 shows the L1 and L2 miss rates for these 10 benchmarks. Although the miss rate for L1 is about 14 times higher than the miss rate for L2, the miss penalty for L2 is comparably higher, and the inability of the microarchitecture to hide these very long misses means that L2 misses likely are responsible for an equal or greater performance loss than L1 misses, especially for benchmarks such as mcf and swim.

How do the effects of misspeculation and cache misses translate to actual performance? Figure 2.31 shows the effective CPI for the 10 SPEC CPU2000 benchmarks. There are three benchmarks whose performance stands out from the pack and are worth examining:

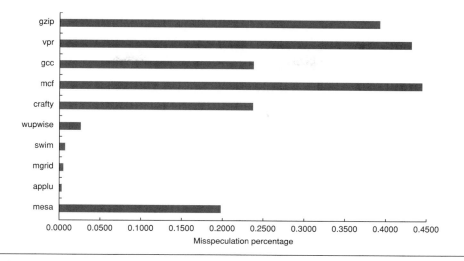

Figure 2.29 The percentage of uop instructions issued that are misspeculated.

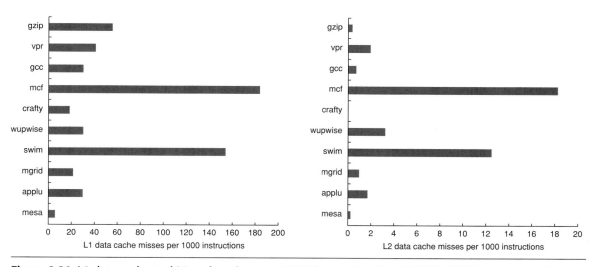

Figure 2.30 **L1 data cache and L2 cache misses per 1000 instructions for 10 SPEC CPU2000 benchmarks.** Note that the scale of the L1 misses is 10 times that of the L2 misses. Because the miss penalty for L2 is likely to be at least 10 times larger than for L1, the relative sizes of the bars are an indication of the relative performance penalty for the misses in each cache. The inability to hide long L2 misses with overlapping execution will further increase the stalls caused by L2 misses relative to L1 misses.

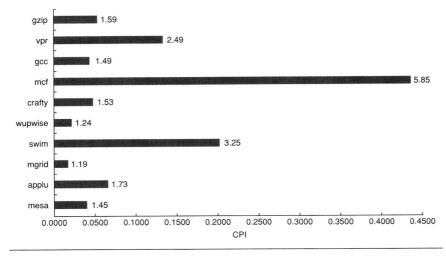

Figure 2.31 The CPI for the 10 SPEC CPU benchmarks. An increase in the CPI by a factor of 1.29 comes from the translation of IA-32 instructions into uops, which results in 1.29 uops per IA-32 instruction on average for these 10 benchmarks.

1. mcf has a CPI that is more than four times higher than that of the four other integer benchmarks. It has the worst misspeculation rate. Equally importantly, mcf has the worst L1 and the worst L2 miss rate among any benchmark, integer or floating point, in the SPEC suite. The high cache miss rates make it impossible for the processor to hide significant amounts of miss latency.

2. vpr achieves a CPI that is 1.6 times higher than three of the five integer benchmarks (excluding mcf). This appears to arise from a branch misprediction that is the worst among the integer benchmarks (although not much worse than the average) together with a high L2 miss rate, second only to mcf among the integer benchmarks.

3. swim is the lowest performing FP benchmark, with a CPI that is more than two times the average of the other four FP benchmarks. swim's problems are high L1 and L2 cache miss rates, second only to mcf. Notice that swim has excellent speculation results, but that success can probably not hide the high miss rates, especially in L2. In contrast, several benchmarks with reasonable L1 miss rates and low L2 miss rates (such as mgrid and gzip) perform well.

To close this section, let's look at the relative performance of the Pentium 4 and AMD Opteron for this subset of the SPEC benchmarks. The AMD Opteron and Intel Pentium 4 share a number of similarities:

- Both use a dynamically scheduled, speculative pipeline capable of issuing and committing three IA-32 instructions per clock.

- Both use a two-level on-chip cache structure, although the Pentium 4 uses a trace cache for the first-level instruction cache and recent Pentium 4 implementations have larger second-level caches.

- They have similar transistor counts, die size, and power, with the Pentium 4 being about 7% to 10% higher on all three measures at the highest clock rates available in 2005 for these two processors.

The most significant difference is the very deep pipeline of the Intel Netburst microarchitecture, which was designed to allow higher clock rates. Although compilers optimized for the two architectures produce slightly different code sequences, comparing CPI measures can provide important insights into how these two processors compare. Remember that differences in the memory hierarchy as well as differences in the pipeline structure will affect these measurements; we analyze the differences in memory system performance in Chapter 5. Figure 2.32 shows the CPI measures for a set of SPEC CPU2000 benchmarks for a 3.2 GHz Pentium 4 and a 2.6 GHz AMD Opteron. At these clock rates, the Opteron processor has an average improvement in CPI by 1.27 over the Pentium 4.

Of course, we should expect the Pentium 4, with its much deeper pipeline, to have a somewhat higher CPI than the AMD Opteron. The key question for the very deeply pipelined Netburst design is whether the increase in clock rate, which the deeper pipelining allows, overcomes the disadvantages of a higher

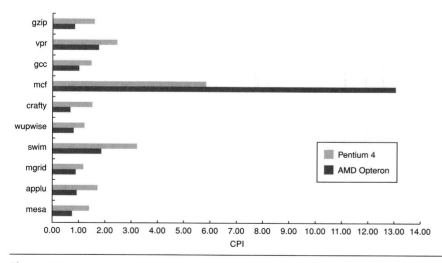

Figure 2.32 A 2.6 GHz AMD Opteron has a lower CPI by a factor of 1.27 versus a 3.2 GHz Pentium 4.

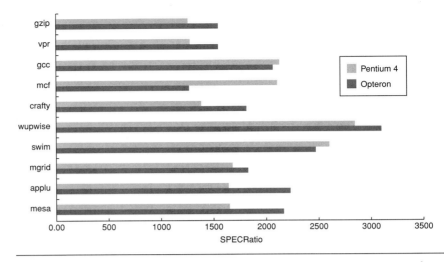

Figure 2.33 The performance of a 2.8 GHz AMD Opteron versus a 3.8 GHz Intel Pentium 4 shows a performance advantage for the Opteron of about 1.08.

CPI. We examine this by showing the SPEC CPU2000 performance for these two processors at their highest available clock rate of these processors in 2005: 2.8 GHz for the Opteron and 3.8 GHz for the Pentium 4. These higher clock rates will increase the effective CPI measurement versus those in Figure 2.32, since the cost of a cache miss will increase. Figure 2.33 shows the relative performance on the same subset of SPEC as Figure 2.32. The Opteron is slightly faster, meaning that the higher clock rate of the Pentium 4 is insufficient to overcome the higher CPI arising from more pipeline stalls.

Hence, while the Pentium 4 performs well, it is clear that the attempt to achieve both high clock rates via a deep pipeline and high instruction throughput via multiple issue is not as successful as the designers once believed it would be. We discuss this topic in depth in the next chapter.

2.11   Fallacies and Pitfalls

Our first fallacy has two parts: First, simple rules do not hold, and, second, the choice of benchmarks plays a major role.

Fallacy   *Processors with lower CPIs will always be faster.*

Fallacy   *Processors with faster clock rates will always be faster.*

Although a lower CPI is certainly better, sophisticated multiple-issue pipelines typically have slower clock rates than processors with simple pipelines. In applications with limited ILP or where the parallelism cannot be exploited by the hardware resources, the faster clock rate often wins. But, when significant ILP exists, a processor that exploits lots of ILP may be better.

The IBM Power5 processor is designed for high-performance integer and FP; it contains two processor cores each capable of sustaining four instructions per clock, including two FP and two load-store instructions. The highest clock rate for a Power5 processor in 2005 is 1.9 GHz. In comparison, the Pentium 4 offers a single processor with multithreading (see the next chapter). The processor can sustain three instructions per clock with a very deep pipeline, and the maximum available clock rate in 2005 is 3.8 GHz.

Thus, the Power5 will be faster if the product of the instruction count and CPI is less than one-half the same product for the Pentium 4. As Figure 2.34 shows the CPI × instruction count advantages of the Power5 are significant for the FP programs, sometimes by more than a factor of 2, while for the integer programs the CPI × instruction count advantage of the Power5 is usually not enough to overcome the clock rate advantage of the Pentium 4. By comparing the SPEC numbers, we find that the product of instruction count and CPI advantage for the Power5 is 3.1 times on the floating-point programs but only 1.5 times on the integer programs. Because the maximum clock rate of the Pentium 4 in 2005 is exactly twice that of the Power5, the Power5 is faster by 1.5 on SPECfp2000 and the Pentium 4 will be faster by 1.3 on SPECint2000.

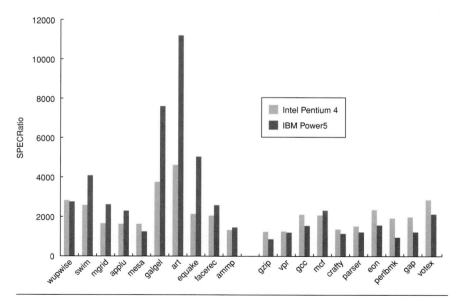

Figure 2.34 A comparison of the 1.9 GHZ IBM Power5 processor versus the 3.8 GHz Intel Pentium 4 for 20 SPEC benchmarks (10 integer on the left and 10 floating point on the right) shows that the higher clock Pentium 4 is generally faster for the integer workload, while the lower CPI Power5 is usually faster for the floating-point workload.

Pitfall *Sometimes bigger and dumber is better.*

Advanced pipelines have focused on novel and increasingly sophisticated schemes for improving CPI. The 21264 uses a sophisticated tournament predictor with a total of 29K bits (see page 88), while the earlier 21164 uses a simple 2-bit predictor with 2K entries (or a total of 4K bits). For the SPEC95 benchmarks, the more sophisticated branch predictor of the 21264 outperforms the simpler 2-bit scheme on all but one benchmark. On average, for SPECint95, the 21264 has 11.5 mispredictions per 1000 instructions committed, while the 21164 has about 16.5 mispredictions.

Somewhat surprisingly, the simpler 2-bit scheme works better for the transaction-processing workload than the sophisticated 21264 scheme (17 mispredictions versus 19 per 1000 completed instructions)! How can a predictor with less than 1/7 the number of bits and a much simpler scheme actually work better? The answer lies in the structure of the workload. The transaction-processing workload has a very large code size (more than an order of magnitude larger than any SPEC95 benchmark) with a large branch frequency. The ability of the 21164 predictor to hold twice as many branch predictions based on purely local behavior (2K versus the 1K local predictor in the 21264) seems to provide a slight advantage.

This pitfall also reminds us that different applications can produce different behaviors. As processors become more sophisticated, including specific microarchitectural features aimed at some particular program behavior, it is likely that different applications will see more divergent behavior.

2.12 Concluding Remarks

The tremendous interest in multiple-issue organizations came about because of an interest in improving performance without affecting the standard uniprocessor programming model. Although taking advantage of ILP is conceptually simple, the design problems are amazingly complex in practice. It is extremely difficult to achieve the performance you might expect from a simple first-level analysis.

Rather than embracing dramatic new approaches in microarchitecture, most of the last 10 years have focused on raising the clock rates of multiple-issue processors and narrowing the gap between peak and sustained performance. The dynamically scheduled, multiple-issue processors announced in the last five years (the Pentium 4, IBM Power5, and the AMD Athlon and Opteron) have the same basic structure and similar sustained issue rates (three to four instructions per clock) as the first dynamically scheduled, multiple-issue processors announced in 1995! But the clock rates are 10–20 times higher, the caches are 4–8 times bigger, there are 2–4 times as many renaming registers, and twice as many load-store units! The result is performance that is 8–16 times higher.

The trade-offs between increasing clock speed and decreasing CPI through multiple issue are extremely hard to quantify. In the 1995 edition of this book, we stated:

> Although you might expect that it is possible to build an advanced multiple-issue processor with a high clock rate, a factor of 1.5 to 2 in clock rate has consistently separated the highest clock rate processors and the most sophisticated multiple-issue processors. It is simply too early to tell whether this difference is due to fundamental implementation trade-offs, or to the difficulty of dealing with the complexities in multiple-issue processors, or simply a lack of experience in implementing such processors.

Given the availability of the Pentium 4 at 3.8 GHz, it has become clear that the limitation was primarily our understanding of how to build such processors. As we will see in the next chapter, however, it appears unclear that the initial success in achieving high-clock-rate processors that issue three to four instructions per clock can be carried much further due to limitations in available ILP, efficiency in exploiting that ILP, and power concerns. In addition, as we saw in the comparison of the Opteron and Pentium 4, it appears that the performance advantage in high clock rates achieved by very deep pipelines (20–30 stages) is largely lost by additional pipeline stalls. We analyze this behavior further in the next chapter.

One insight that was clear in 1995 and has become even more obvious in 2005 is that the peak-to-sustained performance ratios for multiple-issue processors are often quite large and typically grow as the issue rate grows. The lessons to be gleaned by comparing the Power5 and Pentium 4, or the Pentium 4 and Pentium III (which differ primarily in pipeline depth and hence clock rate, rather than issue rates), remind us that it is difficult to generalize about clock rate versus CPI, or about the underlying trade-offs in pipeline depth, issue rate, and other characteristics.

A change in approach is clearly upon us. Higher-clock-rate versions of the Pentium 4 have been abandoned. IBM has shifted to putting two processors on a single chip in the Power4 and Power5 series, and both Intel and AMD have delivered early versions of two-processor chips. We will return to this topic in the next chapter and indicate why the 20-year rapid pursuit of ILP seems to have reached its end.

2.13   Historical Perspective and References

Section K.4 on the companion CD features a discussion on the development of pipelining and instruction-level parallelism. We provide numerous references for further reading and exploration of these topics.

Case Studies with Exercises by Robert P. Colwell

Case Study 1: Exploring the Impact of Microarchitectural Techniques

Concepts illustrated by this case study

■ Basic Instruction Scheduling, Reordering, Dispatch

■ Multiple Issue and Hazards

■ Register Renaming

■ Out-of-Order and Speculative Execution

■ Where to Spend Out-of-Order Resources

You are tasked with designing a new processor microarchitecture, and you are trying to figure out how best to allocate your hardware resources. Which of the hardware and software techniques you learned in Chapter 2 should you apply? You have a list of latencies for the functional units and for memory, as well as some representative code. Your boss has been somewhat vague about the performance requirements of your new design, but you know from experience that, all else being equal, faster is usually better. Start with the basics. Figure 2.35 provides a sequence of instructions and list of latencies.

2.1 [10] <1.8, 2.1, 2.2> What would be the baseline performance (in cycles, per loop iteration) of the code sequence in Figure 2.35 if no new instruction execution could be initiated until the previous instruction execution had completed? Ignore front-end fetch and decode. Assume for now that execution does not stall for lack of the next instruction, but only one instruction/cycle can be issued. Assume the branch is taken, and that there is a 1 cycle branch delay slot.

			Latencies beyond single cycle	
Loop:	LD	F2,0(Rx)	Memory LD	+3
I0:	MULTD	F2,F0,F2	Memory SD	+1
I1:	DIVD	F8,F2,F0	Integer ADD, SUB	+0
I2:	LD	F4,0(Ry)	Branches	+1
I3:	ADDD	F4,F0,F4	ADDD	+2
I4:	ADDD	F10,F8,F2	MULTD	+4
I5:	SD	F4,0(Ry)	DIVD	+10
I6:	ADDI	Rx,Rx,#8		
I7:	ADDI	Ry,Ry,#8		
I8:	SUB	R20,R4,Rx		
I9:	BNZ	R20,Loop		

Figure 2.35 Code and latencies for Exercises 2.1 through 2.6.

2.2 [10] <1.8, 2.1, 2.2> Think about what latency numbers really mean—they indicate the number of cycles a given function requires to produce its output, nothing more. If the overall pipeline stalls for the latency cycles of each functional unit, then you are at least guaranteed that any pair of back-to-back instructions (a "producer" followed by a "consumer") will execute correctly. But not all instruction pairs have a producer/consumer relationship. Sometimes two adjacent instructions have nothing to do with each other. How many cycles would the loop body in the code sequence in Figure 2.35 require if the pipeline detected true data dependences and only stalled on those, rather than blindly stalling everything just because one functional unit is busy? Show the code with `<stall>` inserted where necessary to accommodate stated latencies. (*Hint:* An instruction with latency "+2" needs 2 `<stall>` cycles to be inserted into the code sequence. Think of it this way: a 1-cycle instruction has latency 1 + 0, meaning zero extra wait states. So latency 1 + 1 implies 1 stall cycle; latency 1 + N has N extra stall cycles.)

2.3 [15] <2.6, 2.7> Consider a multiple-issue design. Suppose you have two execution pipelines, each capable of beginning execution of one instruction per cycle, and enough fetch/decode bandwidth in the front end so that it will not stall your execution. Assume results can be immediately forwarded from one execution unit to another, or to itself. Further assume that the only reason an execution pipeline would stall is to observe a true data dependence. Now how many cycles does the loop require?

2.4 [10] <2.6, 2.7> In the multiple-issue design of Exercise 2.3, you may have recognized some subtle issues. Even though the two pipelines have the exact same instruction repertoire, they are not identical nor interchangeable, because there is an implicit ordering between them that must reflect the ordering of the instructions in the original program. If instruction $N + 1$ begins execution in Execution Pipe 1 at the same time that instruction N begins in Pipe 0, and $N + 1$ happens to require a shorter execution latency than N, then $N + 1$ will complete before N (even though program ordering would have implied otherwise). Recite at least two reasons why that could be hazardous and will require special considerations in the microarchitecture. Give an example of two instructions from the code in Figure 2.35 that demonstrate this hazard.

2.5 [20] <2.7> Reorder the instructions to improve performance of the code in Figure 2.35. Assume the two-pipe machine in Exercise 2.3, and that the out-of-order completion issues of Exercise 2.4 have been dealt with successfully. Just worry about observing true data dependences and functional unit latencies for now. How many cycles does your reordered code take?

2.6 [10/10] <2.1, 2.2> Every cycle that does not initiate a new operation in a pipe is a lost opportunity, in the sense that your hardware is not "living up to its potential."

    a. [10] <2.1, 2.2> In your reordered code from Exercise 2.5, what fraction of all cycles, counting both pipes, were wasted (did not initiate a new op)?

    b. [10] <2.1, 2.2> Loop unrolling is one standard compiler technique for finding more parallelism in code, in order to minimize the lost opportunities for performance.

c. Hand-unroll two iterations of the loop in your reordered code from Exercise 2.5. What speedup did you obtain? (For this exercise, just color the $N + 1$ iteration's instructions green to distinguish them from the Nth iteration's; if you were actually unrolling the loop you would have to reassign registers to prevent collisions between the iterations.)

2.7 [15] <2.1> Computers spend most of their time in loops, so multiple loop iterations are great places to speculatively find more work to keep CPU resources busy. Nothing is ever easy, though; the compiler emitted only one copy of that loop's code, so even though multiple iterations are handling distinct data, they will appear to use the same registers. To keep register usages multiple iterations from colliding, we rename their registers. Figure 2.36 shows example code that we would like our hardware to rename.

A compiler could have simply unrolled the loop and used different registers to avoid conflicts, but if we expect our hardware to unroll the loop, it must also do the register renaming. How? Assume your hardware has a pool of temporary registers (call them T registers, and assume there are 64 of them, T0 through T63) that it can substitute for those registers designated by the compiler. This rename hardware is indexed by the source register designation, and the value in the table is the T register of the last destination that targeted that register. (Think of these table values as producers, and the src registers are the consumers; it doesn't much matter where the producer puts its result as long as its consumers can find it.) Consider the code sequence in Figure 2.36. Every time you see a destination register in the code, substitute the next available T, beginning with T9. Then update all the src registers accordingly, so that true data dependences are maintained. Show the resulting code. (*Hint:* See Figure 2.37.)

```
Loop: LD     F2,0(Rx)
I0:   MULTD  F5,F0,F2
I1:   DIVD   F8,F0,F2
I2:   LD     F4,0(Ry)
I3:   ADDD   F6,F0,F4
I4:   ADDD   F10,F8,F2
I5:   SD     F4,0(Ry)
```

Figure 2.36 Sample code for register renaming practice.

```
I0:   LD     T9,0(Rx)
I1:   MULTD  T10,F0,T9
  . . .
```

Figure 2.37 Expected output of register renaming.

```
I0:   MULTD   F5,F0,F2
I1:   ADDD    F9,F5,F4
I2:   ADDD    F5,F5,F2
I3:   DIVD    F2,F9,F0
```

Figure 2.38 Sample code for superscalar register renaming.

2.8   [20] <2.4> Exercise 2.7 explored simple register renaming: when the hardware
       register renamer sees a source register, it substitutes the destination T register of
       the last instruction to have targeted that source register. When the rename table
       sees a destination register, it substitutes the next available T for it. But superscalar
       designs need to handle multiple instructions per clock cycle at every stage in the
       machine, including the register renaming. A simple scalar processor would there-
       fore look up both src register mappings for each instruction, and allocate a new
       destination mapping per clock cycle. Superscalar processors must be able to do
       that as well, but they must also ensure that any dest-to-src relationships between
       the two concurrent instructions are handled correctly. Consider the sample code
       sequence in Figure 2.38. Assume that we would like to simultaneously rename
       the first two instructions. Further assume that the next two available T registers to
       be used are known at the beginning of the clock cycle in which these two instruc-
       tions are being renamed. Conceptually, what we want is for the first instruction to
       do its rename table lookups, and then update the table per its destination's T reg-
       ister. Then the second instruction would do exactly the same thing, and any inter-
       instruction dependency would thereby be handled correctly. But there's not
       enough time to write that T register designation into the renaming table and then
       look it up again for the second instruction, all in the same clock cycle. That regis-
       ter substitution must instead be done live (in parallel with the register rename
       table update). Figure 2.39 shows a circuit diagram, using multiplexers and com-
       parators, that will accomplish the necessary on-the-fly register renaming. Your
       task is to show the cycle-by-cycle state of the rename table for every instruction
       of the code. Assume the table starts out with every entry equal to its index (T0 = 0;
       T1 = 1, . . .).

2.9   [5] <2.4> If you ever get confused about what a register renamer has to do, go
       back to the assembly code you're executing, and ask yourself what has to happen
       for the right result to be obtained. For example, consider a three-way superscalar
       machine renaming these three instructions concurrently:

```
ADDI    R1, R1, R1
ADDI    R1, R1, R1
ADDI    R1, R1, R1
```

       If the value of R1 starts out as 5, what should its value be when this sequence has
       executed?

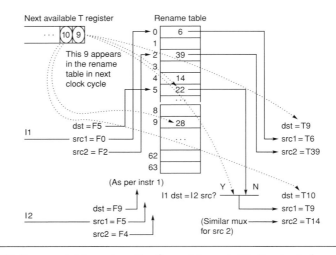

Figure 2.39 Rename table and on-the-fly register substitution logic for superscalar machines. (Note: "src" is source, "dst" is destination.)

```
Loop: LW      R1,0(R2)   ;   LW      R3,8(R2)
      <stall>
      <stall>
      ADDI    R10,R1,#1;  ADDI    R11,R3,#1
      SW      R1,0(R2)  ;  SW      R3,8(R2)
      ADDI    R2,R2,#8
      SUB     R4,R3,R2
      BNZ     R4,Loop
```

Figure 2.40 Sample VLIW code with two adds, two loads, and two stalls.

2.10 [20] <2.4, 2.9> VLIW designers have a few basic choices to make regarding architectural rules for register use. Suppose a VLIW is designed with self-draining execution pipelines: once an operation is initiated, its results will appear in the destination register at most L cycles later (where L is the latency of the operation). There are never enough registers, so there is a temptation to wring maximum use out of the registers that exist. Consider Figure 2.40. If loads have a 1 + 2 cycle latency, unroll this loop once, and show how a VLIW capable of two loads and two adds per cycle can use the minimum number of registers, in the absence of any pipeline interruptions or stalls. Give an example of an event that, in the presence of self-draining pipelines, could disrupt this pipelining and yield wrong results.

2.11 [10/10/10] <2.3> Assume a five-stage single-pipeline microarchitecture (fetch, decode, execute, memory, write back) and the code in Figure 2.41. All ops are 1 cycle except LW and SW, which are 1 + 2 cycles, and branches, which are 1 + 1 cycles. There is no forwarding. Show the phases of each instruction per clock cycle for one iteration of the loop.

    a. [10] <2.3> How many clock cycles per loop iteration are lost to branch overhead?

    b. [10] <2.3> Assume a static branch predictor, capable of recognizing a backwards branch in the decode stage. Now how many clock cycles are wasted on branch overhead?

    c. [10] <2.3> Assume a dynamic branch predictor. How many cycles are lost on a correct prediction?

2.12 [20/20/20/10/20] <2.4, 2.7, 2.10> Let's consider what dynamic scheduling might achieve here. Assume a microarchitecture as shown in Figure 2.42. Assume that the ALUs can do all arithmetic ops (MULTD, DIVD, ADDD, ADDI, SUB) and branches, and that the Reservation Station (RS) can dispatch at most one operation to each functional unit per cycle (one op to each ALU plus one memory op to the LD/ST unit).

```
Loop: LW    R1,0(R2)
      ADDI  R1,R1,#1
      SW    R1,0(R2)
      ADDI  R2,R2,#4
      SUB   R4,R3,R2
      BNZ   R4,Loop
```

Figure 2.41 Code loop for Exercise 2.11.

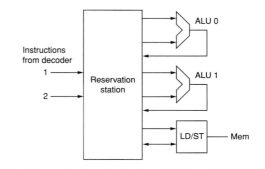

Figure 2.42 An out-of-order microarchitecture.

a. [15] <2.4> Suppose all of the instructions from the sequence in Figure 2.35 are present in the RS, with no renaming having been done. Highlight any instructions in the code where register renaming would improve performance. *Hint:* Look for RAW and WAW hazards. Assume the same functional unit latencies as in Figure 2.35.

b. [20] <2.4> Suppose the register-renamed version of the code from part (a) is resident in the RS in clock cycle *N,* with latencies as given in Figure 2.35. Show how the RS should dispatch these instructions out-of-order, clock by clock, to obtain optimal performance on this code. (Assume the same RS restrictions as in part (a). Also assume that results must be written into the RS before they're available for use; i.e., no bypassing.) How many clock cycles does the code sequence take?

c. [20] <2.4> Part (b) lets the RS try to optimally schedule these instructions. But in reality, the whole instruction sequence of interest is not usually present in the RS. Instead, various events clear the RS, and as a new code sequence streams in from the decoder, the RS must choose to dispatch what it has. Suppose that the RS is empty. In cycle 0 the first two register-renamed instructions of this sequence appear in the RS. Assume it takes 1 clock cycle to dispatch any op, and assume functional unit latencies are as they were for Exercise 2.2. Further assume that the front end (decoder/register-renamer) will continue to supply two new instructions per clock cycle. Show the cycle-by-cycle order of dispatch of the RS. How many clock cycles does this code sequence require now?

d. [10] <2.10> If you wanted to improve the results of part (c), which would have helped most: (1) another ALU; (2) another LD/ST unit; (3) full bypassing of ALU results to subsequent operations; (4) cutting the longest latency in half? What's the speedup?

e. [20] <2.7> Now let's consider speculation, the act of fetching, decoding, and executing beyond one or more conditional branches. Our motivation to do this is twofold: the dispatch schedule we came up with in part (c) had lots of nops, and we know computers spend most of their time executing loops (which implies the branch back to the top of the loop is pretty predictable.) Loops tell us where to find more work to do; our sparse dispatch schedule suggests we have opportunities to do some of that work earlier than before. In part (d) you found the critical path through the loop. Imagine folding a second copy of that path onto the schedule you got in part (b). How many more clock cycles would be required to do two loops' worth of work (assuming all instructions are resident in the RS)? (Assume all functional units are fully pipelined.)

Case Study 2: Modeling a Branch Predictor

Concept illustrated by this case study

■ Modeling a Branch Predictor

Besides studying microarchitecture techniques, to really understand computer architecture you must also program computers. Getting your hands dirty by directly modeling various microarchitectural ideas is better yet. Write a C or Java program to model a 2,1 branch predictor. Your program will read a series of lines from a file named history.txt (available on the companion CD—see Figure Figure 2.43).

Each line of that file has three data items, separated by tabs. The first datum on each line is the address of the branch instruction in hex. The second datum is the branch target address in hex. The third datum is a 1 or a 0; 1 indicates a taken branch, and 0 indicates not taken. The total number of branches your model will consider is, of course, equal to the number of lines in the file. Assume a direct-mapped BTB, and don't worry about instruction lengths or alignment (i.e., if your BTB has four entries, then branch instructions at 0x0, 0x1, 0x2, and 0x3 will reside in those four entries, but a branch instruction at 0x4 will overwrite BTB[0]). For each line in the input file, your model will read the pair of data values, adjust the various tables per the branch predictor being modeled, and collect key performance statistics. The final output of your program will look like that shown in Figure 2.44.

Make the number of BTB entries in your model a command-line option.

2.13 [20/10/10/10/10/10/10] <2.3> Write a model of a simple four-state branch target buffer with 64 entries.

    a. [20] <2.3> What is the overall hit rate in the BTB (the fraction of times a branch was looked up in the BTB and found present)?

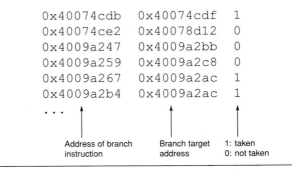

Figure 2.43 Sample history.txt input file format.

b. [10] <2.3> What is the overall branch misprediction rate on a cold start (the fraction of times a branch was correctly predicted taken or not taken, regardless of whether that prediction "belonged to" the branch being predicted)?

c. [10] <2.3> Find the most common branch. What was its contribution to the overall number of correct predictions? (*Hint:* Count the number of times that branch occurs in the history.txt file, then track how each instance of that branch fares within the BTB model.)

d. [10] <2.3> How many capacity misses did your branch predictor suffer?

e. [10] <2.3> What is the effect of a cold start versus a warm start? To find out, run the same input data set once to initialize the history table, and then again to collect the new set of statistics.

f. [10] <2.3> Cold-start the BTB 4 more times, with BTB sizes 16, 32, and 64. Graph the resulting five misprediction rates. Also graph the five hit rates.

g. [10] Submit the well-written, commented source code for your branch target buffer model.

Exercise 2.13 (a)

  Number of hits BTB: 54390. Total brs: 55493. Hit rate: 99.8%

Exercise 2.13 (b)

  Incorrect predictions: 1562 of 55493, or 2.8%

Exercise 2.13 (c)

  <a simple unix command line shell script will give you the most
    common branch...show how you got it here.>
  Most signif. branch seen 15418 times, out of 55493 tot brs ;
    27.8%
  MS branch = 0x80484ef, correct predictions = 19151 (of 36342
    total correct preds) or 52.7%

Exercise 2.13 (d)

  Total unique branches (1 miss per br compulsory): 121
  Total misses seen: 104.
  So total capacity misses = total misses — compulsory misses = 17

Exercise 2.13 (e)

  Number of hits in BTB: 54390. Total brs: 55493. Hit rate: 99.8%
  Incorrect predictions: 1103 of 54493, or 2.0%

Exercise 2.13 (f)

BTB Length	mispredict rate
1	32.91%
2	6.42%
4	0.28%
8	0.23%
16	0.21%
32	0.20%
64	0.20%

Figure 2.44 Sample program output format.

3.1	Introduction	154
3.2	Studies of the Limitations of ILP	154
3.3	Limitations on ILP for Realizable Processors	165
3.4	Crosscutting Issues: Hardware versus Software Speculation	170
3.5	Multithreading: Using ILP Support to Exploit Thread-Level Parallelism	172
3.6	Putting It All Together: Performance and Efficiency in Advanced Multiple-Issue Processors	179
3.7	Fallacies and Pitfalls	183
3.8	Concluding Remarks	184
3.9	Historical Perspective and References	185
	Case Study with Exercises by Wen-mei W. Hwu and John W. Sias	185

3

Limits on Instruction-Level Parallelism

> Processors are being produced with the potential for very many parallel operations on the instruction level.... Far greater extremes in instruction-level parallelism are on the horizon.
>
> **J. Fisher**
> *(1981), in the paper that inaugurated*
> *the term "instruction-level parallelism"*

> One of the surprises about IA-64 is that we hear no claims of high frequency, despite claims that an EPIC processor is less complex than a superscalar processor. It's hard to know why this is so, but one can speculate that the overall complexity involved in focusing on CPI, as IA-64 does, makes it hard to get high megahertz.
>
> **M. Hopkins**
> *(2000), in a commentary on the IA-64 architecture,*
> *a joint development of HP and Intel designed to achieve dra-*
> *matic increases in the exploitation*
> *of ILP while retaining a simple architecture,*
> *which would allow higher performance*

3.1   Introduction

As we indicated in the last chapter, exploiting ILP was the primary focus of processor designs for about 20 years starting in the mid-1980s. For the first 15 years, we saw a progression of successively more sophisticated schemes for pipelining, multiple issue, dynamic scheduling and speculation. Since 2000, designers have focused primarily on optimizing designs or trying to achieve higher clock rates without increasing issue rates. As we indicated in the close of the last chapter, this era of advances in exploiting ILP appears to be coming to an end.

In this chapter we begin by examining the limitations on ILP from program structure, from realistic assumptions about hardware budgets, and from the accuracy of important techniques for speculation such as branch prediction. In Section 3.5, we examine the use of thread-level parallelism as an alternative or addition to instruction-level parallelism. Finally, we conclude the chapter by comparing a set of recent processors both in performance and in efficiency measures per transistor and per watt.

3.2   Studies of the Limitations of ILP

Exploiting ILP to increase performance began with the first pipelined processors in the 1960s. In the 1980s and 1990s, these techniques were key to achieving rapid performance improvements. The question of how much ILP exists was critical to our long-term ability to enhance performance at a rate that exceeds the increase in speed of the base integrated circuit technology. On a shorter scale, the critical question of what is needed to exploit more ILP is crucial to both computer designers and compiler writers. The data in this section also provide us with a way to examine the value of ideas that we have introduced in the last chapter, including memory disambiguation, register renaming, and speculation.

In this section we review one of the studies done of these questions. The historical perspectives section in Appendix K describes several studies, including the source for the data in this section (Wall's 1993 study). All these studies of available parallelism operate by making a set of assumptions and seeing how much parallelism is available under those assumptions. The data we examine here are from a study that makes the fewest assumptions; in fact, the ultimate hardware model is probably unrealizable. Nonetheless, all such studies assume a certain level of compiler technology, and some of these assumptions could affect the results, despite the use of incredibly ambitious hardware.

In the future, advances in compiler technology together with significantly new and different hardware techniques may be able to overcome some limitations assumed in these studies; however, it is unlikely that such advances *when coupled with realistic hardware* will overcome these limits in the near future. For example, value prediction, which we examined in the last chapter, can remove data dependence limits. For value prediction to have a significant impact on performance, however, predictors would need to achieve far higher prediction accuracy than has so far been reported. Indeed for reasons we discuss in Section 3.6, we are likely reaching the limits of how much ILP can be exploited efficiently. This section will lay the groundwork to understand why this is the case.

The Hardware Model

To see what the limits of ILP might be, we first need to define an ideal processor. An ideal processor is one where all constraints on ILP are removed. The only limits on ILP in such a processor are those imposed by the actual data flows through either registers or memory.

The assumptions made for an ideal or perfect processor are as follows:

1. *Register renaming*—There are an infinite number of virtual registers available, and hence all WAW and WAR hazards are avoided and an unbounded number of instructions can begin execution simultaneously.

2. *Branch prediction*—Branch prediction is perfect. All conditional branches are predicted exactly.

3. *Jump prediction*—All jumps (including jump register used for return and computed jumps) are perfectly predicted. When combined with perfect branch prediction, this is equivalent to having a processor with perfect speculation and an unbounded buffer of instructions available for execution.

4. *Memory address alias analysis*—All memory addresses are known exactly, and a load can be moved before a store provided that the addresses are not identical. Note that this implements perfect address alias analysis.

5. *Perfect caches*—All memory accesses take 1 clock cycle. In practice, superscalar processors will typically consume large amounts of ILP hiding cache misses, making these results highly optimistic.

Assumptions 2 and 3 eliminate *all* control dependences. Likewise, assumptions 1 and 4 eliminate *all but the true* data dependences. Together, these four assumptions mean that *any* instruction in the program's execution can be scheduled on the cycle immediately following the execution of the predecessor on which it depends. It is even possible, under these assumptions, for the *last* dynamically executed instruction in the program to be scheduled on the very first cycle! Thus, this set of assumptions subsumes both control and address speculation and implements them as if they were perfect.

Initially, we examine a processor that can issue an unlimited number of instructions at once looking arbitrarily far ahead in the computation. For all the processor models we examine, there are no restrictions on what types of instructions can execute in a cycle. For the unlimited-issue case, this means there may be an unlimited number of loads or stores issuing in 1 clock cycle. In addition, all functional unit latencies are assumed to be 1 cycle, so that any sequence of dependent instructions can issue on successive cycles. Latencies longer than 1 cycle would decrease the number of issues per cycle, although not the number of instructions under execution at any point. (The instructions in execution at any point are often referred to as *in flight*.)

Of course, this processor is on the edge of unrealizable. For example, the IBM Power5 is one of the most advanced superscalar processors announced to date. The Power5 issues up to four instructions per clock and initiates execution on up to six (with significant restrictions on the instruction type, e.g., at most two load-stores), supports a large set of renaming registers (88 integer and 88 floating point, allowing over 200 instructions in flight, of which up to 32 can be loads and 32 can be stores), uses a large aggressive branch predictor, and employs dynamic memory disambiguation. After looking at the parallelism available for the perfect processor, we will examine the impact of restricting various features.

To measure the available parallelism, a set of programs was compiled and optimized with the standard MIPS optimizing compilers. The programs were instrumented and executed to produce a trace of the instruction and data references. Every instruction in the trace is then scheduled as early as possible, limited only by the data dependences. Since a trace is used, perfect branch prediction and perfect alias analysis are easy to do. With these mechanisms, instructions may be scheduled much earlier than they would otherwise, moving across large numbers of instructions on which they are not data dependent, including branches, since branches are perfectly predicted.

Figure 3.1 shows the average amount of parallelism available for six of the SPEC92 benchmarks. Throughout this section the parallelism is measured by the average instruction issue rate. Remember that all instructions have a 1-cycle latency; a longer latency would reduce the average number of instructions per clock. Three of these benchmarks (fpppp, doduc, and tomcatv) are floating-point intensive, and the other three are integer programs. Two of the floating-point benchmarks (fpppp and tomcatv) have extensive parallelism, which could be exploited by a vector computer or by a multiprocessor (the structure in fpppp is quite messy, however, since some hand transformations have been done on the code). The doduc program has extensive parallelism, but the parallelism does not occur in simple parallel loops as it does in fpppp and tomcatv. The program li is a LISP interpreter that has many short dependences.

In the next few sections, we restrict various aspects of this processor to show what the effects of various assumptions are before looking at some ambitious but realizable processors.

Limitations on the Window Size and Maximum Issue Count

To build a processor that even comes close to perfect branch prediction and perfect alias analysis requires extensive dynamic analysis, since static compile time schemes cannot be perfect. Of course, most realistic dynamic schemes will not be perfect, but the use of dynamic schemes will provide the ability to uncover parallelism that cannot be analyzed by static compile time analysis. Thus, a dynamic processor might be able to more closely match the amount of parallelism uncovered by our ideal processor.

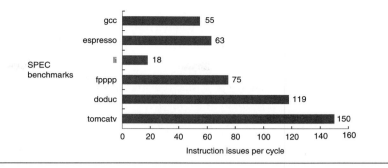

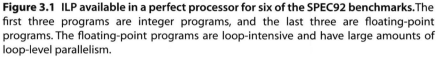

Figure 3.1 ILP available in a perfect processor for six of the SPEC92 benchmarks. The first three programs are integer programs, and the last three are floating-point programs. The floating-point programs are loop-intensive and have large amounts of loop-level parallelism.

How close could a real dynamically scheduled, speculative processor come to the ideal processor? To gain insight into this question, consider what the perfect processor must do:

1. Look arbitrarily far ahead to find a set of instructions to issue, predicting all branches perfectly.

2. Rename all register uses to avoid WAR and WAW hazards.

3. Determine whether there are any data dependences among the instructions in the issue packet; if so, rename accordingly.

4. Determine if any memory dependences exist among the issuing instructions and handle them appropriately.

5. Provide enough replicated functional units to allow all the ready instructions to issue.

Obviously, this analysis is quite complicated. For example, to determine whether n issuing instructions have any register dependences among them, assuming all instructions are register-register and the total number of registers is unbounded, requires

$$2n - 2 + 2n - 4 + \ldots + 2 = 2\sum_{i=1}^{n-1} i = 2\frac{(n-1)n}{2} = n^2 - n$$

comparisons. Thus, to detect dependences among the next 2000 instructions—the default size we assume in several figures—requires almost *4 million* comparisons! Even issuing only 50 instructions requires 2450 comparisons. This cost obviously limits the number of instructions that can be considered for issue at once.

In existing and near-term processors, the costs are not quite so high, since we need only detect dependence pairs and the limited number of registers allows different solutions. Furthermore, in a real processor, issue occurs in order, and dependent instructions are handled by a renaming process that accommodates dependent renaming in 1 clock. Once instructions are issued, the detection of dependences is handled in a distributed fashion by the reservation stations or scoreboard.

The set of instructions that is examined for simultaneous execution is called the *window*. Each instruction in the window must be kept in the processor, and the number of comparisons required every clock is equal to the maximum completion rate times the window size times the number of operands per instruction (today up to $6 \times 200 \times 2 = 2400$), since every pending instruction must look at every completing instruction for either of its operands. Thus, the total window size is limited by the required storage, the comparisons, and a limited issue rate, which makes a larger window less helpful. Remember that even though existing processors allow hundreds of instructions to be in flight, because they cannot issue and rename more than a handful in any clock cycle, the maximum throughout is likely to be limited by the issue rate. For example, if the instruction stream contained totally independent instructions that all hit in the cache, a large window would simply never fill. The value of having a window larger than the issue rate occurs when there are dependences or cache misses in the instruction stream.

The window size directly limits the number of instructions that begin execution in a given cycle. In practice, real processors will have a more limited number of functional units (e.g., no superscalar processor has handled more than two memory references per clock), as well as limited numbers of buses and register access ports, which serve as limits on the number of instructions initiated per clock. Thus, the maximum number of instructions that may issue, begin execution, or commit in the same clock cycle is usually much smaller than the window size.

Obviously, the number of possible implementation constraints in a multiple-issue processor is large, including issues per clock, functional units and unit latency, register file ports, functional unit queues (which may be fewer than units), issue limits for branches, and limitations on instruction commit. Each of these acts as a constraint on the ILP. Rather than try to understand each of these effects, however, we will focus on limiting the size of the window, with the understanding that all other restrictions would further reduce the amount of parallelism that can be exploited.

Figure 3.2 shows the effects of restricting the size of the window from which an instruction can execute. As we can see in Figure 3.2, the amount of parallelism uncovered falls sharply with decreasing window size. In 2005, the most advanced processors have window sizes in the range of 64–200, but these window sizes are not strictly comparable to those shown in Figure 3.2 for two reasons. First, many functional units have multicycle latency, reducing the effective window size compared to the case where all units have single-cycle latency. Second, in real processors the window must also hold any memory references waiting on a cache miss, which are not considered in this model, since it assumes a perfect, single-cycle cache access.

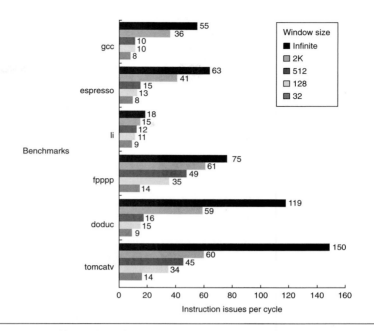

Figure 3.2 **The effect of window size shown by each application by plotting the average number of instruction issues per clock cycle.**

As we can see in Figure 3.2, the integer programs do not contain nearly as much parallelism as the floating-point programs. This result is to be expected. Looking at how the parallelism drops off in Figure 3.2 makes it clear that the parallelism in the floating-point cases is coming from loop-level parallelism. The fact that the amount of parallelism at low window sizes is not that different among the floating-point and integer programs implies a structure where there are dependences within loop bodies, but few dependences between loop iterations in programs such as tomcatv. At small window sizes, the processors simply cannot see the instructions in the next loop iteration that could be issued in parallel with instructions from the current iteration. This case is an example of where better compiler technology (see Appendix G) could uncover higher amounts of ILP, since it could find the loop-level parallelism and schedule the code to take advantage of it, even with small window sizes.

We know that very large window sizes are impractical and inefficient, and the data in Figure 3.2 tells us that instruction throughput will be considerably reduced with realistic implementations. Thus, we will assume a base window size of 2K entries, roughly 10 times as large as the largest implementation in 2005, and a maximum issue capability of 64 instructions per clock, also 10 times the widest issue processor in 2005, for the rest of this analysis. As we will see in the next few sections, when the rest of the processor is not perfect, a 2K window and a 64-issue limitation do not constrain the amount of ILP the processor can exploit.

The Effects of Realistic Branch and Jump Prediction

Our ideal processor assumes that branches can be perfectly predicted: The outcome of any branch in the program is known before the first instruction is executed! Of course, no real processor can ever achieve this. Figure 3.3 shows the effects of more realistic prediction schemes in two different formats. Our data are for several different branch-prediction schemes, varying from perfect to no predictor. We assume a separate predictor is used for jumps. Jump predictors are important primarily with the most accurate branch predictors, since the branch frequency is higher and the accuracy of the branch predictors dominates.

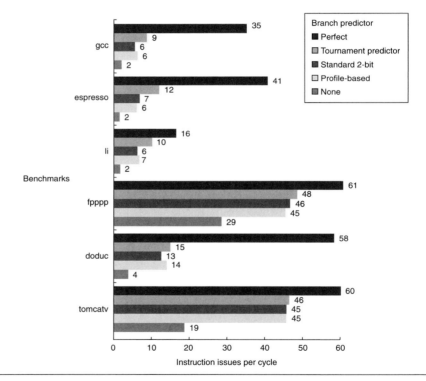

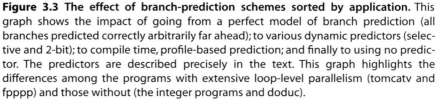

Figure 3.3 The effect of branch-prediction schemes sorted by application. This graph shows the impact of going from a perfect model of branch prediction (all branches predicted correctly arbitrarily far ahead); to various dynamic predictors (selective and 2-bit); to compile time, profile-based prediction; and finally to using no predictor. The predictors are described precisely in the text. This graph highlights the differences among the programs with extensive loop-level parallelism (tomcatv and fpppp) and those without (the integer programs and doduc).

The five levels of branch prediction shown in these figure are

1. *Perfect*—All branches and jumps are perfectly predicted at the start of execution.

2. *Tournament-based branch predictor*—The prediction scheme uses a correlating 2-bit predictor and a noncorrelating 2-bit predictor together with a selector, which chooses the best predictor for each branch. The prediction buffer contains 2^{13} (8K) entries, each consisting of three 2-bit fields, two of which are predictors and the third a selector. The correlating predictor is indexed using the exclusive-or of the branch address and the global branch history. The noncorrelating predictor is the standard 2-bit predictor indexed by the branch address. The selector table is also indexed by the branch address and specifies whether the correlating or noncorrelating predictor should be used. The selector is incremented or decremented just as we would for a standard 2-bit predictor. This predictor, which uses a total of 48K bits, achieves an average misprediction rate of 3% for these six SPEC92 benchmarks and is comparable in strategy and size to the best predictors in use in 2005. Jump prediction is done with a pair of 2K-entry predictors, one organized as a circular buffer for predicting returns and one organized as a standard predictor and used for computed jumps (as in case statements or computed gotos). These jump predictors are nearly perfect.

3. *Standard 2-bit predictor with 512 2-bit entries*—In addition, we assume a 16-entry buffer to predict returns.

4. *Profile-based*—A static predictor uses the profile history of the program and predicts that the branch is always taken or always not taken based on the profile.

5. *None*—No branch prediction is used, though jumps are still predicted. Parallelism is largely limited to within a basic block.

Since we do *not* charge additional cycles for a mispredicted branch, the only effect of varying the branch prediction is to vary the amount of parallelism that can be exploited across basic blocks by speculation. Figure 3.4 shows the accuracy of the three realistic predictors for the conditional branches for the subset of SPEC92 benchmarks we include here.

Figure 3.3 shows that the branch behavior of two of the floating-point programs is much simpler than the other programs, primarily because these two programs have many fewer branches and the few branches that exist are more predictable. This property allows significant amounts of parallelism to be exploited with realistic prediction schemes. In contrast, for all the integer programs and for doduc, the FP benchmark with the least loop-level parallelism, even the difference between perfect branch prediction and the ambitious selective predictor is dramatic. Like the window size data, these figures tell us that to achieve significant amounts of parallelism in integer programs, the processor must select and execute instructions that are widely separated. When branch

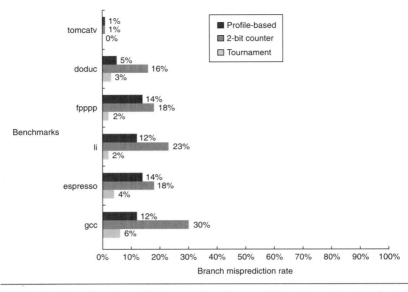

Figure 3.4 Branch misprediction rate for the conditional branches in the SPEC92 subset.

prediction is not highly accurate, the mispredicted branches become a barrier to finding the parallelism.

As we have seen, branch prediction is critical, especially with a window size of 2K instructions and an issue limit of 64. For the rest of this section, in addition to the window and issue limit, we assume as a base a more ambitious tournament predictor that uses two levels of prediction and a total of 8K entries. This predictor, which requires more than 150K bits of storage (roughly four times the largest predictor to date), slightly outperforms the selective predictor described above (by about 0.5–1%). We also assume a pair of 2K jump and return predictors, as described above.

The Effects of Finite Registers

Our ideal processor eliminates all name dependences among register references using an infinite set of virtual registers. To date, the IBM Power5 has provided the largest numbers of virtual registers: 88 additional floating-point and 88 additional integer registers, in addition to the 64 registers available in the base architecture. All 240 registers are shared by two threads when executing in multithreading mode (see Section 3.5), and all are available to a single thread when in single-thread mode. Figure 3.5 shows the effect of reducing the number of registers available for renaming; *both* the FP and GP registers are increased by the number of registers shown in the legend.

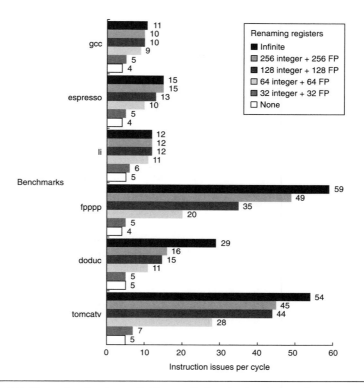

Figure 3.5 The reduction in available parallelism is significant when fewer than an unbounded number of renaming registers are available. *Both* the number of FP registers and the number of GP registers are increased by the number shown on the *x*-axis. So, the entry corresponding to "128 integer + 128 FP" has a total of 128 + 128 + 64 = 320 registers (128 for integer renaming, 128 for FP renaming, and 64 integer and FP registers present in the MIPS architecture). The effect is most dramatic on the FP programs, although having only 32 extra integer and 32 extra FP registers has a significant impact on all the programs. For the integer programs, the impact of having more than 64 extra registers is not seen here. To use more than 64 registers requires uncovering lots of parallelism, which for the integer programs requires essentially perfect branch prediction.

The results in this figure might seem somewhat surprising: You might expect that name dependences should only slightly reduce the parallelism available. Remember though, that exploiting large amounts of parallelism requires evaluating many possible execution paths, speculatively. Thus, many registers are needed to hold live variables from these threads. Figure 3.5 shows that the impact of having only a finite number of registers is significant if extensive parallelism exists. Although this graph shows a large impact on the floating-point programs, the impact on the integer programs is small primarily because the limitations in window size and branch prediction have limited the ILP substantially, making renaming less valuable. In addition, notice that the reduction in available parallelism is significant even if 64 additional integer and 64 additional FP registers are available for renaming, which is comparable to the number of extra registers available on any existing processor as of 2005.

Although register renaming is obviously critical to performance, an infinite number of registers is not practical. Thus, for the next section, we assume that there are 256 integer and 256 FP registers available for renaming—far more than any anticipated processor has as of 2005.

The Effects of Imperfect Alias Analysis

Our optimal model assumes that it can perfectly analyze all memory dependences, as well as eliminate all register name dependences. Of course, perfect alias analysis is not possible in practice: The analysis cannot be perfect at compile time, and it requires a potentially unbounded number of comparisons at run time (since the number of simultaneous memory references is unconstrained). Figure 3.6 shows the impact of three other models of memory alias analysis, in addition to perfect analysis. The three models are

1. *Global/stack perfect*—This model does perfect predictions for global and stack references and assumes all heap references conflict. This model repre-

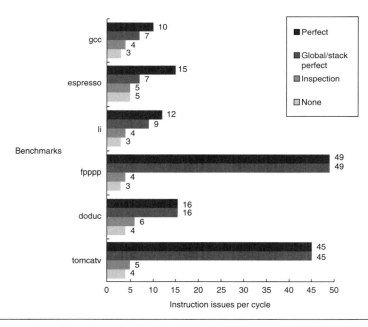

Figure 3.6 The effect of varying levels of alias analysis on individual programs. Anything less than perfect analysis has a dramatic impact on the amount of parallelism found in the integer programs, and global/stack analysis is perfect (and unrealizable) for the FORTRAN programs.

sents an idealized version of the best compiler-based analysis schemes currently in production. Recent and ongoing research on alias analysis for pointers should improve the handling of pointers to the heap in the future.

2. *Inspection*—This model examines the accesses to see if they can be determined not to interfere at compile time. For example, if an access uses R10 as a base register with an offset of 20, then another access that uses R10 as a base register with an offset of 100 cannot interfere, assuming R10 could not have changed. In addition, addresses based on registers that point to different allocation areas (such as the global area and the stack area) are assumed never to alias. This analysis is similar to that performed by many existing commercial compilers, though newer compilers can do better, at least for loop-oriented programs.

3. *None*—All memory references are assumed to conflict.

As you might expect, for the FORTRAN programs (where no heap references exist), there is no difference between perfect and global/stack perfect analysis. The global/stack perfect analysis is optimistic, since no compiler could ever find all array dependences exactly. The fact that perfect analysis of global and stack references is still a factor of two better than inspection indicates that either sophisticated compiler analysis or dynamic analysis on the fly will be required to obtain much parallelism. In practice, dynamically scheduled processors rely on dynamic memory disambiguation. To implement perfect dynamic disambiguation for a given load, we must know the memory addresses of all earlier stores that have not yet committed, since a load may have a dependence through memory on a store. As we mentioned in the last chapter, memory address speculation could be used to overcome this limit.

3.3   Limitations on ILP for Realizable Processors

In this section we look at the performance of processors with ambitious levels of hardware support equal to or better than what is available in 2006 or likely to be available in the next few years. In particular we assume the following fixed attributes:

1. Up to 64 instruction issues per clock with *no* issue restrictions, or roughly 10 times the total issue width of the widest processor in 2005. As we discuss later, the practical implications of very wide issue widths on clock rate, logic complexity, and power may be the most important limitation on exploiting ILP.

2. A tournament predictor with 1K entries and a 16-entry return predictor. This predictor is fairly comparable to the best predictors in 2005; the predictor is not a primary bottleneck.

3. Perfect disambiguation of memory references done dynamically—this is ambitious but perhaps attainable for small window sizes (and hence small issue rates and load-store buffers) or through a memory dependence predictor.

4. Register renaming with 64 additional integer and 64 additional FP registers, which is roughly comparable to the IBM Power5.

Figure 3.7 shows the result for this configuration as we vary the window size. This configuration is more complex and expensive than any existing implementations, especially in terms of the number of instruction issues, which is more than 10 times larger than the largest number of issues available on any processor in 2005. Nonetheless, it gives a useful bound on what future implementations might

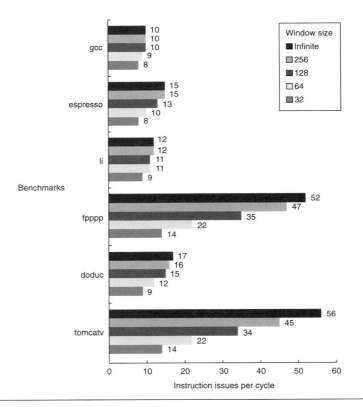

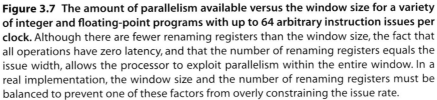

Figure 3.7 The amount of parallelism available versus the window size for a variety of integer and floating-point programs with up to 64 arbitrary instruction issues per clock. Although there are fewer renaming registers than the window size, the fact that all operations have zero latency, and that the number of renaming registers equals the issue width, allows the processor to exploit parallelism within the entire window. In a real implementation, the window size and the number of renaming registers must be balanced to prevent one of these factors from overly constraining the issue rate.

yield. The data in these figures are likely to be very optimistic for another reason. There are no issue restrictions among the 64 instructions: They may all be memory references. No one would even contemplate this capability in a processor in the near future. Unfortunately, it is quite difficult to bound the performance of a processor with reasonable issue restrictions; not only is the space of possibilities quite large, but the existence of issue restrictions requires that the parallelism be evaluated with an accurate instruction scheduler, making the cost of studying processors with large numbers of issues very expensive.

In addition, remember that in interpreting these results, cache misses and nonunit latencies have not been taken into account, and both these effects will have significant impact!

The most startling observation from Figure 3.7 is that with the realistic processor constraints listed above, the effect of the window size for the integer programs is not as severe as for FP programs. This result points to the key difference between these two types of programs. The availability of loop-level parallelism in two of the FP programs means that the amount of ILP that can be exploited is higher, but that for integer programs other factors—such as branch prediction, register renaming, and less parallelism to start with—are all important limitations. This observation is critical because of the increased emphasis on integer performance in the last few years. Indeed, most of the market growth in the last decade—transaction processing, web servers, and the like—depended on integer performance, rather than floating point. As we will see in the next section, for a realistic processor in 2005, the actual performance levels are much lower than those shown in Figure 3.7.

Given the difficulty of increasing the instruction rates with realistic hardware designs, designers face a challenge in deciding how best to use the limited resources available on an integrated circuit. One of the most interesting trade-offs is between simpler processors with larger caches and higher clock rates versus more emphasis on instruction-level parallelism with a slower clock and smaller caches. The following example illustrates the challenges.

Example   Consider the following three hypothetical, but not atypical, processors, which we run with the SPEC gcc benchmark:

1. A simple MIPS two-issue static pipe running at a clock rate of 4 GHz and achieving a pipeline CPI of 0.8. This processor has a cache system that yields 0.005 misses per instruction.

2. A deeply pipelined version of a two-issue MIPS processor with slightly smaller caches and a 5 GHz clock rate. The pipeline CPI of the processor is 1.0, and the smaller caches yield 0.0055 misses per instruction on average.

3. A speculative superscalar with a 64-entry window. It achieves one-half of the ideal issue rate measured for this window size. (Use the data in Figure 3.7.)

This processor has the smallest caches, which lead to 0.01 misses per instruction, but it hides 25% of the miss penalty on every miss by dynamic scheduling. This processor has a 2.5 GHz clock.

Assume that the main memory time (which sets the miss penalty) is 50 ns. Determine the relative performance of these three processors.

Answer First, we use the miss penalty and miss rate information to compute the contribution to CPI from cache misses for each configuration. We do this with the following formula:

$$\text{Cache CPI} = \text{Misses per instruction} \times \text{Miss penalty}$$

We need to compute the miss penalties for each system:

$$\text{Miss penalty} = \frac{\text{Memory access time}}{\text{Clock cycle}}$$

The clock cycle times for the processors are 250 ps, 200 ps, and 400 ps, respectively. Hence, the miss penalties are

$$\text{Miss penalty}_1 = \frac{50 \text{ ns}}{250 \text{ ps}} = 200 \text{ cycles}$$

$$\text{Miss penalty}_2 = \frac{50 \text{ ns}}{200 \text{ ps}} = 250 \text{ cycles}$$

$$\text{Miss penalty}_3 = \frac{0.75 \times 50 \text{ ns}}{400 \text{ ps}} = 94 \text{ cycles}$$

Applying this for each cache:

$$\text{Cache CPI}_1 = 0.005 \times 200 = 1.0$$
$$\text{Cache CPI}_2 = 0.0055 \times 250 = 1.4$$
$$\text{Cache CPI}_3 = 0.01 \times 94 = 0.94$$

We know the pipeline CPI contribution for everything but processor 3; its pipeline CPI is given by

$$\text{Pipeline CPI}_3 = \frac{1}{\text{Issue rate}} = \frac{1}{9 \times 0.5} = \frac{1}{4.5} = 0.22$$

Now we can find the CPI for each processor by adding the pipeline and cache CPI contributions:

$$\text{CPI}_1 = 0.8 + 1.0 = 1.8$$
$$\text{CPI}_2 = 1.0 + 1.4 = 2.4$$
$$\text{CPI}_3 = 0.22 + 0.94 = 1.16$$

Since this is the same architecture, we can compare instruction execution rates in millions of instructions per second (MIPS) to determine relative performance:

$$\text{Instruction execution rate} = \frac{CR}{CPI}$$

$$\text{Instruction execution rate}_1 = \frac{4000 \text{ MHz}}{1.8} = 2222 \text{ MIPS}$$

$$\text{Instruction execution rate}_2 = \frac{5000 \text{ MHz}}{2.4} = 2083 \text{ MIPS}$$

$$\text{Instruction execution rate}_3 = \frac{2500 \text{ MHz}}{1.16} = 2155 \text{ MIPS}$$

In this example, the simple two-issue static superscalar looks best. In practice, performance depends on both the CPI and clock rate assumptions.

Beyond the Limits of This Study

Like any limit study, the study we have examined in this section has its own limitations. We divide these into two classes: limitations that arise even for the perfect speculative processor, and limitations that arise for one or more realistic models. Of course, all the limitations in the first class apply to the second. The most important limitations that apply even to the perfect model are

1. *WAW and WAR hazards through memory*—The study eliminated WAW and WAR hazards through register renaming, but not in memory usage. Although at first glance it might appear that such circumstances are rare (especially WAW hazards), they arise due to the allocation of stack frames. A called procedure reuses the memory locations of a previous procedure on the stack, and this can lead to WAW and WAR hazards that are unnecessarily limiting. Austin and Sohi [1992] examine this issue.

2. *Unnecessary dependences*—With infinite numbers of registers, all but true register data dependences are removed. There are, however, dependences arising from either recurrences or code generation conventions that introduce unnecessary true data dependences. One example of these is the dependence on the control variable in a simple do loop: Since the control variable is incremented on every loop iteration, the loop contains at least one dependence. As we show in Appendix G, loop unrolling and aggressive algebraic optimization can remove such dependent computation. Wall's study includes a limited amount of such optimizations, but applying them more aggressively could lead to increased amounts of ILP. In addition, certain code generation conventions introduce unneeded dependences, in particular the use of return address registers and a register for the stack pointer (which is incremented and decremented in the call/return sequence). Wall removes the effect of the

return address register, but the use of a stack pointer in the linkage convention can cause "unnecessary" dependences. Postiff et al. [1999] explored the advantages of removing this constraint.

3. *Overcoming the data flow limit*—If value prediction worked with high accuracy, it could overcome the data flow limit. As of yet, none of the more than 50 papers on the subject have achieved a significant enhancement in ILP when using a realistic prediction scheme. Obviously, perfect data value prediction would lead to effectively infinite parallelism, since every value of every instruction could be predicted a priori.

For a less-than-perfect processor, several ideas have been proposed that could expose more ILP. One example is to speculate along multiple paths. This idea was discussed by Lam and Wilson [1992] and explored in the study covered in this section. By speculating on multiple paths, the cost of incorrect recovery is reduced and more parallelism can be uncovered. It only makes sense to evaluate this scheme for a limited number of branches because the hardware resources required grow exponentially. Wall [1993] provides data for speculating in both directions on up to eight branches. Given the costs of pursuing both paths, knowing that one will be thrown away (and the growing amount of useless computation as such a process is followed through multiple branches), every commercial design has instead devoted additional hardware to better speculation on the correct path.

It is critical to understand that none of the limits in this section are fundamental in the sense that overcoming them requires a change in the laws of physics! Instead, they are practical limitations that imply the existence of some formidable barriers to exploiting additional ILP. These limitations—whether they be window size, alias detection, or branch prediction—represent challenges for designers and researchers to overcome! As we discuss in Section 3.6, the implications of ILP limitations and the costs of implementing wider issue seem to have created effective limitations on ILP exploitation.

3.4 Crosscutting Issues: Hardware versus Software Speculation

"Crosscutting Issues" is a section that discusses topics that involve subjects from different chapters. The next few chapters include such a section.

The hardware-intensive approaches to speculation in the previous chapter and the software approaches of Appendix G provide alternative approaches to exploiting ILP. Some of the trade-offs, and the limitations, for these approaches are listed below:

■ To speculate extensively, we must be able to disambiguate memory references. This capability is difficult to do at compile time for integer programs that contain pointers. In a hardware-based scheme, dynamic run time disambiguation of memory addresses is done using the techniques we saw earlier for Tomasulo's algorithm. This disambiguation allows us to move loads past stores at run time. Support for speculative memory references can help overcome the conservatism of the compiler, but unless such approaches are used carefully, the overhead of the recovery mechanisms may swamp the advantages.

■ Hardware-based speculation works better when control flow is unpredictable, and when hardware-based branch prediction is superior to software-based branch prediction done at compile time. These properties hold for many integer programs. For example, a good static predictor has a misprediction rate of about 16% for four major integer SPEC92 programs, and a hardware predictor has a misprediction rate of under 10%. Because speculated instructions may slow down the computation when the prediction is incorrect, this difference is significant. One result of this difference is that even statically scheduled processors normally include dynamic branch predictors.

■ Hardware-based speculation maintains a completely precise exception model even for speculated instructions. Recent software-based approaches have added special support to allow this as well.

■ Hardware-based speculation does not require compensation or bookkeeping code, which is needed by ambitious software speculation mechanisms.

■ Compiler-based approaches may benefit from the ability to see further in the code sequence, resulting in better code scheduling than a purely hardware-driven approach.

■ Hardware-based speculation with dynamic scheduling does not require different code sequences to achieve good performance for different implementations of an architecture. Although this advantage is the hardest to quantify, it may be the most important in the long run. Interestingly, this was one of the motivations for the IBM 360/91. On the other hand, more recent explicitly parallel architectures, such as IA-64, have added flexibility that reduces the hardware dependence inherent in a code sequence.

The major disadvantage of supporting speculation in hardware is the complexity and additional hardware resources required. This hardware cost must be evaluated against both the complexity of a compiler for a software-based approach and the amount and usefulness of the simplifications in a processor that relies on such a compiler. We return to this topic in the concluding remarks.

Some designers have tried to combine the dynamic and compiler-based approaches to achieve the best of each. Such a combination can generate interesting and obscure interactions. For example, if conditional moves are combined with register renaming, a subtle side effect appears. A conditional move that is annulled must still copy a value to the destination register, since it was renamed earlier in the instruction pipeline. These subtle interactions complicate the design and verification process and can also reduce performance.

3.5 Multithreading: Using ILP Support to Exploit Thread-Level Parallelism

Although increasing performance by using ILP has the great advantage that it is reasonably transparent to the programmer, as we have seen, ILP can be quite limited or hard to exploit in some applications. Furthermore, there may be significant parallelism occurring naturally at a higher level in the application that cannot be exploited with the approaches discussed in this chapter. For example, an online transaction-processing system has natural parallelism among the multiple queries and updates that are presented by requests. These queries and updates can be processed mostly in parallel, since they are largely independent of one another. Of course, many scientific applications contain natural parallelism since they model the three-dimensional, parallel structure of nature, and that structure can be exploited in a simulation.

This higher-level parallelism is called *thread-level parallelism* (TLP) because it is logically structured as separate threads of execution. A *thread* is a separate process with its own instructions and data. A thread may represent a process that is part of a parallel program consisting of multiple processes, or it may represent an independent program on its own. Each thread has all the state (instructions, data, PC, register state, and so on) necessary to allow it to execute. Unlike instruction-level parallelism, which exploits implicit parallel operations within a loop or straight-line code segment, thread-level parallelism is explicitly represented by the use of multiple threads of execution that are inherently parallel.

Thread-level parallelism is an important alternative to instruction-level parallelism primarily because it could be more cost-effective to exploit than instruction-level parallelism. There are many important applications where thread-level parallelism occurs naturally, as it does in many server applications. In other cases, the software is being written from scratch, and expressing the inherent parallelism is easy, as is true in some embedded applications. Large, established applications written without parallelism in mind, however, pose a significant challenge and can be extremely costly to rewrite to exploit thread-level parallelism. Chapter 4 explores multiprocessors and the support they provide for thread-level parallelism.

Thread-level and instruction-level parallelism exploit two different kinds of parallel structure in a program. One natural question to ask is whether it is possible for a processor oriented at instruction-level parallelism to exploit thread-level parallelism. The motivation for this question comes from the observation that a data path designed to exploit higher amounts of ILP will find that functional units are often idle because of either stalls or dependences in the code. Could the parallelism among threads be used as a source of independent instructions that might keep the processor busy during stalls? Could this thread-level parallelism be used to employ the functional units that would otherwise lie idle when insufficient ILP exists?

Multithreading allows multiple threads to share the functional units of a single processor in an overlapping fashion. To permit this sharing, the processor must duplicate the independent state of each thread. For example, a separate copy of the register file, a separate PC, and a separate page table are required for each thread. The memory itself can be shared through the virtual memory mechanisms, which already support multiprogramming. In addition, the hardware must support the ability to change to a different thread relatively quickly; in particular, a thread switch should be much more efficient than a process switch, which typically requires hundreds to thousands of processor cycles.

There are two main approaches to multithreading. *Fine-grained multithreading* switches between threads on each instruction, causing the execution of multiple threads to be interleaved. This interleaving is often done in a round-robin fashion, skipping any threads that are stalled at that time. To make fine-grained multithreading practical, the CPU must be able to switch threads on every clock cycle. One key advantage of fine-grained multithreading is that it can hide the throughput losses that arise from both short and long stalls, since instructions from other threads can be executed when one thread stalls. The primary disadvantage of fine-grained multithreading is that it slows down the execution of the individual threads, since a thread that is ready to execute without stalls will be delayed by instructions from other threads.

Coarse-grained multithreading was invented as an alternative to fine-grained multithreading. Coarse-grained multithreading switches threads only on costly stalls, such as level 2 cache misses. This change relieves the need to have thread-switching be essentially free and is much less likely to slow the processor down, since instructions from other threads will only be issued when a thread encounters a costly stall.

Coarse-grained multithreading suffers, however, from a major drawback: It is limited in its ability to overcome throughput losses, especially from shorter stalls. This limitation arises from the pipeline start-up costs of coarse-grain multithreading. Because a CPU with coarse-grained multithreading issues instructions from a single thread, when a stall occurs, the pipeline must be emptied or frozen. The new thread that begins executing after the stall must fill the pipeline before instructions will be able to complete. Because of this start-up overhead, coarse-grained multithreading is much more useful for reducing the penalty of high-cost stalls, where pipeline refill is negligible compared to the stall time.

The next subsection explores a variation on fine-grained multithreading that enables a superscalar processor to exploit ILP and multithreading in an integrated and efficient fashion. In Chapter 4, we return to the issue of multithreading when we discuss its integration with multiple CPUs in a single chip.

Simultaneous Multithreading: Converting Thread-Level Parallelism into Instruction-Level Parallelism

Simultaneous multithreading (SMT) is a variation on multithreading that uses the resources of a multiple-issue, dynamically scheduled processor to exploit TLP at the same time it exploits ILP. The key insight that motivates SMT is that modern multiple-issue processors often have more functional unit parallelism available than a single thread can effectively use. Furthermore, with register renaming and dynamic scheduling, multiple instructions from independent threads can be issued without regard to the dependences among them; the resolution of the dependences can be handled by the dynamic scheduling capability.

Figure 3.8 conceptually illustrates the differences in a processor's ability to exploit the resources of a superscalar for the following processor configurations:

- A superscalar with no multithreading support
- A superscalar with coarse-grained multithreading
- A superscalar with fine-grained multithreading
- A superscalar with simultaneous multithreading

In the superscalar without multithreading support, the use of issue slots is limited by a lack of ILP, a topic we discussed in earlier sections. In addition, a major stall, such as an instruction cache miss, can leave the entire processor idle.

In the coarse-grained multithreaded superscalar, the long stalls are partially hidden by switching to another thread that uses the resources of the processor. Although this reduces the number of completely idle clock cycles, within each clock cycle, the ILP limitations still lead to idle cycles. Furthermore, in a coarse-grained multithreaded processor, since thread switching only occurs when there is a stall and the new thread has a start-up period, there are likely to be some fully idle cycles remaining.

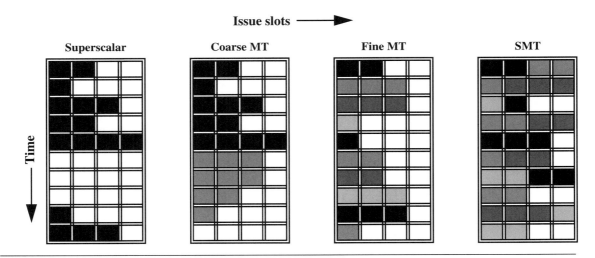

Figure 3.8 How four different approaches use the issue slots of a superscalar processor. The horizontal dimension represents the instruction issue capability in each clock cycle. The vertical dimension represents a sequence of clock cycles. An empty (white) box indicates that the corresponding issue slot is unused in that clock cycle. The shades of grey and black correspond to four different threads in the multithreading processors. Black is also used to indicate the occupied issue slots in the case of the superscalar without multithreading support. The Sun T1 (aka Niagara) processor, which is discussed in the next chapter, is a fine-grained multithreaded architecture.

In the fine-grained case, the interleaving of threads eliminates fully empty slots. Because only one thread issues instructions in a given clock cycle, however, ILP limitations still lead to a significant number of idle slots within individual clock cycles.

In the SMT case, TLP and ILP are exploited simultaneously, with multiple threads using the issue slots in a single clock cycle. Ideally, the issue slot usage is limited by imbalances in the resource needs and resource availability over multiple threads. In practice, other factors—including how many active threads are considered, finite limitations on buffers, the ability to fetch enough instructions from multiple threads, and practical limitations of what instruction combinations can issue from one thread and from multiple threads—can also restrict how many slots are used. Although Figure 3.8 greatly simplifies the real operation of these processors, it does illustrate the potential performance advantages of multithreading in general and SMT in particular.

As mentioned earlier, simultaneous multithreading uses the insight that a dynamically scheduled processor already has many of the hardware mechanisms needed to support the integrated exploitation of TLP through multithreading. In particular, dynamically scheduled superscalars have a large set of virtual registers that can be used to hold the register sets of independent threads (assuming separate renaming tables are kept for each thread). Because register renaming provides unique register identifiers, instructions from multiple threads can be mixed in the data path without confusing sources and destinations across the threads.

This observation leads to the insight that multithreading can be built on top of an out-of-order processor by adding a per-thread renaming table, keeping separate PCs, and providing the capability for instructions from multiple threads to commit.

There are complications in handling instruction commit, since we would like instructions from independent threads to be able to commit independently. The independent commitment of instructions from separate threads can be supported by logically keeping a separate reorder buffer for each thread.

Design Challenges in SMT

Because a dynamically scheduled superscalar processor is likely to have a deep pipeline, SMT will be unlikely to gain much in performance if it were coarse-grained. Since SMT makes sense only in a fine-grained implementation, we must worry about the impact of fine-grained scheduling on single-thread performance. This effect can be minimized by having a preferred thread, which still permits multithreading to preserve some of its performance advantage with a smaller compromise in single-thread performance.

At first glance, it might appear that a preferred-thread approach sacrifices neither throughput nor single-thread performance. Unfortunately, with a preferred thread, the processor is likely to sacrifice some throughput when the preferred thread encounters a stall. The reason is that the pipeline is less likely to have a mix of instructions from several threads, resulting in greater probability that either empty slots or a stall will occur. Throughput is maximized by having a sufficient number of independent threads to hide all stalls in any combination of threads.

Unfortunately, mixing many threads will inevitably compromise the execution time of individual threads. Similar problems exist in instruction fetch. To maximize single-thread performance, we should fetch as far ahead as possible in that single thread and always have the fetch unit free when a branch is mispredicted and a miss occurs in the prefetch buffer. Unfortunately, this limits the number of instructions available for scheduling from other threads, reducing throughput. All multithreaded processors must seek to balance this trade-off.

In practice, the problems of dividing resources and balancing single-thread and multiple-thread performance turn out not to be as challenging as they sound, at least for current superscalar back ends. In particular, for current machines that issue four to eight instructions per cycle, it probably suffices to have a small number of active threads, and an even smaller number of "preferred" threads. Whenever possible, the processor acts on behalf of a preferred thread. This starts with prefetching instructions: whenever the prefetch buffers for the preferred threads are not full, instructions are fetched for those threads. Only when the preferred thread buffers are full is the instruction unit directed to prefetch for other threads. Note that having two preferred threads means that we are simultaneously prefetching for two instruction streams, and this adds complexity to the instruction fetch unit and the instruction cache. Similarly, the instruction issue unit can direct its attention to the preferred threads, considering other threads only if the preferred threads are stalled and cannot issue.

There are a variety of other design challenges for an SMT processor, including the following:

- Dealing with a larger register file needed to hold multiple contexts

- Not affecting the clock cycle, particularly in critical steps such as instruction issue, where more candidate instructions need to be considered, and in instruction completion, where choosing what instructions to commit may be challenging

- Ensuring that the cache and TLB conflicts generated by the simultaneous execution of multiple threads do not cause significant performance degradation

In viewing these problems, two observations are important. First, in many cases, the potential performance overhead due to multithreading is small, and simple choices work well enough. Second, the efficiency of current superscalars is low enough that there is room for significant improvement, even at the cost of some overhead.

The IBM Power5 used the same pipeline as the Power4, but it added SMT support. In adding SMT, the designers found that they had to increase a number of structures in the processor so as to minimize the negative performance consequences from fine-grained thread interaction. These changes included the following:

- Increasing the associativity of the L1 instruction cache and the instruction address translation buffers

- Adding per-thread load and store queues

- Increasing the size of the L2 and L3 caches

- Adding separate instruction prefetch and buffering

- Increasing the number of virtual registers from 152 to 240

- Increasing the size of several issue queues

Because SMT exploits thread-level parallelism on a multiple-issue superscalar, it is most likely to be included in high-end processors targeted at server markets. In addition, it is likely that there will be some mode to restrict the multithreading, so as to maximize the performance of a single thread.

Potential Performance Advantages from SMT

A key question is, How much performance can be gained by implementing SMT? When this question was explored in 2000–2001, researchers assumed that dynamic superscalars would get much wider in the next five years, supporting six to eight issues per clock with speculative dynamic scheduling, many simultaneous loads and stores, large primary caches, and four to eight contexts with simultaneous fetching from multiple contexts. For a variety of reasons, which will become more clear in the next section, no processor of this capability has been built nor is likely to be built in the near future.

As a result, simulation research results that showed gains for multiprogrammed workloads of two or more times are unrealistic. In practice, the existing implementations of SMT offer only two contexts with fetching from only one, as well as more modest issue abilities. The result is that the gain from SMT is also more modest.

For example, in the Pentium 4 Extreme, as implemented in HP-Compaq servers, the use of SMT yields a performance improvement of 1.01 when running the SPECintRate benchmark and about 1.07 when running the SPECfpRate benchmark. In a separate study, Tuck and Tullsen [2003] observe that running a mix of each of the 26 SPEC benchmarks paired with every other SPEC benchmark (that is, 26^2 runs, if a benchmark is also run opposite itself) results in speedups ranging from 0.90 to 1.58, with an average speedup of 1.20. (Note that this measurement is different from SPECRate, which requires that each SPEC benchmark be run against a vendor-selected number of copies of the same benchmark.) On the SPLASH parallel benchmarks, they report multithreaded speedups ranging from 1.02 to 1.67, with an average speedup of about 1.22.

The IBM Power5 is the most aggressive implementation of SMT as of 2005 and has extensive additions to support SMT, as described in the previous subsection. A direct performance comparison of the Power5 in SMT mode, running two copies of an application on a processor, versus the Power5 in single-thread mode, with one process per core, shows speedup across a wide variety of benchmarks of between 0.89 (a performance loss) to 1.41. Most applications, however, showed at least some gain from SMT; floating-point-intensive applications, which suffered the most cache conflicts, showed the least gains.

Figure 3.9 shows the speedup for an 8-processor Power5 multiprocessor with and without SMT for the SPECRate2000 benchmarks, as described in the caption. On average, the SPECintRate is 1.23 times faster, while the SPECfpRate is 1.16 times faster. Note that a few floating-point benchmarks experience a slight decrease in performance in SMT mode, with the maximum reduction in speedup being 0.93.

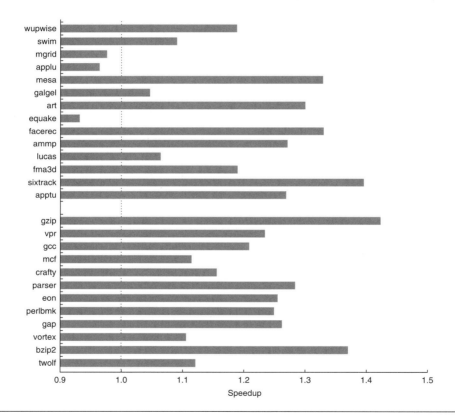

Figure 3.9 A comparison of SMT and single-thread (ST) performance on the 8-processor IBM eServer p5 575. Note that the *y*-axis starts at a speedup of 0.9, a performance loss. Only one processor in each Power5 core is active, which should slightly improve the results from SMT by decreasing destructive interference in the memory system. The SMT results are obtained by creating 16 user threads, while the ST results use only 8 threads; with only one thread per processor, the Power5 is switched to single-threaded mode by the OS. These results were collected by John McCalpin of IBM. As we can see from the data, the standard deviation of the results for the SPECfpRate is higher than for SPECintRate (0.13 versus 0.07), indicating that the SMT improvement for FP programs is likely to vary widely.

These results clearly show the benefit of SMT for an aggressive speculative processor with extensive support for SMT. Because of the costs and diminishing returns in performance, however, rather than implement wider superscalars and more aggressive versions of SMT, many designers are opting to implement multiple CPU cores on a single die with slightly less aggressive support for multiple issue and multithreading; we return to this topic in the next chapter.

3.6 Putting It All Together: Performance and Efficiency in Advanced Multiple-Issue Processors

In this section, we discuss the characteristics of several recent multiple-issue processors and examine their performance and their efficiency in use of silicon, transistors, and energy. We then turn to a discussion of the practical limits of superscalars and the future of high-performance microprocessors.

Figure 3.10 shows the characteristics of four of the most recent high-performance microprocessors. They vary widely in organization, issue rate, functional unit capability, clock rate, die size, transistor count, and power. As Figures 3.11 and 3.12 show, there is no obvious overall leader in performance. The Itanium 2 and Power5, which perform similarly on SPECfp, clearly dominate the Athlon and Pentium 4 on those benchmarks. The AMD Athlon leads on SPECint performance followed by the Pentium 4, Itanium 2, and Power5.

Processor	Microarchitecture	Fetch/ issue/ execute	Func. units	Clock rate (GHz)	Transistors and die size	Power
Intel Pentium 4 Extreme	Speculative dynamically scheduled; deeply pipelined; SMT	3/3/4	7 int. 1 FP	3.8	125M 122 mm^2	115 W
AMD Athlon 64 FX-57	Speculative dynamically scheduled	3/3/4	6 int. 3 FP	2.8	114M 115 mm^2	104 W
IBM Power5 1 processor	Speculative dynamically scheduled; SMT; two CPU cores/chip	8/4/8	6 int. 2 FP	1.9	200M 300 mm^2 (estimated)	80 W (estimated)
Intel Itanium 2	EPIC style; primarily statically scheduled	6/5/11	9 int. 2 FP	1.6	592M 423 mm^2	130 W

Figure 3.10 The characteristics of four recent multiple-issue processors. The Power5 includes two CPU cores, although we only look at the performance of one core in this chapter. The transistor count, area, and power consumption of the Power5 are estimated for one core based on two-core measurements of 276M, 389 mm^2, and 125 W, respectively. The large die and transistor count for the Itanium 2 is partly driven by a 9 MB tertiary cache on the chip. The AMD Opteron and Athlon both share the same core microarchitecture. Athlon is intended for desktops and does not support multiprocessing; Opteron is intended for servers and does. This is similar to the differentiation between Pentium and Xeon in the Intel product line.

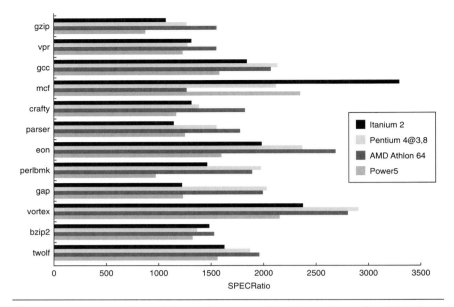

Figure 3.11 A comparison of the performance of the four advanced multiple-issue processors shown in Figure 3.10 for the SPECint2000 benchmarks.

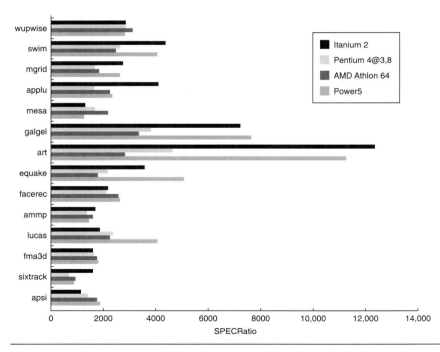

Figure 3.12 A comparison of the performance of the four advanced multiple-issue processors shown in Figure 3.10 for the SPECfp2000 benchmarks.

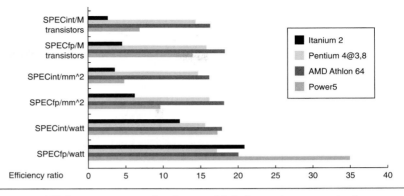

Figure 3.13 Efficiency measures for four multiple-issue processors. In the case of Power5, a single die includes two processor cores, so we estimate the single-core metrics as power = 80 W, area = 290 mm², and transistor count = 200M.

As important as overall performance is, the question of efficiency in terms of silicon area and power is equally critical. As we discussed in Chapter 1, power has become the major constraint on modern processors. Figure 3.13 shows how these processors compare in terms of efficiency, by charting the SPECint and SPECfp performance versus the transistor count, silicon area, and power. The results provide an interesting contrast to the performance results. The Itanium 2 is the most inefficient processor both for floating-point and integer code for all but one measure (SPECfp/watt). The Athlon and Pentium 4 both make good use of transistors and area in terms of efficiency, while the IBM Power5 is the most effective user of energy on SPECfp and essentially tied on SPECint. The fact that none of the processors offer an overwhelming advantage in efficiency across multiple measures leads us to believe that none of these approaches provide a "silver bullet" that will allow the exploitation of ILP to scale easily and efficiently much beyond current levels.

Let's try to understand why this is the case.

What Limits Multiple-Issue Processors?

The limitations explored in Sections 3.1 and 3.3 act as significant barriers to exploiting more ILP, but they are not the only barriers. For example, doubling the issue rates above the current rates of 3–6 instructions per clock, say, to 6–12 instructions, will probably require a processor to issue three or four data memory accesses per cycle, resolve two or three branches per cycle, rename and access more than 20 registers per cycle, and fetch 12–24 instructions per cycle. The complexities of implementing these capabilities is likely to mean sacrifices in the maximum clock rate. For example, the widest-issue processor in Figure 3.10 is the Itanium 2, but it also has the slowest clock rate, despite the fact that it consumes the most power!

It is now widely accepted that modern microprocessors are primarily power limited. Power is a function of both static power, which grows proportionally to the transistor count (whether or not the transistors are switching), and dynamic power, which is proportional to the product of the number of switching transistors and the switching rate. Although static power is certainly a design concern, when operating, dynamic power is usually the dominant energy consumer. A microprocessor trying to achieve both a low CPI and a high CR must switch more transistors and switch them faster, increasing the power consumption as the product of the two.

Of course, most techniques for increasing performance, including multiple cores and multithreading, will increase power consumption. The key question is whether a technique is *energy efficient:* Does it increase power consumption faster than it increases performance? Unfortunately, the techniques we currently have to boost the performance of multiple-issue processors all have this inefficiency, which arises from two primary characteristics.

First, issuing multiple instructions incurs some overhead in logic that grows faster than the issue rate grows. This logic is responsible for instruction issue analysis, including dependence checking, register renaming, and similar functions. The combined result is that, without voltage reductions to decrease power, lower CPIs are likely to lead to lower ratios of performance per watt, simply due to overhead.

Second, and more important, is the growing gap between peak issue rates and sustained performance. Since the number of transistors switching will be proportional to the peak issue rate, and the performance is proportional to the sustained rate, a growing performance gap between peak and sustained performance translates to increasing energy per unit of performance. Unfortunately, this growing gap appears to be quite fundamental and arises from many of the issues we discuss in Sections 3.2 and 3.3. For example, if we want to *sustain* four instructions per clock, we must *fetch* more, *issue* more, and *initiate execution* on more than four instructions. The power will be proportional to the peak rate, but performance will be at the sustained rate. (In many recent processors, provision has been made for decreasing power consumption by shutting down an inactive portion of a processor, including powering off the clock to that portion of the chip. Such techniques, while useful, cannot prevent the long-term decrease in power efficiency.)

Furthermore, the most important technique of the last decade for increasing the exploitation of ILP—namely, speculation—is inherently inefficient. Why? Because it can never be perfect; that is, there is inherently waste in executing computations before we know whether they advance the program.

If speculation were perfect, it could save power, since it would reduce the execution time and save static power, while adding some additional overhead to implement. When speculation is not perfect, it rapidly becomes energy inefficient, since it requires additional dynamic power both for the incorrect speculation and for the resetting of the processor state. Because of the overhead of implementing speculation—register renaming, reorder buffers, more registers, and so on—it is unlikely that any speculative processor could save energy for a significant range of realistic programs.

What about focusing on improving clock rate? Unfortunately, a similar conundrum applies to attempts to increase clock rate: increasing the clock rate will increase transistor switching frequency and directly increase power consumption. To achieve a faster clock rate, we would need to increase pipeline depth. Deeper pipelines, however, incur additional overhead penalties as well as causing higher switching rates.

The best example of this phenomenon comes from comparing the Pentium III and Pentium 4. To a first approximation, the Pentium 4 is a deeply pipelined version of the Pentium III architecture. In a similar process, it consumes roughly an amount of power proportional to the difference in clock rate. Unfortunately, its performance is somewhat less than the ratio of the clock rates because of overhead and ILP limitations.

It appears that we have reached—and, in some cases, possibly even surpassed—the point of diminishing returns in our attempts to exploit ILP. The implications of these limits can be seen over the last few years in the slower performance growth rates (see Chapter 1), in the lack of increase in issue capability, and in the emergence of multicore designs; we return to this issue in the concluding remarks.

3.7   Fallacies and Pitfalls

Fallacy   *There is a simple approach to multiple-issue processors that yields high performance without a significant investment in silicon area or design complexity.*

The last few sections should have made this point obvious. What has been surprising is that many designers have believed that this fallacy was accurate and committed significant effort to trying to find this "silver bullet" approach. Although it is possible to build relatively simple multiple-issue processors, as issue rates increase, diminishing returns appear and the silicon and energy costs of wider issue dominate the performance gains.

In addition to the hardware inefficiency, it has become clear that compiling for processors with significant amounts of ILP has become extremely complex. Not only must the compiler support a wide set of sophisticated transformations, but tuning the compiler to achieve good performance across a wide set of benchmarks appears to be very difficult.

Obtaining good performance is also affected by design decisions at the system level, and such choices can be complex, as the last section clearly illustrated.

Pitfall   *Improving only one aspect of a multiple-issue processor and expecting overall performance improvement.*

This pitfall is simply a restatement of Amdahl's Law. A designer might simply look at a design, see a poor branch-prediction mechanism, and improve it, expecting to see significant performance improvements. The difficulty is that many factors limit the performance of multiple-issue machines, and improving one aspect of a processor often exposes some other aspect that previously did not limit performance.

We can see examples of this in the data on ILP. For example, looking just at the effect of branch prediction in Figure 3.3 on page 160, we can see that going from a standard 2-bit predictor to a tournament predictor significantly improves the parallelism in espresso (from an issue rate of 7 to an issue rate of 12). If the processor provides only 32 registers for renaming, however, the amount of parallelism is limited to 5 issues per clock cycle, even with a branch-prediction scheme better than either alternative.

3.8 Concluding Remarks

The relative merits of software-intensive and hardware-intensive approaches to exploiting ILP continue to be debated, although the debate has shifted in the last five years. Initially, the software-intensive and hardware-intensive approaches were quite different, and the ability to manage the complexity of the hardware-intensive approaches was in doubt. The development of several high-performance dynamic speculation processors, which have high clock rates, has eased this concern.

The complexity of the IA-64 architecture and the Itanium design has signaled to many designers that it is unlikely that a software-intensive approach will produce processors that are significantly faster (especially for integer code), smaller (in transistor count or die size), simpler, or more power efficient. It has become clear in the past five years that the IA-64 architecture does *not* represent a significant breakthrough in scaling ILP or in avoiding the problems of complexity and power consumption in high-performance processors. Appendix H explores this assessment in more detail.

The limits of complexity and diminishing returns for wider issue probably also mean that only limited use of simultaneous multithreading is likely. It simply is not worthwhile to build the very wide issue processors that would justify the most aggressive implementations of SMT. For this reason, existing designs have used modest, two-context versions of SMT or simple multithreading with two contexts, which is the appropriate choice with simple one- or two-issue processors.

Instead of pursuing more ILP, architects are increasingly focusing on TLP implemented with single-chip multiprocessors, which we explore in the next chapter. In 2000, IBM announced the first commercial single-chip, general-purpose multiprocessor, the Power4, which contains two Power3 processors and an integrated second-level cache. Since then, Sun Microsystems, AMD, and Intel have switched to a focus on single-chip multiprocessors rather than more aggressive uniprocessors.

The question of the right balance of ILP and TLP is still open in 2005, and designers are exploring the full range of options, from simple pipelining with more processors per chip, to aggressive ILP and SMT with fewer processors. It may well be that the right choice for the server market, which can exploit more TLP, may differ from the desktop, where single-thread performance may continue to be a primary requirement. We return to this topic in the next chapter.

3.9 Historical Perspective and References

Section K.4 on the companion CD features a discussion on the development of pipelining and instruction-level parallelism. We provide numerous references for further reading and exploration of these topics.

Case Study with Exercises by Wen-mei W. Hwu and John W. Sias

Concepts illustrated by this case study

■ Limited ILP due to software dependences

■ Achievable ILP with hardware resource constraints

■ Variability of ILP due to software and hardware interaction

■ Tradeoffs in ILP techniques at compile time vs. execution time

Case Study: Dependences and Instruction-Level Parallelism

The purpose of this case study is to demonstrate the interaction of hardware and software factors in producing instruction-level parallel execution. This case study presents a concise code example that concretely illustrates the various limits on instruction-level parallelism. By working with this case study, you will gain intuition about how hardware and software factors interact to determine the execution time of a particular type of code on a given system.

A hash table is a popular data structure for organizing a large collection of data items so that one can quickly answer questions such as, "Does an element of value 100 exist in the collection?" This is done by assigning data elements into one of a large number of buckets according to a hash function value generated from the data values. The data items in each bucket are typically organized as a linked list sorted according to a given order. A lookup of the hash table starts by determining the bucket that corresponds to the data value in question. It then traverses the linked list of data elements in the bucket and checks if any element in the list has the value in question. As long as one keeps the number of data elements in each bucket small, the search result can be determined very quickly.

The C source code in Figure 3.14 inserts a large number (N_ELEMENTS) of elements into a hash table, whose 1024 buckets are all linked lists sorted in ascending order according to the value of the elements. The array element[] contains the elements to be inserted, allocated on the heap. Each iteration of the outer (for) loop, starting at line 6, enters one element into the hash table.

Line 9 in Figure 3.14 calculates hash_index, the hash function value, from the data value stored in element[i]. The hashing function used is a very simple

```
1    typedef struct _Element {
2      int value;
3      struct _Element *next;
4    } Element;
5    Element element[N_ELEMENTS], *bucket[1024];
     /* The array element is initialized with the items to be inserted;
        the pointers in the array bucket are initialized to NULL. */

6    for (i = 0; i < N_ELEMENTS; i++)
       {
7      Element *ptrCurr, **ptrUpdate;
8      int hash_index;

       /* Find the location at which the new element is to be inserted. */
9      hash_index = element[i].value & 1023;
10     ptrUpdate = &bucket[hash_index];
11     ptrCurr = bucket[hash_index];
       /* Find the place in the chain to insert the new element. */
12     while (ptrCurr &&
13            ptrCurr->value <= element[i].value)
14       {
15     ptrUpdate = &ptrCurr->next;
16         ptrCurr = ptrCurr->next;
         }

       /* Update pointers to insert the new element into the chain. */
17     element[i].next = *ptrUpdate;
18     *ptrUpdate = &element[i];
       }
```

Figure 3.14 Hash table code example.

one; it consists of the least significant 10 bits of an element's data value. This is done by computing the bitwise logical AND of the element data value and the (binary) bit mask 11 1111 1111 (1023 in decimal).

Figure 3.15 illustrates the hash table data structure used in our C code example. The bucket array on the left side of Figure 3.15 is the hash table. Each entry of the bucket array contains a pointer to the linked list that stores the data elements in the bucket. If bucket i is currently empty, the corresponding bucket[i] entry contains a NULL pointer. In Figure 3.15, the first three buckets contain one data element each; the other buckets are empty.

Variable ptrCurr contains a pointer used to examine the elements in the linked list of a bucket. At Line 11 of Figure 3.14, ptrCurr is set to point to the first element of the linked list stored in the given bucket of the hash table. If the bucket selected by the hash_index is empty, the corresponding bucket array entry contains a NULL pointer.

The while loop starts at line 12. Line 12 tests if there is any more data elements to be examined by checking the contents of variable ptrCurr. Lines 13 through 16 will be skipped if there are no more elements to be examined, either because the bucket is empty, or because all the data elements in the linked list have been examined by previous iterations of the while loop. In the first case, the new data element will be inserted as the first element in the bucket. In the second case, the new element will be inserted as the last element of the linked list.

In the case where there are still more elements to be examined, line 13 tests if the current linked list element contains a value that is smaller than or equal to that of the data element to be inserted into the hash table. If the condition is true, the while loop will continue to move on to the next element in the linked list; lines 15 and 16 advance to the next data element of the linked list by moving ptrCurr to the next element in the linked list. Otherwise, it has found the position in the

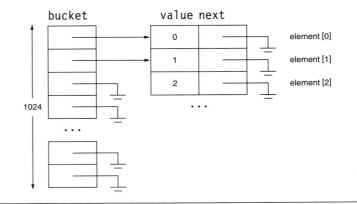

Figure 3.15 Hash table data structure.

linked list where the new data element should be inserted; the `while` loop will terminate and the new data element will be inserted right before the element pointed to by `ptrCurr`.

The variable `ptrUpdate` identifies the pointer that must be updated in order to insert the new data element into the bucket. It is set by line 10 to point to the bucket entry. If the bucket is empty, the `while` loop will be skipped altogether and the new data element is inserted by changing the pointer in `bucket[hash_index]` from NULL to the address of the new data element by line 18. After the `while` loop, `ptrUpdate` points to the pointer that must be updated for the new element to be inserted into the appropriate bucket.

After the execution exits the `while` loop, lines 17 and 18 finish the job of inserting the new data element into the linked list. In the case where the bucket is empty, `ptrUpdate` will point to `bucket[hash_index]`, which contains a NULL pointer. Line 17 will then assign that NULL pointer to the next pointer of the new data element. Line 18 changes `bucket[hash_table]` to point to the new data element. In the case where the new data element is smaller than all elements in the linked list, `ptrUpdate` will also point to `bucket[hash_table]`, which points to the first element of the linked list. In this case, line 17 assigns the pointer to the first element of the linked list to the next pointer of the new data structure.

In the case where the new data element is greater than some of the linked list elements but smaller than the others, `ptrUpdate` will point to the `next` pointer of the element after which the new data element will be inserted. In this case, line 17 makes the new data element to point to the element right after the insertion point. Line 18 makes the original data element right before the insertion point to point to the new data element. The reader should verify that the code works correctly when the new data element is to be inserted to the end of the linked list.

Now that we have a good understanding of the C code, we will proceed with analyzing the amount of instruction-level parallelism available in this piece of code.

3.1 [25/15/10/15/20/20/15] <2.1, 2.2, 3.2, 3.3, App. H> This part of our case study will focus on the amount of instruction-level parallelism available to the *run time hardware scheduler* under the most favorable execution scenarios (the ideal case). (Later, we will consider less ideal scenarios for the run time hardware scheduler as well as the amount of parallelism available to a compiler scheduler.) For the ideal scenario, assume that the hash table is initially empty. Suppose there are 1024 new data elements, whose values are numbered sequentially from 0 to 1023, so that each goes in its own bucket (this reduces the problem to a matter of updating known array locations!). Figure 3.15 shows the hash table contents after the first three elements have been inserted, according to this "ideal case." Since the `value` of `element[ i]` is simply i in this ideal case, each element is inserted into its own bucket.

For the purposes of this case study, assume that each line of code in Figure 3.14 takes one execution cycle (its dependence height is 1) and, for the purposes of computing ILP, takes one instruction. These (unrealistic) assumptions are made to greatly simplify bookkeeping in solving the following exercises. Note that the for and while statements execute on each iteration of their respective loops, to test if the loop should continue. In this ideal case, most of the dependences in the code sequence are relaxed and a high degree of ILP is therefore readily available. We will later examine a general case, in which the realistic dependences in the code segment reduce the amount of parallelism available.

Further suppose that the code is executed on an "ideal" processor with infinite issue width, unlimited renaming, "omniscient" knowledge of memory access disambiguation, branch prediction, and so on, so that the execution of instructions is limited only by data dependence. Consider the following in this context:

a. [25] <2.1> Describe the data (true, anti, and output) and control dependences that govern the parallelism of this code segment, as seen by a run time hardware scheduler. Indicate only the *actual* dependences (i.e., ignore dependences between stores and loads that access different addresses, even if a compiler or processor would not realistically determine this). Draw the *dynamic* dependence graph for six consecutive iterations of the outer loop (for insertion of six elements), under the ideal case. Note that in this dynamic dependence graph, we are identifying data dependences between dynamic instances of instructions: each static instruction in the original program has multiple dynamic instances due to loop execution. *Hint:* The following definitions may help you find the dependences related to each instruction:

- *Data true dependence:* On the results of which previous instructions does each instruction immediately depend?

- *Data antidependence:* Which instructions subsequently write locations read by the instruction?

- *Data output dependence:* Which instructions subsequently write locations written by the instruction?

- *Control dependence:* On what previous decisions does the execution of a particular instruction depend (in what case will it be reached)?

b. [15] <2.1> Assuming the ideal case just described, and using the dynamic dependence graph you just constructed, how many instructions are executed, and in how many cycles?

c. [10] <3.2> What is the average level of ILP available during the execution of the for loop?

d. [15] <2.2, App. H> In part (c) we considered the maximum parallelism achievable by a run-time hardware scheduler using the code as written. How could a compiler increase the available parallelism, assuming that the compiler knows that it is dealing with the ideal case. *Hint:* Think about what is the primary constraint that prevents executing more iterations at once in the ideal case. How can the loop be restructured to relax that constraint?

e. [25] <3.2, 3.3> For simplicity, assume that only variables i, hash_index, ptrCurr, and ptrUpdate need to occupy registers. Assuming general renaming, how many registers are necessary to achieve the maximum achievable parallelism in part (b)?

f. [25] <3.3> Assume that in your answer to part (a) there are 7 instructions in each iteration. Now, assuming a consistent steady-state schedule of the instructions in the example and an issue rate of 3 instructions per cycle, how is execution time affected?

g. [15] <3.3> Finally, calculate the minimal instruction window size needed to achieve the maximal level of parallelism.

3.2 [15/15/15/10/10/15/15/10/10/10/25] <2.1, 3.2, 3.3> Let us now consider less favorable scenarios for extraction of instruction-level parallelism by a run-time hardware scheduler in the hash table code in Figure 3.14 (the general case). Suppose that there is no longer a guarantee that each bucket will receive exactly one item. Let us reevaluate our assessment of the parallelism available, given the more realistic situation, which adds some additional, important dependences.

Recall that in the ideal case, the relatively serial inner loop was not in play, and the outer loop provided ample parallelism. In general, the inner loop is in play: the inner while loop could iterate one or more times. Keep in mind that the inner loop, the while loop, has only a limited amount of instruction-level parallelism. First of all, each iteration of the while loop depends on the result of the previous iteration. Second, within each iteration, only a small number of instructions are executed.

The outer loop is, on the contrary, quite parallel. As long as two elements of the outer loop are hashed into different buckets, they can be entered in parallel. Even when they are hashed to the same bucket, they can still go in parallel as long as some type of memory disambiguation enforces correctness of memory loads and stores performed on behalf of each element.

Note that in reality, the data element values will likely be randomly distributed. Although we aim to provide the reader insight into more realistic execution scenarios, we will begin with some regular but nonideal data value patterns that are amenable to systematic analysis. These value patterns offer some intermediate steps toward understanding the amount of instruction-level parallelism under the most general, random data values.

a. [15] <2.1> Draw a dynamic dependence graph for the hash table code in Figure 3.14 when the values of the 1024 data elements to be inserted are 0, 1, 1024, 1025, 2048, 2049, 3072, 3073, ... Describe the new dependences across iterations for the for loop when the while loop is iterated one or more times. Pay special attention to the fact that the inner while loop now can iterate one or more times. The number of instructions in the outer for loop will therefore likely vary as it iterates. For the purpose of determining dependences between loads and stores, assume a dynamic memory disambiguation that cannot resolve the dependences between two memory accesses based on different base pointer registers. For example, the run time hardware cannot disambiguate between a store based on `ptrUpdate` and a load based on `ptrCurr`.

b. [15] <2.1> Assuming the dynamic dependence graph you derived in part (a), how many instructions will be executed?

c. [15] <2.1> Assuming the dynamic dependence graph you derived in part (a) and an unlimited amount of hardware resources, how many clock cycles will it take to execute all the instructions you calculated in part (b)?

d. [10] <2.1> How much instruction-level parallelism is available in the dynamic dependence graph you derived in part (a)?

e. [10] <2.1, 3.2> Using the same assumption of run time memory disambiguation mechanism as in part (a), identify a sequence of data elements that will cause the worst-case scenario of the way these new dependences affect the level of parallelism available.

f. [15] <2.1, 3.2> Now, assume the worst-case sequence used in part (e), explain the potential effect of a perfect run time memory disambiguation mechanism (i.e., a system that tracks all outstanding stores and allows all nonconflicting loads to proceed). Derive the number of clock cycles required to execute all the instructions in the dynamic dependence graph.

On the basis of what you have learned so far, consider a couple of qualitative questions: What is the effect of allowing loads to issue speculatively, before prior store addresses are known? How does such speculation affect the significance of memory latency in this code?

g. [15] <2.1, 3.2> Continue the same assumptions as in part (f), and calculate the number of instructions executed.

h. [10] <2.1, 3.2> Continue the same assumptions as in part (f), and calculate the amount of instruction-level parallelism available to the run-time hardware.

i. [10] <2.1, 3.2> In part (h), what is the effect of limited instruction window sizes on the level of instruction-level parallelism?

j. [10] <3.2, 3.3> Now, continuing to consider your solution to part (h), describe the cause of branch-prediction misses and the effect of each branch prediction on the level of parallelism available. Reflect briefly on the implications for power and efficiency. What are potential costs and benefits to executing many off-path speculative instructions (i.e., initiating execution of instructions that will later be squashed by branch-misprediction detection)? *Hint:* Think about the effect on the execution of subsequent insertions of mispredicting the number of elements before the insertion point.

k. [25] <3> Consider the concept of a static dependence graph that captures all the worst-case dependences for the purpose of constraining compiler scheduling and optimization. Draw the static dependence graph for the hash table code shown in Figure 3.14.

Compare the static dependence graph with the various dynamic dependence graphs drawn previously. Reflect in a paragraph or two on the implications of this comparison for dynamic and static discovery of instruction-level parallelism in this example's hash table code. In particular, how is the compiler constrained by having to consistently take into consideration the worst case, where a hardware mechanism might be free to take advantage opportunistically of fortuitous cases? What sort of approaches might help the compiler to make better use of this code?

4.1	Introduction	196
4.2	Symmetric Shared-Memory Architectures	205
4.3	Performance of Symmetric Shared-Memory Multiprocessors	218
4.4	Distributed Shared Memory and Directory-Based Coherence	230
4.5	Synchronization: The Basics	237
4.6	Models of Memory Consistency: An Introduction	243
4.7	Crosscutting Issues	246
4.8	Putting It All Together: The Sun T1 Multiprocessor	249
4.9	Fallacies and Pitfalls	257
4.10	Concluding Remarks	262
4.11	Historical Perspective and References	264
	Case Studies with Exercises by David A. Wood	264

4

Multiprocessors and Thread-Level Parallelism

The turning away from the conventional organization came in the middle 1960s, when the law of diminishing returns began to take effect in the effort to increase the operational speed of a computer.... Electronic circuits are ultimately limited in their speed of operation by the speed of light ... and many of the circuits were already operating in the nanosecond range.

W. Jack Bouknight et al.
The Illiac IV System (1972)

We are dedicating all of our future product development to multicore designs. We believe this is a key inflection point for the industry.

Intel President Paul Otellini,
describing Intel's future direction at the
Intel Developers Forum in 2005

4.1   Introduction

As the quotation that opens this chapter shows, the view that advances in uniprocessor architecture were nearing an end has been held by some researchers for many years. Clearly these views were premature; in fact, during the period of 1986–2002, uniprocessor performance growth, driven by the microprocessor, was at its highest rate since the first transistorized computers in the late 1950s and early 1960s.

Nonetheless, the importance of multiprocessors was growing throughout the 1990s as designers sought a way to build servers and supercomputers that achieved higher performance than a single microprocessor, while exploiting the tremendous cost-performance advantages of commodity microprocessors. As we discussed in Chapters 1 and 3, the slowdown in uniprocessor performance arising from diminishing returns in exploiting ILP, combined with growing concern over power, is leading to a new era in computer architecture—an era where multiprocessors play a major role. The second quotation captures this clear inflection point.

This trend toward more reliance on multiprocessing is reinforced by other factors:

- A growing interest in servers and server performance

- A growth in data-intensive applications

- The insight that increasing performance on the desktop is less important (outside of graphics, at least)

- An improved understanding of how to use multiprocessors effectively, especially in server environments where there is significant natural thread-level parallelism

- The advantages of leveraging a design investment by replication rather than unique design—all multiprocessor designs provide such leverage

That said, we are left with two problems. First, multiprocessor architecture is a large and diverse field, and much of the field is in its youth, with ideas coming and going and, until very recently, more architectures failing than succeeding. Full coverage of the multiprocessor design space and its trade-offs would require another volume. (Indeed, Culler, Singh, and Gupta [1999] cover *only* multiprocessors in their 1000-page book!) Second, broad coverage would necessarily entail discussing approaches that may not stand the test of time—something we have largely avoided to this point.

For these reasons, we have chosen to focus on the mainstream of multiprocessor design: multiprocessors with small to medium numbers of processors (4 to 32). Such designs vastly dominate in terms of both units and dollars. We will pay only slight attention to the larger-scale multiprocessor design space (32 or more processors), primarily in Appendix H, which covers more aspects of the design of such processors, as well as the behavior performance for parallel scientific workloads, a primary class of applications for large-scale multiprocessors. In the large-scale multiprocessors, the interconnection networks are a critical part of the design; Appendix E focuses on that topic.

A Taxonomy of Parallel Architectures

We begin this chapter with a taxonomy so that you can appreciate both the breadth of design alternatives for multiprocessors and the context that has led to the development of the dominant form of multiprocessors. We briefly describe the alternatives and the rationale behind them; a longer description of how these different models were born (and often died) can be found in Appendix K.

The idea of using multiple processors both to increase performance and to improve availability dates back to the earliest electronic computers. About 40 years ago, Flynn [1966] proposed a simple model of categorizing all computers that is still useful today. He looked at the parallelism in the instruction and data streams called for by the instructions at the most constrained component of the multiprocessor, and placed all computers into one of four categories:

1. *Single instruction stream, single data stream* (SISD)—This category is the uniprocessor.

2. *Single instruction stream, multiple data streams* (SIMD)—The same instruction is executed by multiple processors using different data streams. SIMD computers exploit *data-level parallelism* by applying the same operations to multiple items of data in parallel. Each processor has its own data memory (hence multiple data), but there is a single instruction memory and control processor, which fetches and dispatches instructions. For applications that display significant data-level parallelism, the SIMD approach can be very efficient. The multimedia extensions discussed in Appendices B and C are a form of SIMD parallelism. Vector architectures, discussed in Appendix F, are the largest class of SIMD architectures. SIMD approaches have experienced a rebirth in the last few years with the growing importance of graphics performance, especially for the game market. SIMD approaches are the favored method for achieving the high performance needed to create realistic three-dimensional, real-time virtual environments.

3. *Multiple instruction streams, single data stream* (MISD)—No commercial multiprocessor of this type has been built to date.

4. *Multiple instruction streams, multiple data streams* (MIMD)—Each processor fetches its own instructions and operates on its own data. MIMD computers exploit *thread-level parallelism*, since multiple threads operate in parallel. In general, thread-level parallelism is more flexible than data-level parallelism and thus more generally applicable.

This is a coarse model, as some multiprocessors are hybrids of these categories. Nonetheless, it is useful to put a framework on the design space.

Because the MIMD model can exploit thread-level parallelism, it is the architecture of choice for general-purpose multiprocessors and our focus in this chapter. Two other factors have also contributed to the rise of the MIMD multiprocessors:

1. MIMDs offer flexibility. With the correct hardware and software support, MIMDs can function as single-user multiprocessors focusing on high performance for one application, as multiprogrammed multiprocessors running many tasks simultaneously, or as some combination of these functions.

2. MIMDs can build on the cost-performance advantages of off-the-shelf processors. In fact, nearly all multiprocessors built today use the same microprocessors found in workstations and single-processor servers. Furthermore, multicore chips leverage the design investment in a single processor core by replicating it.

One popular class of MIMD computers are *clusters*, which often use standard components and often standard network technology, so as to leverage as much commodity technology as possible. In Appendix H we distinguish two different types of clusters: *commodity clusters*, which rely entirely on third-party processors and interconnection technology, and *custom clusters*, in which a designer customizes either the detailed node design or the interconnection network, or both.

In a commodity cluster, the nodes of a cluster are often blades or rack-mounted servers (including small-scale multiprocessor servers). Applications that focus on throughput and require almost no communication among threads, such as Web serving, multiprogramming, and some transaction-processing applications, can be accommodated inexpensively on a cluster. Commodity clusters are often assembled by users or computer center directors, rather than by vendors.

Custom clusters are typically focused on parallel applications that can exploit large amounts of parallelism on a single problem. Such applications require a significant amount of communication during the computation, and customizing the node and interconnect design makes such communication more efficient than in a commodity cluster. Currently, the largest and fastest multiprocessors in existence are custom clusters, such as the IBM Blue Gene, which we discuss in Appendix H.

Starting in the 1990s, the increasing capacity of a single chip allowed designers to place multiple processors on a single die. This approach, initially called *on-chip multiprocessing* or *single-chip multiprocessing*, has come to be called *multicore*, a name arising from the use of multiple processor cores on a single die. In such a design, the multiple cores typically share some resources, such as a second- or third-level cache or memory and I/O buses. Recent processors, including the IBM Power5, the Sun T1, and the Intel Pentium D and Xeon-MP, are multicore and multithreaded. Just as using multiple copies of a microprocessor in a multiprocessor leverages a design investment through replication, a multicore achieves the same advantage relying more on replication than the alternative of building a wider superscalar.

With an MIMD, each processor is executing its own instruction stream. In many cases, each processor executes a different process. A *process* is a segment of code that may be run independently; the state of the process contains all the information necessary to execute that program on a processor. In a multiprogrammed environment, where the processors may be running independent tasks, each process is typically independent of other processes.

It is also useful to be able to have multiple processors executing a single program and sharing the code and most of their address space. When multiple processes share code and data in this way, they are often called *threads*. Today, the term *thread* is often used in a casual way to refer to multiple loci of execution that may run on different processors, even when they do not share an address space. For example, a multithreaded architecture actually allows the simultaneous execution of multiple processes, with potentially separate address spaces, as well as multiple threads that share the same address space.

To take advantage of an MIMD multiprocessor with n processors, we must usually have at least n threads or processes to execute. The independent threads within a single process are typically identified by the programmer or created by the compiler. The threads may come from large-scale, independent processes scheduled and manipulated by the operating system. At the other extreme, a thread may consist of a few tens of iterations of a loop, generated by a parallel compiler exploiting data parallelism in the loop. Although the amount of computation assigned to a thread, called the *grain size,* is important in considering how to exploit thread-level parallelism efficiently, the important qualitative distinction from instruction-level parallelism is that thread-level parallelism is identified at a high level by the software system and that the threads consist of hundreds to millions of instructions that may be executed in parallel.

Threads can also be used to exploit data-level parallelism, although the overhead is likely to be higher than would be seen in an SIMD computer. This overhead means that grain size must be sufficiently large to exploit the parallelism efficiently. For example, although a vector processor (see Appendix F) may be able to efficiently parallelize operations on short vectors, the resulting grain size when the parallelism is split among many threads may be so small that the overhead makes the exploitation of the parallelism prohibitively expensive.

Existing MIMD multiprocessors fall into two classes, depending on the number of processors involved, which in turn dictates a memory organization and interconnect strategy. We refer to the multiprocessors by their memory organization because what constitutes a small or large number of processors is likely to change over time.

The first group, which we call *centralized shared-memory architectures,* has at most a few dozen processor chips (and less than 100 cores) in 2006. For multiprocessors with small processor counts, it is possible for the processors to share a single centralized memory. With large caches, a single memory, possibly with multiple banks, can satisfy the memory demands of a small number of processors. By using multiple point-to-point connections, or a switch, and adding additional memory banks, a centralized shared-memory design can be scaled to a few dozen processors. Although scaling beyond that is technically conceivable, sharing a centralized memory becomes less attractive as the number of processors sharing it increases.

Because there is a single main memory that has a symmetric relationship to all processors and a uniform access time from any processor, these multiprocessors are most often called *symmetric (shared-memory) multiprocessors* (SMPs), and this style of architecture is sometimes called *uniform memory access* (UMA), arising from the fact that all processors have a uniform latency from memory, even if the memory is organized into multiple banks. Figure 4.1 shows what these multiprocessors look like. This type of symmetric shared-memory architecture is currently by far the most popular organization. The architecture of such multiprocessors is the topic of Section 4.2.

The second group consists of multiprocessors with physically distributed memory. Figure 4.2 shows what these multiprocessors look like. To support larger processor counts, memory must be distributed among the processors rather than centralized; otherwise the memory system would not be able to support the bandwidth demands of a larger number of processors without incurring excessively long access latency. With the rapid increase in processor performance and the associated increase in a processor's memory bandwidth requirements, the size of a multiprocessor for which distributed memory is preferred continues to shrink. The larger number of processors also raises the need for a high-bandwidth interconnect, of which we will see examples in Appendix E.

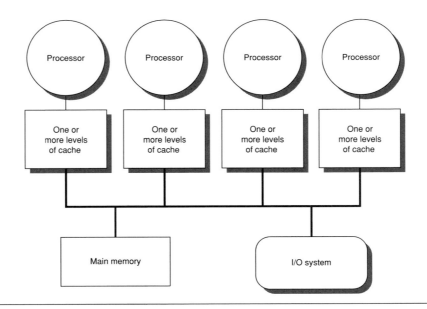

Figure 4.1 Basic structure of a centralized shared-memory multiprocessor. Multiple processor-cache subsystems share the same physical memory, typically connected by one or more buses or a switch. The key architectural property is the uniform access time to all of memory from all the processors.

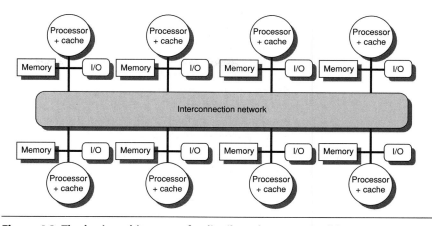

Figure 4.2 The basic architecture of a distributed-memory multiprocessor consists of individual nodes containing a processor, some memory, typically some I/O, and an interface to an interconnection network that connects all the nodes. Individual nodes may contain a small number of processors, which may be interconnected by a small bus or a different interconnection technology, which is less scalable than the global interconnection network.

Both direction networks (i.e., switches) and indirect networks (typically multidimensional meshes) are used.

Distributing the memory among the nodes has two major benefits. First, it is a cost-effective way to scale the memory bandwidth if most of the accesses are to the local memory in the node. Second, it reduces the latency for accesses to the local memory. These two advantages make distributed memory attractive at smaller processor counts as processors get ever faster and require more memory bandwidth and lower memory latency. The key disadvantages for a distributed-memory architecture are that communicating data between processors becomes somewhat more complex, and that it requires more effort in the software to take advantage of the increased memory bandwidth afforded by distributed memories. As we will see shortly, the use of distributed memory also leads to two different paradigms for interprocessor communication.

Models for Communication and Memory Architecture

As discussed earlier, any large-scale multiprocessor must use multiple memories that are physically distributed with the processors. There are two alternative architectural approaches that differ in the method used for communicating data among processors.

In the first method, communication occurs through a shared address space, as it does in a symmetric shared-memory architecture. The physically separate memories can be addressed as one logically shared address space, meaning that a memory reference can be made by any processor to any memory location, assuming it has the correct access rights. These multiprocessors are called *distributed shared-memory* (DSM) architectures. The term *shared memory* refers to the fact that the *address space* is shared; that is, the same physical address on two processors refers to the same location in memory. Shared memory does *not* mean that there is a single, centralized memory. In contrast to the symmetric shared-memory multiprocessors, also known as UMAs (uniform memory access), the DSM multiprocessors are also called NUMAs (nonuniform memory access), since the access time depends on the location of a data word in memory.

Alternatively, the address space can consist of multiple private address spaces that are logically disjoint and cannot be addressed by a remote processor. In such multiprocessors, the same physical address on two different processors refers to two different locations in two different memories. Each processor-memory module is essentially a separate computer. Initially, such computers were built with different processing nodes and specialized interconnection networks. Today, most designs of this type are actually clusters, which we discuss in Appendix H.

With each of these organizations for the address space, there is an associated communication mechanism. For a multiprocessor with a shared address space, that address space can be used to communicate data implicitly via load and store operations—hence the name *shared memory* for such multiprocessors. For a multiprocessor with multiple address spaces, communication of data is done by explicitly passing messages among the processors. Therefore, these multiprocessors are often called *message-passing multiprocessors*. Clusters inherently use message passing.

Challenges of Parallel Processing

The application of multiprocessors ranges from running independent tasks with essentially no communication to running parallel programs where threads must communicate to complete the task. Two important hurdles, both explainable with Amdahl's Law, make parallel processing challenging. The degree to which these hurdles are difficult or easy is determined both by the application and by the architecture.

The first hurdle has to do with the limited parallelism available in programs, and the second arises from the relatively high cost of communications. Limitations in available parallelism make it difficult to achieve good speedups in any parallel processor, as our first example shows.

Example Suppose you want to achieve a speedup of 80 with 100 processors. What fraction of the original computation can be sequential?

Answer Amdahl's Law is

$$\text{Speedup} = \frac{1}{\dfrac{\text{Fraction}_{enhanced}}{\text{Speedup}_{enhanced}} + (1 - \text{Fraction}_{enhanced})}$$

For simplicity in this example, assume that the program operates in only two modes: parallel with all processors fully used, which is the enhanced mode, or serial with only one processor in use. With this simplification, the speedup in enhanced mode is simply the number of processors, while the fraction of enhanced mode is the time spent in parallel mode. Substituting into the previous equation:

$$80 = \frac{1}{\dfrac{\text{Fraction}_{\text{parallel}}}{100} + (1 - \text{Fraction}_{\text{parallel}})}$$

Simplifying this equation yields

$$0.8 \times \text{Fraction}_{\text{parallel}} + 80 \times (1 - \text{Fraction}_{\text{parallel}}) = 1$$

$$80 - 79.2 \times \text{Fraction}_{\text{parallel}} = 1$$

$$\text{Fraction}_{\text{parallel}} = \frac{80 - 1}{79.2}$$

$$\text{Fraction}_{\text{parallel}} = 0.9975$$

Thus, to achieve a speedup of 80 with 100 processors, only 0.25% of original computation can be sequential. Of course, to achieve linear speedup (speedup of n with n processors), the entire program must usually be parallel with no serial portions. In practice, programs do not just operate in fully parallel or sequential mode, but often use less than the full complement of the processors when running in parallel mode.

The second major challenge in parallel processing involves the large latency of remote access in a parallel processor. In existing shared-memory multiprocessors, communication of data between processors may cost anywhere from 50 clock cycles (for multicores) to over 1000 clock cycles (for large-scale multiprocessors), depending on the communication mechanism, the type of interconnection network, and the scale of the multiprocessor. The effect of long communication delays is clearly substantial. Let's consider a simple example.

Example   Suppose we have an application running on a 32-processor multiprocessor, which has a 200 ns time to handle reference to a remote memory. For this application, assume that all the references except those involving communication hit in the local memory hierarchy, which is slightly optimistic. Processors are stalled on a remote request, and the processor clock rate is 2 GHz. If the base CPI (assuming that all references hit in the cache) is 0.5, how much faster is the multiprocessor if there is no communication versus if 0.2% of the instructions involve a remote communication reference?

Answer   It is simpler to first calculate the CPI. The effective CPI for the multiprocessor with 0.2% remote references is

$$CPI = \text{Base CPI} + \text{Remote request rate} \times \text{Remote request cost}$$
$$= 0.5 + 0.2\% \times \text{Remote request cost}$$

The remote request cost is

$$\frac{\text{Remote access cost}}{\text{Cycle time}} = \frac{200 \text{ ns}}{0.5 \text{ ns}} = 400 \text{ cycles}$$

Hence we can compute the CPI:

$$CPI = 0.5 + 0.8 = 1.3$$

The multiprocessor with all local references is 1.3/0.5 = 2.6 times faster. In practice, the performance analysis is much more complex, since some fraction of the noncommunication references will miss in the local hierarchy and the remote access time does not have a single constant value. For example, the cost of a remote reference could be quite a bit worse, since contention caused by many references trying to use the global interconnect can lead to increased delays.

These problems—insufficient parallelism and long-latency remote communication—are the two biggest performance challenges in using multiprocessors. The problem of inadequate application parallelism must be attacked primarily in software with new algorithms that can have better parallel performance. Reducing the impact of long remote latency can be attacked both by the architecture and by the programmer. For example, we can reduce the frequency of remote accesses with either hardware mechanisms, such as caching shared data, or software mechanisms, such as restructuring the data to make more accesses local. We can try to tolerate the latency by using multithreading (discussed in Chapter 3 and later in this chapter) or by using prefetching (a topic we cover extensively in Chapter 5).

Much of this chapter focuses on techniques for reducing the impact of long remote communication latency. For example, Sections 4.2 and 4.3 discuss how caching can be used to reduce remote access frequency, while maintaining a coherent view of memory. Section 4.5 discusses synchronization, which, because it inherently involves interprocessor communication and also can limit parallelism, is a major potential bottleneck. Section 4.6 covers latency-hiding techniques and memory consistency models for shared memory. In Appendix I, we focus primarily on large-scale multiprocessors, which are used predominantly for scientific work. In that appendix, we examine the nature of such applications and the challenges of achieving speedup with dozens to hundreds of processors.

Understanding a modern shared-memory multiprocessor requires a good understanding of the basics of caches. Readers who have covered this topic in our introductory book, *Computer Organization and Design: The Hardware/ Software Interface*, will be well-prepared. If topics such as write-back caches and multilevel caches are unfamiliar to you, you should take the time to review Appendix C.

Symmetric Shared-Memory Architectures

The use of large, multilevel caches can substantially reduce the memory bandwidth demands of a processor. If the main memory bandwidth demands of a single processor are reduced, multiple processors may be able to share the same memory. Starting in the 1980s, this observation, combined with the emerging dominance of the microprocessor, motivated many designers to create small-scale multiprocessors where several processors shared a single physical memory connected by a shared bus. Because of the small size of the processors and the significant reduction in the requirements for bus bandwidth achieved by large caches, such symmetric multiprocessors were extremely cost-effective, provided that a sufficient amount of memory bandwidth existed. Early designs of such multiprocessors were able to place the processor and cache subsystem on a board, which plugged into the bus backplane. Subsequent versions of such designs in the 1990s could achieve higher densities with two to four processors per board, and often used multiple buses and interleaved memories to support the faster processors.

IBM introduced the first on-chip multiprocessor for the general-purpose computing market in 2000. AMD and Intel followed with two-processor versions for the server market in 2005, and Sun introduced T1, an eight-processor multicore in 2006. Section 4.8 looks at the design and performance of T1. The earlier Figure 4.1 on page 200 shows a simple diagram of such a multiprocessor. With the more recent, higher-performance processors, the memory demands have outstripped the capability of reasonable buses. As a result, most recent designs use a small-scale switch or a limited point-to-point network.

Symmetric shared-memory machines usually support the caching of both shared and private data. *Private data* are used by a single processor, while *shared data* are used by multiple processors, essentially providing communication among the processors through reads and writes of the shared data. When a private item is cached, its location is migrated to the cache, reducing the average access time as well as the memory bandwidth required. Since no other processor uses the data, the program behavior is identical to that in a uniprocessor. When shared data are cached, the shared value may be replicated in multiple caches. In addition to the reduction in access latency and required memory bandwidth, this replication also provides a reduction in contention that may exist for shared data items that are being read by multiple processors simultaneously. Caching of shared data, however, introduces a new problem: cache coherence.

What Is Multiprocessor Cache Coherence?

Unfortunately, caching shared data introduces a new problem because the view of memory held by two different processors is through their individual caches, which, without any additional precautions, could end up seeing two different values. Figure 4.3 illustrates the problem and shows how two different processors

Time	Event	Cache contents for CPU A	Cache contents for CPU B	Memory contents for location X
0				1
1	CPU A reads X	1		1
2	CPU B reads X	1	1	1
3	CPU A stores 0 into X	0	1	0

Figure 4.3 The cache coherence problem for a single memory location (X), read and written by two processors (A and B). We initially assume that neither cache contains the variable and that X has the value 1. We also assume a write-through cache; a write-back cache adds some additional but similar complications. After the value of X has been written by A, A's cache and the memory both contain the new value, but B's cache does not, and if B reads the value of X, it will receive 1!

can have two different values for the same location. This difficulty is generally referred to as the *cache coherence problem.*

Informally, we could say that a memory system is coherent if any read of a data item returns the most recently written value of that data item. This definition, although intuitively appealing, is vague and simplistic; the reality is much more complex. This simple definition contains two different aspects of memory system behavior, both of which are critical to writing correct shared-memory programs. The first aspect, called *coherence,* defines what values can be returned by a read. The second aspect, called *consistency,* determines when a written value will be returned by a read. Let's look at coherence first.

A memory system is coherent if

1. A read by a processor P to a location X that follows a write by P to X, with no writes of X by another processor occurring between the write and the read by P, always returns the value written by P.

2. A read by a processor to location X that follows a write by another processor to X returns the written value if the read and write are sufficiently separated in time and no other writes to X occur between the two accesses.

3. Writes to the same location are *serialized;* that is, two writes to the same location by any two processors are seen in the same order by all processors. For example, if the values 1 and then 2 are written to a location, processors can never read the value of the location as 2 and then later read it as 1.

The first property simply preserves program order—we expect this property to be true even in uniprocessors. The second property defines the notion of what it means to have a coherent view of memory: If a processor could continuously read an old data value, we would clearly say that memory was incoherent.

The need for write serialization is more subtle, but equally important. Suppose we did not serialize writes, and processor P1 writes location X followed by

P2 writing location X. Serializing the writes ensures that every processor will see the write done by P2 at some point. If we did not serialize the writes, it might be the case that some processor could see the write of P2 first and then see the write of P1, maintaining the value written by P1 indefinitely. The simplest way to avoid such difficulties is to ensure that all writes to the same location are seen in the same order; this property is called *write serialization*.

Although the three properties just described are sufficient to ensure coherence, the question of when a written value will be seen is also important. To see why, observe that we cannot require that a read of X instantaneously see the value written for X by some other processor. If, for example, a write of X on one processor precedes a read of X on another processor by a very small time, it may be impossible to ensure that the read returns the value of the data written, since the written data may not even have left the processor at that point. The issue of exactly *when* a written value must be seen by a reader is defined by a *memory consistency model*—a topic discussed in Section 4.6.

Coherence and consistency are complementary: Coherence defines the behavior of reads and writes to the same memory location, while consistency defines the behavior of reads and writes with respect to accesses to other memory locations. For now, make the following two assumptions. First, a write does not complete (and allow the next write to occur) until all processors have seen the effect of that write. Second, the processor does not change the order of any write with respect to any other memory access. These two conditions mean that if a processor writes location A followed by location B, any processor that sees the new value of B must also see the new value of A. These restrictions allow the processor to reorder reads, but forces the processor to finish a write in program order. We will rely on this assumption until we reach Section 4.6, where we will see exactly the implications of this definition, as well as the alternatives.

Basic Schemes for Enforcing Coherence

The coherence problem for multiprocessors and I/O, although similar in origin, has different characteristics that affect the appropriate solution. Unlike I/O, where multiple data copies are a rare event—one to be avoided whenever possible—a program running on multiple processors will normally have copies of the same data in several caches. In a coherent multiprocessor, the caches provide both *migration* and *replication* of shared data items.

Coherent caches provide migration, since a data item can be moved to a local cache and used there in a transparent fashion. This migration reduces both the latency to access a shared data item that is allocated remotely and the bandwidth demand on the shared memory.

Coherent caches also provide replication for shared data that are being simultaneously read, since the caches make a copy of the data item in the local cache. Replication reduces both latency of access and contention for a read shared data item. Supporting this migration and replication is critical to performance in accessing shared data. Thus, rather than trying to solve the problem by avoiding it in software, small-scale multiprocessors adopt a hardware solution by introducing a protocol to maintain coherent caches.

The protocols to maintain coherence for multiple processors are called *cache coherence protocols*. Key to implementing a cache coherence protocol is tracking the state of any sharing of a data block. There are two classes of protocols, which use different techniques to track the sharing status, in use:

■ *Directory based*—The sharing status of a block of physical memory is kept in just one location, called the *directory;* we focus on this approach in Section 4.4, when we discuss scalable shared-memory architecture. Directory-based coherence has slightly higher implementation overhead than snooping, but it can scale to larger processor counts. The Sun T1 design, the topic of Section 4.8, uses directories, albeit with a central physical memory.

■ *Snooping*—Every cache that has a copy of the data from a block of physical memory also has a copy of the sharing status of the block, but no centralized state is kept. The caches are all accessible via some broadcast medium (a bus or switch), and all cache controllers monitor or *snoop* on the medium to determine whether or not they have a copy of a block that is requested on a bus or switch access. We focus on this approach in this section.

Snooping protocols became popular with multiprocessors using microprocessors and caches attached to a single shared memory because these protocols can use a preexisting physical connection—the bus to memory—to interrogate the status of the caches. In the following section we explain snoop-based cache coherence as implemented with a shared bus, but any communication medium that broadcasts cache misses to all processors can be used to implement a snooping-based coherence scheme. This broadcasting to all caches is what makes snooping protocols simple to implement but also limits their scalability.

Snooping Protocols

There are two ways to maintain the coherence requirement described in the prior subsection. One method is to ensure that a processor has exclusive access to a data item before it writes that item. This style of protocol is called a *write invalidate protocol* because it invalidates other copies on a write. It is by far the most common protocol, both for snooping and for directory schemes. Exclusive access ensures that no other readable or writable copies of an item exist when the write occurs: All other cached copies of the item are invalidated.

Figure 4.4 shows an example of an invalidation protocol for a snooping bus with write-back caches in action. To see how this protocol ensures coherence, consider a write followed by a read by another processor: Since the write requires exclusive access, any copy held by the reading processor must be invalidated (hence the protocol name). Thus, when the read occurs, it misses in the cache and is forced to fetch a new copy of the data. For a write, we require that the writing processor have exclusive access, preventing any other processor from being able

Processor activity	Bus activity	Contents of CPU A's cache	Contents of CPU B's cache	Contents of memory location X
				0
CPU A reads X	Cache miss for X	0		0
CPU B reads X	Cache miss for X	0	0	0
CPU A writes a 1 to X	Invalidation for X	1		0
CPU B reads X	Cache miss for X	1	1	1

Figure 4.4 An example of an invalidation protocol working on a snooping bus for a single cache block (X) with write-back caches. We assume that neither cache initially holds X and that the value of X in memory is 0. The CPU and memory contents show the value after the processor and bus activity have both completed. A blank indicates no activity or no copy cached. When the second miss by B occurs, CPU A responds with the value canceling the response from memory. In addition, both the contents of B's cache and the memory contents of X are updated. This update of memory, which occurs when a block becomes shared, simplifies the protocol, but it is possible to track the owner-ship and force the write back only if the block is replaced. This requires the introduction of an additional state called "owner," which indicates that a block may be shared, but the owning processor is responsible for updating any other processors and memory when it changes the block or replaces it.

to write simultaneously. If two processors do attempt to write the same data simultaneously, one of them wins the race (we'll see how we decide who wins shortly), causing the other processor's copy to be invalidated. For the other processor to complete its write, it must obtain a new copy of the data, which must now contain the updated value. Therefore, this protocol enforces write serialization.

The alternative to an invalidate protocol is to update all the cached copies of a data item when that item is written. This type of protocol is called a *write update* or *write broadcast* protocol. Because a write update protocol must broadcast all writes to shared cache lines, it consumes considerably more bandwidth. For this reason, all recent multiprocessors have opted to implement a write invalidate protocol, and we will focus only on invalidate protocols for the rest of the chapter.

Basic Implementation Techniques

The key to implementing an invalidate protocol in a small-scale multiprocessor is the use of the bus, or another broadcast medium, to perform invalidates. To perform an invalidate, the processor simply acquires bus access and broadcasts the address to be invalidated on the bus. All processors continuously snoop on the bus, watching the addresses. The processors check whether the address on the bus is in their cache. If so, the corresponding data in the cache are invalidated.

When a write to a block that is shared occurs, the writing processor must acquire bus access to broadcast its invalidation. If two processors attempt to write shared blocks at the same time, their attempts to broadcast an invalidate operation will be serialized when they arbitrate for the bus. The first processor to obtain bus access will cause any other copies of the block it is writing to be invalidated. If the processors were attempting to write the same block, the serialization enforced by the bus also serializes their writes. One implication of this scheme is that a write to a shared data item cannot actually complete until it obtains bus access. All coherence schemes require some method of serializing accesses to the same cache block, either by serializing access to the communication medium or another shared structure.

In addition to invalidating outstanding copies of a cache block that is being written into, we also need to locate a data item when a cache miss occurs. In a write-through cache, it is easy to find the recent value of a data item, since all written data are always sent to the memory, from which the most recent value of a data item can always be fetched. (Write buffers can lead to some additional complexities, which are discussed in the next chapter.) In a design with adequate memory bandwidth to support the write traffic from the processors, using write through simplifies the implementation of cache coherence.

For a write-back cache, the problem of finding the most recent data value is harder, since the most recent value of a data item can be in a cache rather than in memory. Happily, write-back caches can use the same snooping scheme both for cache misses and for writes: Each processor snoops every address placed on the bus. If a processor finds that it has a dirty copy of the requested cache block, it provides that cache block in response to the read request and causes the memory access to be aborted. The additional complexity comes from having to retrieve the cache block from a processor's cache, which can often take longer than retrieving it from the shared memory if the processors are in separate chips. Since write-back caches generate lower requirements for memory bandwidth, they can support larger numbers of faster processors and have been the approach chosen in most multiprocessors, despite the additional complexity of maintaining coherence. Therefore, we will examine the implementation of coherence with write-back caches.

The normal cache tags can be used to implement the process of snooping, and the valid bit for each block makes invalidation easy to implement. Read misses, whether generated by an invalidation or by some other event, are also straightforward since they simply rely on the snooping capability. For writes we'd like to know whether any other copies of the block are cached because, if there are no other cached copies, then the write need not be placed on the bus in a write-back cache. Not sending the write reduces both the time taken by the write and the required bandwidth.

To track whether or not a cache block is shared, we can add an extra state bit associated with each cache block, just as we have a valid bit and a dirty bit. By adding a bit indicating whether the block is shared, we can decide whether a write must generate an invalidate. When a write to a block in the shared state occurs, the cache generates an invalidation on the bus and marks the block as *exclusive*. No further invalidations will be sent by that processor for that block.

The processor with the sole copy of a cache block is normally called the *owner* of the cache block.

When an invalidation is sent, the state of the owner's cache block is changed from shared to unshared (or exclusive). If another processor later requests this cache block, the state must be made shared again. Since our snooping cache also sees any misses, it knows when the exclusive cache block has been requested by another processor and the state should be made shared.

Every bus transaction must check the cache-address tags, which could potentially interfere with processor cache accesses. One way to reduce this interference is to duplicate the tags. The interference can also be reduced in a multilevel cache by directing the snoop requests to the L2 cache, which the processor uses only when it has a miss in the L1 cache. For this scheme to work, every entry in the L1 cache must be present in the L2 cache, a property called the *inclusion property*. If the snoop gets a hit in the L2 cache, then it must arbitrate for the L1 cache to update the state and possibly retrieve the data, which usually requires a stall of the processor. Sometimes it may even be useful to duplicate the tags of the secondary cache to further decrease contention between the processor and the snooping activity. We discuss the inclusion property in more detail in the next chapter.

An Example Protocol

A snooping coherence protocol is usually implemented by incorporating a finite-state controller in each node. This controller responds to requests from the processor and from the bus (or other broadcast medium), changing the state of the selected cache block, as well as using the bus to access data or to invalidate it. Logically, you can think of a separate controller being associated with each block; that is, snooping operations or cache requests for different blocks can proceed independently. In actual implementations, a single controller allows multiple operations to distinct blocks to proceed in interleaved fashion (that is, one operation may be initiated before another is completed, even though only one cache access or one bus access is allowed at a time). Also, remember that, although we refer to a bus in the following description, any interconnection network that supports a broadcast to all the coherence controllers and their associated caches can be used to implement snooping.

The simple protocol we consider has three states: invalid, shared, and modified. The shared state indicates that the block is potentially shared, while the modified state indicates that the block has been updated in the cache; note that the modified state *implies* that the block is exclusive. Figure 4.5 shows the requests generated by the processor-cache module in a node (in the top half of the table) as well as those coming from the bus (in the bottom half of the table). This protocol is for a write-back cache but is easily changed to work for a write-through cache by reinterpreting the modified state as an exclusive state and updating the cache on writes in the normal fashion for a write-through cache. The most common extension of this basic protocol is the addition of an exclusive state, which describes a block that is unmodified but held in only one cache; the caption of Figure 4.5 describes this state and its addition in more detail.

When an invalidate or a write miss is placed on the bus, any processors with copies of the cache block invalidate it. For a write-through cache, the data for a write miss can always be retrieved from the memory. For a write miss in a write-back cache, if the block is exclusive in just one cache, that cache also writes back the block; otherwise, the data can be read from memory.

Figure 4.6 shows a finite-state transition diagram for a single cache block using a write invalidation protocol and a write-back cache. For simplicity, the three states of the protocol are duplicated to represent transitions based on processor requests (on the left, which corresponds to the top half of the table in Figure 4.5), as opposed to transitions based on bus requests (on the right, which corresponds to the bottom half of the table in Figure 4.5). Boldface type is used to distinguish the bus actions, as opposed to the conditions on which a state transition depends. The state in each node represents the state of the selected cache block specified by the processor or bus request.

All of the states in this cache protocol would be needed in a uniprocessor cache, where they would correspond to the invalid, valid (and clean), and dirty states. Most of the state changes indicated by arcs in the left half of Figure 4.6 would be needed in a write-back uniprocessor cache, with the exception being the invalidate on a write hit to a shared block. The state changes represented by the arcs in the right half of Figure 4.6 are needed only for coherence and would not appear at all in a uniprocessor cache controller.

As mentioned earlier, there is only one finite-state machine per cache, with stimuli coming either from the attached processor or from the bus. Figure 4.7 shows how the state transitions in the right half of Figure 4.6 are combined with those in the left half of the figure to form a single state diagram for each cache block.

To understand why this protocol works, observe that any valid cache block is either in the shared state in one or more caches or in the exclusive state in exactly one cache. Any transition to the exclusive state (which is required for a processor to write to the block) requires an invalidate or write miss to be placed on the bus, causing all caches to make the block invalid. In addition, if some other cache had the block in exclusive state, that cache generates a write back, which supplies the block containing the desired address. Finally, if a read miss occurs on the bus to a block in the exclusive state, the cache with the exclusive copy changes its state to shared.

The actions in gray in Figure 4.7, which handle read and write misses on the bus, are essentially the snooping component of the protocol. One other property that is preserved in this protocol, and in most other protocols, is that any memory block in the shared state is always up to date in the memory, which simplifies the implementation.

Although our simple cache protocol is correct, it omits a number of complications that make the implementation much trickier. The most important of these is

Request	Source	State of addressed cache block	Type of cache action	Function and explanation
Read hit	processor	shared or modified	normal hit	Read data in cache.
Read miss	processor	invalid	normal miss	Place read miss on bus.
Read miss	processor	shared	replacement	Address conflict miss: place read miss on bus.
Read miss	processor	modified	replacement	Address conflict miss: write back block, then place read miss on bus.
Write hit	processor	modified	normal hit	Write data in cache.
Write hit	processor	shared	coherence	Place invalidate on bus. These operations are often called upgrade or *ownership* misses, since they do not fetch the data but only change the state.
Write miss	processor	invalid	normal miss	Place write miss on bus.
Write miss	processor	shared	replacement	Address conflict miss: place write miss on bus.
Write miss	processor	modified	replacement	Address conflict miss: write back block, then place write miss on bus.
Read miss	bus	shared	no action	Allow memory to service read miss.
Read miss	bus	modified	coherence	Attempt to share data: place cache block on bus and change state to shared.
Invalidate	bus	shared	coherence	Attempt to write shared block; invalidate the block.
Write miss	bus	shared	coherence	Attempt to write block that is shared; invalidate the cache block.
Write miss	bus	modified	coherence	Attempt to write block that is exclusive elsewhere: write back the cache block and make its state invalid.

Figure 4.5 The cache coherence mechanism receives requests from both the processor and the bus and responds to these based on the type of request, whether it hits or misses in the cache, and the state of the cache block specified in the request. The fourth column describes the type of cache action as normal hit or miss (the same as a uniprocessor cache would see), replacement (a uniprocessor cache replacement miss), or coherence (required to maintain cache coherence); a normal or replacement action may cause a coherence action depending on the state of the block in other caches. For read, misses, write misses, or invalidates snooped from the bus, an action is required *only* if the read or write addresses match a block in the cache and the block is valid. Some protocols also introduce a state to designate when a block is exclusively in one cache but has not yet been written. This state can arise if a write access is broken into two pieces: getting the block exclusively in one cache and then subsequently updating it; in such a protocol this "exclusive unmodified state" is transient, ending as soon as the write is completed. Other protocols use and maintain an exclusive state for an unmodified block. In a snooping protocol, this state can be entered when a processor reads a block that is not resident in any other cache. Because all subsequent accesses are snooped, it is possible to maintain the accuracy of this state. In particular, if another processor issues a read miss, the state is changed from exclusive to shared. The advantage of adding this state is that a subsequent write to a block in the exclusive state by the same processor need not acquire bus access or generate an invalidate, since the block is known to be exclusively in this cache; the processor merely changes the state to modified. This state is easily added by using the bit that encodes the coherent state as an exclusive state and using the dirty bit to indicate that a bock is modified. The popular MESI protocol, which is named for the four states it includes (modified, exclusive, shared, and invalid), uses this structure. The MOESI protocol introduces another extension: the "owned" state, as described in the caption of Figure 4.4.

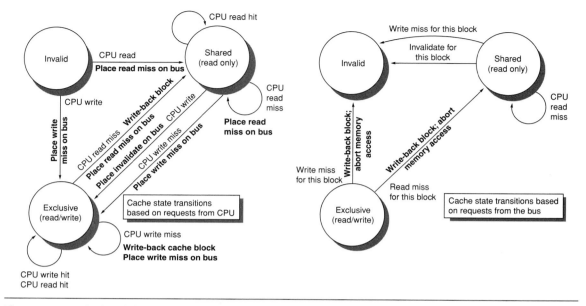

Figure 4.6 A write invalidate, cache coherence protocol for a write-back cache showing the states and state transitions for each block in the cache. The cache states are shown in circles, with any access permitted by the processor without a state transition shown in parentheses under the name of the state. The stimulus causing a state change is shown on the transition arcs in regular type, and any bus actions generated as part of the state transition are shown on the transition arc in bold. The stimulus actions apply to a block in the cache, not to a specific address in the cache. Hence, a read miss to a block in the shared state is a miss for that cache block but for a different address. The left side of the diagram shows state transitions based on actions of the processor associated with this cache; the right side shows transitions based on operations on the bus. A read miss in the exclusive or shared state and a write miss in the exclusive state occur when the address requested by the processor does not match the address in the cache block. Such a miss is a standard cache replacement miss. An attempt to write a block in the shared state generates an invalidate. Whenever a bus transaction occurs, all caches that contain the cache block specified in the bus transaction take the action dictated by the right half of the diagram. The protocol assumes that memory provides data on a read miss for a block that is clean in all caches. In actual implementations, these two sets of state diagrams are combined. In practice, there are many subtle variations on invalidate protocols, including the introduction of the exclusive unmodified state, as to whether a processor or memory provides data on a miss.

that the protocol assumes that operations are *atomic*—that is, an operation can be done in such a way that no intervening operation can occur. For example, the protocol described assumes that write misses can be detected, acquire the bus, and receive a response as a single atomic action. In reality this is not true. Similarly, if we used a switch, as all recent multiprocessors do, then even read misses would also not be atomic.

Nonatomic actions introduce the possibility that the protocol can *deadlock*, meaning that it reaches a state where it cannot continue. We will explore how these protocols are implemented without a bus shortly.

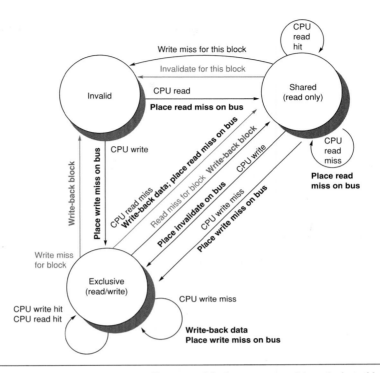

Figure 4.7 Cache coherence state diagram with the state transitions induced by the local processor shown in black and by the bus activities shown in gray. As in Figure 4.6, the activities on a transition are shown in bold.

Constructing small-scale (two to four processors) multiprocessors has become very easy. For example, the Intel Pentium 4 Xeon and AMD Opteron processors are designed for use in cache-coherent multiprocessors and have an external interface that supports snooping and allows two to four processors to be directly connected. They also have larger on-chip caches to reduce bus utilization. In the case of the Opteron processors, the support for interconnecting multiple processors is integrated onto the processor chip, as are the memory interfaces. In the case of the Intel design, a two-processor system can be built with only a few additional external chips to interface with the memory system and I/O. Although these designs cannot be easily scaled to larger processor counts, they offer an extremely cost-effective solution for two to four processors.

The next section examines the performance of these protocols for our parallel and multiprogrammed workloads; the value of these extensions to a basic protocol will be clear when we examine the performance. But before we do that, let's take a brief look at the limitations on the use of a symmetric memory structure and a snooping coherence scheme.

Limitations in Symmetric Shared-Memory Multiprocessors and Snooping Protocols

As the number of processors in a multiprocessor grows, or as the memory demands of each processor grow, any centralized resource in the system can become a bottleneck. In the simple case of a bus-based multiprocessor, the bus must support both the coherence traffic as well as normal memory traffic arising from the caches. Likewise, if there is a single memory unit, it must accommodate all processor requests. As processors have increased in speed in the last few years, the number of processors that can be supported on a single bus or by using a single physical memory unit has fallen.

How can a designer increase the memory bandwidth to support either more or faster processors? To increase the communication bandwidth between processors and memory, designers have used multiple buses as well as interconnection networks, such as crossbars or small point-to-point networks. In such designs, the memory system can be configured into multiple physical banks, so as to boost the effective memory bandwidth while retaining uniform access time to memory. Figure 4.8 shows this approach, which represents a midpoint between the two approaches we discussed in the beginning of the chapter: centralized shared memory and distributed shared memory.

The AMD Opteron represents another intermediate point in the spectrum between a snoopy and a directory protocol. Memory is directly connected to each dual-core processor chip, and up to four processor chips, eight cores in total, can be connected. The Opteron implements its coherence protocol using the point-to-point links to broadcast up to three other chips. Because the interprocessor links are not shared, the only way a processor can know when an invalid operation has

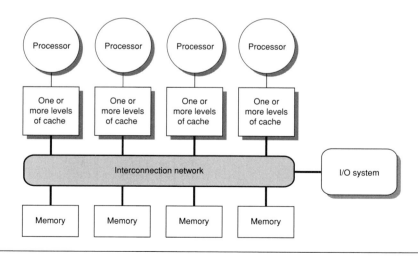

Figure 4.8 A multiprocessor with uniform memory access using an interconnection network rather than a bus.

completed is by an explicit acknowledgment. Thus, the coherence protocol uses a broadcast to find potentially shared copies, like a snoopy protocol, but uses the acknowledgments to order operations, like a directory protocol. Interestingly, the remote memory latency and local memory latency are not dramatically different, allowing the operating system to treat an Opteron multiprocessor as having uniform memory access.

A snoopy cache coherence protocol can be used without a centralized bus, but still requires that a broadcast be done to snoop the individual caches on every miss to a potentially shared cache block. This cache coherence traffic creates another limit on the scale and the speed of the processors. Because coherence traffic is unaffected by larger caches, faster processors will inevitably overwhelm the network and the ability of each cache to respond to snoop requests from *all* the other caches. In Section 4.4, we examine directory-based protocols, which eliminate the need for broadcast to all caches on a miss. As processor speeds and the number of cores per processor increase, more designers are likely to opt for such protocols to avoid the broadcast limit of a snoopy protocol.

Implementing Snoopy Cache Coherence

The devil is in the details.

Classic proverb

When we wrote the first edition of this book in 1990, our final "Putting It All Together" was a 30-processor, single bus multiprocessor using snoop-based coherence; the bus had a capacity of just over 50 MB/sec, which would not be enough bus bandwidth to support even one Pentium 4 in 2006! When we wrote the second edition of this book in 1995, the first cache coherence multiprocessors with more than a single bus had recently appeared, and we added an appendix describing the implementation of snooping in a system with multiple buses. In 2006, *every* multiprocessor system with more than two processors uses an interconnect other than a single bus, and designers must face the challenge of implementing snooping without the simplification of a bus to serialize events.

As we said earlier, the major complication in actually implementing the snooping coherence protocol we have described is that write and upgrade misses are not atomic in any recent multiprocessor. The steps of detecting a write or upgrade miss, communicating with the other processors and memory, getting the most recent value for a write miss and ensuring that any invalidates are processed, and updating the cache cannot be done as if they took a single cycle.

In a simple single-bus system, these steps can be made effectively atomic by arbitrating for the bus first (before changing the cache state) and not releasing the bus until all actions are complete. How can the processor know when all the invalidates are complete? In most bus-based multiprocessors a single line is used to signal when all necessary invalidates have been received and are being processed. Following that signal, the processor that generated the miss can release the bus, knowing that any required actions will be completed before any activity related to the next miss. By holding the bus exclusively during these steps, the processor effectively makes the individual steps atomic.

In a system without a bus, we must find some other method of making the steps in a miss atomic. In particular, we must ensure that two processors that attempt to write the same block at the same time, a situation which is called a *race*, are strictly ordered: one write is processed and precedes before the next is begun. It does not matter which of two writes in a race wins the race, just that there be only a single winner whose coherence actions are completed first. In a snoopy system ensuring that a race has only one winner is ensured by using broadcast for all misses as well as some basic properties of the interconnection network. These properties, together with the ability to restart the miss handling of the loser in a race, are the keys to implementing snoopy cache coherence without a bus. We explain the details in Appendix H.

4.3 Performance of Symmetric Shared-Memory Multiprocessors

In a multiprocessor using a snoopy coherence protocol, several different phenomena combine to determine performance. In particular, the overall cache performance is a combination of the behavior of uniprocessor cache miss traffic and the traffic caused by communication, which results in invalidations and subsequent cache misses. Changing the processor count, cache size, and block size can affect these two components of the miss rate in different ways, leading to overall system behavior that is a combination of the two effects.

Appendix C breaks the uniprocessor miss rate into the three C's classification (capacity, compulsory, and conflict) and provides insight into both application behavior and potential improvements to the cache design. Similarly, the misses that arise from interprocessor communication, which are often called *coherence misses,* can be broken into two separate sources.

The first source is the so-called *true sharing misses* that arise from the communication of data through the cache coherence mechanism. In an invalidation-based protocol, the first write by a processor to a shared cache block causes an invalidation to establish ownership of that block. Additionally, when another processor attempts to read a modified word in that cache block, a miss occurs and the resultant block is transferred. Both these misses are classified as true sharing misses since they directly arise from the sharing of data among processors.

The second effect, called *false sharing,* arises from the use of an invalidation-based coherence algorithm with a single valid bit per cache block. False sharing occurs when a block is invalidated (and a subsequent reference causes a miss) because some word in the block, other than the one being read, is written into. If the word written into is actually used by the processor that received the invalidate, then the reference was a true sharing reference and would have caused a miss independent of the block size. If, however, the word being written and the word read are different and the invalidation does not cause a new value to be communicated, but only causes an extra cache miss, then it is a false sharing miss. In a false sharing miss, the block is shared, but no word in the cache is actually shared, and the miss would not occur if the block size were a single word. The following example makes the sharing patterns clear.

Example   Assume that words x1 and x2 are in the same cache block, which is in the shared state in the caches of both P1 and P2. Assuming the following sequence of events, identify each miss as a true sharing miss, a false sharing miss, or a hit. Any miss that would occur if the block size were one word is designated a true sharing miss.

Time	P1	P2
1	Write x1	
2		Read x2
3	Write x1	
4		Write x2
5	Read x2	

Answer   Here are classifications by time step:

1. This event is a true sharing miss, since x1 was read by P2 and needs to be invalidated from P2.

2. This event is a false sharing miss, since x2 was invalidated by the write of x1 in P1, but that value of x1 is not used in P2.

3. This event is a false sharing miss, since the block containing x1 is marked shared due to the read in P2, but P2 did not read x1. The cache block containing x1 will be in the shared state after the read by P2; a write miss is required to obtain exclusive access to the block. In some protocols this will be handled as an *upgrade request,* which generates a bus invalidate, but does not transfer the cache block.

4. This event is a false sharing miss for the same reason as step 3.

5. This event is a true sharing miss, since the value being read was written by P2.

Although we will see the effects of true and false sharing misses in commercial workloads, the role of coherence misses is more significant for tightly coupled applications that share significant amounts of user data. We examine their effects in detail in Appendix H, when we consider the performance of a parallel scientific workload.

A Commercial Workload

In this section, we examine the memory system behavior of a four-processor shared-memory multiprocessor. The results were collected either on an Alpha-Server 4100 or using a configurable simulator modeled after the AlphaServer 4100. Each processor in the AlphaServer 4100 is an Alpha 21164, which issues up to four instructions per clock and runs at 300 MHz. Although the clock rate of the Alpha processor in this system is considerably slower than processors in recent systems, the basic structure of the system, consisting of a four-issue processor and a three-level cache hierarchy, is comparable to many recent systems. In particular, each processor has a three-level cache hierarchy:

■ L1 consists of a pair of 8 KB direct-mapped on-chip caches, one for instruction and one for data. The block size is 32 bytes, and the data cache is write through to L2, using a write buffer.

■ L2 is a 96 KB on-chip unified three-way set associative cache with a 32-byte block size, using write back.

■ L3 is an off-chip, combined, direct-mapped 2 MB cache with 64-byte blocks also using write back.

The latency for an access to L2 is 7 cycles, to L3 it is 21 cycles, and to main memory it is 80 clock cycles (typical without contention). Cache-to-cache transfers, which occur on a miss to an exclusive block held in another cache, require 125 clock cycles. Although these miss penalties are smaller than today's higher clock systems would experience, the caches are also smaller, meaning that a more recent system would likely have lower miss rates but higher miss penalties.

The workload used for this study consists of three applications:

1. An online transaction-processing workload (OLTP) modeled after TPC-B (which has similar memory behavior to its newer cousin TPC-C) and using Oracle 7.3.2 as the underlying database. The workload consists of a set of client processes that generate requests and a set of servers that handle them. The server processes consume 85% of the user time, with the remaining going to the clients. Although the I/O latency is hidden by careful tuning and enough requests to keep the CPU busy, the server processes typically block for I/O after about 25,000 instructions.

2. A decision support system (DSS) workload based on TPC-D and also using Oracle 7.3.2 as the underlying database. The workload includes only 6 of the 17 read queries in TPC-D, although the 6 queries examined in the benchmark span the range of activities in the entire benchmark. To hide the I/O latency, parallelism is exploited both within queries, where parallelism is detected during a query formulation process, and across queries. Blocking calls are much less frequent than in the OLTP benchmark; the 6 queries average about 1.5 million instructions before blocking.

Benchmark	% time user mode	% time kernel	% time CPU idle
OLTP	71	18	11
DSS (average across all queries)	87	4	9
AltaVista	> 98	< 1	< 1

Figure 4.9 The distribution of execution time in the commercial workloads. The OLTP benchmark has the largest fraction of both OS time and CPU idle time (which is I/O wait time). The DSS benchmark shows much less OS time, since it does less I/O, but still more than 9% idle time. The extensive tuning of the AltaVista search engine is clear in these measurements. The data for this workload were collected by Barroso et al. [1998] on a four-processor AlphaServer 4100.

3. A Web index search (AltaVista) benchmark based on a search of a memory-mapped version of the AltaVista database (200 GB). The inner loop is heavily optimized. Because the search structure is static, little synchronization is needed among the threads.

The percentages of time spent in user mode, in the kernel, and in the idle loop are shown in Figure 4.9. The frequency of I/O increases both the kernel time and the idle time (see the OLTP entry, which has the largest I/O-to-computation ratio). AltaVista, which maps the entire search database into memory and has been extensively tuned, shows the least kernel or idle time.

Performance Measurements of the Commercial Workload

We start by looking at the overall CPU execution for these benchmarks on the four-processor system; as discussed on page 220, these benchmarks include substantial I/O time, which is ignored in the CPU time measurements. We group the six DSS queries as a single benchmark, reporting the average behavior. The effective CPI varies widely for these benchmarks, from a CPI of 1.3 for the AltaVista Web search, to an average CPI of 1.6 for the DSS workload, to 7.0 for the OLTP workload. Figure 4.10 shows how the execution time breaks down into instruction execution, cache and memory system access time, and other stalls (which are primarily pipeline resource stalls, but also include TLB and branch mispredict stalls). Although the performance of the DSS and AltaVista workloads is reasonable, the performance of the OLTP workload is very poor, due to a poor performance of the memory hierarchy.

Since the OLTP workload demands the most from the memory system with large numbers of expensive L3 misses, we focus on examining the impact of L3 cache size, processor count, and block size on the OLTP benchmark. Figure 4.11 shows the effect of increasing the cache size, using two-way set associative caches, which reduces the large number of conflict misses. The execution time is improved as the L3 cache grows due to the reduction in L3 misses. Surprisingly,

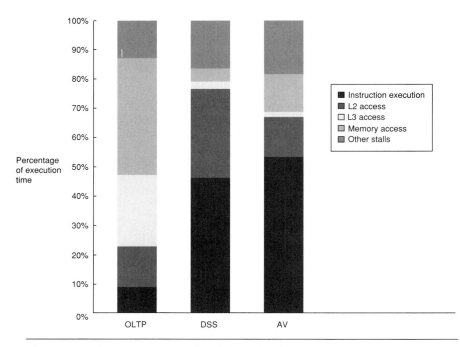

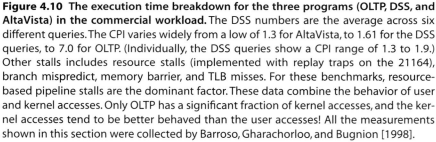

Figure 4.10 The execution time breakdown for the three programs (OLTP, DSS, and AltaVista) in the commercial workload. The DSS numbers are the average across six different queries. The CPI varies widely from a low of 1.3 for AltaVista, to 1.61 for the DSS queries, to 7.0 for OLTP. (Individually, the DSS queries show a CPI range of 1.3 to 1.9.) Other stalls includes resource stalls (implemented with replay traps on the 21164), branch mispredict, memory barrier, and TLB misses. For these benchmarks, resource-based pipeline stalls are the dominant factor. These data combine the behavior of user and kernel accesses. Only OLTP has a significant fraction of kernel accesses, and the kernel accesses tend to be better behaved than the user accesses! All the measurements shown in this section were collected by Barroso, Gharachorloo, and Bugnion [1998].

almost all of the gain occurs in going from 1 to 2 MB, with little additional gain beyond that, despite the fact that cache misses are still a cause of significant performance loss with 2 MB and 4 MB caches. The question is, Why?

To better understand the answer to this question, we need to determine what factors contribute to the L3 miss rate and how they change as the L3 cache grows. Figure 4.12 shows this data, displaying the number of memory access cycles contributed per instruction from five sources. The two largest sources of L3 memory access cycles with a 1 MB L3 are instruction and capacity/conflict misses. With a larger L3 these two sources shrink to be minor contributors. Unfortunately, the compulsory, false sharing, and true sharing misses are unaffected by a larger L3. Thus, at 4 MB and 8 MB, the true sharing misses generate the dominant fraction of the misses; the lack of change in true sharing misses leads to the limited reductions in the overall miss rate when increasing the L3 cache size beyond 2 MB.

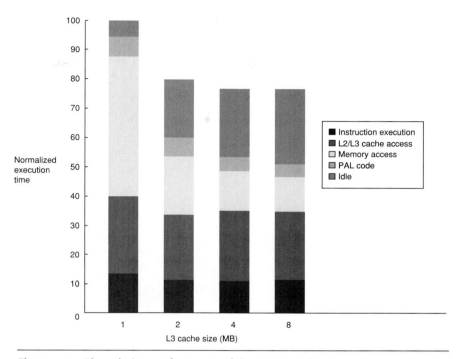

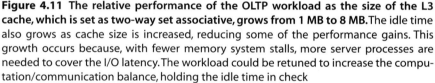

Figure 4.11 The relative performance of the OLTP workload as the size of the L3 cache, which is set as two-way set associative, grows from 1 MB to 8 MB. The idle time also grows as cache size is increased, reducing some of the performance gains. This growth occurs because, with fewer memory system stalls, more server processes are needed to cover the I/O latency. The workload could be retuned to increase the computation/communication balance, holding the idle time in check

Increasing the cache size eliminates most of the uniprocessor misses, while leaving the multiprocessor misses untouched. How does increasing the processor count affect different types of misses? Figure 4.13 shows this data assuming a base configuration with a 2 MB, two-way set associative L3 cache. As we might expect, the increase in the true sharing miss rate, which is not compensated for by any decrease in the uniprocessor misses, leads to an overall increase in the memory access cycles per instruction.

The final question we examine is whether increasing the block size—which should decrease the instruction and cold miss rate and, within limits, also reduce the capacity/conflict miss rate and possibly the true sharing miss rate—is helpful for this workload. Figure 4.14 shows the number of misses per 1000 instructions as the block size is increased from 32 to 256. Increasing the block size from 32 to 256 affects four of the miss rate components:

■   The true sharing miss rate decreases by more than a factor of 2, indicating some locality in the true sharing patterns.

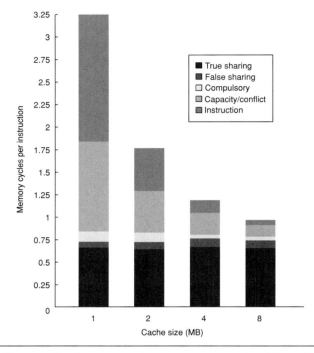

Figure 4.12 The contributing causes of memory access cycles shift as the cache size is increased. The L3 cache is simulated as two-way set associative.

- The compulsory miss rate significantly decreases, as we would expect.

- The conflict/capacity misses show a small decrease (a factor of 1.26 compared to a factor of 8 increase in block size), indicating that the spatial locality is not high in the uniprocessor misses that occur with L3 caches larger than 2 MB.

- The false sharing miss rate, although small in absolute terms, nearly doubles.

The lack of a significant effect on the instruction miss rate is startling. If there were an instruction-only cache with this behavior, we would conclude that the spatial locality is very poor. In the case of a mixed L2 cache, other effects such as instruction-data conflicts may also contribute to the high instruction cache miss rate for larger blocks. Other studies have documented the low spatial locality in the instruction stream of large database and OLTP workloads, which have lots of short basic blocks and special-purpose code sequences. Nonetheless, increasing the block size of the third-level cache to 128 or possibly 256 bytes seems appropriate.

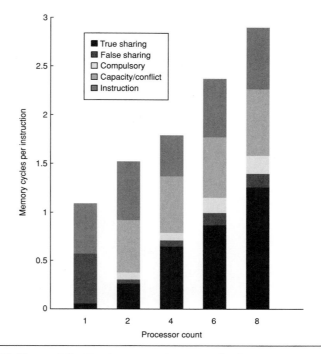

Figure 4.13 The contribution to memory access cycles increases as processor count increases primarily due to increased true sharing. The compulsory misses slightly increase since each processor must now handle more compulsory misses.

A Multiprogramming and OS Workload

Our next study is a multiprogrammed workload consisting of both user activity and OS activity. The workload used is two independent copies of the compile phases of the Andrew benchmark, a benchmark that emulates a software development environment. The compile phase consists of a parallel make using eight processors. The workload runs for 5.24 seconds on eight processors, creating 203 processes and performing 787 disk requests on three different file systems. The workload is run with 128 MB of memory, and no paging activity takes place.

The workload has three distinct phases: compiling the benchmarks, which involves substantial compute activity; installing the object files in a library; and removing the object files. The last phase is completely dominated by I/O and only two processes are active (one for each of the runs). In the middle phase, I/O also plays a major role and the processor is largely idle. The overall workload is much more system and I/O intensive than the highly tuned commercial workload.

For the workload measurements, we assume the following memory and I/O systems:

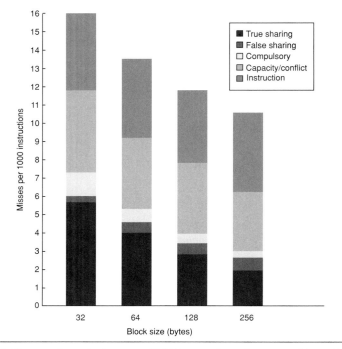

Figure 4.14 **The number of misses per 1000 instructions drops steadily as the block size of the L3 cache is increased, making a good case for an L3 block size of at least 128 bytes.** The L3 cache is 2 MB, two-way set associative.

- *Level 1 instruction cache*—32 KB, two-way set associative with a 64-byte block, 1 clock cycle hit time.

- *Level 1 data cache*—32 KB, two-way set associative with a 32-byte block, 1 clock cycle hit time. We vary the L1 data cache to examine its effect on cache behavior.

- *Level 2 cache*—1 MB unified, two-way set associative with a 128-byte block, hit time 10 clock cycles.

- *Main memory*—Single memory on a bus with an access time of 100 clock cycles.

- *Disk system*—Fixed-access latency of 3 *ms* (less than normal to reduce idle time).

Figure 4.15 shows how the execution time breaks down for the eight processors using the parameters just listed. Execution time is broken into four components:

1. *Idle*—Execution in the kernel mode idle loop

	User execution	Kernel execution	Synchronization wait	CPU idle (waiting for I/O)
% instructions executed	27	3	1	69
% execution time	27	7	2	64

Figure 4.15 The distribution of execution time in the multiprogrammed parallel make workload. The high fraction of idle time is due to disk latency when only one of the eight processors is active. These data and the subsequent measurements for this workload were collected with the SimOS system [Rosenblum et al. 1995]. The actual runs and data collection were done by M. Rosenblum, S. Herrod, and E. Bugnion of Stanford University.

2. *User*—Execution in user code

3. *Synchronization*—Execution or waiting for synchronization variables

4. *Kernel*—Execution in the OS that is neither idle nor in synchronization access

This multiprogramming workload has a significant instruction cache performance loss, at least for the OS. The instruction cache miss rate in the OS for a 64-byte block size, two-way set-associative cache varies from 1.7% for a 32 KB cache to 0.2% for a 256 KB cache. User-level instruction cache misses are roughly one-sixth of the OS rate, across the variety of cache sizes. This partially accounts for the fact that although the user code executes nine times as many instructions as the kernel, those instructions take only about four times as long as the smaller number of instructions executed by the kernel.

Performance of the Multiprogramming and OS Workload

In this subsection we examine the cache performance of the multiprogrammed workload as the cache size and block size are changed. Because of differences between the behavior of the kernel and that of the user processes, we keep these two components separate. Remember, though, that the user processes execute more than eight times as many instructions, so that the overall miss rate is determined primarily by the miss rate in user code, which, as we will see, is often one-fifth of the kernel miss rate.

Although the user code executes more instructions, the behavior of the operating system can cause more cache misses than the user processes for two reasons beyond larger code size and lack of locality. First, the kernel initializes all pages before allocating them to a user, which significantly increases the compulsory component of the kernel's miss rate. Second, the kernel actually shares data and thus has a nontrivial coherence miss rate. In contrast, user processes cause coherence misses only when the process is scheduled on a different processor, and this component of the miss rate is small.

Figure 4.16 shows the data miss rate versus data cache size and versus block size for the kernel and user components. Increasing the data cache size affects the user miss rate more than it affects the kernel miss rate. Increasing the block size has beneficial effects for both miss rates, since a larger fraction of the misses arise from compulsory and capacity, both of which can be potentially improved with larger block sizes. Since coherence misses are relatively rarer, the negative effects of increasing block size are small. To understand why the kernel and user processes behave differently, we can look at the how the kernel misses behave.

Figure 4.17 shows the variation in the kernel misses versus increases in cache size and in block size. The misses are broken into three classes: compulsory misses. coherence misses (from both true and false sharing), and capacity/conflict misses (which include misses caused by interference between the OS and the user process and between multiple user processes). Figure 4.17 confirms that, for the kernel references, increasing the cache size reduces solely the uniprocessor capacity/conflict miss rate. In contrast, increasing the block size causes a reduction in the compulsory miss rate. The absence of large increases in the coherence miss rate as block size is increased means that false sharing effects are probably insignificant, although such misses may be offsetting some of the gains from reducing the true sharing misses.

If we examine the number of bytes needed per data reference, as in Figure 4.18, we see that the kernel has a higher traffic ratio that grows with block size. It

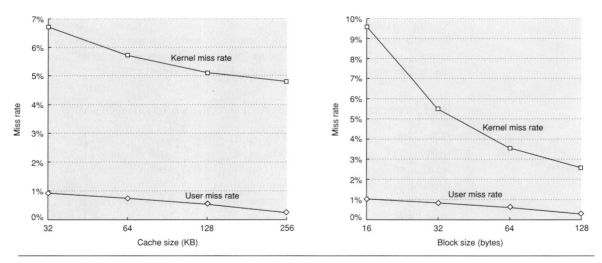

Figure 4.16 **The data miss rates for the user and kernel components behave differently for increases in the L1 data cache size (on the left) versus increases in the L1 data cache block size (on the right).** Increasing the L1 data cache from 32 KB to 256 KB (with a 32-byte block) causes the user miss rate to decrease proportionately more than the kernel miss rate: the user-level miss rate drops by almost a factor of 3, while the kernel-level miss rate drops only by a factor of 1.3. The miss rate for both user and kernel components drops steadily as the L1 block size is increased (while keeping the L1 cache at 32 KB). In contrast to the effects of increasing the cache size, increasing the block size improves the kernel miss rate more significantly (just under a factor of 4 for the kernel references when going from 16-byte to 128-byte blocks versus just under a factor of 3 for the user references).

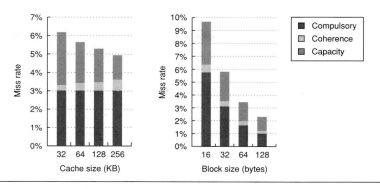

Figure 4.17 The components of the kernel data miss rate change as the L1 data cache size is increased from 32 KB to 256 KB, when the multiprogramming workload is run on eight processors. The compulsory miss rate component stays constant, since it is unaffected by cache size. The capacity component drops by more than a factor of 2, while the coherence component nearly doubles. The increase in coherence misses occurs because the probability of a miss being caused by an invalidation increases with cache size, since fewer entries are bumped due to capacity. As we would expect, the increasing block size of the L1 data cache substantially reduces the compulsory miss rate in the kernel references. It also has a significant impact on the capacity miss rate, decreasing it by a factor of 2.4 over the range of block sizes. The increased block size has a small reduction in coherence traffic, which appears to stabilize at 64 bytes, with no change in the coherence miss rate in going to 128-byte lines. Because there are not significant reductions in the coherence miss rate as the block size increases, the fraction of the miss rate due to coherence grows from about 7% to about 15%.

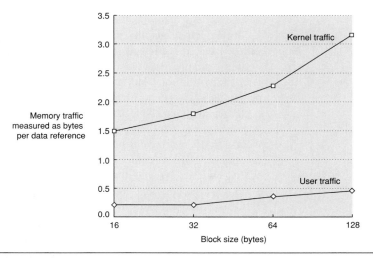

Figure 4.18 The number of bytes needed per data reference grows as block size is increased for both the kernel and user components. It is interesting to compare this chart against the data on scientific programs shown in Appendix H.

is easy to see why this occurs: when going from a 16-byte block to a 128-byte block, the miss rate drops by about 3.7, but the number of bytes transferred per miss increases by 8, so the total miss traffic increases by just over a factor of 2. The user program also more than doubles as the block size goes from 16 to 128 bytes, but it starts out at a much lower level.

For the multiprogrammed workload, the OS is a much more demanding user of the memory system. If more OS or OS-like activity is included in the workload, and the behavior is similar to what was measured for this workload, it will become very difficult to build a sufficiently capable memory system. One possible route to improving performance is to make the OS more cache aware, through either better programming environments or through programmer assistance. For example, the OS reuses memory for requests that arise from different system calls. Despite the fact that the reused memory will be completely overwritten, the hardware, not recognizing this, will attempt to preserve coherency and the possibility that some portion of a cache block may be read, even if it is not. This behavior is analogous to the reuse of stack locations on procedure invocations. The IBM Power series has support to allow the compiler to indicate this type of behavior on procedure invocations. It is harder to detect such behavior by the OS, and doing so may require programmer assistance, but the payoff is potentially even greater.

4.4 Distributed Shared Memory and Directory-Based Coherence

As we saw in Section 4.2, a snooping protocol requires communication with all caches on every cache miss, including writes of potentially shared data. The absence of any centralized data structure that tracks the state of the caches is both the fundamental advantage of a snooping-based scheme, since it allows it to be inexpensive, as well as its Achilles' heel when it comes to scalability.

For example, with only 16 processors, a block size of 64 bytes, and a 512 KB data cache, the total bus bandwidth demand (ignoring stall cycles) for the four programs in the scientific/technical workload of Appendix H ranges from about 4 GB/sec to about 170 GB/sec, assuming a processor that sustains one data reference per clock, which for a 4 GHz clock is four data references per ns, which is what a 2006 superscalar processor with nonblocking caches might generate. In comparison, the memory bandwidth of the highest-performance centralized shared-memory 16-way multiprocessor in 2006 was 2.4 GB/sec per processor. In 2006, multiprocessors with a distributed-memory model are available with over 12 GB/sec per processor to the nearest memory.

We can increase the memory bandwidth and interconnection bandwidth by distributing the memory, as shown in Figure 4.2 on page 201; this immediately separates local memory traffic from remote memory traffic, reducing the bandwidth demands on the memory system and on the interconnection network. Unless we eliminate the need for the coherence protocol to broadcast on every cache miss, distributing the memory will gain us little.

As we mentioned earlier, the alternative to a snoop-based coherence protocol is a *directory protocol*. A directory keeps the state of every block that may be cached. Information in the directory includes which caches have copies of the block, whether it is dirty, and so on. A directory protocol also can be used to reduce the bandwidth demands in a centralized shared-memory machine, as the Sun T1 design does (see Section 4.8.) We explain a directory protocol as if it were implemented with a distributed memory, but the same design also applies to a centralized memory organized into banks.

The simplest directory implementations associate an entry in the directory with each memory block. In such implementations, the amount of information is proportional to the product of the number of memory blocks (where each block is the same size as the level 2 or level 3 cache block) and the number of processors. This overhead is not a problem for multiprocessors with less than about 200 processors because the directory overhead with a reasonable block size will be tolerable. For larger multiprocessors, we need methods to allow the directory structure to be efficiently scaled. The methods that have been used either try to keep information for fewer blocks (e.g., only those in caches rather than all memory blocks) or try to keep fewer bits per entry by using individual bits to stand for a small collection of processors.

To prevent the directory from becoming the bottleneck, the directory is distributed along with the memory (or with the interleaved memory banks in an SMP), so that different directory accesses can go to different directories, just as different memory requests go to different memories. A distributed directory retains the characteristic that the sharing status of a block is always in a single known location. This property is what allows the coherence protocol to avoid broadcast. Figure 4.19 shows how our distributed-memory multiprocessor looks with the directories added to each node.

Directory-Based Cache Coherence Protocols: The Basics

Just as with a snooping protocol, there are two primary operations that a directory protocol must implement: handling a read miss and handling a write to a shared, clean cache block. (Handling a write miss to a block that is currently shared is a simple combination of these two.) To implement these operations, a directory must track the state of each cache block. In a simple protocol, these states could be the following:

■   *Shared*—One or more processors have the block cached, and the value in memory is up to date (as well as in all the caches).

■   *Uncached*—No processor has a copy of the cache block.

■   *Modified*—Exactly one processor has a copy of the cache block, and it has written the block, so the memory copy is out of date. The processor is called the *owner* of the block.

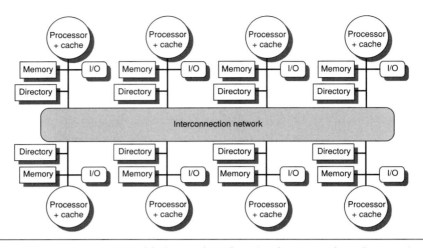

Figure 4.19 A directory is added to each node to implement cache coherence in a distributed-memory multiprocessor. Each directory is responsible for tracking the caches that share the memory addresses of the portion of memory in the node. The directory may communicate with the processor and memory over a common bus, as shown, or it may have a separate port to memory, or it may be part of a central node controller through which all intranode and internode communications pass.

In addition to tracking the state of each potentially shared memory block, we must track which processors have copies of that block, since those copies will need to be invalidated on a write. The simplest way to do this is to keep a bit vector for each memory block. When the block is shared, each bit of the vector indicates whether the corresponding processor has a copy of that block. We can also use the bit vector to keep track of the owner of the block when the block is in the exclusive state. For efficiency reasons, we also track the state of each cache block at the individual caches.

The states and transitions for the state machine at each cache are identical to what we used for the snooping cache, although the actions on a transition are slightly different. The process of invalidating or locating an exclusive copy of a data item are different, since they both involve communication between the requesting node and the directory and between the directory and one or more remote nodes. In a snooping protocol, these two steps are combined through the use of a broadcast to all nodes.

Before we see the protocol state diagrams, it is useful to examine a catalog of the message types that may be sent between the processors and the directories for the purpose of handling misses and maintaining coherence. Figure 4.20 shows the type of messages sent among nodes. The *local node* is the node where a request originates. The *home node* is the node where the memory location and the directory entry of an address reside. The physical address space is statically distributed, so the node that contains the memory and directory for a given physical address is known. For example, the high-order bits may provide the node number,

Message type	Source	Destination	Message contents	Function of this message
Read miss	local cache	home directory	P, A	Processor P has a read miss at address A; request data and make P a read sharer.
Write miss	local cache	home directory	P, A	Processor P has a write miss at address A; request data and make P the exclusive owner.
Invalidate	local cache	home directory	A	Request to send invalidates to all remote caches that are caching the block at address A.
Invalidate	home directory	remote cache	A	Invalidate a shared copy of data at address A.
Fetch	home directory	remote cache	A	Fetch the block at address A and send it to its home directory; change the state of A in the remote cache to shared.
Fetch/invalidate	home directory	remote cache	A	Fetch the block at address A and send it to its home directory; invalidate the block in the cache.
Data value reply	home directory	local cache	D	Return a data value from the home memory.
Data write back	remote cache	home directory	A, D	Write back a data value for address A.

Figure 4.20 The possible messages sent among nodes to maintain coherence, along with the source and destination node, the contents (where P = requesting processor number, A = requested address, and D = data contents), and the function of the message. The first three messages are requests sent by the local cache to the home. The fourth through sixth messages are messages sent to a remote cache by the home when the home needs the data to satisfy a read or write miss request. Data value replies are used to send a value from the home node back to the requesting node. Data value write backs occur for two reasons: when a block is replaced in a cache and must be written back to its home memory, and also in reply to fetch or fetch/invalidate messages from the home. Writing back the data value whenever the block becomes shared simplifies the number of states in the protocol, since any dirty block must be exclusive and any shared block is always available in the home memory.

while the low-order bits provide the offset within the memory on that node. The local node may also be the home node. The directory must be accessed when the home node is the local node, since copies may exist in yet a third node, called a *remote node.*

A remote node is the node that has a copy of a cache block, whether exclusive (in which case it is the only copy) or shared. A remote node may be the same as either the local node or the home node. In such cases, the basic protocol does not change, but interprocessor messages may be replaced with intraprocessor messages.

In this section, we assume a simple model of memory consistency. To minimize the type of messages and the complexity of the protocol, we make an assumption that messages will be received and acted upon in the same order they are sent. This assumption may not be true in practice and can result in additional complications, some of which we address in Section 4.6 when we discuss memory consistency models. In this section, we use this assumption to ensure that invalidates sent by a processor are honored before new messages are transmitted, just as we assumed in the discussion of implementing snooping protocols. As we did in the snooping case, we omit some details necessary to implement the coherence protocol. In particular, the serialization of writes and knowing that the invalidates for a write have completed are not as simple as in the broadcast-based snooping mechanism. Instead, explicit acknowledgements are required in response to write misses and invalidate requests. We discuss these issues in more detail in Appendix H.

An Example Directory Protocol

The basic states of a cache block in a directory-based protocol are exactly like those in a snooping protocol, and the states in the directory are also analogous to those we showed earlier. Thus we can start with simple state diagrams that show the state transitions for an individual cache block and then examine the state diagram for the directory entry corresponding to each block in memory. As in the snooping case, these state transition diagrams do not represent all the details of a coherence protocol; however, the actual controller is highly dependent on a number of details of the multiprocessor (message delivery properties, buffering structures, and so on). In this section we present the basic protocol state diagrams. The knotty issues involved in implementing these state transition diagrams are examined in Appendix H.

Figure 4.21 shows the protocol actions to which an individual cache responds. We use the same notation as in the last section, with requests coming from outside the node in gray and actions in bold. The state transitions for an individual cache are caused by read misses, write misses, invalidates, and data fetch requests; these operations are all shown in Figure 4.21. An individual cache also generates read miss, write miss, and invalidate messages that are sent to the home directory. Read and write misses require data value replies, and these events wait for replies before changing state. Knowing when invalidates complete is a separate problem and is handled separately.

The operation of the state transition diagram for a cache block in Figure 4.21 is essentially the same as it is for the snooping case: The states are identical, and the stimulus is almost identical. The write miss operation, which was broadcast on the bus (or other network) in the snooping scheme, is replaced by the data fetch and invalidate operations that are selectively sent by the directory controller. Like the snooping protocol, any cache block must be in the exclusive state when it is written, and any shared block must be up to date in memory.

In a directory-based protocol, the directory implements the other half of the coherence protocol. A message sent to a directory causes two different types of actions: updating the directory state and sending additional messages to satisfy the request. The states in the directory represent the three standard states for a block; unlike in a snoopy scheme, however, the directory state indicates the state of all the cached copies of a memory block, rather than for a single cache block.

The memory block may be uncached by any node, cached in multiple nodes and readable (shared), or cached exclusively and writable in exactly one node. In addition to the state of each block, the directory must track the set of processors

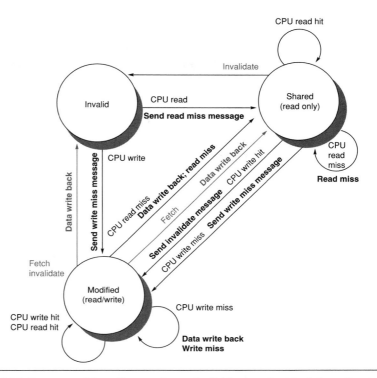

Figure 4.21 State transition diagram for an individual cache block in a directory-based system. Requests by the local processor are shown in black, and those from the home directory are shown in gray. The states are identical to those in the snooping case, and the transactions are very similar, with explicit invalidate and write-back requests replacing the write misses that were formerly broadcast on the bus. As we did for the snooping controller, we assume that an attempt to write a shared cache block is treated as a miss; in practice, such a transaction can be treated as an ownership request or upgrade request and can deliver ownership without requiring that the cache block be fetched.

that have a copy of a block; we use a set called *Sharers* to perform this function. In multiprocessors with less than 64 nodes (each of which may represent two to four times as many processors), this set is typically kept as a bit vector. In larger multiprocessors, other techniques are needed. Directory requests need to update the set Sharers and also read the set to perform invalidations.

Figure 4.22 shows the actions taken at the directory in response to messages received. The directory receives three different requests: read miss, write miss, and data write back. The messages sent in response by the directory are shown in bold, while the updating of the set Sharers is shown in bold italics. Because all the stimulus messages are external, all actions are shown in gray. Our simplified protocol assumes that some actions are atomic, such as requesting a value and sending it to another node; a realistic implementation cannot use this assumption.

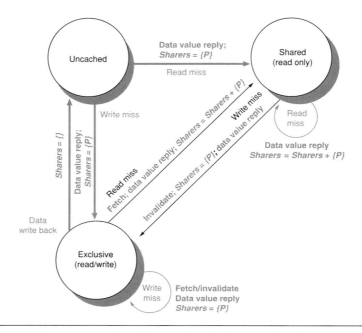

Figure 4.22 The state transition diagram for the directory has the same states and structure as the transition diagram for an individual cache. All actions are in gray because they are all externally caused. Bold indicates the action taken by the directory in response to the request.

To understand these directory operations, let's examine the requests received and actions taken state by state. When a block is in the uncached state, the copy in memory is the current value, so the only possible requests for that block are

■ *Read miss*—The requesting processor is sent the requested data from memory, and the requestor is made the only sharing node. The state of the block is made shared.

■ *Write miss*—The requesting processor is sent the value and becomes the sharing node. The block is made exclusive to indicate that the only valid copy is cached. Sharers indicates the identity of the owner.

When the block is in the shared state, the memory value is up to date, so the same two requests can occur:

■ *Read miss*—The requesting processor is sent the requested data from memory, and the requesting processor is added to the sharing set.

■ *Write miss*—The requesting processor is sent the value. All processors in the set Sharers are sent invalidate messages, and the Sharers set is to contain the identity of the requesting processor. The state of the block is made exclusive.

When the block is in the exclusive state, the current value of the block is held in the cache of the processor identified by the set Sharers (the owner), so there are three possible directory requests:

- *Read miss*—The owner processor is sent a data fetch message, which causes the state of the block in the owner's cache to transition to shared and causes the owner to send the data to the directory, where it is written to memory and sent back to the requesting processor. The identity of the requesting processor is added to the set Sharers, which still contains the identity of the processor that was the owner (since it still has a readable copy).

- *Data write back*—The owner processor is replacing the block and therefore must write it back. This write back makes the memory copy up to date (the home directory essentially becomes the owner), the block is now uncached, and the Sharers set is empty.

- *Write miss*—The block has a new owner. A message is sent to the old owner, causing the cache to invalidate the block and send the value to the directory, from which it is sent to the requesting processor, which becomes the new owner. Sharers is set to the identity of the new owner, and the state of the block remains exclusive.

This state transition diagram in Figure 4.22 is a simplification, just as it was in the snooping cache case. In the case of a directory, as well as a snooping scheme implemented with a network other than a bus, our protocols will need to deal with nonatomic memory transactions. Appendix H explores these issues in depth.

The directory protocols used in real multiprocessors contain additional optimizations. In particular, in this protocol when a read or write miss occurs for a block that is exclusive, the block is first sent to the directory at the home node. From there it is stored into the home memory and also sent to the original requesting node. Many of the protocols in use in commercial multiprocessors forward the data from the owner node to the requesting node directly (as well as performing the write back to the home). Such optimizations often add complexity by increasing the possibility of deadlock and by increasing the types of messages that must be handled.

Implementing a directory scheme requires solving most of the same challenges we discussed for snoopy protocols beginning on page 217. There are, however, new and additional problems, which we describe in Appendix H.

4.5   Synchronization: The Basics

Synchronization mechanisms are typically built with user-level software routines that rely on hardware-supplied synchronization instructions. For smaller multiprocessors or low-contention situations, the key hardware capability is an uninterruptible instruction or instruction sequence capable of atomically retrieving and changing a value. Software synchronization mechanisms are then constructed using this capability. In this section we focus on the implementation of lock and unlock synchronization operations. Lock and unlock can be used straightforwardly to create mutual exclusion, as well as to implement more complex synchronization mechanisms.

In larger-scale multiprocessors or high-contention situations, synchronization can become a performance bottleneck because contention introduces additional delays and because latency is potentially greater in such a multiprocessor. We discuss how the basic synchronization mechanisms of this section can be extended for large processor counts in Appendix H.

Basic Hardware Primitives

The key ability we require to implement synchronization in a multiprocessor is a set of hardware primitives with the ability to atomically read and modify a memory location. Without such a capability, the cost of building basic synchronization primitives will be too high and will increase as the processor count increases. There are a number of alternative formulations of the basic hardware primitives, all of which provide the ability to atomically read and modify a location, together with some way to tell if the read and write were performed atomically. These hardware primitives are the basic building blocks that are used to build a wide variety of user-level synchronization operations, including things such as locks and barriers. In general, architects do not expect users to employ the basic hardware primitives, but instead expect that the primitives will be used by system programmers to build a synchronization library, a process that is often complex and tricky. Let's start with one such hardware primitive and show how it can be used to build some basic synchronization operations.

One typical operation for building synchronization operations is the *atomic exchange,* which interchanges a value in a register for a value in memory. To see how to use this to build a basic synchronization operation, assume that we want to build a simple lock where the value 0 is used to indicate that the lock is free and 1 is used to indicate that the lock is unavailable. A processor tries to set the lock by doing an exchange of 1, which is in a register, with the memory address corresponding to the lock. The value returned from the exchange instruction is 1 if some other processor had already claimed access and 0 otherwise. In the latter case, the value is also changed to 1, preventing any competing exchange from also retrieving a 0.

For example, consider two processors that each try to do the exchange simultaneously: This race is broken since exactly one of the processors will perform the exchange first, returning 0, and the second processor will return 1 when it does the exchange. The key to using the exchange (or swap) primitive to implement synchronization is that the operation is atomic: The exchange is indivisible, and two simultaneous exchanges will be ordered by the write serialization mechanisms. It is impossible for two processors trying to set the synchronization variable in this manner to both think they have simultaneously set the variable.

There are a number of other atomic primitives that can be used to implement synchronization. They all have the key property that they read and update a memory value in such a manner that we can tell whether or not the two operations executed atomically. One operation, present in many older multiprocessors, is *test-and-set*, which tests a value and sets it if the value passes the test. For example, we could define an operation that tested for 0 and set the value to 1, which can be used in a fashion similar to how we used atomic exchange. Another atomic synchronization primitive is *fetch-and-increment:* It returns the value of a memory location and atomically increments it. By using the value 0 to indicate that the synchronization variable is unclaimed, we can use fetch-and-increment, just as we used exchange. There are other uses of operations like fetch-and-increment, which we will see shortly.

Implementing a single atomic memory operation introduces some challenges, since it requires both a memory read and a write in a single, uninterruptible instruction. This requirement complicates the implementation of coherence, since the hardware cannot allow any other operations between the read and the write, and yet must not deadlock.

An alternative is to have a pair of instructions where the second instruction returns a value from which it can be deduced whether the pair of instructions was executed as if the instructions were atomic. The pair of instructions is effectively atomic if it appears as if all other operations executed by any processor occurred before or after the pair. Thus, when an instruction pair is effectively atomic, no other processor can change the value between the instruction pair.

The pair of instructions includes a special load called a *load linked* or *load locked* and a special store called a *store conditional*. These instructions are used in sequence: If the contents of the memory location specified by the load linked are changed before the store conditional to the same address occurs, then the store conditional fails. If the processor does a context switch between the two instructions, then the store conditional also fails. The store conditional is defined to return 1 if it was successful and a 0 otherwise. Since the load linked returns the initial value and the store conditional returns 1 only if it succeeds, the following sequence implements an atomic exchange on the memory location specified by the contents of R1:

```
try:    MOV     R3,R4           ;mov exchange value
        LL      R2,0(R1)        ;load linked
        SC      R3,0(R1)        ;store conditional
        BEQZ    R3,try          ;branch store fails
        MOV     R4,R2           ;put load value in R4
```

At the end of this sequence the contents of R4 and the memory location specified by R1 have been atomically exchanged (ignoring any effect from delayed branches). Any time a processor intervenes and modifies the value in memory between the LL and SC instructions, the SC returns 0 in R3, causing the code sequence to try again.

An advantage of the load linked/store conditional mechanism is that it can be used to build other synchronization primitives. For example, here is an atomic fetch-and-increment:

```
try:    LL      R2,0(R1)   ;load linked
        DADDUI  R3,R2,#1   ;increment
        SC      R3,0(R1)   ;store conditional
        BEQZ    R3,try     ;branch store fails
```

These instructions are typically implemented by keeping track of the address specified in the LL instruction in a register, often called the *link register*. If an interrupt occurs, or if the cache block matching the address in the link register is invalidated (for example, by another SC), the link register is cleared. The SC instruction simply checks that its address matches that in the link register. If so, the SC succeeds; otherwise, it fails. Since the store conditional will fail after either another attempted store to the load linked address or any exception, care must be taken in choosing what instructions are inserted between the two instructions. In particular, only register-register instructions can safely be permitted; otherwise, it is possible to create deadlock situations where the processor can never complete the SC. In addition, the number of instructions between the load linked and the store conditional should be small to minimize the probability that either an unrelated event or a competing processor causes the store conditional to fail frequently.

Implementing Locks Using Coherence

Once we have an atomic operation, we can use the coherence mechanisms of a multiprocessor to implement *spin locks*—locks that a processor continuously tries to acquire, spinning around a loop until it succeeds. Spin locks are used when programmers expect the lock to be held for a very short amount of time and when they want the process of locking to be low latency when the lock is available. Because spin locks tie up the processor, waiting in a loop for the lock to become free, they are inappropriate in some circumstances.

The simplest implementation, which we would use if there were no cache coherence, would keep the lock variables in memory. A processor could continually try to acquire the lock using an atomic operation, say, exchange, and test whether the exchange returned the lock as free. To release the lock, the processor simply stores the value 0 to the lock. Here is the code sequence to lock a spin lock whose address is in R1 using an atomic exchange:

```
        DADDUI  R2,R0,#1
lockit: EXCH    R2,0(R1)   ;atomic exchange
        BNEZ    R2,lockit  ;already locked?
```

If our multiprocessor supports cache coherence, we can cache the locks using the coherence mechanism to maintain the lock value coherently. Caching locks has two advantages. First, it allows an implementation where the process of "spinning" (trying to test and acquire the lock in a tight loop) could be done on a local cached copy rather than requiring a global memory access on each attempt to acquire the lock. The second advantage comes from the observation that there is often locality in lock accesses: that is, the processor that used the lock last will use it again in the near future. In such cases, the lock value may reside in the cache of that processor, greatly reducing the time to acquire the lock.

Obtaining the first advantage—being able to spin on a local cached copy rather than generating a memory request for each attempt to acquire the lock—requires a change in our simple spin procedure. Each attempt to exchange in the loop directly above requires a write operation. If multiple processors are attempting to get the lock, each will generate the write. Most of these writes will lead to write misses, since each processor is trying to obtain the lock variable in an exclusive state.

Thus, we should modify our spin lock procedure so that it spins by doing reads on a local copy of the lock until it successfully sees that the lock is available. Then it attempts to acquire the lock by doing a swap operation. A processor first reads the lock variable to test its state. A processor keeps reading and testing until the value of the read indicates that the lock is unlocked. The processor then races against all other processes that were similarly "spin waiting" to see who can lock the variable first. All processes use a swap instruction that reads the old value and stores a 1 into the lock variable. The single winner will see the 0, and the losers will see a 1 that was placed there by the winner. (The losers will continue to set the variable to the locked value, but that doesn't matter.) The winning processor executes the code after the lock and, when finished, stores a 0 into the lock variable to release the lock, which starts the race all over again. Here is the code to perform this spin lock (remember that 0 is unlocked and 1 is locked):

```
lockit:   LD       R2,0(R1)      ;load of lock
          BNEZ     R2,lockit     ;not available-spin
          DADDUI   R2,R0,#1      ;load locked value
          EXCH     R2,0(R1)      ;swap
          BNEZ     R2,lockit     ;branch if lock wasn't 0
```

Let's examine how this "spin lock" scheme uses the cache coherence mechanisms. Figure 4.23 shows the processor and bus or directory operations for multiple processes trying to lock a variable using an atomic swap. Once the processor with the lock stores a 0 into the lock, all other caches are invalidated and must fetch the new value to update their copy of the lock. One such cache gets the copy of the unlocked value (0) first and performs the swap. When the cache miss of other processors is satisfied, they find that the variable is already locked, so they must return to testing and spinning.

Step	Processor P0	Processor P1	Processor P2	Coherence state of lock	Bus/directory activity
1	Has lock	Spins, testing if lock = 0	Spins, testing if lock = 0	Shared	None
2	Set lock to 0	(Invalidate received)	(Invalidate received)	Exclusive (P0)	Write invalidate of lock variable from P0
3		Cache miss	Cache miss	Shared	Bus/directory services P2 cache miss; write back from P0
4		(Waits while bus/ directory busy)	Lock = 0	Shared	Cache miss for P2 satisfied
5		Lock = 0	Executes swap, gets cache miss	Shared	Cache miss for P1 satisfied
6		Executes swap, gets cache miss	Completes swap: returns 0 and sets Lock = 1	Exclusive (P2)	Bus/directory services P2 cache miss; generates invalidate
7		Swap completes and returns 1, and sets Lock = 1	Enter critical section	Exclusive (P1)	Bus/directory services P1 cache miss; generates write back
8		Spins, testing if lock = 0			None

Figure 4.23 Cache coherence steps and bus traffic for three processors, P0, P1, and P2. This figure assumes write invalidate coherence. P0 starts with the lock (step 1). P0 exits and unlocks the lock (step 2). P1 and P2 race to see which reads the unlocked value during the swap (steps 3–5). P2 wins and enters the critical section (steps 6 and 7), while P1's attempt fails so it starts spin waiting (steps 7 and 8). In a real system, these events will take many more than 8 clock ticks, since acquiring the bus and replying to misses takes much longer.

This example shows another advantage of the load linked/store conditional primitives: The read and write operations are explicitly separated. The load linked need not cause any bus traffic. This fact allows the following simple code sequence, which has the same characteristics as the optimized version using exchange (R1 has the address of the lock, the LL has replaced the LD, and the SC has replaced the EXCH):

```
lockit:  LL      R2,0(R1)      ;load linked
         BNEZ    R2,lockit     ;not available-spin
         DADDUI  R2,R0,#1      ;locked value
         SC      R2,0(R1)      ;store
         BEQZ    R2,lockit     ;branch if store fails
```

The first branch forms the spinning loop; the second branch resolves races when two processors see the lock available simultaneously.

Although our spin lock scheme is simple and compelling, it has difficulty scaling up to handle many processors because of the communication traffic generated when the lock is released. We address this issue and other issues for larger processor counts in Appendix H.

4.6 Models of Memory Consistency: An Introduction

Cache coherence ensures that multiple processors see a consistent view of memory. It does not answer the question of *how* consistent the view of memory must be. By "how consistent" we mean, when must a processor see a value that has been updated by another processor? Since processors communicate through shared variables (used both for data values and for synchronization), the question boils down to this: In what order must a processor observe the data writes of another processor? Since the only way to "observe the writes of another processor" is through reads, the question becomes, What properties must be enforced among reads and writes to different locations by different processors?

Although the question of how consistent memory must be seems simple, it is remarkably complicated, as we can see with a simple example. Here are two code segments from processes P1 and P2, shown side by side:

```
P1:     A = 0;            P2:     B = 0;
        .....                     .....
        A = 1;                    B = 1;
L1:     if (B == 0) ...   L2:     if (A == 0)...
```

Assume that the processes are running on different processors, and that locations A and B are originally cached by both processors with the initial value of 0. If writes always take immediate effect and are immediately seen by other processors, it will be impossible for *both* if statements (labeled L1 and L2) to evaluate their conditions as true, since reaching the if statement means that either A or B must have been assigned the value 1. But suppose the write invalidate is delayed, and the processor is allowed to continue during this delay; then it is possible that both P1 and P2 have not seen the invalidations for B and A (respectively) *before* they attempt to read the values. The question is, Should this behavior be allowed, and if so, under what conditions?

The most straightforward model for memory consistency is called *sequential consistency*. Sequential consistency requires that the result of any execution be the same as if the memory accesses executed by each processor were kept in order and the accesses among different processors were arbitrarily interleaved. Sequential consistency eliminates the possibility of some nonobvious execution in the previous example because the assignments must be completed before the if statements are initiated.

The simplest way to implement sequential consistency is to require a processor to delay the completion of any memory access until all the invalidations caused by that access are completed. Of course, it is equally effective to delay the next memory access until the previous one is completed. Remember that memory consistency involves operations among different variables: the two accesses that must be ordered are actually to different memory locations. In our example, we must delay the read of A or B (A == 0 or B == 0) until the previous write has completed (B = 1 or A = 1). Under sequential consistency, we cannot, for example, simply place the write in a write buffer and continue with the read.

Although sequential consistency presents a simple programming paradigm, it reduces potential performance, especially in a multiprocessor with a large number of processors or long interconnect delays, as we can see in the following example.

Example   Suppose we have a processor where a write miss takes 50 cycles to establish ownership, 10 cycles to issue each invalidate after ownership is established, and 80 cycles for an invalidate to complete and be acknowledged once it is issued. Assuming that four other processors share a cache block, how long does a write miss stall the writing processor if the processor is sequentially consistent? Assume that the invalidates must be explicitly acknowledged before the coherence controller knows they are completed. Suppose we could continue executing after obtaining ownership for the write miss without waiting for the invalidates; how long would the write take?

Answer   When we wait for invalidates, each write takes the sum of the ownership time plus the time to complete the invalidates. Since the invalidates can overlap, we need only worry about the last one, which starts 10 + 10 + 10 + 10 = 40 cycles after ownership is established. Hence the total time for the write is 50 + 40 + 80 = 170 cycles. In comparison, the ownership time is only 50 cycles. With appropriate write buffer implementations, it is even possible to continue before ownership is established.

To provide better performance, researchers and architects have explored two different routes. First, they developed ambitious implementations that preserve sequential consistency but use latency-hiding techniques to reduce the penalty; we discuss these in Section 4.7. Second, they developed less restrictive memory consistency models that allow for faster hardware. Such models can affect how the programmer sees the multiprocessor, so before we discuss these less restrictive models, let's look at what the programmer expects.

The Programmer's View

Although the sequential consistency model has a performance disadvantage, from the viewpoint of the programmer it has the advantage of simplicity. The challenge is to develop a programming model that is simple to explain and yet allows a high-performance implementation.

One such programming model that allows us to have a more efficient implementation is to assume that programs are *synchronized*. A program is synchronized if all access to shared data are ordered by synchronization operations. A data reference is ordered by a synchronization operation if, in every possible execution, a write of a variable by one processor and an access (either a read or a write) of that variable by another processor are separated by a pair of synchronization operations, one executed after the write by the writing processor and one executed before the access by the second processor. Cases where variables may be updated without ordering by synchronization are called *data races* because the execution outcome depends on the relative speed of the processors, and like races in hardware design, the outcome is unpredictable, which leads to another name for synchronized programs: *data-race-free*.

As a simple example, consider a variable being read and updated by two different processors. Each processor surrounds the read and update with a lock and an unlock, both to ensure mutual exclusion for the update and to ensure that the read is consistent. Clearly, every write is now separated from a read by the other processor by a pair of synchronization operations: one unlock (after the write) and one lock (before the read). Of course, if two processors are writing a variable with no intervening reads, then the writes must also be separated by synchronization operations.

It is a broadly accepted observation that most programs are synchronized. This observation is true primarily because if the accesses were unsynchronized, the behavior of the program would likely be unpredictable because the speed of execution would determine which processor won a data race and thus affect the results of the program. Even with sequential consistency, reasoning about such programs is very difficult.

Programmers could attempt to guarantee ordering by constructing their own synchronization mechanisms, but this is extremely tricky, can lead to buggy programs, and may not be supported architecturally, meaning that they may not work in future generations of the multiprocessor. Instead, almost all programmers will choose to use synchronization libraries that are correct and optimized for the multiprocessor and the type of synchronization.

Finally, the use of standard synchronization primitives ensures that even if the architecture implements a more relaxed consistency model than sequential consistency, a synchronized program will behave as if the hardware implemented sequential consistency.

Relaxed Consistency Models: The Basics

The key idea in relaxed consistency models is to allow reads and writes to complete out of order, but to use synchronization operations to enforce ordering, so that a synchronized program behaves as if the processor were sequentially consistent. There are a variety of relaxed models that are classified according to what read and write orderings they relax. We specify the orderings by a set of rules of the form X→Y, meaning that operation X must complete before operation Y is done. Sequential consistency requires maintaining all four possible orderings: R→W, R→R, W→R, and W→W. The relaxed models are defined by which of these four sets of orderings they relax:

1. Relaxing the W→R ordering yields a model known as *total store ordering* or *processor consistency*. Because this ordering retains ordering among writes, many programs that operate under sequential consistency operate under this model, without additional synchronization.

2. Relaxing the W→W ordering yields a model known as *partial store order*.

3. Relaxing the R→W and R→R orderings yields a variety of models including *weak ordering*, the PowerPC consistency model, and *release consistency*, depending on the details of the ordering restrictions and how synchronization operations enforce ordering.

By relaxing these orderings, the processor can possibly obtain significant performance advantages. There are, however, many complexities in describing relaxed consistency models, including the advantages and complexities of relaxing different orders, defining precisely what it means for a write to complete, and deciding when processors can see values that the processor itself has written. For more information about the complexities, implementation issues, and performance potential from relaxed models, we highly recommend the excellent tutorial by Adve and Gharachorloo [1996].

Final Remarks on Consistency Models

At the present time, many multiprocessors being built support some sort of relaxed consistency model, varying from processor consistency to release consistency. Since synchronization is highly multiprocessor specific and error prone, the expectation is that most programmers will use standard synchronization libraries and will write synchronized programs, making the choice of a weak consistency model invisible to the programmer and yielding higher performance.

An alternative viewpoint, which we discuss more extensively in the next section, argues that with speculation much of the performance advantage of relaxed consistency models can be obtained with sequential or processor consistency.

A key part of this argument in favor of relaxed consistency revolves around the role of the compiler and its ability to optimize memory access to potentially shared variables; this topic is also discussed in the next section.

4.7 Crosscutting Issues

Because multiprocessors redefine many system characteristics (e.g., performance assessment, memory latency, and the importance of scalability), they introduce interesting design problems that cut across the spectrum, affecting both hardware and software. In this section we give several examples related to the issue of memory consistency.

Compiler Optimization and the Consistency Model

Another reason for defining a model for memory consistency is to specify the range of legal compiler optimizations that can be performed on shared data. In explicitly parallel programs, unless the synchronization points are clearly defined and the programs are synchronized, the compiler could not interchange a read and a write of two different shared data items because such transformations might affect the semantics of the program. This prevents even relatively simple optimizations, such as register allocation of shared data, because such a process usually interchanges reads and writes. In implicitly parallelized programs—for example, those written in High Performance FORTRAN (HPF)—programs must be synchronized and the synchronization points are known, so this issue does not arise.

Using Speculation to Hide Latency in Strict Consistency Models

As we saw in Chapter 2, speculation can be used to hide memory latency. It can also be used to hide latency arising from a strict consistency model, giving much of the benefit of a relaxed memory model. The key idea is for the processor to use dynamic scheduling to reorder memory references, letting them possibly execute out of order. Executing the memory references out of order may generate violations of sequential consistency, which might affect the execution of the program. This possibility is avoided by using the delayed commit feature of a speculative processor. Assume the coherency protocol is based on invalidation. If the processor receives an invalidation for a memory reference before the memory reference is committed, the processor uses speculation recovery to back out the computation and restart with the memory reference whose address was invalidated.

If the reordering of memory requests by the processor yields an execution order that could result in an outcome that differs from what would have been seen under sequential consistency, the processor will redo the execution. The key to using this approach is that the processor need only guarantee that the result would be the same as if all accesses were completed in order, and it can achieve this by detecting when the results might differ. The approach is attractive because the speculative restart will rarely be triggered. It will only be triggered when there are unsynchronized accesses that actually cause a race [Gharachorloo, Gupta, and Hennessy 1992].

Hill [1998] advocates the combination of sequential or processor consistency together with speculative execution as the consistency model of choice. His argument has three parts. First, an aggressive implementation of either sequential consistency or processor consistency will gain most of the advantage of a more relaxed model. Second, such an implementation adds very little to the implementation cost of a speculative processor. Third, such an approach allows the programmer to reason using the simpler programming models of either sequential or processor consistency.

The MIPS R10000 design team had this insight in the mid-1990s and used the R10000's out-of-order capability to support this type of aggressive implementation of sequential consistency. Hill's arguments are likely to motivate others to follow this approach.

One open question is how successful compiler technology will be in optimizing memory references to shared variables. The state of optimization technology and the fact that shared data are often accessed via pointers or array indexing have limited the use of such optimizations. If this technology became available and led to significant performance advantages, compiler writers would want to be able to take advantage of a more relaxed programming model.

Inclusion and Its Implementation

All multiprocessors use multilevel cache hierarchies to reduce both the demand on the global interconnect and the latency of cache misses. If the cache also provides *multilevel inclusion*—every level of cache hierarchy is a subset of the level further away from the processor—then we can use the multilevel structure to reduce the contention between coherence traffic and processor traffic that occurs when snoops and processor cache accesses must contend for the cache. Many multiprocessors with multilevel caches enforce the inclusion property, although recent multiprocessors with smaller L1 caches and different block sizes have sometimes chosen not to enforce inclusion. This restriction is also called the *subset property* because each cache is a subset of the cache below it in the hierarchy.

At first glance, preserving the multilevel inclusion property seems trivial. Consider a two-level example: any miss in L1 either hits in L2 or generates a miss in L2, causing it to be brought into both L1 and L2. Likewise, any invalidate that hits in L2 must be sent to L1, where it will cause the block to be invalidated if it exists.

The catch is what happens when the block sizes of L1 and L2 are different. Choosing different block sizes is quite reasonable, since L2 will be much larger and have a much longer latency component in its miss penalty, and thus will want to use a larger block size. What happens to our "automatic" enforcement of inclusion when the block sizes differ? A block in L2 represents multiple blocks in L1, and a miss in L2 causes the replacement of data that is equivalent to multiple L1 blocks. For example, if the block size of L2 is four times that of L1, then a miss in L2 will replace the equivalent of four L1 blocks. Let's consider a detailed example.

Example   Assume that L2 has a block size four times that of L1. Show how a miss for an address that causes a replacement in L1 and L2 can lead to violation of the inclusion property.

Answer   Assume that L1 and L2 are direct mapped and that the block size of L1 is b bytes and the block size of L2 is $4b$ bytes. Suppose L1 contains two blocks with starting addresses x and $x + b$ and that $x \bmod 4b = 0$, meaning that x also is the starting address of a block in L2; then that single block in L2 contains the L1 blocks x, $x + b$, $x + 2b$, and $x + 3b$. Suppose the processor generates a reference to block y that maps to the block containing x in both caches and hence misses. Since L2 missed, it fetches $4b$ bytes and replaces the block containing x, $x + b$, $x + 2b$, and $x + 3b$, while L1 takes b bytes and replaces the block containing x. Since L1 still contains $x + b$, but L2 does not, the inclusion property no longer holds.

To maintain inclusion with multiple block sizes, we must probe the higher levels of the hierarchy when a replacement is done at the lower level to ensure that any words replaced in the lower level are invalidated in the higher-level caches; different levels of associativity create the same sort of problems. In 2006, designers appear to be split on the enforcement of inclusion. Baer and Wang [1988] describe the advantages and challenges of inclusion in detail.

4.8 Putting It All Together: The Sun T1 Multiprocessor

T1 is a multicore multiprocessor introduced by Sun in 2005 as a server processor. What makes T1 especially interesting is that it is almost totally focused on exploiting thread-level parallelism (TLP) rather than instruction-level parallelism (ILP). Indeed, it is the only single-issue desktop or server microprocessor introduced in more than five years. Instead of focusing on ILP, T1 puts all its attention on TLP, using both multiple cores and multithreading to produce throughput.

Each T1 processor contains eight processor cores, each supporting four threads. Each processor core consists of a simple six-stage, single-issue pipeline (a standard five-stage RISC pipeline like that of Appendix A, with one stage added for thread switching). T1 uses fine-grained multithreading, switching to a new thread on each clock cycle, and threads that are idle because they are waiting due to a pipeline delay or cache miss are bypassed in the scheduling. The processor is idle only when all four threads are idle or stalled. Both loads and branches incur a 3-cycle delay that can only be hidden by other threads. A single set of floating-point functional units is shared by all eight cores, as floating-point performance was not a focus for T1.

Figure 4.24 shows the organization of the T1 processor. The cores access four level 2 caches via a crossbar switch, which also provides access to the shared floating-point unit. Coherency is enforced among the L1 caches by a directory associated with each L2 cache block. The directory operates analogously to those we discussed in Section 4.4, but is used to track which L1 caches have copies of an L2 block. By associating each L2 cache with a particular memory bank and enforcing the subset property, T1 can place the directory at L2 rather than at the memory, which reduces the directory overhead. Because the L1 data cache is write through, only invalidation messages are required; the data can always be retrieved from the L2 cache.

Figure 4.25 summarizes the T1 processor.

T1 Performance

We look at the performance of T1 using three server-oriented benchmarks: TPC-C, SPECJBB (the SPEC Java Business Benchmark), and SPECWeb99. The SPECWeb99 benchmark is run on a four-core version of T1 because it cannot scale to use the full 32 threads of an eight-core processor; the other two benchmarks are run with eight cores and 4 threads each for a total of 32 threads.

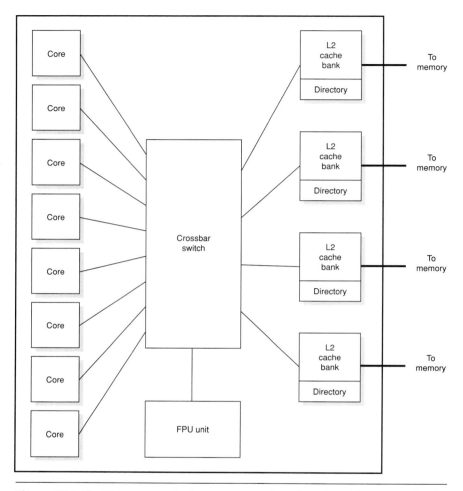

Figure 4.24 The T1 processor. Each core supports four threads and has its own level 1 caches (16 KB for instructions and 8 KB for data). The level 2 caches total 3 MB and are effectively 12-way associative. The caches are interleaved by 64-byte cache lines.

We begin by looking at the effect of multithreading on the performance of the memory system when running in single-threaded versus multithreaded mode. Figure 4.26 shows the relative increase in the miss rate and the observed miss latency when executing with 1 thread per core versus executing 4 threads per core for TPC-C. Both the miss rates and the miss latencies increase, due to increased contention in the memory system. The relatively small increase in miss latency indicates that the memory system still has unused capacity.

As we demonstrated in the previous section, the performance of multiprocessor workloads depends intimately on the memory system and the interaction with

Characteristic	Sun T1
Multiprocessor and multithreading support	Eight cores per chip; four threads per core. Fine-grained thread scheduling. One shared floating-point unit for eight cores. Supports only on-chip multiprocessing.
Pipeline structure	Simple, in-order, six-deep pipeline with 3-cycle delays for loads and branches.
L1 caches	16 KB instructions; 8 KB data. 64-byte block size. Miss to L2 is 23 cycles, assuming no contention.
L2 caches	Four separate L2 caches, each 750 KB and associated with a memory bank. 64-byte block size. Miss to main memory is 110 clock cycles assuming no contention.
Initial implementation	90 nm process; maximum clock rate of 1.2 GHz; power 79 W; 300M transistors, 379 mm^2 die.

Figure 4.25   A summary of the T1 processor.

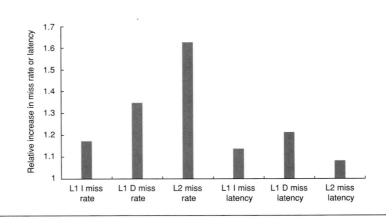

Figure 4.26   The relative change in the miss rates and miss latencies when executing with 1 thread per core versus 4 threads per core on the TPC-C benchmark. The latencies are the actual time to return the requested data after a miss. In the 4-thread case, the execution of other threads could potentially hide much of this latency.

the application. For T1 both the L2 cache size and the block size are key parameters. Figure 4.27 shows the effect on miss rates from varying the L2 cache size by a factor of 2 from the base of 3 MB and by reducing the block size to 32 bytes. The data clearly show a significant advantage of a 3 MB L2 versus a 1.5 MB; further improvements can be gained from a 6 MB L2. As we can see, the choice of a 64-byte block size reduces the miss rate but by considerably less than a factor of 2. Hence, using the larger block size T1 generates more traffic to the memories. Whether this has a significant performance impact depends on the characteristics of the memory system.

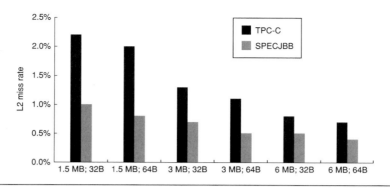

Figure 4.27 Change in the L2 miss rate with variation in cache size and block size. Both TPC-C and SPECJBB are run with all eight cores and four threads per core. Recall that T1 has a 3 MB L2 with 64-byte lines.

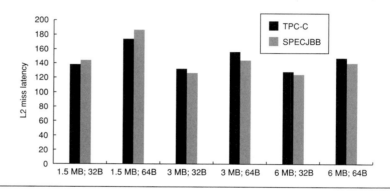

Figure 4.28 The change in the miss latency of the L2 cache as the cache size and block size are changed. Although TPC-C has a significantly higher miss rate, its miss penalty is only slightly higher. This is because SPECJBB has a much higher dirty miss rate, requiring L2 cache lines to be written back with high frequency. Recall that T1 has a 3 MB L2 with 64-byte lines.

As we mentioned earlier, there is some contention at the memory from multiple threads. How do the cache size and block size affect the contention at the memory system? Figure 4.28 shows the effect on the L2 cache miss latency under the same variations as we saw in Figure 4.27. As we can see, for either a 3 MB or 6 MB cache, the larger block size results in a smaller L2 cache miss time. How can this be if the miss rate changes much less than a factor of 2? As we will see in more detail in the next chapter, modern DRAMs provide a block of data for only slightly more time than needed to provide a single word; thus, the miss penalty for the 32-byte block is only slightly less than the 64-byte block.

Overall Performance

Figure 4.29 shows the per-thread and per-core CPI, as well as the effective instructions per clock (IPC) for the eight-processor chip. Because T1 is a fine-grained multithreaded processor with four threads per core, with sufficient parallelism the ideal effective CPI per thread would be 4, since that would mean that each thread was consuming one cycle out of every four. The ideal CPI per core would be 1. The effective IPC for T1 is simply 8 divided by the per-core CPI.

At first glance, one might react that T1 is not very efficient, since the effective throughout is between 56% and 71% of the ideal on these three benchmarks. But, consider the comparative performance of a wide-issue superscalar. Processors such as the Itanium 2 (higher transistor count, much higher power, comparable silicon area) would need to achieve incredible instruction throughput sustaining 4.5–5.7 instructions per clock, well more than double the acknowledged IPC. It appears quite clear that, at least for integer-oriented server applications with thread-level parallelism, a multicore approach is a much better alternative than a single very wide issue processor. The next subsection offers some performance comparisons among multicore processors.

By looking at the behavior of an average thread, we can understand the interaction between multithreading and parallel processing. Figure 4.30 shows the percentage of cycles for which a thread is executing, ready but not executing, and not ready. Remember that not ready does not imply that the core with that thread is stalled; it is only when all four threads are not ready that the core will stall.

Threads can be not ready due to cache misses, pipeline delays (arising from long latency instructions such as branches, loads, floating point, or integer multiply/divide), and a variety of smaller effects. Figure 4.31 shows the relative frequency of these various causes. Cache effects are responsible for the thread not being ready from 50% to 75% of the time, with L1 instruction misses, L1 data misses, and L2 misses contributing roughly equally. Potential delays from the pipeline (called "pipeline delay") are most severe in SPECJBB and may arise from its higher branch frequency.

Benchmark	Per-thread CPI	Per core CPI	Effective CPI for eight cores	Effective IPC for eight cores
TPC-C	7.2	1.8	0.225	4.4
SPECJBB	5.6	1.40	0.175	5.7
SPECWeb99	6.6	1.65	0.206	4.8

Figure 4.29 The per-thread CPI, the per-core CPI, the effective eight-core CPI, and the effective IPC (inverse of CPI) for the eight-core T1 processor.

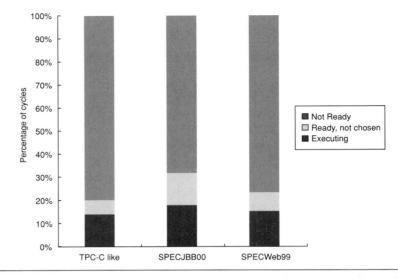

Figure 4.30 Breakdown of the status on an average thread. Executing indicates the thread issues an instruction in that cycle. Ready but not chosen means it could issue, but another thread has been chosen, and *not ready* indicates that the thread is awaiting the completion of an event (a pipeline delay or cache miss, for example).

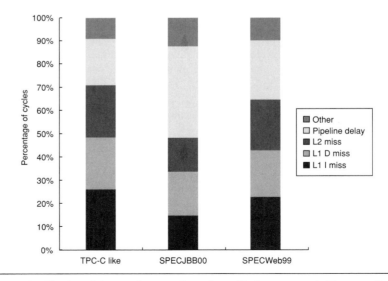

Figure 4.31 The breakdown of causes for a thread being not ready. The contribution to the "other" category varies. In TPC-C, store buffer full is the largest contributor; in SPEC-JBB, atomic instructions are the largest contributor; and in SPECWeb99, both factors contribute.

Performance of Multicore Processors on SPEC Benchmarks

Among recent processors, T1 is uniquely characterized by an intense focus on thread-level parallelism versus instruction-level parallelism. It uses multithreading to achieve performance from a simple RISC pipeline, and it uses multiprocessing with eight cores on a die to achieve high throughput for server applications. In contrast, the dual-core Power5, Opteron, and Pentium D use both multiple issue and multicore. Of course, exploiting significant ILP requires much bigger processors, with the result being that fewer cores fit on a chip in comparison to T1. Figure 4.32 summarizes the features of these multicore chips.

In addition to the differences in emphasis on ILP versus TLP, there are several other fundamental differences in the designs. Among the most important are

- There are significant differences in floating-point support and performance. The Power5 puts a major emphasis on floating-point performance, the Opteron and Pentium allocate significant resources, and the T1 almost ignores it. As a result, Sun is unlikely to provide any benchmark results for floating-point applications. A comparison that included only integer programs would be unfair to the three processors that include significant floating-point hardware (and the silicon and power cost associated with it). In contrast, a comparison using only floating-point applications would be unfair to the T1.

- The multiprocessor expandability of these systems differs and that affects the memory system design and the use of external interfaces. Power5 is designed

Characteristic	SUN T1	AMD Opteron	Intel Pentium D	IBM Power5
Cores	8	2	2	2
Instruction issues per clock per core	1	3	3	4
Multithreading	Fine-grained	No	SMT	SMT
Caches L1 I/D in KB per core L2 per core/shared L3 (off-chip)	16/8 3 MB shared	64/64 1 MB/core	12K uops/16 1 MB/core	64/32 L2: 1.9 MB shared L3: 36 MB
Peak memory bandwidth (DDR2 DRAMs)	34.4 GB/sec	8.6 GB/sec	4.3 GB/sec	17.2 GB/sec
Peak MIPS FLOPS	9600 1200	7200 4800 (w. SSE)	9600 6400 (w. SSE)	7600 7600
Clock rate (GHz)	1.2	2.4	3.2	1.9
Transistor count (M)	300	233	230	276
Die size (mm^2)	379	199	206	389
Power (W)	79	110	130	125

Figure 4.32 Summary of the features and characteristics of four multicore processors.

for the most expandability. The Pentium and Opteron design offer limited multiprocessor support. The T1 is not expandable to a larger system.

■ The implementation technologies vary, making comparisons based on die size and power more difficult.

■ There are significant differences in the assumptions about memory systems and the memory bandwidth available. For benchmarks with high cache miss rates, such as TPC-C and similar programs, the processors with larger memory bandwidth have a significant advantage.

Nonetheless, given the importance of the trade-off between ILP-centric and TLP-centric designs, it would be useful to try to quantify the performance differences as well as the efficacy of the approaches. Figure 4.33 shows the performance of the four multicore processors using the SPECRate CPU benchmarks, the SPECJBB2005 Java business benchmark, the SPECWeb05 Web server benchmark, and a TPC-C-like benchmark.

Figure 4.34 shows efficiency measures in terms of performance per unit die area and per watt for the four dual-core processors, with the results normalized to the measurement on the Pentium D. The most obvious distinction is the significant advantage in terms of performance/watt for the Sun T1 processor on the TPC-C-like and SPECJBB05 benchmarks. These measurements clearly demonstrate that for multithreaded applications, a TLP approach may be much more power efficient than an ILP-intensive approach. This is the strongest evidence to date that the TLP route may provide a way to increase performance in a power-efficient fashion.

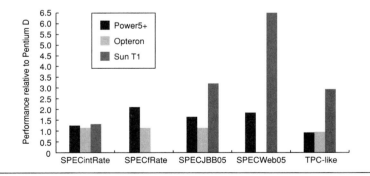

Figure 4.33 Four dual-core processors showing their performance on a variety of SPEC benchmarks and a TPC-C-like benchmark. All the numbers are normalized to the Pentium D (which is therefore at 1 for all the benchmarks). Some results are estimates from slightly larger configurations (e.g., four cores and two processors, rather than two cores and one processor), including the Opteron SPECJBB2005 result, the Power5 SPECWeb05 result, and the TPC-C results for the Power5, Opteron, and Pentium D. At the current time, Sun has refused to release SPECRate results for either the integer or FP portion of the suite.

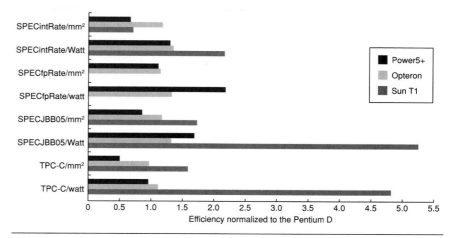

Figure 4.34 Performance efficiency on SPECRate for four dual-core processors, normalized to the Pentium D metric (which is always 1).

It is too early to conclude whether the TLP-intensive approaches will win across the board. If typical server applications have enough threads to keep T1 busy and the per-thread performance is acceptable, the T1 approach will be tough to beat. If single-threaded performance remains important in server or desktop environments, then we may see the market further fracture with significantly different processors for throughput-oriented environments and environments where higher single-thread performance remains important.

4.9 Fallacies and Pitfalls

Given the lack of maturity in our understanding of parallel computing, there are many hidden pitfalls that will be uncovered either by careful designers or by unfortunate ones. Given the large amount of hype that has surrounded multiprocessors, especially at the high end, common fallacies abound. We have included a selection of these.

Pitfall *Measuring performance of multiprocessors by linear speedup versus execution time.*

"Mortar shot" graphs—plotting performance versus number of processors, showing linear speedup, a plateau, and then a falling off—have long been used to judge the success of parallel processors. Although speedup is one facet of a parallel program, it is not a direct measure of performance. The first question is the power of the processors being scaled: A program that linearly improves performance to equal 100 Intel 486s may be slower than the sequential version on a Pentium 4. Be especially careful of floating-point-intensive programs; processing elements without hardware assist may scale wonderfully but have poor collective performance.

Comparing execution times is fair only if you are comparing the best algorithms on each computer. Comparing the identical code on two computers may seem fair, but it is not; the parallel program may be slower on a uniprocessor than a sequential version. Developing a parallel program will sometimes lead to algorithmic improvements, so that comparing the previously best-known sequential program with the parallel code—which seems fair—will not compare equivalent algorithms. To reflect this issue, the terms *relative speedup* (same program) and *true speedup* (best program) are sometimes used.

Results that suggest *superlinear* performance, when a program on *n* processors is more than *n* times faster than the equivalent uniprocessor, may indicate that the comparison is unfair, although there are instances where "real" superlinear speedups have been encountered. For example, some scientific applications regularly achieve superlinear speedup for small increases in processor count (2 or 4 to 8 or 16). These results usually arise because critical data structures that do not fit into the aggregate caches of a multiprocessor with 2 or 4 processors fit into the aggregate cache of a multiprocessor with 8 or 16 processors.

In summary, comparing performance by comparing speedups is at best tricky and at worst misleading. Comparing the speedups for two different multiprocessors does not necessarily tell us anything about the relative performance of the multiprocessors. Even comparing two different algorithms on the same multiprocessor is tricky, since we must use true speedup, rather than relative speedup, to obtain a valid comparison.

Fallacy   *Amdahl's Law doesn't apply to parallel computers.*

In 1987, the head of a research organization claimed that Amdahl's Law (see Section 1.9) had been broken by an MIMD multiprocessor. This statement hardly meant, however, that the law has been overturned for parallel computers; the neglected portion of the program will still limit performance. To understand the basis of the media reports, let's see what Amdahl [1967] originally said:

> A fairly obvious conclusion which can be drawn at this point is that the effort expended on achieving high parallel processing rates is wasted unless it is accompanied by achievements in sequential processing rates of very nearly the same magnitude. [p. 483]

One interpretation of the law was that since portions of every program must be sequential, there is a limit to the useful economic number of processors—say, 100. By showing linear speedup with 1000 processors, this interpretation of Amdahl's Law was disproved.

The basis for the statement that Amdahl's Law had been "overcome" was the use of *scaled speedup*. The researchers scaled the benchmark to have a data set size that is 1000 times larger and compared the uniprocessor and parallel execution times of the scaled benchmark. For this particular algorithm the sequential portion of the program was constant independent of the size of the input, and the rest was fully parallel—hence, linear speedup with 1000 processors. Because the running time grew faster than linear, the program actually ran longer after scaling, even with 1000 processors.

Speedup that assumes scaling of the input is not the same as true speedup and reporting it as if it were misleading. Since parallel benchmarks are often run on different-sized multiprocessors, it is important to specify what type of application scaling is permissible and how that scaling should be done. Although simply scaling the data size with processor count is rarely appropriate, assuming a fixed problem size for a much larger processor count is often inappropriate as well, since it is likely that users given a much larger multiprocessor would opt to run a larger or more detailed version of an application. In Appendix H, we discuss different methods for scaling applications for large-scale multiprocessors, introducing a model called *time-constrained scaling*, which scales the application data size so that execution time remains constant across a range of processor counts.

Fallacy   *Linear speedups are needed to make multiprocessors cost-effective.*

It is widely recognized that one of the major benefits of parallel computing is to offer a "shorter time to solution" than the fastest uniprocessor. Many people, however, also hold the view that parallel processors cannot be as cost-effective as uniprocessors unless they can achieve perfect linear speedup. This argument says that because the cost of the multiprocessor is a linear function of the number of processors, anything less than linear speedup means that the ratio of performance/cost decreases, making a parallel processor less cost-effective than using a uniprocessor.

The problem with this argument is that cost is not only a function of processor count, but also depends on memory, I/O, and the overhead of the system (box, power supply, interconnect, etc.).

The effect of including memory in the system cost was pointed out by Wood and Hill [1995]. We use an example based on more recent data using TPC-C and SPECRate benchmarks, but the argument could also be made with a parallel scientific application workload, which would likely make the case even stronger.

Figure 4.35 shows the speedup for TPC-C, SPECintRate and SPECfpRate on an IBM eserver p5 multiprocessor configured with 4 to 64 processors. The figure shows that only TPC-C achieves better than linear speedup. For SPECintRate and SPECfpRate, speedup is less than linear, but so is the cost, since unlike TPC-C the amount of main memory and disk required both scale less than linearly.

As Figure 4.36 shows, larger processor counts can actually be more cost-effective than the four-processor configuration. In the future, as the cost of multiple processors decreases compared to the cost of the support infrastructure (cabinets, power supplies, fans, etc.), the performance/cost ratio of larger processor configurations will improve further.

In comparing the cost-performance of two computers, we must be sure to include accurate assessments of both total system cost and what performance is achievable. For many applications with larger memory demands, such a comparison can dramatically increase the attractiveness of using a multiprocessor.

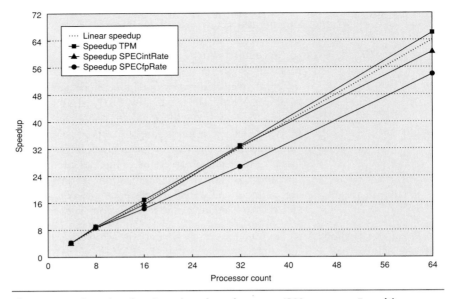

Figure 4.35 Speedup for three benchmarks on an IBM eserver p5 multiprocessor when configured with 4, 8, 16, 32, and 64 processors. The dashed line shows linear speedup.

Fallacy *Scalability is almost free.*

The goal of scalable parallel computing was a focus of much of the research and a significant segment of the high-end multiprocessor development from the mid-1980s through the late 1990s. In the first half of that period, it was widely held that you could build scalability into a multiprocessor and then simply offer the multiprocessor at any point on the scale from a small to large number of processors without sacrificing cost-effectiveness. The difficulty with this view is that multiprocessors that scale to larger processor counts require substantially more investment (in both dollars and design time) in the interprocessor communication network, as well as in aspects such as operating system support, reliability, and reconfigurability.

As an example, consider the Cray T3E, which used a 3D torus capable of scaling to 2048 processors as an interconnection network. At 128 processors, it delivers a peak bisection bandwidth of 38.4 GB/sec, or 300 MB/sec per processor. But for smaller configurations, the contemporaneous Compaq AlphaServer ES40 could accept up to 4 processors and has 5.6 GB/sec of interconnect bandwidth, or almost four times the bandwidth per processor. Furthermore, the cost per processor in a Cray T3E is several times higher than the cost in the ES40.

Scalability is also not free in software: To build software applications that scale requires significantly more attention to load balance, locality, potential contention for shared resources, and the serial (or partly parallel) portions of the

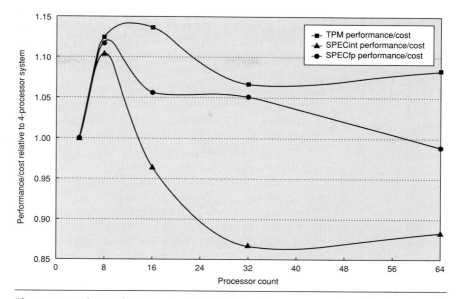

Figure 4.36 The performance/cost relative to a 4-processor system for three bench-marks run on an IBM eserver p5 multiprocessor containing from 4 to 64 processors shows that the larger processor counts can be as cost-effective as the 4-processor configuration. For TPC-C the configurations are those used in the official runs, which means that disk and memory scale nearly linearly with processor count, and a 64-processor machine is approximately twice as expensive as a 32-processor version. In contrast, the disk and memory are scaled more slowly (although still faster than necessary to achieve the best SPECRate at 64 processors). In particular the disk configurations go from one drive for the 4-processor version to four drives (140 GB) for the 64-processor version. Memory is scaled from 8 GB for the 4-processor system to 20 GB for the 64-processor system.

program. Obtaining scalability for real applications, as opposed to toys or small kernels, across factors of more than five in processor count, is a *major* challenge. In the future, new programming approaches, better compiler technology, and performance analysis tools may help with this critical problem, on which little progress has been made in 30 years.

Pitfall *Not developing the software to take advantage of, or optimize for, a multiprocessor architecture.*

There is a long history of software lagging behind on massively parallel processors, possibly because the software problems are much harder. We give one example to show the subtlety of the issues, but there are many examples we could choose from!

One frequently encountered problem occurs when software designed for a uniprocessor is adapted to a multiprocessor environment. For example, the SGI operating system originally protected the page table data structure with a single lock, assuming that page allocation is infrequent. In a uniprocessor, this does not represent a performance problem. In a multiprocessor, it can become a major performance bottleneck for some programs. Consider a program that uses a large number of pages that are initialized at start-up, which UNIX does for statically allocated pages. Suppose the program is parallelized so that multiple processes allocate the pages. Because page allocation requires the use of the page table data structure, which is locked whenever it is in use, even an OS kernel that allows multiple threads in the OS will be serialized if the processes all try to allocate their pages at once (which is exactly what we might expect at initialization time!).

This page table serialization eliminates parallelism in initialization and has significant impact on overall parallel performance. This performance bottleneck persists even under multiprogramming. For example, suppose we split the parallel program apart into separate processes and run them, one process per processor, so that there is no sharing between the processes. (This is exactly what one user did, since he reasonably believed that the performance problem was due to unintended sharing or interference in his application.) Unfortunately, the lock still serializes all the processes—so even the multiprogramming performance is poor. This pitfall indicates the kind of subtle but significant performance bugs that can arise when software runs on multiprocessors. Like many other key software components, the OS algorithms and data structures must be rethought in a multiprocessor context. Placing locks on smaller portions of the page table effectively eliminates the problem. Similar problems exist in memory structures, which increases the coherence traffic in cases where no sharing is actually occurring.

4.10 Concluding Remarks

For more than 30 years, researchers and designers have predicted the end of uniprocessors and their dominance by multiprocessors. During this time period the rise of microprocessors and their rapid performance growth has largely limited the role of multiprocessing to limited market segments. In 2006, we are clearly at an inflection point where multiprocessors and thread-level parallelism will play a greater role across the entire computing spectrum. This change is driven by several phenomena:

1. The use of parallel processing in some domains is much better understood. First among these is the domain of scientific and engineering computation. This application domain has an almost limitless thirst for more computation. It also has many applications that have lots of natural parallelism. Nonetheless, it has not been easy: Programming parallel processors even for these applications remains very challenging, as we discuss further in Appendix H.

2. The growth in server applications for transaction processing and Web services, as well as multiprogrammed environments, has been enormous, and

these applications have inherent and more easily exploited parallelism, through the processing of independent threads

3. After almost 20 years of breakneck performance improvement, we are in the region of diminishing returns for exploiting ILP, at least as we have known it. Power issues, complexity, and increasing inefficiency has forced designers to consider alternative approaches. Exploiting thread-level parallelism is the next natural step.

4. Likewise, for the past 50 years, improvements in clock rate have come from improved transistor speed. As we begin to see reductions in such improvements both from technology limitations and from power consumption, exploiting multiprocessor parallelism is increasingly attractive.

In the 1995 edition of this text, we concluded the chapter with a discussion of two then-current controversial issues:

1. What architecture would very large-scale, microprocessor-based multiprocessors use?

2. What was the role for multiprocessing in the future of microprocessor architecture?

The intervening years have largely resolved these two questions.

Because very large-scale multiprocessors did not become a major and growing market, the only cost-effective way to build such large-scale multiprocessors was to use clusters where the individual nodes are either single microprocessors or moderate-scale, shared-memory multiprocessors, which are simply incorporated into the design. We discuss the design of clusters and their interconnection in Appendices E and H.

The answer to the second question has become clear only recently, but it has become astonishingly clear. The future performance growth in microprocessors, at least for the next five years, will almost certainly come from the exploitation of thread-level parallelism through multicore processors rather than through exploiting more ILP. In fact, we are even seeing designers opt to exploit less ILP in future processors, instead concentrating their attention and hardware resources on more thread-level parallelism. The Sun T1 is a step in this direction, and in March 2006, Intel announced that its next round of multicore processors would be based on a core that is less aggressive in exploiting ILP than the Pentium 4 Netburst core. The best balance between ILP and TLP will probably depend on a variety of factors including the applications mix.

In the 1980s and 1990s, with the birth and development of ILP, software in the form of optimizing compilers that could exploit ILP was key to its success. Similarly, the successful exploitation of thread-level parallelism will depend as much on the development of suitable software systems as it will on the contributions of computer architects. Given the slow progress on parallel software in the past thirty-plus years, it is likely that exploiting thread-level parallelism broadly will remain challenging for years to come.

4.11	# Historical Perspective and References

Section K.5 on the companion CD looks at the history of multiprocessors and parallel processing. Divided by both time period and architecture, the section includes discussions on early experimental multiprocessors and some of the great debates in parallel processing. Recent advances are also covered. References for further reading are included.

Case Studies with Exercises by David A. Wood

Case Study 1: Simple, Bus-Based Multiprocessor

Concepts illustrated by this case study

■ Snooping Coherence Protocol Transitions

■ Coherence Protocol Performance

■ Coherence Protocol Optimizations

■ Synchronization

The simple, bus-based multiprocessor illustrated in Figure 4.37 represents a commonly implemented symmetric shared-memory architecture. Each processor has a single, private cache with coherence maintained using the snooping coherence protocol of Figure 4.7. Each cache is direct-mapped, with four blocks each holding two words. To simplify the illustration, the cache-address tag contains the full address and each word shows only two hex characters, with the least significant word on the right. The coherence states are denoted M, S, and I for Modified, Shared, and Invalid.

4.1 [10/10/10/10/10/10/10] <4.2> For each part of this exercise, assume the initial cache and memory state as illustrated in Figure 4.37. Each part of this exercise specifies a sequence of one or more CPU operations of the form:

```
P#: <op> <address> [ <-- <value> ]
```

where P# designates the CPU (e.g., P0), <op> is the CPU operation (e.g., read or write), <address> denotes the memory address, and <value> indicates the new word to be assigned on a write operation.

Treat each action below as independently applied to the initial state as given in Figure 4.37. What is the resulting state (i.e., coherence state, tags, and data) of the caches and memory after the given action? Show only the blocks that change, for example, P0.B0: (I, 120, 00 01) indicates that CPU P0's block B0 has the final state of I, tag of 120, and data words 00 and 01. Also, what value is returned by each read operation?

a. [10] <4.2> P0: read 120

b. [10] <4.2> P0: write 120 <-- 80

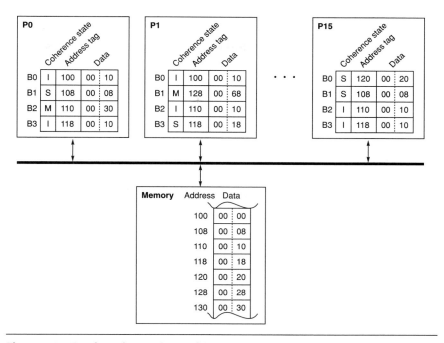

Figure 4.37 Bus-based snooping multiprocessor.

c. [10] <4.2> P15: write 120 <-- 80

d. [10] <4.2> P1: read 110

e. [10] <4.2> P0: write 108 <-- 48

f. [10] <4.2> P0: write 130 <-- 78

g. [10] <4.2> P15: write 130 <-- 78

4.2 [20/20/20/20] <4.3> The performance of a snooping cache-coherent multiprocessor depends on many detailed implementation issues that determine how quickly a cache responds with data in an exclusive or M state block. In some implementations, a CPU read miss to a cache block that is exclusive in another processor's cache is faster than a miss to a block in memory. This is because caches are smaller, and thus faster, than main memory. Conversely, in some implementations, misses satisfied by memory are faster than those satisfied by caches. This is because caches are generally optimized for "front side" or CPU references, rather than "back side" or snooping accesses.

For the multiprocessor illustrated in Figure 4.37, consider the execution of a sequence of operations on a single CPU where

■ CPU read and write hits generate no stall cycles.

■ CPU read and write misses generate N_{memory} and N_{cache} stall cycles if satisfied by memory and cache, respectively.

▪ CPU write hits that generate an invalidate incur $N_{invalidate}$ stall cycles.

▪ a writeback of a block, either due to a conflict or another processor's request to an exclusive block, incurs an additional $N_{writeback}$ stall cycles.

Consider two implementations with different performance characteristics summarized in Figure 4.38.

Consider the following sequence of operations assuming the initial cache state in Figure 4.37. For simplicity, assume that the second operation begins after the first completes (even though they are on different processors):

```
P1:  read 110
P15: read 110
```

For Implementation 1, the first read generates 80 stall cycles because the read is satisfied by P0's cache. P1 stalls for 70 cycles while it waits for the block, and P0 stalls for 10 cycles while it writes the block back to memory in response to P1's request. Thus the second read by P15 generates 100 stall cycles because its miss is satisfied by memory. Thus this sequence generates a total of 180 stall cycles.

For the following sequences of operations, how many stall cycles are generated by each implementation?

a. [20] <4.3>
```
P0:  read  120
P0:  read  128
P0:  read  130
```

b. [20] <4.3>
```
P0:  read  100
P0:  write 108 <-- 48
P0:  write 130 <-- 78
```

c. [20] <4.3>
```
P1:  read  120
P1:  read  128
P1:  read  130
```

d. [20] <4.3>
```
P1:  read  100
P1:  write 108 <-- 48
P1:  write 130 <-- 78
```

Parameter	Implementation 1	Implementation 2
N_{memory}	100	100
N_{cache}	70	130
$N_{invalidate}$	15	15
$N_{writeback}$	10	10

Figure 4.38 Snooping coherence latencies.

4.3 [20] <4.2> Many snooping coherence protocols have additional states, state transitions, or bus transactions to reduce the overhead of maintaining cache coherency. In Implementation 1 of Exercise 4.2, misses are incurring fewer stall cycles when they are supplied by cache than when they are supplied by memory. Some coherence protocols try to improve performance by increasing the frequency of this case.

A common protocol optimization is to introduce an Owned state (usually denoted O). The Owned state behaves like the Shared state, in that nodes may only read Owned blocks. But it behaves like the Modified state, in that nodes must supply data on other nodes' read and write misses to Owned blocks. A read miss to a block in either the Modified or Owned states supplies data to the requesting node and transitions to the Owned state. A write miss to a block in either state Modified or Owned supplies data to the requesting node and transitions to state Invalid. This optimized MOSI protocol only updates memory when a node replaces a block in state Modified or Owned.

Draw new protocol diagrams with the additional state and transitions.

4.4 [20/20/20/20] <4.2> For the following code sequences and the timing parameters for the two implementations in Figure 4.38, compute the total stall cycles for the base MSI protocol and the optimized MOSI protocol in Exercise 4.3. Assume state transitions that do not require bus transactions incur no additional stall cycles.

a. [20] <4.2> P1: read 110

P15: read 110

P0: read 110

b. [20] <4.2> P1: read 120

P15: read 120

P0: read 120

c. [20] <4.2> P0: write 120 <-- 80

P15: read 120

P0: read 120

d. [20] <4.2> P0: write 108 <-- 88

P15: read 108

P0: write 108 <-- 98

4.5 [20] <4.2> Some applications read a large data set first, then modify most or all of it. The base MSI coherence protocol will first fetch all of the cache blocks in the Shared state, and then be forced to perform an invalidate operation to upgrade them to the Modified state. The additional delay has a significant impact on some workloads.

An additional protocol optimization eliminates the need to upgrade blocks that are read and later written by a single processor. This optimization adds the Exclusive (E) state to the protocol, indicating that no other node has a copy of the block, but it has not yet been modified. A cache block enters the Exclusive state when a read miss is satisfied by memory and no other node has a valid copy. CPU reads and writes to that block proceed with no further bus traffic, but CPU writes cause the coherence state to transition to Modified. Exclusive differs from Modified because the node may silently replace Exclusive blocks (while Modified blocks must be written back to memory). Also, a read miss to an Exclusive block results in a transition to Shared, but does not require the node to respond with data (since memory has an up-to-date copy).

Draw new protocol diagrams for a MESI protocol that adds the Exclusive state and transitions to the base MSI protocol's Modified, Shared, and Invalidate states.

4.6 [20/20/20/20/20] <4.2> Assume the cache contents of Figure 4.37 and the timing of Implementation 1 in Figure 4.38. What are the total stall cycles for the following code sequences with both the base protocol and the new MESI protocol in Exercise 4.5? Assume state transitions that do not require bus transactions incur no additional stall cycles.

a. [20] <4.2> P0: read 100

                P0: write 100 <-- 40

b. [20] <4.2> P0: read 120

                P0: write 120 <-- 60

c. [20] <4.2> P0: read 100

                P0: read 120

d. [20] <4.2> P0: read 100

                P1: write 100 <-- 60

e. [20] <4.2> P0: read 100

                P0: write 100 <-- 60

                P1: write 100 <-- 40

4.7 [20/20/20/20] <4.5> The test-and-set spin lock is the simplest synchronization mechanism possible on most commercial shared-memory machines. This spin lock relies on the exchange primitive to atomically load the old value and store a new value. The lock routine performs the exchange operation repeatedly until it finds the lock unlocked (i.e., the returned value is 0).

```
tas:       DADDUI    R2,R0,#1
lockit:    EXCH      R2,0(R1)
           BNEZ      R2, lockit
```

Unlocking a spin lock simply requires a store of the value 0.

```
unlock:    SW        R0,0(R1)
```

As discussed in Section 4.7, the more optimized test-and-test-and-set lock uses a load to check the lock, allowing it to spin with a shared variable in the cache.

```
tatas:    LD        R2, 0(R1)
          BNEZ      R2, tatas
          DADDUI    R2,R0,#1
          EXCH      R2,0(R1)
          BNEZ      R2, tatas
```

Assume that processors P0, P1, and P15 are all trying to acquire a lock at address 0x100 (i.e., register R1 holds the value 0x100). Assume the cache contents from Figure 4.37 and the timing parameters from Implementation 1 in Figure 4.38. For simplicity, assume the critical sections are 1000 cycles long.

a. [20] <4.5> Using the test-and-set spin lock, determine *approximately* how many memory stall cycles each processor incurs before acquiring the lock.

b. [20] <4.5> Using the test-and-test-and-set spin lock, determine *approximately* how many memory stall cycles each processor incurs before acquiring the lock.

c. [20] <4.5> Using the test-and-set spin lock, *approximately* how many bus transactions occur?

d. [20] <4.5> Using the test-and-test-and-set spin lock, *approximately* how many bus transactions occur?

Case Study 2: A Snooping Protocol for a Switched Network

Concepts illustrated by this case study

■ Snooping Coherence Protocol Implementation

■ Coherence Protocol Performance

■ Coherence Protocol Optimizations

■ Memory Consistency Models

The snooping coherence protocols in Case Study 1 describe coherence at an abstract level, but hide many essential details and implicitly assume atomic access to the shared bus to provide correct operation. High-performance snooping systems use one or more pipelined, switched interconnects that greatly improve bandwidth but introduce significant complexity due to transient states and nonatomic transactions. This case study examines a high-performance snooping system, loosely modeled on the Sun E6800, where multiple processor and memory nodes are connected by separate switched address and data networks.

Figure 4.39 illustrates the system organization (middle) with enlargements of a single processor node (left) and a memory module (right). Like most high-

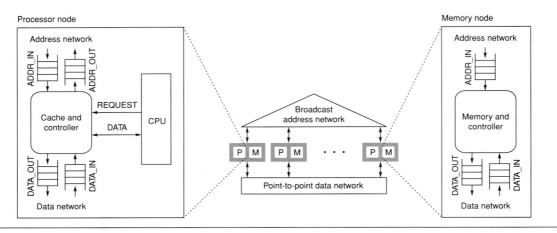

Figure 4.39 Snooping system with switched interconnect.

performance shared-memory systems, this system provides multiple memory modules to increase memory bandwidth. The processor nodes contain a CPU, cache, and a cache controller that implements the coherence protocol. The CPU issues read and write requests to the cache controller over the REQUEST bus and sends/receives data over the DATA bus. The cache controller services these requests locally, (i.e., on cache hits) and on a miss issues a coherence request (e.g., GetShared to request a read-only copy, GetModified to get an exclusive copy) by sending it to the address network via the ADDR_OUT queue. The address network uses a broadcast tree to make sure that all nodes see all coherence requests in a total order. All nodes, including the requesting node, receive this request in the same order (but not necessarily the same cycle) on the ADDR_IN queue. This total order is essential to ensure that all cache controllers act in concert to maintain coherency.

The protocol ensures that at most one node responds, sending a data message on the separate, unordered point-to-point data network.

Figure 4.40 presents a (simplified) coherence protocol for this system in tabular form. Tables are commonly used to specify coherence protocols since the multitude of states makes state diagrams too ungainly. Each row corresponds to a block's coherence state, each column represents an event (e.g., a message arrival or processor operation) affecting that block, and each table entry indicates the action and new next state (if any). Note that there are two types of coherence states. The stable states are the familiar Modified (M), Shared (S), or Invalid (I) and are stored in the cache. Transient states arise because of nonatomic transitions between stable coherence states. An important source of this nonatomicity arises because of races within the pipelined address network and between the address and data networks. For example, two cache controllers may send request messages in the same cycle for the same block, but may not find out for several cycles how the tie is broken (this is done by monitoring the ADDR_IN queue, to

State	Read	Write	Replace-ment	OwnReq	Other GetS	Other GetM	Other Inv	Other PutM	Data
I	send GetS/ IS^{AD}	send GetM/ IM^{AD}	error	error	—	—	—	—	error
S	do Read	send Inv/ SM^A	I	error	—	I	I	—	error
M	do Read	do Write	send PutM/ MI^A	error	send Data/S	send data/I	—	—	error
IS^{AD}	z	z	z	IS^D	—	—	—	—	save Data /IS^A
IM^{AD}	z	z	z	IM^D	—	—	—	—	save Data/IM^A
IS^A	z	z	z	do Read/S	—	—	—	—	error
IM^A	z	z	z	do Write/M	—	—	—	—	error
SM^A	z	z	z	M		II^A	II^A	—	error
MI^A	z	z	z	send Data/I	send Data/II^A	send Data/II^A	—	—	error
II^A	z	z	z	I	—	—	—	—	error
IS^D	z	z	z	error	—	z	z	—	save Data, do Read/S
IM^D	z	z	z	error	z	—	—	—	save Data, do Write/M

Figure 4.40 Broadcast snooping cache controller transitions.

see in which order the requests arrive). Cache controllers use transient states to remember what has transpired in the past while they wait for other actions to occur in the future. Transient states are typically stored in an auxiliary structure such as an MSHR, rather than the cache itself. In this protocol, transient state names encode their initial state, their intended state, and a superscript indicating which messages are still outstanding. For example, the state IS^A indicates that the block was in state I, wants to become state S, but needs to see its own request message (i.e., GetShared) arrive on the ADDR_IN queue before making the transition.

Events at the cache controller depend on CPU requests and incoming request and data messages. The OwnReq event means that a CPU's own request has arrived on the ADDR_IN queue. The Replacement event is a pseudo-CPU event generated when a CPU read or write triggers a cache replacement. Cache controller behavior is detailed in Figure 4.40, where each entry contains an *<action/next state>* tuple. When the current state of a block corresponds to the row of the entry and the next event corresponds to the column of the entry, then the specified action is performed and the state of the block is changed to the specified new state. If only a next state is listed, then no action is required. If no new state is listed, the state remains unchanged. Impossible cases are marked "error" and represent error conditions. "z" means the requested event cannot currently be processed, and "—" means no action or state change is required.

The following example illustrates the basic operation of this protocol. Assume that P0 attempts a read to a block that is in state I (Invalid) in all caches. The cache controller's action—determined by the table entry that corresponds to state I and event "read"—is "send GetS/IS^{AD}," which means that the cache controller should issue a GetS (i.e., GetShared) request to the address network and transition to transient state IS^{AD} to wait for the address and data messages. In the absence of contention, P0's cache controller will normally receive its own GetS message first, indicated by the OwnReq column, causing a transition to state IS^D. Other cache controllers will handle this request as "Other GetS" in state I. When the memory controller sees the request on its ADDR_IN queue, it reads the block from memory and sends a data message to P0. When the data message arrives at P0's DATA_IN queue, indicated by the Data column, the cache controller saves the block in the cache, performs the read, and sets the state to S (i.e., Shared).

A somewhat more complex case arises if node P1 holds the block in state M. In this case, P1's action for "Other GetS" causes it to send the data *both* to P0 and to memory, and then transition to state S. P0 behaves exactly as before, but the memory must maintain enough logic or state to (1) not respond to P0's request (because P1 will respond) and (2) wait to respond to any future requests for this block until it receives the data from P1. This requires the memory controller to implement its own transient states (not shown). Exercise 4.11 explores alternative ways to implement this functionality.

More complex transitions occur when other requests intervene or cause address and data messages to arrive out of order. For example, suppose the cache controller in node P0 initiates a writeback of a block in state Modified. As Figure 4.40 shows, the controller does this by issuing a PutModified coherence request to the ADDR_OUT queue. Because of the pipelined nature of the address network, node P0 cannot send the data until it sees its own request on the ADDR_IN queue and determines its place in the total order. This creates an interval, called a *window of vulnerability,* where another node's request may change the action that should be taken by a cache controller. For example, suppose that node P1 has issued a GetModified request (i.e., requesting an exclusive copy) for the same block that arrives during P0's window of vulnerability for the PutModified request. In this case, P1's GetModified request logically occurs before P0's Put-Modified request, making it incorrect for P0 to complete the writeback. P0's cache controller must respond to P1's GetModified request by sending the block to P1 and invalidating its copy. However, P0's PutModified request remains pending in the address network, and both P0 and P1 must ignore the request when it eventually arrives (node P0 ignores the request since its copy has already been invalidated; node P1 ignores the request since the PutModified was sent by a different node).

4.8   [10/10/10/10/10/10/10] <4.2> Consider the switched network snooping protocol described above and the cache contents from Figure 4.37. What are the sequence of transient states that the affected cache blocks move through in each of the following cases for each of the affected caches? Assume that the address network latency is much less than the data network latency.

a. [10] <4.2> P0: read 120

b. [10] <4.2> P0: write 120 <-- 80

c. [10] <4.2> P15: write 120 <-- 80

d. [10] <4.2> P1: read 110

e. [10] <4.2> P0: write 108 <-- 48

f. [10] <4.2> P0: write 130 <-- 78

g. [10] <4.2> P15: write 130 <-- 78

4.9   [15/15/15/15/15/15/15] <4.2> Consider the switched network snooping protocol described above and the cache contents from Figure 4.37. What are the sequence of transient states that the affected cache blocks move through in each of the following cases? In all cases, assume that the processors issue their requests in the same cycle, but the address network orders the requests in top-down order. Also assume that the data network is much slower than the address network, so that the first data response arrives after all address messages have been seen by all nodes.

a. [15] <4.2> P0: read 120

           P1: read 120

b. [15] <4.2> P0: read 120

           P1: write 120 <-- 80

c. [15] <4.2> P0: write 120 <-- 80
           P1: read 120

d. [15] <4.2> P0: write 120 <-- 80

           P1: write 120 <-- 90

e. [15] <4.2> P0: replace 110

           P1: read 110

f.   [15] <4.2> P1: write 110 <-- 80

           P0: replace 110

g. [15] <4.2> P1: read 110

           P0: replace 110

4.10 [20/20/20/20/20/20/20] <4.2, 4.3> The switched interconnect increases the performance of a snooping cache-coherent multiprocessor by allowing multiple requests to be overlapped. Because the controllers and the networks are pipelined, there is a difference between an operation's latency (i.e., cycles to complete the operation) and overhead (i.e., cycles until the next operation can begin).

For the multiprocessor illustrated in Figure 4.39, assume the following latencies and overheads:

- CPU read and write hits generate no stall cycles.

- A CPU read or write that generates a replacement event issues the corresponding GetShared or GetModified message before the PutModified message (e.g., using a writeback buffer).

- A cache controller event that sends a request message (e.g., GetShared) has latency L_{send_req} and blocks the controller from processing other events for O_{send_req} cycles.

- A cache controller event that reads the cache and sends a data message has latency L_{send_data} and overhead O_{send_data} cycles.

- A cache controller event that receives a data message and updates the cache has latency L_{rcv_data} and overhead O_{rcv_data}.

- A memory controller has latency L_{read_memory} and overhead O_{read_memory} cycles to read memory and send a data message.

- A memory controller has latency L_{write_memory} and overhead O_{write_memory} cycles to write a data message to memory.

- In the absence of contention, a request message has network latency L_{req_msg} and overhead O_{req_msg} cycles.

- In the absence of contention, a data message has network latency L_{data_msg} and overhead O_{data_msg} cycles.

Consider an implementation with the performance characteristics summarized in Figure 4.41.

For the following sequences of operations and the cache contents from Figure Figure 4.37 and the implementation parameters in Figure 4.41, how many stall cycles does each processor incur for each memory request? Similarly, for how many cycles are the different controllers occupied? For simplicity, assume (1) each processor can have only one memory operation outstanding at a time, (2) if two nodes make requests in the same cycle and the one listed first "wins," the

Action	Implementation 1	
	Latency	Overhead
send_req	4	1
send_data	20	4
rcv_data	15	4
read_memory	100	20
write_memory	100	20
req_msg	8	1
data_msg	30	5

Figure 4.41 Switched snooping coherence latencies and overheads.

later node must stall for the request message overhead, and (3) all requests map to the same memory controller.

a. [20] <4.2, 4.3> P0: read 120

b. [20] <4.2, 4.3> P0: write 120 <-- 80

c. [20] <4.2, 4.3> P15: write 120 <-- 80

d. [20] <4.2, 4.3> P1: read 110

e. [20] <4.2, 4.3> P0: read 120

   P15: read 128

f. [20] <4.2, 4.3> P0: read 100

   P1: write 110 <-- 78

g. [20] <4.2, 4.3> P0: write 100 <-- 28

   P1: write 100 <-- 48

4.11 [25/25] <4.2, 4.4> The switched snooping protocol of Figure 4.40 assumes that memory "knows" whether a processor node is in state Modified and thus will respond with data. Real systems implement this in one of two ways. The first way uses a shared "Owned" signal. Processors assert Owned if an "Other GetS" or "Other GetM" event finds the block in state M. A special network ORs the individual Owned signals together; if any processor asserts Owned, the memory controller ignores the request. Note that in a nonpipelined interconnect, this special network is trivial (i.e., it is an OR gate).

However, this network becomes much more complicated with high-performance pipelined interconnects. The second alternative adds a simple directory to the memory controller (e.g., 1 or 2 bits) that tracks whether the memory controller is responsible for responding with data or whether a processor node is responsible for doing so.

a. [25] <4.2, 4.4> Use a table to specify the memory controller protocol needed to implement the second alternative. For this problem, ignore the PUTM message that gets sent on a cache replacement.

b. [25] <4.2, 4.4> Explain what the memory controller must do to support the following sequence, assuming the initial cache contents of Figure 4.37:

   P1: read 110
   P15: read 110

4.12 [30] <4.2> Exercise 4.3 asks you to add the Owned state to the simple MSI snooping protocol. Repeat the question, but with the switched snooping protocol above.

4.13 [30] <4.2> Exercise 4.5 asks you to add the Exclusive state to the simple MSI snooping protocol. Discuss why this is much more difficult to do with the switched snooping protocol. Give an example of the kinds of issues that arise.

4.14   [20/20/20/20] <4.6> Sequential consistency (SC) requires that all reads and writes appear to have executed in some total order. This may require the processor to stall in certain cases before committing a read or write instruction. Consider the following code sequence:

        write A
        read B

where the write A results in a cache miss and the read B results in a cache hit. Under SC, the processor must stall read B until after it can order (and thus perform) write A. Simple implementations of SC will stall the processor until the cache receives the data and can perform the write.

Weaker consistency models relax the ordering constraints on reads and writes, reducing the cases that the processor must stall. The Total Store Order (TSO) consistency model requires that all writes appear to occur in a total order, but allows a processor's reads to pass its own writes. This allows processors to implement write buffers, which hold committed writes that have not yet been ordered with respect to other processor's writes. Reads are allowed to pass (and potentially bypass) the write buffer in TSO (which they could not do under SC).

Assume that one memory operation can be performed per cycle and that operations that hit in the cache or that can be satisfied by the write buffer introduce no stall cycles. Operations that miss incur the latencies listed in Figure 4.41. Assume the cache contents of Figure 4.37 and the base switched protocol of Exercise 4.8. How many stall cycles occur *prior* to each operation for both the SC and TSO consistency models?

a. [20] <4.6> P0: write 110 <-- 80
                P0: read 108

b. [20] <4.6> P0: write 100 <-- 80
                P0: read 108

c. [20] <4.6> P0: write 110 <-- 80
                P0: write 100 <-- 90

d. [20] <4.6> P0: write 100 <-- 80
                P0: write 110 <-- 90

4.15   [20/20] <4.6> The switched snooping protocol above supports sequential consistency in part by making sure that reads are not performed while another node has a writeable block and writes are not performed while another processor has a writeable block. A more aggressive protocol will actually perform a write operation as soon as it receives its own GetModified request, merging the newly written word(s) with the rest of the block when the data message arrives. This may appear illegal, since another node could simultaneously be writing the block. However, the global order required by sequential consistency is determined by the order of coherence requests on the address network, so the other node's write(s) will be ordered before the requester's write(s). Note that this optimization does *not* change the memory consistency model.

Assuming the parameters in Figure 4.41:

a. [20] <4.6> How significant would this optimization be for an in-order core?

b. [20] <4.6> How significant would this optimization be for an out-of-order core?

Case Study 3: Simple Directory-Based Coherence

Concepts illustrated by this case study

■ Directory Coherence Protocol Transitions

■ Coherence Protocol Performance

■ Coherence Protocol Optimizations

Consider the distributed shared-memory system illustrated in Figure 4.42. Each processor has a single direct-mapped cache that holds four blocks each holding two words. To simplify the illustration, the cache address tag contains the full address and each word shows only two hex characters, with the least significant word on the right. The cache states are denoted M, S, and I for Modified, Shared, and Invalid. The directory states are denoted DM, DS, and DI for Directory Modified,

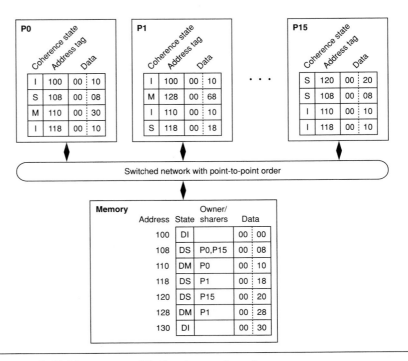

Figure 4.42 Multiprocessor with directory cache coherence.

Directory Shared, and Directory Invalid. The simple directory protocol is described in Figures 4.21 and 4.22.

4.16 [10/10/10/10/15/15/15/15] <4.4> For each part of this exercise, assume the initial cache and memory state in Figure 4.42. Each part of this exercise specifies a sequence of one or more CPU operations of the form:

    P#: <op> <address> [<-- <value>]

where P# designates the CPU (e.g., P0), <op> is the CPU operation (e.g., read or write), <address> denotes the memory address, and <value> indicates the new word to be assigned on a write operation.

What is the final state (i.e., coherence state, tags, and data) of the caches and memory after the given sequence of CPU operations has completed? Also, what value is returned by each read operation?

a. [10] <4.4> P0: read 100

b. [10] <4.4> P0: read 128

c. [10] <4.4> P0: write 128 <-- 78

d. [10] <4.4> P0: read 120

e. [15] <4.4> P0: read 120
              P1: read 120

f. [15] <4.4> P0: read 120
              P1: write 120 <-- 80

g. [15] <4.4> P0: write 120 <-- 80
              P1: read 120

h. [15] <4.4> P0: write 120 <-- 80
              P1: write 120 <-- 90

4.17 [10/10/10/10] <4.4> Directory protocols are more scalable than snooping protocols because they send explicit request and invalidate messages to those nodes that have copies of a block, while snooping protocols broadcast all requests and invalidates to all nodes. Consider the 16-processor system illustrated in Figure 4.42 and assume that all caches not shown have invalid blocks. For each of the sequences below, identify which nodes receive each request and invalidate.

a. [10] <4.4> P0: write 100 <-- 80

b. [10] <4.4> P0: write 108 <-- 88

c. [10] <4.4> P0: write 118 <-- 90

d. [10] <4.4> P1: write 128 <-- 98

4.18 [25] <4.4> Exercise 4.3 asks you to add the Owned state to the simple MSI snooping protocol. Repeat the question, but with the simple directory protocol above.

4.19   [25] <4.4> Exercise 4.5 asks you to add the Exclusive state to the simple MSI snooping protocol. Discuss why this is much more difficult to do with the simple directory protocol. Give an example of the kinds of issues that arise.

Case Study 4: Advanced Directory Protocol

Concepts illustrated by this case study

■   Directory Coherence Protocol Implementation

■   Coherence Protocol Performance

■   Coherence Protocol Optimizations

The directory coherence protocol in Case Study 3 describes directory coherence at an abstract level, but assumes atomic transitions much like the simple snooping system. High-performance directory systems use pipelined, switched interconnects that greatly improve bandwidth but also introduce transient states and non-atomic transactions. Directory cache coherence protocols are more scalable than snooping cache coherence protocols for two reasons. First, snooping cache coherence protocols broadcast requests to all nodes, limiting their scalability. Directory protocols use a level of indirection—a message to the directory—to ensure that requests are only sent to the nodes that have copies of a block. Second, the address network of a snooping system must deliver requests in a total order, while directory protocols can relax this constraint. Some directory protocols assume no network ordering, which is beneficial since it allows adaptive routing techniques to improve network bandwidth. Other protocols rely on point-to-point order (i.e., messages from node P0 to node P1 will arrive in order). Even with this ordering constraint, directory protocols usually have more transient states than snooping protocols. Figure 4.43 presents the cache controller state transitions for a simplified directory protocol that relies on point-to-point network ordering. Figure 4.44 presents the directory controller's state transitions. For each block, the directory maintains a state and a current owner field or a current sharers list (if any).

Like the high-performance snooping protocol presented earlier, indexing the row by the current state and the column by the event determines the *<action/next state>* tuple. If only a next state is listed, then no action is required. Impossible cases are marked "error" and represent error conditions. "z" means the requested event cannot currently be processed.

The following example illustrates the basic operation of this protocol. Suppose a processor attempts a write to a block in state I (Invalid). The corresponding tuple is "send GetM/IM^{AD}" indicating that the cache controller should send a GetM (GetModified) request to the directory and transition to state IM^{AD}. In the simplest case, the request message finds the directory in state DI (Directory Invalid), indicating that no other cache has a copy. The directory responds with a Data message that also contains the number of acks to expect (in this case zero).

State	Read	Write	Replacement	INV	Forwarded_GetS	Forwarded_GetM	PutM_Ack	Data	Last ACK
I	send GetS/ IS^D	send GetM/ IM^{AD}	error	send Ack/I	error	error	error	error	error
S	do Read	send GetM/ IM^{AD}	I	send Ack/I	error	error	error	error	error
M	do Read	do Write	send PutM/ MI^A	error	send Data, send PutMS / MS^A	send Data/I	error	error	error
IS^D	z	z	z	send Ack/ ISI^D	error	error	error	save Data, do Read/S	error
ISI^D	z	z	z	send Ack	error	error	error	save Data, do Read/I	error
IM^{AD}	z	z	z	send Ack	error	error	error	save Data / IM^A	error
IM^A	z	z	z	error	IMS^A	IMI^A	error	error	do Write/M
IMI^A	z	z	z	error	error	error	error	error	do Write, send Data/I
IMS^A	z	z	z	send Ack/ IMI^A	z	z	error	error	do Write, send Data/S
MS^A	do Read	z	z	error	send Data	send Data MI^A	/S	error	error
MI^A	z	z	z	error	send Data	send Data/I	/I	error	error

Figure 4.43 Broadcast snooping cache controller transitions.

State	GetS	GetM	PutM (owner)	PutMS (nonowner)	PutM (owner)	PutMS (nonowner)
DI	send Data, add to sharers/DS	send Data, clear sharers, set owner/ DM	error	send PutM_Ack	error	send PutM_Ack
DS	send Data, add to sharers/DS	send INVs to sharers, clear sharers, set owner, send Data/DM	error	send PutM_Ack	error	send PutM_Ack
DM	forward GetS, add to sharers/ DMS^D	forward GetM, send INVs to sharers, clear sharers, set owner	save Data, send PutM_Ack/DI	send PutM_Ack	save Data, add to sharers, send PutM_Ack/ DS	send PutM_Ack
DMS^D	forward GetS, add to sharers	forward GetM, send INVs to sharers, clear sharers, set owner/ DM	save Data, send PutM_Ack/DS	send PutM_Ack	save Data, add to sharers, send PutM_Ack/ DS	send PutM_Ack

Figure 4.44 Directory controller transitions.

In this simplified protocol, the cache controller treats this single message as two messages: a Data message, followed by a Last Ack event. The Data message is processed first, saving the data and transitioning to IM^A. The Last Ack event is then processed, transitioning to state M. Finally, the write can be performed in state M.

If the GetM finds the directory in state DS (Directory Shared), the directory will send Invalidate (INV) messages to all nodes on the sharers list, send Data to the requester with the number of sharers, and transition to state M. When the INV messages arrive at the sharers, they will either find the block in state S or state I (if they have silently invalidated the block). In either case, the sharer will send an ACK directly to the requesting node. The requester will count the Acks it has received and compare that to the number sent back with the Data message. When all the Acks have arrived, the Last Ack event occurs, triggering the cache to transition to state M and allowing the write to proceed. Note that it is possible for all the Acks to arrive before the Data message, but not for the Last Ack event to occur. This is because the Data message contains the ack count. Thus the protocol assumes that the Data message is processed before the Last Ack event.

4.20 [10/10/10/10/10/10] <4.4> Consider the advanced directory protocol described above and the cache contents from Figure 4.20. What are the sequence of transient states that the affected cache blocks move through in each of the following cases?

a. [10] <4.4> P0: read 100

b. [10] <4.4> P0: read 120

c. [10] <4.4> P0: write 120 <-- 80

d. [10] <4.4> P15: write 120 <-- 80

e. [10] <4.4> P1: read 110

f. [10] <4.4> P0: write 108 <-- 48

4.21 [15/15/15/15/15/15/15] <4.4> Consider the advanced directory protocol described above and the cache contents from Figure 4.42. What are the sequence of transient states that the affected cache blocks move through in each of the following cases? In all cases, assume that the processors issue their requests in the same cycle, but the directory orders the requests in top-down order. Assume that the controllers' actions appear to be atomic (e.g., the directory controller will perform all the actions required for the DS --> DM transition before handling another request for the same block).

a. [15] <4.4> P0: read 120

    P1: read 120

b. [15] <4.4> P0: read 120

    P1: write 120 <-- 80

c. [15] <4.4> P0: write 120

    P1: read 120

    d. [15] <4.4> P0: write 120 <-- 80

                    P1: write 120 <-- 90

    e. [15] <4.4> P0: replace 110

                    P1: read 110

    f. [15] <4.4> P1: write 110 <-- 80

                    P0: replace 110

    g. [15] <4.4> P1: read 110

                    P0: replace 110

4.22 [20/20/20/20/20] <4.4> For the multiprocessor illustrated in Figure 4.42 implementing the protocol described in Figure 4.43 and Figure 4.44, assume the following latencies:

- CPU read and write hits generate no stall cycles.

- Completing a miss (i.e., do Read and do Write) takes L_{ack} cycles *only* if it is performed in response to the Last Ack event (otherwise it gets done while the data is copied to cache).

- A CPU read or write that generates a replacement event issues the corresponding GetShared or GetModified message before the PutModified message (e.g., using a writeback buffer).

- A cache controller event that sends a request or acknowledgment message (e.g., GetShared) has latency L_{send_msg} cycles.

- A cache controller event that reads the cache and sends a data message has latency L_{send_data} cycles.

- A cache controller event that receives a data message and updates the cache has latency L_{rcv_data}.

- A memory controller incurs L_{send_msg} latency when it forwards a request message.

- A memory controller incurs an additional L_{inv} cycles for each invalidate that it must send.

- A cache controller incurs latency L_{send_msg} for each invalidate that it receives (latency is until it sends the Ack message).

- A memory controller has latency L_{read_memory} cycles to read memory and send a data message.

- A memory controller has latency L_{write_memory} to write a data message to memory (latency is until it sends the Ack message).

- A nondata message (e.g., request, invalidate, Ack) has network latency L_{req_msg} cycles

- A data message has network latency L_{data_msg} cycles.

Consider an implementation with the performance characteristics summarized in Figure 4.45.

Action	Implementation 1
	Latency
send_msg	6
send_data	20
rcv_data	15
read_memory	100
write_memory	20
inv	1
ack	4
req_msg	15
data_msg	30

Figure 4.45 Directory coherence latencies.

For the sequences of operations below, the cache contents of Figure 4.42, and the directory protocol above, what is the latency observed by each processor node?

a. [20] <4.4> P0: read 100

b. [20] <4.4> P0: read 128

c. [20] <4.4> P0: write 128 <-- 68

d. [20] <4.4> P0: write 120 <-- 50

e. [20] <4.4> P0: write 108 <-- 80

4.23   [20] <4.4> In the case of a cache miss, both the switched snooping protocol described earlier and the directory protocol in this case study perform the read or write operation as soon as possible. In particular, they do the operation as part of the transition to the stable state, rather than transitioning to the stable state and simply retrying the operation. This is *not* an optimization. Rather, to ensure forward progress, protocol implementations must ensure that they perform at least one CPU operation before relinquishing a block.

Suppose the coherence protocol implementation didn't do this. Explain how this might lead to livelock. Give a simple code example that could stimulate this behavior.

4.24   [20/30] <4.4> Some directory protocols add an Owned (O) state to the protocol, similar to the optimization discussed for snooping protocols. The Owned state behaves like the Shared state, in that nodes may only read Owned blocks. But it behaves like the Modified state, in that nodes must supply data on other nodes' Get requests to Owned blocks. The Owned state eliminates the case where a GetShared request to a block in state Modified requires the node to send the data both to the requesting processor and to the memory. In a MOSI directory protocol, a Get-Shared request to a block in either the Modified or Owned states supplies data to the requesting node and transitions to the Owned state. A GetModified request in state Owned is handled like a request in state Modified. This optimized MOSI protocol only updates memory when a node replaces a block in state Modified or Owned.

a. [20] <4.4> Explain why the MS^A state in the protocol is essentially a "transient" Owned state.

b. [30] <4.4> Modify the cache and directory protocol tables to support a stable Owned state.

4.25   [25/25] <4.4> The advanced directory protocol described above relies on a point-to-point ordered interconnect to ensure correct operation. Assuming the initial cache contents of Figure 4.42 and the following sequences of operations, explain what problem could arise if the interconnect failed to maintain point-to-point ordering. Assume that the processors perform the requests at the same time, but they are processed by the directory in the order shown.

a. [25] <4.4> P1: read 110

P15: write 110 <-- 90

b. [25] <4.4> P1: read 110

P0: replace 110

5.1	Introduction	288
5.2	Eleven Advanced Optimizations of Cache Performance	293
5.3	Memory Technology and Optimizations	310
5.4	Protection: Virtual Memory and Virtual Machines	315
5.5	Crosscutting Issues: The Design of Memory Hierarchies	324
5.6	Putting It All Together: AMD Opteron Memory Hierarchy	326
5.7	Fallacies and Pitfalls	335
5.8	Concluding Remarks	341
5.9	Historical Perspective and References	342
	Case Studies with Exercises by Norman P. Jouppi	342

5

Memory Hierarchy Design

Ideally one would desire an indefinitely large memory capacity such that any particular ... word would be immediately available. ... We are ... forced to recognize the possibility of constructing a hierarchy of memories, each of which has greater capacity than the preceding but which is less quickly accessible.

A. W. Burks, H. H. Goldstine, and J. von Neumann
Preliminary Discussion of the Logical Design of an Electronic Computing Instrument (1946)

Introduction

Computer pioneers correctly predicted that programmers would want unlimited amounts of fast memory. An economical solution to that desire is a *memory hierarchy,* which takes advantage of locality and cost-performance of memory technologies. The *principle of locality,* presented in the first chapter, says that most programs do not access all code or data uniformly. Locality occurs in time (*temporal locality*) and in space (*spatial locality*). This principle, plus the guideline that smaller hardware can be made faster, led to hierarchies based on memories of different speeds and sizes. Figure 5.1 shows a multilevel memory hierarchy, including typical sizes and speeds of access.

Since fast memory is expensive, a memory hierarchy is organized into several levels—each smaller, faster, and more expensive per byte than the next lower level. The goal is to provide a memory system with cost per byte almost as low as the cheapest level of memory and speed almost as fast as the fastest level.

Note that each level maps addresses from a slower, larger memory to a smaller but faster memory higher in the hierarchy. As part of address mapping, the memory hierarchy is given the responsibility of address checking; hence, protection schemes for scrutinizing addresses are also part of the memory hierarchy.

The importance of the memory hierarchy has increased with advances in performance of processors. Figure 5.2 plots processor performance projections against the historical performance improvement in time to access main memory. Clearly, computer architects must try to close the processor-memory gap.

The increasing size and thus importance of this gap led to the migration of the basics of memory hierarchy into undergraduate courses in computer architecture, and even to courses in operating systems and compilers. Thus, we'll start with a quick review of caches. The bulk of the chapter, however, describes more advanced innovations that address the processor-memory performance gap.

When a word is not found in the cache, the word must be fetched from the memory and placed in the cache before continuing. Multiple words, called a

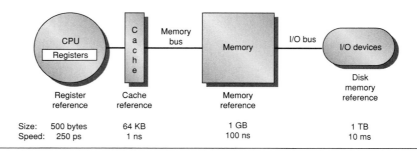

Figure 5.1 The levels in a typical memory hierarchy in embedded, desktop, and server computers. As we move farther away from the processor, the memory in the level below becomes slower and larger. Note that the time units change by factors of 10—from picoseconds to milliseconds—and that the size units change by factors of 1000—from bytes to terabytes.

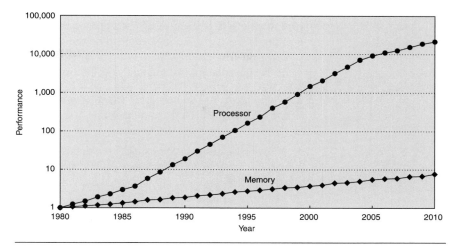

Figure 5.2 Starting with 1980 performance as a baseline, the gap in performance between memory and processors is plotted over time. Note that the vertical axis must be on a logarithmic scale to record the size of the processor-DRAM performance gap. The memory baseline is 64 KB DRAM in 1980, with a 1.07 per year performance improvement in latency (see Figure 5.13 on page 313). The processor line assumes a 1.25 improvement per year until 1986, and a 1.52 improvement until 2004, and a 1.20 improvement thereafter; see Figure 1.1 in Chapter 1.

block (or *line*), are moved for efficiency reasons. Each cache block includes a *tag* to see which memory address it corresponds to.

A key design decision is where blocks (or lines) can be placed in a cache. The most popular scheme is *set associative*, where a *set* is a group of blocks in the cache. A block is first mapped onto a set, and then the block can be placed anywhere within that set. Finding a block consists of first mapping the block address to the set, and then searching the set—usually in parallel—to find the block. The set is chosen by the address of the data:

$$\textit{(Block address)} \; \text{MOD} \; \textit{(Number of sets in cache)}$$

If there are *n* blocks in a set, the cache placement is called *n-way set associative*. The end points of set associativity have their own names. A *direct-mapped* cache has just one block per set (so a block is always placed in the same location), and a *fully associative* cache has just one set (so a block can be placed anywhere).

Caching data that is only read is easy, since the copy in the cache and memory will be identical. Caching writes is more difficult: how can the copy in the cache and memory be kept consistent? There are two main strategies. A *write-through* cache updates the item in the cache *and* writes through to update main memory. A *write-back* cache only updates the copy in the cache. When the block is about to be replaced, it is copied back to memory. Both write strategies can use a *write buffer* to allow the cache to proceed as soon as the data is placed in the buffer rather than wait the full latency to write the data into memory.

One measure of the benefits of different cache organizations is miss rate. *Miss rate* is simply the fraction of cache accesses that result in a miss—that is, the number of accesses that miss divided by the number of accesses.

To gain insights into the causes of high miss rates, which can inspire better cache designs, the three Cs model sorts all misses into three simple categories:

■ *Compulsory*—The very first access to a block *cannot* be in the cache, so the block must be brought into the cache. Compulsory misses are those that occur even if you had an infinite cache.

■ *Capacity*—If the cache cannot contain all the blocks needed during execution of a program, capacity misses (in addition to compulsory misses) will occur because of blocks being discarded and later retrieved.

■ *Conflict*—If the block placement strategy is not fully associative, conflict misses (in addition to compulsory and capacity misses) will occur because a block may be discarded and later retrieved if conflicting blocks map to its set.

Figures C.8 and C.9 on pages C-23 and C-24 show the relative frequency of cache misses broken down by the "three C's." (Chapter 4 adds a fourth C, for *Coherency* misses due to cache flushes to keep multiple caches coherent in a multiprocessor; we won't consider those here.)

Alas, miss rate can be a misleading measure for several reasons. Hence, some designers prefer measuring *misses per instruction* rather than misses per memory reference (miss rate). These two are related:

$$\frac{\text{Misses}}{\text{Instruction}} = \frac{\text{Miss rate} \times \text{Memory accesses}}{\text{Instruction count}} = \text{Miss rate} \times \frac{\text{Memory accesses}}{\text{Instruction}}$$

(It is often reported as misses per 1000 instructions to use integers instead of fractions.) For speculative processors, we only count instructions that commit.

The problem with both measures is that they don't factor in the cost of a miss. A better measure is the *average memory access time:*

$$\text{Average memory access time} = \text{Hit time} + \text{Miss rate} \times \text{Miss penalty}$$

where *Hit time* is the time to hit in the cache and *Miss penalty* is the time to replace the block from memory (that is, the cost of a miss). Average memory access time is still an indirect measure of performance; although it is a better measure than miss rate, it is not a substitute for execution time. For example, in Chapter 2 we saw that speculative processors may execute other instructions during a miss, thereby reducing the effective miss penalty.

If this material is new to you, or if this quick review moves too quickly, see Appendix C. It covers the same introductory material in more depth and includes examples of caches from real computers and quantitative evaluations of their effectiveness.

Section C.3 in Appendix C also presents six basic cache optimizations, which we quickly review here. The appendix also gives quantitative examples of the benefits of these optimizations.

1. *Larger block size to reduce miss rate*—The simplest way to reduce the miss rate is to take advantage of spatial locality and increase the block size. Note that larger blocks also reduce compulsory misses, but they also increase the miss penalty.

2. *Bigger caches to reduce miss rate*—The obvious way to reduce capacity misses is to increase cache capacity. Drawbacks include potentially longer hit time of the larger cache memory and higher cost and power.

3. *Higher associativity to reduce miss rate*—Obviously, increasing associativity reduces conflict misses. Greater associativity can come at the cost of increased hit time.

4. *Multilevel caches to reduce miss penalty*—A difficult decision is whether to make the cache hit time fast, to keep pace with the increasing clock rate of processors, or to make the cache large, to overcome the widening gap between the processor and main memory. Adding another level of cache between the original cache and memory simplifies the decision (see Figure 5.3). The first-level cache can be small enough to match a fast clock cycle time, yet the second-level cache can be large enough to capture many accesses that would go to main memory. The focus on misses in second-level caches leads to larger blocks, bigger capacity, and higher associativity. If L1 and L2 refer, respectively, to first- and second-level caches, we can redefine the average memory access time:

$$\text{Hit time}_{L1} + \text{Miss rate}_{L1} \times (\text{Hit time}_{L2} + \text{Miss rate}_{L2} \times \text{Miss penalty}_{L2})$$

5. *Giving priority to read misses over writes to reduce miss penalty*—A write buffer is a good place to implement this optimization. Write buffers create hazards because they hold the updated value of a location needed on a read miss—that is, a read-after-write hazard through memory. One solution is to check the contents of the write buffer on a read miss. If there are no conflicts, and if the memory system is available, sending the read before the writes reduces the miss penalty. Most processors give reads priority over writes.

6. *Avoiding address translation during indexing of the cache to reduce hit time*—Caches must cope with the translation of a virtual address from the processor to a physical address to access memory. (Virtual memory is covered in Sections 5.4 and C.4.) Figure 5.3 shows a typical relationship between caches, translation lookaside buffers (TLBs), and virtual memory. A common optimization is to use the page offset—the part that is identical in both virtual and physical addresses—to index the cache. The virtual part of the address is translated while the cache is read using that index, so the tag match can use physical addresses. This scheme allows the cache read to begin immediately, and yet the tag comparison still uses physical addresses. The drawback of this *virtually indexed, physically tagged* optimization is that the size of the page limits the size of the cache. For example, a direct-mapped cache can be no bigger than the page size. Higher associativity can keep the cache index in the physical part of the address and yet still support a cache larger than a page.

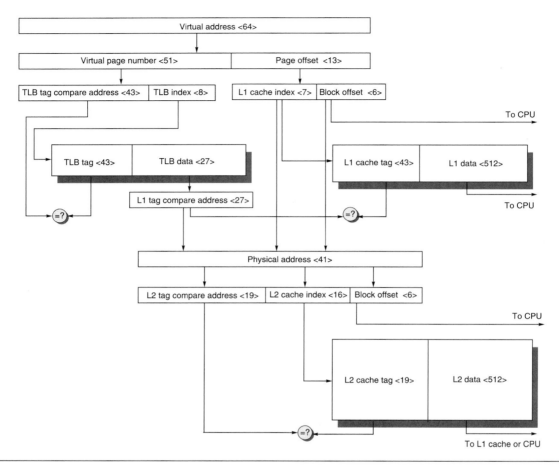

Figure 5.3 The overall picture of a hypothetical memory hierarchy going from virtual address to L2 cache access. The page size is 8 KB. The TLB is direct mapped with 256 entries. The L1 cache is a direct-mapped 8 KB, and the L2 cache is a direct-mapped 4 MB. Both use 64-byte blocks. The virtual address is 64 bits and the physical address is 40 bits. The primary difference between this figure and a real memory hierarchy, as in Figure 5.18 on page 327, is higher associativity for caches and TLBs and a smaller virtual address than 64 bits.

For example, doubling associativity while doubling the cache size maintains the size of the index, since it is controlled by this formula:

$$2^{\text{Index}} = \frac{\text{Cache size}}{\text{Block size} \times \text{Set associativity}}$$

A seemingly obvious alternative is to just use virtual addresses to access the cache, but this can cause extra overhead in the operating system.

Note that each of these six optimizations above has a potential disadvantage that can lead to increased, rather than decreased, average memory access time.

The rest of this chapter assumes familiarity with the material above, including Figure 5.3. To put cache ideas into practice, throughout this chapter (and Appendix C) we show examples from the memory hierarchy of the AMD Opteron microprocessor. Toward the end of the chapter, we evaluate the impact of this hierarchy on performance using the SPEC2000 benchmark programs.

The Opteron is a microprocessor designed for desktops and servers. Even these two related classes of computers have different concerns in a memory hierarchy. Desktop computers are primarily running one application at a time on top of an operating system for a single user, whereas server computers may have hundreds of users running potentially dozens of applications simultaneously. These characteristics result in more context switches, which effectively increase miss rates. Thus, desktop computers are concerned more with average latency from the memory hierarchy, whereas server computers are also concerned about memory bandwidth.

5.2   Eleven Advanced Optimizations of Cache Performance

The average memory access time formula above gives us three metrics for cache optimizations: hit time, miss rate, and miss penalty. Given the popularity of super-scalar processors, we add cache bandwidth to this list. Hence, we group 11 advanced cache optimizations into the following categories:

- Reducing the hit time: small and simple caches, way prediction, and trace caches

- Increasing cache bandwidth: pipelined caches, multibanked caches, and non-blocking caches

- Reducing the miss penalty: critical word first and merging write buffers

- Reducing the miss rate: compiler optimizations

- Reducing the miss penalty or miss rate via parallelism: hardware prefetching and compiler prefetching

We will conclude with a summary of the implementation complexity and the performance benefits of the 11 techniques presented (Figure 5.11 on page 309).

First Optimization: Small and Simple Caches to Reduce Hit Time

A time-consuming portion of a cache hit is using the index portion of the address to read the tag memory and then compare it to the address. Smaller hardware can be faster, so a small cache can help the hit time. It is also critical to keep an L2 cache small enough to fit on the same chip as the processor to avoid the time penalty of going off chip.

The second suggestion is to keep the cache simple, such as using direct mapping. One benefit of direct-mapped caches is that the designer can overlap the tag check with the transmission of the data. This effectively reduces hit time.

Hence, the pressure of a fast clock cycle encourages small and simple cache designs for first-level caches. For lower-level caches, some designs strike a compromise by keeping the tags on chip and the data off chip, promising a fast tag check, yet providing the greater capacity of separate memory chips.

Although the amount of on-chip cache increased with new generations of microprocessors, the size of the L1 caches has recently not increased between generations. The L1 caches are the same size for three generations of AMD microprocessors: K6, Athlon, and Opteron. The emphasis is on fast clock rate while hiding L1 misses with dynamic execution and using L2 caches to avoid going to memory.

One approach to determining the impact on hit time in advance of building a chip is to use CAD tools. CACTI is a program to estimate the access time of alternative cache structures on CMOS microprocessors within 10% of more detailed CAD tools. For a given minimum feature size, it estimates the hit time of caches as you vary cache size, associativity, and number of read/write ports. Figure 5.4 shows the estimated impact on hit time as cache size and associativity are varied. Depending on cache size, for these parameters the model suggests that hit time for direct mapped is 1.2–1.5 times faster than two-way set associative; two-way is 1.02–1.11 times faster than four-way; and four-way is 1.0–1.08 times faster than fully associative.

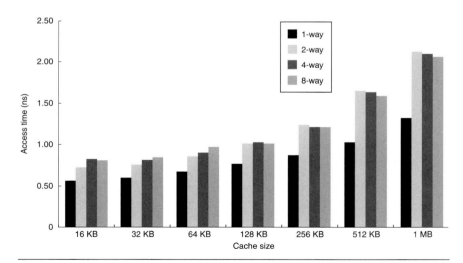

Figure 5.4 Access times as size and associativity vary in a CMOS cache. These data are based on the CACTI model 4 4.0 by Tarjan, Thoziyoor, and Jouppi [2006]. They assumed 90 nm feature size, a single bank, and 64-byte blocks. The median ratios of access time relative to the direct-mapped caches are 1.32, 1.39, and 1.43 for 2-way, 4-way, and 8-way associative caches, respectively.

Example   Assume that the hit time of a two-way set-associative first-level data cache is 1.1 times faster than a four-way set-associative cache of the same size. The miss rate falls from 0.049 to 0.044 for an 8 KB data cache, according to Figure C.8 in Appendix C. Assume a hit is 1 clock cycle and that the cache is the critical path for the clock. Assume the miss penalty is 10 clock cycles to the L2 cache for the two-way set-associative cache, and that the L2 cache does not miss. Which has the faster average memory access time?

Answer   For the two-way cache:

$$\text{Average memory access time}_{2\text{-way}} = \text{Hit time} + \text{Miss rate} \times \text{Miss penalty}$$
$$= 1 + 0.049 \times 10 = 1.49$$

For the four-way cache, the clock time is 1.1 times longer. The elapsed time of the miss penalty should be the same since it's not affected by the processor clock rate, so assume it takes 9 of the longer clock cycles:

$$\text{Average memory access time}_{4\text{-way}} = \text{Hit time} \times 1.1 + \text{Miss rate} \times \text{Miss penalty}$$
$$= 1.1 + 0.044 \times 9 = 1.50$$

If it really stretched the clock cycle time by a factor of 1.1, the performance impact would be even worse than indicated by the average memory access time, as the clock would be slower even when the processor is not accessing the cache.

Despite this advantage, since many processors take at least 2 clock cycles to access the cache, L1 caches today are often at least two-way associative.

Second Optimization: Way Prediction to Reduce Hit Time

Another approach reduces conflict misses and yet maintains the hit speed of direct-mapped cache. In *way prediction,* extra bits are kept in the cache to predict the way, or block within the set of the *next* cache access. This prediction means the multiplexor is set early to select the desired block, and only a single tag comparison is performed that clock cycle in parallel with reading the cache data. A miss results in checking the other blocks for matches in the next clock cycle.

Added to each block of a cache are block predictor bits. The bits select which of the blocks to try on the *next* cache access. If the predictor is correct, the cache access latency is the fast hit time. If not, it tries the other block, changes the way predictor, and has a latency of one extra clock cycle. Simulations suggested set prediction accuracy is in excess of 85% for a two-way set, so way prediction saves pipeline stages more than 85% of the time. Way prediction is a good match to speculative processors, since they must already undo actions when speculation is unsuccessful. The Pentium 4 uses way prediction.

Third Optimization: Trace Caches to Reduce Hit Time

A challenge in the effort to find lots of instruction-level parallelism is to find enough instructions every cycle without use dependencies. To address this challenge, blocks in a *trace cache* contain dynamic traces of the executed instructions rather than static sequences of instructions as determined by layout in memory. Hence, the branch prediction is folded into the cache and must be validated along with the addresses to have a valid fetch.

Clearly, trace caches have much more complicated address-mapping mechanisms, as the addresses are no longer aligned to power-of-two multiples of the word size. However, they can better utilize long blocks in the instruction cache. Long blocks in conventional caches may be entered in the middle from a branch and exited before the end by a branch, so they can have poor space utilization. The downside of trace caches is that conditional branches making different choices result in the same instructions being part of separate traces, which each occupy space in the trace cache and lower its space efficiency.

Note that the trace cache of the Pentium 4 uses decoded micro-operations, which acts as another performance optimization since it saves decode time.

Many optimizations are simple to understand and are widely used, but a trace cache is neither simple nor popular. It is relatively expensive in area, power, and complexity compared to its benefits, so we believe trace caches are likely a one-time innovation. We include them because they appear in the popular Pentium 4.

Fourth Optimization: Pipelined Cache Access to Increase Cache Bandwidth

This optimization is simply to pipeline cache access so that the effective latency of a first-level cache hit can be multiple clock cycles, giving fast clock cycle time and high bandwidth but slow hits. For example, the pipeline for the Pentium took 1 clock cycle to access the instruction cache, for the Pentium Pro through Pentium III it took 2 clocks, and for the Pentium 4 it takes 4 clocks. This split increases the number of pipeline stages, leading to greater penalty on mispredicted branches and more clock cycles between the issue of the load and the use of the data (see Chapter 2).

Fifth Optimization: Nonblocking Caches to Increase Cache Bandwidth

For pipelined computers that allow out-of-order completion (Chapter 2), the processor need not stall on a data cache miss. For example, the processor could continue fetching instructions from the instruction cache while waiting for the data cache to return the missing data. A *nonblocking cache* or *lockup-free cache* escalates the potential benefits of such a scheme by allowing the data cache to continue to supply cache hits during a miss. This "hit under miss" optimization

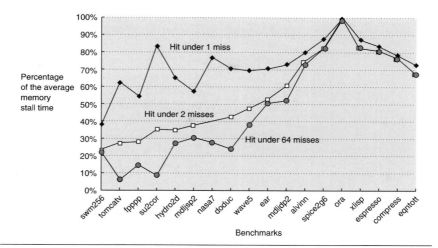

Figure 5.5 Ratio of the average memory stall time for a blocking cache to hit-under-miss schemes as the number of outstanding misses is varied for 18 SPEC92 programs. The hit-under-64-misses line allows one miss for every register in the processor. The first 14 programs are floating-point programs: the average for hit under 1 miss is 76%, for 2 misses is 51%, and for 64 misses is 39%. The final four are integer programs, and the three averages are 81%, 78%, and 78%, respectively. These data were collected for an 8 KB direct-mapped data cache with 32-byte blocks and a 16-clock-cycle miss penalty, which today would imply a second-level cache. These data were generated using the VLIW Multiflow compiler, which scheduled loads away from use [Farkas and Jouppi 1994]. Although it may be a good model for L1 misses to L2 caches, it would be interesting to redo this experiment with SPEC2006 benchmarks and modern assumptions on miss penalty.

reduces the effective miss penalty by being helpful during a miss instead of ignoring the requests of the processor. A subtle and complex option is that the cache may further lower the effective miss penalty if it can overlap multiple misses: a "hit under multiple miss" or "miss under miss" optimization. The second option is beneficial only if the memory system can service multiple misses.

Figure 5.5 shows the average time in clock cycles for cache misses for an 8 KB data cache as the number of outstanding misses is varied. Floating-point programs benefit from increasing complexity, while integer programs get almost all of the benefit from a simple hit-under-one-miss scheme. As pointed out in Chapter 3, the number of simultaneous outstanding misses limits achievable instruction-level parallelism in programs.

Example   Which is more important for floating-point programs: two-way set associativity or hit under one miss? What about integer programs? Assume the following average miss rates for 8 KB data caches: 11.4% for floating-point programs with a direct-mapped cache, 10.7% for these programs with a two-way set-associative cache, 7.4% for integer programs with a direct-mapped cache, and 6.0% for integer programs with a two-way set-associative cache. Assume the average memory stall time is just the product of the miss rate and the miss penalty and the cache described in Figure 5.5, which we assume has a L2 cache.

Answer   The numbers for Figure 5.5 were based on a miss penalty of 16 clock cycles assuming an L2 cache. Although the programs are older and this is low for a miss penalty, let's stick with it for consistency. (To see how well it would work on modern programs and miss penalties, we'd need to redo this experiment.) For floating-point programs, the average memory stall times are

$$\text{Miss rate}_{DM} \times \text{Miss penalty} = 11.4\% \times 16 = 1.84$$

$$\text{Miss rate}_{2\text{-way}} \times \text{Miss penalty} = 10.7\% \times 16 = 1.71$$

The memory stalls for two-way are thus 1.71/1.84 or 93% of direct-mapped cache. The caption of Figure 5.5 says hit under one miss reduces the average memory stall time to 76% of a blocking cache. Hence, for floating-point programs, the direct-mapped data cache supporting hit under one miss gives better performance than a two-way set-associative cache that blocks on a miss.

For integer programs the calculation is

$$\text{Miss rate}_{DM} \times \text{Miss penalty} = 7.4\% \times 16 = 1.18$$

$$\text{Miss rate}_{2\text{-way}} \times \text{Miss penalty} = 6.0\% \times 16 = 0.96$$

The memory stalls of two-way are thus 0.96/1.18 or 81% of direct-mapped cache. The caption of Figure 5.5 says hit under one miss reduces the average memory stall time to 81% of a blocking cache, so the two options give about the same performance for integer programs using this data.

The real difficulty with performance evaluation of nonblocking caches is that a cache miss does not necessarily stall the processor. In this case, it is difficult to judge the impact of any single miss, and hence difficult to calculate the average memory access time. The effective miss penalty is not the sum of the misses but the nonoverlapped time that the processor is stalled. The benefit of nonblocking caches is complex, as it depends upon the miss penalty when there are multiple misses, the memory reference pattern, and how many instructions the processor can execute with a miss outstanding.

In general, out-of-order processors are capable of hiding much of the miss penalty of an L1 data cache miss that hits in the L2 cache, but are not capable of hiding a significant fraction of an L2 cache miss.

Sixth Optimization: Multibanked Caches to Increase Cache Bandwidth

Rather than treat the cache as a single monolithic block, we can divide it into independent banks that can support simultaneous accesses. Banks were origi-

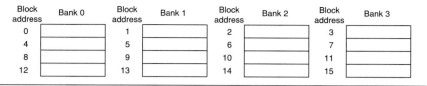

Figure 5.6 Four-way interleaved cache banks using block addressing. Assuming 64 bytes per blocks, each of these addresses would be multiplied by 64 to get byte addressing.

nally used to improve performance of main memory and are now used inside modern DRAM chips as well as with caches. The L2 cache of the AMD Opteron has two banks, and the L2 cache of the Sun Niagara has four banks.

Clearly, banking works best when the accesses naturally spread themselves across the banks, so the mapping of addresses to banks affects the behavior of the memory system. A simple mapping that works well is to spread the addresses of the block sequentially across the banks, called *sequential interleaving*. For example, if there are four banks, bank 0 has all blocks whose address modulo 4 is 0; bank 1 has all blocks whose address modulo 4 is 1; and so on. Figure 5.6 shows this interleaving.

Seventh Optimization: Critical Word First and Early Restart to Reduce Miss Penalty

This technique is based on the observation that the processor normally needs just one word of the block at a time. This strategy is impatience: Don't wait for the full block to be loaded before sending the requested word and restarting the processor. Here are two specific strategies:

- *Critical word first*—Request the missed word first from memory and send it to the processor as soon as it arrives; let the processor continue execution while filling the rest of the words in the block.

- *Early restart*—Fetch the words in normal order, but as soon as the requested word of the block arrives, send it to the processor and let the processor continue execution.

Generally, these techniques only benefit designs with large cache blocks, since the benefit is low unless blocks are large. Note that caches normally continue to satisfy accesses to other blocks while the rest of the block is being filled.

Alas, given spatial locality, there is a good chance that the next reference is to the rest of the block. Just as with nonblocking caches, the miss penalty is not simple to calculate. When there is a second request in critical word first, the effective miss penalty is the nonoverlapped time from the reference until the second piece arrives.

Example   Let's assume a computer has a 64-byte cache block, an L2 cache that takes 7 clock cycles to get the critical 8 bytes, and then 1 clock cycle per 8 bytes + 1 extra clock cycle to fetch the rest of the block. (These parameters are similar to the AMD Opteron.) Without critical word first, it's 8 clock cycles for the first 8 bytes and then 1 clock per 8 bytes for the rest of the block. Calculate the average miss penalty for critical word first, assuming that there will be no other accesses to the rest of the block until it is completely fetched. Then calculate assuming the following instructions read data 8 bytes at a time from the rest of the block. Compare the times with and without critical word first.

Answer   The average miss penalty is 7 clock cycles for critical word first, and without critical word first it takes $8 + (8 - 1) \times 1$ or 15 clock cycles for the processor to read a full cache block. Thus, for one word, the answer is 15 versus 7 clock cycles. The Opteron issues two loads per clock cycle, so it takes 8/2 or 4 clocks to issue the loads. Without critical word first, it would take 19 clock cycles to load and read the full block. With critical word first, it's $7 + 7 \times 1 + 1$ or 15 clock cycles to read the whole block, since the loads are overlapped in critical word first. For the full block, the answer is 19 versus 15 clock cycles.

As this example illustrates, the benefits of critical word first and early restart depend on the size of the block and the likelihood of another access to the portion of the block that has not yet been fetched.

Eighth Optimization: Merging Write Buffer to Reduce Miss Penalty

Write-through caches rely on write buffers, as all stores must be sent to the next lower level of the hierarchy. Even write-back caches use a simple buffer when a block is replaced. If the write buffer is empty, the data and the full address are written in the buffer, and the write is finished from the processor's perspective; the processor continues working while the write buffer prepares to write the word to memory. If the buffer contains other modified blocks, the addresses can be checked to see if the address of this new data matches the address of a valid write buffer entry. If so, the new data are combined with that entry. *Write merging* is the name of this optimization. The Sun Niagara processor, among many others, uses write merging.

If the buffer is full and there is no address match, the cache (and processor) must wait until the buffer has an empty entry. This optimization uses the memory more efficiently since multiword writes are usually faster than writes performed one word at a time. Skadron and Clark [1997] found that about 5% to 10% of performance was lost due to stalls in a four-entry write buffer.

The optimization also reduces stalls due to the write buffer being full. Figure 5.7 shows a write buffer with and without write merging. Assume we had four entries in the write buffer, and each entry could hold four 64-bit words. Without

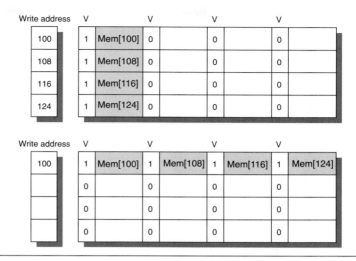

Figure 5.7 To illustrate write merging, the write buffer on top does not use it while the write buffer on the bottom does. The four writes are merged into a single buffer entry with write merging; without it, the buffer is full even though three-fourths of each entry is wasted. The buffer has four entries, and each entry holds four 64-bit words. The address for each entry is on the left, with a valid bit (V) indicating whether the next sequential 8 bytes in this entry are occupied. (Without write merging, the words to the right in the upper part of the figure would only be used for instructions that wrote multiple words at the same time.)

this optimization, four stores to sequential addresses would fill the buffer at one word per entry, even though these four words when merged exactly fit within a single entry of the write buffer.

Note that input/output device registers are often mapped into the physical address space. These I/O addresses cannot allow write merging because separate I/O registers may not act like an array of words in memory. For example, they may require one address and data word per register rather than multiword writes using a single address.

In a write-back cache, the block that is replaced is sometimes called the *victim*. Hence, the AMD Opteron calls its write buffer a *victim buffer*. The write victim buffer or victim buffer contains the dirty blocks that are discarded from a cache because of a miss. Rather than stall on a subsequent cache miss, the contents of the buffer are checked on a miss to see if they have the desired data before going to the next lower-level memory. This name makes it sounds like another optimization called a *victim cache*. In contrast, the victim cache can include any blocks discarded from the cache on a miss, whether they are dirty or not [Jouppi 1990].

While the purpose of the write buffer is to allow the cache to proceed without waiting for dirty blocks to write to memory, the goal of a victim cache is to reduce the impact of conflict misses. Write buffers are far more popular today than victim caches, despite the confusion caused by the use of "victim" in their title.

Ninth Optimization: Compiler Optimizations to Reduce Miss Rate

Thus far, our techniques have required changing the hardware. This next technique reduces miss rates without any hardware changes.

This magical reduction comes from optimized software—the hardware designer's favorite solution! The increasing performance gap between processors and main memory has inspired compiler writers to scrutinize the memory hierarchy to see if compile time optimizations can improve performance. Once again, research is split between improvements in instruction misses and improvements in data misses. The optimizations presented below are found in many modern compilers.

Code and Data Rearrangement

Code can easily be rearranged without affecting correctness; for example, reordering the procedures of a program might reduce instruction miss rates by reducing conflict misses [McFarling 1989]. Another code optimization aims for better efficiency from long cache blocks. Aligning basic blocks so that the entry point is at the beginning of a cache block decreases the chance of a cache miss for sequential code. If the compiler knows that a branch is likely to be taken, it can improve spatial locality by changing the sense of the branch and swapping the basic block at the branch target with the basic block sequentially after the branch. *Branch straightening* is the name of this optimization.

Data have even fewer restrictions on location than code. The goal of such transformations is to try to improve the spatial and temporal locality of the data. For example, array calculations—the cause of most misses in scientific codes—can be changed to operate on all data in a cache block rather than blindly striding through arrays in the order that the programmer wrote the loop.

To give a feeling of this type of optimization, we will show two examples, transforming the C code by hand to reduce cache misses.

Loop Interchange

Some programs have nested loops that access data in memory in nonsequential order. Simply exchanging the nesting of the loops can make the code access the data in the order they are stored. Assuming the arrays do not fit in the cache, this technique reduces misses by improving spatial locality; reordering maximizes use of data in a cache block before they are discarded.

```
/* Before */
for (j = 0; j < 100; j = j+1)
        for (i = 0; i < 5000; i = i+1)
                x[i][j] = 2 * x[i][j];
```

```
/* After */
for (i = 0; i < 5000; i = i+1)
      for (j = 0; j < 100; j = j+1)
            x[i][j] = 2 * x[i][j];
```

The original code would skip through memory in strides of 100 words, while the revised version accesses all the words in one cache block before going to the next block. This optimization improves cache performance without affecting the number of instructions executed.

Blocking

This optimization improves temporal locality to reduce misses. We are again dealing with multiple arrays, with some arrays accessed by rows and some by columns. Storing the arrays row by row (*row major order*) or column by column (*column major order*) does not solve the problem because both rows and columns are used in every loop iteration. Such orthogonal accesses mean that transformations such as loop interchange still leave plenty of room for improvement.

Instead of operating on entire rows or columns of an array, blocked algorithms operate on submatrices or *blocks*. The goal is to maximize accesses to the data loaded into the cache before the data are replaced. The code example below, which performs matrix multiplication, helps motivate the optimization:

```
/* Before */
for (i = 0; i < N; i = i+1)
      for (j = 0; j < N; j = j+1)
            {r = 0;
             for (k = 0; k < N; k = k + 1)
                   r = r + y[i][k]*z[k][j];
             x[i][j] = r;
            };
```

The two inner loops read all N-by-N elements of z, read the same N elements in a row of y repeatedly, and write one row of N elements of x. Figure 5.8 gives a snapshot of the accesses to the three arrays. A dark shade indicates a recent access, a light shade indicates an older access, and white means not yet accessed.

The number of capacity misses clearly depends on N and the size of the cache. If it can hold all three N-by-N matrices, then all is well, provided there are no cache conflicts. If the cache can hold one N-by-N matrix and one row of N, then at least the ith row of y and the array z may stay in the cache. Less than that and misses may occur for both x and z. In the worst case, there would be $2N^3 + N^2$ memory words accessed for N^3 operations.

To ensure that the elements being accessed can fit in the cache, the original code is changed to compute on a submatrix of size B by B. Two inner loops now compute in steps of size B rather than the full length of x and z. B is called the *blocking factor*. (Assume x is initialized to zero.)

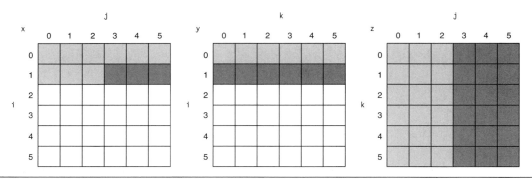

Figure 5.8 A snapshot of the three arrays x, y, and z when *N* = 6 and i = 1. The age of accesses to the array elements is indicated by shade: white means not yet touched, light means older accesses, and dark means newer accesses. Compared to Figure 5.9, elements of y and z are read repeatedly to calculate new elements of x. The variables i, j, and k are shown along the rows or columns used to access the arrays.

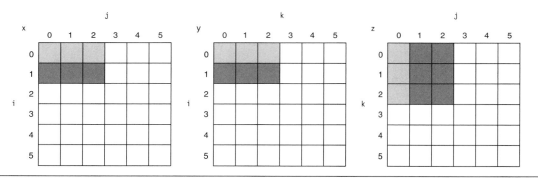

Figure 5.9 The age of accesses to the arrays x, y, and z when *B* = 3. Note in contrast to Figure 5.8 the smaller number of elements accessed.

```
/* After */
for (jj = 0; jj < N; jj = jj+B)
for (kk = 0; kk < N; kk = kk+B)
for (i = 0; i < N; i = i+1)
        for (j = jj; j < min(jj+B,N); j = j+1)
            {r = 0;
             for (k = kk; k < min(kk+B,N); k = k + 1)
                 r = r + y[i][k]*z[k][j];
             x[i][j] = x[i][j] + r;
            };
```

Figure 5.9 illustrates the accesses to the three arrays using blocking. Looking only at capacity misses, the total number of memory words accessed is $2N^3/B + N^2$. This total is an improvement by about a factor of B. Hence, blocking exploits a combination of spatial and temporal locality, since y benefits from spatial locality and z benefits from temporal locality.

Although we have aimed at reducing cache misses, blocking can also be used to help register allocation. By taking a small blocking size such that the block can be held in registers, we can minimize the number of loads and stores in the program.

Tenth Optimization: Hardware Prefetching of Instructions and Data to Reduce Miss Penalty or Miss Rate

Nonblocking caches effectively reduce the miss penalty by overlapping execution with memory access. Another approach is to prefetch items before the processor requests them. Both instructions and data can be prefetched, either directly into the caches or into an external buffer that can be more quickly accessed than main memory.

Instruction prefetch is frequently done in hardware outside of the cache. Typically, the processor fetches two blocks on a miss: the requested block and the next consecutive block. The requested block is placed in the instruction cache when it returns, and the prefetched block is placed into the instruction stream buffer. If the requested block is present in the instruction stream buffer, the original cache request is canceled, the block is read from the stream buffer, and the next prefetch request is issued.

A similar approach can be applied to data accesses [Jouppi 1990]. Palacharla and Kessler [1994] looked at a set of scientific programs and considered multiple stream buffers that could handle either instructions or data. They found that eight stream buffers could capture 50% to 70% of all misses from a processor with two 64 KB four-way set-associative caches, one for instructions and the other for data.

The Intel Pentium 4 can prefetch data into the second-level cache from up to eight streams from eight different 4 KB pages. Prefetching is invoked if there are two successive L2 cache misses to a page, and if the distance between those cache blocks is less than 256 bytes. (The stride limit is 512 bytes on some models of the Pentium 4.) It won't prefetch across a 4 KB page boundary.

Figure 5.10 shows the overall performance improvement for a subset of SPEC2000 programs when hardware prefetching is turned on. Note that this figure includes only 2 of 12 integer programs, while it includes the majority of the SPEC floating-point programs.

Prefetching relies on utilizing memory bandwidth that otherwise would be unused, but if it interferes with demand misses, it can actually lower performance. Help from compilers can reduce useless prefetching.

Eleventh Optimization: Compiler-Controlled Prefetching to Reduce Miss Penalty or Miss Rate

An alternative to hardware prefetching is for the compiler to insert prefetch instructions to request data before the processor needs it. There are two flavors of prefetch:

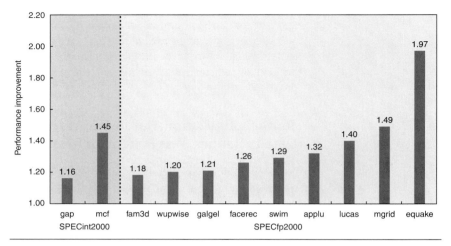

Figure 5.10 Speedup due to hardware prefetching on Intel Pentium 4 with hardware prefetching turned on for 2 of 12 SPECint2000 benchmarks and 9 of 14 SPECfp2000 benchmarks. Only the programs that benefit the most from prefetching are shown; prefetching speeds up the missing 15 SPEC benchmarks by less than 15% [Singhal 2004].

■ *Register prefetch* will load the value into a register.

■ *Cache prefetch* loads data only into the cache and not the register.

Either of these can be *faulting* or *nonfaulting;* that is, the address does or does not cause an exception for virtual address faults and protection violations. Using this terminology, a normal load instruction could be considered a "faulting register prefetch instruction." Nonfaulting prefetches simply turn into no-ops if they would normally result in an exception, which is what we want.

The most effective prefetch is "semantically invisible" to a program: It doesn't change the contents of registers and memory, *and* it cannot cause virtual memory faults. Most processors today offer nonfaulting cache prefetches. This section assumes nonfaulting cache prefetch, also called *nonbinding* prefetch.

Prefetching makes sense only if the processor can proceed while prefetching the data; that is, the caches do not stall but continue to supply instructions and data while waiting for the prefetched data to return. As you would expect, the data cache for such computers is normally nonblocking.

Like hardware-controlled prefetching, the goal is to overlap execution with the prefetching of data. Loops are the important targets, as they lend themselves to prefetch optimizations. If the miss penalty is small, the compiler just unrolls the loop once or twice, and it schedules the prefetches with the execution. If the miss penalty is large, it uses software pipelining (see Appendix G) or unrolls many times to prefetch data for a future iteration.

Issuing prefetch instructions incurs an instruction overhead, however, so compilers must take care to ensure that such overheads do not exceed the benefits. By concentrating on references that are likely to be cache misses, programs can avoid unnecessary prefetches while improving average memory access time significantly.

Example   For the code below, determine which accesses are likely to cause data cache misses. Next, insert prefetch instructions to reduce misses. Finally, calculate the number of prefetch instructions executed and the misses avoided by prefetching. Let's assume we have an 8 KB direct-mapped data cache with 16-byte blocks, and it is a write-back cache that does write allocate. The elements of a and b are 8 bytes long since they are double-precision floating-point arrays. There are 3 rows and 100 columns for a and 101 rows and 3 columns for b. Let's also assume they are not in the cache at the start of the program.

```
for (i = 0; i < 3; i = i+1)
        for (j = 0; j < 100; j = j+1)
                a[i][j] = b[j][0] * b[j+1][0];
```

Answer   The compiler will first determine which accesses are likely to cause cache misses; otherwise, we will waste time on issuing prefetch instructions for data that would be hits. Elements of a are written in the order that they are stored in memory, so a will benefit from spatial locality: The even values of j will miss and the odd values will hit. Since a has 3 rows and 100 columns, its accesses will lead to $3 \times \left\lceil \dfrac{100}{2} \right\rceil$, or 150 misses.

The array b does not benefit from spatial locality since the accesses are not in the order it is stored. The array b does benefit twice from temporal locality: The same elements are accessed for each iteration of i, and each iteration of j uses the same value of b as the last iteration. Ignoring potential conflict misses, the misses due to b will be for b[j+1][0] accesses when i = 0, and also the first access to b[j][0] when j = 0. Since j goes from 0 to 99 when i = 0, accesses to b lead to 100 + 1, or 101 misses.

Thus, this loop will miss the data cache approximately 150 times for a plus 101 times for b, or 251 misses.

To simplify our optimization, we will not worry about prefetching the first accesses of the loop. These may already be in the cache, or we will pay the miss penalty of the first few elements of a or b. Nor will we worry about suppressing the prefetches at the end of the loop that try to prefetch beyond the end of a (a[i][100] ... a[i][106]) and the end of b (b[101][0] ... b[107][0]). If these were faulting prefetches, we could not take this luxury. Let's assume that the miss penalty is so large we need to start prefetching at least, say, seven iterations in advance. (Stated alternatively, we assume prefetching has no benefit until the eighth iteration.) We underline the changes to the code above needed to add prefetching.

```
for (j = 0; j < 100; j = j+1) {
        prefetch(b[j+7][0]);
        /* b(j,0) for 7 iterations later */
        prefetch(a[0][j+7]);
        /* a(0,j) for 7 iterations later */
        a[0][j] = b[j][0] * b[j+1][0];};
    for (i = 1; i < 3; i = i+1)
        for (j = 0; j < 100; j = j+1) {
                prefetch(a[i][j+7]);
                /* a(i,j) for +7 iterations */
                a[i][j] = b[j][0] * b[j+1][0];}
```

This revised code prefetches a[i][7] through a[i][99] and b[7][0] through b[100][0], reducing the number of nonprefetched misses to

- 7 misses for elements b[0][0], b[1][0], ..., b[6][0] in the first loop

- 4 misses ($\lceil 7/2 \rceil$) for elements a[0][0], a[0][1], ..., a[0][6] in the first loop (spatial locality reduces misses to 1 per 16-byte cache block)

- 4 misses ($\lceil 7/2 \rceil$) for elements a[1][0], a[1][1], ..., a[1][6] in the second loop

- 4 misses ($\lceil 7/2 \rceil$) for elements a[2][0], a[2][1], ..., a[2][6] in the second loop

or a total of 19 nonprefetched misses. The cost of avoiding 232 cache misses is executing 400 prefetch instructions, likely a good trade-off.

Example   Calculate the time saved in the example above. Ignore instruction cache misses and assume there are no conflict or capacity misses in the data cache. Assume that prefetches can overlap with each other and with cache misses, thereby transferring at the maximum memory bandwidth. Here are the key loop times ignoring cache misses: The original loop takes 7 clock cycles per iteration, the first prefetch loop takes 9 clock cycles per iteration, and the second prefetch loop takes 8 clock cycles per iteration (including the overhead of the outer for loop). A miss takes 100 clock cycles.

Answer   The original doubly nested loop executes the multiply 3 × 100 or 300 times. Since the loop takes 7 clock cycles per iteration, the total is 300 × 7 or 2100 clock cycles plus cache misses. Cache misses add 251 × 100 or 25,100 clock cycles, giving a total of 27,200 clock cycles. The first prefetch loop iterates 100 times; at 9 clock cycles per iteration the total is 900 clock cycles plus cache misses. They add 11 × 100 or 1100 clock cycles for cache misses, giving a total of 2000. The second loop executes 2 × 100 or 200 times, and at 8 clock cycles per iteration it takes 1600 clock cycles plus 8 × 100 or 800 clock cycles for cache misses. This gives a total of 2400 clock cycles. From the prior example, we know that this code executes 400 prefetch instructions during the 2000 + 2400 or 4400 clock cycles to execute these two loops. If we assume that the prefetches are completely overlapped with the rest of the execution, then the prefetch code is 27,200/4400 or 6.2 times faster.

Although array optimizations are easy to understand, modern programs are more likely to use pointers. Luk and Mowry [1999] have demonstrated that compiler-based prefetching can sometimes be extended to pointers as well. Of 10 programs with recursive data structures, prefetching all pointers when a node is visited improved performance by 4% to 31% in half the programs. On the other hand, the remaining programs were still within 2% of their original performance. The issue is both whether prefetches are to data already in the cache and whether they occur early enough for the data to arrive by the time it is needed.

Cache Optimization Summary

The techniques to improve hit time, bandwidth, miss penalty, and miss rate generally affect the other components of the average memory access equation as well as the complexity of the memory hierarchy. Figure 5.11 summarizes these techniques and estimates the impact on complexity, with + meaning that the technique improves the factor, – meaning it hurts that factor, and blank meaning it has no impact. Generally, no technique helps more than one category.

Technique	Hit time	Band-width	Miss pen-alty	Miss rate	Hardware cost/ complexity	Comment
Small and simple caches	+			–	0	Trivial; widely used
Way-predicting caches	+				1	Used in Pentium 4
Trace caches	+				3	Used in Pentium 4
Pipelined cache access	–	+			1	Widely used
Nonblocking caches		+	+		3	Widely used
Banked caches		+			1	Used in L2 of Opteron and Niagara
Critical word first and early restart			+		2	Widely used
Merging write buffer			+		1	Widely used with write through
Compiler techniques to reduce cache misses				+	0	Software is a challenge; some computers have compiler option
Hardware prefetching of instructions and data			+	+	2 instr., 3 data	Many prefetch instructions; Opteron and Pentium 4 prefetch data
Compiler-controlled prefetching			+	+	3	Needs nonblocking cache; possible instruction overhead; in many CPUs

Figure 5.11 Summary of 11 advanced cache optimizations showing impact on cache performance and complexity. Although generally a technique helps only one factor, prefetching can reduce misses if done sufficiently early; if not, it can reduce miss penalty. + means that the technique improves the factor, – means it hurts that factor, and blank means it has no impact. The complexity measure is subjective, with 0 being the easiest and 3 being a challenge.

Memory Technology and Optimizations

... the one single development that put computers on their feet was the invention of a reliable form of memory, namely, the core memory.... Its cost was reasonable, it was reliable and, because it was reliable, it could in due course be made large. [p. 209]

Maurice Wilkes
Memoirs of a Computer Pioneer (1985)

Main memory is the next level down in the hierarchy. Main memory satisfies the demands of caches and serves as the I/O interface, as it is the destination of input as well as the source for output. Performance measures of main memory emphasize both latency and bandwidth. Traditionally, main memory latency (which affects the cache miss penalty) is the primary concern of the cache, while main memory bandwidth is the primary concern of multiprocessors and I/O. Chapter 4 discusses the relationship of main memory and multiprocessors, and Chapter 6 discusses the relationship of main memory and I/O.

Although caches benefit from low-latency memory, it is generally easier to improve memory bandwidth with new organizations than it is to reduce latency. The popularity of second-level caches, and their larger block sizes, makes main memory bandwidth important to caches as well. In fact, cache designers increase block size to take advantage of the high memory bandwidth.

The previous sections describe what can be done with cache organization to reduce this processor-DRAM performance gap, but simply making caches larger or adding more levels of caches cannot eliminate the gap. Innovations in main memory are needed as well.

In the past, the innovation was how to organize the many DRAM chips that made up the main memory, such as multiple memory banks. Higher bandwidth is available using memory banks, by making memory and its bus wider, or doing both.

Ironically, as capacity per memory chip increases, there are fewer chips in the same-sized memory system, reducing chances for innovation. For example, a 2 GB main memory takes 256 memory chips of 64 Mbit (16M × 4 bits), easily organized into 16 64-bit-wide banks of 16 memory chips. However, it takes only 16 256M × 4-bit memory chips for 2 GB, making one 64-bit-wide bank the limit. Since computers are often sold and benchmarked with small, standard memory configurations, manufacturers cannot rely on very large memories to get bandwidth. This shrinking number of chips in a standard configuration shrinks the importance of innovations at the board level.

Hence, memory innovations are now happening inside the DRAM chips themselves. This section describes the technology inside the memory chips and those innovative, internal organizations. Before describing the technologies and options, let's go over the performance metrics.

Memory latency is traditionally quoted using two measures—access time and cycle time. *Access time* is the time between when a read is requested and when the desired word arrives, while *cycle time* is the minimum time between requests to memory. One reason that cycle time is greater than access time is that the memory needs the address lines to be stable between accesses.

Virtually all desktop or server computers since 1975 used DRAMs for main memory, and virtually all use SRAMs for cache, our first topic.

SRAM Technology

The first letter of SRAM stands for *static*. The dynamic nature of the circuits in DRAM requires data to be written back after being read—hence the difference between the access time and the cycle time as well as the need to refresh. SRAMs don't need to refresh and so the access time is very close to the cycle time. SRAMs typically use six transistors per bit to prevent the information from being disturbed when read. SRAM needs only minimal power to retain the charge in standby mode.

SRAM designs are concerned with speed and capacity, while in DRAM designs the emphasis is on cost per bit and capacity. For memories designed in comparable technologies, the capacity of DRAMs is roughly 4–8 times that of SRAMs. The cycle time of SRAMs is 8–16 times faster than DRAMs, but they are also 8–16 times as expensive.

DRAM Technology

As early DRAMs grew in capacity, the cost of a package with all the necessary address lines was an issue. The solution was to multiplex the address lines, thereby cutting the number of address pins in half. Figure 5.12 shows the basic DRAM organization. One-half of the address is sent first, called the *row access strobe* (RAS). The other half of the address, sent during the *column access strobe* (CAS), follows it. These names come from the internal chip organization, since the memory is organized as a rectangular matrix addressed by rows and columns.

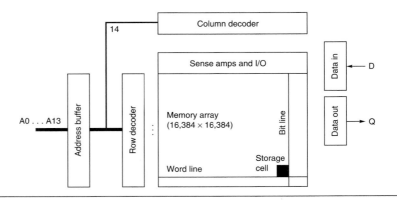

Figure 5.12 Internal organization of a 64M bit DRAM. DRAMs often use banks of memory arrays internally and select between them. For example, instead of one 16,384 × 16,384 memory, a DRAM might use 256 1024 × 1024 arrays or 16 2048 × 2048 arrays.

An additional requirement of DRAM derives from the property signified by its first letter, *D,* for *dynamic.* To pack more bits per chip, DRAMs use only a single transistor to store a bit. Reading that bit destroys the information, so it must be restored. This is one reason the DRAM cycle time is much longer than the access time. In addition, to prevent loss of information when a bit is not read or written, the bit must be "refreshed" periodically. Fortunately, all the bits in a row can be refreshed simultaneously just by reading that row. Hence, every DRAM in the memory system must access every row within a certain time window, such as 8 ms. Memory controllers include hardware to refresh the DRAMs periodically.

This requirement means that the memory system is occasionally unavailable because it is sending a signal telling every chip to refresh. The time for a refresh is typically a full memory access (RAS and CAS) for each row of the DRAM. Since the memory matrix in a DRAM is conceptually square, the number of steps in a refresh is usually the square root of the DRAM capacity. DRAM designers try to keep time spent refreshing to less than 5% of the total time.

So far we have presented main memory as if it operated like a Swiss train, consistently delivering the goods exactly according to schedule. Refresh belies that analogy, since some accesses take much longer than others do. Thus, refresh is another reason for variability of memory latency and hence cache miss penalty.

Amdahl suggested a rule of thumb that memory capacity should grow linearly with processor speed to keep a balanced system, so that a 1000 MIPS processor should have 1000 MB of memory. Processor designers rely on DRAMs to supply that demand: In the past, they expected a fourfold improvement in capacity every three years, or 55% per year. Unfortunately, the performance of DRAMs is growing at a much slower rate. Figure 5.13 shows a performance improvement in row access time, which is related to latency, of about 5% per year. The CAS or data transfer time, which is related to bandwidth, is growing at more than twice that rate.

Although we have been talking about individual chips, DRAMs are commonly sold on small boards called *dual inline memory modules* (DIMMs). DIMMs typically contain 4–16 DRAMs, and they are normally organized to be 8 bytes wide (+ ECC) for desktop systems.

In addition to the DIMM packaging and the new interfaces to improve the data transfer time, discussed in the following subsections, the biggest change to DRAMs has been a slowing down in capacity growth. DRAMs obeyed Moore's Law for 20 years, bringing out a new chip with four times the capacity every three years. Due to a slowing in demand for DRAMs, since 1998 new chips only double capacity every two years. In 2006, this new slower pace shows signs of further deceleration.

Improving Memory Performance inside a DRAM Chip

As Moore's Law continues to supply more transistors and as the processor-memory gap increases pressure on memory performance, the ideas of the previous section have made their way inside the DRAM chip. Generally, innovation

Year of introduction	Chip size	Row access strobe (RAS)		Column access strobe (CAS)/ data transfer time (ns)	Cycle time (ns)
		Slowest DRAM (ns)	Fastest DRAM (ns)		
1980	64K bit	180	150	75	250
1983	256K bit	150	120	50	220
1986	1M bit	120	100	25	190
1989	4M bit	100	80	20	165
1992	16M bit	80	60	15	120
1996	64M bit	70	50	12	110
1998	128M bit	70	50	10	100
2000	256M bit	65	45	7	90
2002	512M bit	60	40	5	80
2004	1G bit	55	35	5	70
2006	2G bit	50	30	2.5	60

Figure 5.13 Times of fast and slow DRAMs with each generation. (Cycle time is defined on page 310.) Performance improvement of row access time is about 5% per year. The improvement by a factor of 2 in column access in 1986 accompanied the switch from NMOS DRAMs to CMOS DRAMs.

has led to greater bandwidth, sometimes at the cost of greater latency. This subsection presents techniques that take advantage of the nature of DRAMs.

As mentioned earlier, a DRAM access is divided into row access and column access. DRAMs must buffer a row of bits inside the DRAM for the column access, and this row is usually the square root of the DRAM size—16K bits for 256M bits, 64K bits for 1G bits, and so on.

Although presented logically as a single monolithic array of memory bits, the internal organization of DRAM actually consists of many memory modules. For a variety of manufacturing reasons, these modules are usually 1–4M bits. Thus, if you were to examine a 1G bit DRAM under a microscope, you might see 512 memory arrays, each of 2M bits, on the chip. This large number of arrays internally presents the opportunity to provide much higher bandwidth off chip.

To improve bandwidth, there has been a variety of evolutionary innovations over time. The first was timing signals that allow repeated accesses to the row buffer without another row access time, typically called *fast page mode*. Such a buffer comes naturally, as each array will buffer 1024–2048 bits for each access.

Conventional DRAMs had an asynchronous interface to the memory controller, and hence every transfer involved overhead to synchronize with the controller. The second major change was to add a clock signal to the DRAM interface, so that the repeated transfers would not bear that overhead. *Synchronous DRAM*

Standard	Clock rate (MHz)	M transfers per second	DRAM name	MB/sec /DIMM	DIMM name
DDR	133	266	DDR266	2128	PC2100
DDR	150	300	DDR300	2400	PC2400
DDR	200	400	DDR400	3200	PC3200
DDR2	266	533	DDR2-533	4264	PC4300
DDR2	333	667	DDR2-667	5336	PC5300
DDR2	400	800	DDR2-800	6400	PC6400
DDR3	533	1066	DDR3-1066	8528	PC8500
DDR3	666	1333	DDR3-1333	10,664	PC10700
DDR3	800	1600	DDR3-1600	12,800	PC12800

Figure 5.14 Clock rates, bandwidth, and names of DDR DRAMS and DIMMs in 2006. Note the numerical relationship between the columns. The third column is twice the second, and the fourth uses the number from the third column in the name of the DRAM chip. The fifth column is eight times the third column, and a rounded version of this number is used in the name of the DIMM. Although not shown in this figure, DDRs also specify latency in clock cycles. The name DDR400 CL3 means that memory delays 3 clock cycles of 5 ns each—the clock period a 200 MHz clock—before starting to deliver the request data. The exercises explore these details further.

(SDRAM) is the name of this optimization. SDRAMs typically also had a programmable register to hold the number of bytes requested, and hence can send many bytes over several cycles per request.

The third major DRAM innovation to increase bandwidth is to transfer data on both the rising edge and falling edge of the DRAM clock signal, thereby doubling the peak data rate. This optimization is called *double data rate* (DDR). To supply data at these high rates, DDR SDRAMs activate multiple banks internally.

The bus speeds for these DRAMs are also 133–200 MHz, but these DDR DIMMs are confusingly labeled by the peak *DIMM* bandwidth. Hence, the DIMM name PC2100 comes from 133 MHz × 2 × 8 bytes or 2100 MB/sec. Sustaining the confusion, the chips themselves are labeled with *the number of bits per second* rather than their clock rate, so a 133 MHz DDR chip is called a DDR266. Figure 5.14 shows the relationship between clock rate, transfers per second per chip, chip name, DIMM bandwidth, and DIMM name.

Example   Suppose you measured a new DDR3 DIMM to transfer at 16000 MB/sec. What do you think its name will be? What is the clock rate of that DIMM? What is your guess of the name of DRAMs used in that DIMM?

Answer   A good guideline is to assume that DRAM marketers picked names with the biggest numbers. The DIMM name is likely PC16000. The clock rate of the DIMM is

$$\text{Clock rate} \times 2 \times 8 = 16000$$
$$\text{Clock rate} = 16000/16$$
$$\text{Clock rate} = 1000$$

or 1000 MHz and 2000 M transfers per second, so the DRAM name is likely to be DDR3-2000.

DDR is now a sequence of standards. DDR2 lowers power by dropping the voltage from 2.5 volts to 1.8 volts and offers higher clock rates: 266 MHz, 333 MHz, and 400 MHz. DDR3 drops voltage to 1.5 volts and has a maximum clock speed of 800 MHz.

In each of these three cases, the advantage of such optimizations is that they add a small amount of logic to exploit the high potential internal DRAM bandwidth, adding little cost to the system while achieving a significant improvement in bandwidth.

5.4   Protection: Virtual Memory and Virtual Machines

A virtual machine is taken to be an efficient, isolated duplicate *of the real machine. We explain these notions through the idea of a* virtual machine monitor *(VMM). . . . a VMM has three essential characteristics. First, the VMM provides an environment for programs which is essentially identical with the original machine; second, programs run in this environment show at worst only minor decreases in speed; and last, the VMM is in complete control of system resources.*

Gerald Popek and Robert Goldberg
"Formal requirements for virtualizable third generation architectures,"
Communications of the ACM (July 1974)

Security and privacy are two of the most vexing challenges for information technology in 2006. Electronic burglaries, often involving lists of credit card numbers, are announced regularly, and it's widely believed that many more go unreported. Hence, both researchers and practitioners are looking for new ways to make computing systems more secure. Although protecting information is not limited to hardware, in our view real security and privacy will likely involve innovation in computer architecture as well as in systems software.

This section starts with a review of the architecture support for protecting processes from each other via virtual memory. It then describes the added protection provided from virtual machines, the architecture requirements of virtual machines, and the performance of a virtual machine.

Protection via Virtual Memory

Page-based virtual memory, including a translation lookaside buffer that caches page table entries, is the primary mechanism that protects processes from each other. Sections C.4 and C.5 in Appendix C review virtual memory, including a detailed description of protection via segmentation and paging in the 80x86. This subsection acts as a quick review; refer to those sections if it's too quick.

Multiprogramming, where several programs running concurrently would share a computer, led to demands for protection and sharing among programs and to the concept of a *process*. Metaphorically, a process is a program's breathing air and living space—that is, a running program plus any state needed to continue running it. At any instant, it must be possible to switch from one process to another. This exchange is called a *process switch* or *context switch*.

The operating system and architecture join forces to allow processes to share the hardware yet not interfere with each other. To do this, the architecture must limit what a process can access when running a user process yet allow an operating system process to access more. At the minimum, the architecture must do the following:

1. Provide at least two modes, indicating whether the running process is a user process or an operating system process. This latter process is sometimes called a *kernel* process or a *supervisor* process.

2. Provide a portion of the processor state that a user process can use but not write. This state includes an user/supervisor mode bit(s), an exception enable/disable bit, and memory protection information. Users are prevented from writing this state because the operating system cannot control user processes if users can give themselves supervisor privileges, disable exceptions, or change memory protection.

3. Provide mechanisms whereby the processor can go from user mode to supervisor mode and vice versa. The first direction is typically accomplished by a *system call,* implemented as a special instruction that transfers control to a dedicated location in supervisor code space. The PC is saved from the point of the system call, and the processor is placed in supervisor mode. The return to user mode is like a subroutine return that restores the previous user/supervisor mode.

4. Provide mechanisms to limit memory accesses to protect the memory state of a process without having to swap the process to disk on a context switch.

Appendix C describes several memory protection schemes, but by far the most popular is adding protection restrictions to each page of virtual memory. Fixed-sized pages, typically 4 KB or 8 KB long, are mapped from the virtual address space into physical address space via a page table. The protection restrictions are included in each page table entry. The protection restrictions might determine whether a user process can read this page, whether a user process can write to this page, and whether code can be executed from this page. In addition, a process can neither read nor write a page if it is not in the page table. Since only the OS can update the page table, the paging mechanism provides total access protection.

Paged virtual memory means that every memory access logically takes at least twice as long, with one memory access to obtain the physical address and a second access to get the data. This cost would be far too dear. The solution is to rely on the principle of locality; if the accesses have locality, then the *address translations* for the accesses must also have locality. By keeping these address translations in a special cache, a memory access rarely requires a second access to translate the data. This special address translation cache is referred to as a *translation lookaside buffer* (TLB).

A TLB entry is like a cache entry where the tag holds portions of the virtual address and the data portion holds a physical page address, protection field, valid bit, and usually a use bit and a dirty bit. The operating system changes these bits by changing the value in the page table and then invalidating the corresponding TLB entry. When the entry is reloaded from the page table, the TLB gets an accurate copy of the bits.

Assuming the computer faithfully obeys the restrictions on pages and maps virtual addresses to physical addresses, it would seem that we are done. Newspaper headlines suggest otherwise.

The reason we're not done is that we depend on the accuracy of the operating system as well as the hardware. Today's operating systems consist of tens of millions of lines of code. Since bugs are measured in number per thousand lines of code, there are thousands of bugs in production operating systems. Flaws in the OS have led to vulnerabilities that are routinely exploited.

This problem, and the possibility that not enforcing protection could be much more costly than in the past, has led some to look for a protection model with a much smaller code base than the full OS, such as Virtual Machines.

Protection via Virtual Machines

An idea related to virtual memory that is almost as old is Virtual Machines (VM). They were first developed in the late 1960s, and they have remained an important part of mainframe computing over the years. Although largely ignored in the domain of single-user computers in the 1980s and 1990s, they have recently gained popularity due to

- the increasing importance of isolation and security in modern systems,
- the failures in security and reliability of standard operating systems,
- the sharing of a single computer among many unrelated users, and
- the dramatic increases in raw speed of processors, which makes the overhead of VMs more acceptable.

The broadest definition of VMs includes basically all emulation methods that provide a standard software interface, such as the Java VM. We are interested in VMs that provide a complete system-level environment at the binary instruction set architecture (ISA) level. Although some VMs run different ISAs in the VM from the native hardware, we assume they always match the hardware. Such VMs are called (Operating) *System Virtual Machines*. IBM VM/370, VMware ESX Server, and Xen are examples. They present the illusion that the users of a VM have an entire computer to themselves, including a copy of the operating system. A single computer runs multiple VMs and can support a number of different operating systems (OSes). On a conventional platform, a single OS "owns" all the hardware resources, but with a VM, multiple OSes all share the hardware resources.

The software that supports VMs is called a *virtual machine monitor* (VMM) or *hypervisor;* the VMM is the heart of Virtual Machine technology. The underlying hardware platform is called the *host*, and its resources are shared among the *guest* VMs. The VMM determines how to map virtual resources to physical resources: A physical resource may be time-shared, partitioned, or even emulated in software. The VMM is much smaller than a traditional OS; the isolation portion of a VMM is perhaps only 10,000 lines of code.

In general, the cost of processor virtualization depends on the workload. User-level processor-bound programs, such as SPEC CPU2006, have zero virtualization overhead because the OS is rarely invoked so everything runs at native speeds. I/O-intensive workloads generally are also OS-intensive, which execute many system calls and privileged instructions that can result in high virtualization overhead. The overhead is determined by the number of instructions that must be emulated by the VMM and how slowly they are emulated. Hence, when the guest VMs run the same ISA as the host, as we assume here, the goal of the architecture and the VMM is to run almost all instructions directly on the native hardware. On the other hand, if the I/O-intensive workload is also *I/O-bound*, the cost of processor virtualization can be completely hidden by low processor utilization since it is often waiting for I/O (as we will see later in Figures 5.15 and 5.16).

Although our interest here is in VMs for improving protection, VMs provide two other benefits that are commercially significant:

1. *Managing software*. VMs provide an abstraction that can run the complete software stack, even including old operating systems like DOS. A typical deployment might be some VMs running legacy OSes, many running the current stable OS release, and a few testing the next OS release.

2. *Managing hardware*. One reason for multiple servers is to have each application running with the compatible version of the operating system on separate computers, as this separation can improve dependability. VMs allow these separate software stacks to run independently yet share hardware, thereby consolidating the number of servers. Another example is that some VMMs support migration of a running VM to a different computer, either to balance load or to evacuate from failing hardware.

Requirements of a Virtual Machine Monitor

What must a VM monitor do? It presents a software interface to guest software, it must isolate the state of guests from each other, and it must protect itself from guest software (including guest OSes). The qualitative requirements are

- Guest software should behave on a VM exactly as if it were running on the native hardware, except for performance-related behavior or limitations of fixed resources shared by multiple VMs.

- Guest software should not be able to change allocation of real system resources directly.

To "virtualize" the processor, the VMM must control just about everything— access to privileged state, address translation, I/O, exceptions and interrupts— even though the guest VM and OS currently running are temporarily using them.

For example, in the case of a timer interrupt, the VMM would suspend the currently running guest VM, save its state, handle the interrupt, determine which guest VM to run next, and then load its state. Guest VMs that rely on a timer interrupt are provided with a virtual timer and an emulated timer interrupt by the VMM.

To be in charge, the VMM must be at a higher privilege level than the guest VM, which generally runs in user mode; this also ensures that the execution of any privileged instruction will be handled by the VMM. The basic requirements of system virtual machines are almost identical to those for paged virtual memory listed above:

- At least two processor modes, system and user.

- A privileged subset of instructions that is available only in system mode, resulting in a trap if executed in user mode. All system resources must be controllable only via these instructions.

(Lack of) Instruction Set Architecture Support for Virtual Machines

If VMs are planned for during the design of the ISA, it's relatively easy to both reduce the number of instructions that must be executed by a VMM and how long it takes to emulate them. An architecture that allows the VM to execute directly on the hardware earns the title *virtualizable,* and the IBM 370 architecture proudly bears that label.

Alas, since VMs have been considered for desktop and PC-based server applications only fairly recently, most instruction sets were created without virtualization in mind. These culprits include 80x86 and most RISC architectures.

Because the VMM must ensure that the guest system only interacts with virtual resources, a conventional guest OS runs as a user mode program on top of the VMM. Then, if a guest OS attempts to access or modify information related to hardware resources via a privileged instruction—for example, reading or writing the page table pointer—it will trap to the VMM. The VMM can then effect the appropriate changes to corresponding real resources.

Hence, if any instruction that tries to read or write such sensitive information traps when executed in user mode, the VMM can intercept it and support a virtual version of the sensitive information as the guest OS expects.

In the absence of such support, other measures must be taken. A VMM must take special precautions to locate all problematic instructions and ensure that they behave correctly when executed by a guest OS, thereby increasing the complexity of the VMM and reducing the performance of running the VM.

Sections 5.5 and 5.7 give concrete examples of problematic instructions in the 80x86 architecture.

Impact of Virtual Machines on Virtual Memory and I/O

Another challenge is virtualization of virtual memory, as each guest OS in every VM manages its own set of page tables. To make this work, the VMM separates the notions of *real* and *physical memory* (which are often treated synonymously), and makes real memory a separate, intermediate level between virtual memory and physical memory. (Some use the terms *virtual memory, physical memory,* and *machine memory* to name the same three levels.) The guest OS maps virtual memory to real memory via its page tables, and the VMM page tables map the guests' real memory to physical memory. The virtual memory architecture is specified either via page tables, as in IBM VM/370 and the 80x86, or via the TLB structure, as in many RISC architectures.

Rather than pay an extra level of indirection on every memory access, the VMM maintains a *shadow page table* that maps directly from the guest virtual address space to the physical address space of the hardware. By detecting all modifications to the guest's page table, the VMM can ensure the shadow page table entries being used by the hardware for translations correspond to those of the guest OS environment, with the exception of the correct physical pages substituted for the real pages in the guest tables. Hence, the VMM must trap any attempt by the guest OS to change its page table or to access the page table pointer. This is commonly done by write protecting the guest page tables and trapping any access to the page table pointer by a guest OS. As noted above, the latter happens naturally if accessing the page table pointer is a privileged operation.

The IBM 370 architecture solved the page table problem in the 1970s with an additional level of indirection that is managed by the VMM. The guest OS keeps its page tables as before, so the shadow pages are unnecessary. AMD has proposed a similar scheme for their Pacifica revision to the 80x86.

To virtualize the TLB architected in many RISC computers, the VMM manages the real TLB and has a copy of the contents of the TLB of each guest VM. To pull this off, any instructions that access the TLB must trap. TLBs with Process ID tags can support a mix of entries from different VMs and the VMM, thereby avoiding flushing of the TLB on a VM switch. Meanwhile, in the background, the VMM supports a mapping between the VMs' virtual Process IDs and the real Process IDs.

The final portion of the architecture to virtualize is I/O. This is by far the most difficult part of system virtualization because of the increasing number of I/O devices attached to the computer *and* the increasing diversity of I/O device types. Another difficulty is the sharing of a real device among multiple VMs, and yet another comes from supporting the myriad of device drivers that are required, especially if different guest OSes are supported on the same VM system. The VM illusion can be maintained by giving each VM generic versions of each type of I/O device driver, and then leaving it to the VMM to handle real I/O.

The method for mapping a virtual to physical I/O device depends on the type of device. For example, physical disks are normally partitioned by the VMM to create virtual disks for guest VMs, and the VMM maintains the mapping of virtual tracks and sectors to the physical ones. Network interfaces are often shared between VMs in very short time slices, and the job of the VMM is to keep track of messages for the virtual network addresses to ensure that guest VMs receive only messages intended for them.

An Example VMM: The Xen Virtual Machine

Early in the development of VMs, a number of inefficiencies became apparent. For example, a guest OS manages its virtual to real page mapping, but this mapping is ignored by the VMM, which performs the actual mapping to physical pages. In other words, a significant amount of wasted effort is expended just to keep the guest OS happy. To reduce such inefficiencies, VMM developers decided that it may be worthwhile to allow the guest OS to be aware that it is running on a VM. For example, a guest OS could assume a real memory as large as its virtual memory so that no memory management is required by the guest OS.

Allowing small modifications to the guest OS to simplify virtualization is referred to as *paravirtualization*, and the open source Xen VMM is a good example. The Xen VMM provides a guest OS with a virtual machine abstraction that is similar to the physical hardware, but it drops many of the troublesome pieces. For example, to avoid flushing the TLB, Xen maps itself into the upper 64 MB of the address space of each VM. It allows the guest OS to allocate pages, just checking to be sure it does not violate protection restrictions. To protect the guest OS from the user programs in the VM, Xen takes advantage of the four protection levels available in the 80x86. The Xen VMM runs at the highest privilege level (0), the guest OS runs at the next level (1), and the applications run at the lowest privilege level (3). Most OSes for the 80x86 keep everything at privilege levels 0 or 3.

For subsetting to work properly, Xen modifies the guest OS to not use problematic portions of the architecture. For example, the port of Linux to Xen changed about 3000 lines, or about 1% of the 80x86-specific code. These changes, however, do not affect the application-binary interfaces of the guest OS.

To simplify the I/O challenge of VMs, Xen recently assigned privileged virtual machines to each hardware I/O device. These special VMs are called *driver domains*. (Xen calls its VMs "domains.") Driver domains run the physical device drivers, although interrupts are still handled by the VMM before being sent to the appropriate driver domain. Regular VMs, called *guest domains*, run simple virtual device drivers that must communicate with the physical device drivers in the driver domains over a channel to access the physical I/O hardware. Data are sent between guest and driver domains by page remapping.

Figure 5.15 compares the relative performance of Xen for six benchmarks. According to these experiments, Xen performs very close to the native performance of Linux. The popularity of Xen, plus such performance results, led standard releases of the Linux kernel to incorporate Xen's paravirtualization changes.

A subsequent study noticed that the experiments in Figure 5.15 were based on a single Ethernet network interface card (NIC), and the single NIC was a performance bottleneck. As a result, the higher processor utilization of Xen did not affect performance. Figure 5.16 compares TCP receive performance as the number of NICs increases from 1 to 4 for native Linux and two configurations of Xen:

1. *Xen privileged VM only (driver domain).* To measure the overhead of Xen without the driver VM scheme, the whole application is run inside the single privileged driver domain.

2. *Xen guest VM + privileged VM.* In the more natural setting, the application and virtual device driver run in the guest VM (guest domain), and the physical device driver runs in the privileged driver VM (driver domain).

Clearly, a single NIC is a bottleneck. Xen driver VM peaks at 1.9 Gbits/sec with 2 NICs while native Linux peaks at 2.5 Gbits/sec with 3 NICs. For guest VMs, the peak receive rate drops under 0.9 Gbits/sec.

After removing the NIC bottleneck, a different Web server workload showed that driver VM Xen achieves less than 80% of the throughput of native Linux, while guest VM + driver VM drops to 34%.

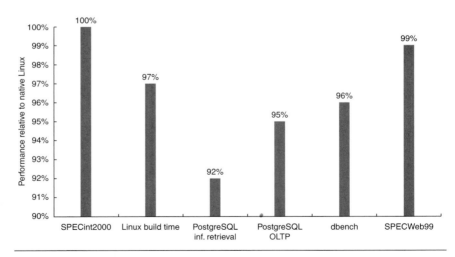

Figure 5.15 **Relative performance for Xen versus native Linux.** The experiments were performed on a Dell 2650 dual processor 2.4 GHz Xeon server with 2 GB RAM, one Broadcom Tigon 3 Gigabit Ethernet NIC, a single Hitachi DK32EJ 146 GB 10K RPM SCSI disk, and running Linux version 2.4.21 [Barham et al. 2003; Clark et al. 2004].

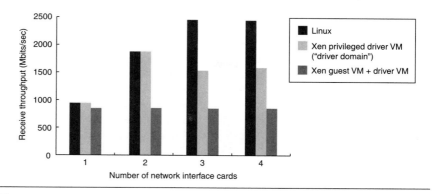

Figure 5.16 **TCP receive performance in Mbits/sec for native Linux versus two configurations of Xen.** Guest VM + driver VM is the conventional configuration [Menon et al. 2005]. The experiments were performed on a Dell PowerEdge 1600SC running a 2.4 GHz Xeon server with 1 GB RAM, and four Intel Pro-1000 Gigabit Ethernet NIC, running Linux version 2.6.10 and Xen version 2.0.3.

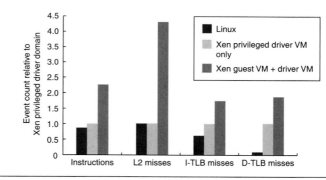

Figure 5.17 **Relative change in instructions executed, L2 cache misses, and I-TLB and D-TLB misses of native Linux versus two configurations of Xen for a Web workload [Menon et al. 2005].** Higher L2 and TLB misses come from the lack of support in Xen for superpages, globally marked PTEs, and gather DMA [Menon 2006].

Figure 5.17 explains this drop in performance by plotting the relative change in instructions executed, L2 cache misses, and instruction and data TLB misses for native Linux and the two Xen configurations. Data TLB misses per instruction are 12–24 times higher for Xen than for native Linux, and this is the primary reason for the slowdown for the privileged driver VM configuration. The higher TLB misses are because of two optimizations that Linux uses that Xen does not: superpages and marking page table entries as global. Linux uses superpages for part of its kernel space, and using 4 MB pages obviously lowers TLB misses versus using 1024 4 KB pages. PTEs marked global are not flushed on a context switch, and Linux uses them for its kernel space.

In addition to higher D-TLB misses, the more natural guest VM + driver VM configuration executes more than twice as many instructions. The increase is due to page remapping and page transfer between the driver and guest VMs and due to communication between the two VMs over a channel. This is also the reason for the lower receive performance of guest VMs in Figure 5.16. In addition, the guest VM configuration has more than four times as many L2 caches misses. The reason is Linux uses a zero-copy network interface that depends on the ability of the NIC to do DMA from different locations in memory. Since Xen does not support "gather DMA" in its virtual network interface, it can't do true zero-copy in the guest VM, resulting in more L2 cache misses.

While future versions of Xen may be able to incorporate support for superpages, globally marked PTEs, and gather DMA, the higher instruction overhead looks to be inherent in the split between guest VM and driver VM.

5.5 Crosscutting Issues: The Design of Memory Hierarchies

This section describes three topics discussed in other chapters that are fundamental to memory hierarchies.

Protection and Instruction Set Architecture

Protection is a joint effort of architecture and operating systems, but architects had to modify some awkward details of existing instruction set architectures when virtual memory became popular. For example, to support virtual memory in the IBM 370, architects had to change the successful IBM 360 instruction set architecture that had been announced just six years before. Similar adjustments are being made today to accommodate virtual machines.

For example, the 80x86 instruction POPF loads the flag registers from the top of the stack in memory. One of the flags is the Interrupt Enable (IE) flag. If you run the POPF instruction in user mode, rather than trap it simply changes all the flags except IE. In system mode, it does change the IE. Since a guest OS runs in user mode inside a VM, this is a problem, as it expects to see a changed IE.

Historically, IBM mainframe hardware and VMM took three steps to improve performance of virtual machines:

1. Reduce the cost of processor virtualization

2. Reduce interrupt overhead cost due to the virtualization

3. Reduce interrupt cost by steering interrupts to the proper VM without invoking VMM

IBM is still the gold standard of virtual machine technology. For example, an IBM mainframe ran thousands of Linux VMs in 2000, while Xen ran 25 VMs in 2004 [Clark et al. 2004].

In 2006, new proposals by AMD and Intel try to address the first point, reducing the cost of processor virtualization (see Section 5.7). It will be interesting how many generations of architecture and VMM modifications it will take to address all three points, and how long before virtual machines of the 21st century will be as efficient as the IBM mainframes and VMMs of the 1970s.

Speculative Execution and the Memory System

Inherent in processors that support speculative execution or conditional instructions is the possibility of generating invalid addresses that would not occur without speculative execution. Not only would this be incorrect behavior if protection exceptions were taken, but the benefits of speculative execution would be swamped by false exception overhead. Hence, the memory system must identify speculatively executed instructions and conditionally executed instructions and suppress the corresponding exception.

By similar reasoning, we cannot allow such instructions to cause the cache to stall on a miss because again unnecessary stalls could overwhelm the benefits of speculation. Hence, these processors must be matched with nonblocking caches.

In reality, the penalty of an L2 miss is so large that compilers normally only speculate on L1 misses. Figure 5.5 on page 297 shows that for some well-behaved scientific programs the compiler can sustain multiple outstanding L2 misses to cut the L2 miss penalty effectively. Once again, for this to work, the memory system behind the cache must match the goals of the compiler in number of simultaneous memory accesses.

I/O and Consistency of Cached Data

Data can be found in memory and in the cache. As long as one processor is the sole device changing or reading the data and the cache stands between the processor and memory, there is little danger in the processor seeing the old or *stale* copy. As mentioned in Chapter 4, multiple processors and I/O devices raise the opportunity for copies to be inconsistent and to read the wrong copy.

The frequency of the cache coherency problem is different for multiprocessors than I/O. Multiple data copies are a rare event for I/O—one to be avoided whenever possible—but a program running on multiple processors will *want* to have copies of the same data in several caches. Performance of a multiprocessor program depends on the performance of the system when sharing data.

The *I/O cache coherency* question is this: Where does the I/O occur in the computer—between the I/O device and the cache or between the I/O device and main memory? If input puts data into the cache and output reads data from the cache, both I/O and the processor see the same data. The difficulty in this approach is that it interferes with the processor and can cause the processor to stall for I/O. Input may also interfere with the cache by displacing some information with new data that is unlikely to be accessed soon.

The goal for the I/O system in a computer with a cache is to prevent the stale-data problem while interfering as little as possible. Many systems, therefore, prefer that I/O occur directly to main memory, with main memory acting as an I/O buffer. If a write-through cache were used, then memory would have an up-to-date copy of the information, and there would be no stale-data issue for output. (This benefit is a reason processors used write through.) Alas, write through is usually found today only in first-level data caches backed by an L2 cache that uses write back.

Input requires some extra work. The software solution is to guarantee that no blocks of the input buffer are in the cache. A page containing the buffer can be marked as noncachable, and the operating system can always input to such a page. Alternatively, the operating system can flush the buffer addresses from the cache before the input occurs. A hardware solution is to check the I/O addresses on input to see if they are in the cache. If there is a match of I/O addresses in the cache, the cache entries are invalidated to avoid stale data. All these approaches can also be used for output with write-back caches.

5.6 Putting It All Together: AMD Opteron Memory Hierarchy

This section unveils the AMD Opteron memory hierarchy and shows the performance of its components for the SPEC2000 programs. The Opteron is an out-of-order execution processor that fetches up to three 80x86 instructions per clock cycle, translates them into RISC-like operations, issues three of them per clock cycle, and it has 11 parallel execution units. In 2006, the 12-stage integer pipeline yields a maximum clock rate of 2.8 GHz, and the fastest memory supported is PC3200 DDR SDRAM. It uses 48-bit virtual addresses and 40-bit physical addresses. Figure 5.18 shows the mapping of the address through the multiple levels of data caches and TLBs, similar to the format of Figure 5.3 on page 292.

We are now ready to follow the memory hierarchy in action: Figure 5.19 is labeled with the steps of this narrative. First, the PC is sent to the instruction cache. It is 64 KB, two-way set associative with a 64-byte block size and LRU replacement. The cache index is

$$2^{\text{Index}} = \frac{\text{Cache size}}{\text{Block size} \times \text{Set associativity}} = \frac{64\text{K}}{64 \times 2} = 512 = 2^9$$

or 9 bits. It is virtually indexed and *physically* tagged. Thus, the page frame of the instruction's data address is sent to the instruction TLB (step 1) at the same time the 9-bit index (plus an additional 2 bits to select the appropriate 16 bytes) from the virtual address is sent to the data cache (step 2). The fully associative TLB simultaneously searches all 40 entries to find a match between the address and a valid PTE (steps 3 and 4). In addition to translating the address, the TLB checks to see if the PTE demands that this access result in an exception due to an access violation.

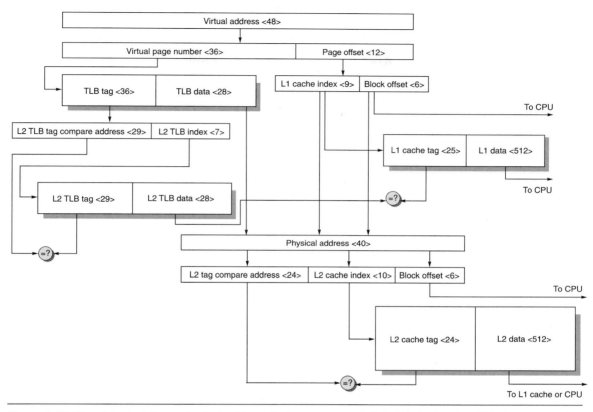

Figure 5.18 The virtual address, physical address, indexes, tags, and data blocks for the AMD Opteron caches and TLBs. Since the instruction and data hierarchies are symmetric, we only show one. The L1 TLB is fully associative with 40 entries. The L2 TLB is 4-way set associative with 512 entries. The L1 cache is 2-way set associative with 64-byte blocks and 64 KB capacity. The L2 cache is 16-way set associative with 64-byte blocks and 1 MB capacity. This figure doesn't show the valid bits and protection bits for the caches and TLBs, as does Figure 5.19.

An I TLB miss first goes to the L2 I TLB, which contains 512 PTEs of 4 KB page sizes and is four-way set associative. It takes 2 clock cycles to load the L1 TLB from the L2 TLB. The traditional 80x86 TLB scheme flushes all TLBs if the page directory pointer register is changed. In contrast, Opteron checks for changes to the actual page directory in memory and flushes only when the data structure is changed, thereby avoiding some flushes.

In the worst case, the page is not in memory, and the operating system gets the page from disk. Since millions of instructions could execute during a page fault, the operating system will swap in another process if one is waiting to run. Otherwise, if there is no TLB exception, the instruction cache access continues.

The index field of the address is sent to both groups of the two-way set-associative data cache (step 5). The instruction cache tag is 40 − 9 bits (index) − 6 bits (block offset) or 25 bits. The four tags and valid bits are compared to the

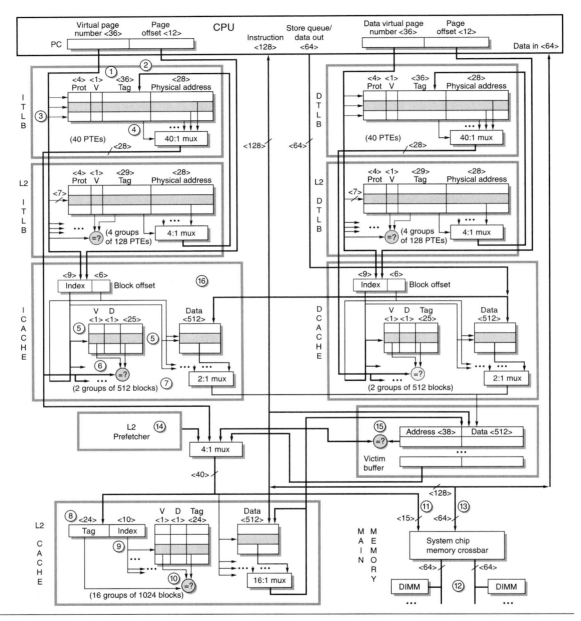

Figure 5.19 The AMD Opteron memory hierarchy. The L1 caches are both 64 KB, 2-way set associative with 64-byte blocks and LRU replacement. The L2 cache is 1 MB, 16-way set associative with 64-byte blocks, and pseudo LRU replacement. The data and L2 caches use write back with write allocation. The L1 instruction and data caches are virtually indexed and physically tagged, so every address must be sent to the instruction or data TLB at the same time as it is sent to a cache. Both TLBs are fully associative and have 40 entries, with 32 entries for 4 KB pages and 8 for 2 MB or 4 MB pages. Each TLB has a 4-way set associative L2 TLB behind it, with 512 entities of 4 KB page sizes. Opteron supports 48-bit virtual addresses and 40-bit physical addresses.

physical page frame from the Instruction TLB (step 6). As the Opteron expects 16 bytes each instruction fetch, an additional 2 bits are used from the 6-bit block offset to select the appropriate 16 bytes. Hence, 9 + 2 or 11 bits are used to send 16 bytes of instructions to the processor. The L1 cache is pipelined, and the latency of a hit is 2 clock cycles. A miss goes to the second-level cache *and* to the memory controller, to lower the miss penalty in case the L2 cache misses.

As mentioned earlier, the instruction cache is virtually addressed and physically tagged. On a miss, the cache controller must check for a synonym (two different virtual addresses that reference the same physical address). Hence, the instruction cache tags are examined for synonyms in parallel with the L2 cache tags during an L2 lookup. As the minimum page size is 4 KB or 12 bits and the cache index plus block offset is 15 bits, the cache must check 2^3 or 8 blocks per way for synonyms. Opteron uses the redundant snooping tags to check all synonyms in 1 clock cycle. If it finds a synonym, the offending block is invalidated and refetched from memory. This guarantees that a cache block can reside in only one of the 16 possible data cache locations at any given time.

The second-level cache tries to fetch the block on a miss. The L2 cache is 1 MB, 16-way set associative with 64-byte blocks. It uses a pseudo-LRU scheme by managing eight pairs of blocks LRU, and then randomly picking one of the LRU pair on a replacement. The L2 index is

$$2^{\text{Index}} = \frac{\text{Cache size}}{\text{Block size} \times \text{Set associativity}} = \frac{1024\text{K}}{64 \times 16} = 1024 = 2^{10}$$

so the 34-bit block address (40-bit physical address – 6-bit block offset) is divided into a 24-bit tag and a 10-bit index (step 8). Once again, the index and tag are sent to all 16 groups of the 16-way set associative data cache (step 9), which are compared in parallel. If one matches and is valid (step 10), it returns the block in sequential order, 8 bytes per clock cycle. The L2 cache also cancels the memory request that the L1 cache sent to the controller. An L1 instruction cache miss that hits in the L2 cache costs 7 processor clock cycles for the first word.

The Opteron has an exclusion policy between the L1 caches and the L2 cache to try to better utilize the resources, which means a block is in L1 or L2 caches but not in both. Hence, it does not simply place a copy of the block in the L2 cache. Instead, the only copy of the new block is placed in the L1 cache. The old L1 block is sent to the L2 cache. If a block knocked out of the L2 cache is dirty, it is sent to the write buffer, called the victim buffer in the Opteron.

In the last chapter, we showed how inclusion allows all coherency traffic to affect only the L2 cache and not the L1 caches. Exclusion means coherency traffic must check both. To reduce interference between coherency traffic and the processor for the L1 caches, the Opteron has a duplicate set of address tags for coherency snooping.

If the instruction is not found in the secondary cache, the on-chip memory controller must get the block from main memory. The Opteron has dual 64-bit memory channels that can act as one 128-bit channel, since there is only one memory controller and the same address is sent on both channels (step 11). Wide transfers happen when both channels have identical DIMMs. Each channel supports up to four DDR DIMMs (step 12).

Since the Opteron provides single-error correction/double-error detection checking on data cache, L2 cache, buses, and main memory, the data buses actually include an additional 8 bits for ECC for every 64 bits of data. To reduce the chances of a second error, the Opteron uses idle cycles to remove single-bit errors by reading and rewriting damaged blocks in the data cache, L2 cache, and memory. Since the instruction cache and TLBs are read-only structures, they are protected by parity, and reread from lower levels if a parity error occurs.

The total latency of the instruction miss that is serviced by main memory is approximately 20 processor cycles plus the DRAM latency for the critical instructions. For a PC3200 DDR SDRAM and 2.8 GHz CPU, the DRAM latency is 140 processor cycles (50 ns) to the first 16 bytes. The memory controller fills the remainder of the 64-byte cache block at a rate of 16 bytes per memory clock cycle. With 200 MHz DDR DRAM, that is three more clock edges and an extra 7.5 ns latency, or 21 more processor cycles with a 2.8 GHz processor (step 13).

Opteron has a prefetch engine associated with the L2 cache (step 14). It looks at patterns for L2 misses to consecutive blocks, either ascending or descending, and then prefetches the next line into the L2 cache.

Since the second-level cache is a write-back cache, any miss can lead to an old block being written back to memory. The Opteron places this "victim" block into a victim buffer (step 15), as it does with a victim dirty block in the data cache. The buffer allows the original instruction fetch read that missed to proceed first. The Opteron sends the address of the victim out the system address bus following the address of the new request. The system chip set later extracts the victim data and writes it to the memory DIMMs.

The victim buffer is size eight, so many victims can be queued before being written back either to L2 or to memory. The memory controller can manage up to 10 simultaneous cache block misses—8 from the data cache and 2 from the instruction cache—allowing it to hit under 10 misses, as described in Appendix C. The data cache and L2 cache check the victim buffer for the missing block, but it stalls until the data is written to memory and then refetched. The new data are loaded into the instruction cache as soon as they arrive (step 16). Once again, because of the exclusion property, the missing block is not loaded into the L2 cache.

If this initial instruction is a load, the data address is sent to the data cache and data TLBs, acting very much like an instruction cache access since the instruction and data caches and TLBs are symmetric. One difference is that the data cache has two banks so that it can support two loads or stores simultaneously, as long as they address different banks. In addition, a write-back victim can be produced on a data cache miss. The victim data are extracted from the data cache simultaneously with the fill of the data cache with the L2 data and sent to the victim buffer.

Suppose the instruction is a store instead of a load. When the store issues, it does a data cache lookup just like a load. A store miss causes the block to be filled into the data cache very much as with a load miss, since the policy is to allocate on writes. The store does not update the cache until later, after it is known to be nonspeculative. During this time the store resides in a load-store queue, part of the out-of-order control mechanism of the processor. It can hold up to 44 entries and supports speculative forwarding results to the execution unit. The data cache is ECC protected, so a read-modify-write operation is required to update the data cache on stores. This is accomplished by assembling the full block in the load/store queue and always writing the entire block.

Performance of the Opteron Memory Hierarchy

How well does the Opteron work? The bottom line in this evaluation is the percentage of time lost while the processor is waiting for the memory hierarchy. The major components are the instruction and data caches, instruction and data TLBs, and the secondary cache. Alas, in an out-of-order execution processor like the Opteron, it is very hard to isolate the time waiting for memory, since a memory stall for one instruction may be completely hidden by successful completion of a later instruction.

Figure 5.20 shows the CPI and various misses per 1000 instructions for a benchmark similar to TPC-C on a database and the SPEC2000 programs. Clearly, most of the SPEC2000 programs do not tax the Opteron memory hierarchy, with mcf being the exception. (SPEC nicknamed it the "cache buster" because of its memory footprint size and its access patterns.) The average SPEC I cache misses per instruction is 0.01% to 0.09%, the average D cache misses per instruction are 1.34% to 1.43%, and the average L2 cache misses per instruction are 0.23% to 0.36%. The commercial benchmark does exercise the memory hierarchy more, with misses per instruction of 1.83%, 1.39%, and 0.62%, respectively.

How do the real CPIs of Opteron compare to the peak rate of 0.33, or 3 instructions per clock cycle? The Opteron completes on average 0.8–0.9 instructions per clock cycle for SPEC2000, with an average CPI of 1.15–1.30. For the database benchmark, the higher miss rates for caches and TLBs yields a CPI of 2.57, or 0.4 instructions per clock cycle. This factor of 2 slowdown in CPI for TPC-C-like benchmarks suggests that microprocessors designed in servers see heavier demands on the memory systems than do microprocessors for desktops. Figure 5.21 estimates the breakdown between the base CPI of 0.33 and the stalls for memory and for the pipeline.

Figure 5.21 assumes none of the memory hierarchy misses are overlapped with the execution pipeline or with each other, so the pipeline stall portion is a lower bound. Using this calculation, the CPI above the base that is attributable to memory averages about 50% for the integer programs (from 1% for eon to 100% for vpr) and about 60% for the floating-point programs (from 12% for sixtrack to 98% for applu). Going deeper into the numbers, about 50% of the memory CPI (25% overall) is due to L2 cache misses for the integer programs and L2 represents about 70% of the memory CPI for the floating-point programs (40% overall). As mentioned earlier, L2 misses are so long that it is difficult to hide them with extra work.

Benchmark	Avg CPI	Misses per 1000 instructions						
		Icache	Dcache	L2	ITLB L1	DTLB L1	ITLB L2	DTLB L2
TPC-C-like	2.57	18.34	13.89	6.18	3.25	9.00	0.09	1.71
SPECint2000 total	1.30	0.90	14.27	3.57	0.25	12.47	0.00	1.06
164.gzip	0.86	0.01	16.03	0.10	0.01	11.06	0.00	0.09
175.vpr	1.78	0.02	23.36	5.73	0.01	50.52	0.00	3.22
176.gcc	1.02	1.94	19.04	0.90	0.79	4.53	0.00	0.19
181.mcf	13.06	0.02	148.90	103.82	0.01	50.49	0.00	26.98
186.crafty	0.72	3.15	4.05	0.06	0.16	18.07	0.00	0.01
197.parser	1.28	0.08	14.80	1.34	0.01	11.56	0.00	0.65
252.eon	0.82	0.06	0.45	0.00	0.01	0.05	0.00	0.00
253.perlbmk	0.70	1.36	2.41	0.43	0.93	3.51	0.00	0.31
254.gap	0.86	0.76	4.27	0.58	0.05	3.38	0.00	0.33
255.vortex	0.88	3.67	5.86	1.17	0.68	15.78	0.00	1.38
256.bzip2	1.00	0.01	10.57	2.94	0.00	8.17	0.00	0.63
300.twolf	1.85	0.08	26.18	4.49	0.02	14.79	0.00	0.01
SPECfp2000 total	1.15	0.08	13.43	2.26	0.01	3.70	0.00	0.79
168.wupwise	0.83	0.00	6.56	1.66	0.00	0.22	0.00	0.17
171.swim	1.88	0.01	30.87	2.02	0.00	0.59	0.00	0.41
172.mgrid	0.89	0.01	16.54	1.35	0.00	0.35	0.00	0.25
173.applu	0.97	0.01	8.48	3.41	0.00	2.42	0.00	0.13
177.mesa	0.78	0.03	1.58	0.13	0.01	8.78	0.00	0.17
178.galgel	1.07	0.01	18.63	2.38	0.00	7.62	0.00	0.67
179.art	3.03	0.00	56.96	8.27	0.00	1.20	0.00	0.41
183.equake	2.35	0.06	37.29	3.30	0.00	1.20	0.00	0.59
187.facerec	1.07	0.01	9.31	3.94	0.00	1.21	0.00	0.20
188.ammp	1.19	0.02	16.58	2.37	0.00	8.61	0.00	3.25
189.lucas	1.73	0.00	17.35	4.36	0.00	4.80	0.00	3.27
191.fma3d	1.34	0.20	11.84	3.02	0.05	0.36	0.00	0.21
200.sixtrack	0.63	0.03	0.53	0.16	0.01	0.66	0.00	0.01
301.apsi	1.17	0.50	13.81	2.48	0.01	10.37	0.00	1.69

Figure 5.20 CPI and misses per 1000 instructions for running a TPC-C-like database workload and the SPEC2000 benchmarks on the AMD Opteron. Since the Opteron uses an out-of-order instruction execution, the statistics are calculated as the number of misses per 1000 instructions successfully committed.

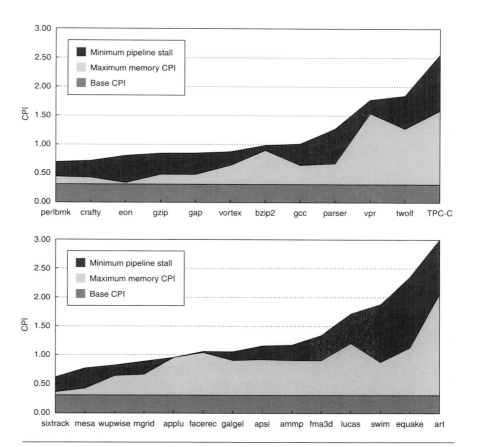

Figure 5.21 Area plots that estimate CPI breakdown into base CPI, memory stalls, and pipeline stalls for SPECint2000 programs (plus a TPC-C-like benchmark) on the top and SPECfp2000 on the bottom. They are sorted from lowest to highest overall CPI. We estimated the memory CPI by multiplying the misses per instruction at the various levels by their miss penalties, and subtracted it and the base CPI from the measured CPI to calculate the pipeline stall CPI. The L2 miss penalty is 140 clock cycles, and all other misses hit in the L2 cache. This estimate assumes no overlapping of memory and execution, so the memory portion is high, as some of it is surely overlapped with pipeline stalls and with other memory accesses. Since it would overwhelm the rest of the data with its CPI of 13.06, mcf is not included. Memory misses must be overlapped in mcf; otherwise the CPI would grow to 18.53.

Finally, Figure 5.22 compares the miss rates of the data caches and the L2 caches of Opteron to the Intel Pentium 4, showing the ratio of the misses per instruction for 10 SPEC2000 benchmarks. Although they are executing the same programs compiled for the same instruction set, the compilers and resulting code

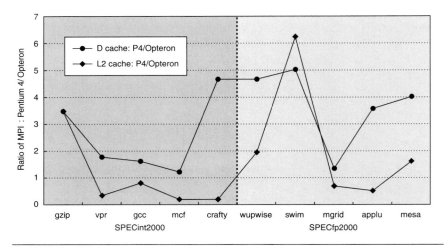

Figure 5.22 Ratio of misses per instruction for Pentium 4 versus Opteron. Bigger means a higher miss rate for Pentium 4. The 10 programs are the first 5 SPECint2000 and the first 5 SPECfp2000. (The two processors and their memory hierarchies are described in the table in the text.) The geometric mean of the ratio of performance of the 5 SPECint programs on the two processors is 1.00 with a standard deviation of 1.42; the geometric mean of the performance of the 5 SPECfp programs suggests Opteron is 1.15 times faster, with a standard deviation of 1.25. Note the clock rate for the Pentium 4 was 3.2 GHz in these experiments; higher-clock-rate Pentium 4s were available but not used in this experiment. Figure 5.10 shows that half of these programs benefit significantly from the prefetching hardware of the Pentium 4: mcf, wupwise, swim, mgrid, and applu.

sequences are different as are the memory hierarchies. The following table summarizes the two memory hierarchies:

Processor	Pentium 4 (3.2 GHz)	Opteron (2.8 GHz)
Data cache	8-way associative, 16 KB, 64-byte block	2-way associative, 64 KB, 64-byte block
L2 cache	8-way associative, 2 MB, 128-byte block, inclusive of D cache	16-way associative, 1 MB, 64-byte block, exclusive of D cache
Prefetch	8 streams to L2	1 stream to L2

Although the Pentium 4 has much higher associativity, the four times larger data cache of Opteron has lower L1 miss rates. The geometric mean of the ratios of L1 miss rates is 2.25 and geometric standard deviation is 1.75 for the five SPECint2000 programs; they are 3.37 and 1.72 for the five SPECfp2000 programs (see Chapter 1 to review geometric means and standard deviations).

With twice the L2 block size and L2 cache capacity and more aggressive prefetching, the Pentium 4 usually has fewer L2 misses per instruction. Surprisingly, the Opteron L2 cache has fewer on 4 of the 10 programs. This variability is reflected in the means and high standard deviations: the geometric mean and standard deviation of the ratios of L2 miss rates is 0.50 and 3.45 for the integer programs and 1.48 and 2.66 for the floating-point programs. As mentioned earlier, this nonintuitive result could simply be the consequence of using different compilers and optimizations. Another possible explanation is that the lower memory latency and higher memory bandwidth of the Opteron helps the effectiveness of its hardware prefetching, which is known to reduce misses on many of these floating-point programs. (See Figure 5.10 on page 306.)

5.7 Fallacies and Pitfalls

As the most naturally quantitative of the computer architecture disciplines, memory hierarchy would seem to be less vulnerable to fallacies and pitfalls. Yet we were limited here not by lack of warnings, but by lack of space!

Fallacy *Predicting cache performance of one program from another.*

Figure 5.23 shows the instruction miss rates and data miss rates for three programs from the SPEC2000 benchmark suite as cache size varies. Depending on the program, the data misses per thousand instructions for a 4096 KB cache is 9, 2, or 90, and the instruction misses per thousand instructions for a 4 KB cache is 55, 19, or 0.0004. Commercial programs such as databases will have significant miss rates even in large second-level caches, which is generally not the case for the SPEC programs. Clearly, generalizing cache performance from one program to another is unwise.

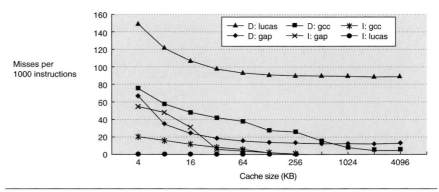

Figure 5.23 Instruction and data misses per 1000 instructions as cache size varies from 4 KB to 4096 KB. Instruction misses for gcc are 30,000 to 40,000 times larger than lucas, and conversely, data misses for lucas are 2 to 60 times larger than gcc. The programs gap, gcc, and lucas are from the SPEC2000 benchmark suite.

Pitfall *Simulating enough instructions to get accurate performance measures of the memory hierarchy.*

There are really three pitfalls here. One is trying to predict performance of a large cache using a small trace. Another is that a program's locality behavior is not constant over the run of the entire program. The third is that a program's locality behavior may vary depending on the input.

Figure 5.24 shows the cumulative average instruction misses per thousand instructions for five inputs to a single SPEC2000 program. For these inputs, the average memory rate for the first 1.9 billion instructions is very different from the average miss rate for the rest of the execution.

The first edition of this book included another example of this pitfall. The compulsory miss ratios were erroneously high (e.g., 1%) because of tracing too few memory accesses. A program with a compulsory cache miss ratio of 1% running on a computer accessing memory 10 million times per second (at the time of the first edition) would access hundreds of megabytes of memory per minute:

$$\frac{10,000,000 \text{ accesses}}{\text{Second}} \times \frac{0.01 \text{ misses}}{\text{Access}} \times \frac{32 \text{ bytes}}{\text{Miss}} \times \frac{60 \text{ seconds}}{\text{Minute}} = \frac{192,000,000 \text{ bytes}}{\text{Minute}}$$

Data on typical page fault rates and process sizes do not support the conclusion that memory is touched at this rate.

Pitfall *Overemphasizing memory bandwidth in DRAMs.*

Several years ago, a startup named RAMBUS innovated on the DRAM interface. Its product, Direct RDRAM, offered up to 1.6 GB/sec of bandwidth from a single DRAM. When announced, the peak bandwidth was eight times faster than individual conventional SDRAM chips. Figure 5.25 compares prices of various versions of DRAM and RDRAM, in memory modules and in systems.

PCs do most memory accesses through a two-level cache hierarchy, so it was unclear how much benefit is gained from high bandwidth without also improving memory latency. According to Pabst [2000], when comparing PCs with 400 MHz DRDRAM to PCs with 133 MHz SDRAM, for office applications they had identical average performance. For games, DRDRAM was 1% to 2% faster. For professional graphics applications, it was 10% to 15% faster. The tests used an 800 MHz Pentium III (which integrates a 256 KB L2 cache), chip sets that support a 133 MHz system bus, and 128 MB of main memory.

One measure of the RDRAM cost is die size; it had about a 20% larger die for the same capacity compared to SDRAM. DRAM designers use redundant rows and columns to improve yield significantly on the memory portion of the DRAM, so a much larger interface might have a disproportionate impact on yield. Yields are a closely guarded secret, but prices are not. Using the evaluation in Figure 5.25, in 2000 the price was about a factor of 2–3 higher for RDRAM. In 2006, the ratio is not less.

RDRAM was at its strongest in small memory systems that need high bandwidth, such as a Sony Playstation.

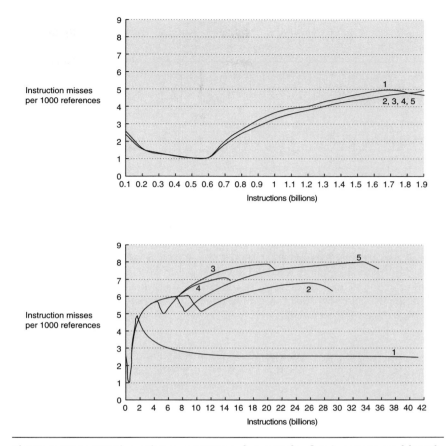

**Figure 5.24 Instruction misses per 1000 references for five inputs to perl bench-
mark from SPEC2000.** There is little variation in misses and little difference between
the five inputs for the first 1.9 billion instructions. Running to completion shows how
misses vary over the life of the program and how they depend on the input. The top
graph shows the running average misses for the first 1.9 billion instructions, which
starts at about 2.5 and ends at about 4.7 misses per 1000 references for all five inputs.
The bottom graph shows the running average misses to run to completion, which takes
16–41 billion instructions depending on the input. After the first 1.9 billion instructions,
the misses per 1000 references vary from 2.4 to 7.9 depending on the input. The simulations were for the Alpha processor using separate L1 caches for instructions and data,
each two-way 64 KB with LRU, and a unified 1 MB direct-mapped L2 cache.

Pitfall   *Not delivering high memory bandwidth in a cache-based system*

Caches help with average cache memory latency but may not deliver high memory bandwidth to an application that must go to main memory. The architect must

	Modules		Dell XPS PCs					
ECC?	No ECC	ECC	No ECC			ECC		
Label	DIMM	RIMM	A	B	B – A	C	D	D – C
Memory or system?	DRAM		System		DRAM	System		DRAM
Memory size (MB)	256	256	128	512	384	128	512	384
SDRAM PC100	$175	$259	$1519	$2139	$620	$1559	$2269	$710
DRDRAM PC700	$725	$826	$1689	$3009	$1320	$1789	$3409	$1620
Price ratio DRDRAM/SDRAM	4.1	3.2	1.1	1.4	2.1	1.1	1.5	2.3

Figure 5.25 Comparison of price of SDRAM versus DRDRAM in memory modules and in systems in 2000. DRDRAM memory modules cost about a factor of 4 more without ECC and 3 more with ECC. Looking at the cost of the extra 384 MB of memory in PCs in going from 128 MB to 512 MB, DRDRAM costs twice as much. Except for differences in bandwidths of the DRAMs, the systems were identically configured. The Dell XPS PCs were identical except for memory: 800 MHz Pentium III, 20 GB ATA disk, 48X CD-ROM, 17-inch monitor, and Microsoft Windows 95/98 and Office 98. The module prices were the lowest found at pricewatch.com in June 2000. By September 2005, PC800 DRDRAM cost $76 for 256 MB, while PC100 to PC150 SDRAM cost $15 to $23, or about a factor of 3.3 to 5.0 less expensive. (In September 2005 Dell did not offer systems whose only difference was type of DRAMs; hence, we stick with the comparison from 2000.)

design a high bandwidth memory behind the cache for such applications. As an extreme example, the NEC SX7 offers up to 16,384 interleaved SDRAM memory banks. It is a vector computer that doesn't rely on data caches for memory performance (see Appendix F). Figure 5.26 shows the top 10 results from the Stream benchmark as of 2005, which measures bandwidth to copy data [McCalpin 2005]. Not surprisingly, the NEC SX7 has the top ranking.

Only four computers rely on data caches for memory performance, and their memory bandwidth is a factor of 7–25 slower than the NEC SX7.

Pitfall *Implementing a virtual machine monitor on an instruction set architecture that wasn't designed to be virtualizable.*

Many architects in the 1970s and 1980s weren't careful to make sure that all instructions reading or writing information related to hardware resource information were privileged. This laissez faire attitude causes problems for VMMs for all of these architectures, including the 80x86, which we use here as an example.

Figure 5.27 describes the 18 instructions that cause problems for virtualization [Robin and Irvine 2000]. The two broad classes are instructions that

- read control registers in user mode that reveals that the guest operating system is running in a virtual machine (such as POPF mentioned earlier), and

- check protection as required by the segmented architecture but assume that the operating system is running at the highest privilege level.

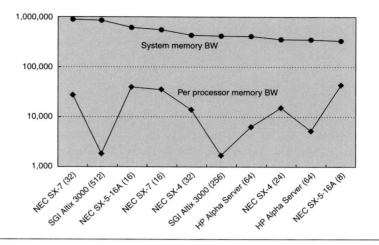

Figure 5.26 Top 10 in memory bandwidth as measured by the untuned copy portion of the stream benchmark [McCalpin 2005]. The number of processors is shown in parentheses. Two are cache-based clusters (SGI), two are cache-based SMPs (HP), but most are NEC vector processors of different generations and number of processors. Systems use between 8 and 512 processors to achieve higher memory bandwidth. System bandwidth is bandwidth of all processors collectively. Processor bandwidth is simply system bandwidth divided by the number of processors. The STREAM benchmark is a simple synthetic benchmark program that measures sustainable memory bandwidth (in MB/sec) for simple vector kernels. It specifically works with data sets much larger than the available cache on any given system.

Virtual memory is also challenging. Because the 80x86 TLBs do not support process ID tags, as do most RISC architectures, it is more expensive for the VMM and guest OSes to share the TLB; each address space change typically requires a TLB flush.

Virtualizing I/O is also a challenge for the 80x86, in part because it both supports memory-mapped I/O and has separate I/O instructions, but more importantly, because there is a very large number and variety of types of devices and device drivers of PCs for the VMM to handle. Third-party vendors supply their own drivers, and they may not properly virtualize. One solution for conventional VM implementations is to load real device drivers directly into the VMM.

To simplify implementations of VMMs on the 80x86, both AMD and Intel have proposed extensions to the architecture. Intel's VT-x provides a new execution mode for running VMs, an architected definition of the VM state, instructions to swap VMs rapidly, and a large set of parameters to select the circumstances where a VMM must be invoked. Altogether, VT-x adds 11 new instructions for the 80x86. AMD's Pacifica makes similar proposals.

After turning on the mode that enables VT-x support (via the new VMXON instruction), VT-x offers four privilege levels for the guest OS that are lower in priority than the original four. VT-x captures all the state of a virtual machine in

Problem category	Problem 80x86 instructions
Access sensitive registers without trapping when running in user mode	Store global descriptor table register (SGDT) Store local descriptor table register (SLDT) Store interrupt descriptor table register (SIDT) Store machine status word (SMSW) Push flags (PUSHF, PUSHFD) Pop flags (POPF, POPFD)
When accessing virtual memory mechanisms in user mode, instructions fail the 80x86 protection checks	Load access rights from segment descriptor (LAR) Load segment limit from segment descriptor (LSL) Verify if segment descriptor is readable (VERR) Verify if segment descriptor is writable (VERW) Pop to segment register (POP CS, POP SS, . . .) Push segment register (PUSH CS, PUSH SS, . . .) Far call to different privilege level (CALL) Far return to different privilege level (RET) Far jump to different privilege level (JMP) Software interrupt (INT) Store segment selector register (STR) Move to/from segment registers (MOVE)

Figure 5.27 Summary of 18 80x86 instructions that cause problems for virtualization [Robin and Irvine 2000]. The first five instructions of the top group allow a program in user mode to read a control register, such as a descriptor table registers, without causing a trap. The pop flags instruction modifies a control register with sensitive information, but fails silently when in user mode. The protection checking of the segmented architecture of the 80x86 is the downfall of the bottom group, as each of these instructions checks the privilege level implicitly as part of instruction execution when reading a control register. The checking assumes that the OS must be at the highest privilege level, which is not the case for guest VMs. Only the MOVE to segment register tries to modify control state, and protection checking foils it as well.

the Virtual Machine Control State (VMCS), and then provides atomic instructions to save and restore a VMCS. In addition to critical state, the VMCS includes configuration information to determine when to invoke the VMM, and then specifically what caused the VMM to be invoked. To reduce the number of times the VMM must be invoked, this mode adds shadow versions of some sensitive registers and adds masks that check to see whether critical bits of a sensitive register will be changed before trapping. To reduce the cost of virtualizing virtual memory, AMD's Pacifica adds an additional level of indirection, called *nested page tables*. It makes shadow page tables unnecessary.

It is ironic that AMD and Intel are proposing a new mode. If operating systems like Linux or Microsoft Windows start using that mode in their kernel, the new mode would cause performance problems for the VMM since it would be about 100 times too slow! Nevertheless, the Xen organization plans to use VT-x to allow it to support Windows as a guest OS.

| | 5.8 | **Concluding Remarks** |

Figure 5.28 compares the memory hierarchy of microprocessors aimed at desktop and server applications. The L1 caches are similar across applications, with the primary differences being L2 cache size, die size, processor clock rate, and instructions issued per clock.

The design decisions at all these levels interact, and the architect must take the whole system view to make wise decisions. The primary challenge for the memory hierarchy designer is in choosing parameters that work well together,

MPU	AMD Opteron	Intel Pentium 4	IBM Power 5	Sun Niagara
Instruction set architecture	80x86 (64b)	80x86	PowerPC	SPARC v9
Intended application	desktop	desktop	server	server
CMOS process (nm)	90	90	130	90
Die size (mm^2)	199	217	389	379
Instructions issued/clock	3	3 RISC ops	8	1
Processors/chip	2	1	2	8
Clock rate (2006)	2.8 GHz	3.6 GHz	2.0 GHz	1.2 GHz
Instruction cache per processor	64 KB, 2-way set associative	12000 RISC op trace cache (~96 KB)	64 KB, 2-way set associative	16 KB, 1-way set associative
Latency L1 I (clocks)	2	4	1	1
Data cache per processor	64 KB, 2-way set associative	16 KB, 8-way set associative	32 KB, 4-way set associative	8 KB, 1-way set associative
Latency L1 D (clocks)	2	2	2	1
TLB entries (I/D/L2 I/L2 D)	40/40/512/512	128/54	1024/1024	64/64
Minimum page size	4 KB	4 KB	4 KB	8 KB
On-chip L2 cache	2 x 1 MB, 16-way set associative	2 MB, 8-way set associative	1.875 MB, 10-way set associative	3 MB, 2-way set associative
L2 banks	2	1	3	4
Latency L2 (clocks)	7	22	13	22 I, 23 D
Off-chip L3 cache	—	—	36 MB, 12-way set associative (tags on chip)	—
Latency L3 (clocks)	—	—	87	—
Block size (L1I/L1D/L2/L3, bytes)	64	64/64/128/—	128/128/128/256	32/16/64/—
Memory bus width (bits)	128	64	64	128
Memory bus clock	200 MHz	200 MHz	400 MHz	400 MHz
Number of memory buses	1	1	4	4

Figure 5.28 Memory hierarchy and chip size of desktop and server microprocessors in 2005.

not in inventing new techniques. The increasingly fast processors are spending a larger fraction of time waiting for memory, which has led to new inventions that have increased the number of choices: prefetching, cache-aware compilers, and increasing page size. Fortunately, there tends to be a few technological "sweet spots" in balancing cost, performance, power, and complexity: Missing a target wastes performance, power, hardware, design time, debug time, or possibly all five. Architects hit a target by careful, quantitative analysis.

5.9 Historical Perspective and References

In Section K.6 on the companion CD we examine the history of caches, virtual memory, and virtual machines. IBM plays a prominent role in the history of all three. References for further reading are included.

Case Studies with Exercises by Norman P. Jouppi

Case Study 1: Optimizing Cache Performance via Simple Hardware

Concepts illustrated by this case study

- Small and Simple Caches
- Way Prediction
- Pipelined Caches
- Banked Caches
- Merging Write Buffers
- Critical Word First and Early Restart
- Nonblocking Caches
- Calculating Impact of Cache Performance on Simple In-Order Processors

Imagine (unrealistically) that you are building a simple in-order processor that has a CPI of 1 for all nondata memory access instructions. In this case study we will consider the performance implications of small and simple caches, way-predicting caches, pipelined cache access, banked caches, merging write buffers, and critical word first and early restart. Figure 5.29 shows SPEC2000 data miss ratios (misses per 1000 instructions) with the harmonic mean of the full execution of all benchmarks.

CACTI is a tool for estimating the access and cycle time, dynamic and leakage power, and area of a cache based on its lithographic feature size and cache organization. Of course there are many different possible circuit designs for a

```
D-cache misses/inst: 2,521,022,899,870 data refs (0.32899--/inst);
1,801,061,937,244 D-cache 64-byte block accesses (0.23289--/inst)
```

Size	Direct	2-way LRU	4-way LRU	8-way LRU	Full LRU
1 KB	0.0863842--	0.0697167--	0.0634309--	0.0563450--	0.0533706--
2 KB	0.0571524--	0.0423833--	0.0360463--	0.0330364--	0.0305213--
4 KB	0.0370053--	0.0260286--	0.0222981--	0.0202763--	0.0190243--
8 KB	0.0247760--	0.0155691--	0.0129609--	0.0107753--	0.0083886--
16 KB	0.0159470--	0.0085658--	0.0063527--	0.0056438--	0.0050068--
32 KB	0.0110603--	0.0056101--	0.0039190--	0.0034628--	0.0030885--
64 KB	0.0066425--	0.0036625--	0.0009874--	0.0002666--	0.0000106--
128 KB	0.0035823--	0.0002341--	0.0000109--	0.0000058--	0.0000058--
256 KB	0.0026345--	0.0000092--	0.0000049--	0.0000051--	0.0000053--
512 KB	0.0014791--	0.0000065--	0.0000029--	0.0000029--	0.0000029--
1 MB	0.0000090--	0.0000058--	0.0000028--	0.0000028--	0.0000028--

Figure 5.29 SPEC2000 data miss ratios (misses per 1000 instructions) [Cantin and Hill 2003].

given cache organization, and many different technologies for a given lithographic feature size, but CACTI assumes a "generic" organization and technology. Thus it may not be accurate for a specific cache design and technology in absolute terms, but it is fairly accurate at quantifying the relative performance of different cache organizations at different feature sizes. CACTI is available in an online form at *http://quid.hpl.hp.com:9081/cacti/.* Assume all cache misses take 20 cycles.

5.1 [12/12/15/15] <5.2> The following questions investigate the impact of small and simple caches using CACTI, and assume a 90 nm (0.09 μm) technology.

a. [12] <5.2> Compare the access times of 32 KB caches with 64-byte blocks and a single bank. What is the relative access times of two-way and four-way set associative caches in comparison to a direct-mapped organization?

b. [12] <5.2> Compare the access times of two-way set-associative caches with 64-byte blocks and a single bank. What is the relative access times of 32 KB and 64 KB caches in comparison to a 16 KB cache?

c. [15] <5.2> Does the access time for a typical level 1 cache organization increase with size roughly as the capacity in bytes *B*, the square root of *B*, or the log of *B*?

d. [15] <5.2> Find the cache organization with the lowest average memory access time given the miss ratio table in Figure 5.29 and a cache access time budget of 0.90 ns. What is this organization, and does it have the lowest miss rate of all organizations for its capacity?

5.2 [12/15/15/10] <5.2> You are investigating the possible benefits of a way-predicting level 1 cache. Assume that the 32 KB two-way set-associative single-banked level 1 data cache is currently the cycle time limiter. As an alternate cache organization you are considering a way-predicted cache modeled as a 16 KB direct-mapped cache with 85% prediction accuracy. Unless stated otherwise, assume a mispredicted way access that hits in the cache takes one more cycle.

a. [12] <5.2> What is the average memory access time of the current cache versus the way-predicted cache?

b. [15] <5.2> If all other components could operate with the faster way-predicted cache cycle time (including the main memory), what would be the impact on performance from using the way-predicted cache?

c. [15] <5.2> Way-predicted caches have usually only been used for instruction caches that feed an instruction queue or buffer. Imagine you want to try out way prediction on a data cache. Assume you have 85% prediction accuracy, and subsequent operations (e.g., data cache access of other instructions, dependent operations, etc.) are issued assuming a correct way prediction. Thus a way misprediction necessitates a pipe flush and replay trap, which requires 15 cycles. Is the change in average memory access time per load instruction with data cache way prediction positive or negative, and how much is it?

d. [10] <5.2> As an alternative to way prediction, many large associative level 2 caches serialize tag and data access, so that only the required data set array needs to be activated. This saves power but increases the access time. Use CACTI's detailed Web interface for a 0.090 μm process 1 MB four-way set-associative cache with 64-byte blocks, 144 bits read out, 1 bank, only 1 read/write port, and 30-bit tags. What are the ratio of the total dynamic read energies per access and ratio of the access times for serializing tag and data access in comparison to parallel access?

5.3 [10/12/15] <5.2> You have been asked to investigate the relative performance of a banked versus pipelined level 1 data cache for a new microprocessor. Assume a 64 KB two-way set-associative cache with 64 B blocks. The pipelined cache would consist of two pipe stages, similar to the Alpha 21264 data cache. A banked implementation would consist of two 32 KB two-way set-associative banks. Use CACTI and assume a 90 nm (0.09 μm) technology in answering the following questions.

a. [10] <5.2> What is the cycle time of the cache in comparison to its access time, and how many pipe stages will the cache take up (to two decimal places)?

b. [12] <5.2> What is the average memory access time if 20% of the cache access pipe stages are empty due to data dependencies introduced by pipelining the cache and pipelining more finely doubles the miss penalty?

c. [15] <5.2> What is the average memory access time of the banked design if there is a memory access each cycle and a random distribution of bank accesses (with no reordering) and bank conflicts cause a one-cycle delay?

5.4 [12/15] <5.2> Inspired by the usage of critical word first and early restart on level 1 cache misses, consider their use on level 2 cache misses. Assume a 1 MB L2 cache with 64-byte blocks and a refill path that is 16 bytes wide. Assume the L2 can be written with 16 bytes every 4 processor cycles, the time to receive the first 16-byte block from the memory controller is 100 cycles, each additional 16 B from main memory requires 16 cycles and data can be bypassed directly into the read port of the L2 cache. Ignore any cycles to transfer the miss request to the level 2 cache and the requested data to the level 1 cache.

    a. [12] <5.2> How many cycles would it take to service a level 2 cache miss with and without critical word first and early restart?

    b. [15] <5.2> Do you think critical word first and early restart would be more important for level 1 caches or level 2 caches, and what factors would contribute to their relative importance?

5.5 [10/12] <5.2> You are designing a write buffer between a write-through level 1 cache and a write-back level 2 cache. The level 2 cache write data bus is 16 bytes wide and can perform a write to an independent cache address every 4 processor cycles.

    a. [10] <5.2> How many bytes wide should each write buffer entry be?

    b. [12] <5.2> What speedup could be expected in the steady state by using a merging write buffer instead of a nonmerging buffer when zeroing memory by the execution of 32-bit stores if all other instructions could be issued in parallel with the stores and the blocks are present in the level 2 cache?

Case Study 2: Optimizing Cache Performance via Advanced Techniques

Concepts illustrated by this case study

■ Nonblocking Caches

■ Compiler Optimizations for Caches

■ Software and Hardware Prefetching

■ Calculating Impact of Cache Performance on More Complex Processors

The transpose of a matrix interchanges its rows and columns and is illustrated below:

$$
\begin{bmatrix}
A11 & A12 & A13 & A14 \\
A21 & A22 & A23 & A24 \\
A31 & A32 & A33 & A34 \\
A41 & A42 & A43 & A44
\end{bmatrix}
\Rightarrow
\begin{bmatrix}
A11 & A21 & A31 & A41 \\
A12 & A22 & A32 & A42 \\
A13 & A23 & A33 & A43 \\
A14 & A24 & A34 & A44
\end{bmatrix}
$$

Here is a simple C loop to show the transpose:

```
for (i = 0; i < 3; i++) {
    for (j = 0; j < 3; j++) {
        output[j][i] = input[i]j];
    }
}
```

Assume both the input and output matrices are stored in the row major order (row major order means row index changes fastest). Assume you are executing a 256×256 double-precision transpose on a processor with a 16 KB fully associative (so you don't have to worry about cache conflicts) LRU replacement level 1 data cache with 64-byte blocks. Assume level 1 cache misses or prefetches require 16 cycles, always hit in the level 2 cache, and the level 2 cache can process a request every 2 processor cycles. Assume each iteration of the inner loop above requires 4 cycles if the data is present in the level 1 cache. Assume the cache has a write-allocate fetch-on-write policy for write misses. Unrealistically assume writing back dirty cache blocks require 0 cycles.

5.6 [10/15/15] <5.2> For the simple implementation given above, this execution order would be nonideal for the input matrix. However, applying a loop interchange optimization would create a nonideal order for the output matrix. Because loop interchange is not sufficient to improve its performance, it must be blocked instead.

   a. [10] <5.2> What block size should be used to completely fill the data cache with one input and output block?

   b. [15] <5.2> How do the relative number of misses of the blocked and unblocked versions compare if the level 1 cache is direct mapped?

   c. [15] <5.2> Write code to perform a transpose with a block size parameter B that uses $B \times B$ blocks.

5.7 [12] <5.2> Assume you are redesigning a hardware prefetcher for the *unblocked* matrix transposition code above. The simplest type of hardware prefetcher only prefetches sequential cache blocks after a miss. More complicated "nonunit stride" hardware prefetchers can analyze a miss reference stream, and detect and prefetch nonunit strides. In contrast, software prefetching can determine nonunit strides as easily as it can determine unit strides. Assume prefetches write directly into the cache and no *pollution* (overwriting data that needs to be used before the data that is prefetched). In the steady state of the inner loop, what is the performance (in cycles per iteration) when using an ideal nonunit stride prefetcher?

5.8 [15/15] <5.2> Assume you are redesigning a hardware prefetcher for the *unblocked* matrix transposition code as in Exercise 5.7. However, in this case we evaluate a simple two-stream sequential prefetcher. If there are level 2 access slots available, this prefetcher will fetch up to 4 sequential blocks after a miss and place them in a stream buffer. Stream buffers that have empty slots obtain access to the level 2 cache on a round-robin basis. On a level 1 miss, the stream buffer that has least recently supplied data on a miss is flushed and reused for the new miss stream.

    a. [15] <5.2> In the steady state of the inner loop, what is the performance (in cycles per iteration) when using a simple two-stream sequential prefetcher assuming performance is limited by prefetching?

    b. [15] <5.2> What percentage of prefetches are useful given the level 2 cache parameters?

5.9   [12/15] <5.2> With software prefetching it is important to be careful to have the prefetches occur in time for use, but also minimize the number of outstanding prefetches, in order to live within the capabilities of the microarchitecture and minimize cache pollution. This is complicated by the fact that different processors have different capabilities and limitations.

    a. [12] <5.2> Modify the unblocked code above to perform prefetching in software.

    b. [15] <5.2> What is the expected performance of unblocked code with software prefetching?

Case Study 3: Main Memory Technology and Optimizations

Concepts illustrated by this case study

■ Memory System Design: Latency, Bandwidth, Cost, and Power

■ Calculating Impact of Memory System Performance

Using Figure 5.14, consider the design of a variety of memory systems. Assume a chip multiprocessor with eight 3 GHz cores and directly attached memory controllers (i.e., integrated northbridge) as in the Opteron. The chip multiprocessor (CMP) contains a single shared level 2 cache, with misses from that level going to main memory (i.e., no level 3 cache). A sample DDR2 SDRAM timing diagram appears in Figure 5.30. t_{RCD} is the time required to activate a row in a bank, while the CAS latency (CL) is the number of cycles required to read out a column in a row.

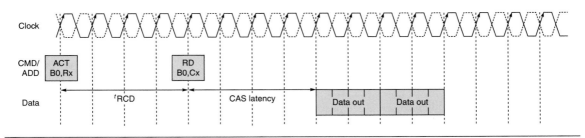

Figure 5.30 DDR2 SDRAM timing diagram.

Assume the RAM is on a standard DDR2 DIMM with ECC, having 72 data lines. Also assume burst lengths of 8 which read out 8 bits per data line, or a total of 32 bytes from the DIMM. Assume the DRAMs have a 1 KB page size, 8 banks, $t_{RCD} =$ CL * Clock_frequency, and Clock_frequency = Transfers_per_second/2. The on-chip latency on a cache miss through levels 1 and 2 and back not including the DRAM access is 20 ns. Assume a DDR2-667 1 GB DIMM with CL = 5 is available for $130 and a DDR2-533 1 GB DIMM with CL = 4 is available for $100. (See *http://download.micron.com/pdf/technotes/ddr2/TN4702.pdf* for more details on DDR2 memory organization and timing.)

5.10 [10/10/10/12/12] <5.3> Assume the system is your desktop PC and only one core on the CMP is active. Assume there is only one memory channel.

a. [10] <5.3> How many DRAMs are on the DIMM if 512 Mbit DRAMs are used, and how many data I/Os must each DRAM have if only one DRAM connects to each DIMM data pin?

b. [10] <5.3> What burst length is required to support 32-byte versus 64-byte level 2 cache blocks?

c. [10] <5.3> What is the peak bandwidth ratio between the DIMMs for reads from an active page?

d. [12] <5.3> How much time is required from the presentation of the activate command until the last requested bit of data from the DRAM transitions from valid to invalid for the DDR2-533 1 GB CL = 4 DIMM?

e. [12] <5.3> What is the relative latency when using the DDR2-533 DIMM of a read requiring a bank activate versus one to an already open page, including the time required to process the miss inside the processor?

5.11 [15] <5.3> Assume just one DIMM is used in a system, and the rest of the system costs $800. Consider the performance of the system using the DDR2-667 and DDR2-533 DIMMs on a workload with 3.33 level 2 misses per 1K instructions, and assume all DRAM reads require an activate. Assume all 8 cores are active with the same workload. What is the cost divided by the performance of the whole system when using the different DIMMs assuming only one level 2 miss is outstanding at a time and an in-order core with a CPI of 1.5 not including level 2 cache miss memory access time?

5.12 [12] <5.3> You are provisioning a server based on the system above. All 8 cores on the CMP will be busy with an overall CPI of 2.0 (assuming level 2 cache miss refills are not delayed). What bandwidth is required to support all 8 cores running a workload with 6.67 level 2 misses per 1K instructions, and optimistically assuming misses from all cores are uniformly distributed in time?

5.13 [12] <5.3> A large amount (more than a third) of DRAM power can be due to page activation (see *http://download.micron.com/pdf/technotes/ddr2/TN4704.pdf* and *http://www.micron.com/systemcalc*). Assume you are building a system with 1 GB of memory using either 4-bank 512 Mbit × 4 DDR2 DRAMs or 8-bank 1 Gbit × 8 DRAMs, both with the same speed grade. Both use a page size of 1 KB. Assume DRAMs that are not active are in precharged standby and dissipate negligible power. Assume the time to transition from standby to active is not significant. Which type of DRAM would be expected to result in lower power? Explain why.

Case Study 4: Virtual Machines

Concepts illustrated by this case study

■ Capabilities Provided by Virtual Machines

■ Impact of Virtualization on Performance

■ Features and Impact of Architectural Extensions to Support Virtualization

Intel and AMD have both created extensions to the x86 architecture to address the shortcomings of the x86 for virtualization. Intel's solution is called VT-x (Virtualization Technology x86) (see IEEE [2005] for more information on VT-x), while AMD's is called Secure Visual Machine (SVM). Intel has a corresponding technology for the Itanium architecture called VT-i. Figure 5.31 lists the early performance of various system calls under native execution, pure virtualization, and paravirtualization for LMbench using Xen on an Itanium system with times measured in microseconds (courtesy of Matthew Chapman of the University of New South Wales).

5.14   [10/10/10/10/10] <5.4> Virtual machines have the potential for adding many beneficial capabilities to computer systems, for example, resulting in improved total cost of ownership (TCO) or availability. Could VMs be used to provide the following capabilities? If so, how could they facilitate this?

   a. [10] <5.4> Make it easy to consolidate a large number of applications running on many old uniprocessor servers onto a single higher-performance CMP-based server?

   b. [10] <5.4> Limit damage caused by computer viruses, worms, or spyware?

   c. [10] <5.4> Higher performance in memory-intensive applications with large memory footprints?

   d. [10] <5.4> Dynamically provision extra capacity for peak application loads?

   e. [10] <5.4> Run a legacy application on old operating systems on modern machines?

5.15   [10/10/12/12] <5.4> Virtual machines can lose performance from a number of events, such as the execution of privileged instructions, TLB misses, traps, and I/O. These events are usually handled in system code. Thus one way of estimating the slowdown when running under a VM is the percentage of application execution time in system versus user mode. For example, an application spending 10% of its execution in system mode might slow down by 60% when running on a VM.

   a. [10] <5.4> What types of programs would be expected to have larger slowdowns when running under VMs?

Benchmark	Native	Pure	Para
Null call	0.04	0.96	0.50
Null I/O	0.27	6.32	2.91
Stat	1.10	10.69	4.14
Open/close	1.99	20.43	7.71
Install sighandler	0.33	7.34	2.89
Handle signal	1.69	19.26	2.36
Fork	56.00	513.00	164.00
Exec	316.00	2084.00	578.00
Fork + exec sh	1451.00	7790.00	2360.00

Figure 5.31 Early performance of various system calls under native execution, pure virtualization, and paravirtualization.

b. [10] <5.4> If slowdowns were linear as a function of system time, given the slowdown above, how much slower would a program spending 30% of its execution in system time be expected to run?

c. [12] <5.4> What is the mean slowdown of the functions in Figure 5.31 under pure and para virtualization?

d. [12] <5.4> Which functions in Figure 5.31 have the smallest slowdowns? What do you think the cause of this could be?

5.16 [12] <5.4> Popek and Goldberg's definition of a virtual machine said that it would be indistinguishable from a real machine except for its performance. In this exercise we'll use that definition to find out if we have access to native execution on a processor or are running on a virtual machine. The Intel VT-x technology effectively provides a second set of privilege levels for the use of the virtual machine. What would happen to relative performance of a virtual machine if it was running on a native machine or on another virtual machine given two sets of privilege levels as in VT-x?

5.17 [15/20] <5.4> With the adoption of virtualization support on the x86 architecture, virtual machines are actively evolving and becoming mainstream. Compare and contrast the Intel VT-x and AMD Secure Virtual Machine (SVM) virtualization technologies. Information on AMD's SVM can be found in *http://www.amd.com/ us-en/assets/content_type/white_papers_and_tech_docs/24593.pdf*.

a. [15] <5.4> How do VT-x and SVM handle privilege-sensitive instructions?

b. [20] <5.4> What do VT-x and SVM do to provide higher performance for memory-intensive applications with large memory footprints?

Case Study 5: Putting It All Together: Highly Parallel Memory Systems

Concept illustrated by this case study

- Understanding the Impact of Memory System Design Tradeoffs on Machine Performance

The program in Figure 5.32 can be used to evaluate the behavior of a memory system. The key is having accurate timing and then having the program stride through memory to invoke different levels of the hierarchy. Figure 5.32 is the code in C. The first part is a procedure that uses a standard utility to get an accurate measure of the user CPU time; this procedure may need to change to work on some systems. The second part is a nested loop to read and write memory at different strides and cache sizes. To get accurate cache timing this code is repeated many times. The third part times the nested loop overhead only so that it can be subtracted from overall measured times to see how long the accesses were. The results are output in .csn file format to facilitate importing into spreadsheets. You may need to change CACHE_MAX depending on the question you are answering and the size of memory on the system you are measuring. Running the program in single-user mode or at least without other active applications will give more consistent results. The code in Figure 5.32 was derived from a program written by Andrea Dusseau of U.C. Berkeley and was based on a detailed description found in Saavedra-Barrera [1992]. It has been modified to fix a number of issues with more modern machines and to run under Microsoft Visual C++.

The program shown in Figure 5.32 assumes that program addresses track physical addresses, which is true on the few machines that use virtually addressed caches, such as the Alpha 21264. In general, virtual addresses tend to follow physical addresses shortly after rebooting, so you may need to reboot the machine in order to get smooth lines in your results. To answer the exercises, assume that the sizes of all components of the memory hierarchy are powers of 2. Assume that the size of the page is much larger than the size of a block in a second-level cache (if there is one), and the size of a second-level cache block is greater than or equal to the size of a block in a first-level cache. An example of the output of the program is plotted in Figure 5.33, with the key listing the size of the array that is exercised.

5.18 [10/12/12/12/12] <5.6> Using the sample program results in Figure 5.33:

a. [10] <5.6> How many levels of cache are there?

b. [12] <5.6> What are the overall size and block size of the first-level cache?

c. [12] <5.6> What is the miss penalty of the first-level cache?

d. [12] <5.6> What is the associativity of the first-level cache?

e. [12] <5.6> What effects can you see when the size of the data used in the array is equal to the size of the second-level cache?

```
#include "stdafx.h"
#include <stdio.h>
#include <time.h>
#define ARRAY_MIN (1024) /* 1/4 smallest cache */
#define ARRAY_MAX (4096*4096) /* 1/4 largest cache */
int x[ARRAY_MAX]; /* array going to stride through */

double get_seconds() { /* routine to read time in seconds */
    __time64_t ltime;
    _time64( &ltime );
    return (double) ltime;
}
int label(int i) {/* generate text labels */
    if (i<1e3) printf("%1dB,",i);
    else if (i<1e6) printf("%1dK,",i/1024);
    else if (i<1e9) printf("%1dM,",i/1048576);
    else printf("%1dG,",i/1073741824);
    return 0;
}
int _tmain(int argc, _TCHAR* argv[]) {
int register nextstep, i, index, stride;
int csize;
double steps, tsteps;
double loadtime, lastsec, sec0, sec1, sec; /* timing variables */

/* Initialize output */
printf(" ,");
for (stride=1; stride <= ARRAY_MAX/2; stride=stride*2)
    label(stride*sizeof(int));
printf("\n");

/* Main loop for each configuration */
for (csize=ARRAY_MIN; csize <= ARRAY_MAX; csize=csize*2) {
    label(csize*sizeof(int)); /* print cache size this loop */
    for (stride=1; stride <= csize/2; stride=stride*2) {

        /* Lay out path of memory references in array */
        for (index=0; index < csize; index=index+stride)
            x[index] = index + stride; /* pointer to next */
        x[index-stride] = 0; /* loop back to beginning */

        /* Wait for timer to roll over */
        lastsec = get_seconds();
        do sec0 = get_seconds(); while (sec0 == lastsec);

        /* Walk through path in array for twenty seconds */
        /* This gives 5% accuracy with second resolution */
        steps = 0.0; /* number of steps taken */
        nextstep = 0; /* start at beginning of path */
        sec0 = get_seconds(); /* start timer */
        do { /* repeat until collect 20 seconds */
            for (i=stride;i!=0;i=i-1) { /* keep samples same */
                nextstep = 0;
                do nextstep = x[nextstep]; /* dependency */
                while (nextstep != 0);
            }
            steps = steps + 1.0; /* count loop iterations */
            sec1 = get_seconds(); /* end timer */
        } while ((sec1 - sec0) < 20.0); /* collect 20 seconds */
        sec = sec1 - sec0;

        /* Repeat empty loop to loop subtract overhead */
        tsteps = 0.0; /* used to match no. while iterations */
        sec0 = get_seconds(); /* start timer */
        do { /* repeat until same no. iterations as above */
            for (i=stride;i!=0;i=i-1) { /* keep samples same */
                index = 0;
                do index = index + stride;
                while (index < csize);
            }
            tsteps = tsteps + 1.0;
            sec1 = get_seconds(); /* - overhead */
        } while (tsteps<steps); /* until = no. iterations */
        sec = sec - (sec1 - sec0);
        loadtime = (sec*1e9)/(steps*csize);
        /* write out results in .csv format for Excel */
        printf("%4.1f,", (loadtime<0.1) ? 0.1 : loadtime);
    }; /* end of inner for loop */
    printf("\n");
}; /* end of outer for loop */
return 0;
}
```

Figure 5.32 C program for evaluating memory systems.

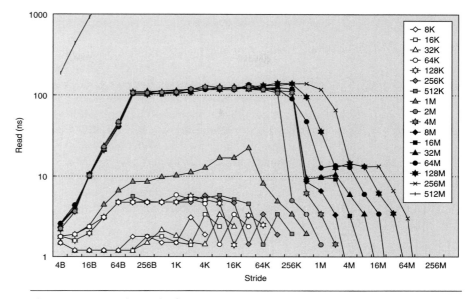

Figure 5.33 Sample results from program in Figure 5.32.

5.19 [15/20/25] <5.6> Modify the code in Figure 5.32 to measure the following system characteristics. Plot the experimental results with elapsed time on the *y*-axis and the memory stride on the *x*-axis. Use logarithmic scales for both axes, and draw a line for each cache size.

 a. [15] <5.6> Is the L1 cache write-through or write-back?

 b. [20] <5.6> Is the memory system blocking or nonblocking?

 c. [25] <5.6> For a nonblocking memory system, how many outstanding memory references can be supported?

5.20 [25/25] <5.6> In multiprocessor memory systems, lower levels of the memory hierarchy may not be able to be saturated by a single processor, but should be able to be saturated by multiple processors working together. Modify the code in Figure 5.32, and run multiple copies at the same time. Can you determine:

 a. [25] <5.6> How much bandwidth does a shared level 2 or level 3 cache (if present) provide?

 b. [25] <5.6> How much bandwidth does the main memory system provide?

5.21 [30] <5.6> Since instruction-level parallelism can also be effectively exploited on in-order superscalar processors and VLIWs with speculation, one important reason for building an out-of-order (OOO) superscalar processor is the ability to tolerate unpredictable memory latency caused by cache misses. Hence, you can think about hardware supporting OOO issue as being part of the memory system! Look at the floorplan of the Alpha 21264 in Figure 5.34 to find the relative area of the integer and floating-point issue queues and mappers versus the caches. The queues schedule instructions for issue, and the mappers rename register specifiers. Hence these are necessary additions to support OOO issue. The 21264 only has level 1 data and instruction caches on chip, and they are both 64 KB two-way set associative. Use an OOO superscalar simulator such as Simplescalar *(www.cs.wisc.edu/~mscalar/simplescalar.html)* on memory-intensive benchmarks to find out how much performance is lost if the area of the issue queues and mappers is used for additional level 1 data cache area in an in-order superscalar processor, instead of OOO issue in a model of the 21264. Make sure the other aspects of the machine are as similar as possible to make the comparison fair. Ignore any increase in access or cycle time from larger caches and effects of the larger data cache on the floorplan of the chip. (Note this comparison will not be totally fair, as the code will not have been scheduled for the in-order processor by the compiler.)

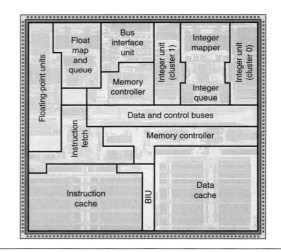

Figure 5.34 Floorplan of the Alpha 21264 [Kessler 1999].

6.1	Introduction	358
6.2	Advanced Topics in Disk Storage	358
6.3	Definition and Examples of Real Faults and Failures	366
6.4	I/O Performance, Reliability Measures, and Benchmarks	371
6.5	A Little Queuing Theory	379
6.6	Crosscutting Issues	390
6.7	Designing and Evaluating an I/O System—The Internet Archive Cluster	392
6.8	Putting It All Together: NetApp FAS6000 Filer	397
6.9	Fallacies and Pitfalls	399
6.10	Concluding Remarks	403
6.11	Historical Perspective and References	404
	Case Studies with Exercises by Andrea C. Arpaci-Dusseau and Remzi H. Arpaci-Dusseau	404

6

Storage Systems

I think Silicon Valley was misnamed. If you look back at the dollars shipped in products in the last decade, there has been more revenue from magnetic disks than from silicon. They ought to rename the place Iron Oxide Valley.

Al Hoagland
a pioneer of magnetic disks
(1982)

Combining bandwidth and storage … enables swift and reliable access to the ever expanding troves of content on the proliferating disks and … repositories of the Internet. … the capacity of storage arrays of all kinds is rocketing ahead of the advance of computer performance.

George Gilder
"The End Is Drawing Nigh,"
Forbes ASAP (April 4, 2000)

6.1 Introduction

The popularity of Internet services like search engines and auctions has enhanced the importance of I/O for computers, since no one would want a desktop computer that couldn't access the Internet. This rise in importance of I/O is reflected by the names of our times. The 1960s to 1980s were called the Computing Revolution; the period since 1990 has been called the Information Age, with concerns focused on advances in information technology versus raw computational power. Internet services depend upon massive storage, which is the focus of this chapter, and networking, which is the focus of Appendix E.

This shift in focus from computation to communication and storage of information emphasizes reliability and scalability as well as cost-performance. Although it is frustrating when a program crashes, people become hysterical if they lose their data. Hence, storage systems are typically held to a higher standard of dependability than the rest of the computer. Dependability is the bedrock of storage, yet it also has its own rich performance theory—queuing theory—that balances throughput versus response time. The software that determines which processor features get used is the compiler, but the operating system usurps that role for storage.

Thus, storage has a different, multifaceted culture from processors, yet it is still found within the architecture tent. We start our exploration with advances in magnetic disks, as they are the dominant storage device today in desktop and server computers. We assume readers are already familiar with the basics of storage devices, some of which were covered in Chapter 1.

6.2 Advanced Topics in Disk Storage

The disk industry historically has concentrated on improving the capacity of disks. Improvement in capacity is customarily expressed as improvement in *areal density,* measured in bits per square inch:

$$\text{Areal density} = \frac{\text{Tracks}}{\text{Inch}} \text{ on a disk surface} \times \frac{\text{Bits}}{\text{Inch}} \text{ on a track}$$

Through about 1988, the rate of improvement of areal density was 29% per year, thus doubling density every three years. Between then and about 1996, the rate improved to 60% per year, quadrupling density every three years and matching the traditional rate of DRAMs. From 1997 to about 2003, the rate increased to 100%, or doubling every year. After the innovations that allowed the renaissances had largely played out, the rate has dropped recently to about 30% per year. In 2006, the highest density in commercial products is 130 billion bits per square inch. Cost per gigabyte has dropped at least as fast as areal density has increased, with smaller diameter drives playing the larger role in this improvement. Costs per gigabyte improved by a factor of 100,000 between 1983 and 2006.

Magnetic disks have been challenged many times for supremacy of secondary storage. Figure 6.1 shows one reason: the fabled *access time gap* between disks and DRAM. DRAM latency is about 100,000 times less than disk, and that performance advantage costs 30–150 times more per gigabyte for DRAM.

The bandwidth gap is more complex. For example, a fast disk in 2006 transfers about 115 MB/sec from the disk media with 37 GB of storage and costs about $150 (as we will see later in Figure 6.3). A 2 GB DRAM module costing about $300 in 2006 could transfer at 3200 MB/sec (see Section 5.3 in Chapter 5), giving the DRAM module about 28 times higher bandwidth than the disk. However, the bandwidth per GB is 500 times higher for DRAM, and the bandwidth per dollar is 14 times higher.

Many have tried to invent a technology cheaper than DRAM but faster than disk to fill that gap, but thus far, all have failed. Challengers have never had a product to market at the right time. By the time a new product would ship, DRAMs and disks have made advances as predicted earlier, costs have dropped accordingly, and the challenging product is immediately obsolete.

The closest challenger is flash memory. This semiconductor memory is non-volatile like disks, and it has about the same bandwidth as disks, but latency is 100–1000 times faster than disk. In 2006, the price per gigabyte of flash was about the same as DRAM. Flash is popular in cameras and portable music players because it comes in much smaller capacities and it is more power efficient than disks, despite the cost per gigabyte being 50 times higher than disks. Unlike

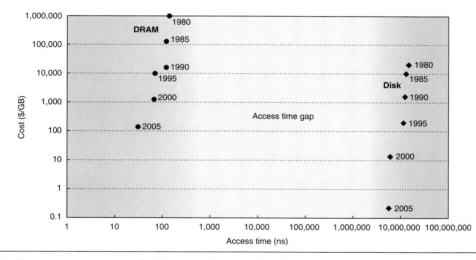

Figure 6.1 **Cost versus access time for DRAM and magnetic disk in 1980, 1985, 1990, 1995, 2000, and 2005.** The two-order-of-magnitude gap in cost and five-order-of-magnitude gap in access times between semiconductor memory and rotating magnetic disks has inspired a host of competing technologies to try to fill them. So far, such attempts have been made obsolete before production by improvements in magnetic disks, DRAMs, or both. Note that between 1990 and 2005 the cost per gigabyte DRAM chips made less improvement, while disk cost made dramatic improvement.

disks and DRAM, flash memory bits wear out—typically limited to 1 million writes—and so they are not popular in desktop and server computers.

While disks will remain viable for the foreseeable future, the conventional sector-track-cylinder model did not. The assumptions of the model are that nearby blocks are on the same track, blocks in the same cylinder take less time to access since there is no seek time, and some tracks are closer than others.

First, disks started offering higher-level intelligent interfaces, like ATA and SCSI, when they included a microprocessor inside a disk. To speed up sequential transfers, these higher-level interfaces organize disks more like tapes than like random access devices. The logical blocks are ordered in serpentine fashion across a single surface, trying to capture all the sectors that are recorded at the same bit density. (Disks vary the recording density since it is hard for the electronics to keep up with the blocks spinning much faster on the outer tracks, and lowering linear density simplifies the task.) Hence, sequential blocks may be on different tracks. We will see later in Figure 6.22 on page 401 an illustration of the fallacy of assuming the conventional sector-track model when working with modern disks.

Second, shortly after the microprocessors appeared inside disks, the disks included buffers to hold the data until the computer was ready to accept it, and later caches to avoid read accesses. They were joined by a command queue that allowed the disk to decide in what order to perform the commands to maximize performance while maintaining correct behavior. Figure 6.2 shows how a queue depth of 50 can double the number of I/Os per second of random I/Os due to better scheduling of accesses. Although it's unlikely that a system would really have 256 commands in a queue, it would triple the number of I/Os per second. Given buffers, caches, and out-of-order accesses, an accurate performance model of a real disk is much more complicated than sector-track-cylinder.

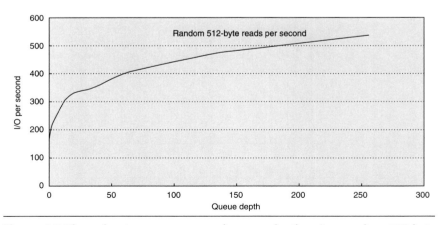

Figure 6.2 Throughput versus command queue depth using random 512-byte reads. The disk performs 170 reads per second starting at no command queue, and doubles performance at 50 and triples at 256 [Anderson 2003].

Finally, the number of platters shrank from 12 in the past to 4 or even 1 today, so the cylinder has less importance than before since the percentage of data in a cylinder is much less.

Disk Power

Power is an increasing concern for disks as well as for processors. A typical ATA disk in 2006 might use 9 watts when idle, 11 watts when reading or writing, and 13 watts when seeking. Because it is more efficient to spin smaller mass, smaller-diameter disks can save power. One formula that indicates the importance of rotation speed and the size of the platters for the power consumed by the disk motor is the following [Gurumurthi 2005]:

$$\text{Power} \approx \text{Diameter}^{4.6} \times \text{RPM}^{2.8} \times \text{Number of platters}$$

Thus, smaller platters, slower rotation, and fewer platters all help reduce disk motor power, and most of the power is in the motor.

Figure 6.3 shows the specifications of two 3.5-inch disks in 2006. The *Serial ATA* (SATA) disks shoot for high capacity and the best cost per gigabyte, and so the 500 GB drives cost less than $1 per gigabyte. They use the widest platters that fit the form factor and use four or five of them, but they spin at 7200 RPM and seek relatively slowly to lower power. The corresponding *Serial Attach SCSI* (SAS) drive aims at performance, and so it spins at 15,000 RPM and seeks much faster. To reduce power, the platter is much narrower than the form factor and it has only a single platter. This combination reduces capacity of the SAS drive to 37 GB.

The cost per gigabyte is about a factor of five better for the SATA drives, and conversely, the cost per I/O per second or MB transferred per second is about a factor of five better for the SAS drives. Despite using smaller platters and many fewer of them, the SAS disks use twice the power of the SATA drives, due to the much faster RPM and seeks.

	Capacity (GB)	Price	Platters	RPM	Diameter (inches)	Average seek (ms)	Power (watts)	I/O/sec	Disk BW (MB/sec)	Buffer BW (MB/sec)	Buffer size (MB)	MTTF (hrs)
SATA	500	$375	4 or 5	7,200	3.7	8–9	12	117	31–65	300	16	0.6M
SAS	37	$150	1	15,000	2.6	3–4	25	285	85–142	300	8	1.2M

Figure 6.3 Serial ATA (SATA) versus Serial Attach SCSI (SAS) drives in 3.5-inch form factor in 2006. The I/Os per second are calculated using the average seek plus the time for one-half rotation plus the time to transfer one sector of 512 KB.

Advanced Topics in Disk Arrays

An innovation that improves both dependability and performance of storage systems is *disk arrays*. One argument for arrays is that potential throughput can be increased by having many disk drives and, hence, many disk arms, rather than fewer large drives. Simply spreading data over multiple disks, called *striping,* automatically forces accesses to several disks if the data files are large. (Although arrays improve throughput, latency is not necessarily improved.) As we saw in Chapter 1, the drawback is that with more devices, dependability decreases: N devices generally have $1/N$ the reliability of a single device.

Although a disk array would have more faults than a smaller number of larger disks when each disk has the same reliability, dependability is improved by adding redundant disks to the array to tolerate faults. That is, if a single disk fails, the lost information is reconstructed from redundant information. The only danger is in having another disk fail during the *mean time to repair* (MTTR). Since the *mean time to failure* (MTTF) of disks is tens of years, and the MTTR is measured in hours, redundancy can make the measured reliability of many disks much higher than that of a single disk.

Such redundant disk arrays have become known by the acronym *RAID,* standing originally for *redundant array of inexpensive disks,* although some prefer the word *independent* for *I* in the acronym. The ability to recover from failures plus the higher throughput, either measured as megabytes per second or as I/Os per second, makes RAID attractive. When combined with the advantages of smaller size and lower power of small-diameter drives, RAIDs now dominate large-scale storage systems.

Figure 6.4 summarizes the five standard RAID levels, showing how eight disks of user data must be supplemented by redundant or check disks at each RAID level, and lists the pros and cons of each level. The standard RAID levels are well documented, so we will just do a quick review here and discuss advanced levels in more depth.

- *RAID 0*—It has no redundancy and is sometimes nicknamed *JBOD,* for "just a bunch of disks," although the data may be striped across the disks in the array. This level is generally included to act as a measuring stick for the other RAID levels in terms of cost, performance, and dependability.

- *RAID 1*—Also called *mirroring* or *shadowing,* there are two copies of every piece of data. It is the simplest and oldest disk redundancy scheme, but it also has the highest cost. Some array controllers will optimize read performance by allowing the mirrored disks to act independently for reads, but this optimization means it may take longer for the mirrored writes to complete.

- *RAID 2*—This organization was inspired by applying memory-style error correcting codes to disks. It was included because there was such a disk array product at the time of the original RAID paper, but none since then as other RAID organizations are more attractive.

RAID level	Disk failures tolerated, check space overhead for 8 data disks	Pros	Cons	Company products
0 Nonredundant striped	0 failures, 0 check disks	No space overhead	No protection	Widely used
1 Mirrored	1 failure, 8 check disks	No parity calculation; fast recovery; small writes faster than higher RAIDs; fast reads	Highest check storage overhead	EMC, HP (Tandem), IBM
2 Memory-style ECC	1 failure, 4 check disks	Doesn't rely on failed disk to self-diagnose	~ Log 2 check storage overhead	Not used
3 Bit-interleaved parity	1 failure, 1 check disk	Low check overhead; high bandwidth for large reads or writes	No support for small, random reads or writes	Storage Concepts
4 Block-interleaved parity	1 failure, 1 check disk	Low check overhead; more bandwidth for small reads	Parity disk is small write bottleneck	Network Appliance
5 Block-interleaved distributed parity	1 failure, 1 check disk	Low check overhead; more bandwidth for small reads and writes	Small writes → 4 disk accesses	Widely used
6 Row-diagonal parity, EVEN-ODD	2 failures, 2 check disks	Protects against 2 disk failures	Small writes → 6 disk accesses; 2X check overhead	Network Appliance

Figure 6.4 RAID levels, their fault tolerance, and their overhead in redundant disks. The paper that introduced the term *RAID* [Patterson, Gibson, and Katz 1987] used a numerical classification that has become popular. In fact, the nonredundant disk array is often called RAID 0, indicating the data are striped across several disks but without redundancy. Note that mirroring (RAID 1) in this instance can survive up to eight disk failures provided only one disk of each mirrored pair fails; worst case is both disks in a mirrored pair. In 2006, there may be no commercial implementations of RAID 2; the rest are found in a wide range of products. RAID 0 + 1, 1 + 0, 01, 10, and 6 are discussed in the text.

- *RAID 3*—Since the higher-level disk interfaces understand the health of a disk, it's easy to figure out which disk failed. Designers realized that if one extra disk contains the parity of the information in the data disks, a single disk allows recovery from a disk failure. The data is organized in stripes, with *N* data blocks and one parity block. When a failure occurs, you just "subtract" the good data from the good blocks, and what remains is the missing data. (This works whether the failed disk is a data disk or the parity disk.) RAID 3 assumes the data is spread across all disks on reads and writes, which is attractive when reading or writing large amounts of data.

- *RAID 4*—Many applications are dominated by small accesses. Since sectors have their own error checking, you can safely increase the number of reads per second by allowing each disk to perform independent reads. It would seem that writes would still be slow, if you have to read every disk to calculate parity. To increase the number of writes per second, an alternative approach involves only two disks. First, the array reads the old data that is about to be overwritten, and then calculates what bits would change before it writes the new data. It then reads the old value of the parity on the check disks, updates parity according to the list of changes, and then writes the new value of parity to the check disk. Hence, these so-called "small writes" are still slower than small reads—they involve four disks accesses—but they are faster than if you had to read all disks on every write. RAID 4 has the same low check disk overhead as RAID 3, and it can still do large reads and writes as fast as RAID 3 in addition to small reads and writes, but control is more complex.

■ *RAID 5*—Note that a performance flaw for small writes in RAID 4 is that they all must read and write the same check disk, so it is a performance bottleneck. RAID 5 simply distributes the parity information across all disks in the array, thereby removing the bottleneck. The parity block in each stripe is rotated so that parity is spread evenly across all disks. The disk array controller must now calculate which disk has the parity for when it wants to write a given block, but that can be a simple calculation. RAID 5 has the same low check disk overhead as RAID 3 and 4, and it can do the large reads and writes of RAID 3 and the small reads of RAID 4, but it has higher small write bandwidth than RAID 4. Nevertheless, RAID 5 requires the most sophisticated controller of the classic RAID levels.

Having completed our quick review of the classic RAID levels, we can now look at two levels that have become popular since RAID was introduced.

RAID 10 versus 01 (or 1 + 0 versus RAID 0+1)

One topic not always described in the RAID literature involves how mirroring in RAID 1 interacts with striping. Suppose you had, say, four disks worth of data to store and eight physical disks to use. Would you create four pairs of disks—each organized as RAID 1—and then stripe data across the four RAID 1 pairs? Alternatively, would you create two sets of four disks—each organized as RAID 0—and then mirror writes to both RAID 0 sets? The RAID terminology has evolved to call the former RAID 1 + 0 or RAID 10 ("striped mirrors") and the latter RAID 0 + 1 or RAID 01 ("mirrored stripes").

RAID 6: Beyond a Single Disk Failure

The parity-based schemes of the RAID 1 to 5 protect against a single self-identifying failure. However, if an operator accidentally replaces the wrong disk during a failure, then the disk array will experience two failures, and data will be lost. Another concern with is that since disk bandwidth is growing more slowly than disk capacity, the MTTR of a disk in a RAID system is increasing, which in turn increases the chances of a second failure. For example, a 500 GB SATA disk could take about 3 hours to read sequentially assuming no interference. Given that the damaged RAID is likely to continue to serve data, reconstruction could be stretched considerably, thereby increasing MTTR. Besides increasing reconstruction time, another concern is that reading much more data during reconstruction means increasing the chance of an uncorrectable media failure, which would result in data loss. Other arguments for concern about simultaneous multiple failures are the increasing number of disks in arrays and the use of ATA disks, which are slower and larger than SCSI disks.

Hence, over the years, there has been growing interest in protecting against more than one failure. Network Appliance, for example, started by building RAID 4 file servers. As double failures were becoming a danger to customers, they created a more robust scheme to protect data, called *row-diagonal parity* or *RAID-DP* [Corbett 2004]. Like the standard RAID schemes, row-diagonal parity uses redundant space based on a parity calculation on a per-stripe basis. Since it is protecting against a double failure, it adds two check blocks per stripe of data. Let's assume there are $p + 1$ disks total, and so $p - 1$ disks have data. Figure 6.5 shows the case when p is 5.

The row parity disk is just like in RAID 4; it contains the even parity across the other four data blocks in its stripe. Each block of the diagonal parity disk contains the even parity of the blocks in the same diagonal. Note that each diagonal does not cover one disk; for example, diagonal 0 does not cover disk 1. Hence, we need just $p - 1$ diagonals to protect the p disks, so the disk only has diagonals 0 to 3 in Figure 6.5.

Let's see how row-diagonal parity works by assuming that data disks 1 and 3 fail in Figure 6.5. We can't perform the standard RAID recovery using the first row using row parity, since it is missing two data blocks from disks 1 and 3. However, we can perform recovery on diagonal 0, since it is only missing the data block associated with disk 3. Thus, row-diagonal parity starts by recovering one of the four blocks on the failed disk in this example using diagonal parity. Since each diagonal misses one disk, and all diagonals miss a different disk, two diagonals are only missing one block. They are diagonals 0 and 2 in this example,

Data disk 0	Data disk 1	Data disk 2	Data disk 3	Row parity	Diagonal parity
0	1	2	3	4	0
1	2	3	4	0	1
2	3	4	0	1	2
3	4	0	1	2	3

Figure 6.5 Row diagonal parity for $p = 5$, which protects four data disks from double failures [Corbett 2004]. This figure shows the diagonal groups for which parity is calculated and stored in the diagonal parity disk. Although this shows all the check data in separate disks for row parity and diagonal parity as in RAID 4, there is a rotated version of row-diagonal parity that is analogous to RAID 5. Parameter p must be prime and greater than 2. However, you can make p larger than the number of data disks by assuming the missing disks have all zeros, and the scheme still works. This trick makes it easy to add disks to an existing system. NetApp picks p to be 257, which allows the system to grow to up to 256 data disks.

so we next restore the block from diagonal 2 from failed disk 1. Once the data for those blocks is recovered, then the standard RAID recovery scheme can be used to recover two more blocks in the standard RAID 4 stripes 0 and 2, which in turn allows us to recover more diagonals. This process continues until two failed disks are completely restored.

The EVEN-ODD scheme developed earlier by researchers at IBM is similar to row diagonal parity, but it has a bit more computation during operation and recovery [Blaum 1995]. Papers that are more recent show how to expand EVEN-ODD to protect against three failures [Blaum 1996; Blaum 2001].

6.3 Definition and Examples of Real Faults and Failures

Although people may be willing to live with a computer that occasionally crashes and forces all programs to be restarted, they insist that their information is never lost. The prime directive for storage is then to remember information, no matter what happens.

Chapter 1 covered the basics of dependability, and this section expands that information to give the standard definitions and examples of failures.

The first step is to clarify confusion over terms. The terms *fault, error,* and *failure* are often used interchangeably, but they have different meanings in the dependability literature. For example, is a programming mistake a fault, error, or failure? Does it matter whether we are talking about when it was designed, or when the program is run? If the running program doesn't exercise the mistake, is it still a fault/error/failure? Try another one. Suppose an alpha particle hits a DRAM memory cell. Is it a fault/error/failure if it doesn't change the value? Is it a fault/error/failure if the memory doesn't access the changed bit? Did a fault/error/failure still occur if the memory had error correction and delivered the corrected value to the CPU? You get the drift of the difficulties. Clearly, we need precise definitions to discuss such events intelligently.

To avoid such imprecision, this subsection is based on the terminology used by Laprie [1985] and Gray and Siewiorek [1991], endorsed by IFIP working group 10.4 and the IEEE Computer Society Technical Committee on Fault Tolerance. We talk about a system as a single module, but the terminology applies to submodules recursively. Let's start with a definition of *dependability*:

> Computer system *dependability* is the quality of delivered service such that reliance can justifiably be placed on this service. The *service* delivered by a system is its observed *actual behavior* as perceived by other system(s) interacting with this system's users. Each module also has an ideal *specified behavior,* where a *service specification* is an agreed description of the expected behavior. A system *failure* occurs when the actual behavior deviates from the specified behavior. The failure occurred because of an *error,* a defect in that module. The cause of an error is a *fault.*
>
> When a fault occurs, it creates a *latent error,* which becomes *effective* when it is activated; when the error actually affects the delivered service, a failure occurs.

The time between the occurrence of an error and the resulting failure is the *error latency*. Thus, an error is the manifestation *in the system* of a fault, and a failure is the manifestation *on the service* of an error. [p. 3]

Let's go back to our motivating examples above. A programming mistake is a *fault*. The consequence is an *error* (or *latent error*) in the software. Upon activation, the error becomes *effective*. When this effective error produces erroneous data that affect the delivered service, a *failure* occurs.

An alpha particle hitting a DRAM can be considered a fault. If it changes the memory, it creates an error. The error will remain latent until the affected memory word is read. If the effective word error affects the delivered service, a failure occurs. If ECC corrected the error, a failure would not occur.

A mistake by a human operator is a fault. The resulting altered data is an error. It is latent until activated, and so on as before.

To clarify, the relation between faults, errors, and failures is as follows:

■ A fault creates one or more latent errors.

■ The properties of errors are (1) a latent error becomes effective once activated; (2) an error may cycle between its latent and effective states; (3) an effective error often propagates from one component to another, thereby creating new errors. Thus, either an effective error is a formerly latent error in that component, or it has propagated from another error in that component or from elsewhere.

■ A component failure occurs when the error affects the delivered service.

■ These properties are recursive and apply to any component in the system.

Gray and Siewiorek classify faults into four categories according to their cause:

1. *Hardware faults*—Devices that fail, such as perhaps due to an alpha particle hitting a memory cell

2. *Design faults*—Faults in software (usually) and hardware design (occasionally)

3. *Operation faults*—Mistakes by operations and maintenance personnel

4. *Environmental faults*—Fire, flood, earthquake, power failure, and sabotage

Faults are also classified by their duration into transient, intermittent, and permanent [Nelson 1990]. *Transient faults* exist for a limited time and are not recurring. *Intermittent faults* cause a system to oscillate between faulty and fault-free operation. *Permanent faults* do not correct themselves with the passing of time.

Now that we have defined the difference between faults, errors, and failures, we are ready to see some real-world examples. Publications of real error rates are rare for two reasons. First, academics rarely have access to significant hardware resources to measure. Second, industrial researchers are rarely allowed to publish failure information for fear that it would be used against their companies in the marketplace. A few exceptions follow.

Berkeley's Tertiary Disk

The Tertiary Disk project at the University of California created an art image server for the Fine Arts Museums of San Francisco. This database consists of high-quality images of over 70,000 artworks. The database was stored on a cluster, which consisted of 20 PCs connected by a switched Ethernet and containing 368 disks. It occupied seven 7-foot-high racks.

Figure 6.6 shows the failure rates of the various components of Tertiary Disk. In advance of building the system, the designers assumed that SCSI data disks would be the least reliable part of the system, as they are both mechanical and plentiful. Next would be the IDE disks, since there were fewer of them, then the power supplies, followed by integrated circuits. They assumed that passive devices like cables would scarcely ever fail.

Figure 6.6 shatters some of those assumptions. Since the designers followed the manufacturer's advice of making sure the disk enclosures had reduced vibration and good cooling, the data disks were very reliable. In contrast, the PC chassis containing the IDE/ATA disks did not afford the same environmental controls. (The IDE/ATA disks did not store data, but helped the application and operating system to boot the PCs.) Figure 6.6 shows that the SCSI backplane, cables, and Ethernet cables were no more reliable than the data disks themselves!

As Tertiary Disk was a large system with many redundant components, it could survive this wide range of failures. Components were connected and mirrored images were placed so that no single failure could make any image unavailable. This strategy, which initially appeared to be overkill, proved to be vital.

This experience also demonstrated the difference between transient faults and hard faults. Virtually all the failures in Figure 6.6 appeared first as transient faults. It was up to the operator to decide if the behavior was so poor that they needed to be replaced or if they could continue. In fact, the word "failure" was not used; instead, the group borrowed terms normally used for dealing with problem employees, with the operator deciding whether a problem component should or should not be "fired."

Tandem

The next example comes from industry. Gray [1990] collected data on faults for Tandem Computers, which was one of the pioneering companies in fault-tolerant computing and used primarily for databases. Figure 6.7 graphs the faults that caused system failures between 1985 and 1989 in absolute faults per system and in percentage of faults encountered. The data show a clear improvement in the reliability of hardware and maintenance. Disks in 1985 needed yearly service by Tandem, but they were replaced by disks that needed no scheduled maintenance. Shrinking numbers of chips and connectors per system plus software's ability to tolerate hardware faults reduced hardware's contribution to only 7% of failures by 1989. Moreover, when hardware was at fault, software embedded in the hardware device (firmware) was often the culprit. The data indicate that software in

Component	Total in system	Total failed	Percentage failed
SCSI controller	44	1	2.3%
SCSI cable	39	1	2.6%
SCSI disk	368	7	1.9%
IDE/ATA disk	24	6	25.0%
Disk enclosure—backplane	46	13	28.3%
Disk enclosure—power supply	92	3	3.3%
Ethernet controller	20	1	5.0%
Ethernet switch	2	1	50.0%
Ethernet cable	42	1	2.3%
CPU/motherboard	20	0	0%

Figure 6.6 Failures of components in Tertiary Disk over 18 months of operation. For each type of component, the table shows the total number in the system, the number that failed, and the percentage failure rate. Disk enclosures have two entries in the table because they had two types of problems: backplane integrity failures and power supply failures. Since each enclosure had two power supplies, a power supply failure did not affect availability. This cluster of 20 PCs, contained in seven 7-foot-high, 19-inch-wide racks, hosts 368 8.4 GB, 7200 RPM, 3.5-inch IBM disks. The PCs are P6-200 MHz with 96 MB of DRAM each. They ran FreeBSD 3.0, and the hosts are connected via switched 100 Mbit/sec Ethernet. All SCSI disks are connected to two PCs via double-ended SCSI chains to support RAID 1. The primary application is called the Zoom Project, which in 1998 was the world's largest art image database, with 72,000 images. See Talagala et al. [2000].

1989 was the major source of reported outages (62%), followed by system operations (15%).

The problem with any such statistics is that these data only refer to what is reported; for example, environmental failures due to power outages were not reported to Tandem because they were seen as a local problem. Data on operation faults is very difficult to collect because it relies on the operators to report personal mistakes, which may affect the opinion of their managers, which in turn can affect job security and pay raises. Gray believes both environmental faults and operator faults are underreported. His study concluded that achieving higher availability requires improvement in software quality and software fault tolerance, simpler operations, and tolerance of operational faults.

Other Studies of the Role of Operators in Dependability

While Tertiary Disk and Tandem are storage-oriented dependability studies, we need to look outside storage to find better measurements on the role of humans in failures. Murphy and Gent [1995] tried to improve the accuracy of data on operator faults by having the system automatically prompt the operator on each

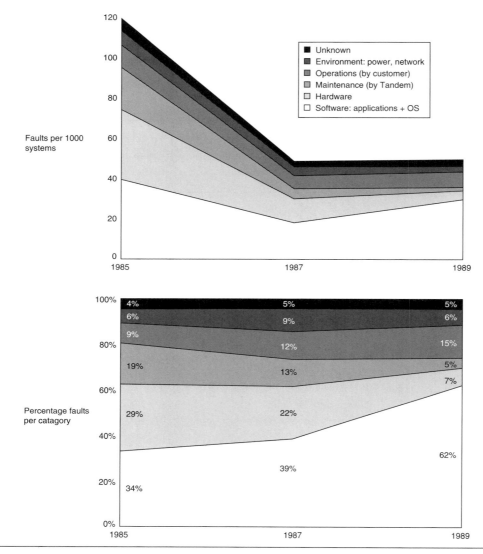

Figure 6.7 Faults in Tandem between 1985 and 1989. Gray [1990] collected these data for the fault-tolerant Tandem computers based on reports of component failures by customers.

boot for the reason for that reboot. They classified consecutive crashes to the same fault as operator fault and included operator actions that directly resulted in crashes, such as giving parameters bad values, bad configurations, and bad application installation. Although they believe operator error is still under-reported, they did get more accurate information than did Gray, who relied on a form that the operator filled out and then sent up the management chain. The hardware/operating system went from causing 70% of the failures in VAX systems in 1985 to 28% in 1993, and failures due to operators rose from 15% to 52% in that same period. Murphy and Gent expected managing systems to be the primary dependability challenge in the future.

The final set of data comes from the government. The Federal Communications Commission (FCC) requires that all telephone companies submit explanations when they experience an outage that affects at least 30,000 people or lasts 30 minutes. These detailed disruption reports do not suffer from the self-reporting problem of earlier figures, as investigators determine the cause of the outage rather than operators of the equipment. Kuhn [1997] studied the causes of outages between 1992 and 1994, and Enriquez [2001] did a follow-up study for the first half of 2001. Although there was a significant improvement in failures due to overloading of the network over the years, failures due to humans increased, from about one-third to two-thirds of the customer-outage minutes.

These four examples and others suggest that the primary cause of failures in large systems today is faults by human operators. Hardware faults have declined due to a decreasing number of chips in systems and fewer connectors. Hardware dependability has improved through fault tolerance techniques such as memory ECC and RAID. At least some operating systems are considering reliability implications before adding new features, so in 2006 the failures largely occurred elsewhere.

Although failures may be initiated due to faults by operators, it is a poor reflection on the state of the art of systems that the process of maintenance and upgrading are so error prone. Most storage vendors claim today that customers spend much more on managing storage over its lifetime than they do on purchasing the storage. Thus, the challenge for dependable storage systems of the future is either to tolerate faults by operators or to avoid faults by simplifying the tasks of system administration. Note that RAID 6 allows the storage system to survive even if the operator mistakenly replaces a good disk.

We have now covered the bedrock issue of dependability, giving definitions, case studies, and techniques to improve it. The next step in the storage tour is performance.

6.4   I/O Performance, Reliability Measures, and Benchmarks

I/O performance has measures that have no counterparts in design. One of these is diversity: which I/O devices can connect to the computer system? Another is capacity: how many I/O devices can connect to a computer system?

In addition to these unique measures, the traditional measures of performance, namely, response time and throughput, also apply to I/O. (I/O throughput is sometimes called *I/O bandwidth,* and response time is sometimes called *latency.*) The next two figures offer insight into how response time and throughput trade off against each other. Figure 6.8 shows the simple producer-server model. The producer creates tasks to be performed and places them in a buffer; the server takes tasks from the first in, first out buffer and performs them.

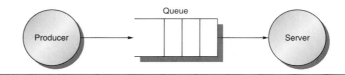

Figure 6.8 The traditional producer-server model of response time and throughput. Response time begins when a task is placed in the buffer and ends when it is completed by the server. Throughput is the number of tasks completed by the server in unit time.

Response time is defined as the time a task takes from the moment it is placed in the buffer until the server finishes the task. Throughput is simply the average number of tasks completed by the server over a time period. To get the highest possible throughput, the server should never be idle, and thus the buffer should never be empty. Response time, on the other hand, counts time spent in the buffer, so an empty buffer shrinks it.

Another measure of I/O performance is the interference of I/O with processor execution. Transferring data may interfere with the execution of another process. There is also overhead due to handling I/O interrupts. Our concern here is how much longer a process will take because of I/O for another process.

Throughput versus Response Time

Figure 6.9 shows throughput versus response time (or latency) for a typical I/O system. The knee of the curve is the area where a little more throughput results in much longer response time or, conversely, a little shorter response time results in much lower throughput.

How does the architect balance these conflicting demands? If the computer is interacting with human beings, Figure 6.10 suggests an answer. An interaction, or *transaction,* with a computer is divided into three parts:

1. *Entry time*—The time for the user to enter the command.

2. *System response time*—The time between when the user enters the command and the complete response is displayed.

3. *Think time*—The time from the reception of the response until the user begins to enter the next command.

The sum of these three parts is called the *transaction time.* Several studies report that user productivity is inversely proportional to transaction time. The results in Figure 6.10 show that cutting system response time by 0.7 seconds saves 4.9 seconds (34%) from the conventional transaction and 2.0 seconds (70%) from the graphics transaction. This implausible result is explained by human nature: People need less time to think when given a faster response. Although this study is 20 years old, response times are often still much slower than 1 second, even if

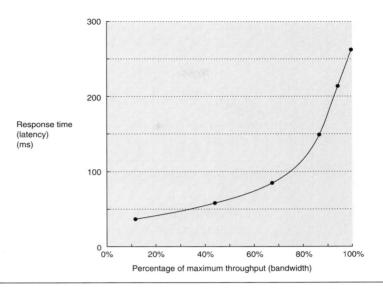

Figure 6.9　Throughput versus response time. Latency is normally reported as response time. Note that the minimum response time achieves only 11% of the throughput, while the response time for 100% throughput takes seven times the minimum response time. Note that the independent variable in this curve is implicit: to trace the curve, you typically vary load (concurrency). Chen et al. [1990] collected these data for an array of magnetic disks.

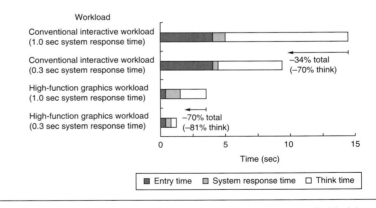

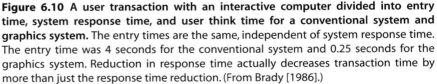

Figure 6.10　A user transaction with an interactive computer divided into entry time, system response time, and user think time for a conventional system and graphics system. The entry times are the same, independent of system response time. The entry time was 4 seconds for the conventional system and 0.25 seconds for the graphics system. Reduction in response time actually decreases transaction time by more than just the response time reduction. (From Brady [1986].)

I/O benchmark	Response time restriction	Throughput metric
TPC-C: Complex Query OLTP	≥ 90% of transaction must meet response time limit; 5 seconds for most types of transactions	new order transactions per minute
TPC-W: Transactional Web benchmark	≥ 90% of Web interactions must meet response time limit; 3 seconds for most types of Web interactions	Web interactions per second
SPECsfs97	average response time ≤ 40 ms	NFS operations per second

Figure 6.11 Response time restrictions for three I/O benchmarks.

processors are 1000 times faster. Examples of long delays include starting an application on a desktop PC due to many disk I/Os, or network delays when clicking on Web links.

To reflect the importance of response time to user productivity, I/O benchmarks also address the response time versus throughput trade-off. Figure 6.11 shows the response time bounds for three I/O benchmarks. They report maximum throughput given either that 90% of response times must be less than a limit or that the average response time must be less than a limit.

Let's next look at these benchmarks in more detail.

Transaction-Processing Benchmarks

Transaction processing (TP, or OLTP for online transaction processing) is chiefly concerned with *I/O rate* (the number of disk accesses per second), as opposed to *data rate* (measured as bytes of data per second). TP generally involves changes to a large body of shared information from many terminals, with the TP system guaranteeing proper behavior on a failure. Suppose, for example, a bank's computer fails when a customer tries to withdraw money from an ATM. The TP system would guarantee that the account is debited if the customer received the money *and* that the account is unchanged if the money was not received. Airline reservations systems as well as banks are traditional customers for TP.

As mentioned in Chapter 1, two dozen members of the TP community conspired to form a benchmark for the industry and, to avoid the wrath of their legal departments, published the report anonymously [Anon. et al. 1985]. This report led to the *Transaction Processing Council,* which in turn has led to eight benchmarks since its founding. Figure 6.12 summarizes these benchmarks.

Let's describe TPC-C to give a flavor of these benchmarks. TPC-C uses a database to simulate an order-entry environment of a wholesale supplier, including entering and delivering orders, recording payments, checking the status of orders, and monitoring the level of stock at the warehouses. It runs five concurrent transactions of varying complexity, and the database includes nine tables with a scalable range of records and customers. TPC-C is measured in transac-

Benchmark	Data size (GB)	Performance metric	Date of first results
A: debit credit (retired)	0.1–10	transactions per second	July 1990
B: batch debit credit (retired)	0.1–10	transactions per second	July 1991
C: complex query OLTP	100–3000 (minimum 0.07 * TPM)	new order transactions per minute (TPM)	September 1992
D: decision support (retired)	100, 300, 1000	queries per hour	December 1995
H: ad hoc decision support	100, 300, 1000	queries per hour	October 1999
R: business reporting decision support (retired)	1000	queries per hour	August 1999
W: transactional Web benchmark	≈ 50, 500	Web interactions per second	July 2000
App: application server and Web services benchmark	≈ 2500	Web service interactions per second (SIPS)	June 2005

Figure 6.12 Transaction Processing Council benchmarks. The summary results include both the performance metric and the price-performance of that metric. TPC-A, TPC-B, TPC-D, and TPC-R were retired.

tions per minute (tpmC) and in price of system, including hardware, software, and three years of maintenance support. Figure 1.16 on page 46 in Chapter 1 describes the top systems in performance and cost-performance for TPC-C.

These TPC benchmarks were the first—and in some cases still the only ones—that have these unusual characteristics:

■ *Price is included with the benchmark results.* The cost of hardware, software, and maintenance agreements is included in a submission, which enables evaluations based on price-performance as well as high performance.

■ *The data set generally must scale in size as the throughput increases.* The benchmarks are trying to model real systems, in which the demand on the system and the size of the data stored in it increase together. It makes no sense, for example, to have thousands of people per minute access hundreds of bank accounts.

■ *The benchmark results are audited.* Before results can be submitted, they must be approved by a certified TPC auditor, who enforces the TPC rules that try to make sure that only fair results are submitted. Results can be challenged and disputes resolved by going before the TPC.

■ *Throughput is the performance metric, but response times are limited.* For example, with TPC-C, 90% of the New-Order transaction response times must be less than 5 seconds.

■ *An independent organization maintains the benchmarks.* Dues collected by TPC pay for an administrative structure including a Chief Operating Office. This organization settles disputes, conducts mail ballots on approval of changes to benchmarks, holds board meetings, and so on.

SPEC System-Level File Server, Mail, and Web Benchmarks

The SPEC benchmarking effort is best known for its characterization of processor performance, but it has created benchmarks for file servers, mail servers, and Web servers.

Seven companies agreed on a synthetic benchmark, called SFS, to evaluate systems running the Sun Microsystems network file service (NFS). This benchmark was upgraded to SFS 3.0 (also called SPEC SFS97_R1) to include support for NFS version 3, using TCP in addition to UDP as the transport protocol, and making the mix of operations more realistic. Measurements on NFS systems led to a synthetic mix of reads, writes, and file operations. SFS supplies default parameters for comparative performance. For example, half of all writes are done in 8 KB blocks and half are done in partial blocks of 1, 2, or 4 KB. For reads, the mix is 85% full blocks and 15% partial blocks.

Like TPC-C, SFS scales the amount of data stored according to the reported throughput: For every 100 NFS operations per second, the capacity must increase by 1 GB. It also limits the average response time, in this case to 40 ms. Figure 6.13 shows average response time versus throughput for two NetApp systems. Unfortunately, unlike the TPC benchmarks, SFS does not normalize for different price configurations.

SPECMail is a benchmark to help evaluate performance of mail servers at an Internet service provider. SPECMail2001 is based on the standard Internet protocols SMTP and POP3, and it measures throughput and user response time while scaling the number of users from 10,000 to 1,000,000.

SPECWeb is a benchmark for evaluating the performance of World Wide Web servers, measuring number of simultaneous user sessions. The SPECWeb2005

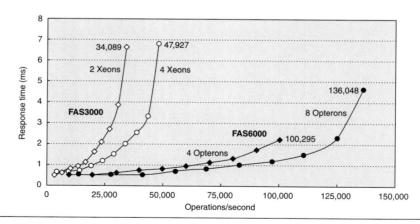

Figure 6.13 SPEC SFS97_R1 performance for the NetApp FAS3050c NFS servers in two configurations. Two processors reached 34,089 operations per second and four processors did 47,927. Reported in May 2005, these systems used the Data ONTAP 7.0.1R1 operating system, 2.8 GHz Pentium Xeon microprocessors, 2 GB of DRAM per processor, 1 GB of nonvolatile memory per system, and 168 15K RPM, 72 GB, fibre channel disks. These disks were connected using two or four QLogic ISP-2322 FC disk controllers.

workload simulates accesses to a Web service provider, where the server supports home pages for several organizations. It has three workloads: Banking (HTTPS), E-commerce (HTTP and HTTPS), and Support (HTTP).

Examples of Benchmarks of Dependability

The TPC-C benchmark does in fact have a dependability requirement. The benchmarked system must be able to handle a single disk failure, which means in practice that all submitters are running some RAID organization in their storage system.

Efforts that are more recent have focused on the effectiveness of fault tolerance in systems. Brown and Patterson [2000] propose that availability be measured by examining the variations in system quality-of-service metrics over time as faults are injected into the system. For a Web server the obvious metrics are performance (measured as requests satisfied per second) and degree of fault tolerance (measured as the number of faults that can be tolerated by the storage subsystem, network connection topology, and so forth).

The initial experiment injected a single fault—such as a write error in disk sector—and recorded the system's behavior as reflected in the quality-of-service metrics. The example compared software RAID implementations provided by Linux, Solaris, and Windows 2000 Server. SPECWeb99 was used to provide a workload and to measure performance. To inject faults, one of the SCSI disks in the software RAID volume was replaced with an emulated disk. It was a PC running software using a SCSI controller that appears to other devices on the SCSI bus as a disk. The disk emulator allowed the injection of faults. The faults injected included a variety of transient disk faults, such as correctable read errors, and permanent faults, such as disk media failures on writes.

Figure 6.14 shows the behavior of each system under different faults. The two top graphs show Linux (on the left) and Solaris (on the right). As RAID systems can lose data if a second disk fails before reconstruction completes, the longer the reconstruction (MTTR), the lower the availability. Faster reconstruction implies decreased application performance, however, as reconstruction steals I/O resources from running applications. Thus, there is a policy choice between taking a performance hit during reconstruction, or lengthening the window of vulnerability and thus lowering the predicted MTTF.

Although none of the tested systems documented their reconstruction policies outside of the source code, even a single fault injection was able to give insight into those policies. The experiments revealed that both Linux and Solaris initiate automatic reconstruction of the RAID volume onto a hot spare when an active disk is taken out of service due to a failure. Although Windows supports RAID reconstruction, the reconstruction must be initiated manually. Thus, without human intervention, a Windows system that did not rebuild after a first failure remains susceptible to a second failure, which increases the window of vulnerability. It does repair quickly once told to do so.

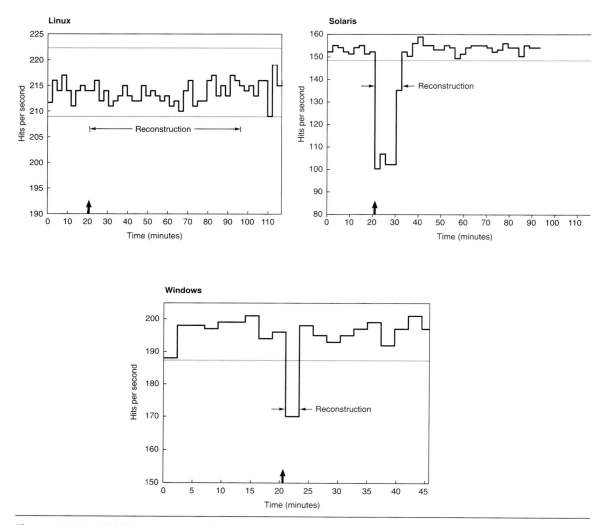

Figure 6.14 Availability benchmark for software RAID systems on the same computer running Red Hat 6.0 Linux, Solaris 7, and Windows 2000 operating systems. Note the difference in philosophy on speed of reconstruction of Linux versus Windows and Solaris. The *y*-axis is behavior in hits per second running SPECWeb99. The arrow indicates time of fault insertion. The lines at the top give the 99% confidence interval of performance before the fault is inserted. A 99% confidence interval means that if the variable is outside of this range, the probability is only 1% that this value would appear.

The fault injection experiments also provided insight into other availability policies of Linux, Solaris, and Windows 2000 concerning automatic spare utilization, reconstruction rates, transient errors, and so on. Again, no system documented their policies.

In terms of managing transient faults, the fault injection experiments revealed that Linux's software RAID implementation takes an opposite approach than do the RAID implementations in Solaris and Windows. The Linux implementation is paranoid—it would rather shut down a disk in a controlled manner at the first error, rather than wait to see if the error is transient. In contrast, Solaris and Windows are more forgiving—they ignore most transient faults with the expectation that they will not recur. Thus, these systems are substantially more robust to transients than the Linux system. Note that both Windows and Solaris do log the transient faults, ensuring that the errors are reported even if not acted upon. When faults were permanent, the systems behaved similarly.

6.5   A Little Queuing Theory

In processor design, we have simple back-of-the-envelope calculations of performance associated with the CPI formula in Chapter 1, or we can use full scale simulation for greater accuracy at greater cost. In I/O systems, we also have a best-case analysis as a back-of-the-envelope calculation. Full-scale simulation is also much more accurate and much more work to calculate expected performance.

With I/O systems, however, we also have a mathematical tool to guide I/O design that is a little more work and much more accurate than best-case analysis, but much less work than full-scale simulation. Because of the probabilistic nature of I/O events and because of sharing of I/O resources, we can give a set of simple theorems that will help calculate response time and throughput of an entire I/O system. This helpful field is called *queuing theory*. Since there are many books and courses on the subject, this section serves only as a first introduction to the topic. However, even this small amount can lead to better design of I/O systems.

Let's start with a black-box approach to I/O systems, as in Figure 6.15. In our example, the processor is making I/O requests that arrive at the I/O device, and the requests "depart" when the I/O device fulfills them.

We are usually interested in the long term, or steady state, of a system rather than in the initial start-up conditions. Suppose we weren't. Although there is a mathematics that helps (Markov chains), except for a few cases, the only way to solve the resulting equations is simulation. Since the purpose of this section is to show something a little harder than back-of-the-envelope calculations but less

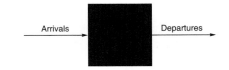

Figure 6.15 Treating the I/O system as a black box. This leads to a simple but important observation: If the system is in steady state, then the number of tasks entering the system must equal the number of tasks leaving the system. This *flow-balanced* state is necessary but not sufficient for steady state. If the system has been observed or measured for a sufficiently long time and mean waiting times stabilize, then we say that the system has reached steady state.

than simulation, we won't cover such analyses here. (See the references in Appendix K for more details.)

Hence, in this section we make the simplifying assumption that we are evaluating systems with multiple independent requests for I/O service that are in equilibrium: the input rate must be equal to the output rate. We also assume there is a steady supply of tasks independent for how long they wait for service. In many real systems, such as TPC-C, the task consumption rate is determined by other system characteristics, such as memory capacity.

This leads us to *Little's Law,* which relates the average number of tasks in the system, the average arrival rate of new tasks, and the average time to perform a task:

$$\text{Mean number of tasks in system} = \text{Arrival rate} \times \text{Mean response time}$$

Little's Law applies to any system in equilibrium, as long as nothing inside the black box is creating new tasks or destroying them. Note that the arrival rate and the response time must use the same time unit; inconsistency in time units is a common cause of errors.

Let's try to derive Little's Law. Assume we observe a system for $\text{Time}_{observe}$ minutes. During that observation, we record how long it took each task to be serviced, and then sum those times. The number of tasks completed during $\text{Time}_{observe}$ is Number_{task}, and the sum of the times each task spends in the system is $\text{Time}_{accumulated}$. Note that the tasks can overlap in time, so $\text{Time}_{accumulated} \geq \text{Time}_{observed}$. Then

$$\text{Mean number of tasks in system} = \frac{\text{Time}_{accumulated}}{\text{Time}_{observe}}$$

$$\text{Mean response time} = \frac{\text{Time}_{accumulated}}{\text{Number}_{tasks}}$$

$$\text{Arrival rate} = \frac{\text{Number}_{tasks}}{\text{Time}_{observe}}$$

Algebra lets us split the first formula:

$$\frac{\text{Time}_{accumulated}}{\text{Time}_{observe}} = \frac{\text{Time}_{accumulated}}{\text{Number}_{tasks}} \times \frac{\text{Number}_{tasks}}{\text{Time}_{observe}}$$

If we substitute the three definitions above into this formula, and swap the resulting two terms on the right-hand side, we get Little's Law:

$$\text{Mean number of tasks in system} = \text{Arrival rate} \times \text{Mean response time}$$

This simple equation is surprisingly powerful, as we shall see.

If we open the black box, we see Figure 6.16. The area where the tasks accumulate, waiting to be serviced, is called the *queue,* or *waiting line.* The device performing the requested service is called the *server.* Until we get to the last two pages of this section, we assume a single server.

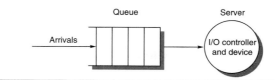

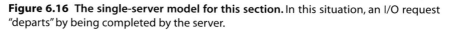

Figure 6.16 The single-server model for this section. In this situation, an I/O request "departs" by being completed by the server.

Little's Law and a series of definitions lead to several useful equations:

■ $Time_{server}$—Average time to service a task; average service rate is $1/Time_{server}$, traditionally represented by the symbol μ in many queuing texts.

■ $Time_{queue}$—Average time per task in the queue.

■ $Time_{system}$—Average time/task in the system, or the response time, which is the sum of $Time_{queue}$ and $Time_{server}$.

■ Arrival rate—Average number of arriving tasks/second, traditionally represented by the symbol λ in many queuing texts.

■ $Length_{server}$—Average number of tasks in service.

■ $Length_{queue}$—Average length of queue.

■ $Length_{system}$—Average number of tasks in system, which is the sum of $Length_{queue}$ and $Length_{server}$.

One common misunderstanding can be made clearer by these definitions: whether the question is how long a task must wait in the queue before service starts ($Time_{queue}$) or how long a task takes until it is completed ($Time_{system}$). The latter term is what we mean by response time, and the relationship between the terms is $Time_{system} = Time_{queue} + Time_{server}$.

The mean number of tasks in service ($Length_{server}$) is simply Arrival rate $\times$ $Time_{server}$, which is Little's Law. Server utilization is simply the mean number of tasks being serviced divided by the service rate. For a single server, the service rate is $1/Time_{server}$. Hence, server utilization (and, in this case, the mean number of tasks per server) is simply

$$Server\ utilization\ =\ Arrival\ rate \times Time_{server}$$

Service utilization must be between 0 and 1; otherwise, there would be more tasks arriving than could be serviced, violating our assumption that the system is in equilibrium. Note that this formula is just a restatement of Little's Law. Utilization is also called *traffic intensity* and is represented by the symbol ρ in many queuing theory texts.

Example   Suppose an I/O system with a single disk gets on average 50 I/O requests per second. Assume the average time for a disk to service an I/O request is 10 ms. What is the utilization of the I/O system?

Answer   Using the equation above, with 10 ms represented as 0.01 seconds; we get:

$$\text{Server utilization} = \text{Arrival rate} \times \text{Time}_{server} = \frac{50}{\text{sec}} \times 0.01\,\text{sec} = 0.50$$

Therefore, the I/O system utilization is 0.5.

How the queue delivers tasks to the server is called the *queue discipline*. The simplest and most common discipline is *first in, first out* (FIFO). If we assume FIFO, we can relate time waiting in the queue to the mean number of tasks in the queue:

$$\text{Time}_{queue} = \text{Length}_{queue} \times \text{Time}_{server} + \text{Mean time to complete service of task when new task arrives if server is busy}$$

That is, the time in the queue is the number of tasks in the queue times the mean service time plus the time it takes the server to complete whatever task is being serviced when a new task arrives. (There is one more restriction about the arrival of tasks, which we reveal on page 384.)

The last component of the equation is not as simple as it first appears. A new task can arrive at any instant, so we have no basis to know how long the existing task has been in the server. Although such requests are random events, if we know something about the distribution of events, we can predict performance.

Poisson Distribution of Random Variables

To estimate the last component of the formula we need to know a little about distributions of *random variables*. A variable is random if it takes one of a specified set of values with a specified probability; that is, you cannot know exactly what its next value will be, but you may know the probability of all possible values.

Requests for service from an I/O system can be modeled by a random variable because the operating system is normally switching between several processes that generate independent I/O requests. We also model I/O service times by a random variable given the probabilistic nature of disks in terms of seek and rotational delays.

One way to characterize the distribution of values of a random variable with discrete values is a *histogram*, which divides the range between the minimum and maximum values into subranges called *buckets*. Histograms then plot the number in each bucket as columns.

Histograms work well for distributions that are discrete values—for example, the number of I/O requests. For distributions that are not discrete values, such as time waiting for an I/O request, we have two choices. Either we need a curve to plot the values over the full range, so that we can estimate accurately the value, or we need a very fine time unit so that we get a very large number of buckets to estimate time accurately. For example, a histogram can be built of disk service times measured in intervals of 10 μs although disk service times are truly continuous.

Hence, to be able to solve the last part of the previous equation we need to characterize the distribution of this random variable. The mean time and some measure of the variance are sufficient for that characterization.

For the first term, we use the *weighted arithmetic mean time*. Let's first assume that after measuring the number of occurrences, say, n_i, of tasks, you could compute frequency of occurrence of task i:

$$f_i = \frac{n_i}{\left(\sum_{i=1}^{n} n_i\right)}$$

Then weighted arithmetic mean is

$$\text{Weighted arithmetic mean time} = f_1 \times T_1 + f_2 \times T_2 + \ldots + f_n \times T_n$$

where T_i is the time for task i and f_i is the frequency of occurrence of task i.

To characterize variability about the mean, many people use the standard deviation. Let's use the *variance* instead, which is simply the square of the standard deviation, as it will help us with characterizing the probability distribution. Given the weighted arithmetic mean, the variance can be calculated as

$$\text{Variance} = (f_1 \times T_1^2 + f_2 \times T_2^2 + \ldots + f_n \times T_n^2) - \text{Weighted arithmetic mean time}^2$$

It is important to remember the units when computing variance. Let's assume the distribution is of time. If time is about 100 milliseconds, then squaring it yields 10,000 square milliseconds. This unit is certainly unusual. It would be more convenient if we had a unitless measure.

To avoid this unit problem, we use the *squared coefficient of variance*, traditionally called C^2:

$$C^2 = \frac{\text{Variance}}{\text{Weighted arithmetic mean time}^2}$$

We can solve for C, the coefficient of variance, as

$$C = \frac{\sqrt{\text{Variance}}}{\text{Weighted arithmetic mean time}} = \frac{\text{Standard deviation}}{\text{Weighted arithmetic mean time}}$$

We are trying to characterize random events, but to be able to predict performance we need a distribution of random events where the mathematics is tractable. The most popular such distribution is the *exponential distribution*, which has a C value of 1.

Note that we are using a constant to characterize variability about the mean. The invariance of C over time reflects the property that the history of events has no impact on the probability of an event occurring now. This forgetful property is called *memoryless,* and this property is an important assumption used to predict behavior using these models. (Suppose this memoryless property did not exist; then we would have to worry about the exact arrival times of requests relative to each other, which would make the mathematics considerably less tractable!)

One of the most widely used exponential distributions is called a *Poisson distribution,* named after the mathematician Simeon Poisson. It is used to characterize random events in a given time interval and has several desirable mathematical properties. The Poisson distribution is described by the following equation (called the probability mass function):

$$\text{Probability}(k) = \frac{e^{-a} \times a^{k}}{k!}$$

where a = Rate of events × Elapsed time. If interarrival times are exponentially distributed and we use arrival rate from above for rate of events, the number of arrivals in a time interval t is a *Poisson process,* which has the Poisson distribution with a = Arrival rate × t. As mentioned on page 382, the equation for $\text{Time}_{\text{server}}$ has another restriction on task arrival: It holds only for Poisson processes.

Finally, we can answer the question about the length of time a new task must wait for the server to complete a task, called the *average residual service time,* which again assumes Poisson arrivals:

$$\text{Average residual service time} = 1/2 \times \text{Arithemtic mean} \times (1 + C^{2})$$

Although we won't derive this formula, we can appeal to intuition. When the distribution is not random and all possible values are equal to the average, the standard deviation is 0 and so C is 0. The average residual service time is then just half the average service time, as we would expect. If the distribution is random and it is Poisson, then C is 1 and the average residual service time equals the weighted arithmetic mean time.

Example Using the definitions and formulas above, derive the average time waiting in the queue ($\text{Time}_{\text{queue}}$) in terms of the average service time ($\text{Time}_{\text{server}}$) and server utilization.

Answer All tasks in the queue ($\text{Length}_{\text{queue}}$) ahead of the new task must be completed before the task can be serviced; each takes on average $\text{Time}_{\text{server}}$. If a task is at the server, it takes average residual service time to complete. The chance the server is busy is *server utilization;* hence the expected time for service is Server utilization × Average residual service time. This leads to our initial formula:

$$\text{Time}_{\text{queue}} = \text{Length}_{\text{queue}} \times \text{Time}_{\text{server}}$$
$$+ \text{Server utilization} \times \text{Average residual service time}$$

Replacing average residual service time by its definition and Length$_{queue}$ by Arrival rate × Time$_{queue}$ yields

$$\text{Time}_{queue} = \text{Server utilization} \times (1/2 \times \text{Time}_{server} \times (1 + C^2))$$
$$+ (\text{Arrival rate} \times \text{Time}_{queue}) \times \text{Time}_{server}$$

Since this section is concerned with exponential distributions, C^2 is 1. Thus

$$\text{Time}_{queue} = \text{Server utilization} \times \text{Time}_{server} + (\text{Arrival rate} \times \text{Time}_{queue}) \times \text{Time}_{server}$$

Rearranging the last term, let us replace Arrival rate × Time$_{server}$ by Server utilization:

$$\text{Time}_{queue} = \text{Server utilization} \times \text{Time}_{server} + (\text{Arrival rate} \times \text{Time}_{server}) \times \text{Time}_{queue}$$
$$= \text{Server utilization} \times \text{Time}_{server} + \text{Server utilization} \times \text{Time}_{queue}$$

Rearranging terms and simplifying gives us the desired equation:

$$\text{Time}_{queue} = \text{Server utilization} \times \text{Time}_{server} + \text{Server utilization} \times \text{Time}_{queue}$$
$$\text{Time}_{queue} - \text{Server utilization} \times \text{Time}_{queue} = \text{Server utilization} \times \text{Time}_{server}$$
$$\text{Time}_{queue} \times (1 - \text{Server utilization}) = \text{Server utilization} \times \text{Time}_{server}$$
$$\text{Time}_{queue} = \text{Time}_{server} \times \frac{\text{Server utilization}}{(1 - \text{Server utilization})}$$

Little's Law can be applied to the components of the black box as well, since they must also be in equilibrium:

$$\text{Length}_{queue} = \text{Arrival rate} \times \text{Time}_{queue}$$

If we substitute for Time$_{queue}$ from above, we get

$$\text{Length}_{queue} = \text{Arrival rate} \times \text{Time}_{server} \times \frac{\text{Server utilization}}{(1 - \text{Server utilization})}$$

Since Arrival rate × Time$_{server}$ = Server utilization, we can simplify further:

$$\text{Length}_{queue} = \text{Server utilization} \times \frac{\text{Server utilization}}{(1 - \text{Server utilization})} = \frac{\text{Server utilization}^2}{(1 - \text{Server utilization})}$$

This relates number of items in queue to service utilization.

Example   For the system in the example on page 382, which has a server utilization of 0.5, what is the mean number of I/O requests in the queue?

Answer   Using the equation above,

$$\text{Length}_{queue} = \frac{\text{Server utilization}^2}{(1 - \text{Server utilization})} = \frac{0.5^2}{(1 - 0.5)} = \frac{0.25}{0.50} = 0.5$$

Therefore, there are 0.5 requests on average in the queue.

As mentioned earlier, these equations and this section are based on an area of applied mathematics called queuing theory, which offers equations to predict behavior of such random variables. Real systems are too complex for queuing theory to provide exact analysis, and hence queuing theory works best when only approximate answers are needed.

Queuing theory makes a sharp distinction between past events, which can be characterized by measurements using simple arithmetic, and future events, which are predictions requiring more sophisticated mathematics. In computer systems, we commonly predict the future from the past; one example is least-recently used block replacement (see Chapter 5). Hence, the distinction between measurements and predicted distributions is often blurred; we use measurements to verify the type of distribution and then rely on the distribution thereafter.

Let's review the assumptions about the queuing model:

- The system is in equilibrium.

- The times between two successive requests arriving, called the *interarrival times,* are exponentially distributed, which characterizes the arrival rate mentioned earlier.

- The number of sources of requests is unlimited. (This is called an *infinite population model* in queuing theory; finite population models are used when arrival rates vary with the number of jobs already in the system.)

- The server can start on the next job immediately after finishing the prior one.

- There is no limit to the length of the queue, and it follows the first in, first out order discipline, so all tasks in line must be completed.

- There is one server.

Such a queue is called *M/M/1:*

> M = exponentially random request arrival ($C^2 = 1$), with M standing for A. A. Markov, the mathematician who defined and analyzed the memoryless processes mentioned earlier
>
> M = exponentially random service time ($C^2 = 1$), with M again for Markov
>
> 1 = single server

The M/M/1 model is a simple and widely used model.

The assumption of exponential distribution is commonly used in queuing examples for three reasons—one good, one fair, and one bad. The good reason is that a superposition of many arbitrary distributions acts as an exponential distribution. Many times in computer systems, a particular behavior is the result of many components interacting, so an exponential distribution of interarrival times is the right model. The fair reason is that when variability is unclear, an exponential distribution with intermediate variability ($C = 1$) is a safer guess than low variability ($C \approx 0$) or high variability (large C). The bad reason is that the math is simpler if you assume exponential distributions.

Let's put queuing theory to work in a few examples.

Example   Suppose a processor sends 40 disk I/Os per second, these requests are exponentially distributed, and the average service time of an older disk is 20 ms. Answer the following questions:

1. On average, how utilized is the disk?

2. What is the average time spent in the queue?

3. What is the average response time for a disk request, including the queuing time and disk service time?

Answer   Let's restate these facts:

Average number of arriving tasks/second is 40.

Average disk time to service a task is 20 ms (0.02 sec).

The server utilization is then

$$\text{Server utilization} = \text{Arrival rate} \times \text{Time}_{\text{server}} = 40 \times 0.02 = 0.8$$

Since the service times are exponentially distributed, we can use the simplified formula for the average time spent waiting in line:

$$\text{Time}_{\text{queue}} = \text{Time}_{\text{server}} \times \frac{\text{Server utilization}}{(1 - \text{Server utilization})}$$

$$= 20 \text{ ms} \times \frac{0.8}{1 - 0.8} = 20 \times \frac{0.8}{0.2} = 20 \times 4 = 80 \text{ ms}$$

The average response time is

$$\text{Time system} = \text{Time}_{\text{queue}} + \text{Time}_{\text{server}} = 80 + 20 \text{ ms} = 100 \text{ ms}$$

Thus, on average we spend 80% of our time waiting in the queue!

Example   Suppose we get a new, faster disk. Recalculate the answers to the questions above, assuming the disk service time is 10 ms.

Answer   The disk utilization is then

$$\text{Server utilization} = \text{Arrival rate} \times \text{Time}_{\text{server}} = 40 \times 0.01 = 0.4$$

The formula for the average time spent waiting in line:

$$\text{Time}_{\text{queue}} = \text{Time}_{\text{server}} \times \frac{\text{Server utilization}}{(1 - \text{Server utilization})}$$

$$= 10 \text{ ms} \times \frac{0.4}{1 - 0.4} = 10 \times \frac{0.4}{0.6} = 10 \times \frac{2}{3} = 6.7 \text{ ms}$$

The average response time is 10 + 6.7 ms or 16.7 ms, 6.0 times faster than the old response time even though the new service time is only 2.0 times faster.

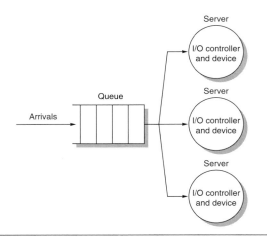

Figure 6.17 The M/M/m multiple-server model.

Thus far, we have been assuming a single server, such as a single disk. Many real systems have multiple disks and hence could use multiple servers, as in Figure 6.17. Such a system is called an *M/M/m* model in queuing theory.

Let's give the same formulas for the M/M/m queue, using $N_{servers}$ to represent the number of servers. The first two formulas are easy:

$$\text{Utilization} = \frac{\text{Arrival rate} \times \text{Time}_{server}}{N_{servers}}$$

$$\text{Length}_{queue} = \text{Arrival rate} \times \text{Time}_{queue}$$

The time waiting in the queue is

$$\text{Time}_{queue} = \text{Time}_{server} \times \frac{P_{tasks \geq N_{servers}}}{N_{servers} \times (1 - \text{Utilization})}$$

This formula is related to the one for M/M/1, except we replace utilization of a single server with the probability that a task will be queued as opposed to being immediately serviced, and divide the time in queue by the number of servers. Alas, calculating the probability of jobs being in the queue is much more complicated when there are $N_{servers}$. First, the probability that there are no tasks in the system is

$$\text{Prob}_{0 \text{ tasks}} = \left[1 + \frac{(N_{servers} \times \text{Utilization})^{N_{servers}}}{N_{servers}! \times (1 - \text{Utilization})} + \sum_{n=1}^{N_{servers}-1} \frac{(N_{servers} \times \text{Utilization})^{n}}{n!} \right]^{-1}$$

Then the probability there are as many or more tasks than we have servers is

$$\text{Prob}_{tasks \geq N_{servers}} = \frac{N_{servers} \times \text{Utilization}^{N_{servers}}}{N_{servers}! \times (1 - \text{Utilization})} \times \text{Prob}_{0 \text{ tasks}}$$

Note that if $N_{servers}$ is 1, $Prob_{task \geq N_{servers}}$ simplifies back to Utilization, and we get the same formula as for M/M/1. Let's try an example.

Example   Suppose instead of a new, faster disk, we add a second slow disk and duplicate the data so that reads can be serviced by either disk. Let's assume that the requests are all reads. Recalculate the answers to the earlier questions, this time using an M/M/m queue.

Answer   The average utilization of the two disks is then

$$\text{Server utilization} = \frac{\text{Arrival rate} \times \text{Time}_{server}}{N_{servers}} = \frac{40 \times 0.02}{2} = 0.4$$

We first calculate the probability of no tasks in the queue:

$$Prob_{0 \text{ tasks}} = \left[1 + \frac{(2 \times \text{Utilization})^2}{2! \times (1 - \text{Utilization})} + \sum_{n=1}^{1} \frac{(2 \times \text{Utilization})^n}{n!} \right]^{-1}$$

$$= \left[1 + \frac{(2 \times 0.4)^2}{2 \times (1 - 0.4)} + (2 \times 0.4) \right]^{-1} = \left[1 + \frac{0.640}{1.2} + 0.800 \right]^{-1}$$

$$= [1 + 0.533 + 0.800]^{-1} = 2.333^{-1}$$

We use this result to calculate the probability of tasks in the queue:

$$Prob_{tasks \geq N_{servers}} = \frac{2 \times \text{Utilization}^2}{2! \times (1 - \text{Utilization})} \times Prob_{0 \text{ tasks}}$$

$$= \frac{(2 \times 0.4)^2}{2 \times (1 - 0.4)} \times 2.333^{-1} = \frac{0.640}{1.2} \times 2.333^{-1}$$

$$= 0.533 / 2.333 = 0.229$$

Finally, the time waiting in the queue:

$$\text{Time}_{queue} = \text{Time}_{server} \times \frac{Prob_{tasks \geq N_{servers}}}{N_{servers} \times (1 - \text{Utilization})}$$

$$= 0.020 \times \frac{0.229}{2 \times (1 - 0.4)} = 0.020 \times \frac{0.229}{1.2}$$

$$= 0.020 \times 0.190 = 0.0038$$

The average response time is 20 + 3.8 ms or 23.8 ms. For this workload, two disks cut the queue waiting time by a factor of 21 over a single slow disk and a factor of 1.75 versus a single fast disk. The mean service time of a system with a single fast disk, however, is still 1.4 times faster than one with two disks since the disk service time is 2.0 times faster.

It would be wonderful if we could generalize the M/M/m model to multiple queues and multiple servers, as this step is much more realistic. Alas, these models are very hard to solve and to use, and so we won't cover them here.

6.6 Crosscutting Issues

Point-to-Point Links and Switches Replacing Buses

Point-to-point links and switches are increasing in popularity as Moore's Law continues to reduce the cost of components. Combined with the higher I/O bandwidth demands from faster processors, faster disks, and faster local area networks, the decreasing cost advantage of buses means the days of buses in desktop and server computers are numbered. This trend started in high-performance computers in the last edition of the book, and by 2006 has spread itself throughout the storage. Figure 6.18 shows the old bus-based standards and their replacements.

The number of bits and bandwidth for the new generation is per direction, so they double for both directions. Since these new designs use many fewer wires, a common way to increase bandwidth is to offer versions with several times the number of wires and bandwidth.

Block Servers versus Filers

Thus far, we have largely ignored the role of the operating system in storage. In a manner analogous to the way compilers use an instruction set, operating systems determine what I/O techniques implemented by the hardware will actually be used. The operating system typically provides the file abstraction on top of blocks stored on the disk. The terms *logical units, logical volumes,* and *physical volumes* are related terms used in Microsoft and UNIX systems to refer to subset collections of disk blocks.

A logical unit is the element of storage exported from a disk array, usually constructed from a subset of the array's disks. A logical unit appears to the server

Standard	Width (bits)	Length (meters)	Clock rate	MB/sec	Max I/O devices
(Parallel) ATA	8	0.5	133 MHz	133	2
Serial ATA	2	2	3 GHz	300	?
SCSI	16	12	80 MHz	320	15
Serial Attach SCSI	1	10	(DDR)	375	16,256
PCI	32/64	0.5	33/66 MHz	533	?
PCI Express	2	0.5	3 GHz	250	?

Figure 6.18 Parallel I/O buses and their point-to-point replacements. Note the bandwidth and wires are per direction, so bandwidth doubles when sending both directions.

as a single virtual "disk." In a RAID disk array, the logical unit is configured as a particular RAID layout, such as RAID 5. A physical volume is the device file used by the file system to access a logical unit. A logical volume provides a level of virtualization that enables the file system to split the physical volume across multiple pieces or to stripe data across multiple physical volumes. A logical unit is an abstraction of a disk array that presents a virtual disk to the operating system, while physical and logical volumes are abstractions used by the operating system to divide these virtual disks into smaller, independent file systems.

Having covered some of the terms for collections of blocks, the question arises, Where should the file illusion be maintained: in the server or at the other end of the storage area network?

The traditional answer is the server. It accesses storage as disk blocks and maintains the metadata. Most file systems use a file cache, so the server must maintain consistency of file accesses. The disks may be *direct attached*—found inside a server connected to an I/O bus—or attached over a storage area network, but the server transmits data blocks to the storage subsystem.

The alternative answer is that the disk subsystem itself maintains the file abstraction, and the server uses a file system protocol to communicate with storage. Example protocols are Network File System (NFS) for UNIX systems and Common Internet File System (CIFS) for Windows systems. Such devices are called *network attached storage* (NAS) devices since it makes no sense for storage to be directly attached to the server. The name is something of a misnomer because a storage area network like FC-AL can also be used to connect to block servers. The term *filer* is often used for NAS devices that only provide file service and file storage. Network Appliances was one of the first companies to make filers.

The driving force behind placing storage on the network is to make it easier for many computers to share information and for operators to maintain the shared system.

Asynchronous I/O and Operating Systems

Disks typically spend much more time in mechanical delays than in transferring data. Thus, a natural path to higher I/O performance is parallelism, trying to get many disks to simultaneously access data for a program.

The straightforward approach to I/O is to request data and then start using it. The operating system then switches to another process until the desired data arrive, and then the operating system switches back to the requesting process. Such a style is called *synchronous I/O*—the process waits until the data have been read from disk.

The alternative model is for the process to continue after making a request, and it is not blocked until it tries to read the requested data. Such *asynchronous I/O* allows the process to continue making requests so that many I/O requests can be operating simultaneously. Asynchronous I/O shares the same philosophy as caches in out-of-order CPUs, which achieve greater bandwidth by having multiple outstanding events.

**Designing and Evaluating an I/O System—
The Internet Archive Cluster**

The art of I/O system design is to find a design that meets goals for cost, dependability, and variety of devices while avoiding bottlenecks in I/O performance and dependability. Avoiding bottlenecks means that components must be balanced between main memory and the I/O device, because performance and dependability—and hence effective cost-performance or cost-dependability—can only be as good as the weakest link in the I/O chain. The architect must also plan for expansion so that customers can tailor the I/O to their applications. This expansibility, both in numbers and types of I/O devices, has its costs in longer I/O buses and networks, larger power supplies to support I/O devices, and larger cabinets.

In designing an I/O system, we analyze performance, cost, capacity, and availability using varying I/O connection schemes and different numbers of I/O devices of each type. Here is one series of steps to follow in designing an I/O system. The answers for each step may be dictated by market requirements or simply by cost, performance, and availability goals.

1. List the different types of I/O devices to be connected to the machine, or list the standard buses and networks that the machine will support.

2. List the physical requirements for each I/O device. Requirements include size, power, connectors, bus slots, expansion cabinets, and so on.

3. List the cost of each I/O device, including the portion of cost of any controller needed for this device.

4. List the reliability of each I/O device.

5. Record the processor resource demands of each I/O device. This list should include

   ▪ Clock cycles for instructions used to initiate an I/O, to support operation of an I/O device (such as handling interrupts), and to complete I/O

   ▪ Processor clock stalls due to waiting for I/O to finish using the memory, bus, or cache

   ▪ Processor clock cycles to recover from an I/O activity, such as a cache flush

6. List the memory and I/O bus resource demands of each I/O device. Even when the processor is not using memory, the bandwidth of main memory and the I/O connection is limited.

7. The final step is assessing the performance and availability of the different ways to organize these I/O devices. When you can afford it, try to avoid single points of failure. Performance can only be properly evaluated with simulation, although it may be estimated using queuing theory. Reliability can be calculated assuming I/O devices fail independently and that the times to failure are

exponentially distributed. Availability can be computed from reliability by estimating MTTF for the devices, taking into account the time from failure to repair.

Given your cost, performance, and availability goals, you then select the best organization,

Cost-performance goals affect the selection of the I/O scheme and physical design. Performance can be measured either as megabytes per second or I/Os per second, depending on the needs of the application. For high performance, the only limits should be speed of I/O devices, number of I/O devices, and speed of memory and processor. For low cost, most of the cost should be the I/O devices themselves. Availability goals depend in part on the cost of unavailability to an organization.

Rather than create a paper design, let's evaluate a real system.

The Internet Archive Cluster

To make these ideas clearer, we'll estimate the cost, performance, and availability of a large storage-oriented cluster at the Internet Archive. The Internet Archive began in 1996 with the goal of making a historical record of the Internet as it changed over time. You can use the Wayback Machine interface to the Internet Archive to perform time travel to see what the Web site at a URL looked like some time in the past. In 2006 it contains over a petabyte (10^{15} bytes) and is growing by 20 terabytes (10^{12} bytes) of new data per month, so expansible storage is a requirement. In addition to storing the historical record, the same hardware is used to crawl the Web every few months to get snapshots of the Internet.

Clusters of computers connected by local area networks have become a very economical computation engine that work well for some applications. Clusters also play an important role in Internet services such the Google search engine, where the focus is more on storage than it is on computation, as is the case here.

Although it has used a variety of hardware over the years, the Internet Archive is moving to a new cluster to become more efficient in power and in floor space. The basic building block is a 1U storage node called the PetaBox GB2000 from Capricorn Technologies. In 2006 it contains four 500 GB Parallel ATA (PATA) disk drives, 512 MB of DDR266 DRAM, one 10/100/1000 Ethernet interface, and a 1 GHz C3 Processor from VIA, which executes the 80x86 instruction set. This node dissipates about 80 watts in typical configurations.

Figure 6.19 shows the cluster in a standard VME rack. Forty of the GB2000s fit in a standard VME rack, which gives the rack 80 TB of raw capacity. The 40 nodes are connected together with a 48-port 10/100 or 10/100/1000 switch, and it dissipates about 3 KW. The limit is usually 10 KW per rack in computer facilities, so it is well within the guidelines.

A petabyte needs 12 of these racks, connected by a higher-level switch that connects the Gbit links coming from the switches in each of the racks.

Figure 6.19 The TB-80 VME rack from Capricorn Systems used by the Internet Archive. All cables, switches, and displays are accessible from the front side, and so the back side is only used for airflow. This allows two racks to be placed back-to-back, which reduces the floor space demands in machine rooms.

Estimating Performance, Dependability, and Cost of the Internet Archive Cluster

To illustrate how to evaluate an I/O system, we'll make some guesses about the cost, performance, and reliability of the components of this cluster. We make the following assumptions about cost and performance:

- The VIA processor, 512 MB of DDR266 DRAM, ATA disk controller, power supply, fans, and enclosure costs $500.

- Each of the four 7200 RPM Parallel ATA drives holds 500 GB, has an average time seek of 8.5 ms, transfers at 50 MB/sec from the disk, and costs $375. The PATA link speed is 133 MB/sec.

- The 48-port 10/100/1000 Ethernet switch and all cables for a rack costs $3000.

- The performance of the VIA processor is 1000 MIPS.

- The ATA controller adds 0.1 ms of overhead to perform a disk I/O.

- The operating system uses 50,000 CPU instructions for a disk I/O.

- The network protocol stacks use 100,000 CPU instructions to transmit a data block between the cluster and the external world.

- The average I/O size is 16 KB for accesses to the historical record via the Wayback interface, and 50 KB when collecting a new snapshot.

Example   Evaluate the cost per I/O per second (IOPS) of the 80 TB rack. Assume that every disk I/O requires an average seek and average rotational delay. Assume the workload is evenly divided among all disks and that all devices can be used at 100% of capacity; that is, the system is limited only by the weakest link, and it can operate that link at 100% utilization. Calculate for both average I/O sizes.

Answer   I/O performance is limited by the weakest link in the chain, so we evaluate the maximum performance of each link in the I/O chain for each organization to determine the maximum performance of that organization.

Let's start by calculating the maximum number of IOPS for the CPU, main memory, and I/O bus of one GB2000. The CPU I/O performance is determined by the speed of the CPU and the number of instructions to perform a disk I/O and to send it over the network:

$$\text{Maximum IOPS for CPU} = \frac{1000 \text{ MIPS}}{50,000 \text{ instructions per I/O} + 100,000 \text{ instructions per message}} = 6667 \text{ IOPS}$$

The maximum performance of the memory system is determined by the memory bandwidth and the size of the I/O transfers:

$$\text{Maximum IOPS for main memory} = \frac{266 \times 8}{16 \text{ KB per I/O}} \approx 133,000 \text{ IOPS}$$

$$\text{Maximum IOPS for main memory} = \frac{266 \times 8}{50 \text{ KB per I/O}} \approx 42,500 \text{ IOPS}$$

The Parallel ATA link performance is limited by the bandwidth and the size of the I/O:

$$\text{Maximum IOPS for the I/O bus} = \frac{133 \text{ MB/sec}}{16 \text{ KB per I/O}} \approx 8300 \text{ IOPS}$$

$$\text{Maximum IOPS for the I/O bus} = \frac{133 \text{ MB/sec}}{50 \text{ KB per I/O}} \approx 2700 \text{ IOPS}$$

Since the box has two buses, the I/O bus limits the maximum performance to no more than 18,600 IOPS for 16 KB blocks and 5400 IOPS for 50 KB blocks.

Now it's time to look at the performance of the next link in the I/O chain, the ATA controllers. The time to transfer a block over the PATA channel is

$$\text{Parallel ATA transfer time} = \frac{16 \text{ KB}}{133 \text{ MB/sec}} = 0.1 \text{ ms}$$

$$\text{Parallel ATA transfer time} = \frac{50 \text{ KB}}{133 \text{ MB/sec}} = 0.4 \text{ ms}$$

Adding the 0.1 ms ATA controller overhead means 0.2 ms to 0.5 ms per I/O, making the maximum rate per controller

$$\text{Maximum IOPS per ATA controller} = \frac{1}{0.2 \text{ ms}} = 5000 \text{ IOPS}$$

$$\text{Maximum IOPS per ATA controller} = \frac{1}{0.5 \text{ ms}} = 2000 \text{ IOPS}$$

The next link in the chain is the disks themselves. The time for an average disk I/O is

$$\text{I/O time} = 8.5 \text{ ms} + \frac{0.5}{7200 \text{ RPM}} + \frac{16 \text{ KB}}{50 \text{ MB/sec}} = 8.5 + 4.2 + 0.3 = 13.0 \text{ ms}$$

$$\text{I/O time} = 8.5 \text{ ms} + \frac{0.5}{7200 \text{ RPM}} + \frac{50 \text{ KB}}{50 \text{ MB/sec}} = 8.5 + 4.2 + 1.0 = 13.7 \text{ ms}$$

Therefore, disk performance is

$$\text{Maximum IOPS (using average seeks) per disk} = \frac{1}{13.0 \text{ ms}} \approx 77 \text{ IOPS}$$

$$\text{Maximum IOPS (using average seeks) per disk} = \frac{1}{13.7 \text{ ms}} \approx 73 \text{ IOPS}$$

or 292–308 IOPS for the four disks.

The final link in the chain is the network that connects the computers to the outside world. The link speed determines the limit

$$\text{Maximum IOPS per 1000 Mbit Ethernet link} = \frac{1000 \text{ Mbit}}{16K \times 8} = 7812 \text{ IOPS}$$

$$\text{Maximum IOPS per 1000 Mbit Ethernet link} = \frac{1000 \text{ Mbit}}{50K \times 8} = 2500 \text{ IOPS}$$

Clearly, the performance bottleneck of the GB2000 is the disks. The IOPS for the whole rack is 40×308 or 12,320 IOPS to 40×292 or 11,680 IOPS. The network switch would be the bottleneck if it couldn't support $12,320 \times 16K \times 8$ or 1.6 Gbits/sec for 16 KB blocks and $11,680 \times 50K \times 8$ or 4.7 Gbits/sec for 50 KB blocks. We assume that the extra 8 Gbit ports of the 48-port switch connects the rack to the rest of the world, so it could support the full IOPS of the collective 160 disks in the rack.

Using these assumptions, the cost is $40 \times (\$500 + 4 \times \$375) + \$3000 + \$1500$ or \$84,500 for an 80 TB rack. The disks themselves are almost 60% of the cost. The cost per terabyte is almost \$1000, which is about a factor of 10–15 better than storage cluster from the prior edition in 2001. The cost per IOPS is about \$7.

Calculating MTTF of the TB-80 Cluster

Internet services like Google rely on many copies of the data at the application level to provide dependability, often at different geographic sites to protect against environmental faults as well as hardware faults. Hence, the Internet Archive has two copies of the data in each site and has sites in San Francisco, Amsterdam, and Alexandria, Egypt. Each site maintains a duplicate copy of the high-value content—music, books, film, and video—and a single copy of the historical Web crawls. To keep costs low, there is no redundancy in the 80 TB rack.

Example Let's look at the resulting mean time to fail of the rack. Rather than use the manufacturer's quoted MTTF of 600,000 hours, we'll use data from a recent survey of disk drives [Gray and van Ingen 2005]. As mentioned in Chapter 1, about 3% to 7% of ATA drives fail per year, or an MTTF of about 125,000–300,000 hours. Make the following assumptions, again assuming exponential lifetimes:

- CPU/memory/enclosure MTTF is 1,000,000 hours.
- PATA Disk MTTF is 125,000 hours.
- PATA controller MTTF is 500,000 hours.
- Ethernet Switch MTTF is 500,000 hours.
- Power supply MTTF is 200,000 hours.
- Fan MTTF is 200,000 hours.
- PATA cable MTTF is 1,000,000 hours.

Answer Collecting these together, we compute these failure rates:

$$\text{Failure rate} = \frac{40}{1,000,000} + \frac{160}{125,000} + \frac{40}{500,000} + \frac{1}{500,000} + \frac{40}{200,000} + \frac{40}{200,000} + \frac{80}{1,000,000}$$

$$= \frac{40 + 1280 + 80 + 2 + 200 + 200 + 80}{1,000,000 \text{ hours}} = \frac{1882}{1,000,000 \text{ hours}}$$

The MTTF for the system is just the inverse of the failure rate:

$$\text{MTTF} = \frac{1}{\text{Failure rate}} = \frac{1,000,000 \text{ hours}}{1882} = 531 \text{ hours}$$

That is, given these assumptions about the MTTF of components, something in a rack fails on average every 3 weeks. About 70% of the failures would be the disks, and about 20% would be fans or power supplies.

6.8 Putting It All Together: NetApp FAS6000 Filer

Network Appliance entered the storage market in 1992 with a goal of providing an easy-to-operate file server running NSF using their own log-structured file system and a RAID 4 disk array. The company later added support for the Windows CIFS file system and a RAID 6 scheme called row-diagonal parity or RAID-DP (see page 364). To support applications that want access to raw data blocks without the overhead of a file system, such as database systems, NetApp filers can serve data blocks over a standard Fibre Channel interface. NetApp also supports *iSCSI*, which allows SCSI commands to run over a TCP/IP network, thereby allowing the use of standard networking gear to connect servers to storage, such as Ethernet, and hence greater distance.

The latest hardware product is the FAS6000. It is a multiprocessor based on the AMD Opteron microprocessor connected using its Hypertransport links. The microprocessors run the NetApp software stack, including NSF, CIFS, RAID-DP, SCSI, and so on. The FAS6000 comes as either a dual processor (FAS6030) or a quad processor (FAS6070). As mentioned in Chapter 4, DRAM is distributed to each microprocessor in the Opteron. The FAS6000 connects 8 GB of DDR2700 to each Opteron, yielding 16 GB for the FAS6030 and 32 GB for the FAS6070. As mentioned in Chapter 5, the DRAM bus is 128 bits wide, plus extra bits for SEC/DED memory. Both models dedicate four Hypertransport links to I/O.

As a filer, the FAS6000 needs a lot of I/O to connect to the disks and to connect to the servers. The integrated I/O consists of

- 8 Fibre Channel (FC) controllers and ports,

- 6 Gigabit Ethernet links,

- 6 slots for x8 (2 GB/sec) PCI Express cards,

- 3 slots for PCI-X 133 MHz, 64-bit cards,

- plus standard I/O options like IDE, USB, and 32-bit PCI.

The 8 Fibre Channel controllers can each be attached to 6 shelves containing 14 3.5-inch FC disks. Thus, the maximum number of drives for the integrated I/O is $8 \times 6 \times 14$ or 672 disks. Additional FC controllers can be added to the option slots to connect up to 1008 drives, to reduce the number of drives per FC network so as to reduce contention, and so on. At 500 GB per FC drive in 2006, if we assume the RAID RDP group is 14 data disks and 2 check disks, the available data capacity is 294 TB for 672 disks and 441 TB for 1008 disks.

It can also connect to Serial ATA disks via a Fibre Channel to SATA bridge controller, which, as its name suggests, allows FC and SATA to communicate.

The six 1-gigabit Ethernet links connect to servers to make the FAS6000 look like a file server running if NTFS or CIFS, or like a block server if running iSCSI.

For greater dependability, FAS6000 filers can be paired so that if one fails, the other can take over. Clustered failover requires that both filers have access to all disks in the pair of filers using the FC interconnect. This interconnect also allows each filer to have a copy of the log data in the NVRAM of the other filer and to keep the clocks of the pair synchronized. The health of the filers is constantly monitored, and failover happens automatically. The healthy filer maintains its own network identity and its own primary functions, but it also assumes the network identity of the failed filer and handles all its data requests via a virtual filer until an administrator restores the data service to the original state.

| 6.9 | **Fallacies and Pitfalls** |

Fallacy   *Components fail fast.*

A good deal of the fault-tolerant literature is based on the simplifying assumption that a component operates perfectly until a latent error becomes effective, and then a failure occurs that stops the component.

The Tertiary Disk project had the opposite experience. Many components started acting strangely long before they failed, and it was generally up to the system operator to determine whether to declare a component as failed. The component would generally be willing to continue to act in violation of the service agreement until an operator "terminated" that component.

Figure 6.20 shows the history of four drives that were terminated, and the number of hours they started acting strangely before they were replaced.

Fallacy   *Computers systems achieve 99.999% availability ("five nines"), as advertised.*

Marketing departments of companies making servers started bragging about the availability of their computer hardware; in terms of Figure 6.21, they claim availability of 99.999%, nicknamed *five nines*. Even the marketing departments of operating system companies tried to give this impression.

Five minutes of unavailability per year is certainly impressive, but given the failure data collected in surveys, it's hard to believe. For example, Hewlett-Packard claims that the HP-9000 server hardware and HP-UX operating system can deliver a 99.999% availability guarantee "in certain pre-defined, pre-tested customer environments" (see Hewlett-Packard [1998]). This guarantee does not include failures due to operator faults, application faults, or environmental faults,

Messages in system log for failed disk	Number of log messages	Duration (hours)
Hardware Failure (Peripheral device write fault [for] Field Replaceable Unit)	1763	186
Not Ready (Diagnostic failure: ASCQ = Component ID [of] Field Replaceable Unit)	1460	90
Recovered Error (Failure Prediction Threshold Exceeded [for] Field Replaceable Unit)	1313	5
Recovered Error (Failure Prediction Threshold Exceeded [for] Field Replaceable Unit)	431	17

Figure 6.20 Record in system log for 4 of the 368 disks in Tertiary Disk that were replaced over 18 months. See Talagala and Patterson [1999]. These messages, matching the SCSI specification, were placed into the system log by device drivers. Messages started occurring as much as a week before one drive was replaced by the operator. The third and fourth messages indicate that the drive's failure prediction mechanism detected and predicted imminent failure, yet it was still hours before the drives were replaced by the operator.

Unavailability (minutes per year)	Availability (percent)	Availability class ("number of nines")
50,000	90%	1
5,000	99%	2
500	99.9%	3
50	99.99%	4
5	99.999%	5
0.5	99.9999%	6
0.05	99.99999%	7

Figure 6.21 Minutes unavailable per year to achieve availability class (from Gray and Siewiorek [1991]). Note that five nines mean unavailable five minutes per year.

which are likely the dominant fault categories today. Nor does it include scheduled downtime. It is also unclear what the financial penalty is to a company if a system does not match its guarantee.

Microsoft also promulgated a five nines marketing campaign. In January 2001, *www.microsoft.com* was unavailable for 22 hours. For its Web site to achieve 99.999% availability, it will require a clean slate for 250 years.

In contrast to marketing suggestions, well-managed servers in 2006 typically achieve 99% to 99.9% availability.

Pitfall   *Where a function is implemented affects its reliability.*

In theory, it is fine to move the RAID function into software. In practice, it is very difficult to make it work reliably.

The software culture is generally based on eventual correctness via a series of releases and patches. It is also difficult to isolate from other layers of software. For example, proper software behavior is often based on having the proper version and patch release of the operating system. Thus, many customers have lost data due to software bugs or incompatibilities in environment in software RAID systems.

Obviously, hardware systems are not immune to bugs, but the hardware culture tends to place a greater emphasis on testing correctness in the initial release. In addition, the hardware is more likely to be independent of the version of the operating system.

Fallacy   *Operating systems are the best place to schedule disk accesses.*

Higher-level interfaces like ATA and SCSI offer logical block addresses to the host operating system. Given this high-level abstraction, the best an OS can do is to try to sort the logical block addresses into increasing order. Since only the disk knows the mapping of the logical addresses onto the physical geometry of sectors, tracks, and surfaces, it can reduce the rotational and seek latencies.

For example, suppose the workload is four reads [Anderson 2003]:

Operation	Starting LBA	Length
Read	724	8
Read	100	16
Read	9987	1
Read	26	128

The host might reorder the four reads into logical block order:

Read	26	128
Read	100	16
Read	724	8
Read	9987	1

Depending on the relative location of the data on the disk, reordering could make it worse, as Figure 6.22 shows. The disk-scheduled reads complete in three-quarters of a disk revolution, but the OS-scheduled reads take three revolutions.

Fallacy   *The time of an average seek of a disk in a computer system is the time for a seek of one-third the number of cylinders.*

This fallacy comes from confusing the way manufacturers market disks with the expected performance, and from the false assumption that seek times are linear in distance. The one-third-distance rule of thumb comes from calculating the distance of a seek from one random location to another random location, not including the current track and assuming there are a large number of tracks. In

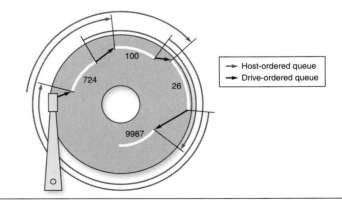

Figure 6.22 Example showing OS versus disk schedule accesses, labeled host-ordered versus drive-ordered. The former takes 3 revolutions to complete the 4 reads, while the latter completes them in just 3/4 of a revolution. From Anderson [2003].

the past, manufacturers listed the seek of this distance to offer a consistent basis for comparison. (Today they calculate the "average" by timing all seeks and dividing by the number.) Assuming (incorrectly) that seek time is linear in distance, and using the manufacturer's reported minimum and "average" seek times, a common technique to predict seek time is

$$\text{Time}_{\text{seek}} = \text{Time}_{\text{minimum}} + \frac{\text{Distance}}{\text{Distance}_{\text{average}}} \times (\text{Time}_{\text{average}} - \text{Time}_{\text{minimum}})$$

The fallacy concerning seek time is twofold. First, seek time is *not* linear with distance; the arm must accelerate to overcome inertia, reach its maximum traveling speed, decelerate as it reaches the requested position, and then wait to allow the arm to stop vibrating (*settle time*). Moreover, sometimes the arm must pause to control vibrations. For disks with more than 200 cylinders, Chen and Lee [1995] modeled the seek distance as

$$\text{Seek time(Distance)} = a \times \sqrt{\text{Distance} - 1} + b \times (\text{Distance} - 1) + c$$

where *a, b,* and *c* are selected for a particular disk so that this formula will match the quoted times for Distance = 1, Distance = max, and Distance = 1/3 max. Figure 6.23 plots this equation versus the fallacy equation. Unlike the first equation, the square root of the distance reflects acceleration and deceleration.

The second problem is that the average in the product specification would only be true if there were no locality to disk activity. Fortunately, there is both

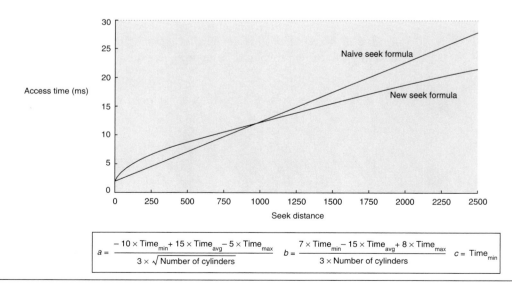

Figure 6.23 Seek time versus seek distance for sophisticated model versus naive model. Chen and Lee [1995] found that the equations shown above for parameters *a, b,* and *c* worked well for several disks.

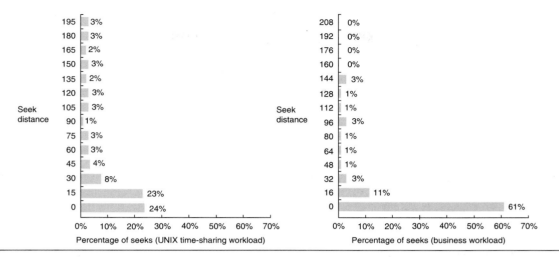

Figure 6.24 Sample measurements of seek distances for two systems. The measurements on the left were taken on a UNIX time-sharing system. The measurements on the right were taken from a business-processing application in which the disk seek activity was scheduled to improve throughput. Seek distance of 0 means the access was made to the same cylinder. The rest of the numbers show the collective percentage for distances between numbers on the y-axis. For example, 11% for the bar labeled 16 in the business graph means that the percentage of seeks between 1 and 16 cylinders was 11%. The UNIX measurements stopped at 200 of the 1000 cylinders, but this captured 85% of the accesses. The business measurements tracked all 816 cylinders of the disks. The only seek distances with 1% or greater of the seeks that are not in the graph are 224 with 4%, and 304, 336, 512, and 624, each having 1%. This total is 94%, with the difference being small but nonzero distances in other categories. Measurements courtesy of Dave Anderson of Seagate.

temporal and spatial locality (see page C-2 in Appendix C). For example, Figure 6.24 shows sample measurements of seek distances for two workloads: a UNIX time-sharing workload and a business-processing workload. Notice the high percentage of disk accesses to the same cylinder, labeled distance 0 in the graphs, in both workloads. Thus, this fallacy couldn't be more misleading.

6.10 Concluding Remarks

Storage is one of those technologies that we tend to take for granted. And yet, if we look at the true status of things today, storage is king. One can even argue that servers, which have become commodities, are now becoming peripheral to storage devices. Driving that point home are some estimates from IBM, which expects storage sales to surpass server sales in the next two years.

Michael Vizard
editor in chief, *Infoworld,* August 11, 2001

As their value is becoming increasingly evident, storage systems have become the target of innovation and investment.

The challenge for storage systems today is dependability and maintainability. Not only do users want to be sure their data are never lost (reliability), applications today increasingly demand that the data are always available to access (availability). Despite improvements in hardware and software reliability and fault tolerance, the awkwardness of maintaining such systems is a problem both for cost and for availability. A widely mentioned statistic is that customers spend $6 to $8 operating a storage system for every $1 of purchase price. When dependability is attacked by having many redundant copies at a higher level of the system—such as for search—then very large systems can be sensitive to the price-performance of the storage components.

Today, challenges in storage dependability and maintainability dominate the challenges of I/O.

6.11   Historical Perspective and References

Section K.7 on the companion CD covers the development of storage devices and techniques, including who invented disks, the story behind RAID, and the history of operating systems and databases. References for further reading are included.

Case Studies with Exercises by Andrea C. Arpaci-Dusseau and Remzi H. Arpaci-Dusseau

Case Study 1: Deconstructing a Disk

Concepts illustrated by this case study

- Performance Characteristics
- Microbenchmarks

The internals of a storage system tend to be hidden behind a simple interface, that of a linear array of blocks. There are many advantages to having a common interface for all storage systems: an operating system can use any storage system without modification, and yet the storage system is free to innovate behind this interface. For example, a single disk can map its internal <sector, track, surface> geometry to the linear array in whatever way achieves the best performance; similarly, a multidisk RAID system can map the blocks on any number of disks to this same linear array. However, this fixed interface has a number of disadvantages as well; in particular, the operating system is not able to perform some performance, reliability, and security optimizations without knowing the precise layout of its blocks inside the underlying storage system.

In this case study, we will explore how software can be used to uncover the internal structure of a storage system hidden behind a block-based interface. The basic idea is to *fingerprint* the storage system: by running a well-defined workload on top of the storage system and measuring the amount of time required for different requests, one is able to infer a surprising amount of detail about the underlying system.

The Skippy algorithm, from work by Nisha Talagala and colleagues at U.C. Berkeley, uncovers the parameters of a single disk. The key is to factor out disk rotational effects by making consecutive seeks to individual sectors with addresses that differ by a linearly increasing amount (increasing by 1, 2, 3, and so forth). Thus, the basic algorithm skips through the disk, increasing the distance of the seek by one sector before every write, and outputs the distance and time for each write. The raw device interface is used to avoid file system optimizations. The SECTOR SIZE is set equal to the minimum amount of data that can be read at once from the disk (e.g., 512 bytes). (Skippy is described in more detail in Talagala et al. [1999].)

```
fd = open("raw disk device");
for (i = 0; i < measurements; i++) {
    begin_time = gettime();
    lseek(fd, i*SECTOR_SIZE, SEEK_CUR);
    write(fd, buffer, SECTOR_SIZE);
    interval_time = gettime() -begin_time;

    printf("Stride: %d Time: %d\n", i, interval_time);
}
close(fd);
```

By graphing the time required for each write as a function of the seek distance, one can infer the minimal transfer time (with no seek or rotational latency), head switch time, cylinder switch time, rotational latency, and the number of heads in the disk. A typical graph will have four distinct lines, each with the same slope, but with different offsets. The highest and lowest lines correspond to requests that incur different amounts of rotational delay, but no cylinder or head switch costs; the difference between these two lines reveals the rotational latency of the disk. The second lowest line corresponds to requests that incur a head switch (in addition to increasing amounts of rotational delay). Finally, the third line corresponds to requests that incur a cylinder switch (in addition to rotational delay).

6.1 [10/10/10/10/10] <6.2> The results of running Skippy are shown for a mock disk (Disk Alpha) in Figure 6.25.

a. [10] <6.2> What is the minimal transfer time?

b. [10] <6.2> What is the rotational latency?

c. [10] <6.2> What is the head switch time?

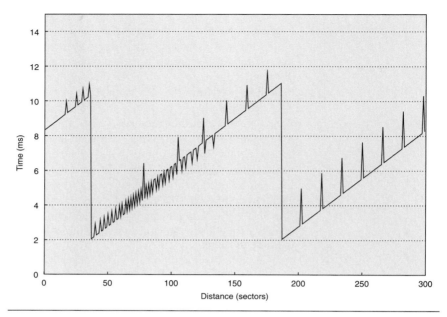

Figure 6.25 Results from running Skippy on Disk Alpha.

    d. [10] <6.2> What is the cylinder switch time?

    e. [10] <6.2> What is the number of disk heads?

6.2 [25] <6.2> Draw an approximation of the graph that would result from running Skippy on Disk Beta, a disk with the following parameters:

    ■ Minimal transfer time: 2.0 ms

    ■ Rotational latency: 6.0 ms

    ■ Head switch time: 1.0 ms

    ■ Cylinder switch time: 1.5 ms

    ■ Number of disk heads: 4

    ■ Sectors per track: 100

6.3 [10/10/10/10/10/10/10] <6.2> Implement and run the Skippy algorithm on a disk drive of your choosing.

    a. [10] <6.2> Graph the results of running Skippy. Report the manufacturer and model of your disk.

    b. [10] <6.2> What is the minimal transfer time?

    c. [10] <6.2> What is the rotational latency?

    d. [10] <6.2> What is the head switch time?

    e. [10] <6.2> What is the cylinder switch time?

    f.   [10] <6.2> What is the number of disk heads?

    g.   [10] <6.2> Do the results of running Skippy on a real disk differ in any qualitative way from that of the mock disk?

Case Study 2: Deconstructing a Disk Array

Concepts illustrated by this case study

- Performance Characteristics
- Microbenchmarks

The Shear algorithm, from work by Timothy Denehy and colleagues at the University of Wisconsin [Denehy et al. 2004], uncovers the parameters of a RAID system. The basic idea is to generate a workload of requests to the RAID array and time those requests; by observing which sets of requests take longer, one can infer which blocks are allocated to the same disk.

    We define RAID properties as follows. Data is allocated to disks in the RAID at the block level, where a *block* is the minimal unit of data that the file system reads or writes from the storage system; thus, block size is known by the file system and the fingerprinting software. A *chunk* is a set of blocks that is allocated contiguously within a disk. A *stripe* is a set of chunks across each of D data disks. Finally, a *pattern* is the minimum sequence of data blocks such that block offset i within the pattern is always located on disk j.

6.4   [20/20] <6.2> One can uncover the pattern size with the following code. The code accesses the raw device to avoid file system optimizations. The key to all of the Shear algorithms is to use random requests to avoid triggering any of the prefetch or caching mechanisms within the RAID or within individual disks. The basic idea of this code sequence is to access N random blocks at a fixed interval p within the RAID array and to measure the completion time of each interval.

```
for (p = BLOCKSIZE; p <= testsize; p += BLOCKSIZE) {
    for (i = 0; i < N; i++) {
        request[i] = random()*p;
    }
    begin_time = gettime();
    issues all request[N] to raw device in parallel;
    wait for all request[N] to complete;
    interval_time = gettime() - begin_time;
    printf("PatternSize: %d Time: %d\n", p,
        interval_time);
}
```

If you run this code on a RAID array and plot the measured time for the N requests as a function of p, then you will see that the time is highest when all N

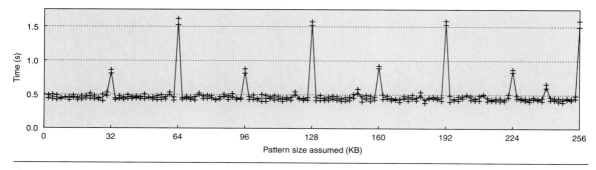

Figure 6.26 Results from running the pattern size algorithm of Shear on a mock storage system.

requests fall on the same disk; thus, the value of p with the highest time corresponds to the pattern size of the RAID.

a. [20] <6.2> Figure 6.26 shows the results of running the pattern size algorithm on an unknown RAID system.

■ What is the pattern size of this storage system?

■ What do the measured times of 0.4, 0.8, and 1.6 seconds correspond to in this storage system?

■ If this is a RAID 0 array, then how many disks are present?

■ If this is a RAID 0 array, then what is the chunk size?

b. [20] <6.2> Draw the graph that would result from running this Shear code on a storage system with the following characteristics:

■ Number of requests: $N = 1000$

■ Time for a random read on disk: 5 ms

■ RAID level: RAID 0

■ Number of disks: 4

■ Chunk size: 8 KB

6.5 [20/20] <6.2> One can uncover the chunk size with the following code. The basic idea is to perform reads from N patterns chosen at random, but always at controlled offsets, c and $c - 1$, within the pattern.

```
for (c = 0; c < patternsize; c += BLOCKSIZE) {
    for (i = 0; i < N; i++) {
        requestA[i] = random()*patternsize + c;
        requestB[i] = random()*patternsize +
            (c-1)%patternsize;
    }
```

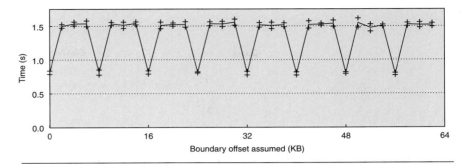

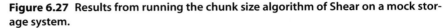

Figure 6.27 Results from running the chunk size algorithm of Shear on a mock storage system.

```
begin_time = gettime();
issue all requestA[N] and requestB[N] to raw device
    in parallel;
wait for requestA[N] and requestB[N] to complete;

interval_time = gettime() - begin_time;
printf("ChunkSize: %d Time: %d\n", c, interval_time);
}
```

If you run this code and plot the measured time as a function of c, then you will see that the measured time is lowest when the *requestA* and *requestB* reads fall on two different disks. Thus, the values of c with low times correspond to the chunk boundaries between disks of the RAID.

a. [20] <6.2> Figure 6.27 shows the results of running the chunk size algorithm on an unknown RAID system.

   ■ What is the chunk size of this storage system?

   ■ What do the measured times of 0.75 and 1.5 seconds correspond to in this storage system?

b. [20] <6.2> Draw the graph that would result from running this Shear code on a storage system with the following characteristics:

   ■ Number of requests: $N = 1000$

   ■ Time for a random read on disk: 5 ms

   ■ RAID level: RAID 0

   ■ Number of disks: 8

   ■ Chunk size: 12 KB

6.6 [10/10/10/10] <6.2> Finally, one can determine the layout of chunks to disks with the following code. The basic idea is to select N random patterns, and to exhaustively read together all pairwise combinations of the chunks within the pattern.

```
for (a = 0; a < numchunks; a += chunksize) {

    for (b = a; b < numchunks; b += chunksize) {

        for (i = 0; i < N; i++) {
            requestA[i] = random()*patternsize + a;
            requestB[i] = random()*patternsize + b;
        }

        begin_time = gettime();
        issue all requestA[N] and requestB[N] to raw device
        in parallel;
        wait for all requestA[N] and requestB[N] to
            complete;

        interval_time = gettime() - begin_time;
        printf("A: %d B: %d Time: %d\n", a, b,
            interval_time);
    }
}
```

After running this code, you can report the measured time as a function of *a* and *b*. The simplest way to graph this is to create a two-dimensional table with *a* and *b* as the parameters, and the time scaled to a shaded value; we use darker shadings for faster times and lighter shadings for slower times. Thus, a light shading indicates that the two offsets of *a* and *b* within the pattern fall on the same disk.

Figure 6.28 shows the results of running the layout algorithm on a storage system that is known to have a pattern size of 384 KB and a chunk size of 32 KB.

a. [20] <6.2> How many chunks are in a pattern?

b. [20] <6.2> Which chunks of each pattern appear to be allocated on the same disks?

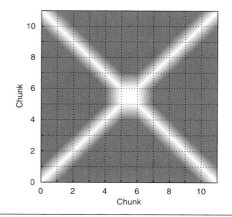

Figure 6.28 Results from running the layout algorithm of Shear on a mock storage system.

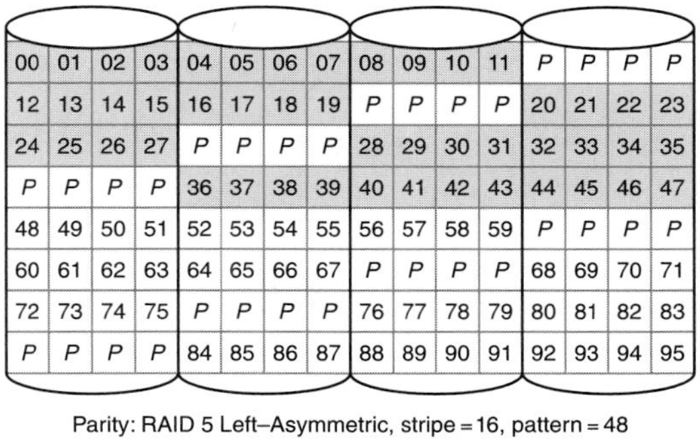

00	01	02	03	04	05	06	07	08	09	10	11	P	P	P	P
12	13	14	15	16	17	18	19	P	P	P	P	20	21	22	23
24	25	26	27	P	P	P	P	28	29	30	31	32	33	34	35
P	P	P	P	36	37	38	39	40	41	42	43	44	45	46	47
48	49	50	51	52	53	54	55	56	57	58	59	P	P	P	P
60	61	62	63	64	65	66	67	P	P	P	P	68	69	70	71
72	73	74	75	P	P	P	P	76	77	78	79	80	81	82	83
P	P	P	P	84	85	86	87	88	89	90	91	92	93	94	95

Parity: RAID 5 Left–Asymmetric, stripe = 16, pattern = 48

Figure 6.29 A storage system with 4 disks, a chunk size of four 4 KB blocks, and using a RAID 5 Left-Asymmetric layout. Two repetitions of the pattern are shown.

c. [20] <6.2> How many disks appear to be in this storage system?

d. [20] <6.2> Draw the likely layout of blocks across the disks.

6.7 [20] <6.2> Draw the graph that would result from running the layout algorithm on the storage system shown in Figure 6.29. This storage system has 4 disks, a chunk size of four 4 KB blocks (16 KB), and is using a RAID 5 Left-Asymmetric layout.

Case Study 3: RAID Reconstruction

Concepts illustrated by this case study

- RAID Systems
- RAID Reconstruction
- Mean Time to Failure (MTTF)
- Mean Time until Data Loss (MTDL)
- Performability
- Double Failures

A RAID system ensures that data is not lost when a disk fails. Thus, one of the key responsibilities of a RAID is to reconstruct the data that was on a disk when it failed; this process is called *reconstruction* and is what you will explore in this case study. You will consider both a RAID system that can tolerate one disk failure, and a RAID-DP, which can tolerate two disk failures.

Reconstruction is commonly performed in two different ways. In *off-line reconstruction,* the RAID devotes all of its resources to performing reconstruction and does not service any requests from the workload. In *on-line reconstruction,* the RAID continues to service workload requests while performing the reconstruction; the reconstruction process is often limited to use some fraction of the total bandwidth of the RAID system.

How reconstruction is performed impacts both the *reliability* and the *performability* of the system. In a RAID 5, data is lost if a second disk fails before the data from the first disk is recovered; therefore, the longer the reconstruction time (MTTR), the lower the reliability or the *mean time until data loss* (MTDL). Performability is a metric meant to combine both the performance of a system and its availability; it is defined as the performance of the system in a given state multiplied by the probability of that state. For a RAID array, possible states include normal operation with no disk failures, reconstruction with one disk failure, and shutdown due to multiple disk failures.

For these exercises, assume that you have built a RAID system with six disks, plus a sufficient number of hot spares. Assume each disk is the 37 GB SCSI disk shown in Figure 6.3; assume each disk can sequentially read data at a peak of 142 MB/sec and sequentially write data at a peak of 85 MB/sec. Assume that the disks are connected to an Ultra320 SCSI bus that can transfer a total of 320 MB/ sec. You can assume that each disk failure is independent and ignore other potential failures in the system. For the reconstruction process, you can assume that the overhead for any XOR computation or memory copying is negligible. During online reconstruction, assume that the reconstruction process is limited to use a total bandwidth of 10 MB/sec from the RAID system.

6.8 [10] <6.2> Assume that you have a RAID 4 system with six disks. Draw a simple diagram showing the layout of blocks across disks for this RAID system.

6.9 [10] <6.2, 6.4> When a single disk fails, the RAID 4 system will perform reconstruction. What is the expected time until a reconstruction is needed?

6.10 [10/10/10] <6.2, 6.4> Assume that reconstruction of the RAID 4 array begins at time *t*.

a. [10] <6.2, 6.4> What read and write operations are required to perform the reconstruction?

b. [10] <6.2, 6.4> For offline reconstruction, when will the reconstruction process be complete?

c. [10] <6.2, 6.4> For online reconstruction, when will the reconstruction process be complete?

6.11 [10/10/10/10] <6.2, 6.4> In this exercise, we will investigate the mean time until data loss (MTDL). In RAID 4, data is lost only if a second disk fails before the first failed disk is repaired.

a. [10] <6.2, 6.4> What is the likelihood of having a second failure during offline reconstruction?

b. [10] <6.2, 6.4> Given this likelihood of a second failure during reconstruction, what is the MTDL for offline reconstruction?

c. [10] <6.2, 6.4> What is the likelihood of having a second failure during online reconstruction?

d. [10] <6.2, 6.4> Given this likelihood of a second failure during reconstruction, what is the MTDL for online reconstruction?

6.12 [10] <6.2, 6.4> What is performability for the RAID 4 array for offline reconstruction? Calculate the performability using IOPS, assuming a random read-only workload that is evenly distributed across the disks of the RAID 4 array.

6.13 [10] <6.2, 6.4> What is the performability for the RAID 4 array for online reconstruction? During online repair, you can assume that the IOPS drop to 70% of their peak rate. Does offline or online reconstruction lead to better performability?

6.14 [10] <6.2, 6.4> RAID 6 is used to tolerate up to two simultaneous disk failures. Assume that you have a RAID 6 system based on row-diagonal parity, or RAID-DP; your six-disk RAID-DP system is based on RAID 4, with $p = 5$, as shown in Figure 6.5. If data disk 0 and data disk 3 fail, how can those disks be reconstructed? Show the sequence of steps that are required to compute the missing blocks in the first four stripes.

Case Study 4: Performance Prediction for RAIDs

Concepts illustrated by this case study

■ RAID Levels

■ Queuing Theory

■ Impact of Workloads

■ Impact of Disk Layout

In this case study, you will explore how simple queuing theory can be used to predict the performance of the I/O system. You will investigate how both storage system configuration and the workload influence service time, disk utilization, and average response time.

The configuration of the storage system has a large impact on performance. Different RAID levels can be modeled using queuing theory in different ways. For example, a RAID 0 array containing N disks can be modeled as N separate systems of M/M/1 queues, assuming that requests are appropriately distributed across the N disks. The behavior of a RAID 1 array depends upon the workload: a read operation can be sent to either mirror, whereas a write operation must be sent to both disks. Therefore, for a read-only workload, a two-disk RAID 1 array can be modeled as an M/M/2 queue, whereas for a write-only workload, it can be modeled as an M/M/1 queue. The behavior of a RAID 4 array containing N disks also depends upon the workload: a read will be sent to a particular data disk, whereas writes must all update the parity disk, which becomes the bottleneck of the system. Therefore, for a read-only workload, RAID 4 can be modeled as $N - 1$ separate systems, whereas for a write-only workload, it can be modeled as one M/M/1 queue.

The layout of blocks within the storage system can have a significant impact on performance. Consider a single disk with a 40 GB capacity. If the workload randomly accesses 40 GB of data, then the layout of those blocks to the disk does not have much of an impact on performance. However, if the workload randomly accesses only half of the disk's capacity (i.e., 20 GB of data on that disk), then layout does matter: to reduce seek time, the 20 GB of data can be compacted within 20 GB of consecutive tracks instead of allocated uniformly distributed over the entire 40 GB capacity.

For this problem, we will use a rather simplistic model to estimate the service time of a disk. In this basic model, the average positioning and transfer time for a small random request is a linear function of the seek distance. For the 40 GB disk in this problem, assume that the service time is 5 *ms* * space utilization. Thus, if the entire 40 GB disk is used, then the average positioning and transfer time for a random request is 5 ms; if only the first 20 GB of the disk is used, then the average positioning and transfer time is 2.5 ms.

Throughout this case study, you can assume that the processor sends 167 small random disk requests per second and that these requests are exponentially distributed. You can assume that the size of the requests is equal to the block size of 8 KB. Each disk in the system has a capacity of 40 GB. Regardless of the storage system configuration, the workload accesses a total of 40 GB of data; you should allocate the 40 GB of data across the disks in the system in the most efficient manner.

6.15 [10/10/10/10/10] <6.5> Begin by assuming that the storage system consists of a single 40 GB disk.

    a. [10] <6.5> Given this workload and storage system, what is the average service time?

    b. [10] <6.5> On average, what is the utilization of the disk?

    c. [10] <6.5> On average, how much time does each request spend waiting for the disk?

    d. [10] <6.5> What is the mean number of requests in the queue?

    e. [10] <6.5> Finally, what is the average response time for the disk requests?

6.16 [10/10/10/10/10/10] <6.2, 6.5> Imagine that the storage system is now configured to contain two 40 GB disks in a RAID 0 array; that is, the data is striped in blocks of 8 KB equally across the two disks with no redundancy.

    a. [10] <6.2, 6.5> How will the 40 GB of data be allocated across the disks? Given a random request workload over a total of 40 GB, what is the expected service time of each request?

    b. [10] <6.2, 6.5> How can queuing theory be used to model this storage system?

    c. [10] <6.2, 6.5> What is the average utilization of each disk?

    d. [10] <6.2, 6.5> On average, how much time does each request spend waiting for the disk?

    e. [10] <6.2, 6.5> What is the mean number of requests in each queue?

    f. [10] <6.2, 6.5> Finally, what is the average response time for the disk requests?

6.17 [20/20/20/20/20] <6.2, 6.5> Instead imagine that the storage system is configured to contain two 40 GB disks in a RAID 1 array; that is, the data is mirrored across the two disks. Use queuing theory to model this system for a read-only workload.

    a. [20] <6.2, 6.5> How will the 40 GB of data be allocated across the disks? Given a random request workload over a total of 40 GB, what is the expected service time of each request?

    b. [20] <6.2, 6.5> How can queuing theory be used to model this storage system?

    c. [20] <6.2, 6.5> What is the average utilization of each disk?

    d. [20] <6.2, 6.5> On average, how much time does each request spend waiting for the disk?

    e. [20] <6.2, 6.5> Finally, what is the average response time for the disk requests?

6.18 [10/10] <6.2, 6.5> Imagine that instead of a read-only workload, you now have a write-only workload on a RAID 1 array.

    a. [10] <6.2, 6.5> Describe how you can use queuing theory to model this system and workload.

    b. [10] <6.2, 6.5> Given this system and workload, what is the average utilization, average waiting time, and average response time?

Case Study 5: I/O Subsystem Design

Concepts illustrated by this case study

- RAID Systems
- Mean Time to Failure (MTTF)
- Performance and Reliability Trade-offs

In this case study, you will design an I/O subsystem, given a monetary budget. Your system will have a minimum required capacity and you will optimize for performance, reliability, or both. You are free to use as many disks and controllers as fit within your budget.

Here are your building blocks:

- A 10,000 MIPS CPU costing $1000. Its MTTF is 1,000,000 hours.
- A 1000 MB/sec I/O bus with room for 20 Ultra320 SCSI buses and controllers.
- Ultra320 SCSI buses that can transfer 320 MB/sec and support up to 15 disks per bus (these are also called SCSI strings). The SCSI cable MTTF is 1,000,000 hours.

- An Ultra320 SCSI controller that is capable of 50,000 IOPS, costs $250, and has an MTTF of 500,000 hours.

- A $2000 enclosure supplying power and cooling to up to eight disks. The enclosure MTTF is 1,000,000 hours, the fan MTTF is 200,000 hours, and the power supply MTTF is 200,000 hours.

- The SCSI disks described in Figure 6.3.

- Replacing any failed component requires 24 hours.

You may make the following assumptions about your workload:

- The operating system requires 70,000 CPU instructions for each disk I/O.

- The workload consists of many concurrent, random I/Os, with an average size of 16 KB.

All of your constructed systems must have the following properties:

- You have a monetary budget of $28,000.

- You must provide at least 1 TB of capacity.

6.19 [10] <6.2> You will begin by designing an I/O subsystem that is optimized only for capacity and performance (and not reliability), specifically IOPS. Discuss the RAID level and block size that will deliver the best performance.

6.20 [20/20/20/20] <6.2, 6.4, 6.7> What configuration of SCSI disks, controllers, and enclosures results in the best performance given your monetary and capacity constraints?

a. [20] <6.2, 6.4, 6.7> How many IOPS do you expect to deliver with your system?

b. [20] <6.2, 6.4, 6.7> How much does your system cost?

c. [20] <6.2, 6.4, 6.7> What is the capacity of your system?

d. [20] <6.2, 6.4, 6.7> What is the MTTF of your system?

6.21 [10] <6.2, 6.4, 6.7> You will now redesign your system to optimize for reliability, by creating a RAID 10 or RAID 01 array. Your storage system should be robust not only to disk failures, but to controller, cable, power supply, and fan failures as well; specifically, a single component failure should not prohibit accessing both replicas of a pair. Draw a diagram illustrating how blocks are allocated across disks in the RAID 10 and RAID 01 configurations. Is RAID 10 or RAID 01 more appropriate in this environment?

6.22 [20/20/20/20/20] <6.2, 6.4, 6.7> Optimizing your RAID 10 or RAID 01 array only for reliability (but keeping within your capacity and monetary constraints), what is your RAID configuration?

a. [20] <6.2, 6.4, 6.7> What is the overall MTTF of the components in your system?

b. [20] <6.2, 6.4, 6.7> What is the MTDL of your system?

c. [20] <6.2, 6.4, 6.7> What is the usable capacity of this system?

d. [20] <6.2, 6.4, 6.7> How much does your system cost?

e. [20] <6.2, 6.4, 6.7> Assuming a write-only workload, how many IOPS can you expect to deliver?

6.23 [10] <6.2, 6.4, 6.7> Assume that you now have access to a disk that has twice the capacity, for the same price. If you continue to design only for reliability, how would you change the configuration of your storage system? Why?

Case Study 6: Dirty Rotten Bits

Concepts illustrated by this case study

- Partial Disk Failure
- Failure Analysis
- Performance Analysis
- Parity Protection
- Checksumming

You are put in charge of avoiding the problem of "bit rot"—bits or blocks in a file going bad over time. This problem is particularly important in archival scenarios, where data is written once and perhaps accessed many years later; without taking extra measures to protect the data, the bits or blocks of a file may slowly change or become unavailable due to media errors or other I/O faults.

Dealing with bit rot requires two specific components: detection and recovery. To detect bit rot efficiently, one can use checksums over each block of the file in question; a checksum is just a function of some kind that takes a (potentially long) string of data as input and outputs a fixed-size string (the checksum) of the data as output. The property you will exploit is that if the data changes, the computed checksum is very likely to change as well.

Once detected, recovering from bit rot requires some form of redundancy. Examples include mirroring (keeping multiple copies of each block) and parity (some extra redundant information, usually more space efficient than mirroring).

In this case study, you will analyze how effective these techniques are given various scenarios. You will also write code to implement data integrity protection over a set of files.

6.24 [20/20/20] <6.2> Assume that you will use simple parity protection in Exercises 6.24 through 6.27. Specifically, assume that you will be computing *one* parity block for each file in the file system. Further, assume that you will also use a 20-byte MD5 checksum per 4 KB block of each file.

We first tackle the problem of space overhead. According to recent studies [Douceur and Bolosky 1999], these file size distributions are what is found in modern PCs:

≤1 KB	2 KB	4 KB	8 KB	16 KB	32 KB	64 KB	128 KB	256 KB	512 KB	≥1 MB
26.6%	11.0%	11.2%	10.9%	9.5%	8.5%	7.1%	5.1%	3.7%	2.4%	4.0%

The study also finds that file systems are usually about half full. Assume you have a 37 GB disk volume that is roughly half full and follows that same distribution, and answer the following questions:

a. [20] <6.2> How much extra information (both in bytes and as a percent of the volume) must you keep on disk to be able to detect a single error with checksums?

b. [20] <6.2> How much extra information (both in bytes and as a percent of the volume) would you need to be able to both detect a single error with checksums as well as correct it?

c. [20] <6.2> Given this file distribution, is the block size you are using to compute checksums too big, too little, or just right?

6.25 [10/10] <6.2, 6.3> One big problem that arises in data protection is error detection. One approach is to perform error detection *lazily*—that is, wait until a file is accessed, and at that point, check it and make sure the correct data is there. The problem with this approach is that files that are not accessed frequently may thus slowly rot away, and when finally accessed, have too many errors to be corrected. Hence, an eager approach is to perform what is sometimes called *disk scrubbing*—periodically go through all data and find errors proactively.

a. [10] <6.2, 6.3> Assume that bit flips occur independently, at a rate of 1 flip per GB of data per month. Assuming the same 20 GB volume that is half full, and assuming that you are using the SCSI disk as specified in Figure 6.3 (4 ms seek, roughly 100 MB/sec transfer), how often should you scan through files to check and repair their integrity?

b. [10] <6.2, 6.3> At what bit flip rate does it become impossible to maintain data integrity? Again assume the 20 GB volume and the SCSI disk.

6.26 [10/10/10/10] <6.2, 6.4> Another potential cost of added data protection is found in performance overhead. We now study the performance overhead of this data protection approach.

a. [10] <6.2, 6.4> Assume we write a 40 MB file to the SCSI disk sequentially, and then write out the extra information to implement our data protection scheme to disk once. How much *write traffic* (both in total volume of bytes and as a percentage of total traffic) does our scheme generate?

b. [10] <6.2, 6.4> Assume we now are updating the file randomly, similar to a database table. That is, assume we perform a series of 4 KB random writes to the file, and each time we perform a single write, we must update the on-disk protection information. Assuming that we perform 10,000 random writes, how much *I/O traffic* (both in total volume of bytes and as a percentage of total traffic) does our scheme generate?

c. [10] <6.2, 6.4> Now assume that the data protection information is always kept in a separate portion of the disk, away from the file it is guarding (that is, assume for each file A, there is another file $A_{checksums}$ that holds all the checksums for A). Hence, one potential overhead we must incur arises upon reads—that is, upon each read, we will use the checksum to detect data corruption.

Assume you read 10,000 blocks of 4 KB each sequentially from disk. Assuming a 4 ms average seek cost and a 100 MB/sec transfer rate (like the SCSI disk in Figure 6.3), how long will it take to read the file (and corresponding checksums) from disk? What is the time penalty due to adding checksums?

d. [10] <6.2, 6.4> Again assuming that the data protection information is kept separate as in part (c), now assume you have to read 10,000 random blocks of 4 KB each from a very large file (much bigger than 10,000 blocks, that is). For each read, you must again use the checksum to ensure data integrity. How long will it take to read the 10,000 blocks from disk, again assuming the same disk characteristics? What is the time penalty due to adding checksums?

6.27 [40] <6.2, 6.3, 6.4> Finally, we put theory into practice by developing a user-level tool to guard against file corruption. Assume you are to write a simple set of tools to detect and repair data integrity. The first tool is used to checksums and parity. It should be called `build` and used like this:

```
build <filename>
```

The `build` program should then store the needed checksum and redundancy information for the file `filename` in a file in the same directory called `.filename.cp` (so it is easy to find later).

A second program is then used to check and potentially repair damaged files. It should be called `repair` and used like this:

```
repair <filename>
```

The `repair` program should consult the `.cp` file for the filename in question and verify that all the stored checksums match the computed checksums for the data. If the checksums don't match for a single block, `repair` should use the redundant information to reconstruct the correct data and fix the file. However, if two or more blocks are bad, `repair` should simply report that the file has been corrupted beyond repair. To test your system, we will provide a tool to corrupt files called `corrupt`. It works as follows:

```
corrupt <filename> <blocknumber>
```

All `corrupt` does is fill the specified block number of the file with random noise. For checksums you will be using MD5. MD5 takes an input string and gives you a 128-bit "fingerprint" or checksum as an output. A great and simple implementation of MD5 is available here:

```
http://sourceforge.net/project/showfiles.php?group_id=42360
```

Parity is computed with the XOR operator. In C code, you can compute the parity of two blocks, each of size BLOCKSIZE, as follows:

```c
unsigned char block1[BLOCKSIZE];
unsigned char block2[BLOCKSIZE];

unsigned char parity[BLOCKSIZE];

// first, clear parity block
for (int i = 0; i < BLOCKSIZE; i++)
    parity[i] = 0;

// then compute parity; carat symbol does XOR in C
for (int i = 0; i < BLOCKSIZE; i++) {
    parity[i] = block1[i] ^ block2[i];
}
```

Case Study 7: Sorting Things Out

Concepts illustrated by this case study

■ Benchmarking

■ Performance Analysis

■ Cost/Performance Analysis

■ Amortization of Overhead

■ Balanced Systems

The database field has a long history of using benchmarks to compare systems. In this question, you will explore one of the benchmarks introduced by Anonymous et al. [1985] (see Chapter 1): external, or disk-to-disk, sorting.

Sorting is an exciting benchmark for a number of reasons. First, sorting exercises a computer system across all its components, including disk, memory, and processors. Second, sorting at the highest possible performance requires a great deal of expertise about how the CPU caches, operating systems, and I/O subsystems work. Third, it is simple enough to be implemented by a student (see below!).

Depending on how much data you have, sorting can be done in one or multiple passes. Simply put, if you have enough memory to hold the entire data set in memory, you can read the entire data set into memory, sort it, and then write it out; this is called a "one-pass" sort.

If you do not have enough memory, you must sort the data in multiple passes. There are many different approaches possible. One simple approach is to sort each chunk of the input file and write it to disk; this leaves (input file size)/(memory size) sorted files on disk. Then, you have to merge each sorted temporary file into a final sorted output. This is called a "two-pass" sort. More passes are needed in the unlikely case that you cannot merge all the streams in the second pass.

In this case study you will analyze various aspects of sorting, determining its effectiveness and cost-effectiveness in different scenarios. You will also write your own version of an external sort, measuring its performance on real hardware.

6.28 [20/20/20] <6.4> We will start by configuring a system to complete a sort in the least possible time, with no limits on how much we can spend. To get peak bandwidth from the sort, we have to make sure all the paths through the system have sufficient bandwidth.

Assume for simplicity that the time to perform the in-memory sort of keys is linearly proportional to the CPU rate and memory bandwidth of the given machine (e.g., sorting 1 MB of records on a machine with 1 MB/sec of memory bandwidth and a 1 MIPS processor will take 1 second). Assume further that you have carefully written the I/O phases of the sort so as to achieve sequential bandwidth. And of course realize that if you don't have enough memory to hold all of the data at once that sort will take two passes.

One problem you may encounter in performing I/O is that systems often perform extra *memory copies;* for example, when the read() system call is invoked, data may first be read from disk into a system buffer, and then subsequently copied into the specified user buffer. Hence, memory bandwidth during I/O can be an issue.

Finally, for simplicity, assume that there is no overlap of reading, sorting, or writing. That is, when you are reading data from disk, that is all you are doing; when sorting, you are just using the CPU and memory bandwidth; when writing, you are just writing data to disk.

Your job in this task is to configure a system to extract peak performance when sorting 1 GB of data (i.e., roughly 10 million 100-byte records). Use the following table to make choices about which machine, memory, I/O interconnect, and disks to buy.

CPU			I/O interconnect		
Slow	1 GIPS	$200	Slow	80 MB/sec	$50
Standard	2 GIPS	$1000	Standard	160 MB/sec	$100
Fast	4 GIPS	$2000	Fast	320 MB/sec	$400
Memory			**Disks**		
Slow	512 MB/sec	$100/GB	Slow	30 MB/sec	$70
Standard	1 GB/sec	$200/GB	Standard	60 MB/sec	$120
Fast	2 GB/sec	$500/GB	Fast	110 MB/sec	$300

Note: Assume you are buying a single-processor system, and that you can have up to two I/O interconnects. However, the amount of memory and number of disks is up to you (assume there is no limit on disks per I/O interconnect).

a. [20] <6.4> What is the total cost of your machine? (Break this down by part, including the cost of the CPU, amount of memory, number of disks, and I/O bus.)

b. [20] <6.4> How much time does it take to complete the sort of 1 GB worth of records? (Break this down into time spent doing reads from disk, writes to disk, and time spent sorting.)

c. [20] <6.4> What is the bottleneck in your system?

6.29 [25/25/25] <6.4> We will now examine cost-performance issues in sorting. After all, it is easy to buy a high-performing machine; it is much harder to buy a cost-effective one.

One place where this issue arises is with the PennySort competition (*research.microsoft.com/barc/SortBenchmark/*). PennySort asks that you sort as many records as you can for a single penny. To compute this, you should assume that a system you buy will last for 3 years (94,608,000 seconds), and divide this by the total cost in pennies of the machine. The result is your time budget per penny.

Our task here will be a little simpler. Assume you have a fixed budget of $2000 (or less). What is the fastest sorting machine you can build? Use the same hardware table as in Exercise 6.28 to configure the winning machine.

(*Hint:* You might want to write a little computer program to generate all the possible configurations.)

a. [25] <6.4> What is the total cost of your machine? (Break this down by part, including the cost of the CPU, amount of memory, number of disks, and I/O bus.)

b. [25] <6.4> How does the reading, writing, and sorting time break down with this configuration?

c. [25] <6.4> What is the bottleneck in your system?

6.30 [20/20/20] <6.4, 6.6> Getting good disk performance often requires *amortization of overhead*. The idea is simple: if you must incur an overhead of some kind, do as much useful work as possible after paying the cost, and hence reduce its impact. This idea is quite general and can be applied to many areas of computer systems; with disks, it arises with the seek and rotational costs (overheads) that you must incur before transferring data. You can amortize an expensive seek and rotation by transferring a large amount of data.

In this exercise, we focus on how to amortize seek and rotational costs during the second pass of a two-pass sort. Assume that when the second pass begins, there are *N* sorted runs on the disk, each of a size that fits within main memory. Our task here is to read in a chunk from each sorted run and merge the results into a final sorted output. Note that a read from one run will incur a seek and rotation, as it is very likely that the last read was from a different run.

a. [20] <6.4, 6.6> Assume that you have a disk that can transfer at 100 MB/sec, with an average seek cost of 7 ms, and a rotational rate of 10,000 RPM. Assume further that every time you read from a run, you read 1 MB of data, and that there are 100 runs each of size 1 GB. Also assume that writes (to the final sorted output) take place in large 1 GB chunks. How long will the merge phase take, assuming I/O is the dominant (i.e., only) cost?

b. [20] <6.4, 6.6> Now assume that you change the read size from 1 MB to 10 MB. How is the total time to perform the second pass of the sort affected?

c. [20] <6.4, 6.6> In both cases, assume that what we wish to maximize is *disk efficiency*. We compute disk efficiency as the ratio of the time spent transferring data over the total time spent accessing the disk. What is the disk efficiency in each of the scenarios mentioned above?

6.31 [40] <6.2, 6.4, 6.6> In this exercise, you will write your own external sort. To generate the data set, we provide a tool `generate` that works as follows:

```
generate <filename> <size (in MB)>
```

By running `generate`, you create a file named `filename` of size `size` MB. The file consists of 100 byte keys, with 10-byte records (the part that must be sorted).

We also provide a tool called `check` that checks whether a given input file is sorted or not. It is run as follows:

```
check <filename>
```

The basic one-pass sort does the following: reads in the data, sorts it, and then writes it out. However, numerous optimizations are available to you: overlapping reading and sorting, separating keys from the rest of the record for better cache behavior and hence faster sorting, overlapping sorting and writing, and so forth. Neuberg et al. [1994] is a terrific place to look for some hints.

One important rule is that data must always start on disk (and not in the file system cache. The easiest way to ensure this is to unmount and remount the file system.

One goal: beat the Datamation sort record. Currently, the record for sorting 1 million 100-byte records is 0.44 seconds, which was obtained on a cluster of 32 machines. If you are careful, you might be able to beat this on a single PC configured with a few disks.

A.1	Introduction	A-2
A.2	The Major Hurdle of Pipelining—Pipeline Hazards	A-11
A.3	How Is Pipelining Implemented?	A-26
A.4	What Makes Pipelining Hard to Implement?	A-37
A.5	Extending the MIPS Pipeline to Handle Multicycle Operations	A-47
A.6	Putting It All Together: The MIPS R4000 Pipeline	A-56
A.7	Crosscutting Issues	A-65
A.8	Fallacies and Pitfalls	A-75
A.9	Concluding Remarks	A-76
A.10	Historical Perspective and References	A-77

A

Pipelining: Basic and Intermediate Concepts

It is quite a three-pipe problem.

Sir Arthur Conan Doyle
The Adventures of Sherlock Holmes

A.1   Introduction

Many readers of this text will have covered the basics of pipelining in another text (such as our more basic text *Computer Organization and Design*) or in another course. Because Chapters 2 and 3 build heavily on this material, readers should ensure that they are familiar with the concepts discussed in this appendix before proceeding. As you read Chapter 2, you may find it helpful to turn to this material for a quick review.

We begin the appendix with the basics of pipelining, including discussing the data path implications, introducing hazards, and examining the performance of pipelines. This section describes the basic five-stage RISC pipeline that is the basis for the rest of the appendix. Section A.2 describes the issue of hazards, why they cause performance problems and how they can be dealt with. Section A.3 discusses how the simple five-stage pipeline is actually implemented, focusing on control and how hazards are dealt with.

Section A.4 discusses the interaction between pipelining and various aspects of instruction set design, including discussing the important topic of exceptions and their interaction with pipelining. Readers unfamiliar with the concepts of precise and imprecise interrupts and resumption after exceptions will find this material useful, since they are key to understanding the more advanced approaches in Chapter 2.

Section A.5 discusses how the five-stage pipeline can be extended to handle longer-running floating-point instructions. Section A.6 puts these concepts together in a case study of a deeply pipelined processor, the MIPS R4000/4400, including both the eight-stage integer pipeline and the floating-point pipeline.

Section A.7 introduces the concept of dynamic scheduling and the use of scoreboards to implement dynamic scheduling. It is introduced as a crosscutting issue, since it can be used to serve as an introduction to the core concepts in Chapter 2, which focused on dynamically scheduled approaches. Section A.7 is also a gentle introduction to the more complex Tomasulo's algorithm covered in Chapter 2. Although Tomasulo's algorithm can be covered and understood without introducing scoreboarding, the scoreboarding approach is simpler and easier to comprehend.

What Is Pipelining?

Pipelining is an implementation technique whereby multiple instructions are overlapped in execution; it takes advantage of parallelism that exists among the actions needed to execute an instruction. Today, pipelining is the key implementation technique used to make fast CPUs.

A pipeline is like an assembly line. In an automobile assembly line, there are many steps, each contributing something to the construction of the car. Each step operates in parallel with the other steps, although on a different car. In a computer pipeline, each step in the pipeline completes a part of an instruction. Like the assembly line, different steps are completing different parts of different instructions in parallel. Each of these steps is called a *pipe stage* or a *pipe segment*. The stages are connected one to the next to form a pipe—instructions enter at one end, progress through the stages, and exit at the other end, just as cars would in an assembly line.

In an automobile assembly line, *throughput* is defined as the number of cars per hour and is determined by how often a completed car exits the assembly line. Likewise, the throughput of an instruction pipeline is determined by how often an instruction exits the pipeline. Because the pipe stages are hooked together, all the stages must be ready to proceed at the same time, just as we would require in an assembly line. The time required between moving an instruction one step down the pipeline is a *processor cycle*. Because all stages proceed at the same time, the length of a processor cycle is determined by the time required for the slowest pipe stage, just as in an auto assembly line, the longest step would determine the time between advancing the line. In a computer, this processor cycle is usually 1 clock cycle (sometimes it is 2, rarely more).

The pipeline designer's goal is to balance the length of each pipeline stage, just as the designer of the assembly line tries to balance the time for each step in the process. If the stages are perfectly balanced, then the time per instruction on the pipelined processor—assuming ideal conditions—is equal to

$$\frac{\text{Time per instruction on unpipelined machine}}{\text{Number of pipe stages}}$$

Under these conditions, the speedup from pipelining equals the number of pipe stages, just as an assembly line with n stages can ideally produce cars n times as fast. Usually, however, the stages will not be perfectly balanced; furthermore, pipelining does involve some overhead. Thus, the time per instruction on the pipelined processor will not have its minimum possible value, yet it can be close.

Pipelining yields a reduction in the average execution time per instruction. Depending on what you consider as the baseline, the reduction can be viewed as decreasing the number of clock cycles per instruction (CPI), as decreasing the clock cycle time, or as a combination. If the starting point is a processor that takes multiple clock cycles per instruction, then pipelining is usually viewed as reducing the CPI. This is the primary view we will take. If the starting point is a processor that takes 1 (long) clock cycle per instruction, then pipelining decreases the clock cycle time.

Pipelining is an implementation technique that exploits parallelism among the instructions in a sequential instruction stream. It has the substantial advantage that, unlike some speedup techniques (see Chapter 4), it is not visible to the programmer. In this appendix we will first cover the concept of pipelining using a classic five-stage pipeline; other chapters investigate the more sophisticated pipelining techniques in use in modern processors. Before we say more about pipelining and its use in a processor, we need a simple instruction set, which we introduce next.

The Basics of a RISC Instruction Set

Throughout this book we use a RISC (reduced instruction set computer) architecture or load-store architecture to illustrate the basic concepts, although nearly all the ideas we introduce in this book are applicable to other processors. In this section we introduce the core of a typical RISC architecture. In this appendix, and throughout the book, our default RISC architecture is MIPS. In many places, the concepts are significantly similar that they will apply to any RISC. RISC architectures are characterized by a few key properties, which dramatically simplify their implementation:

- All operations on data apply to data in registers and typically change the entire register (32 or 64 bits per register).

- The only operations that affect memory are load and store operations that move data from memory to a register or to memory from a register, respectively. Load and store operations that load or store less than a full register (e.g., a byte, 16 bits, or 32 bits) are often available.

- The instruction formats are few in number with all instructions typically being one size.

These simple properties lead to dramatic simplifications in the implementation of pipelining, which is why these instruction sets were designed this way.

For consistency with the rest of the text, we use MIPS64, the 64-bit version of the MIPS instruction set. The extended 64-bit instructions are generally designated by having a D on the start or end of the mnemonic. For example DADD is the 64-bit version of an add instruction, while LD is the 64-bit version of a load instruction.

Like other RISC architectures, the MIPS instruction set provides 32 registers, although register 0 always has the value 0. Most RISC architectures, like MIPS, have three classes of instructions (see Appendix B for more detail):

1. *ALU instructions*—These instructions take either two registers or a register and a sign-extended immediate (called ALU immediate instructions, they have a 16-bit offset in MIPS), operate on them, and store the result into a third register. Typical operations include add (DADD), subtract (DSUB), and logical operations (such as AND or OR), which do not differentiate between 32-bit and 64-bit versions. Immediate versions of these instructions use the same mnemonics with a suffix of I. In MIPS, there are both signed and unsigned forms of the arithmetic instructions; the unsigned forms, which do not generate overflow exceptions—and thus are the same in 32-bit and 64-bit mode—have a U at the end (e.g., DADDU, DSUBU, DADDIU).

2. *Load and store instructions*—These instructions take a register source, called the *base register,* and an immediate field (16-bit in MIPS), called the *offset,* as operands. The sum—called the *effective address*—of the contents of the base register and the sign-extended offset is used as a memory address. In the case of a load instruction, a second register operand acts as the destination for the

data loaded from memory. In the case of a store, the second register operand is the source of the data that is stored into memory. The instructions load word (LD) and store word (SD) load or store the entire 64-bit register contents.

3. *Branches and jumps*—Branches are conditional transfers of control. There are usually two ways of specifying the branch condition in RISC architectures: with a set of condition bits (sometimes called a condition code) or by a limited set of comparisons between a pair of registers or between a register and zero. MIPS uses the latter. For this appendix, we consider only comparisons for equality between two registers. In all RISC architectures, the branch destination is obtained by adding a sign-extended offset (16 bits in MIPS) to the current PC. Unconditional jumps are provided in many RISC architectures, but we will not cover jumps in this appendix.

A Simple Implementation of a RISC Instruction Set

To understand how a RISC instruction set can be implemented in a pipelined fashion, we need to understand how it is implemented *without* pipelining. This section shows a simple implementation where every instruction takes at most 5 clock cycles. We will extend this basic implementation to a pipelined version, resulting in a much lower CPI. Our unpipelined implementation is not the most economical or the highest-performance implementation without pipelining. Instead, it is designed to lead naturally to a pipelined implementation. Implementing the instruction set requires the introduction of several temporary registers that are not part of the architecture; these are introduced in this section to simplify pipelining. Our implementation will focus only on a pipeline for an integer subset of a RISC architecture that consists of load-store word, branch, and integer ALU operations.

Every instruction in this RISC subset can be implemented in at most 5 clock cycles. The 5 clock cycles are as follows.

1. *Instruction fetch cycle* (IF):

   Send the program counter (PC) to memory and fetch the current instruction from memory. Update the PC to the next sequential PC by adding 4 (since each instruction is 4 bytes) to the PC.

2. *Instruction decode/register fetch cycle* (ID):

   Decode the instruction and read the registers corresponding to register source specifiers from the register file. Do the equality test on the registers as they are read, for a possible branch. Sign-extend the offset field of the instruction in case it is needed. Compute the possible branch target address by adding the sign-extended offset to the incremented PC. In an aggressive implementation, which we explore later, the branch can be completed at the end of this stage, by storing the branch-target address into the PC, if the condition test yielded true.

   Decoding is done in parallel with reading registers, which is possible because the register specifiers are at a fixed location in a RISC architecture.

This technique is known as *fixed-field decoding*. Note that we may read a register we don't use, which doesn't help but also doesn't hurt performance. (It does waste energy to read an unneeded register, and power-sensitive designs might avoid this.) Because the immediate portion of an instruction is also located in an identical place, the sign-extended immediate is also calculated during this cycle in case it is needed.

3. *Execution/effective address cycle* (EX):

   The ALU operates on the operands prepared in the prior cycle, performing one of three functions depending on the instruction type.

   ■ Memory reference: The ALU adds the base register and the offset to form the effective address.

   ■ Register-Register ALU instruction: The ALU performs the operation specified by the ALU opcode on the values read from the register file.

   ■ Register-Immediate ALU instruction: The ALU performs the operation specified by the ALU opcode on the first value read from the register file and the sign-extended immediate.

   In a load-store architecture the effective address and execution cycles can be combined into a single clock cycle, since no instruction needs to simultaneously calculate a data address and perform an operation on the data.

4. *Memory access* (MEM):

   If the instruction is a load, memory does a read using the effective address computed in the previous cycle. If it is a store, then the memory writes the data from the second register read from the register file using the effective address.

5. *Write-back cycle* (WB):

   ■ Register-Register ALU instruction or Load instruction:

   Write the result into the register file, whether it comes from the memory system (for a load) or from the ALU (for an ALU instruction).

In this implementation, branch instructions require 2 cycles, store instructions require 4 cycles, and all other instructions require 5 cycles. Assuming a branch frequency of 12% and a store frequency of 10%, a typical instruction distribution leads to an overall CPI of 4.54. This implementation, however, is not optimal either in achieving the best performance or in using the minimal amount of hardware given the performance level; we leave the improvement of this design as an exercise for you and instead focus on pipelining this version.

The Classic Five-Stage Pipeline for a RISC Processor

We can pipeline the execution described above with almost no changes by simply starting a new instruction on each clock cycle. (See why we chose this design!)

Each of the clock cycles from the previous section becomes a *pipe stage*—a cycle in the pipeline. This results in the execution pattern shown in Figure A.1, which is the typical way a pipeline structure is drawn. Although each instruction takes 5 clock cycles to complete, during each clock cycle the hardware will initiate a new instruction and will be executing some part of the five different instructions.

You may find it hard to believe that pipelining is as simple as this; it's not. In this and the following sections, we will make our RISC pipeline "real" by dealing with problems that pipelining introduces.

To start with, we have to determine what happens on every clock cycle of the processor and make sure we don't try to perform two different operations with the same data path resource on the same clock cycle. For example, a single ALU cannot be asked to compute an effective address and perform a subtract operation at the same time. Thus, we must ensure that the overlap of instructions in the pipeline cannot cause such a conflict. Fortunately, the simplicity of a RISC instruction set makes resource evaluation relatively easy. Figure A.2 shows a simplified version of a RISC data path drawn in pipeline fashion. As you can see, the major functional units are used in different cycles, and hence overlapping the execution of multiple instructions introduces relatively few conflicts. There are three observations on which this fact rests.

First, we use separate instruction and data memories, which we would typically implement with separate instruction and data caches (discussed in Chapter 5). The use of separate caches eliminates a conflict for a single memory that would arise between instruction fetch and data memory access. Notice that if our pipelined processor has a clock cycle that is equal to that of the unpipelined version, the memory system must deliver five times the bandwidth. This increased demand is one cost of higher performance.

Second, the register file is used in the two stages: one for reading in ID and one for writing in WB. These uses are distinct, so we simply show the register file in two places. Hence, we need to perform two reads and one write every clock cycle. To handle reads and a write to the same register (and for another reason,

					Clock number				
Instruction number	**1**	**2**	**3**	**4**	**5**	**6**	**7**	**8**	**9**
Instruction *i*	IF	ID	EX	MEM	WB				
Instruction *i* + 1		IF	ID	EX	MEM	WB			
Instruction *i* + 2			IF	ID	EX	MEM	WB		
Instruction *i* + 3				IF	ID	EX	MEM	WB	
Instruction *i* + 4					IF	ID	EX	MEM	WB

Figure A.1 Simple RISC pipeline. On each clock cycle, another instruction is fetched and begins its 5-cycle execution. If an instruction is started every clock cycle, the performance will be up to five times that of a processor that is not pipelined. The names for the stages in the pipeline are the same as those used for the cycles in the unpipelined implementation: IF = instruction fetch, ID = instruction decode, EX = execution, MEM = memory access, and WB = write back.

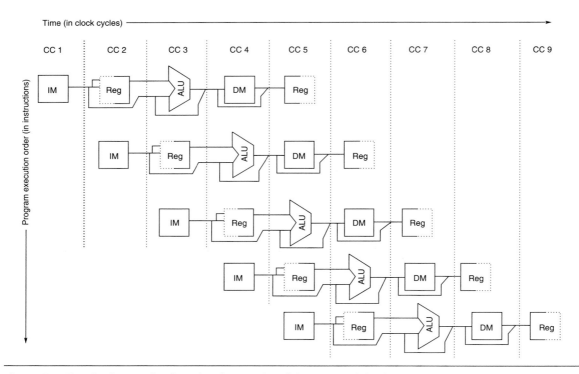

Figure A.2 The pipeline can be thought of as a series of data paths shifted in time. This shows the overlap among the parts of the data path, with clock cycle 5 (CC 5) showing the steady-state situation. Because the register file is used as a source in the ID stage and as a destination in the WB stage, it appears twice. We show that it is read in one part of the stage and written in another by using a solid line, on the right or left, respectively, and a dashed line on the other side. The abbreviation IM is used for instruction memory, DM for data memory, and CC for clock cycle.

which will become obvious shortly), we perform the register write in the first half of the clock cycle and the read in the second half.

Third, Figure A.2 does not deal with the PC. To start a new instruction every clock, we must increment and store the PC every clock, and this must be done during the IF stage in preparation for the next instruction. Furthermore, we must also have an adder to compute the potential branch target during ID. One further problem is that a branch does not change the PC until the ID stage. This causes a problem, which we ignore for now, but will handle shortly.

Although it is critical to ensure that instructions in the pipeline do not attempt to use the hardware resources at the same time, we must also ensure that instructions in different stages of the pipeline do not interfere with one another. This separation is done by introducing *pipeline registers* between successive stages of the pipeline, so that at the end of a clock cycle all the results from a given stage are stored into a register that is used as the input to the next stage on the next clock cycle. Figure A.3 shows the pipeline drawn with these pipeline registers.

Time (in clock cycles)

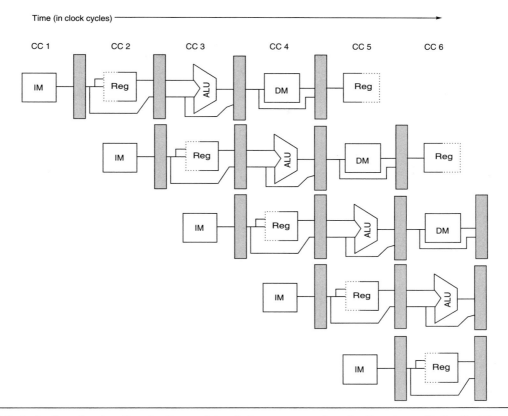

Figure A.3 A pipeline showing the pipeline registers between successive pipeline stages. Notice that the registers prevent interference between two different instructions in adjacent stages in the pipeline. The registers also play the critical role of carrying data for a given instruction from one stage to the other. The edge-triggered property of registers—that is, that the values change instantaneously on a clock edge—is critical. Otherwise, the data from one instruction could interfere with the execution of another!

Although many figures will omit such registers for simplicity, they are required to make the pipeline operate properly and must be present. Of course, similar registers would be needed even in a multicycle data path that had no pipelining (since only values in registers are preserved across clock boundaries). In the case of a pipelined processor, the pipeline registers also play the key role of carrying intermediate results from one stage to another where the source and destination may not be directly adjacent. For example, the register value to be stored during a store instruction is read during ID, but not actually used until MEM; it is passed through two pipeline registers to reach the data memory during the MEM stage. Likewise, the result of an ALU instruction is computed during EX, but not actually stored until WB; it arrives there by passing through two pipeline registers. It is sometimes useful to name the pipeline registers, and we follow the convention of naming them by the pipeline stages they connect, so that the registers are called IF/ID, ID/EX, EX/MEM, and MEM/WB.

Basic Performance Issues in Pipelining

Pipelining increases the CPU instruction throughput—the number of instructions completed per unit of time—but it does not reduce the execution time of an individual instruction. In fact, it usually slightly increases the execution time of each instruction due to overhead in the control of the pipeline. The increase in instruction throughput means that a program runs faster and has lower total execution time, even though no single instruction runs faster!

The fact that the execution time of each instruction does not decrease puts limits on the practical depth of a pipeline, as we will see in the next section. In addition to limitations arising from pipeline latency, limits arise from imbalance among the pipe stages and from pipelining overhead. Imbalance among the pipe stages reduces performance since the clock can run no faster than the time needed for the slowest pipeline stage. Pipeline overhead arises from the combination of pipeline register delay and clock skew. The pipeline registers add setup time, which is the time that a register input must be stable before the clock signal that triggers a write occurs, plus propagation delay to the clock cycle. Clock skew, which is maximum delay between when the clock arrives at any two registers, also contributes to the lower limit on the clock cycle. Once the clock cycle is as small as the sum of the clock skew and latch overhead, no further pipelining is useful, since there is no time left in the cycle for useful work. The interested reader should see Kunkel and Smith [1986]. As we will see in Chapter 2, this overhead affected the performance gains achieved by the Pentium 4 versus the Pentium III.

Example Consider the unpipelined processor in the previous section. Assume that it has a 1 ns clock cycle and that it uses 4 cycles for ALU operations and branches and 5 cycles for memory operations. Assume that the relative frequencies of these operations are 40%, 20%, and 40%, respectively. Suppose that due to clock skew and setup, pipelining the processor adds 0.2 ns of overhead to the clock. Ignoring any latency impact, how much speedup in the instruction execution rate will we gain from a pipeline?

Answer The average instruction execution time on the unpipelined processor is

$$
\begin{aligned}
\text{Average instruction execution time} &= \text{Clock cycle} \times \text{Average CPI} \\
&= 1 \text{ ns} \times ((40\% + 20\%) \times 4 + 40\% \times 5) \\
&= 1 \text{ ns} \times 4.4 \\
&= 4.4 \text{ ns}
\end{aligned}
$$

In the pipelined implementation, the clock must run at the speed of the slowest stage plus overhead, which will be $1 + 0.2$ or 1.2 ns; this is the average instruction execution time. Thus, the speedup from pipelining is

This leads to the following:

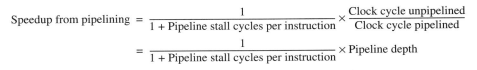

$$\text{Speedup from pipelining} = \frac{1}{1 + \text{Pipeline stall cycles per instruction}} \times \frac{\text{Clock cycle unpipelined}}{\text{Clock cycle pipelined}}$$

$$= \frac{1}{1 + \text{Pipeline stall cycles per instruction}} \times \text{Pipeline depth}$$

Thus, if there are no stalls, the speedup is equal to the number of pipeline stages, matching our intuition for the ideal case.

Structural Hazards

When a processor is pipelined, the overlapped execution of instructions requires pipelining of functional units and duplication of resources to allow all possible combinations of instructions in the pipeline. If some combination of instructions cannot be accommodated because of resource conflicts, the processor is said to have a *structural hazard.*

The most common instances of structural hazards arise when some functional unit is not fully pipelined. Then a sequence of instructions using that unpipelined unit cannot proceed at the rate of one per clock cycle. Another common way that structural hazards appear is when some resource has not been duplicated enough to allow all combinations of instructions in the pipeline to execute. For example, a processor may have only one register-file write port, but under certain circumstances, the pipeline might want to perform two writes in a clock cycle. This will generate a structural hazard.

When a sequence of instructions encounters this hazard, the pipeline will stall one of the instructions until the required unit is available. Such stalls will increase the CPI from its usual ideal value of 1.

Some pipelined processors have shared a single-memory pipeline for data and instructions. As a result, when an instruction contains a data memory reference, it will conflict with the instruction reference for a later instruction, as shown in Figure A.4. To resolve this hazard, we stall the pipeline for 1 clock cycle when the data memory access occurs. A stall is commonly called a *pipeline bubble* or just *bubble,* since it floats through the pipeline taking space but carrying no useful work. We will see another type of stall when we talk about data hazards.

Designers often indicate stall behavior using a simple diagram with only the pipe stage names, as in Figure A.5. The form of Figure A.5 shows the stall by indicating the cycle when no action occurs and simply shifting instruction 3 to the right (which delays its execution start and finish by 1 cycle). The effect of the pipeline bubble is actually to occupy the resources for that instruction slot as it travels through the pipeline.

Example Let's see how much the load structural hazard might cost. Suppose that data references constitute 40% of the mix, and that the ideal CPI of the pipelined processor, ignoring the structural hazard, is 1. Assume that the processor with the structural hazard has a clock rate that is 1.05 times higher than the clock rate of

Time (in clock cycles)

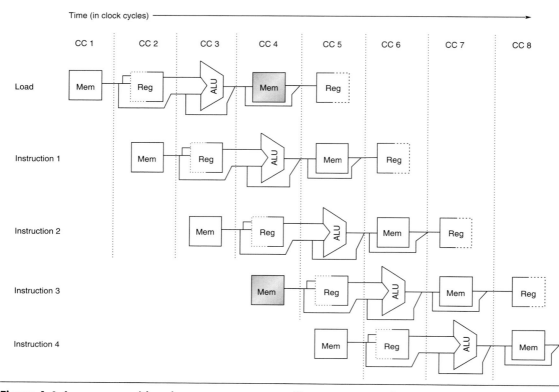

Figure A.4 A processor with only one memory port will generate a conflict whenever a memory reference occurs. In this example the load instruction uses the memory for a data access at the same time instruction 3 wants to fetch an instruction from memory.

the processor without the hazard. Disregarding any other performance losses, is the pipeline with or without the structural hazard faster, and by how much?

Answer   There are several ways we could solve this problem. Perhaps the simplest is to compute the average instruction time on the two processors:

$$\text{Average instruction time} = \text{CPI} \times \text{Clock cycle time}$$

Since it has no stalls, the average instruction time for the ideal processor is simply the Clock cycle time$_{ideal}$. The average instruction time for the processor with the structural hazard is

$$\text{Average instruction time} = \text{CPI} \times \text{Clock cycle time}$$

$$= (1 + 0.4 \times 1) \times \frac{\text{Clock cycle time}_{ideal}}{1.05}$$

$$= 1.3 \times \text{Clock cycle time}_{ideal}$$

	Clock cycle number								
Instruction	**1**	**2**	**3**	**4**	**5**	**6**	**7**	**8**	**9**	**10**
Load instruction	IF	ID	EX	MEM	WB					
Instruction $i + 1$		IF	ID	EX	MEM	WB				
Instruction $i + 2$			IF	ID	EX	MEM	WB			
Instruction $i + 3$				stall	IF	ID	EX	MEM	WB	
Instruction $i + 4$						IF	ID	EX	MEM	WB
Instruction $i + 5$							IF	ID	EX	MEM
Instruction $i + 6$								IF	ID	EX

Figure A.5 A pipeline stalled for a structural hazard—a load with one memory port. As shown here, the load instruction effectively steals an instruction-fetch cycle, causing the pipeline to stall—no instruction is initiated on clock cycle 4 (which normally would initiate instruction $i + 3$). Because the instruction being fetched is stalled, all other instructions in the pipeline before the stalled instruction can proceed normally. The stall cycle will continue to pass through the pipeline, so that no instruction completes on clock cycle 8. Sometimes these pipeline diagrams are drawn with the stall occupying an entire horizontal row and instruction 3 being moved to the next row; in either case, the effect is the same, since instruction $i + 3$ does not begin execution until cycle 5. We use the form above, since it takes less space in the figure. Note that this figure assumes that instruction $i + 1$ and $i + 2$ are not memory references.

Clearly, the processor without the structural hazard is faster; we can use the ratio of the average instruction times to conclude that the processor without the hazard is 1.3 times faster.

As an alternative to this structural hazard, the designer could provide a separate memory access for instructions, either by splitting the cache into separate instruction and data caches, or by using a set of buffers, usually called *instruction buffers,* to hold instructions. Chapter 5 discusses both the split cache and instruction buffer ideas.

If all other factors are equal, a processor without structural hazards will always have a lower CPI. Why, then, would a designer allow structural hazards? The primary reason is to reduce cost of the unit, since pipelining all the functional units, or duplicating them, may be too costly. For example, processors that support both an instruction and a data cache access every cycle (to prevent the structural hazard of the above example) require twice as much total memory bandwidth and often have higher bandwidth at the pins. Likewise, fully pipelining a floating-point multiplier consumes lots of gates. If the structural hazard is rare, it may not be worth the cost to avoid it.

Data Hazards

A major effect of pipelining is to change the relative timing of instructions by overlapping their execution. This overlap introduces data and control hazards.

Data hazards occur when the pipeline changes the order of read/write accesses to operands so that the order differs from the order seen by sequentially executing instructions on an unpipelined processor. Consider the pipelined execution of these instructions:

```
DADD    R1,R2,R3
DSUB    R4,R1,R5
AND     R6,R1,R7
OR      R8,R1,R9
XOR     R10,R1,R11
```

All the instructions after the DADD use the result of the DADD instruction. As shown in Figure A.6, the DADD instruction writes the value of R1 in the WB pipe stage, but the DSUB instruction reads the value during its ID stage. This problem is called a *data hazard*. Unless precautions are taken to prevent it, the DSUB instruction will read the wrong value and try to use it. In fact, the value used by the DSUB

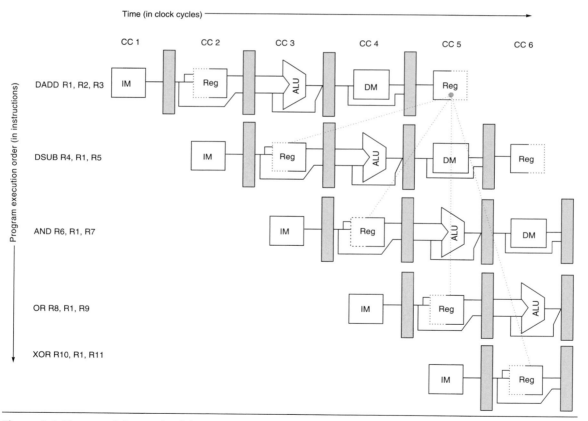

Figure A.6 The use of the result of the DADD instruction in the next three instructions causes a hazard, since the register is not written until after those instructions read it.

instruction is not even deterministic: Though we might think it logical to assume that DSUB would always use the value of R1 that was assigned by an instruction prior to DADD, this is not always the case. If an interrupt should occur between the DADD and DSUB instructions, the WB stage of the DADD will complete, and the value of R1 at that point will be the result of the DADD. This unpredictable behavior is obviously unacceptable.

The AND instruction is also affected by this hazard. As we can see from Figure A.6, the write of R1 does not complete until the end of clock cycle 5. Thus, the AND instruction that reads the registers during clock cycle 4 will receive the wrong results.

The XOR instruction operates properly because its register read occurs in clock cycle 6, after the register write. The OR instruction also operates without incurring a hazard because we perform the register file reads in the second half of the cycle and the writes in the first half.

The next subsection discusses a technique to eliminate the stalls for the hazard involving the DSUB and AND instructions.

Minimizing Data Hazard Stalls by Forwarding

The problem posed in Figure A.6 can be solved with a simple hardware technique called *forwarding* (also called *bypassing* and sometimes *short-circuiting*). The key insight in forwarding is that the result is not really needed by the DSUB until after the DADD actually produces it. If the result can be moved from the pipeline register where the DADD stores it to where the DSUB needs it, then the need for a stall can be avoided. Using this observation, forwarding works as follows:

1. The ALU result from both the EX/MEM and MEM/WB pipeline registers is always fed back to the ALU inputs.

2. If the forwarding hardware detects that the previous ALU operation has written the register corresponding to a source for the current ALU operation, control logic selects the forwarded result as the ALU input rather than the value read from the register file.

Notice that with forwarding, if the DSUB is stalled, the DADD will be completed and the bypass will not be activated. This relationship is also true for the case of an interrupt between the two instructions.

As the example in Figure A.6 shows, we need to forward results not only from the immediately previous instruction, but possibly from an instruction that started 2 cycles earlier. Figure A.7 shows our example with the bypass paths in place and highlighting the timing of the register read and writes. This code sequence can be executed without stalls.

Forwarding can be generalized to include passing a result directly to the functional unit that requires it: A result is forwarded from the pipeline register corresponding to the output of one unit to the input of another, rather than just from

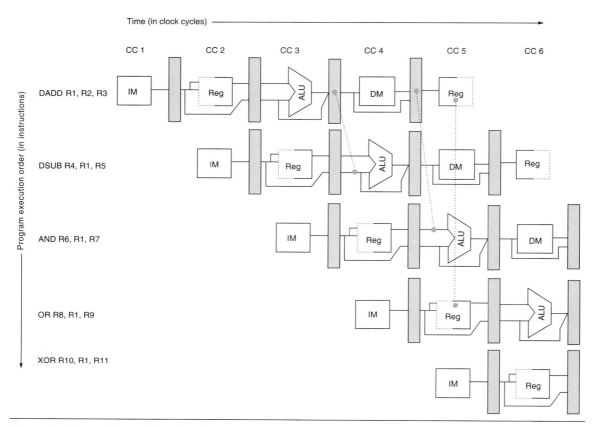

Figure A.7 A set of instructions that depends on the DADD result uses forwarding paths to avoid the data hazard. The inputs for the DSUB and AND instructions forward from the pipeline registers to the first ALU input. The OR receives its result by forwarding through the register file, which is easily accomplished by reading the registers in the second half of the cycle and writing in the first half, as the dashed lines on the registers indicate. Notice that the forwarded result can go to either ALU input; in fact, both ALU inputs could use forwarded inputs from either the same pipeline register or from different pipeline registers. This would occur, for example, if the AND instruction was AND R6,R1,R4.

the result of a unit to the input of the same unit. Take, for example, the following sequence:

```
DADD    R1,R2,R3
LD      R4,0(R1)
SD      R4,12(R1)
```

To prevent a stall in this sequence, we would need to forward the values of the ALU output and memory unit output from the pipeline registers to the ALU and data memory inputs. Figure A.8 shows all the forwarding paths for this example.

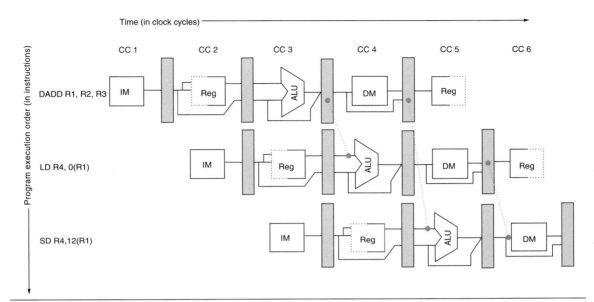

Figure A.8 Forwarding of operand required by stores during MEM. The result of the load is forwarded from the memory output to the memory input to be stored. In addition, the ALU output is forwarded to the ALU input for the address calculation of both the load and the store (this is no different than forwarding to another ALU operation). If the store depended on an immediately preceding ALU operation (not shown above), the result would need to be forwarded to prevent a stall.

Data Hazards Requiring Stalls

Unfortunately, not all potential data hazards can be handled by bypassing. Consider the following sequence of instructions:

```
LD        R1,0(R2)
DSUB      R4,R1,R5
AND       R6,R1,R7
OR        R8,R1,R9
```

The pipelined data path with the bypass paths for this example is shown in Figure A.9. This case is different from the situation with back-to-back ALU operations. The LD instruction does not have the data until the end of clock cycle 4 (its MEM cycle), while the DSUB instruction needs to have the data by the beginning of that clock cycle. Thus, the data hazard from using the result of a load instruction cannot be completely eliminated with simple hardware. As Figure A.9 shows, such a forwarding path would have to operate backward in time—a capability not yet available to computer designers! We *can* forward the result immediately to the ALU from the pipeline registers for use in the AND operation, which begins 2 clock cycles after the load. Likewise, the OR instruction has no problem, since it receives the value through the register file. For the DSUB

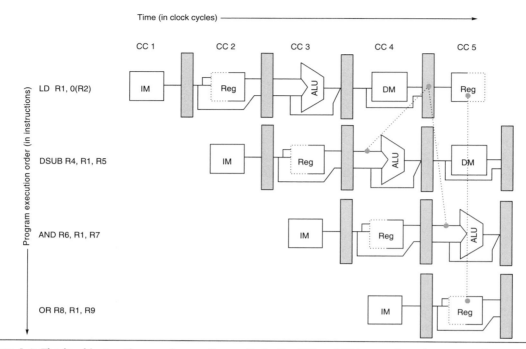

Figure A.9 The load instruction can bypass its results to the AND and OR instructions, but not to the DSUB, since that would mean forwarding the result in "negative time."

instruction, the forwarded result arrives too late—at the end of a clock cycle, when it is needed at the beginning.

The load instruction has a delay or latency that cannot be eliminated by forwarding alone. Instead, we need to add hardware, called a *pipeline interlock,* to preserve the correct execution pattern. In general, a pipeline interlock detects a hazard and stalls the pipeline until the hazard is cleared. In this case, the interlock stalls the pipeline, beginning with the instruction that wants to use the data until the source instruction produces it. This pipeline interlock introduces a stall or bubble, just as it did for the structural hazard. The CPI for the stalled instruction increases by the length of the stall (1 clock cycle in this case).

Figure A.10 shows the pipeline before and after the stall using the names of the pipeline stages. Because the stall causes the instructions starting with the DSUB to move 1 cycle later in time, the forwarding to the AND instruction now goes through the register file, and no forwarding at all is needed for the OR instruction. The insertion of the bubble causes the number of cycles to complete this sequence to grow by one. No instruction is started during clock cycle 4 (and none finishes during cycle 6).

LD	R1,0(R2)	IF	ID	EX	MEM	WB				
DSUB	R4,R1,R5		IF	ID	EX	MEM	WB			
AND	R6,R1,R7			IF	ID	EX	MEM	WB		
OR	R8,R1,R9				IF	ID	EX	MEM	WB	

LD	R1,0(R2)	IF	ID	EX	MEM	WB				
DSUB	R4,R1,R5		IF	ID	stall	EX	MEM	WB		
AND	R6,R1,R7			IF	stall	ID	EX	MEM	WB	
OR	R8,R1,R9				stall	IF	ID	EX	MEM	WB

Figure A.10 In the top half, we can see why a stall is needed: The MEM cycle of the load produces a value that is needed in the EX cycle of the DSUB, which occurs at the same time. This problem is solved by inserting a stall, as shown in the bottom half.

Branch Hazards

Control hazards can cause a greater performance loss for our MIPS pipeline than do data hazards. When a branch is executed, it may or may not change the PC to something other than its current value plus 4. Recall that if a branch changes the PC to its target address, it is a *taken* branch; if it falls through, it is *not taken,* or *untaken.* If instruction *i* is a taken branch, then the PC is normally not changed until the end of ID, after the completion of the address calculation and comparison.

Figure A.11 shows that the simplest method of dealing with branches is to redo the fetch of the instruction following a branch, once we detect the branch during ID (when instructions are decoded). The first IF cycle is essentially a stall, because it never performs useful work. You may have noticed that if the branch is untaken, then the repetition of the IF stage is unnecessary since the correct instruction was indeed fetched. We will develop several schemes to take advantage of this fact shortly.

One stall cycle for every branch will yield a performance loss of 10% to 30% depending on the branch frequency, so we will examine some techniques to deal with this loss.

Branch instruction	IF	ID	EX	MEM	WB			
Branch successor		IF	IF	ID	EX	MEM	WB	
Branch successor + 1				IF	ID	EX	MEM	
Branch successor + 2					IF	ID	EX	

Figure A.11 A branch causes a 1-cycle stall in the five-stage pipeline. The instruction after the branch is fetched, but the instruction is ignored, and the fetch is restarted once the branch target is known. It is probably obvious that if the branch is not taken, the second IF for branch successor is redundant. This will be addressed shortly.

Reducing Pipeline Branch Penalties

There are many methods for dealing with the pipeline stalls caused by branch delay; we discuss four simple compile time schemes in this subsection. In these four schemes the actions for a branch are static—they are fixed for each branch during the entire execution. The software can try to minimize the branch penalty using knowledge of the hardware scheme and of branch behavior. Chapters 2 and 3 look at more powerful hardware and software techniques for both static and dynamic branch prediction.

The simplest scheme to handle branches is to *freeze* or *flush* the pipeline, holding or deleting any instructions after the branch until the branch destination is known. The attractiveness of this solution lies primarily in its simplicity both for hardware and software. It is the solution used earlier in the pipeline shown in Figure A.11. In this case the branch penalty is fixed and cannot be reduced by software.

A higher-performance, and only slightly more complex, scheme is to treat every branch as not taken, simply allowing the hardware to continue as if the branch were not executed. Here, care must be taken not to change the processor state until the branch outcome is definitely known. The complexity of this scheme arises from having to know when the state might be changed by an instruction and how to "back out" such a change.

In the simple five-stage pipeline, this *predicted-not-taken* or *predicted-untaken* scheme is implemented by continuing to fetch instructions as if the branch were a normal instruction. The pipeline looks as if nothing out of the ordinary is happening. If the branch is taken, however, we need to turn the fetched instruction into a no-op and restart the fetch at the target address. Figure A.12 shows both situations.

Untaken branch instruction	IF	ID	EX	MEM	WB				
Instruction $i + 1$		IF	ID	EX	MEM	WB			
Instruction $i + 2$			IF	ID	EX	MEM	WB		
Instruction $i + 3$				IF	ID	EX	MEM	WB	
Instruction $i + 4$					IF	ID	EX	MEM	WB

Taken branch instruction	IF	ID	EX	MEM	WB				
Instruction $i + 1$		IF	**idle**	**idle**	**idle**	**idle**			
Branch target			IF	ID	EX	MEM	WB		
Branch target $+ 1$				IF	ID	EX	MEM	WB	
Branch target $+ 2$					IF	ID	EX	MEM	WB

Figure A.12 The predicted-not-taken scheme and the pipeline sequence when the branch is untaken (top) and taken (bottom). When the branch is untaken, determined during ID, we have fetched the fall-through and just continue. If the branch is taken during ID, we restart the fetch at the branch target. This causes all instructions following the branch to stall 1 clock cycle.

An alternative scheme is to treat every branch as taken. As soon as the branch is decoded and the target address is computed, we assume the branch to be taken and begin fetching and executing at the target. Because in our five-stage pipeline we don't know the target address any earlier than we know the branch outcome, there is no advantage in this approach for this pipeline. In some processors—especially those with implicitly set condition codes or more powerful (and hence slower) branch conditions—the branch target is known before the branch outcome, and a predicted-taken scheme might make sense. In either a predicted-taken or predicted-not-taken scheme, the compiler can improve performance by organizing the code so that the most frequent path matches the hardware's choice. Our fourth scheme provides more opportunities for the compiler to improve performance.

A fourth scheme in use in some processors is called *delayed branch*. This technique was heavily used in early RISC processors and works reasonably well in the five-stage pipeline. In a delayed branch, the execution cycle with a branch delay of one is

```
branch instruction
sequential successor₁
branch target if taken
```

The sequential successor is in the *branch delay slot*. This instruction is executed whether or not the branch is taken. The pipeline behavior of the five-stage pipeline with a branch delay is shown in Figure A.13. Although it is possible to have a branch delay longer than one, in practice, almost all processors with delayed branch have a single instruction delay; other techniques are used if the pipeline has a longer potential branch penalty.

Untaken branch instruction	IF	ID	EX	MEM	WB			
Branch delay instruction ($i + 1$)		IF	ID	EX	MEM	WB		
Instruction $i + 2$			IF	ID	EX	MEM	WB	
Instruction $i + 3$				IF	ID	EX	MEM	WB
Instruction $i + 4$					IF	ID	EX	MEM	WB
Taken branch instruction	IF	ID	EX	MEM	WB			
Branch delay instruction ($i + 1$)		IF	ID	EX	MEM	WB		
Branch target			IF	ID	EX	MEM	WB	
Branch target + 1				IF	ID	EX	MEM	WB
Branch target + 2					IF	ID	EX	MEM	WB

Figure A.13 The behavior of a delayed branch is the same whether or not the branch is taken. The instructions in the delay slot (there is only one delay slot for MIPS) are executed. If the branch is untaken, execution continues with the instruction after the branch delay instruction; if the branch is taken, execution continues at the branch target. When the instruction in the branch delay slot is also a branch, the meaning is unclear: If the branch is not taken, what should happen to the branch in the branch delay slot? Because of this confusion, architectures with delay branches often disallow putting a branch in the delay slot.

The job of the compiler is to make the successor instructions valid and useful. A number of optimizations are used. Figure A.14 shows the three ways in which the branch delay can be scheduled.

The limitations on delayed-branch scheduling arise from (1) the restrictions on the instructions that are scheduled into the delay slots and (2) our ability to predict at compile time whether a branch is likely to be taken or not. To improve the ability of the compiler to fill branch delay slots, most processors with conditional branches have introduced a *canceling* or *nullifying* branch. In a canceling branch, the instruction includes the direction that the branch was predicted. When the branch behaves as predicted, the instruction in the branch delay slot is simply executed as it would

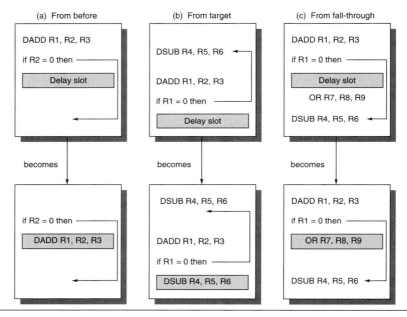

Figure A.14 Scheduling the branch delay slot. The top box in each pair shows the code before scheduling; the bottom box shows the scheduled code. In (a) the delay slot is scheduled with an independent instruction from before the branch. This is the best choice. Strategies (b) and (c) are used when (a) is not possible. In the code sequences for (b) and (c), the use of R1 in the branch condition prevents the DADD instruction (whose destination is R1) from being moved after the branch. In (b) the branch delay slot is scheduled from the target of the branch; usually the target instruction will need to be copied because it can be reached by another path. Strategy (b) is preferred when the branch is taken with high probability, such as a loop branch. Finally, the branch may be scheduled from the not-taken fall-through as in (c). To make this optimization legal for (b) or (c), it must be OK to execute the moved instruction when the branch goes in the unexpected direction. By OK we mean that the work is wasted, but the program will still execute correctly. This is the case, for example, in (c) if R7 were an unused temporary register when the branch goes in the unexpected direction.

normally be with a delayed branch. When the branch is incorrectly predicted, the instruction in the branch delay slot is simply turned into a no-op.

Performance of Branch Schemes

What is the effective performance of each of these schemes? The effective pipeline speedup with branch penalties, assuming an ideal CPI of 1, is

$$\text{Pipeline speedup} = \frac{\text{Pipeline depth}}{1 + \text{Pipeline stall cycles from branches}}$$

Because of the following:

$$\text{Pipeline stall cycles from branches} = \text{Branch frequency} \times \text{Branch penalty}$$

we obtain

$$\text{Pipeline speedup} = \frac{\text{Pipeline depth}}{1 + \text{Branch frequency} \times \text{Branch penalty}}$$

The branch frequency and branch penalty can have a component from both unconditional and conditional branches. However, the latter dominate since they are more frequent.

Example   For a deeper pipeline, such as that in a MIPS R4000, it takes at least three pipeline stages before the branch-target address is known and an additional cycle before the branch condition is evaluated, assuming no stalls on the registers in the conditional comparison. A three-stage delay leads to the branch penalties for the three simplest prediction schemes listed in Figure A.15.

Find the effective addition to the CPI arising from branches for this pipeline, assuming the following frequencies:

Unconditional branch	4%
Conditional branch, untaken	6%
Conditional branch, taken	10%

Branch scheme	Penalty unconditional	Penalty untaken	Penalty taken
Flush pipeline	2	3	3
Predicted taken	2	3	2
Predicted untaken	2	0	3

Figure A.15 Branch penalties for the three simplest prediction schemes for a deeper pipeline.

Branch scheme	Additions to the CPI from branch costs			
	Unconditional branches	Untaken conditional branches	Taken conditional branches	All branches
Frequency of event	4%	6%	10%	20%
Stall pipeline	0.08	0.18	0.30	0.56
Predicted taken	0.08	0.18	0.20	0.46
Predicted untaken	0.08	0.00	0.30	0.38

Figure A.16 CPI penalties for three branch-prediction schemes and a deeper pipeline.

Answer We find the CPIs by multiplying the relative frequency of unconditional, conditional untaken, and conditional taken branches by the respective penalties. The results are shown in Figure A.16.

The differences among the schemes are substantially increased with this longer delay. If the base CPI were 1 and branches were the only source of stalls, the ideal pipeline would be 1.56 times faster than a pipeline that used the stall-pipeline scheme. The predicted-untaken scheme would be 1.13 times better than the stall-pipeline scheme under the same assumptions.

A.3 How Is Pipelining Implemented?

Before we proceed to basic pipelining, we need to review a simple implementation of an unpipelined version of MIPS.

A Simple Implementation of MIPS

In this section we follow the style of Section A.1, showing first a simple unpipelined implementation and then the pipelined implementation. This time, however, our example is specific to the MIPS architecture.

In this subsection we focus on a pipeline for an integer subset of MIPS that consists of load-store word, branch equal zero, and integer ALU operations. Later in this appendix, we will incorporate the basic floating-point operations. Although we discuss only a subset of MIPS, the basic principles can be extended to handle all the instructions. We initially used a less aggressive implementation of a branch instruction. We show how to implement the more aggressive version at the end of this section.

Every MIPS instruction can be implemented in at most 5 clock cycles. The 5 clock cycles are as follows.

1. *Instruction fetch cycle* (IF):

```
IR ← Mem[PC];
NPC ← PC + 4;
```

Operation: Send out the PC and fetch the instruction from memory into the instruction register (IR); increment the PC by 4 to address the next sequential instruction. The IR is used to hold the instruction that will be needed on subsequent clock cycles; likewise the register NPC is used to hold the next sequential PC.

2. *Instruction decode/register fetch cycle* (ID):

```
A ← Regs[rs];
B ← Regs[rt];
Imm ← sign-extended immediate field of IR;
```

Operation: Decode the instruction and access the register file to read the registers (rs and rt are the register specifiers). The outputs of the general-purpose registers are read into two temporary registers (A and B) for use in later clock cycles. The lower 16 bits of the IR are also sign extended and stored into the temporary register Imm, for use in the next cycle.

Decoding is done in parallel with reading registers, which is possible because these fields are at a fixed location in the MIPS instruction format (see Figure B.22 on page B-35). Because the immediate portion of an instruction is located in an identical place in every MIPS format, the sign-extended immediate is also calculated during this cycle in case it is needed in the next cycle.

3. *Execution/effective address cycle* (EX):

The ALU operates on the operands prepared in the prior cycle, performing one of four functions depending on the MIPS instruction type.

- Memory reference:

```
ALUOutput ← A + Imm;
```

Operation: The ALU adds the operands to form the effective address and places the result into the register ALUOutput.

- Register-Register ALU instruction:

```
ALUOutput ← A func B;
```

Operation: The ALU performs the operation specified by the function code on the value in register A and on the value in register B. The result is placed in the temporary register ALUOutput.

- Register-Immediate ALU instruction:

```
ALUOutput ← A op Imm;
```

Operation: The ALU performs the operation specified by the opcode on the value in register A and on the value in register Imm. The result is placed in the temporary register ALUOutput.

- Branch:

```
ALUOutput ← NPC + (Imm << 2);
Cond ← (A == 0)
```

Operation: The ALU adds the NPC to the sign-extended immediate value in Imm, which is shifted left by 2 bits to create a word offset, to compute the address of the branch target. Register A, which has been read in the prior cycle, is checked to determine whether the branch is taken. Since we are considering only one form of branch (BEQZ), the comparison is against 0. Note that BEQZ is actually a pseudoinstruction that translates to a BEQ with R0 as an operand. For simplicity, this is the only form of branch we consider.

The load-store architecture of MIPS means that effective address and execution cycles can be combined into a single clock cycle, since no instruction needs to simultaneously calculate a data address, calculate an instruction target address, and perform an operation on the data. The other integer instructions not included above are jumps of various forms, which are similar to branches.

4. *Memory access/branch completion cycle* (MEM):

   The PC is updated for all instructions: PC ← NPC;

   ■ Memory reference:

   LMD ← Mem[ALUOutput] or
   Mem[ALUOutput] ← B;

   Operation: Access memory if needed. If instruction is a load, data returns from memory and is placed in the LMD (load memory data) register; if it is a store, then the data from the B register is written into memory. In either case the address used is the one computed during the prior cycle and stored in the register ALUOutput.

   ■ Branch:

   if (cond) PC ← ALUOutput

   Operation: If the instruction branches, the PC is replaced with the branch destination address in the register ALUOutput.

5. *Write-back cycle* (WB):

   ■ Register-Register ALU instruction:

   Regs[rd] ← ALUOutput;

   ■ Register-Immediate ALU instruction:

   Regs[rt] ← ALUOutput;

   ■ Load instruction:

   Regs[rt] ← LMD;

   Operation: Write the result into the register file, whether it comes from the memory system (which is in LMD) or from the ALU (which is in ALUOutput); the register destination field is also in one of two positions (rd or rt) depending on the effective opcode.

Figure A.17 shows how an instruction flows through the data path. At the end of each clock cycle, every value computed during that clock cycle and required on a later clock cycle (whether for this instruction or the next) is written into a storage device, which may be memory, a general-purpose register, the PC, or a temporary register (i.e., LMD, Imm, A, B, IR, NPC, ALUOutput, or Cond). The temporary registers hold values between clock cycles for one instruction, while the other storage elements are visible parts of the state and hold values between successive instructions.

Although all processors today are pipelined, this multicycle implementation is a reasonable approximation of how most processors would have been implemented in earlier times. A simple finite-state machine could be used to implement the control following the 5-cycle structure shown above. For a much more complex processor, microcode control could be used. In either event, an instruction sequence like that above would determine the structure of the control.

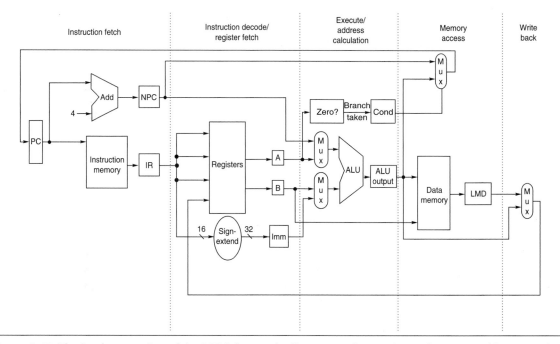

Figure A.17   The implementation of the MIPS data path allows every instruction to be executed in 4 or 5 clock cycles. Although the PC is shown in the portion of the data path that is used in instruction fetch and the registers are shown in the portion of the data path that is used in instruction decode/register fetch, both of these functional units are read as well as written by an instruction. Although we show these functional units in the cycle corresponding to where they are read, the PC is written during the memory access clock cycle and the registers are written during the write-back clock cycle. In both cases, the writes in later pipe stages are indicated by the multiplexer output (in memory access or write back), which carries a value back to the PC or registers. These backward-flowing signals introduce much of the complexity of pipelining, since they indicate the possibility of hazards.

There are some hardware redundancies that could be eliminated in this multi-cycle implementation. For example, there are two ALUs: one to increment the PC and one used for effective address and ALU computation. Since they are not needed on the same clock cycle, we could merge them by adding additional multiplexers and sharing the same ALU. Likewise, instructions and data could be stored in the same memory, since the data and instruction accesses happen on different clock cycles.

Rather than optimize this simple implementation, we will leave the design as it is in Figure A.17, since this provides us with a better base for the pipelined implementation.

As an alternative to the multicycle design discussed in this section, we could also have implemented the CPU so that every instruction takes 1 long clock cycle. In such cases, the temporary registers would be deleted, since there would not be any communication across clock cycles within an instruction. Every instruction would execute in 1 long clock cycle, writing the result into the data memory, registers, or PC at the end of the clock cycle. The CPI would be one for such a processor. The clock cycle, however, would be roughly equal to five times the clock cycle of the multicycle processor, since every instruction would need to traverse all the functional units. Designers would never use this single-cycle implementation for two reasons. First, a single-cycle implementation would be very inefficient for most CPUs that have a reasonable variation among the amount of work, and hence in the clock cycle time, needed for different instructions. Second, a single-cycle implementation requires the duplication of functional units that could be shared in a multicycle implementation. Nonetheless, this single-cycle data path allows us to illustrate how pipelining can improve the clock cycle time, as opposed to the CPI, of a processor.

A Basic Pipeline for MIPS

As before, we can pipeline the data path of Figure A.17 with almost no changes by starting a new instruction on each clock cycle. Because every pipe stage is active on every clock cycle, all operations in a pipe stage must complete in 1 clock cycle and any combination of operations must be able to occur at once. Furthermore, pipelining the data path requires that values passed from one pipe stage to the next must be placed in registers. Figure A.18 shows the MIPS pipeline with the appropriate registers, called *pipeline registers* or *pipeline latches,* between each pipeline stage. The registers are labeled with the names of the stages they connect. Figure A.18 is drawn so that connections through the pipeline registers from one stage to another are clear.

All of the registers needed to hold values temporarily between clock cycles within one instruction are subsumed into these pipeline registers. The fields of the instruction register (IR), which is part of the IF/ID register, are labeled when they are used to supply register names. The pipeline registers carry both data and control from one pipeline stage to the next. Any value needed on a later pipeline stage must be placed in such a register and copied from one pipeline register to

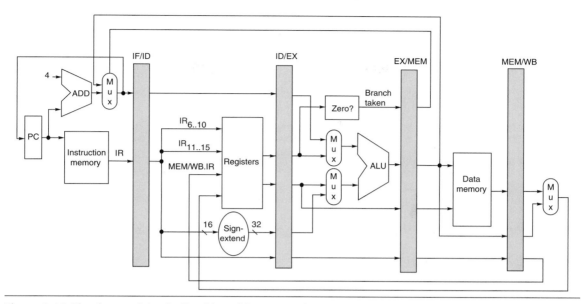

Figure A.18 The data path is pipelined by adding a set of registers, one between each pair of pipe stages. The registers serve to convey values and control information from one stage to the next. We can also think of the PC as a pipeline register, which sits before the IF stage of the pipeline, leading to one pipeline register for each pipe stage. Recall that the PC is an edge-triggered register written at the end of the clock cycle; hence there is no race condition in writing the PC. The selection multiplexer for the PC has been moved so that the PC is written in exactly one stage (IF). If we didn't move it, there would be a conflict when a branch occurred, since two instructions would try to write different values into the PC. Most of the data paths flow from left to right, which is from earlier in time to later. The paths flowing from right to left (which carry the register write-back information and PC information on a branch) introduce complications into our pipeline.

the next, until it is no longer needed. If we tried to just use the temporary registers we had in our earlier unpipelined data path, values could be overwritten before all uses were completed. For example, the field of a register operand used for a write on a load or ALU operation is supplied from the MEM/WB pipeline register rather than from the IF/ID register. This is because we want a load or ALU operation to write the register designated by that operation, not the register field of the instruction currently transitioning from IF to ID! This destination register field is simply copied from one pipeline register to the next, until it is needed during the WB stage.

Any instruction is active in exactly one stage of the pipeline at a time; therefore, any actions taken on behalf of an instruction occur between a pair of pipeline registers. Thus, we can also look at the activities of the pipeline by examining what has to happen on any pipeline stage depending on the instruction type. Figure A.19 shows this view. Fields of the pipeline registers are named so as to show the flow of data from one stage to the next. Notice that the actions in the first two stages are independent of the current instruction type; they must be independent because the instruction is not decoded until the end of the ID stage. The IF activity

Stage	Any instruction		
IF	IF/ID.IR ← Mem[PC]; IF/ID.NPC,PC ← (if ((EX/MEM.opcode == branch) & EX/MEM.cond){EX/MEM.ALUOutput} else {PC+4});		
ID	ID/EX.A ← Regs[IF/ID.IR[rs]]; ID/EX.B ← Regs[IF/ID.IR[rt]]; ID/EX.NPC ← IF/ID.NPC; ID/EX.IR ← IF/ID.IR; ID/EX.Imm ← sign-extend(IF/ID.IR[immediate field]);		
	ALU instruction	**Load or store instruction**	**Branch instruction**
EX	EX/MEM.IR ← ID/EX.IR; EX/MEM.ALUOutput ← ID/EX.A func ID/EX.B; or EX/MEM.ALUOutput ← ID/EX.A op ID/EX.Imm;	EX/MEM.IR to ID/EX.IR EX/MEM.ALUOutput ← ID/EX.A + ID/EX.Imm; EX/MEM.B ← ID/EX.B;	EX/MEM.ALUOutput ← ID/EX.NPC + (ID/EX.Imm << 2); EX/MEM.cond ← (ID/EX.A == 0);
MEM	MEM/WB.IR ← EX/MEM.IR; MEM/WB.ALUOutput ← EX/MEM.ALUOutput;	MEM/WB.IR ← EX/MEM.IR; MEM/WB.LMD ← Mem[EX/MEM.ALUOutput]; or Mem[EX/MEM.ALUOutput] ← EX/MEM.B;	
WB	Regs[MEM/WB.IR[rd]] ← MEM/WB.ALUOutput; or Regs[MEM/WB.IR[rt]] ← MEM/WB.ALUOutput;	For load only: Regs[MEM/WB.IR[rt]] ← MEM/WB.LMD;	

Figure A.19 Events on every pipe stage of the MIPS pipeline. Let's review the actions in the stages that are specific to the pipeline organization. In IF, in addition to fetching the instruction and computing the new PC, we store the incremented PC both into the PC and into a pipeline register (NPC) for later use in computing the branch-target address. This structure is the same as the organization in Figure A.18, where the PC is updated in IF from one of two sources. In ID, we fetch the registers, extend the sign of the lower 16 bits of the IR (the immediate field), and pass along the IR and NPC. During EX, we perform an ALU operation or an address calculation; we pass along the IR and the B register (if the instruction is a store). We also set the value of cond to 1 if the instruction is a taken branch. During the MEM phase, we cycle the memory, write the PC if needed, and pass along values needed in the final pipe stage. Finally, during WB, we update the register field from either the ALU output or the loaded value. For simplicity we always pass the entire IR from one stage to the next, although as an instruction proceeds down the pipeline, less and less of the IR is needed.

depends on whether the instruction in EX/MEM is a taken branch. If so, then the branch-target address of the branch instruction in EX/MEM is written into the PC at the end of IF; otherwise the incremented PC will be written back. (As we said earlier, this effect of branches leads to complications in the pipeline that we deal with in the next few sections.) The fixed-position encoding of the register source operands is critical to allowing the registers to be fetched during ID.

To control this simple pipeline we need only determine how to set the control for the four multiplexers in the data path of Figure A.18. The two multiplexers in the ALU stage are set depending on the instruction type, which is dictated by the IR field of the ID/EX register. The top ALU input multiplexer is set by whether the instruction is a branch or not, and the bottom multiplexer is set by whether the instruction is a register-register ALU operation or any other type of operation. The multiplexer in the IF stage chooses whether to use the value of the incremented PC or the value of the EX/MEM.ALUOutput (the branch target) to write into the PC. This multiplexer is controlled by the field EX/MEM.cond. The fourth multiplexer is controlled by whether the instruction in the WB stage is a load or an ALU operation. In addition to these four multiplexers, there is one additional multiplexer needed that is not drawn in Figure A.18, but whose existence is clear from looking at the WB stage of an ALU operation. The destination register field is in one of two different places depending on the instruction type (register-register ALU versus either ALU immediate or load). Thus, we will need a multiplexer to choose the correct portion of the IR in the MEM/WB register to specify the register destination field, assuming the instruction writes a register.

Implementing the Control for the MIPS Pipeline

The process of letting an instruction move from the instruction decode stage (ID) into the execution stage (EX) of this pipeline is usually called *instruction issue;* an instruction that has made this step is said to have *issued*. For the MIPS integer pipeline, all the data hazards can be checked during the ID phase of the pipeline. If a data hazard exists, the instruction is stalled before it is issued. Likewise, we can determine what forwarding will be needed during ID and set the appropriate controls then. Detecting interlocks early in the pipeline reduces the hardware complexity because the hardware never has to suspend an instruction that has updated the state of the processor, unless the entire processor is stalled. Alternatively, we can detect the hazard or forwarding at the beginning of a clock cycle that uses an operand (EX and MEM for this pipeline). To show the differences in these two approaches, we will show how the interlock for a RAW hazard with the source coming from a load instruction (called a *load interlock*) can be implemented by a check in ID, while the implementation of forwarding paths to the ALU inputs can be done during EX. Figure A.20 lists the variety of circumstances that we must handle.

Let's start with implementing the load interlock. If there is a RAW hazard with the source instruction being a load, the load instruction will be in the EX stage when an instruction that needs the load data will be in the ID stage. Thus, we can describe all the possible hazard situations with a small table, which can be directly translated to an implementation. Figure A.21 shows a table that detects all load interlocks when the instruction using the load result is in the ID stage.

Once a hazard has been detected, the control unit must insert the pipeline stall and prevent the instructions in the IF and ID stages from advancing. As we said earlier, all the control information is carried in the pipeline registers. (Carrying

Situation	Example code sequence	Action
No dependence	LD **R1**,45(R2) DADD R5,R6,R7 DSUB R8,R6,R7 OR R9,R6,R7	No hazard possible because no dependence exists on R1 in the immediately following three instructions.
Dependence requiring stall	LD **R1**,45(R2) DADD R5,**R1**,R7 DSUB R8,R6,R7 OR R9,R6,R7	Comparators detect the use of R1 in the DADD and stall the DADD (and DSUB and OR) before the DADD begins EX.
Dependence overcome by forwarding	LD **R1**,45(R2) DADD R5,R6,R7 DSUB R8,**R1**,R7 OR R9,R6,R7	Comparators detect use of R1 in DSUB and forward result of load to ALU in time for DSUB to begin EX.
Dependence with accesses in order	LD **R1**,45(R2) DADD R5,R6,R7 DSUB R8,R6,R7 OR R9,**R1**,R7	No action required because the read of R1 by OR occurs in the second half of the ID phase, while the write of the loaded data occurred in the first half.

Figure A.20 Situations that the pipeline hazard detection hardware can see by comparing the destination and sources of adjacent instructions. This table indicates that the only comparison needed is between the destination and the sources on the two instructions following the instruction that wrote the destination. In the case of a stall, the pipeline dependences will look like the third case once execution continues. Of course hazards that involve R0 can be ignored since the register always contains 0, and the test above could be extended to do this.

Opcode field of ID/EX (ID/EX.IR$_{0..5}$)	Opcode field of IF/ID (IF/ID.IR$_{0..5}$)	Matching operand fields
Load	Register-register ALU	ID/EX.IR[rt] == IF/ID.IR[rs]
Load	Register-register ALU	ID/EX.IR[rt] == IF/ID.IR[rt]
Load	Load, store, ALU immediate, or branch	ID/EX.IR[rt] == IF/ID.IR[rs]

Figure A.21 The logic to detect the need for load interlocks during the ID stage of an instruction requires three comparisons. Lines 1 and 2 of the table test whether the load destination register is one of the source registers for a register-register operation in ID. Line 3 of the table determines if the load destination register is a source for a load or store effective address, an ALU immediate, or a branch test. Remember that the IF/ID register holds the state of the instruction in ID, which potentially uses the load result, while ID/EX holds the state of the instruction in EX, which is the load instruction.

the instruction along is enough, since all control is derived from it.) Thus, when we detect a hazard we need only change the control portion of the ID/EX pipeline register to all 0s, which happens to be a no-op (an instruction that does nothing, such as DADD R0,R0,R0). In addition, we simply recirculate the contents of the IF/ID registers to hold the stalled instruction. In a pipeline with more complex hazards, the same ideas would apply: We can detect the hazard by comparing some set of pipeline registers and shift in no-ops to prevent erroneous execution.

Implementing the forwarding logic is similar, although there are more cases to consider. The key observation needed to implement the forwarding logic is that the pipeline registers contain both the data to be forwarded as well as the source and destination register fields. All forwarding logically happens from the ALU or data memory output to the ALU input, the data memory input, or the zero detection unit. Thus, we can implement the forwarding by a comparison of the destination registers of the IR contained in the EX/MEM and MEM/WB stages against the source registers of the IR contained in the ID/EX and EX/MEM registers. Figure A.22 shows the comparisons and possible forwarding operations where the destination of the forwarded result is an ALU input for the instruction currently in EX.

In addition to the comparators and combinational logic that we need to determine when a forwarding path needs to be enabled, we also need to enlarge the multiplexers at the ALU inputs and add the connections from the pipeline registers that are used to forward the results. Figure A.23 shows the relevant segments of the pipelined data path with the additional multiplexers and connections in place.

For MIPS, the hazard detection and forwarding hardware is reasonably simple; we will see that things become somewhat more complicated when we extend this pipeline to deal with floating point. Before we do that, we need to handle branches.

Dealing with Branches in the Pipeline

In MIPS, the branches (BEQ and BNE) require testing a register for equality to another register, which may be R0. If we consider only the cases of BEQZ and BNEZ, which require a zero test, it is possible to complete this decision by the end of the ID cycle by moving the zero test into that cycle. To take advantage of an early decision on whether the branch is taken, both PCs (taken and untaken) must be computed early. Computing the branch-target address during ID requires an additional adder because the main ALU, which has been used for this function so far, is not usable until EX. Figure A.24 shows the revised pipelined data path. With the separate adder and a branch decision made during ID, there is only a 1-clock-cycle stall on branches. Although this reduces the branch delay to 1 cycle, it means that an ALU instruction followed by a branch on the result of the instruction will incur a data hazard stall. Figure A.25 shows the branch portion of the revised pipeline table from Figure A.19.

In some processors, branch hazards are even more expensive in clock cycles than in our example, since the time to evaluate the branch condition and compute the destination can be even longer. For example, a processor with separate decode and register fetch stages will probably have a *branch delay*—the length of the control hazard—that is at least 1 clock cycle longer. The branch delay, unless it is

Pipeline register containing source instruction	Opcode of source instruction	Pipeline register containing destination instruction	Opcode of destination instruction	Destination of the forwarded result	Comparison (if equal then forward)
EX/MEM	Register-register ALU	ID/EX	Register-register ALU, ALU immediate, load, store, branch	Top ALU input	EX/MEM.IR[rd] == ID/EX.IR[rs]
EX/MEM	Register-register ALU	ID/EX	Register-register ALU	Bottom ALU input	EX/MEM.IR[rd] == ID/EX.IR[rt]
MEM/WB	Register-register ALU	ID/EX	Register-register ALU, ALU immediate, load, store, branch	Top ALU input	MEM/WB.IR[rd] == ID/EX.IR[rs]
MEM/WB	Register-register ALU	ID/EX	Register-register ALU	Bottom ALU input	MEM/WB.IR[rd] == ID/EX.IR[rt]
EX/MEM	ALU immediate	ID/EX	Register-register ALU, ALU immediate, load, store, branch	Top ALU input	EX/MEM.IR[rt] == ID/EX.IR[rs]
EX/MEM	ALU immediate	ID/EX	Register-register ALU	Bottom ALU input	EX/MEM.IR[rt] == ID/EX.IR[rt]
MEM/WB	ALU immediate	ID/EX	Register-register ALU, ALU immediate, load, store, branch	Top ALU input	MEM/WB.IR[rt] == ID/EX.IR[rs]
MEM/WB	ALU immediate	ID/EX	Register-register ALU	Bottom ALU input	MEM/WB.IR[rt] == ID/EX.IR[rt]
MEM/WB	Load	ID/EX	Register-register ALU, ALU immediate, load, store, branch	Top ALU input	MEM/WB.IR[rt] == ID/EX.IR[rs]
MEM/WB	Load	ID/EX	Register-register ALU	Bottom ALU input	MEM/WB.IR[rt] == ID/EX.IR[rt]

Figure A.22 Forwarding of data to the two ALU inputs (for the instruction in EX) can occur from the ALU result (in EX/MEM or in MEM/WB) or from the load result in MEM/WB. There are 10 separate comparisons needed to tell whether a forwarding operation should occur. The top and bottom ALU inputs refer to the inputs corresponding to the first and second ALU source operands, respectively, and are shown explicitly in Figure A.17 on page A-29 and in Figure A.23 on page A-37. Remember that the pipeline latch for destination instruction in EX is ID/EX, while the source values come from the ALUOutput portion of EX/MEM or MEM/WB or the LMD portion of MEM/WB. There is one complication not addressed by this logic: dealing with multiple instructions that write the same register. For example, during the code sequence DADD R1, R2, R3; DADDI R1, R1, #2; DSUB R4, R3, R1, the logic must ensure that the DSUB instruction uses the result of the DADDI instruction rather than the result of the DADD instruction. The logic shown above can be extended to handle this case by simply testing that forwarding from MEM/WB is enabled only when forwarding from EX/MEM is not enabled for the same input. Because the DADDI result will be in EX/MEM, it will be forwarded, rather than the DADD result in MEM/WB.

dealt with, turns into a branch penalty. Many older CPUs that implement more complex instruction sets have branch delays of 4 clock cycles or more, and large, deeply pipelined processors often have branch penalties of 6 or 7. In general, the

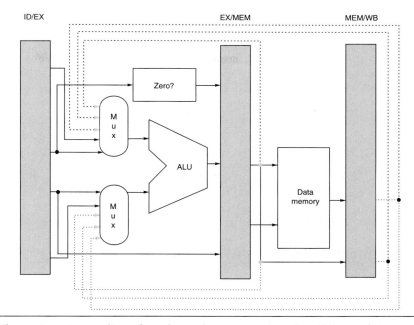

Figure A.23 Forwarding of results to the ALU requires the addition of three extra inputs on each ALU multiplexer and the addition of three paths to the new inputs. The paths correspond to a bypass of (1) the ALU output at the end of the EX, (2) the ALU output at the end of the MEM stage, and (3) the memory output at the end of the MEM stage.

deeper the pipeline, the worse the branch penalty in clock cycles. Of course, the relative performance effect of a longer branch penalty depends on the overall CPI of the processor. A low-CPI processor can afford to have more expensive branches because the percentage of the processor's performance that will be lost from branches is less.

A.4   What Makes Pipelining Hard to Implement?

Now that we understand how to detect and resolve hazards, we can deal with some complications that we have avoided so far. The first part of this section considers the challenges of exceptional situations where the instruction execution order is changed in unexpected ways. In the second part of this section, we discuss some of the challenges raised by different instruction sets.

Dealing with Exceptions

Exceptional situations are harder to handle in a pipelined CPU because the overlapping of instructions makes it more difficult to know whether an instruction can

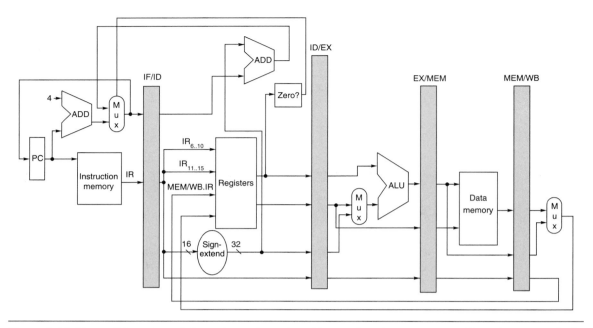

Figure A.24 The stall from branch hazards can be reduced by moving the zero test and branch-target calcula-tion into the ID phase of the pipeline. Notice that we have made two important changes, each of which removes 1 cycle from the 3-cycle stall for branches. The first change is to move both the branch-target address calculation and the branch condition decision to the ID cycle. The second change is to write the PC of the instruction in the IF phase, using either the branch-target address computed during ID or the incremented PC computed during IF. In compari-son, Figure A.18 obtained the branch-target address from the EX/MEM register and wrote the result during the MEM clock cycle. As mentioned in Figure A.18, the PC can be thought of as a pipeline register (e.g., as part of ID/IF), which is written with the address of the next instruction at the end of each IF cycle.

safely change the state of the CPU. In a pipelined CPU, an instruction is executed piece by piece and is not completed for several clock cycles. Unfortunately, other instructions in the pipeline can raise exceptions that may force the CPU to abort the instructions in the pipeline before they complete. Before we discuss these problems and their solutions in detail, we need to understand what types of situa-tions can arise and what architectural requirements exist for supporting them.

Types of Exceptions and Requirements

The terminology used to describe exceptional situations where the normal execu-tion order of instruction is changed varies among CPUs. The terms *interrupt, fault,* and *exception* are used, although not in a consistent fashion. We use the term *exception* to cover all these mechanisms, including the following:

■ I/O device request

■ Invoking an operating system service from a user program

Pipe stage	Branch instruction
IF	IF/ID.IR ← Mem[PC]; **IF/ID.NPC,PC ← (if ((IF/ID.opcode == branch) & (Regs[IF/ID.IR$_{6..10}$]** **op 0)) {IF/ID.NPC + sign-extended (IF/ID.IR[immediate field] <<2) else {PC+4});**
ID	ID/EX.A ← Regs[IF/ID.IR$_{6..10}$]; ID/EX.B ← Regs[IF/ID.IR$_{11..15}$]; ID/EX.IR ← IF/ID.IR; ID/EX.Imm ← (IF/ID.IR$_{16}$)^{16}##IF/ID.IR$_{16..31}$
EX	
MEM	
WB	

Figure A.25 This revised pipeline structure is based on the original in Figure A.19. It uses a separate adder, as in Figure A.24, to compute the branch-target address during ID. The operations that are new or have changed are in bold. Because the branch-target address addition happens during ID, it will happen for all instructions; the branch condition (Regs[IF/ID.IR$_{6..10}$] *op* 0) will also be done for all instructions. The selection of the sequential PC or the branch-target PC still occurs during IF, but it now uses values from the ID stage, which correspond to the values set by the previous instruction. This change reduces the branch penalty by 2 cycles: one from evaluating the branch target and condition earlier and one from controlling the PC selection on the same clock rather than on the next clock. Since the value of cond is set to 0, unless the instruction in ID is a taken branch, the processor must decode the instruction before the end of ID. Because the branch is done by the end of ID, the EX, MEM, and WB stages are unused for branches. An additional complication arises for jumps that have a longer offset than branches. We can resolve this by using an additional adder that sums the PC and lower 26 bits of the IR after shifting left by 2 bits.

- Tracing instruction execution
- Breakpoint (programmer-requested interrupt)
- Integer arithmetic overflow
- FP arithmetic anomaly
- Page fault (not in main memory)
- Misaligned memory accesses (if alignment is required)
- Memory protection violation
- Using an undefined or unimplemented instruction
- Hardware malfunctions
- Power failure

When we wish to refer to some particular class of such exceptions, we will use a longer name, such as I/O interrupt, floating-point exception, or page fault. Figure A.26 shows the variety of different names for the common exception events above.

Although we use the term *exception* to cover all of these events, individual events have important characteristics that determine what action is needed in the hardware. The requirements on exceptions can be characterized on five semi-independent axes:

Exception event	IBM 360	VAX	Motorola 680x0	Intel 80x86
I/O device request	Input/output interruption	Device interrupt	Exception (level 0...7 autovector)	Vectored interrupt
Invoking the operating system service from a user program	Supervisor call interruption	Exception (change mode supervisor trap)	Exception (unimplemented instruction)— on Macintosh	Interrupt (INT instruction)
Tracing instruction execution	Not applicable	Exception (trace fault)	Exception (trace)	Interrupt (single-step trap)
Breakpoint	Not applicable	Exception (breakpoint fault)	Exception (illegal instruction or breakpoint)	Interrupt (breakpoint trap)
Integer arithmetic overflow or underflow; FP trap	Program interruption (overflow or underflow exception)	Exception (integer overflow trap or floating underflow fault)	Exception (floating-point coprocessor errors)	Interrupt (overflow trap or math unit exception)
Page fault (not in main memory)	Not applicable (only in 370)	Exception (translation not valid fault)	Exception (memory-management unit errors)	Interrupt (page fault)
Misaligned memory accesses	Program interruption (specification exception)	Not applicable	Exception (address error)	Not applicable
Memory protection violations	Program interruption (protection exception)	Exception (access control violation fault)	Exception (bus error)	Interrupt (protection exception)
Using undefined instructions	Program interruption (operation exception)	Exception (opcode privileged/reserved fault)	Exception (illegal instruction or break-point/unimplemented instruction)	Interrupt (invalid opcode)
Hardware malfunctions	Machine-check interruption	Exception (machine-check abort)	Exception (bus error)	Not applicable
Power failure	Machine-check interruption	Urgent interrupt	Not applicable	Nonmaskable interrupt

Figure A.26 The names of common exceptions vary across four different architectures. Every event on the IBM 360 and 80x86 is called an *interrupt,* while every event on the 680x0 is called an *exception.* VAX divides events into *interrupts* or *exceptions.* Adjectives *device, software,* and *urgent* are used with VAX interrupts, while VAX exceptions are subdivided into *faults, traps,* and *aborts.*

1. *Synchronous versus asynchronous*—If the event occurs at the same place every time the program is executed with the same data and memory allocation, the event is *synchronous.* With the exception of hardware malfunctions, *asynchronous* events are caused by devices external to the CPU and memory. Asynchronous events usually can be handled after the completion of the current instruction, which makes them easier to handle.

2. *User requested versus coerced*—If the user task directly asks for it, it is a *user-requested* event. In some sense, user-requested exceptions are not really

exceptions, since they are predictable. They are treated as exceptions, however, because the same mechanisms that are used to save and restore the state are used for these user-requested events. Because the only function of an instruction that triggers this exception is to cause the exception, user-requested exceptions can always be handled after the instruction has completed. *Coerced* exceptions are caused by some hardware event that is not under the control of the user program. Coerced exceptions are harder to implement because they are not predictable.

3. *User maskable versus user nonmaskable*—If an event can be masked or disabled by a user task, it is *user maskable*. This mask simply controls whether the hardware responds to the exception or not.

4. *Within versus between instructions*—This classification depends on whether the event prevents instruction completion by occurring in the middle of execution—no matter how short—or whether it is recognized *between* instructions. Exceptions that occur *within* instructions are usually synchronous, since the instruction triggers the exception. It's harder to implement exceptions that occur within instructions than those between instructions, since the instruction must be stopped and restarted. Asynchronous exceptions that occur within instructions arise from catastrophic situations (e.g., hardware malfunction) and always cause program termination.

5. *Resume versus terminate*—If the program's execution always stops after the interrupt, it is a *terminating* event. If the program's execution continues after the interrupt, it is a *resuming* event. It is easier to implement exceptions that terminate execution, since the CPU need not be able to restart execution of the same program after handling the exception.

Figure A.27 classifies the examples from Figure A.26 according to these five categories. The difficult task is implementing interrupts occurring within instructions where the instruction must be resumed. Implementing such exceptions requires that another program must be invoked to save the state of the executing program, correct the cause of the exception, and then restore the state of the program before the instruction that caused the exception can be tried again. This process must be effectively invisible to the executing program. If a pipeline provides the ability for the processor to handle the exception, save the state, and restart without affecting the execution of the program, the pipeline or processor is said to be *restartable*. While early supercomputers and microprocessors often lacked this property, almost all processors today support it, at least for the integer pipeline, because it is needed to implement virtual memory (see Chapter 5).

Stopping and Restarting Execution

As in unpipelined implementations, the most difficult exceptions have two properties: (1) they occur within instructions (that is, in the middle of the instruction execution corresponding to EX or MEM pipe stages), and (2) they must be restartable. In our MIPS pipeline, for example, a virtual memory page fault resulting from a data fetch cannot occur until sometime in the MEM stage of the

Exception type	Synchronous vs. asynchronous	User request vs. coerced	User maskable vs. nonmaskable	Within vs. between instructions	Resume vs. terminate
I/O device request	Asynchronous	Coerced	Nonmaskable	Between	Resume
Invoke operating system	Synchronous	User request	Nonmaskable	Between	Resume
Tracing instruction execution	Synchronous	User request	User maskable	Between	Resume
Breakpoint	Synchronous	User request	User maskable	Between	Resume
Integer arithmetic overflow	Synchronous	Coerced	User maskable	Within	Resume
Floating-point arithmetic overflow or underflow	Synchronous	Coerced	User maskable	Within	Resume
Page fault	Synchronous	Coerced	Nonmaskable	Within	Resume
Misaligned memory accesses	Synchronous	Coerced	User maskable	Within	Resume
Memory protection violations	Synchronous	Coerced	Nonmaskable	Within	Resume
Using undefined instructions	Synchronous	Coerced	Nonmaskable	Within	Terminate
Hardware malfunctions	Asynchronous	Coerced	Nonmaskable	Within	Terminate
Power failure	Asynchronous	Coerced	Nonmaskable	Within	Terminate

Figure A.27 Five categories are used to define what actions are needed for the different exception types shown in Figure A.26. Exceptions that must allow resumption are marked as resume, although the software may often choose to terminate the program. Synchronous, coerced exceptions occurring within instructions that can be resumed are the most difficult to implement. We might expect that memory protection access violations would always result in termination; however, modern operating systems use memory protection to detect events such as the first attempt to use a page or the first write to a page. Thus, CPUs should be able to resume after such exceptions.

instruction. By the time that fault is seen, several other instructions will be in execution. A page fault must be restartable and requires the intervention of another process, such as the operating system. Thus, the pipeline must be safely shut down and the state saved so that the instruction can be restarted in the correct state. Restarting is usually implemented by saving the PC of the instruction at which to restart. If the restarted instruction is not a branch, then we will continue to fetch the sequential successors and begin their execution in the normal fashion. If the restarted instruction is a branch, then we will reevaluate the branch condition and begin fetching from either the target or the fall-through. When an exception occurs, the pipeline control can take the following steps to save the pipeline state safely:

1. Force a trap instruction into the pipeline on the next IF.

2. Until the trap is taken, turn off all writes for the faulting instruction and for all instructions that follow in the pipeline; this can be done by placing zeros into the pipeline latches of all instructions in the pipeline, starting with the instruction that generates the exception, but not those that precede that instruction. This prevents any state changes for instructions that will not be completed before the exception is handled.

3. After the exception-handling routine in the operating system receives control, it immediately saves the PC of the faulting instruction. This value will be used to return from the exception later.

When we use delayed branches, as mentioned in the last section, it is no longer possible to re-create the state of the processor with a single PC because the instructions in the pipeline may not be sequentially related. So we need to save and restore as many PCs as the length of the branch delay plus one. This is done in the third step above.

After the exception has been handled, special instructions return the processor from the exception by reloading the PCs and restarting the instruction stream (using the instruction RFE in MIPS). If the pipeline can be stopped so that the instructions just before the faulting instruction are completed and those after it can be restarted from scratch, the pipeline is said to have *precise exceptions*. Ideally, the faulting instruction would not have changed the state, and correctly handling some exceptions requires that the faulting instruction have no effects. For other exceptions, such as floating-point exceptions, the faulting instruction on some processors writes its result before the exception can be handled. In such cases, the hardware must be prepared to retrieve the source operands, even if the destination is identical to one of the source operands. Because floating-point operations may run for many cycles, it is highly likely that some other instruction may have written the source operands (as we will see in the next section, floating-point operations often complete out of order). To overcome this, many recent high-performance CPUs have introduced two modes of operation. One mode has precise exceptions and the other (fast or performance mode) does not. Of course, the precise exception mode is slower, since it allows less overlap among floating-point instructions. In some high-performance CPUs, including Alpha 21064, Power2, and MIPS R8000, the precise mode is often much slower (> 10 times) and thus useful only for debugging of codes.

Supporting precise exceptions is a requirement in many systems, while in others it is "just" valuable because it simplifies the operating system interface. At a minimum, any processor with demand paging or IEEE arithmetic trap handlers must make its exceptions precise, either in the hardware or with some software support. For integer pipelines, the task of creating precise exceptions is easier, and accommodating virtual memory strongly motivates the support of precise exceptions for memory references. In practice, these reasons have led designers and architects to always provide precise exceptions for the integer pipeline. In this section we describe how to implement precise exceptions for the MIPS integer pipeline. We will describe techniques for handling the more complex challenges arising in the FP pipeline in Section A.5.

Exceptions in MIPS

Figure A.28 shows the MIPS pipeline stages and which "problem" exceptions might occur in each stage. With pipelining, multiple exceptions may occur in the

Pipeline stage	Problem exceptions occurring
IF	Page fault on instruction fetch; misaligned memory access; memory protection violation
ID	Undefined or illegal opcode
EX	Arithmetic exception
MEM	Page fault on data fetch; misaligned memory access; memory protection violation
WB	None

Figure A.28 Exceptions that may occur in the MIPS pipeline. Exceptions raised from instruction or data memory access account for six out of eight cases.

same clock cycle because there are multiple instructions in execution. For example, consider this instruction sequence:

LD	IF	ID	EX	MEM	WB	
DADD		IF	ID	EX	MEM	WB

This pair of instructions can cause a data page fault and an arithmetic exception at the same time, since the LD is in the MEM stage while the DADD is in the EX stage. This case can be handled by dealing with only the data page fault and then restarting the execution. The second exception will reoccur (but not the first, if the software is correct), and when the second exception occurs, it can be handled independently.

In reality, the situation is not as straightforward as this simple example. Exceptions may occur out of order; that is, an instruction may cause an exception before an earlier instruction causes one. Consider again the above sequence of instructions, LD followed by DADD. The LD can get a data page fault, seen when the instruction is in MEM, and the DADD can get an instruction page fault, seen when the DADD instruction is in IF. The instruction page fault will actually occur first, even though it is caused by a later instruction!

Since we are implementing precise exceptions, the pipeline is required to handle the exception caused by the LD instruction first. To explain how this works, let's call the instruction in the position of the LD instruction i, and the instruction in the position of the DADD instruction $i + 1$. The pipeline cannot simply handle an exception when it occurs in time, since that will lead to exceptions occurring out of the unpipelined order. Instead, the hardware posts all exceptions caused by a given instruction in a status vector associated with that instruction. The exception status vector is carried along as the instruction goes down the pipeline. Once an exception indication is set in the exception status vector, any control signal that may cause a data value to be written is turned off (this includes both register writes and memory writes). Because a store can cause an exception during MEM, the hardware must be prepared to prevent the store from completing if it raises an exception.

When an instruction enters WB (or is about to leave MEM), the exception status vector is checked. If any exceptions are posted, they are handled in the order in which they would occur in time on an unpipelined processor—the exception corresponding to the earliest instruction (and usually the earliest pipe stage for that instruction) is handled first. This guarantees that all exceptions will be seen on instruction i before any are seen on $i + 1$. Of course, any action taken in earlier pipe stages on behalf of instruction i may be invalid, but since writes to the register file and memory were disabled, no state could have been changed. As we will see in Section A.5, maintaining this precise model for FP operations is much harder.

In the next subsection we describe problems that arise in implementing exceptions in the pipelines of processors with more powerful, longer-running instructions.

Instruction Set Complications

No MIPS instruction has more than one result, and our MIPS pipeline writes that result only at the end of an instruction's execution. When an instruction is guaranteed to complete, it is called *committed*. In the MIPS integer pipeline, all instructions are committed when they reach the end of the MEM stage (or beginning of WB) and no instruction updates the state before that stage. Thus, precise exceptions are straightforward. Some processors have instructions that change the state in the middle of the instruction execution, before the instruction and its predecessors are guaranteed to complete. For example, autoincrement addressing modes in the IA-32 architecture cause the update of registers in the middle of an instruction execution. In such a case, if the instruction is aborted because of an exception, it will leave the processor state altered. Although we know which instruction caused the exception, without additional hardware support the exception will be imprecise because the instruction will be half finished. Restarting the instruction stream after such an imprecise exception is difficult. Alternatively, we could avoid updating the state before the instruction commits, but this may be difficult or costly, since there may be dependences on the updated state: Consider a VAX instruction that autoincrements the same register multiple times. Thus, to maintain a precise exception model, most processors with such instructions have the ability to back out any state changes made before the instruction is committed. If an exception occurs, the processor uses this ability to reset the state of the processor to its value before the interrupted instruction started. In the next section, we will see that a more powerful MIPS floating-point pipeline can introduce similar problems, and Section A.7 introduces techniques that substantially complicate exception handling.

A related source of difficulties arises from instructions that update memory state during execution, such as the string copy operations on the VAX or IBM 360 (see Appendix J). To make it possible to interrupt and restart these instructions, the instructions are defined to use the general-purpose registers as working registers. Thus the state of the partially completed instruction is always in the registers, which are saved on an exception and restored after the exception, allowing the instruction to continue. In the VAX an additional bit of state records when an instruction has started updating the memory state, so that when the pipeline is restarted, the CPU knows whether to restart the instruction from the beginning or from the middle of the instruction. The IA-32 string instructions also use the registers as working storage, so that saving and restoring the registers saves and restores the state of such instructions.

A different set of difficulties arises from odd bits of state that may create additional pipeline hazards or may require extra hardware to save and restore. Condition codes are a good example of this. Many processors set the condition codes implicitly as part of the instruction. This approach has advantages, since condition codes decouple the evaluation of the condition from the actual branch. However, implicitly set condition codes can cause difficulties in scheduling any pipeline delays between setting the condition code and the branch, since most instructions set the condition code and cannot be used in the delay slots between the condition evaluation and the branch.

Additionally, in processors with condition codes, the processor must decide when the branch condition is fixed. This involves finding out when the condition code has been set for the last time before the branch. In most processors with implicitly set condition codes, this is done by delaying the branch condition evaluation until all previous instructions have had a chance to set the condition code.

Of course, architectures with explicitly set condition codes allow the delay between condition test and the branch to be scheduled; however, pipeline control must still track the last instruction that sets the condition code to know when the branch condition is decided. In effect, the condition code must be treated as an operand that requires hazard detection for RAW hazards with branches, just as MIPS must do on the registers.

A final thorny area in pipelining is multicycle operations. Imagine trying to pipeline a sequence of VAX instructions such as this:

```
MOVL     R1,R2                      ;moves between registers
ADDL3    42(R1),56(R1)+,@(R1)       ;adds memory locations
SUBL2    R2,R3                      ;subtracts registers
MOVC3    @(R1)[R2],74(R2),R3        ;moves a character string
```

These instructions differ radically in the number of clock cycles they will require, from as low as one up to hundreds of clock cycles. They also require different numbers of data memory accesses, from zero to possibly hundreds. The data hazards are very complex and occur both between and within instructions. The simple solution of making all instructions execute for the same number of clock cycles is unacceptable because it introduces an enormous number of hazards and bypass conditions and makes an immensely long pipeline. Pipelining the VAX at the instruction level is difficult, but a clever solution was found by the VAX 8800 designers. They pipeline the *microinstruction* execution: a microinstruction is a simple instruction used in sequences to implement a more complex instruction set. Because the microinstructions are simple (they look a lot like MIPS), the pipeline control is much easier. Since 1995, all Intel IA-32 microprocessors have used this strategy of converting the IA-32 instructions into microoperations, and then pipelining the microoperations.

In comparison, load-store processors have simple operations with similar amounts of work and pipeline more easily. If architects realize the relationship between instruction set design and pipelining, they can design architectures for more efficient pipelining. In the next section we will see how the MIPS pipeline deals with long-running instructions, specifically floating-point operations.

For many years the interaction between instruction sets and implementations was believed to be small, and implementation issues were not a major focus in designing instruction sets. In the 1980s it became clear that the difficulty and inefficiency of pipelining could both be increased by instruction set complications. In the 1990s, all companies moved to simpler instructions sets with the goal of reducing the complexity of aggressive implementations.

A.5   Extending the MIPS Pipeline to Handle Multicycle Operations

We now want to explore how our MIPS pipeline can be extended to handle floating-point operations. This section concentrates on the basic approach and the design alternatives, closing with some performance measurements of a MIPS floating-point pipeline.

It is impractical to require that all MIPS floating-point operations complete in 1 clock cycle, or even in 2. Doing so would mean accepting a slow clock, or using enormous amounts of logic in the floating-point units, or both. Instead, the floating-point pipeline will allow for a longer latency for operations. This is easier to grasp if we imagine the floating-point instructions as having the same pipeline as the integer instructions, with two important changes. First, the EX cycle may be repeated as many times as needed to complete the operation—the number of repetitions can vary for different operations. Second, there may be multiple floating-point functional units. A stall will occur if the instruction to be issued will either cause a structural hazard for the functional unit it uses or cause a data hazard.

For this section, let's assume that there are four separate functional units in our MIPS implementation:

1. The main integer unit that handles loads and stores, integer ALU operations, and branches

2. FP and integer multiplier

3. FP adder that handles FP add, subtract, and conversion

4. FP and integer divider

If we also assume that the execution stages of these functional units are not pipelined, then Figure A.29 shows the resulting pipeline structure. Because EX is not pipelined, no other instruction using that functional unit may issue until the previous instruction leaves EX. Moreover, if an instruction cannot proceed to the EX stage, the entire pipeline behind that instruction will be stalled.

In reality, the intermediate results are probably not cycled around the EX unit as Figure A.29 suggests; instead, the EX pipeline stage has some number of clock delays larger than 1. We can generalize the structure of the FP pipeline shown in Figure A.29 to allow pipelining of some stages and multiple ongoing operations. To describe such a pipeline, we must define both the latency of the functional units and also the *initiation interval* or *repeat interval.* We define latency the same way we defined it earlier: the number of intervening cycles between an instruction that produces a result and an instruction that uses the result. The initiation or repeat interval is the number of cycles that must elapse between issuing two operations of a given type. For example, we will use the latencies and initiation intervals shown in Figure A.30.

With this definition of latency, integer ALU operations have a latency of 0, since the results can be used on the next clock cycle, and loads have a latency of 1, since their results can be used after one intervening cycle. Since most operations consume their operands at the beginning of EX, the latency is usually the number of stages after EX that an instruction produces a result—for example, zero stages for ALU operations and one stage for loads. The primary exception is stores, which consume the value being stored 1 cycle later. Hence the latency to a store for the value being stored, but not for the base address register, will be

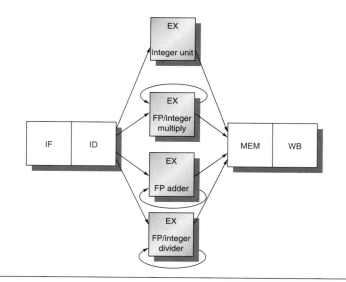

Figure A.29 The MIPS pipeline with three additional unpipelined, floating-point, functional units. Because only one instruction issues on every clock cycle, all instructions go through the standard pipeline for integer operations. The floating-point operations simply loop when they reach the EX stage. After they have finished the EX stage, they proceed to MEM and WB to complete execution.

Functional unit	Latency	Initiation interval
Integer ALU	0	1
Data memory (integer and FP loads)	1	1
FP add	3	1
FP multiply (also integer multiply)	6	1
FP divide (also integer divide)	24	25

Figure A.30 Latencies and initiation intervals for functional units.

1 cycle less. Pipeline latency is essentially equal to 1 cycle less than the depth of the execution pipeline, which is the number of stages from the EX stage to the stage that produces the result. Thus, for the example pipeline just above, the number of stages in an FP add is four, while the number of stages in an FP multiply is seven. To achieve a higher clock rate, designers need to put fewer logic levels in each pipe stage, which makes the number of pipe stages required for more complex operations larger. The penalty for the faster clock rate is thus longer latency for operations.

The example pipeline structure in Figure A.30 allows up to four outstanding FP adds, seven outstanding FP/integer multiplies, and one FP divide. Figure A.31 shows how this pipeline can be drawn by extending Figure A.29. The repeat interval is implemented in Figure A.31 by adding additional pipeline stages, which will be separated by additional pipeline registers. Because the units are independent, we name the stages differently. The pipeline stages that take multiple clock cycles, such as the divide unit, are further subdivided to show the latency of those stages. Because they are not complete stages, only one operation may be active. The pipeline structure can also be shown using the familiar diagrams from earlier in the appendix, as Figure A.32 shows for a set of independent FP operations and FP loads and stores. Naturally, the longer latency of the FP operations increases the frequency of RAW hazards and resultant stalls, as we will see later in this section.

The structure of the pipeline in Figure A.31 requires the introduction of the additional pipeline registers (e.g., A1/A2, A2/A3, A3/A4) and the modification of the connections to those registers. The ID/EX register must be expanded to connect ID to EX, DIV, M1, and A1; we can refer to the portion of the register associated with one of the next stages with the notation ID/EX, ID/DIV, ID/M1, or ID/A1. The pipeline register between ID and all the other stages may be thought of as logically separate registers and may, in fact, be implemented as separate registers. Because only one operation can be in a pipe stage at a time, the control information can be associated with the register at the head of the stage.

Hazards and Forwarding in Longer Latency Pipelines

There are a number of different aspects to the hazard detection and forwarding for a pipeline like that in Figure A.31.

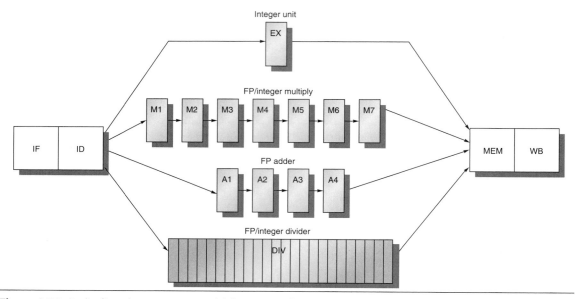

Figure A.31 A pipeline that supports multiple outstanding FP operations. The FP multiplier and adder are fully pipelined and have a depth of seven and four stages, respectively. The FP divider is not pipelined, but requires 24 clock cycles to complete. The latency in instructions between the issue of an FP operation and the use of the result of that operation without incurring a RAW stall is determined by the number of cycles spent in the execution stages. For example, the fourth instruction after an FP add can use the result of the FP add. For integer ALU operations, the depth of the execution pipeline is always one and the next instruction can use the results.

MUL.D	IF	ID	*M1*	M2	M3	M4	M5	M6	**M7**	MEM	WB
ADD.D		IF	ID	*A1*	A2	A3	**A4**	**MEM**	WB		
L.D			IF	ID	*EX*	**MEM**	WB				
S.D				IF	ID	*EX*	*MEM*	WB			

Figure A.32 The pipeline timing of a set of independent FP operations. The stages in italics show where data are needed, while the stages in bold show where a result is available. The ".D" extension on the instruction mnemonic indicates double-precision (64-bit) floating-point operations. FP loads and stores use a 64-bit path to memory so that the pipelining timing is just like an integer load or store.

1. Because the divide unit is not fully pipelined, structural hazards can occur. These will need to be detected and issuing instructions will need to be stalled.

2. Because the instructions have varying running times, the number of register writes required in a cycle can be larger than 1.

3. WAW hazards are possible, since instructions no longer reach WB in order. Note that WAR hazards are not possible, since the register reads always occur in ID.

4. Instructions can complete in a different order than they were issued, causing problems with exceptions; we deal with this in the next subsection.

5. Because of longer latency of operations, stalls for RAW hazards will be more frequent.

The increase in stalls arising from longer operation latencies is fundamentally the same as that for the integer pipeline. Before describing the new problems that arise in this FP pipeline and looking at solutions, let's examine the potential impact of RAW hazards. Figure A.33 shows a typical FP code sequence and the resultant stalls. At the end of this section, we'll examine the performance of this FP pipeline for our SPEC subset.

Now look at the problems arising from writes, described as (2) and (3) in the earlier list. If we assume the FP register file has one write port, sequences of FP operations, as well as an FP load together with FP operations, can cause conflicts for the register write port. Consider the pipeline sequence shown in Figure A.34. In

	Clock cycle number																
Instruction	1	2	3	4	5	6	7	8	9	10	11	12	13	14	15	16	17
L.D F4,0(R2)	IF	ID	EX	MEM	WB												
MUL.D F0,F4,F6		IF	ID	stall	M1	M2	M3	M4	M5	M6	M7	MEM	WB				
ADD.D F2,F0,F8			IF	stall	ID	stall	stall	stall	stall	stall	stall	A1	A2	A3	A4	MEM	WB
S.D F2,0(R2)				IF	stall	stall	stall	stall	stall	stall	stall	ID	EX	stall	stall	stall	MEM

Figure A.33 A typical FP code sequence showing the stalls arising from RAW hazards. The longer pipeline substantially raises the frequency of stalls versus the shallower integer pipeline. Each instruction in this sequence is dependent on the previous and proceeds as soon as data are available, which assumes the pipeline has full bypassing and forwarding. The S.D must be stalled an extra cycle so that its MEM does not conflict with the ADD.D. Extra hardware could easily handle this case.

	Clock cycle number										
Instruction	1	2	3	4	5	6	7	8	9	10	11
MUL.D F0,F4,F6	IF	ID	M1	M2	M3	M4	M5	M6	M7	MEM	WB
...		IF	ID	EX	MEM	WB					
...			IF	ID	EX	MEM	WB				
ADD.D F2,F4,F6				IF	ID	A1	A2	A3	A4	MEM	WB
...					IF	ID	EX	MEM	WB		
...						IF	ID	EX	MEM	WB	
L.D F2,0(R2)							IF	ID	EX	MEM	WB

Figure A.34 Three instructions want to perform a write back to the FP register file simultaneously, as shown in clock cycle 11. This is *not* the worst case, since an earlier divide in the FP unit could also finish on the same clock. Note that although the MUL.D, ADD.D, and L.D all are in the MEM stage in clock cycle 10, only the L.D actually uses the memory, so no structural hazard exists for MEM.

clock cycle 11, all three instructions will reach WB and want to write the register file. With only a single register file write port, the processor must serialize the instruction completion. This single register port represents a structural hazard. We could increase the number of write ports to solve this, but that solution may be unattractive since the additional write ports would be used only rarely. This is because the maximum steady-state number of write ports needed is 1. Instead, we choose to detect and enforce access to the write port as a structural hazard.

There are two different ways to implement this interlock. The first is to track the use of the write port in the ID stage and to stall an instruction before it issues, just as we would for any other structural hazard. Tracking the use of the write port can be done with a shift register that indicates when already-issued instructions will use the register file. If the instruction in ID needs to use the register file at the same time as an instruction already issued, the instruction in ID is stalled for a cycle. On each clock the reservation register is shifted 1 bit. This implementation has an advantage: It maintains the property that all interlock detection and stall insertion occurs in the ID stage. The cost is the addition of the shift register and write conflict logic. We will assume this scheme throughout this section.

An alternative scheme is to stall a conflicting instruction when it tries to enter either the MEM or WB stage. If we wait to stall the conflicting instructions until they want to enter the MEM or WB stage, we can choose to stall either instruction. A simple, though sometimes suboptimal, heuristic is to give priority to the unit with the longest latency, since that is the one most likely to have caused another instruction to be stalled for a RAW hazard. The advantage of this scheme is that it does not require us to detect the conflict until the entrance of the MEM or WB stage, where it is easy to see. The disadvantage is that it complicates pipeline control, as stalls can now arise from two places. Notice that stalling before entering MEM will cause the EX, A4, or M7 stage to be occupied, possibly forcing the stall to trickle back in the pipeline. Likewise, stalling before WB would cause MEM to back up.

Our other problem is the possibility of WAW hazards. To see that these exist, consider the example in Figure A.34. If the L.D instruction were issued one cycle earlier and had a destination of F2, then it would create a WAW hazard, because it would write F2 one cycle earlier than the ADD.D. Note that this hazard only occurs when the result of the ADD.D is overwritten *without* any instruction ever using it! If there were a use of F2 between the ADD.D and the L.D, the pipeline would need to be stalled for a RAW hazard, and the L.D would not issue until the ADD.D was completed. We could argue that, for our pipeline, WAW hazards only occur when a useless instruction is executed, but we must still detect them and make sure that the result of the L.D appears in F2 when we are done. (As we will see in Section A.8, such sequences sometimes *do* occur in reasonable code.)

There are two possible ways to handle this WAW hazard. The first approach is to delay the issue of the load instruction until the ADD.D enters MEM. The second approach is to stamp out the result of the ADD.D by detecting the hazard and changing the control so that the ADD.D does not write its result. Then the L.D can issue right away. Because this hazard is rare, either scheme will work fine—you can pick whatever is simpler to implement. In either case, the hazard can be detected during ID when the L.D is issuing. Then stalling the L.D or making the ADD.D a no-op is easy. The difficult situation is to detect that the L.D might finish before the ADD.D, because that requires knowing the length of the pipeline and the current position of the ADD.D. Luckily, this code sequence (two writes with no intervening read) will be very rare, so we can use a simple solution: If an instruction in ID wants to write the same register as an instruction already issued, do not issue the instruction to EX. In Section A.7, we will see how additional hardware can eliminate stalls for such hazards. First, let's put together the pieces for implementing the hazard and issue logic in our FP pipeline.

In detecting the possible hazards, we must consider hazards among FP instructions, as well as hazards between an FP instruction and an integer instruction. Except for FP loads-stores and FP-integer register moves, the FP and integer registers are distinct. All integer instructions operate on the integer registers, while the floating-point operations operate only on their own registers. Thus, we need only consider FP loads-stores and FP register moves in detecting hazards between FP and integer instructions. This simplification of pipeline control is an additional advantage of having separate register files for integer and floating-point data. (The main advantages are a doubling of the number of registers, without making either set larger, and an increase in bandwidth without adding more ports to either set. The main disadvantage, beyond the need for an extra register file, is the small cost of occasional moves needed between the two register sets.) Assuming that the pipeline does all hazard detection in ID, there are three checks that must be performed before an instruction can issue:

1. *Check for structural hazards*—Wait until the required functional unit is not busy (this is only needed for divides in this pipeline) and make sure the register write port is available when it will be needed.

2. *Check for a RAW data hazard*—Wait until the source registers are not listed as pending destinations in a pipeline register that will not be available when this instruction needs the result. A number of checks must be made here, depending on both the source instruction, which determines when the result will be available, and the destination instruction, which determines when the value is needed. For example, if the instruction in ID is an FP operation with source register F2, then F2 cannot be listed as a destination in ID/A1, A1/A2, or A2/A3, which correspond to FP add instructions that will not be finished when the instruction in ID needs a result. (ID/A1 is the portion of the output register of ID that is sent to A1.) Divide is somewhat more tricky, if we want to allow the last few cycles of a divide to be overlapped, since we need to handle the case when a divide is close to finishing as special. In practice, designers might ignore this optimization in favor of a simpler issue test.

3. *Check for a WAW data hazard*—Determine if any instruction in A1, . . . , A4, D, M1, . . . , M7 has the same register destination as this instruction. If so, stall the issue of the instruction in ID.

Although the hazard detection is more complex with the multicycle FP operations, the concepts are the same as for the MIPS integer pipeline. The same is true for the forwarding logic. The forwarding can be implemented by checking if the destination register in any of EX/MEM, A4/MEM, M7/MEM, D/MEM, or MEM/WB registers is one of the source registers of a floating-point instruction. If so, the appropriate input multiplexer will have to be enabled so as to choose the forwarded data. In the exercises, you will have the opportunity to specify the logic for the RAW and WAW hazard detection as well as for forwarding.

Multicycle FP operations also introduce problems for our exception mechanisms, which we deal with next.

Maintaining Precise Exceptions

Another problem caused by these long-running instructions can be illustrated with the following sequence of code:

```
DIV.D    F0,F2,F4
ADD.D    F10,F10,F8
SUB.D    F12,F12,F14
```

This code sequence looks straightforward; there are no dependences. A problem arises, however, because an instruction issued early may complete after an instruction issued later. In this example, we can expect ADD.D and SUB.D to complete *before* the DIV.D completes. This is called *out-of-order completion* and is common in pipelines with long-running operations (see Section A.7). Because hazard detection will prevent any dependence among instructions from being violated, why is out-of-order completion a problem? Suppose that the SUB.D causes a floating-point arithmetic exception at a point where the ADD.D has completed but the DIV.D has not. The result will be an imprecise exception, something we are trying to avoid. It may appear that this could be handled by letting the floating-point pipeline drain, as we do for the integer pipeline. But the exception may be in a position where this is not possible. For example, if the DIV.D decided to take a floating-point-arithmetic exception after the add completed, we could not have a precise exception at the hardware level. In fact, because the ADD.D destroys one of its operands, we could not restore the state to what it was before the DIV.D, even with software help.

This problem arises because instructions are completing in a different order than they were issued. There are four possible approaches to dealing with out-of-order completion. The first is to ignore the problem and settle for imprecise exceptions. This approach was used in the 1960s and early 1970s. It is still used in some supercomputers, where certain classes of exceptions are not allowed or are handled by the hardware without stopping the pipeline. It is difficult to use this approach in most processors built today because of features such as virtual memory and the IEEE floating-point standard, which essentially require precise exceptions through a combination of hardware and software. As mentioned earlier, some recent processors have solved this problem by introducing two modes of execution: a fast, but possibly imprecise mode and a slower, precise mode. The slower precise mode is implemented either with a mode switch or by insertion of explicit instructions that test for FP exceptions. In either case the amount of overlap and reordering permitted in the FP pipeline is significantly restricted so that effectively only one FP instruction is active at a time. This solution is used in the DEC Alpha 21064 and 21164, in the IBM Power1 and Power2, and in the MIPS R8000.

A second approach is to buffer the results of an operation until all the operations that were issued earlier are complete. Some CPUs actually use this solution, but it becomes expensive when the difference in running times among operations is large, since the number of results to buffer can become large. Furthermore, results from the queue must be bypassed to continue issuing instructions while waiting for the longer instruction. This requires a large number of comparators and a very large multiplexer.

There are two viable variations on this basic approach. The first is a *history file,* used in the CYBER 180/990. The history file keeps track of the original values of registers. When an exception occurs and the state must be rolled back earlier than some instruction that completed out of order, the original value of the register can be restored from the history file. A similar technique is used for autoincrement and autodecrement addressing on processors like VAXes. Another approach, the *future file,* proposed by Smith and Pleszkun [1988], keeps the newer value of a register; when all earlier instructions have completed, the main register file is updated from the future file. On an exception, the main register file has the precise values for the interrupted state. In Chapter 2, we will see extensions of this idea, which are used in processors such as the PowerPC 620 and the MIPS R10000 to allow overlap and reordering while preserving precise exceptions.

A third technique in use is to allow the exceptions to become somewhat imprecise, but to keep enough information so that the trap-handling routines can create a precise sequence for the exception. This means knowing what operations were in the pipeline and their PCs. Then, after handling the exception, the software finishes any instructions that precede the latest instruction completed, and the sequence can restart. Consider the following worst-case code sequence:

$Instruction_1$—A long-running instruction that eventually interrupts execution.

$Instruction_2$, . . . , $Instruction_{n-1}$—A series of instructions that are not completed.

$Instruction_n$—An instruction that is finished.

Given the PCs of all the instructions in the pipeline and the exception return PC, the software can find the state of $instruction_1$ and $instruction_n$. Because $instruction_n$ has completed, we will want to restart execution at $instruction_{n+1}$. After handling the exception, the software must simulate the execution of $instruction_1$, . . . , $instruction_{n-1}$. Then we can return from the exception and restart at $instruction_{n+1}$. The complexity of executing these instructions properly by the handler is the major difficulty of this scheme.

There is an important simplification for simple MIPS-like pipelines: If instruction$_2$, . . . , instruction$_n$ are all integer instructions, then we know that if instruction$_n$ has completed, all of instruction$_2$, . . . , instruction$_{n-1}$ have also completed. Thus, only floating-point operations need to be handled. To make this scheme tractable, the number of floating-point instructions that can be overlapped in execution can be limited. For example, if we only overlap two instructions, then only the interrupting instruction need be completed by software. This restriction may reduce the potential throughput if the FP pipelines are deep or if there are a significant number of FP functional units. This approach is used in the SPARC architecture to allow overlap of floating-point and integer operations.

The final technique is a hybrid scheme that allows the instruction issue to continue only if it is certain that all the instructions before the issuing instruction will complete without causing an exception. This guarantees that when an exception occurs, no instructions after the interrupting one will be completed and all of the instructions before the interrupting one can be completed. This sometimes means stalling the CPU to maintain precise exceptions. To make this scheme work, the floating-point functional units must determine if an exception is possible early in the EX stage (in the first 3 clock cycles in the MIPS pipeline), so as to prevent further instructions from completing. This scheme is used in the MIPS R2000/3000, the R4000, and the Intel Pentium. It is discussed further in Appendix I.

Performance of a MIPS FP Pipeline

The MIPS FP pipeline of Figure A.31 on page A-50 can generate both structural stalls for the divide unit and stalls for RAW hazards (it also can have WAW hazards, but this rarely occurs in practice). Figure A.35 shows the number of stall cycles for each type of floating-point operation on a per-instance basis (i.e., the first bar for each FP benchmark shows the number of FP result stalls for each FP add, subtract, or convert). As we might expect, the stall cycles per operation track the latency of the FP operations, varying from 46% to 59% of the latency of the functional unit.

Figure A.36 gives the complete breakdown of integer and floating-point stalls for five SPECfp benchmarks. There are four classes of stalls shown: FP result stalls, FP compare stalls, load and branch delays, and floating-point structural delays. The compiler tries to schedule both load and FP delays before it schedules branch delays. The total number of stalls per instruction varies from 0.65 to 1.21.

A.6   Putting It All Together: The MIPS R4000 Pipeline

In this section we look at the pipeline structure and performance of the MIPS R4000 processor family, which includes the 4400. The R4000 implements MIPS64 but uses a deeper pipeline than that of our five-stage design both for integer and FP programs. This deeper pipeline allows it to achieve higher clock rates by decomposing the five-stage integer pipeline into eight stages. Because

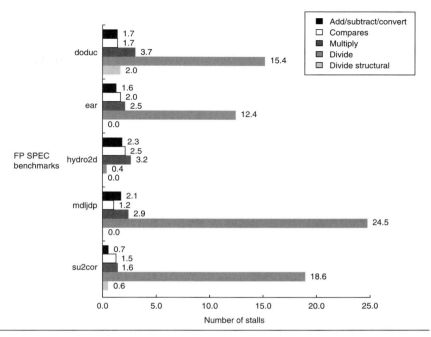

Figure A.35 Stalls per FP operation for each major type of FP operation for the SPEC89 FP benchmarks. Except for the divide structural hazards, these data do not depend on the frequency of an operation, only on its latency and the number of cycles before the result is used. The number of stalls from RAW hazards roughly tracks the latency of the FP unit. For example, the average number of stalls per FP add, subtract, or convert is 1.7 cycles, or 56% of the latency (3 cycles). Likewise, the average number of stalls for multiplies and divides are 2.8 and 14.2, respectively, or 46% and 59% of the corresponding latency. Structural hazards for divides are rare, since the divide frequency is low.

cache access is particularly time critical, the extra pipeline stages come from decomposing the memory access. This type of deeper pipelining is sometimes called *superpipelining*.

Figure A.37 shows the eight-stage pipeline structure using an abstracted version of the data path. Figure A.38 shows the overlap of successive instructions in the pipeline. Notice that although the instruction and data memory occupy multiple cycles, they are fully pipelined, so that a new instruction can start on every clock. In fact, the pipeline uses the data before the cache hit detection is complete; Chapter 5 discusses how this can be done in more detail.

The function of each stage is as follows:

■ IF—First half of instruction fetch; PC selection actually happens here, together with initiation of instruction cache access.

■ IS—Second half of instruction fetch, complete instruction cache access.

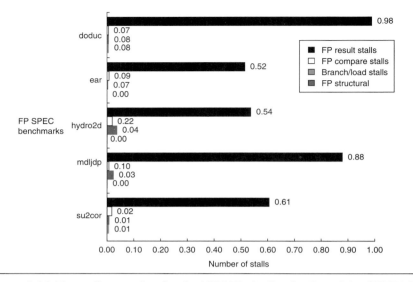

Figure A.36 The stalls occurring for the MIPS FP pipeline for five of the SPEC89 FP benchmarks. The total number of stalls per instruction ranges from 0.65 for su2cor to 1.21 for doduc, with an average of 0.87. FP result stalls dominate in all cases, with an average of 0.71 stalls per instruction, or 82% of the stalled cycles. Compares generate an average of 0.1 stalls per instruction and are the second largest source. The divide structural hazard is only significant for doduc.

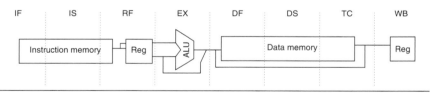

Figure A.37 The eight-stage pipeline structure of the R4000 uses pipelined instruction and data caches. The pipe stages are labeled and their detailed function is described in the text. The vertical dashed lines represent the stage boundaries as well as the location of pipeline latches. The instruction is actually available at the end of IS, but the tag check is done in RF, while the registers are fetched. Thus, we show the instruction memory as operating through RF. The TC stage is needed for data memory access, since we cannot write the data into the register until we know whether the cache access was a hit or not.

■ RF—Instruction decode and register fetch, hazard checking, and also instruction cache hit detection.

■ EX—Execution, which includes effective address calculation, ALU operation, and branch-target computation and condition evaluation.

■ DF—Data fetch, first half of data cache access.

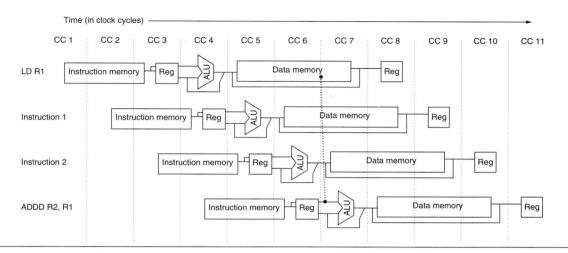

Figure A.38 The structure of the R4000 integer pipeline leads to a 2-cycle load delay. A 2-cycle delay is possible because the data value is available at the end of DS and can be bypassed. If the tag check in TC indicates a miss, the pipeline is backed up a cycle, when the correct data are available.

					Clock number				
Instruction number	**1**	**2**	**3**	**4**	**5**	**6**	**7**	**8**	**9**
LD R1,...	IF	IS	RF	EX	DF	DS	TC	WB	
DADD R2,R1,...		IF	IS	RF	stall	stall	EX	DF	DS
DSUB R3,R1,...			IF	IS	stall	stall	RF	EX	DF
OR R4,R1,...				IF	stall	stall	IS	RF	EX

Figure A.39 A load instruction followed by an immediate use results in a 2-cycle stall. Normal forwarding paths can be used after two cycles, so the DADD and DSUB get the value by forwarding after the stall. The OR instruction gets the value from the register file. Since the two instructions after the load could be independent and hence not stall, the bypass can be to instructions that are 3 or 4 cycles after the load.

- DS—Second half of data fetch, completion of data cache access.
- TC—Tag check, determine whether the data cache access hit.
- WB—Write back for loads and register-register operations.

In addition to substantially increasing the amount of forwarding required, this longer-latency pipeline increases both the load and branch delays. Figure A.38 shows that load delays are 2 cycles, since the data value is available at the end of DS. Figure A.39 shows the shorthand pipeline schedule when a use immediately follows a load. It shows that forwarding is required for the result of a load instruction to a destination that is 3 or 4 cycles later.

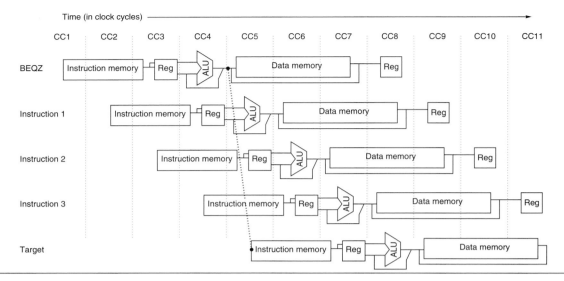

Figure A.40 **The basic branch delay is 3 cycles, since the condition evaluation is performed during EX.**

Figure A.40 shows that the basic branch delay is 3 cycles, since the branch condition is computed during EX. The MIPS architecture has a single-cycle delayed branch. The R4000 uses a predicted-not-taken strategy for the remaining 2 cycles of the branch delay. As Figure A.41 shows untaken branches are simply 1-cycle delayed branches, while taken branches have a 1-cycle delay slot followed by 2 idle cycles. The instruction set provides a branch-likely instruction, which we described earlier and which helps in filling the branch delay slot. Pipeline interlocks enforce both the 2-cycle branch stall penalty on a taken branch and any data hazard stall that arises from use of a load result.

In addition to the increase in stalls for loads and branches, the deeper pipeline increases the number of levels of forwarding for ALU operations. In our MIPS five-stage pipeline, forwarding between two register-register ALU instructions could happen from the ALU/MEM or the MEM/WB registers. In the R4000 pipeline, there are four possible sources for an ALU bypass: EX/DF, DF/DS, DS/TC, and TC/WB.

The Floating-Point Pipeline

The R4000 floating-point unit consists of three functional units: a floating-point divider, a floating-point multiplier, and a floating-point adder. The adder logic is used on the final step of a multiply or divide. Double-precision FP operations can take from 2 cycles (for a negate) up to 112 cycles for a square root. In addition, the various units have different initiation rates. The floating-point functional unit can be thought of as having eight different stages, listed in Figure A.42; these stages are combined in different orders to execute various FP operations.

Instruction number	Clock number								
	1	2	3	4	5	6	7	8	9
Branch instruction	IF	IS	RF	EX	DF	DS	TC	WB	
Delay slot		IF	IS	RF	EX	DF	DS	TC	WB
Stall			stall	stall	stall	stall	stall	stall	stall
Stall			stall	stall	stall	stall	stall	stall	stall
Branch target					IF	IS	RF	EX	DF

Instruction number	Clock number								
	1	2	3	4	5	6	7	8	9
Branch instruction	IF	IS	RF	EX	DF	DS	TC	WB	
Delay slot		IF	IS	RF	EX	DF	DS	TC	WB
Branch instruction + 2			IF	IS	RF	EX	DF	DS	TC
Branch instruction + 3				IF	IS	RF	EX	DF	DS

Figure A.41 A taken branch, shown in the top portion of the figure, has a 1-cycle delay slot followed by a 2-cycle stall, while an untaken branch, shown in the bottom portion, has simply a 1-cycle delay slot. The branch instruction can be an ordinary delayed branch or a branch-likely, which cancels the effect of the instruction in the delay slot if the branch is untaken.

Stage	Functional unit	Description
A	FP adder	Mantissa ADD stage
D	FP divider	Divide pipeline stage
E	FP multiplier	Exception test stage
M	FP multiplier	First stage of multiplier
N	FP multiplier	Second stage of multiplier
R	FP adder	Rounding stage
S	FP adder	Operand shift stage
U		Unpack FP numbers

Figure A.42 The eight stages used in the R4000 floating-point pipelines.

There is a single copy of each of these stages, and various instructions may use a stage zero or more times and in different orders. Figure A.43 shows the latency, initiation rate, and pipeline stages used by the most common double-precision FP operations.

From the information in Figure A.43, we can determine whether a sequence of different, independent FP operations can issue without stalling. If the timing of the sequence is such that a conflict occurs for a shared pipeline stage, then a stall

FP instruction	Latency	Initiation interval	Pipe stages
Add, subtract	4	3	U, S + A, A + R, R + S
Multiply	8	4	U, E + M, M, M, M, N, N + A, R
Divide	36	35	U, A, R, D²⁷, D + A, D + R, D + A, D + R, A, R
Square root	112	111	U, E, (A+R)¹⁰⁸, A, R
Negate	2	1	U, S
Absolute value	2	1	U, S
FP compare	3	2	U, A, R

Figure A.43 The latencies and initiation intervals for the FP operations both depend on the FP unit stages that a given operation must use. The latency values assume that the destination instruction is an FP operation; the latencies are 1 cycle less when the destination is a store. The pipe stages are shown in the order in which they are used for any operation. The notation S + A indicates a clock cycle in which both the S and A stages are used. The notation D^{28} indicates that the D stage is used 28 times in a row.

							Clock cycle						
Operation	Issue/stall	0	1	2	3	4	5	6	7	8	9	10	11 12
Multiply	Issue	U	E + M	M	M	M	N	N + A	R				
Add	Issue		U	S + A	A + R	R + S							
	Issue			U	S + A	A + R	R + S						
	Issue				U	S + A	A + R	R + S					
	Stall					U	S + A	**A + R**	**R + S**				
	Stall						U	**S + A**	**A + R**	R + S			
	Issue							U	S + A	A + R	R + S		
	Issue								U	S + A	A + R	R + S	

Figure A.44 An FP multiply issued at clock 0 is followed by a single FP add issued between clocks 1 and 7. The second column indicates whether an instruction of the specified type stalls when it is issued *n* cycles later, where *n* is the clock cycle number in which the U stage of the second instruction occurs. The stage or stages that cause a stall are highlighted. Note that this table deals with only the interaction between the multiply and *one* add issued between clocks 1 and 7. In this case, the add will stall if it is issued 4 or 5 cycles after the multiply; otherwise, it issues without stalling. Notice that the add will be stalled for 2 cycles if it issues in cycle 4 since on the next clock cycle it will still conflict with the multiply; if, however, the add issues in cycle 5, it will stall for only 1 clock cycle, since that will eliminate the conflicts.

will be needed. Figures A.44, A.45, A.46, and A.47 show four common possible two-instruction sequences: a multiply followed by an add, an add followed by a multiply, a divide followed by an add, and an add followed by a divide. The figures show all the interesting starting positions for the second instruction and whether that second instruction will issue or stall for each position. Of course, there could be three instructions active, in which case the possibilities for stalls are much higher and the figures more complex.

Operation	Issue/stall	Clock cycle												
		0	1	2	3	4	5	6	7	8	9	10	11	12
Add	Issue	U	S + A	A + R	R + S									
Multiply	Issue		U	E + M	M	M	M	N	N + A	R				
	Issue			U	M	M	M	M	N	N + A	R			

Figure A.45 A multiply issuing after an add can always proceed without stalling, since the shorter instruction clears the shared pipeline stages before the longer instruction reaches them.

Operation	Issue/stall	Clock cycle										
		25	26	27	28	29	30	31	32	33	34	35	36
Divide	Issued in cycle 0...	D	D	D	D	D	D + A	D + R	D + A	D + R	A	R	
Add	Issue		U	S + A	A + R	R + S							
	Issue			U	S + A	A + R	R + S						
	Stall				U	S + A	A + R	R + S					
	Stall					U	S + A	A + R	R + S				
	Stall						U	S + A	A + R	R + S			
	Stall							U	S + A	A + R	R + S		
	Stall								U	S + A	A + R	R + S	
	Stall									U	S + A	A + R	R + S
	Issue										U	S + A	A + R
	Issue											U	S + A
	Issue												U

Figure A.46 An FP divide can cause a stall for an add that starts near the end of the divide. The divide starts at cycle 0 and completes at cycle 35; the last 10 cycles of the divide are shown. Since the divide makes heavy use of the rounding hardware needed by the add, it stalls an add that starts in any of cycles 28–33. Notice the add starting in cycle 28 will be stalled until cycle 36. If the add started right after the divide, it would not conflict, since the add could complete before the divide needed the shared stages, just as we saw in Figure A.45 for a multiply and add. As in the earlier figure, this example assumes *exactly* one add that reaches the U stage between clock cycles 26 and 35.

Performance of the R4000 Pipeline

In this section we examine the stalls that occur for the SPEC92 benchmarks when running on the R4000 pipeline structure. There are four major causes of pipeline stalls or losses:

1. *Load stalls*—Delays arising from the use of a load result 1 or 2 cycles after the load

Operation	Issue/stall	Clock cycle												
		0	1	2	3	4	5	6	7	8	9	10	11	12
Add	Issue	U	S + A	A + R	R + S									
Divide	Stall		U	A	R	D	D	D	D	D	D	D	D	D
	Issue			U	A	R	D	D	D	D	D	D	D	D
	Issue				U	A	R	D	D	D	D	D	D	D

Figure A.47 A double-precision add is followed by a double-precision divide. If the divide starts 1 cycle after the add, the divide stalls, but after that there is no conflict.

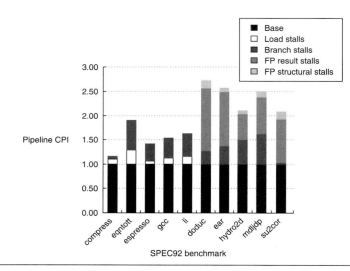

Figure A.48 The pipeline CPI for 10 of the SPEC92 benchmarks, assuming a perfect cache. The pipeline CPI varies from 1.2 to 2.8. The leftmost five programs are integer programs, and branch delays are the major CPI contributor for these. The rightmost five programs are FP, and FP result stalls are the major contributor for these. Figure A.49 shows the numbers used to construct this plot.

2. *Branch stalls*—2-cycle stall on every taken branch plus unfilled or canceled branch delay slots

3. *FP result stalls*—Stalls because of RAW hazards for an FP operand

4. *FP structural stalls*—Delays because of issue restrictions arising from conflicts for functional units in the FP pipeline

Figure A.48 shows the pipeline CPI breakdown for the R4000 pipeline for the 10 SPEC92 benchmarks. Figure A.49 shows the same data but in tabular form.

From the data in Figures A.48 and A.49, we can see the penalty of the deeper pipelining. The R4000's pipeline has much longer branch delays than the classic

Benchmark	Pipeline CPI	Load stalls	Branch stalls	FP result stalls	FP structural stalls
compress	1.20	0.14	0.06	0.00	0.00
eqntott	1.88	0.27	0.61	0.00	0.00
espresso	1.42	0.07	0.35	0.00	0.00
gcc	1.56	0.13	0.43	0.00	0.00
li	1.64	0.18	0.46	0.00	0.00
Integer average	1.54	0.16	0.38	0.00	0.00
doduc	2.84	0.01	0.22	1.39	0.22
mdljdp2	2.66	0.01	0.31	1.20	0.15
ear	2.17	0.00	0.46	0.59	0.12
hydro2d	2.53	0.00	0.62	0.75	0.17
su2cor	2.18	0.02	0.07	0.84	0.26
FP average	2.48	0.01	0.33	0.95	0.18
Overall average	2.00	0.10	0.36	0.46	0.09

Figure A.49 The total pipeline CPI and the contributions of the four major sources of stalls are shown. The major contributors are FP result stalls (both for branches and for FP inputs) and branch stalls, with loads and FP structural stalls adding less.

five-stage pipeline. The longer branch delay substantially increases the cycles spent on branches, especially for the integer programs with a higher branch frequency. An interesting effect for the FP programs is that the latency of the FP functional units leads to more result stalls than the structural hazards, which arise both from the initiation interval limitations and from conflicts for functional units from different FP instructions. Thus, reducing the latency of FP operations should be the first target, rather than more pipelining or replication of the functional units. Of course, reducing the latency would probably increase the structural stalls, since many potential structural stalls are hidden behind data hazards.

A.7 Crosscutting Issues

RISC Instruction Sets and Efficiency of Pipelining

We have already discussed the advantages of instruction set simplicity in building pipelines. Simple instruction sets offer another advantage: They make it easier to schedule code to achieve efficiency of execution in a pipeline. To see this, consider a simple example: Suppose we need to add two values in memory and store the result back to memory. In some sophisticated instruction sets this will take only a single instruction; in others it will take two or three. A typical RISC architecture would require four instructions (two loads, an add, and a store). These instructions cannot be scheduled sequentially in most pipelines without intervening stalls.

With a RISC instruction set, the individual operations are separate instructions and may be individually scheduled either by the compiler (using the techniques we discussed earlier and more powerful techniques discussed in Chapter 2) or using dynamic hardware scheduling techniques (which we discuss next and in further detail in Chapter 2). These efficiency advantages, coupled with the greater ease of implementation, appear to be so significant that almost all recent pipelined implementations of complex instruction sets actually translate their complex instructions into simple RISC-like operations, and then schedule and pipeline those operations. Chapter 2 shows that both the Pentium III and Pentium 4 use this approach.

Dynamically Scheduled Pipelines

Simple pipelines fetch an instruction and issue it, unless there is a data dependence between an instruction already in the pipeline and the fetched instruction that cannot be hidden with bypassing or forwarding. Forwarding logic reduces the effective pipeline latency so that certain dependences do not result in hazards. If there is an unavoidable hazard, then the hazard detection hardware stalls the pipeline (starting with the instruction that uses the result). No new instructions are fetched or issued until the dependence is cleared. To overcome these performance losses, the compiler can attempt to schedule instructions to avoid the hazard; this approach is called *compiler* or *static scheduling*.

Several early processors used another approach, called *dynamic scheduling,* whereby the hardware rearranges the instruction execution to reduce the stalls. This section offers a simpler introduction to dynamic scheduling by explaining the scoreboarding technique of the CDC 6600. Some readers will find it easier to read this material before plunging into the more complicated Tomasulo scheme, which is covered in Chapter 2.

All the techniques discussed in this appendix so far use in-order instruction issue, which means that if an instruction is stalled in the pipeline, no later instructions can proceed. With in-order issue, if two instructions have a hazard between them, the pipeline will stall, even if there are later instructions that are independent and would not stall.

In the MIPS pipeline developed earlier, both structural and data hazards were checked during instruction decode (ID): When an instruction could execute properly, it was issued from ID. To allow an instruction to begin execution as soon as its operands are available, even if a predecessor is stalled, we must separate the issue process into two parts: checking the structural hazards and waiting for the absence of a data hazard. We decode and issue instructions in order. However, we want the instructions to begin execution as soon as their data operands are available. Thus, the pipeline will do *out-of-order execution,* which implies *out-of-order completion.* To implement out-of-order execution, we must split the ID pipe stage into two stages:

1. *Issue*—Decode instructions, check for structural hazards.

2. *Read operands*—Wait until no data hazards, then read operands.

The IF stage proceeds the issue stage, and the EX stage follows the read operands stage, just as in the MIPS pipeline. As in the MIPS floating-point pipeline, execution may take multiple cycles, depending on the operation. Thus, we may need to distinguish when an instruction *begins execution* and when it *completes execution;* between the two times, the instruction is *in execution.* This allows multiple instructions to be in execution at the same time. In addition to these changes to the pipeline structure, we will also change the functional unit design by varying the number of units, the latency of operations, and the functional unit pipelining, so as to better explore these more advanced pipelining techniques.

Dynamic Scheduling with a Scoreboard

In a dynamically scheduled pipeline, all instructions pass through the issue stage in order (in-order issue); however, they can be stalled or bypass each other in the second stage (read operands) and thus enter execution out of order. *Scoreboarding* is a technique for allowing instructions to execute out of order when there are sufficient resources and no data dependences; it is named after the CDC 6600 scoreboard, which developed this capability.

Before we see how scoreboarding could be used in the MIPS pipeline, it is important to observe that WAR hazards, which did not exist in the MIPS floating-point or integer pipelines, may arise when instructions execute out of order. For example, consider the following code sequence:

```
DIV.D     F0,F2,F4
ADD.D     F10,F0,F8
SUB.D     F8,F8,F14
```

There is an antidependence between the ADD.D and the SUB.D: If the pipeline executes the SUB.D before the ADD.D, it will violate the antidependence, yielding incorrect execution. Likewise, to avoid violating output dependences, WAW hazards (e.g., as would occur if the destination of the SUB.D were F10) must also be detected. As we will see, both these hazards are avoided in a scoreboard by stalling the later instruction involved in the antidependence.

The goal of a scoreboard is to maintain an execution rate of one instruction per clock cycle (when there are no structural hazards) by executing an instruction as early as possible. Thus, when the next instruction to execute is stalled, other instructions can be issued and executed if they do not depend on any active or stalled instruction. The scoreboard takes full responsibility for instruction issue and execution, including all hazard detection. Taking advantage of out-of-order execution requires multiple instructions to be in their EX stage simultaneously. This can be achieved with multiple functional units, with pipelined functional units, or with both. Since these two capabilities—pipelined functional units and multiple functional units—are essentially equivalent for the purposes of pipeline control, we will assume the processor has multiple functional units.

The CDC 6600 had 16 separate functional units, including 4 floating-point units, 5 units for memory references, and 7 units for integer operations. On a processor for the MIPS architecture, scoreboards make sense primarily on the floating-point unit since the latency of the other functional units is very small. Let's assume that there are two multipliers, one adder, one divide unit, and a single integer unit for all memory references, branches, and integer operations. Although this example is simpler than the CDC 6600, it is sufficiently powerful to demonstrate the principles without having a mass of detail or needing very long examples. Because both MIPS and the CDC 6600 are load-store architectures, the techniques are nearly identical for the two processors. Figure A.50 shows what the processor looks like.

Every instruction goes through the scoreboard, where a record of the data dependences is constructed; this step corresponds to instruction issue and replaces part of the ID step in the MIPS pipeline. The scoreboard then determines when the instruction can read its operands and begin execution. If the scoreboard decides the instruction cannot execute immediately, it monitors every change in the hardware and decides when the instruction *can* execute. The scoreboard also controls when an instruction can write its result into the destination register. Thus, all hazard detection and resolution is centralized in the scoreboard. We will

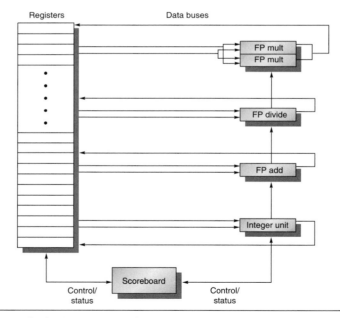

Figure A.50 The basic structure of a MIPS processor with a scoreboard. The scoreboard's function is to control instruction execution (vertical control lines). All data flows between the register file and the functional units over the buses (the horizontal lines, called trunks in the CDC 6600). There are two FP multipliers, an FP divider, an FP adder, and an integer unit. One set of buses (two inputs and one output) serves a group of functional units. The details of the scoreboard are shown in Figures A.51–A.54.

see a picture of the scoreboard later (Figure A.51 on page A-71), but first we need to understand the steps in the issue and execution segment of the pipeline.

Each instruction undergoes four steps in executing. (Since we are concentrating on the FP operations, we will not consider a step for memory access.) Let's first examine the steps informally and then look in detail at how the scoreboard keeps the necessary information that determines when to progress from one step to the next. The four steps, which replace the ID, EX, and WB steps in the standard MIPS pipeline, are as follows:

1. *Issue*—If a functional unit for the instruction is free and no other active instruction has the same destination register, the scoreboard issues the instruction to the functional unit and updates its internal data structure. This step replaces a portion of the ID step in the MIPS pipeline. By ensuring that no other active functional unit wants to write its result into the destination register, we guarantee that WAW hazards cannot be present. If a structural or WAW hazard exists, then the instruction issue stalls, and no further instructions will issue until these hazards are cleared. When the issue stage stalls, it causes the buffer between instruction fetch and issue to fill; if the buffer is a single entry, instruction fetch stalls immediately. If the buffer is a queue with multiple instructions, it stalls when the queue fills.

2. *Read operands*—The scoreboard monitors the availability of the source operands. A source operand is available if no earlier issued active instruction is going to write it. When the source operands are available, the scoreboard tells the functional unit to proceed to read the operands from the registers and begin execution. The scoreboard resolves RAW hazards dynamically in this step, and instructions may be sent into execution out of order. This step, together with issue, completes the function of the ID step in the simple MIPS pipeline.

3. *Execution*—The functional unit begins execution upon receiving operands. When the result is ready, it notifies the scoreboard that it has completed execution. This step replaces the EX step in the MIPS pipeline and takes multiple cycles in the MIPS FP pipeline.

4. *Write result*—Once the scoreboard is aware that the functional unit has completed execution, the scoreboard checks for WAR hazards and stalls the completing instruction, if necessary.

A WAR hazard exists if there is a code sequence like our earlier example with ADD.D and SUB.D that both use F8. In that example we had the code

```
DIV.D     F0,F2,F4
ADD.D     F10,F0,F8
SUB.D     F8,F8,F14
```

ADD.D has a source operand F8, which is the same register as the destination of SUB.D. But ADD.D actually depends on an earlier instruction. The scoreboard will still stall the SUB.D in its Write Result stage until ADD.D reads its operands. In general, then, a completing instruction cannot be allowed to write its results when

■ there is an instruction that has not read its operands that precedes (i.e., in order of issue) the completing instruction, and

■ one of the operands is the same register as the result of the completing instruction.

If this WAR hazard does not exist, or when it clears, the scoreboard tells the functional unit to store its result to the destination register. This step replaces the WB step in the simple MIPS pipeline.

At first glance, it might appear that the scoreboard will have difficulty separating RAW and WAR hazards.

Because the operands for an instruction are read only when both operands are available in the register file, this scoreboard does not take advantage of forwarding. Instead registers are only read when they are both available. This is not as large a penalty as you might initially think. Unlike our simple pipeline of earlier, instructions will write their result into the register file as soon as they complete execution (assuming no WAR hazards), rather than wait for a statically assigned write slot that may be several cycles away. The effect is reduced pipeline latency and benefits of forwarding. There is still one additional cycle of latency that arises since the write result and read operand stages cannot overlap. We would need additional buffering to eliminate this overhead.

Based on its own data structure, the scoreboard controls the instruction progression from one step to the next by communicating with the functional units. There is a small complication, however. There are only a limited number of source operand buses and result buses to the register file, which represents a structural hazard. The scoreboard must guarantee that the number of functional units allowed to proceed into steps 2 and 4 do not exceed the number of buses available. We will not go into further detail on this, other than to mention that the CDC 6600 solved this problem by grouping the 16 functional units together into four groups and supplying a set of buses, called *data trunks,* for each group. Only one unit in a group could read its operands or write its result during a clock.

Now let's look at the detailed data structure maintained by a MIPS scoreboard with five functional units. Figure A.51 shows what the scoreboard's information looks like partway through the execution of this simple sequence of instructions:

```
L.D     F6,34(R2)
L.D     F2,45(R3)
MUL.D   F0,F2,F4
SUB.D   F8,F6,F2
DIV.D   F10,F0,F6
ADD.D   F6,F8,F2
```

	Instruction status			
Instruction	**Issue**	**Read operands**	**Execution complete**	**Write result**
L.D F6,34(R2)	√	√	√	√
L.D F2,45(R3)	√	√	√	
MUL.D F0,F2,F4	√			
SUB.D F8,F6,F2	√			
DIV.D F10,F0,F6	√			
ADD.D F6,F8,F2				

	Functional unit status							
Name	**Busy**	**Op**	**Fi**	**Fj**	**Fk**	**Qj**	**Qk**	**Rj**	**Rk**
Integer	Yes	Load	F2	R3				No	
Mult1	Yes	Mult	F0	F2	F4	Integer		No	Yes
Mult2	No								
Add	Yes	Sub	F8	F6	F2		Integer	Yes	No
Divide	Yes	Div	F10	F0	F6	Mult1		No	Yes

	Register result status								
	F0	**F2**	**F4**	**F6**	**F8**	**F10**	**F12**	**...**	**F30**
FU	Mult1	Integer			Add	Divide			

Figure A.51 Components of the scoreboard. Each instruction that has issued or is pending issue has an entry in the instruction status table. There is one entry in the functional unit status table for each functional unit. Once an instruction issues, the record of its operands is kept in the functional unit status table. Finally, the register result table indicates which unit will produce each pending result; the number of entries is equal to the number of registers. The instruction status table says that (1) the first L.D has completed and written its result, and (2) the second L.D has completed execution but has not yet written its result. The MUL.D, SUB.D, and DIV.D have all issued but are stalled, waiting for their operands. The functional unit status says that the first multiply unit is waiting for the integer unit, the add unit is waiting for the integer unit, and the divide unit is waiting for the first multiply unit. The ADD.D instruction is stalled because of a structural hazard; it will clear when the SUB.D completes. If an entry in one of these scoreboard tables is not being used, it is left blank. For example, the Rk field is not used on a load and the Mult2 unit is unused, hence their fields have no meaning. Also, once an operand has been read, the Rj and Rk fields are set to No. Figure A.54 shows why this last step is crucial.

There are three parts to the scoreboard:

1. *Instruction status*—Indicates which of the four steps the instruction is in.

2. *Functional unit status*—Indicates the state of the functional unit (FU). There are nine fields for each functional unit:

■ Busy—Indicates whether the unit is busy or not.

■ Op—Operation to perform in the unit (e.g., add or subtract).

■ Fi—Destination register.

■ Fj, Fk—Source-register numbers.

■ Qj, Qk—Functional units producing source registers Fj, Fk.

■ Rj, Rk—Flags indicating when Fj, Fk are ready and not yet read. Set to No after operands are read.

3. *Register result status*—Indicates which functional unit will write each register, if an active instruction has the register as its destination. This field is set to blank whenever there are no pending instructions that will write that register.

Now let's look at how the code sequence begun in Figure A.51 continues execution. After that, we will be able to examine in detail the conditions that the scoreboard uses to control execution.

Example   Assume the following EX cycle latencies (chosen to illustrate the behavior and not representative) for the floating-point functional units: Add is 2 clock cycles, multiply is 10 clock cycles, and divide is 40 clock cycles. Using the code segment in Figure A.51 and beginning with the point indicated by the instruction status in Figure A.51, show what the status tables look like when MUL.D and DIV.D are each ready to go to the Write Result state.

Answer   There are RAW data hazards from the second L.D to MUL.D, ADD.D, and SUB.D, from MUL.D to DIV.D, and from SUB.D to ADD.D. There is a WAR data hazard between DIV.D and ADD.D and SUB.D. Finally, there is a structural hazard on the add functional unit for ADD.D and SUB.D. What the tables look like when MUL.D and DIV.D are ready to write their results is shown in Figures A.52 and A.53, respectively.

Now we can see how the scoreboard works in detail by looking at what has to happen for the scoreboard to allow each instruction to proceed. Figure A.54 shows what the scoreboard requires for each instruction to advance and the bookkeeping action necessary when the instruction does advance. The scoreboard records operand specifier information, such as register numbers. For example, we must record the source registers when an instruction is issued. Because we refer to the contents of a register as Regs[D], where D is a register name, there is no ambiguity. For example, Fj[FU] ← S1 causes the register *name* S1 to be placed in Fj[FU], rather than the *contents* of register S1.

The costs and benefits of scoreboarding are interesting considerations. The CDC 6600 designers measured a performance improvement of 1.7 for FORTRAN programs and 2.5 for hand-coded assembly language. However, this was measured in the days before software pipeline scheduling, semiconductor main memory, and caches (which lower memory access time). The scoreboard on the CDC 6600 had about as much logic as one of the functional units, which is sur-

	Instruction status			
Instruction	Issue	Read operands	Execution complete	Write result
L.D F6,34(R2)	√	√	√	√
L.D F2,45(R3)	√	√	√	√
MUL.D F0,F2,F4	√	√	√	
SUB.D F8,F6,F2	√	√	√	√
DIV.D F10,F0,F6	√			
ADD.D F6,F8,F2	√	√	√	

				Functional unit status					
Name	Busy	Op	Fi	Fj	Fk	Qj	Qk	Rj	Rk
Integer	No								
Mult1	Yes	Mult	F0	F2	F4			No	No
Mult2	No								
Add	Yes	Add	F6	F8	F2			No	No
Divide	Yes	Div	F10	F0	F6	Mult1		No	Yes

				Register result status				
	F0	F2	F4	F6	F8	F10	F12	...	F30
FU	Mult 1			Add		Divide			

Figure A.52 Scoreboard tables just before the MUL.D goes to write result. The DIV.D has not yet read either of its operands, since it has a dependence on the result of the multiply. The ADD.D has read its operands and is in execution, although it was forced to wait until the SUB.D finished to get the functional unit. ADD.D cannot proceed to write result because of the WAR hazard on F6, which is used by the DIV.D. The Q fields are only relevant when a functional unit is waiting for another unit.

prisingly low. The main cost was in the large number of buses—about four times as many as would be required if the CPU only executed instructions in order (or if it only initiated one instruction per execute cycle). The recently increasing interest in dynamic scheduling is motivated by attempts to issue more instructions per clock (so the cost of more buses must be paid anyway) and by ideas like speculation (explored in Section 4.7) that naturally build on dynamic scheduling.

A scoreboard uses the available ILP to minimize the number of stalls arising from the program's true data dependences. In eliminating stalls, a scoreboard is limited by several factors:

	Instruction status			
Instruction	**Issue**	**Read operands**	**Execution complete**	**Write result**
L.D F6,34(R2)	√	√	√	√
L.D F2,45(R3)	√	√	√	√
MUL.D F0,F2,F4	√	√	√	√
SUB.D F8,F6,F2	√	√	√	√
DIV.D F10,F0,F6	√	√	√	
ADD.D F6,F8,F2	√	√	√	√

	Functional unit status								
Name	**Busy**	**Op**	**Fi**	**Fj**	**Fk**	**Qj**	**Qk**	**Rj**	**Rk**
Integer	No								
Mult1	No								
Mult2	No								
Add	No								
Divide	Yes	Div	F10	F0	F6			No	No

	Register result status								
	F0	**F2**	**F4**	**F6**	**F8**	**F10**	**F12**	**...**	**F30**
FU						Divide			

Figure A.53 Scoreboard tables just before the DIV.D goes to write result. ADD.D was able to complete as soon as DIV.D passed through read operands and got a copy of F6. Only the DIV.D remains to finish.

1. *The amount of parallelism available among the instructions*—This determines whether independent instructions can be found to execute. If each instruction depends on its predecessor, no dynamic scheduling scheme can reduce stalls. If the instructions in the pipeline simultaneously must be chosen from the same basic block (as was true in the 6600), this limit is likely to be quite severe.

2. *The number of scoreboard entries*—This determines how far ahead the pipeline can look for independent instructions. The set of instructions examined as candidates for potential execution is called the *window*. The size of the scoreboard determines the size of the window. In this section, we assume a window does not extend beyond a branch, so the window (and the scoreboard) always contains straight-line code from a single basic block. Chapter 2 shows how the window can be extended beyond a branch.

Instruction status	Wait until	Bookkeeping

Issue	Not Busy [FU] and not Result [D]	`Busy[FU]←yes; Op[FU]←op; Fi[FU]←D;`
		`Fj[FU]←S1; Fk[FU]←S2;`
		`Qj←Result[S1]; Qk← Result[S2];`
		`Rj← not Qj; Rk← not Qk; Result[D]←FU;`

Read operands	Rj and Rk	`Rj← No; Rk← No; Qj←0; Qk←0`
Execution complete	Functional unit done	

Write result	$\forall f((\text{Fj}[f] \neq \text{Fi[FU]}$ or $\text{Rj}[f] = \text{No})$ &
	$(\text{Fk}[f] \neq \text{Fi[FU]}$ or $\text{Rk}[f] = \text{No}))$
		`∀f(if Qj[f]=FU then Rj[f]←Yes);`
		`∀f(if Qk[f]=FU then Rk[f]←Yes);`
		`Result[Fi[FU]]← 0; Busy[FU]← No`

Figure A.54 Required checks and bookkeeping actions for each step in instruction execution. FU stands for the functional unit used by the instruction, D is the destination register name, S1 and S2 are the source register names, and op is the operation to be done. To access the scoreboard entry named Fj for functional unit FU we use the notation Fj[FU]. Result[D] is the name of the functional unit that will write register D. The test on the write result case prevents the write when there is a WAR hazard, which exists if another instruction has this instruction's destination (Fi[FU]) as a source (Fj[f] or Fk[f]) and if some other instruction has written the register (Rj = Yes or Rk = Yes). The variable f is used for any functional unit.

3. *The number and types of functional units*—This determines the importance of structural hazards, which can increase when dynamic scheduling is used.

4. *The presence of antidependences and output dependences*—These lead to WAR and WAW stalls.

Chapters 2 and 3 focus on techniques that attack the problem of exposing and better utilizing available ILP. The second and third factors can be attacked by increasing the size of the scoreboard and the number of functional units; however, these changes have cost implications and may also affect cycle time. WAW and WAR hazards become more important in dynamically scheduled processors because the pipeline exposes more name dependences. WAW hazards also become more important if we use dynamic scheduling with a branch-prediction scheme that allows multiple iterations of a loop to overlap.

A.8   Fallacies and Pitfalls

Pitfall   *Unexpected execution sequences may cause unexpected hazards.*

At first glance, WAW hazards look like they should never occur in a code sequence because no compiler would ever generate two writes to the same register without an intervening read. But they can occur when the sequence is unexpected. For example, the first write might be in the delay slot of a taken branch when the scheduler thought the branch would not be taken. Here is the code sequence that could cause this:

```
                    BNEZ    R1,foo
                    DIV.D   F0,F2,F4; moved into delay slot
                            ;from fall through
                    .....
                    .....
        foo:        L.D     F0,qrs
```

If the branch is taken, then before the DIV.D can complete, the L.D will reach WB, causing a WAW hazard. The hardware must detect this and may stall the issue of the L.D. Another way this can happen is if the second write is in a trap routine. This occurs when an instruction that traps and is writing results continues and completes after an instruction that writes the same register in the trap handler. The hardware must detect and prevent this as well.

Pitfall *Extensive pipelining can impact other aspects of a design, leading to overall worse cost-performance.*

The best example of this phenomenon comes from two implementations of the VAX, the 8600 and the 8700. When the 8600 was initially delivered, it had a cycle time of 80 ns. Subsequently, a redesigned version, called the 8650, with a 55 ns clock was introduced. The 8700 has a much simpler pipeline that operates at the microinstruction level, yielding a smaller CPU with a faster clock cycle of 45 ns. The overall outcome is that the 8650 has a CPI advantage of about 20%, but the 8700 has a clock rate that is about 20% faster. Thus, the 8700 achieves the same performance with much less hardware.

Pitfall *Evaluating dynamic or static scheduling on the basis of unoptimized code.*

Unoptimized code—containing redundant loads, stores, and other operations that might be eliminated by an optimizer—is much easier to schedule than "tight" optimized code. This holds for scheduling both control delays (with delayed branches) and delays arising from RAW hazards. In gcc running on an R3000, which has a pipeline almost identical to that of Section A.1, the frequency of idle clock cycles increases by 18% from the unoptimized and scheduled code to the optimized and scheduled code. Of course, the optimized program is much faster, since it has fewer instructions. To fairly evaluate a compile time scheduler or run time dynamic scheduling, you must use optimized code, since in the real system you will derive good performance from other optimizations in addition to scheduling.

A.9   Concluding Remarks

At the beginning of the 1980s, pipelining was a technique reserved primarily for supercomputers and large multimillion dollar mainframes. By the mid-1980s, the first pipelined microprocessors appeared and helped transform the world of computing, allowing microprocessors to bypass minicomputers in performance and eventually to take on and outperform mainframes. By the early 1990s, high-end embedded microprocessors embraced pipelining, and desktops were headed toward the use of the sophisticated dynamically scheduled, multiple-issue approaches discussed in Chapter 2. The material in this appendix, which was considered reasonably advanced for graduate students when this text first appeared in 1990, is now considered basic undergraduate material and can be found in processors costing less than $10!

A.10   Historical Perspective and References

Section K.4 on the companion CD features a discussion on the development of pipelining and instruction-level parallelism. We provide numerous references for further reading and exploration of these topics.

B.1	Introduction	B-2
B.2	Classifying Instruction Set Architectures	B-3
B.3	Memory Addressing	B-7
B.4	Type and Size of Operands	B-13
B.5	Operations in the Instruction Set	B-14
B.6	Instructions for Control Flow	B-16
B.7	Encoding an Instruction Set	B-21
B.8	Crosscutting Issues: The Role of Compilers	B-24
B.9	Putting It All Together: The MIPS Architecture	B-32
B.10	Fallacies and Pitfalls	B-39
B.11	Concluding Remarks	B-45
B.12	Historical Perspective and References	B-47

B

Instruction Set Principles and Examples

A n   Add the number in storage location *n* into the accumulator.

E n   If the number in the accumulator is greater than or equal to zero execute next the order which stands in storage location *n;* otherwise proceed serially.

Z   Stop the machine and ring the warning bell.

Wilkes and Renwick
Selection from the List of 18 Machine
Instructions for the EDSAC (1949)

B.1 | Introduction

In this appendix we concentrate on instruction set architecture—the portion of the computer visible to the programmer or compiler writer. Most of this material should be review for readers of this book; we include it here for background. This appendix introduces the wide variety of design alternatives available to the instruction set architect. In particular, we focus on four topics. First, we present a taxonomy of instruction set alternatives and give some qualitative assessment of the advantages and disadvantages of various approaches. Second, we present and analyze some instruction set measurements that are largely independent of a specific instruction set. Third, we address the issue of languages and compilers and their bearing on instruction set architecture. Finally, the "Putting It All Together" section shows how these ideas are reflected in the MIPS instruction set, which is typical of RISC architectures. We conclude with fallacies and pitfalls of instruction set design.

To illustrate the principles further, Appendix J also gives four examples of general-purpose RISC architectures (MIPS, PowerPC, Precision Architecture, SPARC), four embedded RISC processors (ARM, Hitachi SH, MIPS 16, Thumb), and three older architectures (80x86, IBM 360/370, and VAX). Before we discuss how to classify architectures, we need to say something about instruction set measurement.

Throughout this appendix, we examine a wide variety of architectural measurements. Clearly, these measurements depend on the programs measured and on the compilers used in making the measurements. The results should not be interpreted as absolute, and you might see different data if you did the measurement with a different compiler or a different set of programs. We believe that the measurements in this appendix are reasonably indicative of a class of typical applications. Many of the measurements are presented using a small set of benchmarks, so that the data can be reasonably displayed and the differences among programs can be seen. An architect for a new computer would want to analyze a much larger collection of programs before making architectural decisions. The measurements shown are usually *dynamic*—that is, the frequency of a measured event is weighed by the number of times that event occurs during execution of the measured program.

Before starting with the general principles, let's review the three application areas from Chapter 1. *Desktop computing* emphasizes performance of programs with integer and floating-point data types, with little regard for program size or processor power consumption. For example, code size has never been reported in the five generations of SPEC benchmarks. *Servers* today are used primarily for database, file server, and Web applications, plus some time-sharing applications for many users. Hence, floating-point performance is much less important for performance than integers and character strings, yet virtually every server processor still includes floating-point instructions. *Embedded applications* value cost and power, so code size is important because less memory is both cheaper and lower power, and some classes of instructions (such as floating point) may be optional to reduce chip costs.

Thus, instruction sets for all three applications are very similar. In fact, the MIPS architecture that drives this appendix has been used successfully in desktops, servers, and embedded applications.

One successful architecture very different from RISC is the 80x86 (see Appendix J). Surprisingly, its success does not necessarily belie the advantages of a RISC instruction set. The commercial importance of binary compatibility with PC software combined with the abundance of transistors provided by Moore's Law led Intel to use a RISC instruction set internally while supporting an 80x86 instruction set externally. Recent 80x86 microprocessors, such as the Pentium 4, use hardware to translate from 80x86 instructions to RISC-like instructions and then execute the translated operations inside the chip. They maintain the illusion of 80x86 architecture to the programmer while allowing the computer designer to implement a RISC-style processor for performance.

Now that the background is set, we begin by exploring how instruction set architectures can be classified.

B.2   Classifying Instruction Set Architectures

The type of internal storage in a processor is the most basic differentiation, so in this section we will focus on the alternatives for this portion of the architecture. The major choices are a stack, an accumulator, or a set of registers. Operands may be named explicitly or implicitly: The operands in a *stack architecture* are implicitly on the top of the stack, and in an *accumulator architecture* one operand is implicitly the accumulator. The *general-purpose register architectures* have only explicit operands—either registers or memory locations. Figure B.1 shows a block diagram of such architectures, and Figure B.2 shows how the code sequence C = A + B would typically appear in these three classes of instruction sets. The explicit operands may be accessed directly from memory or may need to be first loaded into temporary storage, depending on the class of architecture and choice of specific instruction.

As the figures show, there are really two classes of register computers. One class can access memory as part of any instruction, called *register-memory* architecture, and the other can access memory only with load and store instructions, called *load-store* architecture. A third class, not found in computers shipping today, keeps all operands in memory and is called a *memory-memory* architecture. Some instruction set architectures have more registers than a single accumulator, but place restrictions on uses of these special registers. Such an architecture is sometimes called an *extended accumulator* or *special-purpose register* computer.

Although most early computers used stack or accumulator-style architectures, virtually every new architecture designed after 1980 uses a load-store register architecture. The major reasons for the emergence of general-purpose register (GPR) computers are twofold. First, registers—like other forms of storage internal to the processor—are faster than memory. Second, registers are more

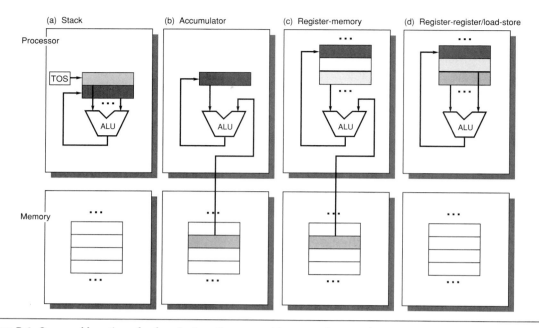

Figure B.1 Operand locations for four instruction set architecture classes. The arrows indicate whether the operand is an input or the result of the ALU operation, or both an input and result. Lighter shades indicate inputs, and the dark shade indicates the result. In (a), a Top Of Stack register (TOS), points to the top input operand, which is combined with the operand below. The first operand is removed from the stack, the result takes the place of the second operand, and TOS is updated to point to the result. All operands are implicit. In (b), the Accumulator is both an implicit input operand and a result. In (c), one input operand is a register, one is in memory, and the result goes to a register. All operands are registers in (d) and, like the stack architecture, can be transferred to memory only via separate instructions: push or pop for (a) and load or store for (d).

Stack	Accumulator	Register (register-memory)	Register (load-store)
Push A	Load A	Load R1,A	Load R1,A
Push B	Add B	Add R3,R1,B	Load R2,B
Add	Store C	Store R3,C	Add R3,R1,R2
Pop C			Store R3,C

Figure B.2 The code sequence for C = A + B for four classes of instruction sets. Note that the **Add** instruction has implicit operands for stack and accumulator architectures, and explicit operands for register architectures. It is assumed that A, B, and C all belong in memory and that the values of A and B cannot be destroyed. Figure B.1 shows the **Add** operation for each class of architecture.

efficient for a compiler to use than other forms of internal storage. For example, on a register computer the expression $(A*B) - (B*C) - (A*D)$ may be evaluated by doing the multiplications in any order, which may be more efficient because of the location of the operands or because of pipelining concerns (see Chapter 2). Nevertheless, on a stack computer the hardware must evaluate the expression in only one order, since operands are hidden on the stack, and it may have to load an operand multiple times.

More importantly, registers can be used to hold variables. When variables are allocated to registers, the memory traffic reduces, the program speeds up (since registers are faster than memory), and the code density improves (since a register can be named with fewer bits than can a memory location).

As explained in Section B.8, compiler writers would prefer that all registers be equivalent and unreserved. Older computers compromise this desire by dedicating registers to special uses, effectively decreasing the number of general-purpose registers. If the number of truly general-purpose registers is too small, trying to allocate variables to registers will not be profitable. Instead, the compiler will reserve all the uncommitted registers for use in expression evaluation.

How many registers are sufficient? The answer, of course, depends on the effectiveness of the compiler. Most compilers reserve some registers for expression evaluation, use some for parameter passing, and allow the remainder to be allocated to hold variables. Modern compiler technology and its ability to effectively use larger number of registers has led to an increase in register counts in more recent architectures.

Two major instruction set characteristics divide GPR architectures. Both characteristics concern the nature of operands for a typical arithmetic or logical instruction (ALU instruction). The first concerns whether an ALU instruction has two or three operands. In the three-operand format, the instruction contains one result operand and two source operands. In the two-operand format, one of the operands is both a source and a result for the operation. The second distinction among GPR architectures concerns how many of the operands may be memory addresses in ALU instructions. The number of memory operands supported by a typical ALU instruction may vary from none to three. Figure B.3 shows combinations of these two attributes with examples of computers. Although there are seven possible combinations, three serve to classify nearly all existing computers. As we mentioned earlier, these three are load-store (also called register-register), register-memory, and memory-memory.

Figure B.4 shows the advantages and disadvantages of each of these alternatives. Of course, these advantages and disadvantages are not absolutes: They are qualitative and their actual impact depends on the compiler and implementation strategy. A GPR computer with memory-memory operations could easily be ignored by the compiler and used as a load-store computer. One of the most pervasive architectural impacts is on instruction encoding and the number of instructions needed to perform a task. We see the impact of these architectural alternatives on implementation approaches in Appendix A and Chapter 2.

Number of memory addresses	Maximum number of operands allowed	Type of architecture	Examples
0	3	Load-store	Alpha, ARM, MIPS, PowerPC, SPARC, SuperH, TM32
1	2	Register-memory	IBM 360/370, Intel 80x86, Motorola 68000, TI TMS320C54x
2	2	Memory-memory	VAX (also has three-operand formats)
3	3	Memory-memory	VAX (also has two-operand formats)

Figure B.3 Typical combinations of memory operands and total operands per typical ALU instruction with examples of computers. Computers with no memory reference per ALU instruction are called load-store or register-register computers. Instructions with multiple memory operands per typical ALU instruction are called register-memory or memory-memory, according to whether they have one or more than one memory operand.

Type	Advantages	Disadvantages
Register-register (0, 3)	Simple, fixed-length instruction encoding. Simple code generation model. Instructions take similar numbers of clocks to execute (see App. A).	Higher instruction count than architectures with memory references in instructions. More instructions and lower instruction density leads to larger programs.
Register-memory (1, 2)	Data can be accessed without a separate load instruction first. Instruction format tends to be easy to encode and yields good density.	Operands are not equivalent since a source operand in a binary operation is destroyed. Encoding a register number and a memory address in each instruction may restrict the number of registers. Clocks per instruction vary by operand location.
Memory-memory (2, 2) or (3, 3)	Most compact. Doesn't waste registers for temporaries.	Large variation in instruction size, especially for three-operand instructions. In addition, large variation in work per instruction. Memory accesses create memory bottleneck. (Not used today.)

Figure B.4 Advantages and disadvantages of the three most common types of general-purpose register computers. The notation (*m, n*) means *m* memory operands and *n* total operands. In general, computers with fewer alternatives simplify the compiler's task since there are fewer decisions for the compiler to make (see Section B.8). Computers with a wide variety of flexible instruction formats reduce the number of bits required to encode the program. The number of registers also affects the instruction size since you need $\log_2$ (number of registers) for each register specifier in an instruction. Thus, doubling the number of registers takes 3 extra bits for a register-register architecture, or about 10% of a 32-bit instruction.

Summary: Classifying Instruction Set Architectures

Here and at the end of Sections B.3 through B.8 we summarize those characteristics we would expect to find in a new instruction set architecture, building the foundation for the MIPS architecture introduced in Section B.9. From this section we should clearly expect the use of general-purpose registers. Figure B.4, combined with Appendix A on pipelining, leads to the expectation of a load-store version of a general-purpose register architecture.

With the class of architecture covered, the next topic is addressing operands.

Memory Addressing

Independent of whether the architecture is load-store or allows any operand to be a memory reference, it must define how memory addresses are interpreted and how they are specified. The measurements presented here are largely, but not completely, computer independent. In some cases the measurements are significantly affected by the compiler technology. These measurements have been made using an optimizing compiler, since compiler technology plays a critical role.

Interpreting Memory Addresses

How is a memory address interpreted? That is, what object is accessed as a function of the address and the length? All the instruction sets discussed in this book are byte addressed and provide access for bytes (8 bits), half words (16 bits), and words (32 bits). Most of the computers also provide access for double words (64 bits).

There are two different conventions for ordering the bytes within a larger object. *Little Endian* byte order puts the byte whose address is "x . . . x000" at the least-significant position in the double word (the little end). The bytes are numbered

| 7 | 6 | 5 | 4 | 3 | 2 | 1 | 0 |

Big Endian byte order puts the byte whose address is "x . . . x000" at the most-significant position in the double word (the big end). The bytes are numbered

| 0 | 1 | 2 | 3 | 4 | 5 | 6 | 7 |

When operating within one computer, the byte order is often unnoticeable—only programs that access the same locations as both, say, words and bytes can notice the difference. Byte order is a problem when exchanging data among computers with different orderings, however. Little Endian ordering also fails to match normal ordering of words when strings are compared. Strings appear "SDRAWKCAB" (backwards) in the registers.

A second memory issue is that in many computers, accesses to objects larger than a byte must be *aligned*. An access to an object of size s bytes at byte address A is aligned if $A \bmod s = 0$. Figure B.5 shows the addresses at which an access is aligned or misaligned.

Why would someone design a computer with alignment restrictions? Misalignment causes hardware complications, since the memory is typically aligned on a multiple of a word or double-word boundary. A misaligned memory access

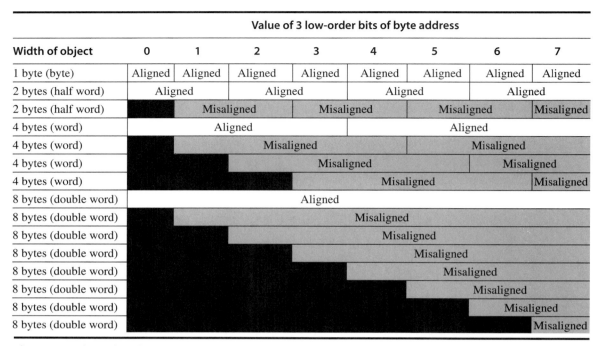

	Value of 3 low-order bits of byte address							
Width of object	0	1	2	3	4	5	6	7
1 byte (byte)	Aligned	Aligned	Aligned	Aligned	Aligned	Aligned	Aligned	Aligned
2 bytes (half word)	Aligned		Aligned		Aligned		Aligned	
2 bytes (half word)		Misaligned		Misaligned		Misaligned		Misaligned
4 bytes (word)	Aligned				Aligned			
4 bytes (word)		Misaligned				Misaligned		
4 bytes (word)			Misaligned				Misaligned	
4 bytes (word)				Misaligned				Misaligned
8 bytes (double word)	Aligned							
8 bytes (double word)		Misaligned						
8 bytes (double word)			Misaligned					
8 bytes (double word)				Misaligned				
8 bytes (double word)					Misaligned			
8 bytes (double word)						Misaligned		
8 bytes (double word)							Misaligned	
8 bytes (double word)								Misaligned

Figure B.5 Aligned and misaligned addresses of byte, half-word, word, and double-word objects for byte-addressed computers. For each misaligned example some objects require two memory accesses to complete. Every aligned object can always complete in one memory access, as long as the memory is as wide as the object. The figure shows the memory organized as 8 bytes wide. The byte offsets that label the columns specify the low-order 3 bits of the address.

may, therefore, take multiple aligned memory references. Thus, even in computers that allow misaligned access, programs with aligned accesses run faster.

Even if data are aligned, supporting byte, half-word, and word accesses requires an alignment network to align bytes, half words, and words in 64-bit registers. For example, in Figure B.5, suppose we read a byte from an address with its 3 low-order bits having the value 4. We will need to shift right 3 bytes to align the byte to the proper place in a 64-bit register. Depending on the instruction, the computer may also need to sign-extend the quantity. Stores are easy: Only the addressed bytes in memory may be altered. On some computers a byte, half-word, and word operation does not affect the upper portion of a register. Although all the computers discussed in this book permit byte, half-word, and word accesses to memory, only the IBM 360/370, Intel 80x86, and VAX support ALU operations on register operands narrower than the full width.

Now that we have discussed alternative interpretations of memory addresses, we can discuss the ways addresses are specified by instructions, called *addressing modes*.

Addressing Modes

Given an address, we now know what bytes to access in memory. In this subsection we will look at addressing modes—how architectures specify the address of an object they will access. Addressing modes specify constants and registers in addition to locations in memory. When a memory location is used, the actual memory address specified by the addressing mode is called the *effective address*.

Figure B.6 shows all the data addressing modes that have been used in recent computers. Immediates or literals are usually considered memory addressing

Addressing mode	Example instruction	Meaning	When used
Register	Add R4,R3	Regs[R4] ← Regs[R4] + Regs[R3]	When a value is in a register.
Immediate	Add R4,#3	Regs[R4] ← Regs[R4] + 3	For constants.
Displacement	Add R4,100(R1)	Regs[R4] ← Regs[R4] + Mem[100+Regs[R1]]	Accessing local variables (+ simulates register indirect, direct addressing modes).
Register indirect	Add R4,(R1)	Regs[R4] ← Regs[R4] + Mem[Regs[R1]]	Accessing using a pointer or a computed address.
Indexed	Add R3,(R1+R2)	Regs[R3] ← Regs[R3] + Mem[Regs[R1]+Regs[R2]]	Sometimes useful in array addressing: R1 = base of array; R2 = index amount.
Direct or absolute	Add R1,(1001)	Regs[R1] ← Regs[R1] + Mem[1001]	Sometimes useful for accessing static data; address constant may need to be large.
Memory indirect	Add R1,@(R3)	Regs[R1] ← Regs[R1] + Mem[Mem[Regs[R3]]]	If R3 is the address of a pointer p, then mode yields $*p$.
Autoincrement	Add R1,(R2)+	Regs[R1] ← Regs[R1] + Mem[Regs[R2]] Regs[R2] ← Regs[R2] + d	Useful for stepping through arrays within a loop. R2 points to start of array; each reference increments R2 by size of an element, d.
Autodecrement	Add R1,-(R2)	Regs[R2] ← Regs[R2] - d Regs[R1] ← Regs[R1] + Mem[Regs[R2]]	Same use as autoincrement. Autodecrement/-increment can also act as push/pop to implement a stack.
Scaled	Add R1,100(R2)[R3]	Regs[R1] ← Regs[R1] + Mem[100+Regs[R2] + Regs[R3]*d]	Used to index arrays. May be applied to any indexed addressing mode in some computers.

Figure B.6 Selection of addressing modes with examples, meaning, and usage. In autoincrement/-decrement and scaled addressing modes, the variable d designates the size of the data item being accessed (i.e., whether the instruction is accessing 1, 2, 4, or 8 bytes). These addressing modes are only useful when the elements being accessed are adjacent in memory. RISC computers use displacement addressing to simulate register indirect with 0 for the address and to simulate direct addressing using 0 in the base register. In our measurements, we use the first name shown for each mode. The extensions to C used as hardware descriptions are defined on page B-36.

modes (even though the value they access is in the instruction stream), although registers are often separated since they don't normally have memory addresses. We have kept addressing modes that depend on the program counter, called *PC-relative addressing,* separate. PC-relative addressing is used primarily for specifying code addresses in control transfer instructions, discussed in Section B.6.

Figure B.6 shows the most common names for the addressing modes, though the names differ among architectures. In this figure and throughout the book, we will use an extension of the C programming language as a hardware description notation. In this figure, only one non-C feature is used: The left arrow ($\leftarrow$) is used for assignment. We also use the array Mem as the name for main memory and the array Regs for registers. Thus, Mem[Regs[R1]] refers to the contents of the memory location whose address is given by the contents of register 1 (R1). Later, we will introduce extensions for accessing and transferring data smaller than a word.

Addressing modes have the ability to significantly reduce instruction counts; they also add to the complexity of building a computer and may increase the average CPI (clock cycles per instruction) of computers that implement those modes. Thus, the usage of various addressing modes is quite important in helping the architect choose what to include.

Figure B.7 shows the results of measuring addressing mode usage patterns in three programs on the VAX architecture. We use the old VAX architecture for a few measurements in this appendix because it has the richest set of addressing modes and the fewest restrictions on memory addressing. For example, Figure B.6 on page B-9 shows all the modes the VAX supports. Most measurements in this appendix, however, will use the more recent register-register architectures to show how programs use instruction sets of current computers.

As Figure B.7 shows, displacement and immediate addressing dominate addressing mode usage. Let's look at some properties of these two heavily used modes.

Displacement Addressing Mode

The major question that arises for a displacement-style addressing mode is that of the range of displacements used. Based on the use of various displacement sizes, a decision of what sizes to support can be made. Choosing the displacement field sizes is important because they directly affect the instruction length. Figure B.8 shows the measurements taken on the data access on a load-store architecture using our benchmark programs. We look at branch offsets in Section B.6—data accessing patterns and branches are different; little is gained by combining them, although in practice the immediate sizes are made the same for simplicity.

Immediate or Literal Addressing Mode

Immediates can be used in arithmetic operations, in comparisons (primarily for branches), and in moves where a constant is wanted in a register. The last case occurs for constants written in the code—which tend to be small—and for

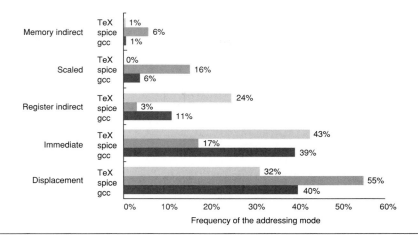

Figure B.7 Summary of use of memory addressing modes (including immediates). These major addressing modes account for all but a few percent (0% to 3%) of the memory accesses. Register modes, which are not counted, account for one-half of the operand references, while memory addressing modes (including immediate) account for the other half. Of course, the compiler affects what addressing modes are used; see Section B.8. The memory indirect mode on the VAX can use displacement, autoincrement, or autodecrement to form the initial memory address; in these programs, almost all the memory indirect references use displacement mode as the base. Displacement mode includes all displacement lengths (8, 16, and 32 bits). The PC-relative addressing modes, used almost exclusively for branches, are not included. Only the addressing modes with an average frequency of over 1% are shown.

address constants, which tend to be large. For the use of immediates it is important to know whether they need to be supported for all operations or for only a subset. Figure B.9 shows the frequency of immediates for the general classes of integer and floating-point operations in an instruction set.

Another important instruction set measurement is the range of values for immediates. Like displacement values, the size of immediate values affects instruction length. As Figure B.10 shows, small immediate values are most heavily used. Large immediates are sometimes used, however, most likely in addressing calculations.

Summary: Memory Addressing

First, because of their popularity, we would expect a new architecture to support at least the following addressing modes: displacement, immediate, and register indirect. Figure B.7 shows that they represent 75% to 99% of the addressing modes used in our measurements. Second, we would expect the size of the address for displacement mode to be at least 12–16 bits, since the caption in Figure B.8 suggests these sizes would capture 75% to 99% of the displacements.

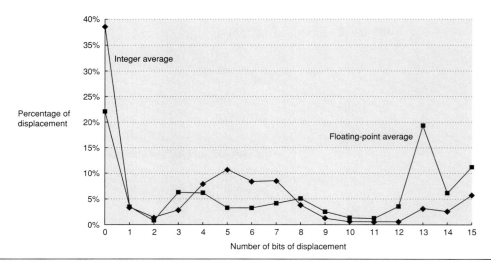

Figure B.8 Displacement values are widely distributed. There are both a large number of small values and a fair number of large values. The wide distribution of displacement values is due to multiple storage areas for variables and different displacements to access them (see Section B.8) as well as the overall addressing scheme the compiler uses. The x-axis is $\log_2$ of the displacement; that is, the size of a field needed to represent the magnitude of the displacement. Zero on the x-axis shows the percentage of displacements of value 0. The graph does not include the sign bit, which is heavily affected by the storage layout. Most displacements are positive, but a majority of the largest displacements (14+ bits) are negative. Since these data were collected on a computer with 16-bit displacements, they cannot tell us about longer displacements. These data were taken on the Alpha architecture with full optimization (see Section B.8) for SPEC CPU2000, showing the average of integer programs (CINT2000) and the average of floating-point programs (CFP2000).

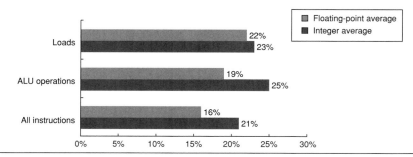

Figure B.9 About one-quarter of data transfers and ALU operations have an immediate operand. The bottom bars show that integer programs use immediates in about one-fifth of the instructions, while floating-point programs use immediates in about one-sixth of the instructions. For loads, the load immediate instruction loads 16 bits into either half of a 32-bit register. Load immediates are not loads in a strict sense because they do not access memory. Occasionally a pair of load immediates is used to load a 32-bit constant, but this is rare. (For ALU operations, shifts by a constant amount are included as operations with immediate operands.) The programs and computer used to collect these statistics are the same as in Figure B.8.

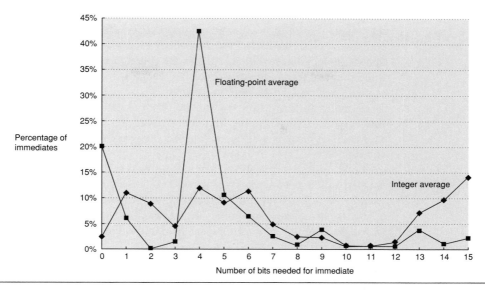

Figure B.10 The distribution of immediate values. The *x*-axis shows the number of bits needed to represent the magnitude of an immediate value—0 means the immediate field value was 0. The majority of the immediate values are positive. About 20% were negative for CINT2000, and about 30% were negative for CFP2000. These measurements were taken on an Alpha, where the maximum immediate is 16 bits, for the same programs as in Figure B.8. A similar measurement on the VAX, which supported 32-bit immediates, showed that about 20% to 25% of immediates were longer than 16 bits. Thus, 16 bits would capture about 80% and 8 bits about 50%.

Third, we would expect the size of the immediate field to be at least 8–16 bits. This claim is not substantiated by the captions of the figure to which it refers.

Having covered instruction set classes and decided on register-register architectures, plus the previous recommendations on data addressing modes, we next cover the sizes and meanings of data.

B.4   Type and Size of Operands

How is the type of an operand designated? Normally, encoding in the opcode designates the type of an operand—this is the method used most often. Alternatively, the data can be annotated with tags that are interpreted by the hardware. These tags specify the type of the operand, and the operation is chosen accordingly. Computers with tagged data, however, can only be found in computer museums.

Let's start with desktop and server architectures. Usually the type of an operand—integer, single-precision floating point, character, and so on—effectively gives its size. Common operand types include character (8 bits), half word (16 bits), word (32 bits), single-precision floating point (also 1 word), and double-precision floating point (2 words). Integers are almost universally represented as two's complement binary numbers. Characters are usually in ASCII, but the 16-bit Unicode (used in Java) is gaining popularity with the internationalization of computers. Until the early 1980s, most computer manufacturers chose their own floating-point representation. Almost all computers since that time follow the same standard for floating point, the IEEE standard 754. The IEEE floating-point standard is discussed in detail in Appendix I.

Some architectures provide operations on character strings, although such operations are usually quite limited and treat each byte in the string as a single character. Typical operations supported on character strings are comparisons and moves.

For business applications, some architectures support a decimal format, usually called *packed decimal* or *binary-coded decimal*—4 bits are used to encode the values 0–9, and 2 decimal digits are packed into each byte. Numeric character strings are sometimes called *unpacked decimal,* and operations—called *packing* and *unpacking*—are usually provided for converting back and forth between them.

One reason to use decimal operands is to get results that exactly match decimal numbers, as some decimal fractions do not have an exact representation in binary. For example, 0.10_{10} is a simple fraction in decimal, but in binary it requires an infinite set of repeating digits: $0.0001100110\overline{0011}\ldots_2$. Thus, calculations that are exact in decimal can be close but inexact in binary, which can be a problem for financial transactions. (See Appendix I to learn more about precise arithmetic.)

Our SPEC benchmarks use byte or character, half-word (short integer), word (integer), double-word (long integer), and floating-point data types. Figure B.11 shows the dynamic distribution of the sizes of objects referenced from memory for these programs. The frequency of access to different data types helps in deciding what types are most important to support efficiently. Should the computer have a 64-bit access path, or would taking two cycles to access a double word be satisfactory? As we saw earlier, byte accesses require an alignment network: How important is it to support bytes as primitives? Figure B.11 uses memory references to examine the types of data being accessed.

In some architectures, objects in registers may be accessed as bytes or half words. However, such access is very infrequent—on the VAX, it accounts for no more than 12% of register references, or roughly 6% of all operand accesses in these programs.

B.5 Operations in the Instruction Set

The operators supported by most instruction set architectures can be categorized as in Figure B.12. One rule of thumb across all architectures is that the most widely executed instructions are the simple operations of an instruction set. For example, Figure B.13 shows 10 simple instructions that account for 96% of

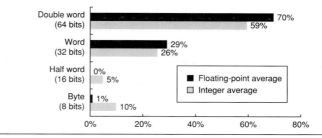

Figure B.11 Distribution of data accesses by size for the benchmark programs. The double-word data type is used for double-precision floating point in floating-point programs and for addresses, since the computer uses 64-bit addresses. On a 32-bit address computer the 64-bit addresses would be replaced by 32-bit addresses, and so almost all double-word accesses in integer programs would become single-word accesses.

Operator type	Examples
Arithmetic and logical	Integer arithmetic and logical operations: add, subtract, and, or, multiply, divide
Data transfer	Loads-stores (move instructions on computers with memory addressing)
Control	Branch, jump, procedure call and return, traps
System	Operating system call, virtual memory management instructions
Floating point	Floating-point operations: add, multiply, divide, compare
Decimal	Decimal add, decimal multiply, decimal-to-character conversions
String	String move, string compare, string search
Graphics	Pixel and vertex operations, compression/decompression operations

Figure B.12 Categories of instruction operators and examples of each. All computers generally provide a full set of operations for the first three categories. The support for system functions in the instruction set varies widely among architectures, but all computers must have some instruction support for basic system functions. The amount of support in the instruction set for the last four categories may vary from none to an extensive set of special instructions. Floating-point instructions will be provided in any computer that is intended for use in an application that makes much use of floating point. These instructions are sometimes part of an optional instruction set. Decimal and string instructions are sometimes primitives, as in the VAX or the IBM 360, or may be synthesized by the compiler from simpler instructions. Graphics instructions typically operate on many smaller data items in parallel, for example, performing eight 8-bit additions on two 64-bit operands.

Rank	80x86 instruction	Integer average (% total executed)
1	load	22%
2	conditional branch	20%
3	compare	16%
4	store	12%
5	add	8%
6	and	6%
7	sub	5%
8	move register-register	4%
9	call	1%
10	return	1%
Total		96%

Figure B.13 The top 10 instructions for the 80x86. Simple instructions dominate this list and are responsible for 96% of the instructions executed. These percentages are the average of the five SPECint92 programs.

instructions executed for a collection of integer programs running on the popular Intel 80x86. Hence, the implementor of these instructions should be sure to make these fast, as they are the common case.

As mentioned before, the instructions in Figure B.13 are found in every computer for every application—desktop, server, embedded—with the variations of operations in Figure B.12 largely depending on which data types that the instruction set includes.

B.6   Instructions for Control Flow

Because the measurements of branch and jump behavior are fairly independent of other measurements and applications, we now examine the use of control flow instructions, which have little in common with the operations of the previous sections.

There is no consistent terminology for instructions that change the flow of control. In the 1950s they were typically called *transfers*. Beginning in 1960 the name *branch* began to be used. Later, computers introduced additional names. Throughout this book we will use *jump* when the change in control is unconditional and *branch* when the change is conditional.

We can distinguish four different types of control flow change:

- Conditional branches
- Jumps

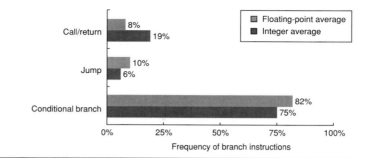

Figure B.14 Breakdown of control flow instructions into three classes: calls or returns, jumps, and conditional branches. Conditional branches clearly dominate. Each type is counted in one of three bars. The programs and computer used to collect these statistics are the same as those in Figure B.8.

■ Procedure calls

■ Procedure returns

We want to know the relative frequency of these events, as each event is different, may use different instructions, and may have different behavior. Figure B.14 shows the frequencies of these control flow instructions for a load-store computer running our benchmarks.

Addressing Modes for Control Flow Instructions

The destination address of a control flow instruction must always be specified. This destination is specified explicitly in the instruction in the vast majority of cases—procedure return being the major exception, since for return the target is not known at compile time. The most common way to specify the destination is to supply a displacement that is added to the *program counter* (PC). Control flow instructions of this sort are called *PC-relative*. PC-relative branches or jumps are advantageous because the target is often near the current instruction, and specifying the position relative to the current PC requires fewer bits. Using PC-relative addressing also permits the code to run independently of where it is loaded. This property, called *position independence,* can eliminate some work when the program is linked and is also useful in programs linked dynamically during execution.

To implement returns and indirect jumps when the target is not known at compile time, a method other than PC-relative addressing is required. Here, there must be a way to specify the target dynamically, so that it can change at run time. This dynamic address may be as simple as naming a register that contains the target address; alternatively, the jump may permit any addressing mode to be used to supply the target address.

These register indirect jumps are also useful for four other important features:

- *Case* or *switch* statements, found in most programming languages (which select among one of several alternatives)

- *Virtual functions* or *methods* in object-oriented languages like C++ or Java (which allow different routines to be called depending on the type of the argument)

- *High-order functions* or *function pointers* in languages like C or C++ (which allow functions to be passed as arguments, giving some of the flavor of object-oriented programming)

- *Dynamically shared libraries* (which allow a library to be loaded and linked at run time only when it is actually invoked by the program rather than loaded and linked statically before the program is run)

In all four cases the target address is not known at compile time, and hence is usually loaded from memory into a register before the register indirect jump.

As branches generally use PC-relative addressing to specify their targets, an important question concerns how far branch targets are from branches. Knowing the distribution of these displacements will help in choosing what branch offsets to support, and thus will affect the instruction length and encoding. Figure B.15 shows the distribution of displacements for PC-relative branches in instructions. About 75% of the branches are in the forward direction.

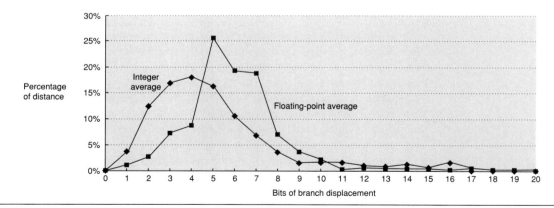

Figure B.15 Branch distances in terms of number of instructions between the target and the branch instruction. The most frequent branches in the integer programs are to targets that can be encoded in 4–8 bits. This result tells us that short displacement fields often suffice for branches and that the designer can gain some encoding density by having a shorter instruction with a smaller branch displacement. These measurements were taken on a load-store computer (Alpha architecture) with all instructions aligned on word boundaries. An architecture that requires fewer instructions for the same program, such as a VAX, would have shorter branch distances. However, the number of bits needed for the displacement may increase if the computer has variable-length instructions to be aligned on any byte boundary. The programs and computer used to collect these statistics are the same as those in Figure B.8.

Conditional Branch Options

Since most changes in control flow are branches, deciding how to specify the branch condition is important. Figure B.16 shows the three primary techniques in use today and their advantages and disadvantages.

One of the most noticeable properties of branches is that a large number of the comparisons are simple tests, and a large number are comparisons with zero. Thus, some architectures choose to treat these comparisons as special cases, especially if a *compare and branch* instruction is being used. Figure B.17 shows the frequency of different comparisons used for conditional branching.

Procedure Invocation Options

Procedure calls and returns include control transfer and possibly some state saving; at a minimum the return address must be saved somewhere, sometimes in a special link register or just a GPR. Some older architectures provide a mechanism to save many registers, while newer architectures require the compiler to generate stores and loads for each register saved and restored.

There are two basic conventions in use to save registers: either at the call site or inside the procedure being called. *Caller saving* means that the calling procedure must save the registers that it wants preserved for access after the call, and thus the called procedure need not worry about registers. *Callee saving* is the opposite: the called procedure must save the registers it wants to use, leaving the caller unrestrained. There are times when caller save must be used because of

Name	Examples	How condition is tested	Advantages	Disadvantages
Condition code (CC)	80x86, ARM, PowerPC, SPARC, SuperH	Tests special bits set by ALU operations, possibly under program control.	Sometimes condition is set for free.	CC is extra state. Condition codes constrain the ordering of instructions since they pass information from one instruction to a branch.
Condition register	Alpha, MIPS	Tests arbitrary register with the result of a comparison.	Simple.	Uses up a register.
Compare and branch	PA-RISC, VAX	Compare is part of the branch. Often compare is limited to subset.	One instruction rather than two for a branch.	May be too much work per instruction for pipelined execution.

Figure B.16 The major methods for evaluating branch conditions, their advantages, and their disadvantages. Although condition codes can be set by ALU operations that are needed for other purposes, measurements on programs show that this rarely happens. The major implementation problems with condition codes arise when the condition code is set by a large or haphazardly chosen subset of the instructions, rather than being controlled by a bit in the instruction. Computers with compare and branch often limit the set of compares and use a condition register for more complex compares. Often, different techniques are used for branches based on floating-point comparison versus those based on integer comparison. This dichotomy is reasonable since the number of branches that depend on floating-point comparisons is much smaller than the number depending on integer comparisons.

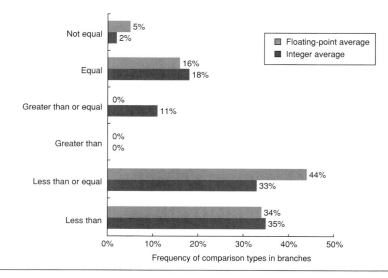

Figure B.17 Frequency of different types of compares in conditional branches. Less than (or equal) branches dominate this combination of compiler and architecture. These measurements include both the integer and floating-point compares in branches. The programs and computer used to collect these statistics are the same as those in Figure B.8.

access patterns to globally visible variables in two different procedures. For example, suppose we have a procedure P1 that calls procedure P2, and both procedures manipulate the global variable x. If P1 had allocated x to a register, it must be sure to save x to a location known by P2 before the call to P2. A compiler's ability to discover when a called procedure may access register-allocated quantities is complicated by the possibility of separate compilation. Suppose P2 may not touch x but can call another procedure, P3, that may access x, yet P2 and P3 are compiled separately. Because of these complications, most compilers will conservatively caller save *any* variable that may be accessed during a call.

In the cases where either convention could be used, some programs will be more optimal with callee save and some will be more optimal with caller save. As a result, most real systems today use a combination of the two mechanisms. This convention is specified in an application binary interface (ABI) that sets down the basic rules as to which registers should be caller saved and which should be callee saved. Later in this appendix we will examine the mismatch between sophisticated instructions for automatically saving registers and the needs of the compiler.

Summary: Instructions for Control Flow

Control flow instructions are some of the most frequently executed instructions. Although there are many options for conditional branches, we would expect branch addressing in a new architecture to be able to jump to hundreds of instructions either above or below the branch. This requirement suggests a PC-relative branch displacement of at least 8 bits. We would also expect to see register indirect and PC-relative addressing for jump instructions to support returns as well as many other features of current systems.

We have now completed our instruction architecture tour at the level seen by an assembly language programmer or compiler writer. We are leaning toward a load-store architecture with displacement, immediate, and register indirect addressing modes. These data are 8-, 16-, 32-, and 64-bit integers and 32- and 64-bit floating-point data. The instructions include simple operations, PC-relative conditional branches, jump and link instructions for procedure call, and register indirect jumps for procedure return (plus a few other uses).

Now we need to select how to represent this architecture in a form that makes it easy for the hardware to execute.

B.7	## Encoding an Instruction Set

Clearly, the choices mentioned above will affect how the instructions are encoded into a binary representation for execution by the processor. This representation affects not only the size of the compiled program; it affects the implementation of the processor, which must decode this representation to quickly find the operation and its operands. The operation is typically specified in one field, called the *opcode*. As we shall see, the important decision is how to encode the addressing modes with the operations.

This decision depends on the range of addressing modes and the degree of independence between opcodes and modes. Some older computers have one to five operands with 10 addressing modes for each operand (see Figure B.6). For such a large number of combinations, typically a separate *address specifier* is needed for each operand: The address specifier tells what addressing mode is used to access the operand. At the other extreme are load-store computers with only one memory operand and only one or two addressing modes; obviously, in this case, the addressing mode can be encoded as part of the opcode.

When encoding the instructions, the number of registers and the number of addressing modes both have a significant impact on the size of instructions, as the register field and addressing mode field may appear many times in a single instruction. In fact, for most instructions many more bits are consumed in encoding addressing modes and register fields than in specifying the opcode. The architect must balance several competing forces when encoding the instruction set:

1. The desire to have as many registers and addressing modes as possible.

2. The impact of the size of the register and addressing mode fields on the average instruction size and hence on the average program size.

3. A desire to have instructions encoded into lengths that will be easy to handle in a pipelined implementation. (The value of easily decoded instructions is

discussed in Appendix A and Chapter 2.) As a minimum, the architect wants instructions to be in multiples of bytes, rather than an arbitrary bit length. Many desktop and server architects have chosen to use a fixed-length instruction to gain implementation benefits while sacrificing average code size.

Figure B.18 shows three popular choices for encoding the instruction set. The first we call *variable,* since it allows virtually all addressing modes to be with all operations. This style is best when there are many addressing modes and operations. The second choice we call *fixed,* since it combines the operation and the addressing mode into the opcode. Often fixed encoding will have only a single size for all instructions; it works best when there are few addressing modes and operations. The trade-off between variable encoding and fixed encoding is size of programs versus ease of decoding in the processor. Variable tries to use as few bits as possible to represent the program, but individual instructions can vary widely in both size and the amount of work to be performed.

Let's look at an 80x86 instruction to see an example of the variable encoding:

```
add EAX,1000(EBX)
```

Operation and no. of operands	Address specifier 1	Address field 1	...	Address specifier *n*	Address field *n*

(a) Variable (e.g., Intel 80x86, VAX)

Operation	Address field 1	Address field 2	Address field 3

(b) Fixed (e.g., Alpha, ARM, MIPS, PowerPC, SPARC, SuperH)

Operation	Address specifier	Address field

Operation	Address specifier 1	Address specifier 2	Address field

Operation	Address specifier	Address field 1	Address field 2

(c) Hybrid (e.g., IBM 360/370, MIPS16, Thumb, TI TMS320C54x)

Figure B.18 Three basic variations in instruction encoding: variable length, fixed length, and hybrid. The variable format can support any number of operands, with each address specifier determining the addressing mode and the length of the specifier for that operand. It generally enables the smallest code representation, since unused fields need not be included. The fixed format always has the same number of operands, with the addressing modes (if options exist) specified as part of the opcode. It generally results in the largest code size. Although the fields tend not to vary in their location, they will be used for different purposes by different instructions. The hybrid approach has multiple formats specified by the opcode, adding one or two fields to specify the addressing mode and one or two fields to specify the operand address.

The name add means a 32-bit integer add instruction with two operands, and this opcode takes 1 byte. An 80x86 address specifier is 1 or 2 bytes, specifying the source/destination register (EAX) and the addressing mode (displacement in this case) and base register (EBX) for the second operand. This combination takes 1 byte to specify the operands. When in 32-bit mode (see Appendix J), the size of the address field is either 1 byte or 4 bytes. Since 1000 is bigger than 2^8, the total length of the instruction is

$$1 + 1 + 4 = 6 \text{ bytes}$$

The length of 80x86 instructions varies between 1 and 17 bytes. 80x86 programs are generally smaller than the RISC architectures, which use fixed formats (see Appendix J).

Given these two poles of instruction set design of variable and fixed, the third alternative immediately springs to mind: Reduce the variability in size and work of the variable architecture but provide multiple instruction lengths to reduce code size. This *hybrid* approach is the third encoding alternative, and we'll see examples shortly.

Reduced Code Size in RISCs

As RISC computers started being used in embedded applications, the 32-bit fixed format became a liability since cost and hence smaller code are important. In response, several manufacturers offered a new hybrid version of their RISC instruction sets, with both 16-bit and 32-bit instructions. The narrow instructions support fewer operations, smaller address and immediate fields, fewer registers, and two-address format rather than the classic three-address format of RISC computers. Appendix J gives two examples, the ARM Thumb and MIPS MIPS16, which both claim a code size reduction of up to 40%.

In contrast to these instruction set extensions, IBM simply compresses its standard instruction set, and then adds hardware to decompress instructions as they are fetched from memory on an instruction cache miss. Thus, the instruction cache contains full 32-bit instructions, but compressed code is kept in main memory, ROMs, and the disk. The advantage of MIPS16 and Thumb is that instruction caches act as if they are about 25% larger, while IBM's CodePack means that compilers need not be changed to handle different instruction sets and instruction decoding can remain simple.

CodePack starts with run-length encoding compression on any PowerPC program, and then loads the resulting compression tables in a 2 KB table on chip. Hence, every program has its own unique encoding. To handle branches, which are no longer to an aligned word boundary, the PowerPC creates a hash table in memory that maps between compressed and uncompressed addresses. Like a TLB (see Chapter 5), it caches the most recently used address maps to reduce the number of memory accesses. IBM claims an overall performance cost of 10%, resulting in a code size reduction of 35% to 40%.

Hitachi simply invented a RISC instruction set with a fixed 16-bit format, called SuperH, for embedded applications (see Appendix J). It has 16 rather than

32 registers to make it fit the narrower format and fewer instructions, but otherwise looks like a classic RISC architecture.

Summary: Encoding an Instruction Set

Decisions made in the components of instruction set design discussed in previous sections determine whether the architect has the choice between variable and fixed instruction encodings. Given the choice, the architect more interested in code size than performance will pick variable encoding, and the one more interested in performance than code size will pick fixed encoding. Appendix D gives 13 examples of the results of architects' choices. In Appendix A and Chapter 2, the impact of variability on performance of the processor will be discussed further.

We have almost finished laying the groundwork for the MIPS instruction set architecture that will be introduced in Section B.9. Before we do that, however, it will be helpful to take a brief look at compiler technology and its effect on program properties.

B.8   Crosscutting Issues: The Role of Compilers

Today almost all programming is done in high-level languages for desktop and server applications. This development means that since most instructions executed are the output of a compiler, an instruction set architecture is essentially a compiler target. In earlier times for these applications, architectural decisions were often made to ease assembly language programming or for a specific kernel. Because the compiler will significantly affect the performance of a computer, understanding compiler technology today is critical to designing and efficiently implementing an instruction set.

Once it was popular to try to isolate the compiler technology and its effect on hardware performance from the architecture and its performance, just as it was popular to try to separate architecture from its implementation. This separation is essentially impossible with today's desktop compilers and computers. Architectural choices affect the quality of the code that can be generated for a computer and the complexity of building a good compiler for it, for better or for worse.

In this section, we discuss the critical goals in the instruction set primarily from the compiler viewpoint. It starts with a review of the anatomy of current compilers. Next we discuss how compiler technology affects the decisions of the architect, and how the architect can make it hard or easy for the compiler to produce good code. We conclude with a review of compilers and multimedia operations, which unfortunately is a bad example of cooperation between compiler writers and architects.

The Structure of Recent Compilers

To begin, let's look at what optimizing compilers are like today. Figure B.19 shows the structure of recent compilers.

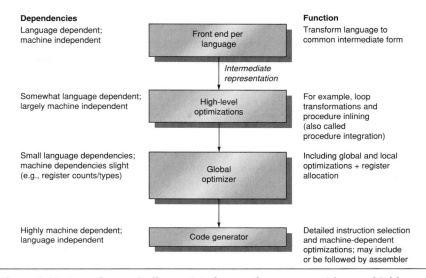

Dependencies

Language dependent;
machine independent

Somewhat language dependent;
largely machine independent

Small language dependencies;
machine dependencies slight
(e.g., register counts/types)

Highly machine dependent;
language independent

Front end per
language

*Intermediate
representation*

High-level
optimizations

Global
optimizer

Code generator

Function

Transform language to
common intermediate form

For example, loop
transformations and
procedure inlining
(also called
procedure integration)

Including global and local
optimizations + register
allocation

Detailed instruction selection
and machine-dependent
optimizations; may include
or be followed by assembler

Figure B.19 Compilers typically consist of two to four passes, with more highly optimizing compilers having more passes. This structure maximizes the probability that a program compiled at various levels of optimization will produce the same output when given the same input. The optimizing passes are designed to be optional and may be skipped when faster compilation is the goal and lower-quality code is acceptable. A *pass* is simply one phase in which the compiler reads and transforms the entire program. (The term *phase* is often used interchangeably with *pass*.) Because the optimizing passes are separated, multiple languages can use the same optimizing and code generation passes. Only a new front end is required for a new language.

A compiler writer's first goal is correctness—all valid programs must be compiled correctly. The second goal is usually speed of the compiled code. Typically, a whole set of other goals follows these two, including fast compilation, debugging support, and interoperability among languages. Normally, the passes in the compiler transform higher-level, more abstract representations into progressively lower-level representations. Eventually it reaches the instruction set. This structure helps manage the complexity of the transformations and makes writing a bug-free compiler easier.

The complexity of writing a correct compiler is a major limitation on the amount of optimization that can be done. Although the multiple-pass structure helps reduce compiler complexity, it also means that the compiler must order and perform some transformations before others. In the diagram of the optimizing compiler in Figure B.19, we can see that certain high-level optimizations are performed long before it is known what the resulting code will look like. Once such a transformation is made, the compiler can't afford to go back and revisit all steps, possibly undoing transformations. Such iteration would be prohibitive, both in compilation time and in complexity. Thus, compilers make assumptions about the ability of later steps to deal with certain problems. For example, compilers usually have to choose which procedure calls to expand inline before they know the exact size of the procedure being called. Compiler writers call this problem the *phase-ordering problem.*

How does this ordering of transformations interact with the instruction set architecture? A good example occurs with the optimization called *global common subexpression elimination.* This optimization finds two instances of an expression that compute the same value and saves the value of the first computation in a temporary. It then uses the temporary value, eliminating the second computation of the common expression.

For this optimization to be significant, the temporary must be allocated to a register. Otherwise, the cost of storing the temporary in memory and later reloading it may negate the savings gained by not recomputing the expression. There are, in fact, cases where this optimization actually slows down code when the temporary is not register allocated. Phase ordering complicates this problem because register allocation is typically done near the end of the global optimization pass, just before code generation. Thus, an optimizer that performs this optimization must *assume* that the register allocator will allocate the temporary to a register.

Optimizations performed by modern compilers can be classified by the style of the transformation, as follows:

- *High-level optimizations* are often done on the source with output fed to later optimization passes.

- *Local optimizations* optimize code only within a straight-line code fragment (called a *basic block* by compiler people).

- *Global optimizations* extend the local optimizations across branches and introduce a set of transformations aimed at optimizing loops.

- *Register allocation* associates registers with operands.

- *Processor-dependent optimizations* attempt to take advantage of specific architectural knowledge.

Register Allocation

Because of the central role that register allocation plays, both in speeding up the code and in making other optimizations useful, it is one of the most important—if not the most important—of the optimizations. Register allocation algorithms today are based on a technique called *graph coloring.* The basic idea behind graph coloring is to construct a graph representing the possible candidates for allocation to a register and then to use the graph to allocate registers. Roughly speaking, the problem is how to use a limited set of colors so that no two adjacent nodes in a dependency graph have the same color. The emphasis in the approach is to achieve 100% register allocation of active variables. The problem of coloring a graph in general can take exponential time as a function of the size of the graph (NP-complete). There are heuristic algorithms, however, that work well in practice, yielding close allocations that run in near-linear time.

Graph coloring works best when there are at least 16 (and preferably more) general-purpose registers available for global allocation for integer variables and additional registers for floating point. Unfortunately, graph coloring does not work very well when the number of registers is small because the heuristic algorithms for coloring the graph are likely to fail.

Impact of Optimizations on Performance

It is sometimes difficult to separate some of the simpler optimizations—local and processor-dependent optimizations—from transformations done in the code generator. Examples of typical optimizations are given in Figure B.20. The last column of Figure B.20 indicates the frequency with which the listed optimizing transforms were applied to the source program.

Figure B.21 shows the effect of various optimizations on instructions executed for two programs. In this case, optimized programs executed roughly 25% to 90% fewer instructions than unoptimized programs. The figure illustrates the importance of looking at optimized code before suggesting new instruction set features, since a compiler might completely remove the instructions the architect was trying to improve.

The Impact of Compiler Technology on the Architect's Decisions

The interaction of compilers and high-level languages significantly affects how programs use an instruction set architecture. There are two important questions: How are variables allocated and addressed? How many registers are needed to allocate variables appropriately? To address these questions, we must look at the three separate areas in which current high-level languages allocate their data:

- The *stack* is used to allocate local variables. The stack is grown or shrunk on procedure call or return, respectively. Objects on the stack are addressed relative to the stack pointer and are primarily scalars (single variables) rather than arrays. The stack is used for activation records, *not* as a stack for evaluating expressions. Hence, values are almost never pushed or popped on the stack.

- The *global data area* is used to allocate statically declared objects, such as global variables and constants. A large percentage of these objects are arrays or other aggregate data structures.

- The *heap* is used to allocate dynamic objects that do not adhere to a stack discipline. Objects in the heap are accessed with pointers and are typically not scalars.

Register allocation is much more effective for stack-allocated objects than for global variables, and register allocation is essentially impossible for heap-allocated objects because they are accessed with pointers. Global variables and some stack variables are impossible to allocate because they are *aliased*—there

Optimization name	Explanation	Percentage of the total number of optimizing transforms
High-level	*At or near the source level; processor-independent*	
Procedure integration	Replace procedure call by procedure body	N.M.
Local	*Within straight-line code*	
Common subexpression elimination	Replace two instances of the same computation by single copy	18%
Constant propagation	Replace all instances of a variable that is assigned a constant with the constant	22%
Stack height reduction	Rearrange expression tree to minimize resources needed for expression evaluation	N.M.
Global	*Across a branch*	
Global common subexpression elimination	Same as local, but this version crosses branches	13%
Copy propagation	Replace all instances of a variable A that has been assigned X (i.e., $A = X$) with X	11%
Code motion	Remove code from a loop that computes same value each iteration of the loop	16%
Induction variable elimination	Simplify/eliminate array addressing calculations within loops	2%
Processor-dependent	*Depends on processor knowledge*	
Strength reduction	Many examples, such as replace multiply by a constant with adds and shifts	N.M.
Pipeline scheduling	Reorder instructions to improve pipeline performance	N.M.
Branch offset optimization	Choose the shortest branch displacement that reaches target	N.M.

Figure B.20 Major types of optimizations and examples in each class. These data tell us about the relative frequency of occurrence of various optimizations. The third column lists the static frequency with which some of the common optimizations are applied in a set of 12 small FORTRAN and Pascal programs. There are nine local and global optimizations done by the compiler included in the measurement. Six of these optimizations are covered in the figure, and the remaining three account for 18% of the total static occurrences. The abbreviation *N.M.* means that the number of occurrences of that optimization was not measured. Processor-dependent optimizations are usually done in a code generator, and none of those was measured in this experiment. The percentage is the portion of the static optimizations that are of the specified type. Data from Chow [1983] (collected using the Stanford UCODE compiler).

are multiple ways to refer to the address of a variable, making it illegal to put it into a register. (Most heap variables are effectively aliased for today's compiler technology.)

For example, consider the following code sequence, where & returns the address of a variable and * dereferences a pointer:

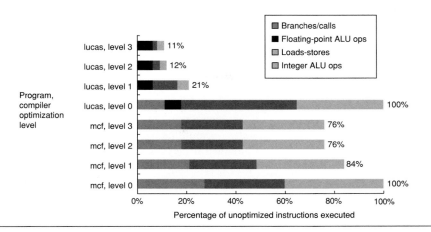

Figure B.21 Change in instruction count for the programs lucas and mcf from the SPEC2000 as compiler optimization levels vary. Level 0 is the same as unoptimized code. Level 1 includes local optimizations, code scheduling, and local register allocation. Level 2 includes global optimizations, loop transformations (software pipelining), and global register allocation. Level 3 adds procedure integration. These experiments were performed on the Alpha compilers.

```
p = &a          -- gets address of a in p
a = ...          -- assigns to a directly
*p = ...         -- uses p to assign to a
...a...          -- accesses a
```

The variable a could not be register allocated across the assignment to *p without generating incorrect code. Aliasing causes a substantial problem because it is often difficult or impossible to decide what objects a pointer may refer to. A compiler must be conservative; some compilers will not allocate *any* local variables of a procedure in a register when there is a pointer that may refer to *one* of the local variables.

How the Architect Can Help the Compiler Writer

Today, the complexity of a compiler does not come from translating simple statements like A = B + C. Most programs are *locally simple,* and simple translations work fine. Rather, complexity arises because programs are large and globally complex in their interactions, and because the structure of compilers means decisions are made one step at a time about which code sequence is best.

Compiler writers often are working under their own corollary of a basic principle in architecture: *Make the frequent cases fast and the rare case correct.* That is, if we know which cases are frequent and which are rare, and if generating code for both is straightforward, then the quality of the code for the rare case may not be very important—but it must be correct!

Some instruction set properties help the compiler writer. These properties should not be thought of as hard-and-fast rules, but rather as guidelines that will make it easier to write a compiler that will generate efficient and correct code.

- *Provide regularity*—Whenever it makes sense, the three primary components of an instruction set—the operations, the data types, and the addressing modes—should be *orthogonal*. Two aspects of an architecture are said to be orthogonal if they are independent. For example, the operations and addressing modes are orthogonal if, for every operation to which one addressing mode can be applied, all addressing modes are applicable. This regularity helps simplify code generation and is particularly important when the decision about what code to generate is split into two passes in the compiler. A good counterexample of this property is restricting what registers can be used for a certain class of instructions. Compilers for special-purpose register architectures typically get stuck in this dilemma. This restriction can result in the compiler finding itself with lots of available registers, but none of the right kind!

- *Provide primitives, not solutions*—Special features that "match" a language construct or a kernel function are often unusable. Attempts to support high-level languages may work only with one language, or do more or less than is required for a correct and efficient implementation of the language. An example of how such attempts have failed is given in Section B.10.

- *Simplify trade-offs among alternatives*—One of the toughest jobs a compiler writer has is figuring out what instruction sequence will be best for every segment of code that arises. In earlier days, instruction counts or total code size might have been good metrics, but—as we saw in Chapter 1—this is no longer true. With caches and pipelining, the trade-offs have become very complex. Anything the designer can do to help the compiler writer understand the costs of alternative code sequences would help improve the code. One of the most difficult instances of complex trade-offs occurs in a register-memory architecture in deciding how many times a variable should be referenced before it is cheaper to load it into a register. This threshold is hard to compute and, in fact, may vary among models of the same architecture.

- *Provide instructions that bind the quantities known at compile time as constants*—A compiler writer hates the thought of the processor interpreting at run time a value that was known at compile time. Good counterexamples of this principle include instructions that interpret values that were fixed at compile time. For instance, the VAX procedure call instruction (`calls`) dynamically interprets a mask saying what registers to save on a call, but the mask is fixed at compile time (see Section B.10).

Compiler Support (or Lack Thereof) for Multimedia Instructions

Alas, the designers of the SIMD instructions that operate on several narrow data items in a single clock cycle consciously ignored the previous subsection. These instructions tend to be solutions, not primitives; they are short of registers; and the data types do not match existing programming languages. Architects hoped to find an inexpensive solution that would help some users, but in reality, only a few low-level graphics library routines use them.

The SIMD instructions are really an abbreviated version of an elegant architecture style that has its own compiler technology. As explained in Appendix F, *vector architectures* operate on vectors of data. Invented originally for scientific codes, multimedia kernels are often vectorizable as well, albeit often with shorter vectors. Hence, we can think of Intel's MMX and SSE or PowerPC's AltiVec as simply short vector computers: MMX with vectors of eight 8-bit elements, four 16-bit elements, or two 32-bit elements, and AltiVec with vectors twice that length. They are implemented as simply adjacent, narrow elements in wide registers.

These microprocessor architectures build the vector register size into the architecture: the sum of the sizes of the elements is limited to 64 bits for MMX and 128 bits for AltiVec. When Intel decided to expand to 128-bit vectors, it added a whole new set of instructions, called Streaming SIMD Extension (SSE).

A major advantage of vector computers is hiding latency of memory access by loading many elements at once and then overlapping execution with data transfer. The goal of vector addressing modes is to collect data scattered about memory, place them in a compact form so that they can be operated on efficiently, and then place the results back where they belong.

Over the years traditional vector computers added *strided addressing* and *gather/scatter addressing* to increase the number of programs that can be vectorized. Strided addressing skips a fixed number of words between each access, so sequential addressing is often called *unit stride addressing*. Gather and scatter find their addresses in another vector register: Think of it as register indirect addressing for vector computers. From a vector perspective, in contrast, these short-vector SIMD computers support only unit strided accesses: Memory accesses load or store all elements at once from a single wide memory location. Since the data for multimedia applications are often streams that start and end in memory, strided and gather/scatter addressing modes are essential to successful vectorization.

Example   As an example, compare a vector computer to MMX for color representation conversion of pixels from RGB (red green blue) to YUV (luminosity chrominance), with each pixel represented by 3 bytes. The conversion is just three lines of C code placed in a loop:

```
Y = (9798*R + 19235*G + 3736*B)/ 32768;
U = (-4784*R - 9437*G + 4221*B)/ 32768 + 128;
V = (20218*R - 16941*G - 3277*B)/ 32768 + 128;
```

A 64-bit-wide vector computer can calculate 8 pixels simultaneously. One vector computer for media with strided addresses takes

- 3 vector loads (to get RGB)
- 3 vector multiplies (to convert R)
- 6 vector multiply adds (to convert G and B)
- 3 vector shifts (to divide by 32,768)
- 2 vector adds (to add 128)
- 3 vector stores (to store YUV)

The total is 20 instructions to perform the 20 operations in the previous C code to convert 8 pixels [Kozyrakis 2000]. (Since a vector might have 32 64-bit elements, this code actually converts up to 32×8 or 256 pixels.)

In contrast, Intel's Web site shows that a library routine to perform the same calculation on 8 pixels takes 116 MMX instructions plus 6 80x86 instructions [Intel 2001]. This sixfold increase in instructions is due to the large number of instructions to load and unpack RGB pixels and to pack and store YUV pixels, since there are no strided memory accesses.

Having short, architecture-limited vectors with few registers and simple memory addressing modes makes it more difficult to use vectorizing compiler technology. Another challenge is that no programming language (yet) has support for operations on these narrow data. Hence, these SIMD instructions are likely to be found in hand-coded libraries than in compiled code.

Summary: The Role of Compilers

This section leads to several recommendations. First, we expect a new instruction set architecture to have at least 16 general-purpose registers—not counting separate registers for floating-point numbers—to simplify allocation of registers using graph coloring. The advice on orthogonality suggests that all supported addressing modes apply to all instructions that transfer data. Finally, the last three pieces of advice—provide primitives instead of solutions, simplify trade-offs between alternatives, don't bind constants at run time—all suggest that it is better to err on the side of simplicity. In other words, understand that less is more in the design of an instruction set. Alas, SIMD extensions are more an example of good marketing than of outstanding achievement of hardware-software co-design.

B.9   Putting It All Together: The MIPS Architecture

In this section we describe a simple 64-bit load-store architecture called MIPS. The instruction set architecture of MIPS and RISC relatives was based on observations similar to those covered in the last sections. (In Section K.3 we discuss how and why these architectures became popular.) Reviewing our expectations from each section, for desktop applications:

- *Section B.2*—Use general-purpose registers with a load-store architecture.

- *Section B.3*—Support these addressing modes: displacement (with an address offset size of 12–16 bits), immediate (size 8–16 bits), and register indirect.

- *Section B.4*—Support these data sizes and types: 8-, 16-, 32-, and 64-bit integers and 64-bit IEEE 754 floating-point numbers.

- *Section B.5*—Support these simple instructions, since they will dominate the number of instructions executed: load, store, add, subtract, move register-register, and shift.

- *Section B.6*—Compare equal, compare not equal, compare less, branch (with a PC-relative address at least 8 bits long), jump, call, and return.

- *Section B.7*—Use fixed instruction encoding if interested in performance, and use variable instruction encoding if interested in code size.

- *Section B.8*—Provide at least 16 general-purpose registers, be sure all addressing modes apply to all data transfer instructions, and aim for a minimalist instruction set. This section didn't cover floating-point programs, but they often use separate floating-point registers. The justification is to increase the total number of registers without raising problems in the instruction format or in the speed of the general-purpose register file. This compromise, however, is not orthogonal.

We introduce MIPS by showing how it follows these recommendations. Like most recent computers, MIPS emphasizes

- a simple load-store instruction set

- design for pipelining efficiency (discussed in Appendix A), including a fixed instruction set encoding

- efficiency as a compiler target

MIPS provides a good architectural model for study, not only because of the popularity of this type of processor, but also because it is an easy architecture to understand. We will use this architecture again in Appendix A and in Chapters 2 and 3, and it forms the basis for a number of exercises and programming projects.

In the years since the first MIPS processor in 1985, there have been many versions of MIPS (see Appendix J). We will use a subset of what is now called MIPS64, which will often abbreviate to just MIPS, but the full instruction set is found in Appendix J.

Registers for MIPS

MIPS64 has 32 64-bit general-purpose registers (GPRs), named R0, R1, ... , R31. GPRs are also sometimes known as *integer registers.* Additionally, there is a set of 32 floating-point registers (FPRs), named F0, F1, . . . , F31, which can hold 32 single-precision (32-bit) values or 32 double-precision (64-bit) values. (When holding one single-precision number, the other half of the FPR is unused.) Both single- and double-precision floating-point operations (32-bit and 64-bit) are provided. MIPS also includes instructions that operate on two single-precision operands in a single 64-bit floating-point register.

The value of R0 is always 0. We shall see later how we can use this register to synthesize a variety of useful operations from a simple instruction set.

A few special registers can be transferred to and from the general-purpose registers. An example is the floating-point status register, used to hold information about the results of floating-point operations. There are also instructions for moving between an FPR and a GPR.

Data Types for MIPS

The data types are 8-bit bytes, 16-bit half words, 32-bit words, and 64-bit double words for integer data and 32-bit single precision and 64-bit double precision for floating point. Half words were added because they are found in languages like C and are popular in some programs, such as the operating systems, concerned about size of data structures. They will also become more popular if Unicode becomes widely used. Single-precision floating-point operands were added for similar reasons. (Remember the early warning that you should measure many more programs before designing an instruction set.)

The MIPS64 operations work on 64-bit integers and 32- or 64-bit floating point. Bytes, half words, and words are loaded into the general-purpose registers with either zeros or the sign bit replicated to fill the 64 bits of the GPRs. Once loaded, they are operated on with the 64-bit integer operations.

Addressing Modes for MIPS Data Transfers

The only data addressing modes are immediate and displacement, both with 16-bit fields. Register indirect is accomplished simply by placing 0 in the 16-bit displacement field, and absolute addressing with a 16-bit field is accomplished by using register 0 as the base register. Embracing zero gives us four effective modes, although only two are supported in the architecture.

MIPS memory is byte addressable with a 64-bit address. It has a mode bit that allows software to select either Big Endian or Little Endian. As it is a load-store architecture, all references between memory and either GPRs or FPRs are through loads or stores. Supporting the data types mentioned above, memory accesses involving GPRs can be to a byte, half word, word, or double word. The

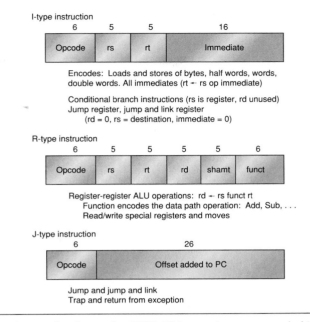

Encodes: Loads and stores of bytes, half words, words, double words. All immediates (rt ← rs op immediate)

Conditional branch instructions (rs is register, rd unused)
Jump register, jump and link register
(rd = 0, rs = destination, immediate = 0)

Register-register ALU operations: rd ← rs funct rt
Function encodes the data path operation: Add, Sub, . . .
Read/write special registers and moves

Jump and jump and link
Trap and return from exception

Figure B.22 Instruction layout for MIPS. All instructions are encoded in one of three types, with common fields in the same location in each format.

FPRs may be loaded and stored with single-precision or double-precision numbers. All memory accesses must be aligned.

MIPS Instruction Format

Since MIPS has just two addressing modes, these can be encoded into the opcode. Following the advice on making the processor easy to pipeline and decode, all instructions are 32 bits with a 6-bit primary opcode. Figure B.22 shows the instruction layout. These formats are simple while providing 16-bit fields for displacement addressing, immediate constants, or PC-relative branch addresses.

Appendix J shows a variant of MIPS—called MIPS16—which has 16-bit and 32-bit instructions to improve code density for embedded applications. We will stick to the traditional 32-bit format in this book.

MIPS Operations

MIPS supports the list of simple operations recommended above plus a few others. There are four broad classes of instructions: loads and stores, ALU operations, branches and jumps, and floating-point operations.

Any of the general-purpose or floating-point registers may be loaded or stored, except that loading R0 has no effect. Figure B.23 gives examples of the load and store instructions. Single-precision floating-point numbers occupy half a floating-point register. Conversions between single and double precision must be done explicitly. The floating-point format is IEEE 754 (see Appendix I). A list of all the MIPS instructions in our subset appears in Figure B.26 (page B-40).

To understand these figures we need to introduce a few additional extensions to our C description language used initially on page B-9:

- A subscript is appended to the symbol $\leftarrow$ whenever the length of the datum being transferred might not be clear. Thus, $\leftarrow_n$ means transfer an n-bit quantity. We use $x, y \leftarrow z$ to indicate that z should be transferred to x and y.

- A subscript is used to indicate selection of a bit from a field. Bits are labeled from the most-significant bit starting at 0. The subscript may be a single digit (e.g., Regs[R4]$_0$ yields the sign bit of R4) or a subrange (e.g., Regs[R3]$_{56..63}$ yields the least-significant byte of R3).

- The variable Mem, used as an array that stands for main memory, is indexed by a byte address and may transfer any number of bytes.

- A superscript is used to replicate a field (e.g., 0^{48} yields a field of zeros of length 48 bits).

- The symbol ## is used to concatenate two fields and may appear on either side of a data transfer.

Example instruction	Instruction name	Meaning
LD R1,30(R2)	Load double word	Regs[R1] $\leftarrow_{64}$ Mem[30+Regs[R2]]
LD R1,1000(R0)	Load double word	Regs[R1] $\leftarrow_{64}$ Mem[1000+0]
LW R1,60(R2)	Load word	Regs[R1] $\leftarrow_{64}$ (Mem[60+Regs[R2]]$_0$)^{32} ## Mem[60+Regs[R2]]
LB R1,40(R3)	Load byte	Regs[R1] $\leftarrow_{64}$ (Mem[40+Regs[R3]]$_0$)^{56} ## Mem[40+Regs[R3]]
LBU R1,40(R3)	Load byte unsigned	Regs[R1] $\leftarrow_{64}$ 0^{56} ## Mem[40+Regs[R3]]
LH R1,40(R3)	Load half word	Regs[R1] $\leftarrow_{64}$ (Mem[40+Regs[R3]]$_0$)^{48} ## Mem[40+Regs[R3]] ## Mem[41+Regs[R3]]
L.S F0,50(R3)	Load FP single	Regs[F0] $\leftarrow_{64}$ Mem[50+Regs[R3]] ## 0^{32}
L.D F0,50(R2)	Load FP double	Regs[F0] $\leftarrow_{64}$ Mem[50+Regs[R2]]
SD R3,500(R4)	Store double word	Mem[500+Regs[R4]] $\leftarrow_{64}$ Regs[R3]
SW R3,500(R4)	Store word	Mem[500+Regs[R4]] $\leftarrow_{32}$ Regs[R3]$_{32..63}$
S.S F0,40(R3)	Store FP single	Mem[40+Regs[R3]] $\leftarrow_{32}$ Regs[F0]$_{0..31}$
S.D F0,40(R3)	Store FP double	Mem[40+Regs[R3]] $\leftarrow_{64}$ Regs[F0]
SH R3,502(R2)	Store half	Mem[502+Regs[R2]] $\leftarrow_{16}$ Regs[R3]$_{48..63}$
SB R2,41(R3)	Store byte	Mem[41+Regs[R3]] $\leftarrow_{8}$ Regs[R2]$_{56..63}$

Figure B.23 The load and store instructions in MIPS. All use a single addressing mode and require that the memory value be aligned. Of course, both loads and stores are available for all the data types shown.

Example instruction	Instruction name	Meaning
DADDU R1,R2,R3	Add unsigned	Regs[R1]←Regs[R2]+Regs[R3]
DADDIU R1,R2,#3	Add immediate unsigned	Regs[R1]←Regs[R2]+3
LUI R1,#42	Load upper immediate	Regs[R1]←0^{32}##42##0^{16}
DSLL R1,R2,#5	Shift left logical	Regs[R1]←Regs[R2]<<5
SLT R1,R2,R3	Set less than	if (Regs[R2]<Regs[R3]) Regs[R1]←1 else Regs[R1]←0

Figure B.24 Examples of arithmetic/logical instructions on MIPS, both with and without immediates.

As an example, assuming that R8 and R10 are 64-bit registers:

$$\text{Regs}[\text{R10}]_{32..63} \leftarrow {}_{32}(\text{Mem}[\text{Regs}[\text{R8}]]_0)^{24} \text{ \#\# Mem}[\text{Regs}[\text{R8}]]$$

means that the byte at the memory location addressed by the contents of register R8 is sign-extended to form a 32-bit quantity that is stored into the lower half of register R10. (The upper half of R10 is unchanged.)

All ALU instructions are register-register instructions. Figure B.24 gives some examples of the arithmetic/logical instructions. The operations include simple arithmetic and logical operations: add, subtract, AND, OR, XOR, and shifts. Immediate forms of all these instructions are provided using a 16-bit sign-extended immediate. The operation LUI (load upper immediate) loads bits 32 through 47 of a register, while setting the rest of the register to 0. LUI allows a 32-bit constant to be built in two instructions, or a data transfer using any constant 32-bit address in one extra instruction.

As mentioned above, R0 is used to synthesize popular operations. Loading a constant is simply an add immediate where the source operand is R0, and a register-register move is simply an add where one of the sources is R0. (We sometimes use the mnemonic LI, standing for load immediate, to represent the former, and the mnemonic MOV for the latter.)

MIPS Control Flow Instructions

MIPS provides compare instructions, which compare two registers to see if the first is less than the second. If the condition is true, these instructions place a 1 in the destination register (to represent true); otherwise they place the value 0. Because these operations "set" a register, they are called set-equal, set-not-equal, set-less-than, and so on. There are also immediate forms of these compares.

Control is handled through a set of jumps and a set of branches. Figure B.25 gives some typical branch and jump instructions. The four jump instructions are differentiated by the two ways to specify the destination address and by whether or not a link is made. Two jumps use a 26-bit offset shifted 2 bits and then replace

Example instruction	Instruction name	Meaning
J name	Jump	$PC_{36..63} \leftarrow$ name
JAL name	Jump and link	$Regs[R31] \leftarrow PC+8$; $PC_{36..63} \leftarrow$ name; $((PC+4)-2^{27}) \leq$ name $< ((PC+4)+2^{27})$
JALR R2	Jump and link register	$Regs[R31] \leftarrow PC+8$; $PC \leftarrow Regs[R2]$
JR R3	Jump register	$PC \leftarrow Regs[R3]$
BEQZ R4,name	Branch equal zero	if $(Regs[R4]==0)$ $PC \leftarrow$ name; $((PC+4)-2^{17}) \leq$ name $< ((PC+4)+2^{17})$
BNE R3,R4,name	Branch not equal zero	if $(Regs[R3] != Regs[R4])$ $PC \leftarrow$ name; $((PC+4)-2^{17}) \leq$ name $< ((PC+4)+2^{17})$
MOVZ R1,R2,R3	Conditional move if zero	if $(Regs[R3]==0)$ $Regs[R1] \leftarrow Regs[R2]$

Figure B.25 Typical control flow instructions in MIPS. All control instructions, except jumps to an address in a register, are PC-relative. Note that the branch distances are longer than the address field would suggest; since MIPS instructions are all 32 bits long, the byte branch address is multiplied by 4 to get a longer distance.

the lower 28 bits of the program counter (of the instruction sequentially following the jump) to determine the destination address. The other two jump instructions specify a register that contains the destination address. There are two flavors of jumps: plain jump and jump and link (used for procedure calls). The latter places the return address—the address of the next sequential instruction—in R31.

All branches are conditional. The branch condition is specified by the instruction, which may test the register source for zero or nonzero; the register may contain a data value or the result of a compare. There are also conditional branch instructions to test for whether a register is negative and for equality between two registers. The branch-target address is specified with a 16-bit signed offset that is shifted left two places and then added to the program counter, which is pointing to the next sequential instruction. There is also a branch to test the floating-point status register for floating-point conditional branches, described later.

Appendix A and Chapter 2 show that conditional branches are a major challenge to pipelined execution; hence many architectures have added instructions to convert a simple branch into a conditional arithmetic instruction. MIPS included conditional move on zero or not zero. The value of the destination register either is left unchanged or is replaced by a copy of one of the source registers depending on whether or not the value of the other source register is zero.

MIPS Floating-Point Operations

Floating-point instructions manipulate the floating-point registers and indicate whether the operation to be performed is single or double precision. The operations MOV.S and MOV.D copy a single-precision (MOV.S) or double-precision (MOV.D) floating-point register to another register of the same type. The operations MFC1, MTC1, DMFC1, DMTC1 move data between a single or double floating-point register and an integer register. Conversions from integer to floating point are also provided, and vice versa.

The floating-point operations are add, subtract, multiply, and divide; a suffix D is used for double precision, and a suffix S is used for single precision (e.g., ADD.D, ADD.S, SUB.D, SUB.S, MUL.D, MUL.S, DIV.D, DIV.S). Floating-point compares set a bit in the special floating-point status register that can be tested with a pair of branches: BC1T and BC1F, branch floating-point true and branch floating-point false.

To get greater performance for graphics routines, MIPS64 has instructions that perform two 32-bit floating-point operations on each half of the 64-bit floating-point register. These *paired single* operations include ADD.PS, SUB.PS, MUL.PS, and DIV.PS. (They are loaded and stored using double-precision loads and stores.)

Giving a nod toward the importance of multimedia applications, MIPS64 also includes both integer and floating-point multiply-add instructions: MADD, MADD.S, MADD.D, and MADD.PS. The registers are all the same width in these combined operations. Figure B.26 contains a list of a subset of MIPS64 operations and their meaning.

MIPS Instruction Set Usage

To give an idea which instructions are popular, Figure B.27 shows the frequency of instructions and instruction classes for five SPECint2000 programs, and Figure B.28 shows the same data for five SPECfp2000 programs.

B.10   Fallacies and Pitfalls

Architects have repeatedly tripped on common, but erroneous, beliefs. In this section we look at a few of them.

Pitfall   *Designing a "high-level" instruction set feature specifically oriented to supporting a high-level language structure.*

Attempts to incorporate high-level language features in the instruction set have led architects to provide powerful instructions with a wide range of flexibility. However, often these instructions do more work than is required in the frequent case, or they don't exactly match the requirements of some languages. Many such efforts have been aimed at eliminating what in the 1970s was called the *semantic gap*. Although the idea is to supplement the instruction set with

Instruction type/opcode	Instruction meaning
Data transfers	*Move data between registers and memory, or between the integer and FP or special registers; only memory address mode is 16-bit displacement + contents of a GPR*
LB,LBU,SB	Load byte, load byte unsigned, store byte (to/from integer registers)
LH,LHU,SH	Load half word, load half word unsigned, store half word (to/from integer registers)
LW,LWU,SW	Load word, load word unsigned, store word (to/from integer registers)
LD,SD	Load double word, store double word (to/from integer registers)
L.S,L.D,S.S,S.D	Load SP float, load DP float, store SP float, store DP float
MFC0,MTC0	Copy from/to GPR to/from a special register
MOV.S,MOV.D	Copy one SP or DP FP register to another FP register
MFC1,MTC1	Copy 32 bits to/from FP registers from/to integer registers
Arithmetic/logical	*Operations on integer or logical data in GPRs; signed arithmetic trap on overflow*
DADD,DADDI,DADDU,DADDIU	Add, add immediate (all immediates are 16 bits); signed and unsigned
DSUB,DSUBU	Subtract; signed and unsigned
DMUL,DMULU,DDIV, DDIVU,MADD	Multiply and divide, signed and unsigned; multiply-add; all operations take and yield 64-bit values
AND,ANDI	And, and immediate
OR,ORI,XOR,XORI	Or, or immediate, exclusive or, exclusive or immediate
LUI	Load upper immediate; loads bits 32 to 47 of register with immediate, then sign-extends
DSLL,DSRL,DSRA,DSLLV, DSRLV,DSRAV	Shifts: both immediate (DS__) and variable form (DS_V); shifts are shift left logical, right logical, right arithmetic
SLT,SLTI,SLTU,SLTIU	Set less than, set less than immediate; signed and unsigned
Control	*Conditional branches and jumps; PC-relative or through register*
BEQZ,BNEZ	Branch GPRs equal/not equal to zero; 16-bit offset from PC + 4
BEQ,BNE	Branch GPR equal/not equal; 16-bit offset from PC + 4
BC1T,BC1F	Test comparison bit in the FP status register and branch; 16-bit offset from PC + 4
MOVN,MOVZ	Copy GPR to another GPR if third GPR is negative, zero
J,JR	Jumps: 26-bit offset from PC + 4 (J) or target in register (JR)
JAL,JALR	Jump and link: save PC + 4 in R31, target is PC-relative (JAL) or a register (JALR)
TRAP	Transfer to operating system at a vectored address
ERET	Return to user code from an exception; restore user mode
Floating point	*FP operations on DP and SP formats*
ADD.D,ADD.S,ADD.PS	Add DP, SP numbers, and pairs of SP numbers
SUB.D,SUB.S,SUB.PS	Subtract DP, SP numbers, and pairs of SP numbers
MUL.D,MUL.S,MUL.PS	Multiply DP, SP floating point, and pairs of SP numbers
MADD.D,MADD.S,MADD.PS	Multiply-add DP, SP numbers and pairs of SP numbers
DIV.D,DIV.S,DIV.PS	Divide DP, SP floating point, and pairs of SP numbers
CVT._._	Convert instructions: CVT.x.y converts from type x to type y, where x and y are L (64-bit integer), W (32-bit integer), D (DP), or S (SP). Both operands are FPRs.
C.__.D,C.__.S	DP and SP compares: "__" = LT,GT,LE,GE,EQ,NE; sets bit in FP status register

Figure B.26 Subset of the instructions in MIPS64. Figure B.22 lists the formats of these instructions. SP = single precision; DP = double precision. This list can also be found on the back inside cover.

Instruction	gap	gcc	gzip	mcf	perlbmk	Integer average
load	26.5%	25.1%	20.1%	30.3%	28.7%	26%
store	10.3%	13.2%	5.1%	4.3%	16.2%	10%
add	21.1%	19.0%	26.9%	10.1%	16.7%	19%
sub	1.7%	2.2%	5.1%	3.7%	2.5%	3%
mul	1.4%	0.1%				0%
compare	2.8%	6.1%	6.6%	6.3%	3.8%	5%
load imm	4.8%	2.5%	1.5%	0.1%	1.7%	2%
cond branch	9.3%	12.1%	11.0%	17.5%	10.9%	12%
cond move	0.4%	0.6%	1.1%	0.1%	1.9%	1%
jump	0.8%	0.7%	0.8%	0.7%	1.7%	1%
call	1.6%	0.6%	0.4%	3.2%	1.1%	1%
return	1.6%	0.6%	0.4%	3.2%	1.1%	1%
shift	3.8%	1.1%	2.1%	1.1%	0.5%	2%
and	4.3%	4.6%	9.4%	0.2%	1.2%	4%
or	7.9%	8.5%	4.8%	17.6%	8.7%	9%
xor	1.8%	2.1%	4.4%	1.5%	2.8%	3%
other logical	0.1%	0.4%	0.1%	0.1%	0.3%	0%
load FP						0%
store FP						0%
add FP						0%
sub FP						0%
mul FP						0%
div FP						0%
mov reg-reg FP						0%
compare FP						0%
cond mov FP						0%
other FP						0%

Figure B.27 MIPS dynamic instruction mix for five SPECint2000 programs. Note that integer register-register move instructions are included in the or instruction. Blank entries have the value 0.0%.

additions that bring the hardware up to the level of the language, the additions can generate what Wulf [1981] has called a *semantic clash:*

> . . . by giving too much semantic content to the instruction, the computer designer made it possible to use the instruction only in limited contexts. [p. 43]

More often the instructions are simply overkill—they are too general for the most frequent case, resulting in unneeded work and a slower instruction. Again, the VAX CALLS is a good example. CALLS uses a callee save strategy (the registers

Instruction	applu	art	equake	lucas	swim	FP average
load	13.8%	18.1%	22.3%	10.6%	9.1%	15%
store	2.9%		0.8%	3.4%	1.3%	2%
add	30.4%	30.1%	17.4%	11.1%	24.4%	23%
sub	2.5%		0.1%	2.1%	3.8%	2%
mul	2.3%			1.2%		1%
compare		7.4%	2.1%			2%
load imm	13.7%		1.0%	1.8%	9.4%	5%
cond branch	2.5%	11.5%	2.9%	0.6%	1.3%	4%
cond mov		0.3%	0.1%			0%
jump			0.1%			0%
call			0.7%			0%
return			0.7%			0%
shift	0.7%		0.2%	1.9%		1%
and			0.2%	1.8%		0%
or	0.8%	1.1%	2.3%	1.0%	7.2%	2%
xor		3.2%	0.1%			1%
other logical			0.1%			0%
load FP	11.4%	12.0%	19.7%	16.2%	16.8%	15%
store FP	4.2%	4.5%	2.7%	18.2%	5.0%	7%
add FP	2.3%	4.5%	9.8%	8.2%	9.0%	7%
sub FP	2.9%		1.3%	7.6%	4.7%	3%
mul FP	8.6%	4.1%	12.9%	9.4%	6.9%	8%
div FP	0.3%	0.6%	0.5%		0.3%	0%
mov reg-reg FP	0.7%	0.9%	1.2%	1.8%	0.9%	1%
compare FP		0.9%	0.6%	0.8%		0%
cond mov FP		0.6%		0.8%		0%
other FP				1.6%		0%

Figure B.28 **MIPS dynamic instruction mix for five programs from SPECfp2000.** Note that integer register-register move instructions are included in the or instruction. Blank entries have the value 0.0%.

to be saved are specified by the callee), *but* the saving is done by the call instruction in the caller. The CALLS instruction begins with the arguments pushed on the stack, and then takes the following steps:

1. Align the stack if needed.

2. Push the argument count on the stack.

3. Save the registers indicated by the procedure call mask on the stack (as mentioned in Section B.8). The mask is kept in the called procedure's code—this

permits the callee to specify the registers to be saved by the caller even with separate compilation.

4. Push the return address on the stack, and then push the top and base of stack pointers (for the activation record).

5. Clear the condition codes, which sets the trap enable to a known state.

6. Push a word for status information and a zero word on the stack.

7. Update the two stack pointers.

8. Branch to the first instruction of the procedure.

The vast majority of calls in real programs do not require this amount of overhead. Most procedures know their argument counts, and a much faster linkage convention can be established using registers to pass arguments rather than the stack in memory. Furthermore, the CALLS instruction forces two registers to be used for linkage, while many languages require only one linkage register. Many attempts to support procedure call and activation stack management have failed to be useful, either because they do not match the language needs or because they are too general and hence too expensive to use.

The VAX designers provided a simpler instruction, JSB, that is much faster since it only pushes the return PC on the stack and jumps to the procedure. However, most VAX compilers use the more costly CALLS instructions. The call instructions were included in the architecture to standardize the procedure linkage convention. Other computers have standardized their calling convention by agreement among compiler writers and without requiring the overhead of a complex, very general procedure call instruction.

Fallacy   *There is such a thing as a typical program.*

Many people would like to believe that there is a single "typical" program that could be used to design an optimal instruction set. For example, see the synthetic benchmarks discussed in Chapter 1. The data in this appendix clearly show that programs can vary significantly in how they use an instruction set. For example, Figure B.29 shows the mix of data transfer sizes for four of the SPEC2000 programs: It would be hard to say what is typical from these four programs. The variations are even larger on an instruction set that supports a class of applications, such as decimal instructions, that are unused by other applications.

Pitfall   *Innovating at the instruction set architecture to reduce code size without accounting for the compiler.*

Figure B.30 shows the relative code sizes for four compilers for the MIPS instruction set. Whereas architects struggle to reduce code size by 30% to 40%, different compiler strategies can change code size by much larger factors. Similar to performance optimization techniques, the architect should start with the tightest code the compilers can produce before proposing hardware innovations to save space.

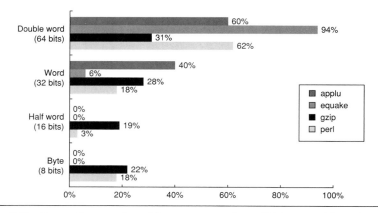

Figure B.29 Data reference size of four programs from SPEC2000. Although you can calculate an average size, it would be hard to claim the average is typical of programs.

Compiler	Apogee Software Version 4.1	Green Hills Multi2000 Version 2.0	Algorithmics SDE4.0B	IDT/c 7.2.1
Architecture	MIPS IV	MIPS IV	MIPS 32	MIPS 32
Processor	NEC VR5432	NEC VR5000	IDT 32334	IDT 79RC32364
Autocorrelation kernel	1.0	2.1	1.1	2.7
Convolutional encoder kernel	1.0	1.9	1.2	2.4
Fixed-point bit allocation kernel	1.0	2.0	1.2	2.3
Fixed-point complex FFT kernel	1.0	1.1	2.7	1.8
Viterbi GSM decoder kernel	1.0	1.7	0.8	1.1
Geometric mean of five kernels	1.0	1.7	1.4	2.0

Figure B.30   Code size relative to Apogee Software Version 4.1 C compiler for Telecom application of EEMBC benchmarks. The instruction set architectures are virtually identical, yet the code sizes vary by factors of 2. These results were reported February–June 2000.

Fallacy   *An architecture with flaws cannot be successful.*

The 80x86 provides a dramatic example: The instruction set architecture is one only its creators could love (see Appendix J). Succeeding generations of Intel engineers have tried to correct unpopular architectural decisions made in designing the 80x86. For example, the 80x86 supports segmentation, whereas all others picked paging; it uses extended accumulators for integer data, but other processors use general-purpose registers; and it uses a stack for floating-point data, when everyone else abandoned execution stacks long before.

Despite these major difficulties, the 80x86 architecture has been enormously successful. The reasons are threefold: first, its selection as the microprocessor in the initial IBM PC makes 80x86 binary compatibility extremely valuable. Second, Moore's Law provided sufficient resources for 80x86 microprocessors to translate to an internal RISC instruction set and then execute RISC-like instructions. This mix enables binary compatibility with the valuable PC software base and performance on par with RISC processors. Third, the very high volumes of PC microprocessors means Intel can easily pay for the increased design cost of hardware translation. In addition, the high volumes allow the manufacturer to go up the learning curve, which lowers the cost of the product.

The larger die size and increased power for translation may be a liability for embedded applications, but it makes tremendous economic sense for the desktop. And its cost-performance in the desktop also makes it attractive for servers, with its main weakness for servers being 32-bit addresses; which was resolved with the 64-bit addresses of AMD64 (see Chapter 5).

Fallacy *You can design a flawless architecture.*

All architecture design involves trade-offs made in the context of a set of hardware and software technologies. Over time those technologies are likely to change, and decisions that may have been correct at the time they were made look like mistakes. For example, in 1975 the VAX designers overemphasized the importance of code size efficiency, underestimating how important ease of decoding and pipelining would be five years later. An example in the RISC camp is delayed branch (see Appendix J). It was a simple matter to control pipeline hazards with five-stage pipelines, but a challenge for processors with longer pipelines that issue multiple instructions per clock cycle. In addition, almost all architectures eventually succumb to the lack of sufficient address space.

In general, avoiding such flaws in the long run would probably mean compromising the efficiency of the architecture in the short run, which is dangerous, since a new instruction set architecture must struggle to survive its first few years.

B.11   Concluding Remarks

The earliest architectures were limited in their instruction sets by the hardware technology of that time. As soon as the hardware technology permitted, computer architects began looking for ways to support high-level languages. This search led to three distinct periods of thought about how to support programs efficiently. In the 1960s, stack architectures became popular. They were viewed as being a good match for high-level languages—and they probably were, given the compiler technology of the day. In the 1970s, the main concern of architects was how to reduce software costs. This concern was met primarily by replacing software with hardware, or by providing high-level architectures that could simplify the task of software designers. The result was both the high-level language computer architecture movement and powerful architectures like the VAX, which has a large number of addressing modes, multiple data types, and a highly orthogonal architecture. In the 1980s, more sophisticated compiler technology and a renewed emphasis on processor performance saw a return to simpler architectures, based mainly on the load-store style of computer.

The following instruction set architecture changes occurred in the 1990s:

- *Address size doubles*—The 32-bit address instruction sets for most desktop and server processors were extended to 64-bit addresses, expanding the width of the registers (among other things) to 64 bits. Appendix J gives three examples of architectures that have gone from 32 bits to 64 bits.

- *Optimization of conditional branches via conditional execution*—In Chapters 2 and 3, we see that conditional branches can limit the performance of aggressive computer designs. Hence, there was interest in replacing conditional branches with conditional completion of operations, such as conditional move (see Appendix G), which was added to most instruction sets.

- *Optimization of cache performance via prefetch*—Chapter 5 explains the increasing role of memory hierarchy in performance of computers, with a cache miss on some computers taking as many instruction times as page faults took on earlier computers. Hence, prefetch instructions were added to try to hide the cost of cache misses by prefetching (see Chapter 5).

- *Support for multimedia*—Most desktop and embedded instruction sets were extended with support for multimedia applications.

- *Faster floating-point operations*—Appendix I describes operations added to enhance floating-point performance, such as operations that perform a multiply and an add and paired single execution. (We include them in MIPS.)

Between 1970 and 1985 many thought the primary job of the computer architect was the design of instruction sets. As a result, textbooks of that era emphasize instruction set design, much as computer architecture textbooks of the 1950s and 1960s emphasized computer arithmetic. The educated architect was expected to have strong opinions about the strengths and especially the weaknesses of the popular computers. The importance of binary compatibility in quashing innovations in instruction set design was unappreciated by many researchers and textbook writers, giving the impression that many architects would get a chance to design an instruction set.

The definition of computer architecture today has been expanded to include design and evaluation of the full computer system—not just the definition of the instruction set and not just the processor—and hence there are plenty of topics for the architect to study. In fact, the material in this appendix was a central point of the book in its first edition in 1990, but now is included in an appendix primarily as reference material!

Appendix J may satisfy readers interested in instruction set architecture: it describes a variety of instruction sets, which are either important in the marketplace today or historically important, and compares nine popular load-store computers with MIPS.

B.12   Historical Perspective and References

Section K.3 (available on the companion CD) features a discussion on the evolution of instruction sets and includes references for further reading and exploration of related topics.

C.1	Introduction	C-2
C.2	Cache Performance	C-15
C.3	Six Basic Cache Optimizations	C-22
C.4	Virtual Memory	C-38
C.5	Protection and Examples of Virtual Memory	C-47
C.6	Fallacies and Pitfalls	C-56
C.7	Concluding Remarks	C-57
C.8	Historical Perspective and References	C-58

C

Review of Memory Hierarchy

Cache: a safe place for hiding or storing things.

Webster's New World Dictionary of the
American Language
Second College Edition (1976)

Introduction

This appendix is a quick refresher of the memory hierarchy, including the basics of cache and virtual memory, performance equations, and simple optimizations. This first section reviews the following 36 terms:

cache	*fully associative*	*write allocate*
virtual memory	*dirty bit*	*unified cache*
memory stall cycles	*block offset*	*misses per instruction*
direct mapped	*write back*	*block*
valid bit	*data cache*	*locality*
block address	*hit time*	*address trace*
write through	*cache miss*	*set*
instruction cache	*page fault*	*random replacement*
average memory access time	*miss rate*	*index field*
cache hit	*n-way set associative*	*no-write allocate*
page	*least-recently used*	*write buffer*
miss penalty	*tag field*	*write stall*

If this review goes too quickly, you might want to look at Chapter 7 in *Computer Organization and Design,* which we wrote for readers with less experience.

   Cache is the name given to the highest or first level of the memory hierarchy encountered once the address leaves the processor. Since the principle of locality applies at many levels, and taking advantage of locality to improve performance is popular, the term *cache* is now applied whenever buffering is employed to reuse commonly occurring items. Examples include *file caches, name caches,* and so on.

   When the processor finds a requested data item in the cache, it is called a *cache hit.* When the processor does not find a data item it needs in the cache, a *cache miss* occurs. A fixed-size collection of data containing the requested word, called a *block* or line run, is retrieved from the main memory and placed into the cache. *Temporal locality* tells us that we are likely to need this word again in the near future, so it is useful to place it in the cache where it can be accessed quickly. Because of *spatial locality,* there is a high probability that the other data in the block will be needed soon.

   The time required for the cache miss depends on both the latency and bandwidth of the memory. Latency determines the time to retrieve the first word of the block, and bandwidth determines the time to retrieve the rest of this block. A cache miss is handled by hardware and causes processors using in-order execu-

Level	1	2	3	4
Name	registers	cache	main memory	disk storage
Typical size	< 1 KB	< 16 MB	< 512 GB	> 1 TB
Implementation technology	custom memory with multiple ports, CMOS	on-chip or off-chip CMOS SRAM	CMOS DRAM	magnetic disk
Access time (ns)	0.25–0.5	0.5–25	50–250	5,000,000
Bandwidth (MB/sec)	50,000–500,000	5000–20,000	2500–10,000	50–500
Managed by	compiler	hardware	operating system	operating system/ operator
Backed by	cache	main memory	disk	CD or tape

Figure C.1 The typical levels in the hierarchy slow down and get larger as we move away from the processor for a large workstation or small server. Embedded computers might have no disk storage, and much smaller memories and caches. The access times increase as we move to lower levels of the hierarchy, which makes it feasible to manage the transfer less responsively. The implementation technology shows the typical technology used for these functions. The access time is given in nanoseconds for typical values in 2006; these times will decrease over time. Bandwidth is given in megabytes per second between levels in the memory hierarchy. Bandwidth for disk storage includes both the media and the buffered interfaces.

tion to pause, or stall, until the data are available. With out-of-order execution, an instruction using the result must still wait, but other instructions may proceed during the miss.

Similarly, not all objects referenced by a program need to reside in main memory. *Virtual memory* means some objects may reside on disk. The address space is usually broken into fixed-size blocks, called *pages*. At any time, each page resides either in main memory or on disk. When the processor references an item within a page that is not present in the cache or main memory, a *page fault* occurs, and the entire page is moved from the disk to main memory. Since page faults take so long, they are handled in software and the processor is not stalled. The processor usually switches to some other task while the disk access occurs. From a high-level perspective, the reliance on locality of references and the relative relationships in size and relative cost per bit of cache versus main memory are similar to those of main memory versus disk.

Figure C.1 shows the range of sizes and access times of each level in the memory hierarchy for computers ranging from high-end desktops to low-end servers.

Cache Performance Review

Because of locality and the higher speed of smaller memories, a memory hierarchy can substantially improve performance. One method to evaluate cache performance is to expand our processor execution time equation from Chapter 1. We now account for the number of cycles during which the processor is stalled waiting for a memory access, which we call the *memory stall cycles*. The performance is then the product of the clock cycle time and the sum of the processor cycles and the memory stall cycles:

$$\text{CPU execution time} = (\text{CPU clock cycles} + \text{Memory stall cycles}) \times \text{Clock cycle time}$$

This equation assumes that the CPU clock cycles include the time to handle a cache hit, and that the processor is stalled during a cache miss. Section C.2 reexamines this simplifying assumption.

The number of memory stall cycles depends on both the number of misses and the cost per miss, which is called the *miss penalty:*

$$
\begin{aligned}
\text{Memory stall cycles} &= \text{Number of misses} \times \text{Miss penalty} \\
&= \text{IC} \times \frac{\text{Misses}}{\text{Instruction}} \times \text{Miss penalty} \\
&= \text{IC} \times \frac{\text{Memory accesses}}{\text{Instruction}} \times \text{Miss rate} \times \text{Miss penalty}
\end{aligned}
$$

The advantage of the last form is that the components can be easily measured. We already know how to measure instruction count. (For speculative processors, we only count instructions that commit.) Measuring the number of memory references per instruction can be done in the same fashion; every instruction requires an instruction access, and it is easy to decide if it also requires a data access.

Note that we calculated miss penalty as an average, but we will use it below as if it were a constant. The memory behind the cache may be busy at the time of the miss because of prior memory requests or memory refresh (see Section 5.3). The number of clock cycles also varies at interfaces between different clocks of the processor, bus, and memory. Thus, please remember that using a single number for miss penalty is a simplification.

The component *miss rate* is simply the fraction of cache accesses that result in a miss (i.e., number of accesses that miss divided by number of accesses). Miss rates can be measured with cache simulators that take an *address trace* of the instruction and data references, simulate the cache behavior to determine which references hit and which miss, and then report the hit and miss totals. Many microprocessors today provide hardware to count the number of misses and memory references, which is a much easier and faster way to measure miss rate.

The formula above is an approximation since the miss rates and miss penalties are often different for reads and writes. Memory stall clock cycles could then be defined in terms of the number of memory accesses per instruction, miss penalty (in clock cycles) for reads and writes, and miss rate for reads and writes:

$$
\begin{aligned}
\text{Memory stall clock cycles} = {}&\text{IC} \times \text{Reads per instruction} \times \text{Read miss rate} \times \text{Read miss penalty} \\
&+ \text{IC} \times \text{Writes per instruction} \times \text{Write miss rate} \times \text{Write miss penalty}
\end{aligned}
$$

We normally simplify the complete formula by combining the reads and writes and finding the average miss rates and miss penalty for reads *and* writes:

$$\text{Memory stall clock cycles} = \text{IC} \times \frac{\text{Memory accesses}}{\text{Instruction}} \times \text{Miss rate} \times \text{Miss penalty}$$

The miss rate is one of the most important measures of cache design, but, as we will see in later sections, not the only measure.

Example   Assume we have a computer where the clocks per instruction (CPI) is 1.0 when all memory accesses hit in the cache. The only data accesses are loads and stores, and these total 50% of the instructions. If the miss penalty is 25 clock cycles and the miss rate is 2%, how much faster would the computer be if all instructions were cache hits?

Answer   First compute the performance for the computer that always hits:

$$
\begin{aligned}
\text{CPU execution time} &= (\text{CPU clock cycles} + \text{Memory stall cycles}) \times \text{Clock cycle} \\
&= (\text{IC} \times \text{CPI} + 0) \times \text{Clock cycle} \\
&= \text{IC} \times 1.0 \times \text{Clock cycle}
\end{aligned}
$$

Now for the computer with the real cache, first we compute memory stall cycles:

$$
\begin{aligned}
\text{Memory stall cycles} &= \text{IC} \times \frac{\text{Memory accesses}}{\text{Instruction}} \times \text{Miss rate} \times \text{Miss penalty} \\
&= \text{IC} \times (1 + 0.5) \times 0.02 \times 25 \\
&= \text{IC} \times 0.75
\end{aligned}
$$

where the middle term $(1 + 0.5)$ represents one instruction access and 0.5 data accesses per instruction. The total performance is thus

$$
\begin{aligned}
\text{CPU execution time}_{\text{cache}} &= (\text{IC} \times 1.0 + \text{IC} \times 0.75) \times \text{Clock cycle} \\
&= 1.75 \times \text{IC} \times \text{Clock cycle}
\end{aligned}
$$

The performance ratio is the inverse of the execution times:

$$
\begin{aligned}
\frac{\text{CPU execution time}_{\text{cache}}}{\text{CPU execution time}} &= \frac{1.75 \times \text{IC} \times \text{Clock cycle}}{1.0 \times \text{IC} \times \text{Clock cycle}} \\
&= 1.75
\end{aligned}
$$

The computer with no cache misses is 1.75 times faster.

Some designers prefer measuring miss rate as *misses per instruction* rather than misses per memory reference. These two are related:

$$
\frac{\text{Misses}}{\text{Instruction}} = \frac{\text{Miss rate} \times \text{Memory accesses}}{\text{Instruction count}} = \text{Miss rate} \times \frac{\text{Memory accesses}}{\text{Instruction}}
$$

The latter formula is useful when you know the average number of memory accesses per instruction because it allows you to convert miss rate into misses per instruction, and vice versa. For example, we can turn the miss rate per memory reference in the previous example into misses per instruction:

$$
\frac{\text{Misses}}{\text{Instruction}} = \text{Miss rate} \times \frac{\text{Memory accesses}}{\text{Instruction}} = 0.02 \times 1.5 = 0.030
$$

By the way, misses per instruction are often reported as misses per 1000 instructions to show integers instead of fractions. Thus, the answer above could also be expressed as 30 misses per 1000 instructions.

The advantage of misses per instruction is that it is independent of the hardware implementation. For example, speculative processors fetch about twice as many instructions as are actually committed, which can artificially reduce the miss rate if measured as misses per memory reference rather than per instruction. The drawback is that misses per instruction is architecture dependent; for example, the average number of memory accesses per instruction may be very different for an 80x86 versus MIPS. Thus, misses per instruction are most popular with architects working with a single computer family, although the similarity of RISC architectures allows one to give insights into others.

Example   To show equivalency between the two miss rate equations, let's redo the example above, this time assuming a miss rate per 1000 instructions of 30. What is memory stall time in terms of instruction count?

Answer   Recomputing the memory stall cycles:

$$\text{Memory stall cycles} = \text{Number of misses} \times \text{Miss penalty}$$

$$= IC \times \frac{\text{Misses}}{\text{Instruction}} \times \text{Miss penalty}$$

$$= IC/1000 \times \frac{\text{Misses}}{\text{Instruction} \times 1000} \times \text{Miss penalty}$$

$$= IC/1000 \times 30 \times 25$$

$$= IC/1000 \times 750$$

$$= IC \times 0.75$$

We get the same answer as on page C-5, showing equivalence of the two equations.

Four Memory Hierarchy Questions

We continue our introduction to caches by answering the four common questions for the first level of the memory hierarchy:

Q1: Where can a block be placed in the upper level? (*block placement*)

Q2: How is a block found if it is in the upper level? (*block identification*)

Q3: Which block should be replaced on a miss? (*block replacement*)

Q4: What happens on a write? (*write strategy*)

The answers to these questions help us understand the different trade-offs of memories at different levels of a hierarchy; hence we ask these four questions on every example.

Q1: Where Can a Block Be Placed in a Cache?

Figure C.2 shows that the restrictions on where a block is placed create three categories of cache organization:

- If each block has only one place it can appear in the cache, the cache is said to be *direct mapped*. The mapping is usually

  (Block address) MOD *(Number of blocks in cache)*

- If a block can be placed anywhere in the cache, the cache is said to be *fully associative*.

- If a block can be placed in a restricted set of places in the cache, the cache is *set associative*. A *set* is a group of blocks in the cache. A block is first mapped onto a set, and then the block can be placed anywhere within that set. The set is usually chosen by *bit selection;* that is,

  (Block address) MOD *(Number of sets in cache)*

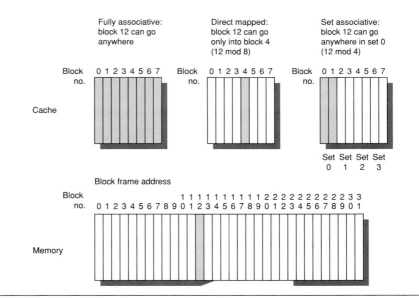

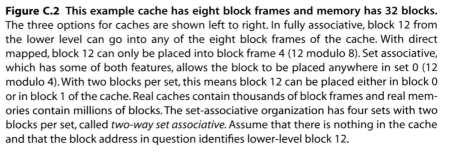

Figure C.2 This example cache has eight block frames and memory has 32 blocks. The three options for caches are shown left to right. In fully associative, block 12 from the lower level can go into any of the eight block frames of the cache. With direct mapped, block 12 can only be placed into block frame 4 (12 modulo 8). Set associative, which has some of both features, allows the block to be placed anywhere in set 0 (12 modulo 4). With two blocks per set, this means block 12 can be placed either in block 0 or in block 1 of the cache. Real caches contain thousands of block frames and real memories contain millions of blocks. The set-associative organization has four sets with two blocks per set, called *two-way set associative*. Assume that there is nothing in the cache and that the block address in question identifies lower-level block 12.

If there are *n* blocks in a set, the cache placement is called *n-way set associative*.

The range of caches from direct mapped to fully associative is really a continuum of levels of set associativity. Direct mapped is simply one-way set associative, and a fully associative cache with *m* blocks could be called "*m*-way set associative." Equivalently, direct mapped can be thought of as having *m* sets, and fully associative as having one set.

The vast majority of processor caches today are direct mapped, two-way set associative, or four-way set associative, for reasons we will see shortly.

Q2: How Is a Block Found If It Is in the Cache?

Caches have an address tag on each block frame that gives the block address. The tag of every cache block that might contain the desired information is checked to see if it matches the block address from the processor. As a rule, all possible tags are searched in parallel because speed is critical.

There must be a way to know that a cache block does not have valid information. The most common procedure is to add a *valid bit* to the tag to say whether or not this entry contains a valid address. If the bit is not set, there cannot be a match on this address.

Before proceeding to the next question, let's explore the relationship of a processor address to the cache. Figure C.3 shows how an address is divided. The first division is between the *block address* and the *block offset*. The block frame address can be further divided into the *tag field* and the *index field*. The block offset field selects the desired data from the block, the index field selects the set, and the tag field is compared against it for a hit. Although the comparison could be made on more of the address than the tag, there is no need because of the following:

■ The offset should not be used in the comparison, since the entire block is present or not, and hence all block offsets result in a match by definition.

■ Checking the index is redundant, since it was used to select the set to be checked. An address stored in set 0, for example, must have 0 in the index field or it couldn't be stored in set 0; set 1 must have an index value of 1; and so on. This optimization saves hardware and power by reducing the width of memory size for the cache tag.

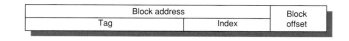

Figure C.3 The three portions of an address in a set-associative or direct-mapped cache. The tag is used to check all the blocks in the set, and the index is used to select the set. The block offset is the address of the desired data within the block. Fully associative caches have no index field.

If the total cache size is kept the same, increasing associativity increases the number of blocks per set, thereby decreasing the size of the index and increasing the size of the tag. That is, the tag-index boundary in Figure C.3 moves to the right with increasing associativity, with the end point of fully associative caches having no index field.

Q3: Which Block Should Be Replaced on a Cache Miss?

When a miss occurs, the cache controller must select a block to be replaced with the desired data. A benefit of direct-mapped placement is that hardware decisions are simplified—in fact, so simple that there is no choice: Only one block frame is checked for a hit, and only that block can be replaced. With fully associative or set-associative placement, there are many blocks to choose from on a miss. There are three primary strategies employed for selecting which block to replace:

- *Random*—To spread allocation uniformly, candidate blocks are randomly selected. Some systems generate pseudorandom block numbers to get reproducible behavior, which is particularly useful when debugging hardware.

- *Least-recently used* (LRU)—To reduce the chance of throwing out information that will be needed soon, accesses to blocks are recorded. Relying on the past to predict the future, the block replaced is the one that has been unused for the longest time. LRU relies on a corollary of locality: If recently used blocks are likely to be used again, then a good candidate for disposal is the least-recently used block.

- *First in, first out* (FIFO)—Because LRU can be complicated to calculate, this approximates LRU by determining the *oldest* block rather than the LRU.

A virtue of random replacement is that it is simple to build in hardware. As the number of blocks to keep track of increases, LRU becomes increasingly expensive and is frequently only approximated. Figure C.4 shows the difference in miss rates between LRU, random, and FIFO replacement.

Q4: What Happens on a Write?

Reads dominate processor cache accesses. All instruction accesses are reads, and most instructions don't write to memory. Figure B.27 in Appendix B suggests a mix of 10% stores and 26% loads for MIPS programs, making writes 10%/(100% + 26% + 10%) or about 7% of the overall memory traffic. Of the *data cache* traffic, writes are 10%/(26% + 10%) or about 28%. Making the common case fast means optimizing caches for reads, especially since processors traditionally wait for reads to complete but need not wait for writes. Amdahl's Law (Section 1.9) reminds us, however, that high-performance designs cannot neglect the speed of writes.

Fortunately, the common case is also the easy case to make fast. The block can be read from the cache at the same time that the tag is read and compared, so

	Associativity								
	Two-way			**Four-way**			**Eight-way**		
Size	LRU	Random	FIFO	LRU	Random	FIFO	LRU	Random	FIFO
16 KB	114.1	117.3	115.5	111.7	115.1	113.3	109.0	111.8	110.4
64 KB	103.4	104.3	103.9	102.4	102.3	103.1	99.7	100.5	100.3
256 KB	92.2	92.1	92.5	92.1	92.1	92.5	92.1	92.1	92.5

Figure C.4 Data cache misses per 1000 instructions comparing least-recently used, random, and first in, first out replacement for several sizes and associativities. There is little difference between LRU and random for the largest-size cache, with LRU outperforming the others for smaller caches. FIFO generally outperforms random in the smaller cache sizes. These data were collected for a block size of 64 bytes for the Alpha architecture using 10 SPEC2000 benchmarks. Five are from SPECint2000 (gap, gcc, gzip, mcf, and perl) and five are from SPECfp2000 (applu, art, equake, lucas, and swim). We will use this computer and these benchmarks in most figures in this appendix.

the block read begins as soon as the block address is available. If the read is a hit, the requested part of the block is passed on to the processor immediately. If it is a miss, there is no benefit—but also no harm except more power in desktop and server computers; just ignore the value read.

Such optimism is not allowed for writes. Modifying a block cannot begin until the tag is checked to see if the address is a hit. Because tag checking cannot occur in parallel, writes normally take longer than reads. Another complexity is that the processor also specifies the size of the write, usually between 1 and 8 bytes; only that portion of a block can be changed. In contrast, reads can access more bytes than necessary without fear.

The write policies often distinguish cache designs. There are two basic options when writing to the cache:

■ *Write through*—The information is written to both the block in the cache *and* to the block in the lower-level memory.

■ *Write back*—The information is written only to the block in the cache. The modified cache block is written to main memory only when it is replaced.

To reduce the frequency of writing back blocks on replacement, a feature called the *dirty bit* is commonly used. This status bit indicates whether the block is *dirty* (modified while in the cache) or *clean* (not modified). If it is clean, the block is not written back on a miss, since identical information to the cache is found in lower levels.

Both write back and write through have their advantages. With write back, writes occur at the speed of the cache memory, and multiple writes within a block require only one write to the lower-level memory. Since some writes don't go to memory, write back uses less memory bandwidth, making write back attractive in multiprocessors. Since write back uses the rest of the memory hierarchy and memory interconnect less than write through, it also saves power, making it attractive for embedded applications.

Write through is easier to implement than write back. The cache is always clean, so unlike write back read misses never result in writes to the lower level. Write through also has the advantage that the next lower level has the most current copy of the data, which simplifies data coherency. Data coherency is important for multiprocessors and for I/O, which we examine in Chapters 4 and 6. Multilevel caches make write through more viable for the upper-level caches, as the writes need only propagate to the next lower level rather than all the way to main memory.

As we will see, I/O and multiprocessors are fickle: They want write back for processor caches to reduce the memory traffic and write through to keep the cache consistent with lower levels of the memory hierarchy.

When the processor must wait for writes to complete during write through, the processor is said to *write stall.* A common optimization to reduce write stalls is a *write buffer,* which allows the processor to continue as soon as the data are written to the buffer, thereby overlapping processor execution with memory updating. As we will see shortly, write stalls can occur even with write buffers.

Since the data are not needed on a write, there are two options on a write miss:

■ *Write allocate* —The block is allocated on a write miss, followed by the write hit actions above. In this natural option, write misses act like read misses.

■ *No-write allocate*—This apparently unusual alternative is write misses do *not* affect the cache. Instead, the block is modified only in the lower-level memory.

Thus, blocks stay out of the cache in no-write allocate until the program tries to read the blocks, but even blocks that are only written will still be in the cache with write allocate. Let's look at an example.

Example   Assume a fully associative write-back cache with many cache entries that starts empty. Below is a sequence of five memory operations (the address is in square brackets):

```
Write Mem[100];
WriteMem[100];
Read Mem[200];
WriteMem[200];
WriteMem[100].
```

What are the number of hits and misses when using no-write allocate versus write allocate?

Answer   For no-write allocate, the address 100 is not in the cache, and there is no allocation on write, so the first two writes will result in misses. Address 200 is also not in the cache, so the read is also a miss. The subsequent write to address 200 is a hit. The last write to 100 is still a miss. The result for no-write allocate is four misses and one hit.

For write allocate, the first accesses to 100 and 200 are misses, and the rest are hits since 100 and 200 are both found in the cache. Thus, the result for write allocate is two misses and three hits.

Either write miss policy could be used with write through or write back. Normally, write-back caches use write allocate, hoping that subsequent writes to that block will be captured by the cache. Write-through caches often use no-write allocate. The reasoning is that even if there are subsequent writes to that block, the writes must still go to the lower-level memory, so what's to be gained?

An Example: The Opteron Data Cache

To give substance to these ideas, Figure C.5 shows the organization of the data cache in the AMD Opteron microprocessor. The cache contains 65,536 (64K) bytes of data in 64-byte blocks with two-way set-associative placement, least-recently used replacement, write back, and write allocate on a write miss.

Let's trace a cache hit through the steps of a hit as labeled in Figure C.5. (The four steps are shown as circled numbers.) As described in Section C.5, the Opteron presents a 48-bit virtual address to the cache for tag comparison, which is simultaneously translated into a 40-bit physical address.

The reason Opteron doesn't use all 64 bits of virtual address is that its designers don't think anyone needs that big of a virtual address space yet, and the smaller size simplifies the Opteron virtual address mapping. The designers plan to grow the virtual address in future microprocessors.

The physical address coming into the cache is divided into two fields: the 34-bit block address and the 6-bit block offset ($64 = 2^6$ and $34 + 6 = 40$). The block address is further divided into an address tag and cache index. Step 1 shows this division.

The cache index selects the tag to be tested to see if the desired block is in the cache. The size of the index depends on cache size, block size, and set associativity. For the Opteron cache the set associativity is set to two, and we calculate the index as follows:

$$2^{\text{Index}} = \frac{\text{Cache size}}{\text{Block size} \times \text{Set associativity}} = \frac{65,536}{64 \times 2} = 512 = 2^9$$

Hence, the index is 9 bits wide, and the tag is $34 - 9$ or 25 bits wide. Although that is the index needed to select the proper block, 64 bytes is much more than the processor wants to consume at once. Hence, it makes more sense to organize the data portion of the cache memory 8 bytes wide, which is the natural data word of the 64-bit Opteron processor. Thus, in addition to 9 bits to index the proper cache block, 3 more bits from the block offset are used to index the proper 8 bytes. Index selection is step 2 in Figure C.5.

After reading the two tags from the cache, they are compared to the tag portion of the block address from the processor. This comparison is step 3 in the fig-

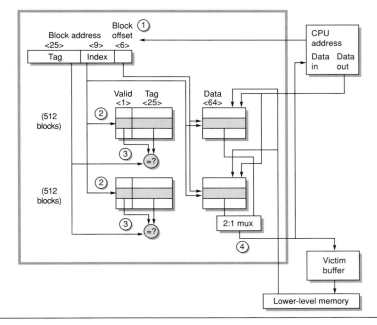

Figure C.5 The organization of the data cache in the Opteron microprocessor. The 64 KB cache is two-way set associative with 64-byte blocks. The 9-bit index selects among 512 sets. The four steps of a read hit, shown as circled numbers in order of occurrence, label this organization. Three bits of the block offset join the index to supply the RAM address to select the proper 8 bytes. Thus, the cache holds two groups of 4096 64-bit words, with each group containing half of the 512 sets. Although not exercised in this example, the line from lower-level memory to the cache is used on a miss to load the cache. The size of address leaving the processor is 40 bits because it is a physical address and not a virtual address. Figure C.23 on page C-45 explains how the Opteron maps from virtual to physical for a cache access.

ure. To be sure the tag contains valid information, the valid bit must be set or else the results of the comparison are ignored.

Assuming one tag does match, the final step is to signal the processor to load the proper data from the cache by using the winning input from a 2:1 multiplexor. The Opteron allows 2 clock cycles for these four steps, so the instructions in the following 2 clock cycles would wait if they tried to use the result of the load.

Handling writes is more complicated than handling reads in the Opteron, as it is in any cache. If the word to be written is in the cache, the first three steps are the same. Since the Opteron executes out of order, only after it signals that the instruction has committed and the cache tag comparison indicates a hit are the data written to the cache.

So far we have assumed the common case of a cache hit. What happens on a miss? On a read miss, the cache sends a signal to the processor telling it the data are not yet available, and 64 bytes are read from the next level of the hierarchy. The latency is 7 clock cycles to the first 8 bytes of the block, and then 2 clock cycles per 8 bytes for the rest of the block. Since the data cache is set associative, there is a choice on which block to replace. Opteron uses LRU, which selects the block that was referenced longest ago, so every access must update the LRU bit. Replacing a block means updating the data, the address tag, the valid bit, and the LRU bit.

Since the Opteron uses write back, the old data block could have been modified, and hence it cannot simply be discarded. The Opteron keeps 1 dirty bit per block to record if the block was written. If the "victim" was modified, its data and address are sent to the Victim Buffer. (This structure is similar to a *write buffer* in other computers.) The Opteron has space for eight victim blocks. In parallel with other cache actions, it writes victim blocks to the next level of the hierarchy. If the Victim Buffer is full, the cache must wait.

A write miss is very similar to a read miss, since the Opteron allocates a block on a read or a write miss.

We have seen how it works, but the *data* cache cannot supply all the memory needs of the processor: The processor also needs instructions. Although a single cache could try to supply both, it can be a bottleneck. For example, when a load or store instruction is executed, the pipelined processor will simultaneously request both a data word *and* an instruction word. Hence, a single cache would present a structural hazard for loads and stores, leading to stalls. One simple way to conquer this problem is to divide it: One cache is dedicated to instructions and another to data. Separate caches are found in most recent processors, including the Opteron. Hence, it has a 64 KB instruction cache as well as the 64 KB data cache.

The processor knows whether it is issuing an instruction address or a data address, so there can be separate ports for both, thereby doubling the bandwidth between the memory hierarchy and the processor. Separate caches also offer the opportunity of optimizing each cache separately: Different capacities, block sizes, and associativities may lead to better performance. (In contrast to the instruction caches and data caches of the Opteron, the terms *unified* or *mixed* are applied to caches that can contain either instructions or data.)

Figure C.6 shows that instruction caches have lower miss rates than data caches. Separating instructions and data removes misses due to conflicts between instruction blocks and data blocks, but the split also fixes the cache space devoted to each type. Which is more important to miss rates? A fair comparison of separate instruction and data caches to unified caches requires the total cache size to be the same. For example, a separate 16 KB instruction cache and 16 KB data cache should be compared to a 32 KB unified cache. Calculating the average miss rate with separate instruction and data caches necessitates knowing the percentage of memory references to each cache. Figure B.27 on page B-41 suggests the split is 100%/(100% + 26% + 10%) or about 74% instruction references to (26% + 10%)/(100% + 26% + 10%) or about 26% data references. Splitting affects performance beyond what is indicated by the change in miss rates, as we will see shortly.

Size	Instruction cache	Data cache	Unified cache
8 KB	8.16	44.0	63.0
16 KB	3.82	40.9	51.0
32 KB	1.36	38.4	43.3
64 KB	0.61	36.9	39.4
128 KB	0.30	35.3	36.2
256 KB	0.02	32.6	32.9

Figure C.6 Miss per 1000 instructions for instruction, data, and unified caches of different sizes. The percentage of instruction references is about 74%. The data are for two-way associative caches with 64-byte blocks for the same computer and benchmarks as Figure C.4.

C.2 Cache Performance

Because instruction count is independent of the hardware, it is tempting to evaluate processor performance using that number. Such indirect performance measures have waylaid many a computer designer. The corresponding temptation for evaluating memory hierarchy performance is to concentrate on miss rate because it, too, is independent of the speed of the hardware. As we will see, miss rate can be just as misleading as instruction count. A better measure of memory hierarchy performance is the *average memory access time:*

$$\text{Average memory access time} = \text{Hit time} + \text{Miss rate} \times \text{Miss penalty}$$

where *Hit time* is the time to hit in the cache; we have seen the other two terms before. The components of average access time can be measured either in absolute time—say, 0.25 to 1.0 nanoseconds on a hit—or in the number of clock cycles that the processor waits for the memory—such as a miss penalty of 150 to 200 clock cycles. Remember that average memory access time is still an indirect measure of performance; although it is a better measure than miss rate, it is not a substitute for execution time.

This formula can help us decide between split caches and a unified cache.

Example Which has the lower miss rate: a 16 KB instruction cache with a 16 KB data cache or a 32 KB unified cache? Use the miss rates in Figure C.6 to help calculate the correct answer, assuming 36% of the instructions are data transfer instructions. Assume a hit takes 1 clock cycle and the miss penalty is 100 clock cycles. A load or store hit takes 1 extra clock cycle on a unified cache if there is only one cache port to satisfy two simultaneous requests. Using the pipelining terminology of Chapter 2, the unified cache leads to a structural hazard. What is the average memory access time in each case? Assume write-through caches with a write buffer and ignore stalls due to the write buffer.

Answer   First let's convert misses per 1000 instructions into miss rates. Solving the general formula from above, the miss rate is

$$\text{Miss rate} = \frac{\dfrac{\text{Misses}}{1000 \text{ Instructions}}/1000}{\dfrac{\text{Memory accesses}}{\text{Instruction}}}$$

Since every instruction access has exactly one memory access to fetch the instruction, the instruction miss rate is

$$\text{Miss rate}_{16 \text{ KB instruction}} = \frac{3.82/1000}{1.00} = 0.004$$

Since 36% of the instructions are data transfers, the data miss rate is

$$\text{Miss rate}_{16 \text{ KB data}} = \frac{40.9/1000}{0.36} = 0.114$$

The unified miss rate needs to account for instruction and data accesses:

$$\text{Miss rate}_{32 \text{ KB unified}} = \frac{43.3/1000}{1.00 + 0.36} = 0.0318$$

As stated above, about 74% of the memory accesses are instruction references. Thus, the overall miss rate for the split caches is

$$(74\% \times 0.004) + (26\% \times 0.114) = 0.0326$$

Thus, a 32 KB unified cache has a slightly lower effective miss rate than two 16 KB caches.

The average memory access time formula can be divided into instruction and data accesses:

Average memory access time
= % instructions × (Hit time + Instruction miss rate × Miss penalty)
+ % data × (Hit time + Data miss rate × Miss penalty)

Therefore, the time for each organization is

Average memory access time$_{\text{split}}$
= 74% × (1 + 0.004 × 200) + 26% × (1 + 0.114 × 200)
= (74% × 1.80) + (26% × 23.80) = 1.332 + 6.188 = 7.52
Average memory access time$_{\text{unified}}$
= 74% × (1 + 0.0318 × 200) + 26% × (1 + 1 + 0.0318 × 200)
= (74% × 7.36) + (26% × 8.36) = 5.446 + 2.174 = 7.62

Hence, the split caches in this example—which offer two memory ports per clock cycle, thereby avoiding the structural hazard—have a better average memory access time than the single-ported unified cache despite having a worse effective miss rate.

Average Memory Access Time and Processor Performance

An obvious question is whether average memory access time due to cache misses predicts processor performance.

First, there are other reasons for stalls, such as contention due to I/O devices using memory. Designers often assume that all memory stalls are due to cache misses, since the memory hierarchy typically dominates other reasons for stalls. We use this simplifying assumption here, but beware to account for *all* memory stalls when calculating final performance.

Second, the answer depends also on the processor. If we have an in-order execution processor (see Chapter 2), then the answer is basically yes. The processor stalls during misses, and the memory stall time is strongly correlated to average memory access time. Let's make that assumption for now, but we'll return to out-of-order processors in the next subsection.

As stated in the previous section, we can model CPU time as

$$\text{CPU time} = (\text{CPU execution clock cycles} + \text{Memory stall clock cycles}) \times \text{Clock cycle time}$$

This formula raises the question of whether the clock cycles for a cache hit should be considered part of CPU execution clock cycles or part of memory stall clock cycles. Although either convention is defensible, the most widely accepted is to include hit clock cycles in CPU execution clock cycles.

We can now explore the impact of caches on performance.

Example   Let's use an in-order execution computer for the first example. Assume the cache miss penalty is 200 clock cycles, and all instructions normally take 1.0 clock cycles (ignoring memory stalls). Assume the average miss rate is 2%, there is an average of 1.5 memory references per instruction, and the average number of cache misses per 1000 instructions is 30. What is the impact on performance when behavior of the cache is included? Calculate the impact using both misses per instruction and miss rate.

Answer $$\text{CPU time} = \text{IC} \times \left(\text{CPI}_{\text{execution}} + \frac{\text{Memory stall clock cycles}}{\text{Instruction}} \right) \times \text{Clock cycle time}$$

The performance, including cache misses, is

$$\begin{aligned} \text{CPU time}_{\text{with cache}} &= \text{IC} \times (1.0 + (30/1000 \times 200)) \times \text{Clock cycle time} \\ &= \text{IC} \times 7.00 \times \text{Clock cycle time} \end{aligned}$$

Now calculating performance using miss rate:

$$\text{CPU time} = \text{IC} \times \left(\text{CPI}_{\text{execution}} + \text{Miss rate} \times \frac{\text{Memory accesses}}{\text{Instruction}} \times \text{Miss penalty}\right) \times \text{Clock cycle time}$$

$$\text{CPU time}_{\text{with cache}} = \text{IC} \times (1.0 + (1.5 \times 2\% \times 200)) \times \text{Clock cycle time}$$
$$= \text{IC} \times 7.00 \times \text{Clock cycle time}$$

The clock cycle time and instruction count are the same, with or without a cache. Thus, CPU time increases sevenfold, with CPI from 1.00 for a "perfect cache" to 7.00 with a cache that can miss. Without any memory hierarchy at all the CPI would increase again to $1.0 + 200 \times 1.5$ or 301—a factor of more than 40 times longer than a system with a cache!

As this example illustrates, cache behavior can have enormous impact on performance. Furthermore, cache misses have a double-barreled impact on a processor with a low CPI and a fast clock:

1. The lower the $\text{CPI}_{\text{execution}}$, the higher the *relative* impact of a fixed number of cache miss clock cycles.

2. When calculating CPI, the cache miss penalty is measured in processor clock cycles for a miss. Therefore, even if memory hierarchies for two computers are identical, the processor with the higher clock rate has a larger number of clock cycles per miss and hence a higher memory portion of CPI.

The importance of the cache for processors with low CPI and high clock rates is thus greater, and, consequently, greater is the danger of neglecting cache behavior in assessing performance of such computers. Amdahl's Law strikes again!

Although minimizing average memory access time is a reasonable goal—and we will use it in much of this appendix—keep in mind that the final goal is to reduce processor execution time. The next example shows how these two can differ.

Example   What is the impact of two different cache organizations on the performance of a processor? Assume that the CPI with a perfect cache is 1.6, the clock cycle time is 0.35 ns, there are 1.4 memory references per instruction, the size of both caches is 128 KB, and both have a block size of 64 bytes. One cache is direct mapped and the other is two-way set associative. Figure C.5 shows that for set-associative caches we must add a multiplexor to select between the blocks in the set depending on the tag match. Since the speed of the processor can be tied directly to the speed of a cache hit, assume the processor clock cycle time must be stretched 1.35 times to accommodate the selection multiplexor of the set-associative cache. To the first approximation, the cache miss penalty is 65 ns for either cache organization. (In practice, it is normally rounded up or down to an integer number of clock cycles.) First, calculate the average memory access time and then processor performance. Assume the hit time is 1 clock cycle, the miss rate of a direct-mapped 128 KB cache is 2.1%, and the miss rate for a two-way set-associative cache of the same size is 1.9%.

Answer   Average memory access time is

$$\text{Average memory access time} = \text{Hit time} + \text{Miss rate} \times \text{Miss penalty}$$

Thus, the time for each organization is

$$\text{Average memory access time}_{1\text{-way}} = 0.35 + (.021 \times 65) = 1.72 \text{ ns}$$
$$\text{Average memory access time}_{2\text{-way}} = 0.35 \times 1.35 + (.019 \times 65) = 1.71 \text{ ns}$$

The average memory access time is better for the two-way set-associative cache. The processor performance is

$$\text{CPU time} = \text{IC} \times \left(\text{CPI}_{\text{execution}} + \frac{\text{Misses}}{\text{Instruction}} \times \text{Miss penalty} \right) \times \text{Clock cycle time}$$

$$= \text{IC} \times \left[(\text{CPI}_{\text{execution}} \times \text{Clock cycle time}) \right.$$

$$\left. + \left(\text{Miss rate} \times \frac{\text{Memory accesses}}{\text{Instruction}} \times \text{Miss penalty} \times \text{Clock cycle time} \right) \right]$$

Substituting 65 ns for (Miss penalty × Clock cycle time), the performance of each cache organization is

$$\text{CPU time}_{1\text{-way}} = \text{IC} \times (1.6 \times 0.35 + (0.021 \times 1.4 \times 65)) = 2.47 \times \text{IC}$$
$$\text{CPU time}_{2\text{-way}} = \text{IC} \times (1.6 \times 0.35 \times 1.35 + (0.019 \times 1.4 \times 65)) = 2.49 \times \text{IC}$$

and relative performance is

$$\frac{\text{CPU time}_{2\text{-way}}}{\text{CPU time}_{1\text{-way}}} = \frac{2.49 \times \text{Instruction count}}{2.47 \times \text{Instruction count}} = \frac{2.49}{2.47} = 1.01$$

In contrast to the results of average memory access time comparison, the direct-mapped cache leads to slightly better average performance because the clock cycle is stretched for *all* instructions for the two-way set-associative case, even if there are fewer misses. Since CPU time is our bottom-line evaluation, and since direct mapped is simpler to build, the preferred cache is direct mapped in this example.

Miss Penalty and Out-of-Order Execution Processors

For an out-of-order execution processor, how do you define "miss penalty"? Is it the full latency of the miss to memory, or is it just the "exposed" or nonoverlapped latency when the processor must stall? This question does not arise in processors that stall until the data miss completes.

Let's redefine memory stalls to lead to a new definition of miss penalty as nonoverlapped latency:

$$\frac{\text{Memory stall cycles}}{\text{Instruction}} = \frac{\text{Misses}}{\text{Instruction}} \times (\text{Total miss latency} - \text{Overlapped miss latency})$$

Similarly, as some out-of-order processors stretch the hit time, that portion of the performance equation could be divided by total hit latency less overlapped hit latency. This equation could be further expanded to account for contention for memory resources in an out-of-order processor by dividing total miss latency into latency without contention and latency due to contention. Let's just concentrate on miss latency.

We now have to decide the following:

■ *Length of memory latency*—What to consider as the start and the end of a memory operation in an out-of-order processor

■ *Length of latency overlap*—What is the start of overlap with the processor (or equivalently, when do we say a memory operation is stalling the processor)

Given the complexity of out-of-order execution processors, there is no single correct definition.

Since only committed operations are seen at the retirement pipeline stage, we say a processor is stalled in a clock cycle if it does not retire the maximum possible number of instructions in that cycle. We attribute that stall to the first instruction that could not be retired. This definition is by no means foolproof. For example, applying an optimization to improve a certain stall time may not always improve execution time because another type of stall—hidden behind the targeted stall—may now be exposed.

For latency, we could start measuring from the time the memory instruction is queued in the instruction window, or when the address is generated, or when the instruction is actually sent to the memory system. Any option works as long as it is used in a consistent fashion.

Example   Let's redo the example above, but this time we assume the processor with the longer clock cycle time supports out-of-order execution yet still has a direct-mapped cache. Assume 30% of the 65 ns miss penalty can be overlapped; that is, the average CPU memory stall time is now 45.5 ns.

Answer   Average memory access time for the out-of-order (OOO) computer is

$$\text{Average memory access time}_{\text{1-way,OOO}} = 0.35 \times 1.35 + (0.021 \times 45.5) = 1.43 \text{ ns}$$

The performance of the OOO cache is

$$\text{CPU time}_{\text{1-way,OOO}} = \text{IC} \times (1.6 \times 0.35 \times 1.35 + (0.021 \times 1.4 \times 45.5)) = 2.09 \times \text{IC}$$

Cache size (KB)	Degree associative	Total miss rate	Miss rate components (relative percent) (sum = 100% of total miss rate)					
			Compulsory		Capacity		Conflict	
4	1-way	0.098	0.0001	0.1%	0.070	72%	0.027	28%
4	2-way	0.076	0.0001	0.1%	0.070	93%	0.005	7%
4	4-way	0.071	0.0001	0.1%	0.070	99%	0.001	1%
4	8-way	0.071	0.0001	0.1%	0.070	100%	0.000	0%
8	1-way	0.068	0.0001	0.1%	0.044	65%	0.024	35%
8	2-way	0.049	0.0001	0.1%	0.044	90%	0.005	10%
8	4-way	0.044	0.0001	0.1%	0.044	99%	0.000	1%
8	8-way	0.044	0.0001	0.1%	0.044	100%	0.000	0%
16	1-way	0.049	0.0001	0.1%	0.040	82%	0.009	17%
16	2-way	0.041	0.0001	0.2%	0.040	98%	0.001	2%
16	4-way	0.041	0.0001	0.2%	0.040	99%	0.000	0%
16	8-way	0.041	0.0001	0.2%	0.040	100%	0.000	0%
32	1-way	0.042	0.0001	0.2%	0.037	89%	0.005	11%
32	2-way	0.038	0.0001	0.2%	0.037	99%	0.000	0%
32	4-way	0.037	0.0001	0.2%	0.037	100%	0.000	0%
32	8-way	0.037	0.0001	0.2%	0.037	100%	0.000	0%
64	1-way	0.037	0.0001	0.2%	0.028	77%	0.008	23%
64	2-way	0.031	0.0001	0.2%	0.028	91%	0.003	9%
64	4-way	0.030	0.0001	0.2%	0.028	95%	0.001	4%
64	8-way	0.029	0.0001	0.2%	0.028	97%	0.001	2%
128	1-way	0.021	0.0001	0.3%	0.019	91%	0.002	8%
128	2-way	0.019	0.0001	0.3%	0.019	100%	0.000	0%
128	4-way	0.019	0.0001	0.3%	0.019	100%	0.000	0%
128	8-way	0.019	0.0001	0.3%	0.019	100%	0.000	0%
256	1-way	0.013	0.0001	0.5%	0.012	94%	0.001	6%
256	2-way	0.012	0.0001	0.5%	0.012	99%	0.000	0%
256	4-way	0.012	0.0001	0.5%	0.012	99%	0.000	0%
256	8-way	0.012	0.0001	0.5%	0.012	99%	0.000	0%
512	1-way	0.008	0.0001	0.8%	0.005	66%	0.003	33%
512	2-way	0.007	0.0001	0.9%	0.005	71%	0.002	28%
512	4-way	0.006	0.0001	1.1%	0.005	91%	0.000	8%
512	8-way	0.006	0.0001	1.1%	0.005	95%	0.000	4%

Figure C.8 Total miss rate for each size cache and percentage of each according to the "three C's." Compulsory misses are independent of cache size, while capacity misses decrease as capacity increases, and conflict misses decrease as associativity increases. Figure C.9 shows the same information graphically. Note that a direct-mapped cache of size N has about the same miss rate as a two-way set-associative cache of size N/2 up through 128 K. Caches larger than 128 KB do not prove that rule. Note that the Capacity column is also the fully associative miss rate. Data were collected as in Figure C.4 using LRU replacement.

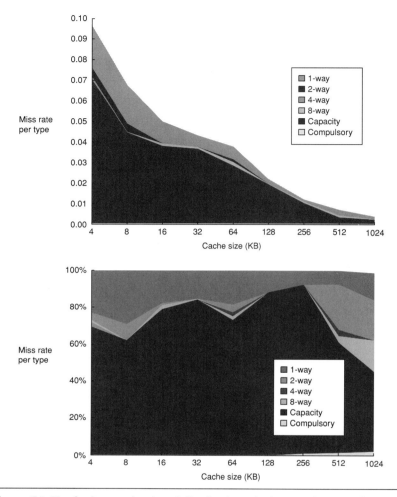

Figure C.9 Total miss rate (top) and distribution of miss rate (bottom) for each size cache according to the three C's for the data in Figure C.8. The top diagram is the actual data cache miss rates, while the bottom diagram shows the percentage in each category. (Space allows the graphs to show one extra cache size than can fit in Figure C.8.)

To show the benefit of associativity, conflict misses are divided into misses caused by each decrease in associativity. Here are the four divisions of conflict misses and how they are calculated:

- *Eight-way*—Conflict misses due to going from fully associative (no conflicts) to eight-way associative

- *Four-way*—Conflict misses due to going from eight-way associative to four-way associative

- *Two-way*—Conflict misses due to going from four-way associative to two-way associative

- *One-way*—Conflict misses due to going from two-way associative to one-way associative (direct mapped)

As we can see from the figures, the compulsory miss rate of the SPEC2000 programs is very small, as it is for many long-running programs.

Having identified the three C's, what can a computer designer do about them? Conceptually, conflicts are the easiest: Fully associative placement avoids all conflict misses. Full associativity is expensive in hardware, however, and may slow the processor clock rate (see the example on page C-28), leading to lower overall performance.

There is little to be done about capacity except to enlarge the cache. If the upper-level memory is much smaller than what is needed for a program, and a significant percentage of the time is spent moving data between two levels in the hierarchy, the memory hierarchy is said to *thrash*. Because so many replacements are required, thrashing means the computer runs close to the speed of the lower-level memory, or maybe even slower because of the miss overhead.

Another approach to improving the three C's is to make blocks larger to reduce the number of compulsory misses, but, as we will see shortly, large blocks can increase other kinds of misses.

The three C's give insight into the cause of misses, but this simple model has its limits; it gives you insight into average behavior but may not explain an individual miss. For example, changing cache size changes conflict misses as well as capacity misses, since a larger cache spreads out references to more blocks. Thus, a miss might move from a capacity miss to a conflict miss as cache size changes. Note that the three C's also ignore replacement policy, since it is difficult to model and since, in general, it is less significant. In specific circumstances the replacement policy can actually lead to anomalous behavior, such as poorer miss rates for larger associativity, which contradicts the three C's model. (Some have proposed using an address trace to determine optimal placement in memory to avoid placement misses from the three C's model; we've not followed that advice here.)

Alas, many of the techniques that reduce miss rates also increase hit time or miss penalty. The desirability of reducing miss rates using the three optimizations must be balanced against the goal of making the whole system fast. This first example shows the importance of a balanced perspective.

First Optimization: Larger Block Size to Reduce Miss Rate

The simplest way to reduce miss rate is to increase the block size. Figure C.10 shows the trade-off of block size versus miss rate for a set of programs and cache sizes. Larger block sizes will reduce also compulsory misses. This reduction occurs because the principle of locality has two components: temporal locality and spatial locality. Larger blocks take advantage of spatial locality.

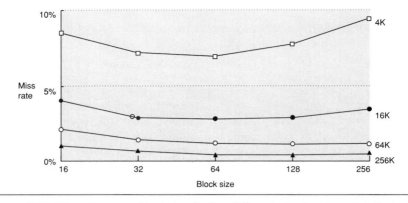

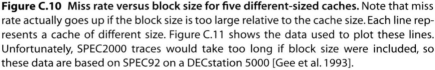

Figure C.10 Miss rate versus block size for five different-sized caches. Note that miss rate actually goes up if the block size is too large relative to the cache size. Each line represents a cache of different size. Figure C.11 shows the data used to plot these lines. Unfortunately, SPEC2000 traces would take too long if block size were included, so these data are based on SPEC92 on a DECstation 5000 [Gee et al. 1993].

At the same time, larger blocks increase the miss penalty. Since they reduce the number of blocks in the cache, larger blocks may increase conflict misses and even capacity misses if the cache is small. Clearly, there is little reason to increase the block size to such a size that it *increases* the miss rate. There is also no benefit to reducing miss rate if it increases the average memory access time. The increase in miss penalty may outweigh the decrease in miss rate.

Example Figure C.11 shows the actual miss rates plotted in Figure C.10. Assume the memory system takes 80 clock cycles of overhead and then delivers 16 bytes every 2 clock cycles. Thus, it can supply 16 bytes in 82 clock cycles, 32 bytes in 84 clock cycles, and so on. Which block size has the smallest average memory access time for each cache size in Figure C.11?

Answer Average memory access time is

$$\text{Average memory access time} = \text{Hit time} + \text{Miss rate} \times \text{Miss penalty}$$

If we assume the hit time is 1 clock cycle independent of block size, then the access time for a 16-byte block in a 4 KB cache is

$$\text{Average memory access time} = 1 + (8.57\% \times 82) = 8.027 \text{ clock cycles}$$

and for a 256-byte block in a 256 KB cache the average memory access time is

$$\text{Average memory access time} = 1 + (0.49\% \times 112) = 1.549 \text{ clock cycles}$$

Block size	Cache size			
	4K	16K	64K	256K
16	8.57%	3.94%	2.04%	1.09%
32	7.24%	2.87%	1.35%	0.70%
64	7.00%	2.64%	1.06%	0.51%
128	7.78%	2.77%	1.02%	0.49%
256	9.51%	3.29%	1.15%	0.49%

Figure C.11 Actual miss rate versus block size for five different-sized caches in Figure C.10. Note that for a 4 KB cache, 256-byte blocks have a higher miss rate than 32-byte blocks. In this example, the cache would have to be 256 KB in order for a 256-byte block to decrease misses.

Block size	Miss penalty	Cache size			
		4K	16K	64K	256K
16	82	8.027	4.231	2.673	1.894
32	84	**7.082**	3.411	2.134	1.588
64	88	7.160	**3.323**	**1.933**	**1.449**
128	96	8.469	3.659	1.979	1.470
256	112	11.651	4.685	2.288	1.549

Figure C.12 Average memory access time versus block size for five different-sized caches in Figure C.10. Block sizes of 32 and 64 bytes dominate. The smallest average time per cache size is boldfaced.

Figure C.12 shows the average memory access time for all block and cache sizes between those two extremes. The boldfaced entries show the fastest block size for a given cache size: 32 bytes for 4 KB and 64 bytes for the larger caches. These sizes are, in fact, popular block sizes for processor caches today.

As in all of these techniques, the cache designer is trying to minimize both the miss rate and the miss penalty. The selection of block size depends on both the latency and bandwidth of the lower-level memory. High latency and high bandwidth encourage large block size since the cache gets many more bytes per miss for a small increase in miss penalty. Conversely, low latency and low bandwidth encourage smaller block sizes since there is little time saved from a larger block. For example, twice the miss penalty of a small block may be close to the penalty of a block twice the size. The larger number of small blocks may also reduce conflict misses. Note that Figures C.10 and C.12 show the difference between selecting a block size based on minimizing miss rate versus minimizing average memory access time.

After seeing the positive and negative impact of larger block size on compulsory and capacity misses, the next two subsections look at the potential of higher capacity and higher associativity.

Second Optimization: Larger Caches to Reduce Miss Rate

The obvious way to reduce capacity misses in Figures C.8 and C.9 is to increase capacity of the cache. The obvious drawback is potentially longer hit time and higher cost and power. This technique has been especially popular in off-chip caches.

Third Optimization: Higher Associativity to Reduce Miss Rate

Figures C.8 and C.9 show how miss rates improve with higher associativity. There are two general rules of thumb that can be gleaned from these figures. The first is that eight-way set associative is for practical purposes as effective in reducing misses for these sized caches as fully associative. You can see the difference by comparing the eight-way entries to the capacity miss column in Figure C.8, since capacity misses are calculated using fully associative caches.

The second observation, called the *2:1 cache rule of thumb*, is that a direct-mapped cache of size N has about the same miss rate as a two-way set-associative cache of size $N/2$. This held in three C's figures for cache sizes less than 128 KB.

Like many of these examples, improving one aspect of the average memory access time comes at the expense of another. Increasing block size reduces miss rate while increasing miss penalty, and greater associativity can come at the cost of increased hit time. Hence, the pressure of a fast processor clock cycle encourages simple cache designs, but the increasing miss penalty rewards associativity, as the following example suggests.

Example   Assume higher associativity would increase the clock cycle time as listed below:

$$\text{Clock cycle time}_{2\text{-way}} = 1.36 \times \text{Clock cycle time}_{1\text{-way}}$$
$$\text{Clock cycle time}_{4\text{-way}} = 1.44 \times \text{Clock cycle time}_{1\text{-way}}$$
$$\text{Clock cycle time}_{8\text{-way}} = 1.52 \times \text{Clock cycle time}_{1\text{-way}}$$

Assume that the hit time is 1 clock cycle, that the miss penalty for the direct-mapped case is 25 clock cycles to a level 2 cache (see next subsection) that never misses, and that the miss penalty need not be rounded to an integral number of clock cycles. Using Figure C.8 for miss rates, for which cache sizes are each of these three statements true?

$$\text{Average memory access time}_{8\text{-way}} < \text{Average memory access time}_{4\text{-way}}$$
$$\text{Average memory access time}_{4\text{-way}} < \text{Average memory access time}_{2\text{-way}}$$
$$\text{Average memory access time}_{2\text{-way}} < \text{Average memory access time}_{1\text{-way}}$$

| | Associativity | | | |
Cache size (KB)	One-way	Two-way	Four-way	Eight-way
4	3.44	3.25	3.22	**3.28**
8	2.69	2.58	2.55	**2.62**
16	2.23	**2.40**	**2.46**	**2.53**
32	2.06	**2.30**	**2.37**	**2.45**
64	1.92	**2.14**	**2.18**	**2.25**
128	1.52	**1.84**	**1.92**	**2.00**
256	1.32	**1.66**	**1.74**	**1.82**
512	1.20	**1.55**	**1.59**	**1.66**

Figure C.13 Average memory access time using miss rates in Figure C.8 for parameters in the example. Boldface type means that this time is higher than the number to the left; that is, higher associativity *increases* average memory access time.

Answer Average memory access time for each associativity is

$$\text{Average memory access time}_{8\text{-way}} = \text{Hit time}_{8\text{-way}} + \text{Miss rate}_{8\text{-way}} \times \text{Miss penalty}_{8\text{-way}} = 1.52 + \text{Miss rate}_{8\text{-way}} \times 25$$
$$\text{Average memory access time}_{4\text{-way}} = 1.44 + \text{Miss rate}_{4\text{-way}} \times 25$$
$$\text{Average memory access time}_{2\text{-way}} = 1.36 + \text{Miss rate}_{2\text{-way}} \times 25$$
$$\text{Average memory access time}_{1\text{-way}} = 1.00 + \text{Miss rate}_{1\text{-way}} \times 25$$

The miss penalty is the same time in each case, so we leave it as 25 clock cycles. For example, the average memory access time for a 4 KB direct-mapped cache is

$$\text{Average memory access time}_{1\text{-way}} = 1.00 + (0.098 \times 25) = 3.44$$

and the time for a 512 KB, eight-way set-associative cache is

$$\text{Average memory access time}_{8\text{-way}} = 1.52 + (0.006 \times 25) = 1.66$$

Using these formulas and the miss rates from Figure C.8, Figure C.13 shows the average memory access time for each cache and associativity. The figure shows that the formulas in this example hold for caches less than or equal to 8 KB for up to four-way associativity. Starting with 16 KB, the greater hit time of larger associativity outweighs the time saved due to the reduction in misses.

Note that we did not account for the slower clock rate on the rest of the program in this example, thereby understating the advantage of direct-mapped cache.

Fourth Optimization: Multilevel Caches to Reduce Miss Penalty

Reducing cache misses had been the traditional focus of cache research, but the cache performance formula assures us that improvements in miss penalty can be just as beneficial as improvements in miss rate. Moreover, Figure 5.2 on page 289 shows that technology trends have improved the speed of processors faster than DRAMs, making the relative cost of miss penalties increase over time.

This performance gap between processors and memory leads the architect to this question: Should I make the cache faster to keep pace with the speed of processors, or make the cache larger to overcome the widening gap between the processor and main memory?

One answer is, do both. Adding another level of cache between the original cache and memory simplifies the decision. The first-level cache can be small enough to match the clock cycle time of the fast processor. Yet the second-level cache can be large enough to capture many accesses that would go to main memory, thereby lessening the effective miss penalty.

Although the concept of adding another level in the hierarchy is straightforward, it complicates performance analysis. Definitions for a second level of cache are not always straightforward. Let's start with the definition of *average memory access time* for a two-level cache. Using the subscripts L1 and L2 to refer, respectively, to a first-level and a second-level cache, the original formula is

$$\text{Average memory access time} = \text{Hit time}_{L1} + \text{Miss rate}_{L1} \times \text{Miss penalty}_{L1}$$

and

$$\text{Miss penalty}_{L1} = \text{Hit time}_{L2} + \text{Miss rate}_{L2} \times \text{Miss penalty}_{L2}$$

so

$$\text{Average memory access time} = \text{Hit time}_{L1} + \text{Miss rate}_{L1}$$
$$\times (\text{Hit time}_{L2} + \text{Miss rate}_{L2} \times \text{Miss penalty}_{L2})$$

In this formula, the second-level miss rate is measured on the leftovers from the first-level cache. To avoid ambiguity, these terms are adopted here for a two-level cache system:

■ *Local miss rate*—This rate is simply the number of misses in a cache divided by the total number of memory accesses to this cache. As you would expect, for the first-level cache it is equal to Miss rate$_{L1}$, and for the second-level cache it is Miss rate$_{L2}$.

■ *Global miss rate*—The number of misses in the cache divided by the total number of memory accesses generated by the processor. Using the terms above, the global miss rate for the first-level cache is still just Miss rate$_{L1}$, but for the second-level cache it is Miss rate$_{L1}$ × Miss rate$_{L2}$.

This local miss rate is large for second-level caches because the first-level cache skims the cream of the memory accesses. This is why the global miss rate is the more useful measure: It indicates what fraction of the memory accesses that leave the processor go all the way to memory.

Here is a place where the misses per instruction metric shines. Instead of confusion about local or global miss rates, we just expand memory stalls per instruction to add the impact of a second-level cache.

$$\text{Average memory stalls per instruction} = \text{Misses per instruction}_{L1} \times \text{Hit time}_{L2}$$
$$+ \text{Misses per instruction}_{L2} \times \text{Miss penalty}_{L2}$$

Example   Suppose that in 1000 memory references there are 40 misses in the first-level cache and 20 misses in the second-level cache. What are the various miss rates? Assume the miss penalty from the L2 cache to memory is 200 clock cycles, the hit time of the L2 cache is 10 clock cycles, the hit time of L1 is 1 clock cycle, and there are 1.5 memory references per instruction. What is the average memory access time and average stall cycles per instruction? Ignore the impact of writes.

Answer   The miss rate (either local or global) for the first-level cache is 40/1000 or 4%. The local miss rate for the second-level cache is 20/40 or 50%. The global miss rate of the second-level cache is 20/1000 or 2%. Then

$$\text{Average memory access time} = \text{Hit time}_{L1} + \text{Miss rate}_{L1} \times (\text{Hit time}_{L2} + \text{Miss rate}_{L2} \times \text{Miss penalty}_{L2})$$
$$= 1 + 4\% \times (10 + 50\% \times 200) = 1 + 4\% \times 110 = 5.4 \text{ clock cycles}$$

To see how many misses we get per instruction, we divide 1000 memory references by 1.5 memory references per instruction, which yields 667 instructions. Thus, we need to multiply the misses by 1.5 to get the number of misses per 1000 instructions. We have 40×1.5 or 60 L1 misses, and 20×1.5 or 30 L2 misses, per 1000 instructions. For average memory stalls per instruction, assuming the misses are distributed uniformly between instructions and data:

$$\text{Average memory stalls per instruction} = \text{Misses per instruction}_{L1} \times \text{Hit time}_{L2} + \text{Misses per instruction}_{L2}$$
$$\times \text{Miss penalty}_{L2}$$
$$= (60/1000) \times 10 + (30/1000) \times 200$$
$$= 0.060 \times 10 + 0.030 \times 200 = 6.6 \text{ clock cycles}$$

If we subtract the L1 hit time from AMAT and then multiply by the average number of memory references per instruction, we get the same average memory stalls per instruction:

$$(5.4 - 1.0) \times 1.5 = 4.4 \times 1.5 = 6.6 \text{ clock cycles}$$

As this example shows, there may be less confusion with multilevel caches when calculating using misses per instruction versus miss rates.

Note that these formulas are for combined reads and writes, assuming a write-back first-level cache. Obviously, a write-through first-level cache will send *all* writes to the second level, not just the misses, and a write buffer might be used.

Figures C.14 and C.15 show how miss rates and relative execution time change with the size of a second-level cache for one design. From these figures we can gain two insights. The first is that the global cache miss rate is very similar to the single cache miss rate of the second-level cache, provided that the second-level cache is much larger than the first-level cache. Hence, our intuition and knowledge about

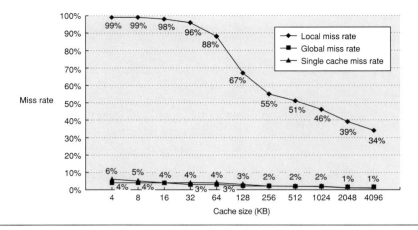

Figure C.14 Miss rates versus cache size for multilevel caches. Second-level caches *smaller* than the sum of the two 64 KB first-level caches make little sense, as reflected in the high miss rates. After 256 KB the single cache is within 10% of the global miss rates. The miss rate of a single-level cache versus size is plotted against the local miss rate and global miss rate of a second-level cache using a 32 KB first-level cache. The L2 caches (unified) were two-way set associative with LRU replacement. Each had split L1 instruction and data caches that were 64 KB two-way set associative with LRU replacement. The block size for both L1 and L2 caches was 64 bytes. Data were collected as in Figure C.4.

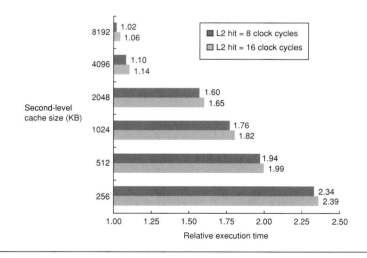

Figure C.15 Relative execution time by second-level cache size. The two bars are for different clock cycles for an L2 cache hit. The reference execution time of 1.00 is for an 8192 KB second-level cache with a 1-clock-cycle latency on a second-level hit. These data were collected the same way as in Figure C.14, using a simulator to imitate the Alpha 21264.

the first-level caches apply. The second insight is that the local cache miss rate is *not* a good measure of secondary caches; it is a function of the miss rate of the first-level cache, and hence can vary by changing the first-level cache. Thus, the global cache miss rate should be used when evaluating second-level caches.

With these definitions in place, we can consider the parameters of second-level caches. The foremost difference between the two levels is that the speed of the first-level cache affects the clock rate of the processor, while the speed of the second-level cache only affects the miss penalty of the first-level cache. Thus, we can consider many alternatives in the second-level cache that would be ill chosen for the first-level cache. There are two major questions for the design of the second-level cache: Will it lower the average memory access time portion of the CPI, and how much does it cost?

The initial decision is the size of a second-level cache. Since everything in the first-level cache is likely to be in the second-level cache, the second-level cache should be much bigger than the first. If second-level caches are just a little bigger, the local miss rate will be high. This observation inspires the design of huge second-level caches—the size of main memory in older computers!

One question is whether set associativity makes more sense for second-level caches.

Example Given the data below, what is the impact of second-level cache associativity on its miss penalty?

- Hit time$_{L2}$ for direct mapped = 10 clock cycles.
- Two-way set associativity increases hit time by 0.1 clock cycles to 10.1 clock cycles.
- Local miss rate$_{L2}$ for direct mapped = 25%.
- Local miss rate$_{L2}$ for two-way set associative = 20%.
- Miss penalty$_{L2}$ = 200 clock cycles.

Answer For a direct-mapped second-level cache, the first-level cache miss penalty is

$$\text{Miss penalty}_{1\text{-way L2}} = 10 + 25\% \times 200 = 60.0 \text{ clock cycles}$$

Adding the cost of associativity increases the hit cost only 0.1 clock cycles, making the new first-level cache miss penalty

$$\text{Miss penalty}_{2\text{-way L2}} = 10.1 + 20\% \times 200 = 50.1 \text{ clock cycles}$$

In reality, second-level caches are almost always synchronized with the first-level cache and processor. Accordingly, the second-level hit time must be an integral number of clock cycles. If we are lucky, we shave the second-level hit time to

10 cycles; if not, we round up to 11 cycles. Either choice is an improvement over the direct-mapped second-level cache:

$$\text{Miss penalty}_{2\text{-way L2}} = 10 + 20\% \times 200 = 50.0 \text{ clock cycles}$$
$$\text{Miss penalty}_{2\text{-way L2}} = 11 + 20\% \times 200 = 51.0 \text{ clock cycles}$$

Now we can reduce the miss penalty by reducing the *miss rate* of the second-level caches.

Another consideration concerns whether data in the first-level cache is in the second-level cache. *Multilevel inclusion* is the natural policy for memory hierarchies: L1 data are always present in L2. Inclusion is desirable because consistency between I/O and caches (or among caches in a multiprocessor) can be determined just by checking the second-level cache.

One drawback to inclusion is that measurements can suggest smaller blocks for the smaller first-level cache and larger blocks for the larger second-level cache. For example, the Pentium 4 has 64-byte blocks in its L1 caches and 128-byte blocks in its L2 cache. Inclusion can still be maintained with more work on a second-level miss. The second-level cache must invalidate all first-level blocks that map onto the second-level block to be replaced, causing a slightly higher first-level miss rate. To avoid such problems, many cache designers keep the block size the same in all levels of caches.

However, what if the designer can only afford an L2 cache that is slightly bigger than the L1 cache? Should a significant portion of its space be used as a redundant copy of the L1 cache? In such cases a sensible opposite policy is *multilevel exclusion*: L1 data is *never* found in an L2 cache. Typically, with exclusion a cache miss in L1 results in a swap of blocks between L1 and L2 instead of a replacement of an L1 block with an L2 block. This policy prevents wasting space in the L2 cache. For example, the AMD Opteron chip obeys the exclusion property using two 64 KB L1 caches and 1 MB L2 cache.

As these issues illustrate, although a novice might design the first- and second-level caches independently, the designer of the first-level cache has a simpler job given a compatible second-level cache. It is less of a gamble to use a write through, for example, if there is a write-back cache at the next level to act as a backstop for repeated writes and it uses multilevel inclusion.

The essence of all cache designs is balancing fast hits and few misses. For second-level caches, there are many fewer hits than in the first-level cache, so the emphasis shifts to fewer misses. This insight leads to much larger caches and techniques to lower the miss rate, such as higher associativity and larger blocks.

Fifth Optimization: Giving Priority to Read Misses over Writes to Reduce Miss Penalty

This optimization serves reads before writes have been completed. We start with looking at the complexities of a write buffer.

With a write-through cache the most important improvement is a write buffer of the proper size. Write buffers, however, do complicate memory accesses because they might hold the updated value of a location needed on a read miss.

Example   Look at this code sequence:

```
SW R3, 512(R0)   ;M[512] ← R3      (cache index 0)
LW R1, 1024(R0)  ;R1 ← M[1024]     (cache index 0)
LW R2, 512(R0)   ;R2 ← M[512]      (cache index 0)
```

Assume a direct-mapped, write-through cache that maps 512 and 1024 to the same block, and a four-word write buffer that is not checked on a read miss. Will the value in R2 always be equal to the value in R3?

Answer   Using the terminology from Chapter 2, this is a read-after-write data hazard in memory. Let's follow a cache access to see the danger. The data in R3 are placed into the write buffer after the store. The following load uses the same cache index and is therefore a miss. The second load instruction tries to put the value in location 512 into register R2; this also results in a miss. If the write buffer hasn't completed writing to location 512 in memory, the read of location 512 will put the old, wrong value into the cache block, and then into R2. Without proper precautions, R3 would not be equal to R2!

The simplest way out of this dilemma is for the read miss to wait until the write buffer is empty. The alternative is to check the contents of the write buffer on a read miss, and if there are no conflicts and the memory system is available, let the read miss continue. Virtually all desktop and server processors use the latter approach, giving reads priority over writes.

The cost of writes by the processor in a write-back cache can also be reduced. Suppose a read miss will replace a dirty memory block. Instead of writing the dirty block to memory, and then reading memory, we could copy the dirty block to a buffer, then read memory, and *then* write memory. This way the processor read, for which the processor is probably waiting, will finish sooner. Similar to the previous situation, if a read miss occurs, the processor can either stall until the buffer is empty or check the addresses of the words in the buffer for conflicts.

Now that we have five optimizations that reduce cache miss penalties or miss rates, it is time to look at reducing the final component of average memory access time. Hit time is critical because it can affect the clock rate of the processor; in many processors today the cache access time limits the clock cycle rate, even for processors that take multiple clock cycles to access the cache. Hence, a fast hit time is multiplied in importance beyond the average memory access time formula because it helps everything.

Sixth Optimization: Avoiding Address Translation during Indexing of the Cache to Reduce Hit Time

Even a small and simple cache must cope with the translation of a virtual address from the processor to a physical address to access memory. As described in Section C.4, processors treat main memory as just another level of the memory hierarchy, and thus the address of the virtual memory that exists on disk must be mapped onto the main memory.

The guideline of making the common case fast suggests that we use virtual addresses for the cache, since hits are much more common than misses. Such caches are termed *virtual caches,* with *physical cache* used to identify the traditional cache that uses physical addresses. As we will shortly see, it is important to distinguish two tasks: indexing the cache and comparing addresses. Thus, the issues are whether a virtual or physical address is used to index the cache and whether a virtual or physical address is used in the tag comparison. Full virtual addressing for both indices and tags eliminates address translation time from a cache hit. Then why doesn't everyone build virtually addressed caches?

One reason is protection. Page-level protection is checked as part of the virtual to physical address translation, and it must be enforced no matter what. One solution is to copy the protection information from the TLB on a miss, add a field to hold it, and check it on every access to the virtually addressed cache.

Another reason is that every time a process is switched, the virtual addresses refer to different physical addresses, requiring the cache to be flushed. Figure C.16 shows the impact on miss rates of this flushing. One solution is to increase the width of the cache address tag with a *process-identifier tag* (PID). If the operating system assigns these tags to processes, it only need flush the cache when a PID is recycled; that is, the PID distinguishes whether or not the data in the cache are for this program. Figure C.16 shows the improvement in miss rates by using PIDs to avoid cache flushes.

A third reason why virtual caches are not more popular is that operating systems and user programs may use two different virtual addresses for the same physical address. These duplicate addresses, called *synonyms* or *aliases,* could result in two copies of the same data in a virtual cache; if one is modified, the other will have the wrong value. With a physical cache this wouldn't happen, since the accesses would first be translated to the same physical cache block.

Hardware solutions to the synonym problem, called *antialiasing,* guarantee every cache block a unique physical address. The Opteron uses a 64 KB instruction cache with an 4 KB page and two-way set associativity, hence the hardware must handle aliases involved with the three virtual address bits in the set index. It avoids aliases by simply checking all eight possible locations on a miss—two blocks in each of four sets—to be sure that none match the physical address of the data being fetched. If one is found, it is invalidated, so when the new data are loaded into the cache their physical address is guaranteed to be unique.

Software can make this problem much easier by forcing aliases to share some address bits. An older version of UNIX from Sun Microsystems, for example,

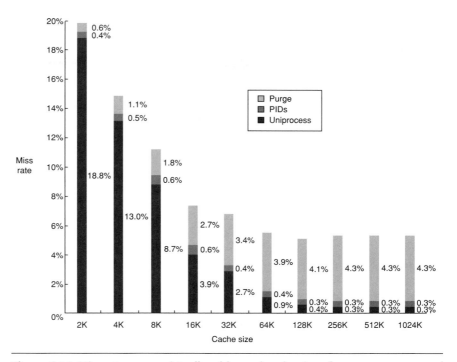

Figure C.16 Miss rate versus virtually addressed cache size of a program measured three ways: without process switches (uniprocess), with process switches using a process-identifier tag (PID), and with process switches but without PIDs (purge). PIDs increase the uniprocess absolute miss rate by 0.3% to 0.6% and save 0.6% to 4.3% over purging. Agarwal [1987] collected these statistics for the Ultrix operating system running on a VAX, assuming direct-mapped caches with a block size of 16 bytes. Note that the miss rate goes up from 128K to 256K. Such nonintuitive behavior can occur in caches because changing size changes the mapping of memory blocks onto cache blocks, which can change the conflict miss rate.

required all aliases to be identical in the last 18 bits of their addresses; this restriction is called *page coloring*. Note that page coloring is simply set-associative mapping applied to virtual memory: The 4 KB (2^{12}) pages are mapped using 64 (2^6) sets to ensure that the physical and virtual addresses match in the last 18 bits. This restriction means a direct-mapped cache that is 2^{18} (256K) bytes or smaller can never have duplicate physical addresses for blocks. From the perspective of the cache, page coloring effectively increases the page offset, as software guarantees that the last few bits of the virtual and physical page address are identical.

The final area of concern with virtual addresses is I/O. I/O typically uses physical addresses and thus would require mapping to virtual addresses to interact with a virtual cache. (The impact of I/O on caches is further discussed in Chapter 6.)

One alternative to get the best of both virtual and physical caches is to use part of the page offset—the part that is identical in both virtual and physical addresses—to index the cache. At the same time as the cache is being read using that index, the virtual part of the address is translated, and the tag match uses physical addresses.

This alternative allows the cache read to begin immediately, and yet the tag comparison is still with physical addresses. The limitation of this *virtually indexed, physically tagged* alternative is that a direct-mapped cache can be no bigger than the page size. For example, in the data cache in Figure C.5 on page C-13, the index is 9 bits and the cache block offset is 6 bits. To use this trick, the virtual page size would have to be at least $2^{(9+6)}$ bytes or 32 KB. If not, a portion of the index must be translated from virtual to physical address.

Associativity can keep the index in the physical part of the address and yet still support a large cache. Recall that the size of the index is controlled by this formula:

$$2^{\text{Index}} = \frac{\text{Cache size}}{\text{Block size} \times \text{Set associativity}}$$

For example, doubling associativity and doubling the cache size does not change the size of the index. The IBM 3033 cache, as an extreme example, is 16-way set associative, even though studies show there is little benefit to miss rates above 8-way set associativity. This high associativity allows a 64 KB cache to be addressed with a physical index, despite the handicap of 4 KB pages in the IBM architecture.

Summary of Basic Cache Optimization

The techniques in this section to improve miss rate, miss penalty, and hit time generally impact the other components of the average memory access equation as well as the complexity of the memory hierarchy. Figure C.17 summarizes these techniques and estimates the impact on complexity, with + meaning that the technique improves the factor, – meaning it hurts that factor, and blank meaning it has no impact. No optimization in this figure helps more than one category.

C.4 Virtual Memory

. . . a system has been devised to make the core drum combination appear to the programmer as a single level store, the requisite transfers taking place automatically.

Kilburn et al. [1962]

At any instant in time computers are running multiple processes, each with its own address space. (Processes are described in the next section.) It would be too expensive to dedicate a full address space worth of memory for each process, especially since many processes use only a small part of their address space.

Technique	Hit time	Miss penalty	Miss rate	Hardware complexity	Comment
Larger block size		–	+	0	Trivial; Pentium 4 L2 uses 128 bytes
Larger cache size	–		+	1	Widely used, especially for L2 caches
Higher associativity	–		+	1	Widely used
Multilevel caches		+		2	Costly hardware; harder if L1 block size ≠ L2 block size; widely used
Read priority over writes		+		1	Widely used
Avoiding address translation during cache indexing	+			1	Widely used

Figure C.17 Summary of basic cache optimizations showing impact on cache performance and complexity for the techniques in this appendix. Generally a technique helps only one factor. + means that the technique improves the factor, – means it hurts that factor, and blank means it has no impact. The complexity measure is subjective, with 0 being the easiest and 3 being a challenge.

Hence, there must be a means of sharing a smaller amount of physical memory among many processes.

One way to do this, *virtual memory,* divides physical memory into blocks and allocates them to different processes. Inherent in such an approach must be a *protection* scheme that restricts a process to the blocks belonging only to that process. Most forms of virtual memory also reduce the time to start a program, since not all code and data need be in physical memory before a program can begin.

Although protection provided by virtual memory is essential for current computers, sharing is not the reason that virtual memory was invented. If a program became too large for physical memory, it was the programmer's job to make it fit. Programmers divided programs into pieces, then identified the pieces that were mutually exclusive, and loaded or unloaded these *overlays* under user program control during execution. The programmer ensured that the program never tried to access more physical main memory than was in the computer, and that the proper overlay was loaded at the proper time. As you can well imagine, this responsibility eroded programmer productivity.

Virtual memory was invented to relieve programmers of this burden; it automatically manages the two levels of the memory hierarchy represented by main memory and secondary storage. Figure C.18 shows the mapping of virtual memory to physical memory for a program with four pages.

In addition to sharing protected memory space and automatically managing the memory hierarchy, virtual memory also simplifies loading the program for execution. Called *relocation,* this mechanism allows the same program to run in any location in physical memory. The program in Figure C.18 can be placed anywhere in physical memory or disk just by changing the mapping between them. (Prior to the popularity of virtual memory, processors would include a relocation register just for that purpose.) An alternative to a hardware solution would be software that changed all addresses in a program each time it was run.

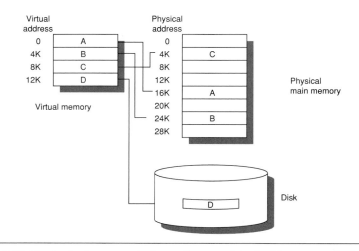

Figure C.18 The logical program in its contiguous virtual address space is shown on the left. It consists of four pages A, B, C, and D. The actual location of three of the blocks is in physical main memory and the other is located on the disk.

Several general memory hierarchy ideas from Chapter 1 about caches are analogous to virtual memory, although many of the terms are different. *Page* or *segment* is used for block, and *page fault* or *address fault* is used for miss. With virtual memory, the processor produces *virtual addresses* that are translated by a combination of hardware and software to *physical addresses,* which access main memory. This process is called *memory mapping* or *address translation*. Today, the two memory hierarchy levels controlled by virtual memory are DRAMs and magnetic disks. Figure C.19 shows a typical range of memory hierarchy parameters for virtual memory.

There are further differences between caches and virtual memory beyond those quantitative ones mentioned in Figure C.19:

■ Replacement on cache misses is primarily controlled by hardware, while virtual memory replacement is primarily controlled by the operating system. The longer miss penalty means it's more important to make a good decision, so the operating system can be involved and take time deciding what to replace.

■ The size of the processor address determines the size of virtual memory, but the cache size is independent of the processor address size.

■ In addition to acting as the lower-level backing store for main memory in the hierarchy, secondary storage is also used for the file system. In fact, the file system occupies most of secondary storage. It is not normally in the address space.

Virtual memory also encompasses several related techniques. Virtual memory systems can be categorized into two classes: those with fixed-size blocks, called

Parameter	First-level cache	Virtual memory
Block (page) size	16–128 bytes	4096–65,536 bytes
Hit time	1–3 clock cycles	100–200 clock cycles
Miss penalty	8–200 clock cycles	1,000,000–10,000,000 clock cycles
(access time)	(6–160 clock cycles)	(800,000–8,000,000 clock cycles)
(transfer time)	(2–40 clock cycles)	(200,000–2,000,000 clock cycles)
Miss rate	0.1–10%	0.00001–0.001%
Address mapping	25–45 bit physical address to 14–20 bit cache address	32–64 bit virtual address to 25–45 bit physical address

Figure C.19 Typical ranges of parameters for caches and virtual memory. Virtual memory parameters represent increases of 10–1,000,000 times over cache parameters. Normally first-level caches contain at most 1 MB of data, while physical memory contains 256 MB to 1 TB.

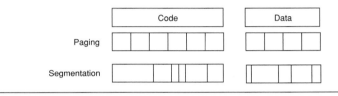

Figure C.20 Example of how paging and segmentation divide a program.

pages, and those with variable-size blocks, called *segments*. Pages are typically fixed at 4096 to 8192 bytes, while segment size varies. The largest segment supported on any processor ranges from 2^{16} bytes up to 2^{32} bytes; the smallest segment is 1 byte. Figure C.20 shows how the two approaches might divide code and data.

The decision to use paged virtual memory versus segmented virtual memory affects the processor. Paged addressing has a single fixed-size address divided into page number and offset within a page, analogous to cache addressing. A single address does not work for segmented addresses; the variable size of segments requires 1 word for a segment number and 1 word for an offset within a segment, for a total of 2 words. An unsegmented address space is simpler for the compiler.

The pros and cons of these two approaches have been well documented in operating systems textbooks; Figure C.21 summarizes the arguments. Because of the replacement problem (the third line of the figure), few computers today use pure segmentation. Some computers use a hybrid approach, called *paged segments,* in which a segment is an integral number of pages. This simplifies replacement because memory need not be contiguous, and the full segments need not be in main memory. A more recent hybrid is for a computer to offer multiple page sizes, with the larger sizes being powers of 2 times the smallest page size.

	Page	**Segment**
Words per address	One	Two (segment and offset)
Programmer visible?	Invisible to application programmer	May be visible to application programmer
Replacing a block	Trivial (all blocks are the same size)	Hard (must find contiguous, variable-size, unused portion of main memory)
Memory use inefficiency	Internal fragmentation (unused portion of page)	External fragmentation (unused pieces of main memory)
Efficient disk traffic	Yes (adjust page size to balance access time and transfer time)	Not always (small segments may transfer just a few bytes)

Figure C.21 Paging versus segmentation. Both can waste memory, depending on the block size and how well the segments fit together in main memory. Programming languages with unrestricted pointers require both the segment and the address to be passed. A hybrid approach, called *paged segments,* shoots for the best of both worlds: Segments are composed of pages, so replacing a block is easy, yet a segment may be treated as a logical unit.

The IBM 405CR embedded processor, for example, allows 1 KB, 4 KB ($2^2 \times$ 1 KB), 16 KB ($2^4 \times$ 1 KB), 64 KB ($2^6 \times$ 1 KB), 256 KB ($2^8 \times$ 1 KB), 1024 KB ($2^{10} \times$ 1 KB), and 4096 KB ($2^{12} \times$ 1 KB) to act as a single page.

Four Memory Hierarchy Questions Revisited

We are now ready to answer the four memory hierarchy questions for virtual memory.

Q1: Where Can a Block Be Placed in Main Memory?

The miss penalty for virtual memory involves access to a rotating magnetic storage device and is therefore quite high. Given the choice of lower miss rates or a simpler placement algorithm, operating systems designers normally pick lower miss rates because of the exorbitant miss penalty. Thus, operating systems allow blocks to be placed anywhere in main memory. According to the terminology in Figure C.2 on page C-7, this strategy would be labeled fully associative.

Q2: How Is a Block Found If It Is in Main Memory?

Both paging and segmentation rely on a data structure that is indexed by the page or segment number. This data structure contains the physical address of the block. For segmentation, the offset is added to the segment's physical address to obtain the final physical address. For paging, the offset is simply concatenated to this physical page address (see Figure C.22).

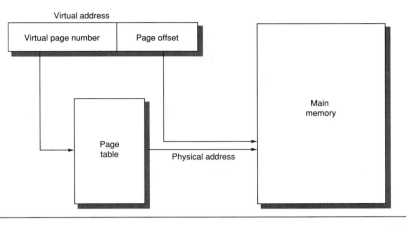

Figure C.22 The mapping of a virtual address to a physical address via a page table.

This data structure, containing the physical page addresses, usually takes the form of a *page table*. Indexed by the virtual page number, the size of the table is the number of pages in the virtual address space. Given a 32-bit virtual address, 4 KB pages, and 4 bytes per Page Table Entry (PTE), the size of the page table would be $(2^{32}/2^{12}) \times 2^2 = 2^{22}$ or 4 MB.

To reduce the size of this data structure, some computers apply a hashing function to the virtual address. The hash allows the data structure to be the length of the number of *physical* pages in main memory. This number could be much smaller than the number of virtual pages. Such a structure is called an *inverted page table*. Using the previous example, a 512 MB physical memory would only need 1 MB (8 × 512 MB/4 KB) for an inverted page table; the extra 4 bytes per page table entry are for the virtual address. The HP/Intel IA-64 covers both bases by offering both traditional pages tables *and* inverted page tables, leaving the choice of mechanism to the operating system programmer.

To reduce address translation time, computers use a cache dedicated to these address translations, called a *translation lookaside buffer,* or simply *translation buffer,* described in more detail shortly.

Q3: Which Block Should Be Replaced on a Virtual Memory Miss?

As mentioned earlier, the overriding operating system guideline is minimizing page faults. Consistent with this guideline, almost all operating systems try to replace the least-recently used (LRU) block because if the past predicts the future, that is the one less likely to be needed.

To help the operating system estimate LRU, many processors provide a *use bit* or *reference bit,* which is logically set whenever a page is accessed. (To reduce work, it is actually set only on a translation buffer miss, which is described shortly.) The operating system periodically clears the use bits and later records them so it can determine which pages were touched during a particular time period. By keeping track in this way, the operating system can select a page that is among the least-recently referenced.

Q4: What Happens on a Write?

The level below main memory contains rotating magnetic disks that take millions of clock cycles to access. Because of the great discrepancy in access time, no one has yet built a virtual memory operating system that writes through main memory to disk on every store by the processor. (This remark should not be interpreted as an opportunity to become famous by being the first to build one!) Thus, the write strategy is always write back.

Since the cost of an unnecessary access to the next-lower level is so high, virtual memory systems usually include a dirty bit. It allows blocks to be written to disk only if they have been altered since being read from the disk.

Techniques for Fast Address Translation

Page tables are usually so large that they are stored in main memory and are sometimes paged themselves. Paging means that every memory access logically takes at least twice as long, with one memory access to obtain the physical address and a second access to get the data. As mentioned in Chapter 5, we use locality to avoid the extra memory access. By keeping address translations in a special cache, a memory access rarely requires a second access to translate the data. This special address translation cache is referred to as a *translation lookaside buffer* (TLB), also called a *translation buffer* (TB).

A TLB entry is like a cache entry where the tag holds portions of the virtual address and the data portion holds a physical page frame number, protection field, valid bit, and usually a use bit and dirty bit. To change the physical page frame number or protection of an entry in the page table, the operating system must make sure the old entry is not in the TLB; otherwise, the system won't behave properly. Note that this dirty bit means the corresponding *page* is dirty, not that the address translation in the TLB is dirty nor that a particular block in the data cache is dirty. The operating system resets these bits by changing the value in the page table and then invalidates the corresponding TLB entry. When the entry is reloaded from the page table, the TLB gets an accurate copy of the bits.

Figure C.23 shows the Opteron data TLB organization, with each step of the translation labeled. This TLB uses fully associative placement; thus, the translation begins (steps 1 and 2) by sending the virtual address to all tags. Of course, the tag must be marked valid to allow a match. At the same time, the type of memory access is checked for a violation (also in step 2) against protection information in the TLB.

For reasons similar to those in the cache case, there is no need to include the 12 bits of the page offset in the TLB. The matching tag sends the corresponding

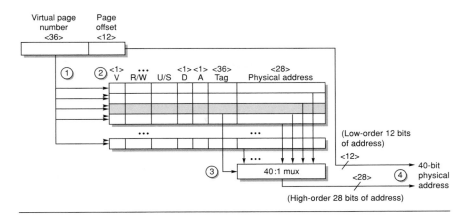

Figure C.23 Operation of the Opteron data TLB during address translation. The four steps of a TLB hit are shown as circled numbers. This TLB has 40 entries. Section C.5 describes the various protection and access fields of an Opteron page table entry.

physical address through effectively a 40:1 multiplexor (step 3). The page offset is then combined with the physical page frame to form a full physical address (step 4). The address size is 40 bits.

Address translation can easily be on the critical path determining the clock cycle of the processor, so the Opteron uses virtually addressed, physically tagged L1 caches.

Selecting a Page Size

The most obvious architectural parameter is the page size. Choosing the page is a question of balancing forces that favor a larger page size versus those favoring a smaller size. The following favor a larger size:

- The size of the page table is inversely proportional to the page size; memory (or other resources used for the memory map) can therefore be saved by making the pages bigger.

- As mentioned in Section C.3, a larger page size can allow larger caches with fast cache hit times.

- Transferring larger pages to or from secondary storage, possibly over a network, is more efficient than transferring smaller pages.

- The number of TLB entries is restricted, so a larger page size means that more memory can be mapped efficiently, thereby reducing the number of TLB misses.

It is for this final reason that recent microprocessors have decided to support multiple page sizes; for some programs, TLB misses can be as significant on CPI as the cache misses.

The main motivation for a smaller page size is conserving storage. A small page size will result in less wasted storage when a contiguous region of virtual memory is not equal in size to a multiple of the page size. The term for this unused memory in a page is *internal fragmentation*. Assuming that each process has three primary segments (text, heap, and stack), the average wasted storage per process will be 1.5 times the page size. This amount is negligible for computers with hundreds of megabytes of memory and page sizes of 4 KB to 8 KB. Of course, when the page sizes become very large (more than 32 KB), storage (both main and secondary) could be wasted, as well as I/O bandwidth. A final concern is process start-up time; many processes are small, so a large page size would lengthen the time to invoke a process.

Summary of Virtual Memory and Caches

With virtual memory, TLBs, first-level caches, and second-level caches all mapping portions of the virtual and physical address space, it can get confusing what bits go where. Figure C.24 gives a hypothetical example going from a 64-bit virtual address to a 41-bit physical address with two levels of cache. This L1 cache is virtually indexed, physically tagged since both the cache size and the page size are 8 KB. The L2 cache is 4 MB. The block size for both is 64 bytes.

First, the 64-bit virtual address is logically divided into a virtual page number and page offset. The former is sent to the TLB to be translated into a physical address, and the high bit of the latter is sent to the L1 cache to act as an index. If the TLB match is a hit, then the physical page number is sent to the L1 cache tag to check for a match. If it matches, it's an L1 cache hit. The block offset then selects the word for the processor.

If the L1 cache check results in a miss, the physical address is then used to try the L2 cache. The middle portion of the physical address is used as an index to the 4 MB L2 cache. The resulting L2 cache tag is compared to the upper part of the physical address to check for a match. If it matches, we have an L2 cache hit, and the data are sent to the processor, which uses the block offset to select the desired word. On an L2 miss, the physical address is then used to get the block from memory.

Although this is a simple example, the major difference between this drawing and a real cache is replication. First, there is only one L1 cache. When there are two L1 caches, the top half of the diagram is duplicated. Note this would lead to two TLBs, which is typical. Hence, one cache and TLB is for instructions, driven from the PC, and one cache and TLB is for data, driven from the effective address.

The second simplification is that all the caches and TLBs are direct mapped. If any were *n*-way set associative, then we would replicate each set of tag memory, comparators, and data memory *n* times and connect data memories with an *n*:1 multiplexor to select a hit. Of course, if the total cache size remained the same, the cache index would also shrink by $\log 2n$ bits according to the formula in Figure C.7 on page C-21.

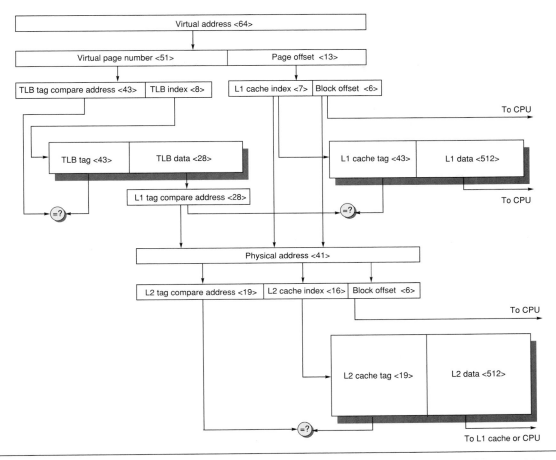

Figure C.24 The overall picture of a hypothetical memory hierarchy going from virtual address to L2 cache access. The page size is 8 KB. The TLB is direct mapped with 256 entries. The L1 cache is a direct-mapped 8 KB, and the L2 cache is a direct-mapped 4 MB. Both use 64-byte blocks. The virtual address is 64 bits and the physical address is 41 bits. The primary difference between this simple figure and a real cache is replication of pieces of this figure.

C.5   Protection and Examples of Virtual Memory

The invention of multiprogramming, where a computer would be shared by several programs running concurrently, led to new demands for protection and sharing among programs. These demands are closely tied to virtual memory in computers today, and so we cover the topic here along with two examples of virtual memory.

Multiprogramming leads to the concept of a *process*. Metaphorically, a process is a program's breathing air and living space—that is, a running program plus any state needed to continue running it. Time-sharing is a variation of multiprogramming that shares the processor and memory with several interactive users at the same time, giving the illusion that all users have their own computers. Thus, at any instant it must be possible to switch from one process to another. This exchange is called a *process switch* or *context switch*.

A process must operate correctly whether it executes continuously from start to finish, or it is interrupted repeatedly and switched with other processes. The responsibility for maintaining correct process behavior is shared by designers of the computer and the operating system. The computer designer must ensure that the processor portion of the process state can be saved and restored. The operating system designer must guarantee that processes do not interfere with each others' computations.

The safest way to protect the state of one process from another would be to copy the current information to disk. However, a process switch would then take seconds—far too long for a time-sharing environment.

This problem is solved by operating systems partitioning main memory so that several different processes have their state in memory at the same time. This division means that the operating system designer needs help from the computer designer to provide protection so that one process cannot modify another. Besides protection, the computers also provide for sharing of code and data between processes, to allow communication between processes or to save memory by reducing the number of copies of identical information.

Protecting Processes

Processes can be protected from one another by having their own page tables, each pointing to distinct pages of memory. Obviously, user programs must be prevented from modifying their page tables or protection would be circumvented.

Protection can be escalated, depending on the apprehension of the computer designer or the purchaser. *Rings* added to the processor protection structure expand memory access protection from two levels (user and kernel) to many more. Like a military classification system of top secret, secret, confidential, and unclassified, concentric rings of security levels allow the most trusted to access anything, the second most trusted to access everything except the innermost level, and so on. The "civilian" programs are the least trusted and, hence, have the most limited range of accesses. There may also be restrictions on what pieces of memory can contain code—execute protection—and even on the entrance point between the levels. The Intel 80x86 protection structure, which uses rings, is described later in this section. It is not clear whether rings are an improvement in practice over the simple system of user and kernel modes.

As the designer's apprehension escalates to trepidation, these simple rings may not suffice. Restricting the freedom given a program in the inner sanctum requires a new classification system. Instead of a military model, the analogy of this system is to keys and locks: A program can't unlock access to the data unless it has the key. For these keys, or *capabilities,* to be useful, the hardware and operating system must be able to explicitly pass them from one program to another without allowing a program itself to forge them. Such checking requires a great deal of hardware support if time for checking keys is to be kept low.

The 80x86 architecture has tried several of these alternatives over the years. Since backwards compatibility is one of the guidelines of this architecture, the most recent versions of the architecture include all of its experiments in virtual memory. We'll go over two of the options here: first, the older segmented address space and then the newer flat, 64-bit address space.

A Segmented Virtual Memory Example: Protection in the Intel Pentium

The second system is the most dangerous system a man ever designs. . . . The general tendency is to over-design the second system, using all the ideas and frills that were cautiously sidetracked on the first one.

F. P. Brooks, Jr.
The Mythical Man-Month (1975)

The original 8086 used segments for addressing, yet it provided nothing for virtual memory or for protection. Segments had base registers but no bound registers and no access checks, and before a segment register could be loaded the corresponding segment had to be in physical memory. Intel's dedication to virtual memory and protection is evident in the successors to the 8086, with a few fields extended to support larger addresses. This protection scheme is elaborate, with many details carefully designed to try to avoid security loopholes. We'll refer to it as IA-32. The next few pages highlight a few of the Intel safeguards; if you find the reading difficult, imagine the difficulty of implementing them!

The first enhancement is to double the traditional two-level protection model: the IA-32 has four levels of protection. The innermost level (0) corresponds to the traditional kernel mode, and the outermost level (3) is the least privileged mode. The IA-32 has separate stacks for each level to avoid security breaches between the levels. There are also data structures analogous to traditional page tables that contain the physical addresses for segments, as well as a list of checks to be made on translated addresses.

The Intel designers did not stop there. The IA-32 divides the address space, allowing both the operating system and the user access to the full space. The IA-32 user can call an operating system routine in this space and even pass parameters to it while retaining full protection. This safe call is not a trivial action, since the stack for the operating system is different from the user's stack. Moreover, the IA-32 allows the operating system to maintain the protection level of the *called* routine for the parameters that are passed to it. This potential loophole in protection is prevented by not allowing the user process to ask the operating system to access something indirectly that it would not have been able to access itself. (Such security loopholes are called *Trojan horses*.)

The Intel designers were guided by the principle of trusting the operating system as little as possible, while supporting sharing and protection. As an example of the use of such protected sharing, suppose a payroll program writes checks and also updates the year-to-date information on total salary and benefits payments. Thus, we want to give the program the ability to read the salary and year-to-date information, and modify the year-to-date information but not the salary. We will see the mechanism to support such features shortly. In the rest of this subsection, we will look at the big picture of the IA-32 protection and examine its motivation.

Adding Bounds Checking and Memory Mapping

The first step in enhancing the Intel processor was getting the segmented addressing to check bounds as well as supply a base. Rather than a base address, the segment registers in the IA-32 contain an index to a virtual memory data structure called a *descriptor table*. Descriptor tables play the role of traditional page tables. On the IA-32 the equivalent of a page table entry is a *segment descriptor*. It contains fields found in PTEs:

- *Present bit*—Equivalent to the PTE valid bit, used to indicate this is a valid translation

- *Base field*—Equivalent to a page frame address, containing the physical address of the first byte of the segment

- *Access bit*—Like the reference bit or use bit in some architectures that is helpful for replacement algorithms

- *Attributes field*—Specifies the valid operations and protection levels for operations that use this segment

There is also a *limit field,* not found in paged systems, which establishes the upper bound of valid offsets for this segment. Figure C.25 shows examples of IA-32 segment descriptors.

IA-32 provides an optional paging system in addition to this segmented addressing. The upper portion of the 32-bit address selects the segment descriptor, and the middle portion is an index into the page table selected by the descriptor. We describe below the protection system that does not rely on paging.

Adding Sharing and Protection

To provide for protected sharing, half of the address space is shared by all processes and half is unique to each process, called *global address space* and *local address space,* respectively. Each half is given a descriptor table with the appropriate name. A descriptor pointing to a shared segment is placed in the global descriptor table, while a descriptor for a private segment is placed in the local descriptor table.

A program loads an IA-32 segment register with an index to the table *and* a bit saying which table it desires. The operation is checked according to the

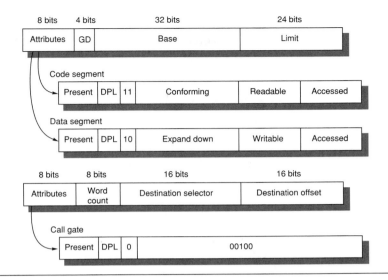

Figure C.25 The IA-32 segment descriptors are distinguished by bits in the attributes field. *Base, limit, present, readable,* and *writable* are all self-explanatory. D gives the default addressing size of the instructions: 16 bits or 32 bits. G gives the granularity of the segment limit: 0 means in bytes and 1 means in 4 KB pages. G is set to 1 when paging is turned on to set the size of the page tables. DPL means *descriptor privilege level*—this is checked against the code privilege level to see if the access will be allowed. *Conforming* says the code takes on the privilege level of the code being called rather than the privilege level of the caller; it is used for library routines. The *expand-down field* flips the check to let the base field be the high-water mark and the limit field be the low-water mark. As you might expect, this is used for stack segments that grow down. *Word count* controls the number of words copied from the current stack to the new stack on a call gate. The other two fields of the call gate descriptor, *destination selector* and *destination offset,* select the descriptor of the destination of the call and the offset into it, respectively. There are many more than these three segment descriptors in the IA-32 protection model.

attributes in the descriptor, the physical address being formed by adding the offset in the processor to the base in the descriptor, provided the offset is less than the limit field. Every segment descriptor has a separate 2-bit field to give the legal access level of this segment. A violation occurs only if the program tries to use a segment with a lower protection level in the segment descriptor.

We can now show how to invoke the payroll program mentioned above to update the year-to-date information without allowing it to update salaries. The program could be given a descriptor to the information that has the writable field clear, meaning it can read but not write the data. A trusted program can then be supplied that will only write the year-to-date information. It is given a descriptor with the writable field set (Figure C.25). The payroll program invokes the trusted code using a code segment descriptor with the conforming field set. This setting means the called program takes on the privilege level of the code being called rather than the privilege level of the caller. Hence, the payroll program can read the salaries and call a trusted program to update the year-to-date totals, yet the payroll program cannot modify the salaries. If a Trojan horse exists in this system, to be effective it must be located in the trusted code whose only job is to update the year-to-date information. The argument for this style of protection is that limiting the scope of the vulnerability enhances security.

Adding Safe Calls from User to OS Gates and Inheriting Protection Level for Parameters

Allowing the user to jump into the operating system is a bold step. How, then, can a hardware designer increase the chances of a safe system without trusting the operating system or any other piece of code? The IA-32 approach is to restrict where the user can enter a piece of code, to safely place parameters on the proper stack, and to make sure the user parameters don't get the protection level of the called code.

To restrict entry into others' code, the IA-32 provides a special segment descriptor, or *call gate,* identified by a bit in the attributes field. Unlike other descriptors, call gates are full physical addresses of an object in memory; the offset supplied by the processor is ignored. As stated above, their purpose is to prevent the user from randomly jumping anywhere into a protected or more privileged code segment. In our programming example, this means the only place the payroll program can invoke the trusted code is at the proper boundary. This restriction is needed to make conforming segments work as intended.

What happens if caller and callee are "mutually suspicious," so that neither trusts the other? The solution is found in the word count field in the bottom descriptor in Figure C.25. When a call instruction invokes a call gate descriptor, the descriptor copies the number of words specified in the descriptor from the local stack onto the stack corresponding to the level of this segment. This copying allows the user to pass parameters by first pushing them onto the local stack. The hardware then safely transfers them onto the correct stack. A return from a call gate will pop the parameters off both stacks and copy any return values to the proper stack. Note that this model is incompatible with the current practice of passing parameters in registers.

This scheme still leaves open the potential loophole of having the operating system use the user's address, passed as parameters, with the operating system's security level, instead of with the user's level. The IA-32 solves this problem by dedicating 2 bits in every processor segment register to the *requested protection level.* When an operating system routine is invoked, it can execute an instruction that sets this 2-bit field in all address parameters with the protection level of the user that called the routine. Thus, when these address parameters are loaded into the segment registers, they will set the requested protection level to the proper value. The IA-32 hardware then uses the requested protection level to prevent any foolishness: No segment can be accessed from the system routine using those parameters if it has a more privileged protection level than requested.

A Paged Virtual Memory Example: The 64-Bit Opteron Memory Management

AMD engineers found few uses of the elaborate protection model described above. The popular model is a flat, 32-bit address space, introduced by the 80386, which sets all the base values of the segment registers to zero. Hence, AMD dispensed with the multiple segments in the 64-bit mode. It assumes that the segment base is zero and ignores the limit field. The page sizes are 4 KB, 2 MB, and 4 MB.

The 64-bit virtual address of the AMD64 architecture is mapped onto 52-bit physical addresses, although implementations can implement fewer bits to simplify hardware. The Opteron, for example, uses 48-bit virtual addresses and 40-bit physical addresses. AMD64 requires that the upper 16 bits of the virtual address be just the sign extension of the lower 48 bits, which it calls *canonical form*.

The size of page tables for the 64-bit address space is alarming. Hence, AMD64 uses a multilevel hierarchical page table to map the address space to keep the size reasonable. The number of levels depends on the size of the virtual address space. Figure C.26 shows the four-level translation of the 48-bit virtual addresses of the Opteron.

The offsets for each of these page tables come from four 9-bit fields. Address translation starts with adding the first offset to the page-map level 4 base register and then reading memory from this location to get the base of the next-level page table. The next address offset is in turn added to this newly fetched address, and memory is accessed again to determine the base of the third page table. It happens again in the same fashion. The last address field is added to this final base address, and memory is read using this sum to (finally) get the physical address of the page being referenced. This address is concatenated with the 12-bit page offset to get the full physical address. Note that page table in the Opteron architecture fits within a single 4 KB page.

The Opteron uses a 64-bit entry in each of these page tables. The first 12 bits are reserved for future use, the next 52 bits contain the physical page frame number, and the last 12 bits give the protection and use information. Although the fields vary some between the page table levels, here are the basic ones:

- *Presence*—Says that page is present in memory.
- *Read/write*—Says whether page is read-only or read-write.
- *User/supervisor*—Says whether a user can access the page or if it is limited to upper three privilege levels.
- *Dirty*—Says if page has been modified.
- *Accessed*—Says if page has been read or written since the bit was last cleared.
- *Page size*—Says whether last level is for 4 KB pages or 4 MB pages; if it's the latter, then the Opteron only uses three instead of four levels of pages.

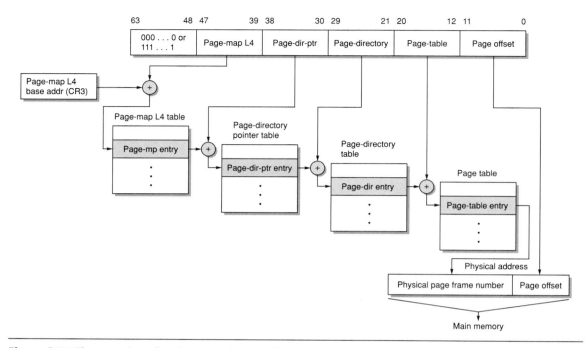

Figure C.26 The mapping of an Opteron virtual address. The Opteron virtual memory implementation with four page table levels supports an effective physical address size of 40 bits. Each page table has 512 entries, so each level field is 9 bits wide. The AMD64 architecture document allows the virtual address size to grow from the current 48 bits to 64 bits, and the physical address size to grow from the current 40 bits to 52 bits.

- *No execute*—Not found in the 80386 protection scheme, this bit was added to prevent code from executing in some pages.

- *Page level cache disable*—Says whether the page can be cached or not.

- *Page level write through*—Says whether the page allows write back or write through for data caches.

Since the Opteron normally goes through four levels of tables on a TLB miss, there are three potential places to check protection restrictions. The Opteron obeys only the bottom-level Page Table Entry, checking the others only to be sure the valid bit is set.

As the entry is 8 bytes long, each page table has 512 entries, and the Opteron has 4 KB pages, the page tables are exactly one page long. Each of the four level fields are 9 bits long and the page offset is 12 bits. This derivation leaves 64 − (4 × 9 + 12) or 16 bits to be sign extended to ensure canonical addresses

Although we have explained translation of legal addresses, what prevents the user from creating illegal address translations and getting into mischief? The

Parameter	Description
Block size	1 PTE (8 bytes)
L1 hit time	1 clock cycle
L2 hit time	7 clock cycles
L1 TLB size	same for instruction and data TLBs: 40 PTEs per TLBs, with 32 4 KB pages and 8 for 2M or 4M pages
L2 TLB size	same for instruction and data TLBs: 512 PTEs of 4 KB pages
Block selection	LRU
Write strategy	(not applicable)
L1 block placement	fully associative
L2 block placement	4-way set associative

Figure C.27 Memory hierarchy parameters of the Opteron L1 and L2 instruction and data TLBs.

page tables themselves are protected from being written by user programs. Thus, the user can try any virtual address, but by controlling the page table entries the operating system controls what physical memory is accessed. Sharing of memory between processes is accomplished by having a page table entry in each address space point to the same physical memory page.

The Opteron employs four TLBs to reduce address translation time, two for instruction accesses and two for data accesses. Like multilevel caches, the Opteron reduces TLB misses by having two larger L2 TLBs: one for instructions and one for data. Figure C.27 describes the data TLB.

Summary: Protection on the 32-Bit Intel Pentium vs. the 64-Bit AMD Opteron

Memory management in the Opteron is typical of most desktop or server computers today, relying on page-level address translation and correct operation of the operating system to provide safety to multiple processes sharing the computer. Although presented as alternatives, Intel has followed AMD's lead and embraced the AMD64 architecture. Hence, both AMD and Intel support the 64-bit extension of 80x86, yet, for compatibility reasons, both support the elaborate segmented protection scheme.

If the segmented protection model looks harder to build than the AMD64 model, that's because it is. This effort must be especially frustrating for the engineers, since few customers use the elaborate protection mechanism. In addition, the fact that the protection model is a mismatch to the simple paging protection of UNIX-like systems means it will be used only by someone writing an operating system especially for this computer, which hasn't happened yet.

C.6 Fallacies and Pitfalls

Even a review of memory hierarchy has fallacies and pitfalls!

Pitfall *Too small an address space.*

Just five years after DEC and Carnegie Mellon University collaborated to design the new PDP-11 computer family, it was apparent that their creation had a fatal flaw. An architecture announced by IBM six years *before* the PDP-11 was still thriving, with minor modifications, 25 years later. And the DEC VAX, criticized for including unnecessary functions, sold millions of units after the PDP-11 went out of production. Why?

The fatal flaw of the PDP-11 was the size of its addresses (16 bits) as compared to the address sizes of the IBM 360 (24 to 31 bits) and the VAX (32 bits). Address size limits the program length, since the size of a program and the amount of data needed by the program must be less than $2^{\text{Address size}}$. The reason the address size is so hard to change is that it determines the minimum width of anything that can contain an address: PC, register, memory word, and effective-address arithmetic. If there is no plan to expand the address from the start, then the chances of successfully changing address size are so slim that it normally means the end of that computer family. Bell and Strecker [1976] put it like this:

> There is only one mistake that can be made in computer design that is difficult to recover from—not having enough address bits for memory addressing and memory management. The PDP-11 followed the unbroken tradition of nearly every known computer. [p. 2]

A partial list of successful computers that eventually starved to death for lack of address bits includes the PDP-8, PDP-10, PDP-11, Intel 8080, Intel 8086, Intel 80186, Intel 80286, Motorola 6800, AMI 6502, Zilog Z80, CRAY-1, and CRAY X-MP.

The venerable 80x86 line bears the distinction of having been extended twice, first to 32 bits with the Intel 80386 in 1985 and recently to 64 bits with the AMD Opteron.

Pitfall *Ignoring the impact of the operating system on the performance of the memory hierarchy.*

Figure C.28 shows the memory stall time due to the operating system spent on three large workloads. About 25% of the stall time is either spent in misses in the operating system or results from misses in the application programs because of interference with the operating system.

Pitfall *Relying on the operating systems to change the page size over time.*

The Alpha architects had an elaborate plan to grow the architecture over time by growing its page size, even building it into the size of its virtual address. When it

	Misses		% time due to application misses		% time due directly to OS misses				% time OS misses and application conflicts
Workload	% in applications	% in OS	Inherent application misses	OS conflicts with applications	OS instruction misses	Data misses for migration	Data misses in block operations	Rest of OS misses	
Pmake	47%	53%	14.1%	4.8%	10.9%	1.0%	6.2%	2.9%	25.8%
Multipgm	53%	47%	21.6%	3.4%	9.2%	4.2%	4.7%	3.4%	24.9%
Oracle	73%	27%	25.7%	10.2%	10.6%	2.6%	0.6%	2.8%	26.8%

Figure C.28 Misses and time spent in misses for applications and operating system. The operating system adds about 25% to the execution time of the application. Each processor has a 64 KB instruction cache and a two-level data cache with 64 KB in the first level and 256 KB in the second level; all caches are direct mapped with 16-byte blocks. Collected on Silicon Graphics POWER station 4D/340, a multiprocessor with four 33 MHz R3000 processors running three application workloads under a UNIX System V—Pmake: a parallel compile of 56 files; Multipgm: the parallel numeric program MP3D running concurrently with Pmake and a five-screen edit session; and Oracle: running a restricted version of the TP-1 benchmark using the Oracle database. (Data from Torrellas, Gupta, and Hennessy [1992].)

came time to grow page sizes with later Alphas, the operating system designers balked and the virtual memory system was revised to grow the address space while maintaining the 8 KB page.

Architects of other computers noticed very high TLB miss rates, and so added multiple, larger page sizes to the TLB. The hope was that operating systems programmers would allocate an object to the largest page that made sense, thereby preserving TLB entries. After a decade of trying, most operating systems use these "superpages" only for handpicked functions: mapping the display memory or other I/O devices, or using very large pages for the database code.

C.7 Concluding Remarks

The difficulty of building a memory system to keep pace with faster processors is underscored by the fact that the raw material for main memory is the same as that found in the cheapest computer. It is the principle of locality that helps us here— its soundness is demonstrated at all levels of the memory hierarchy in current computers, from disks to TLBs.

However, the increasing relative latency to memory, taking hundreds of clock cycles in 2006, means that programmers and compiler writers must be aware of the parameters of the caches and TLBs if they want their programs to perform well.

C.8 Historical Perspective and References

In Section K.6 on the companion CD we examine the history of caches, virtual memory, and virtual machines. IBM plays a prominent role in this history. References for further reading are included.

References

Adve, S. V., and K. Gharachorloo [1996]. "Shared memory consistency models: A tutorial," *IEEE Computer* 29:12 (December), 66–76.

Adve, S. V., and M. D. Hill [1990]. "Weak ordering—a new definition," *Proc. 17th Int'l Symposium on Computer Architecture* (June), Seattle, Wash., 2–14.

Agarwal, A. [1987]. *Analysis of Cache Performance for Operating Systems and Multiprogramming*, Ph.D. thesis, Stanford Univ., Tech. Rep. No. CSL-TR-87-332 (May).

Agarwal, A. [1991]. "Limits on interconnection network performance," *IEEE Trans. on Parallel and Distributed Systems* 2:4 (April), 398–412.

Agarwal, A., R. Bianchini, D. Chaiken, K. Johnson, and D. Kranz [1995]. "The MIT Alewife machine: Architecture and performance," *Int'l Symposium on Computer Architecture* (Denver, Colo.), June, 2–13.

Agarwal, A., J. L. Hennessy, R. Simoni, and M. A. Horowitz [1988]. "An evaluation of directory schemes for cache coherence," *Proc. 15th Int'l Symposium on Computer Architecture* (June), 280–289.

Agarwal, A., J. Kubiatowicz, D. Kranz, B.-H. Lim, D. Yeung, G. D'Souza, and M. Parkin [1993]. "Sparcle: An evolutionary processor design for large-scale multiprocessors," *IEEE Micro* 13 (June), 48–61.

Agarwal, A., and S. D. Pudar [1993]. "Column-associative caches: A technique for reducing the miss rate of direct-mapped caches," 20th Annual Int'l Symposium on Computer Architecture ISCA '20, San Diego, Calif., May 16–19, *Computer Architecture News* 21:2 (May), 179–190.

Agerwala, T., and J. Cocke [1987]. "High performance reduced instruction set processors," IBM Tech. Rep. (March).

Alexander, W. G., and D. B. Wortman [1975]. "Static and dynamic characteristics of XPL programs," *IEEE Computer* 8:11 (November), 41–46.

Alles, A. [1995]. "ATM internetworking" (May), *www.cisco.com/warp/public/614/12.html.*

Alliant Computer Systems Corp. [1987]. *Alliant FX/Series: Product Summary* (June), Acton, Mass.

Almasi, G. S., and A. Gottlieb [1989]. *Highly Parallel Computing,* Benjamin/Cummings, Redwood City, Calif.

Alverson, G., R. Alverson, D. Callahan, B. Koblenz, A. Porterfield, and B. Smith [1992]. "Exploiting heterogeneous parallelism on a multithreaded multiprocessor," *Proc. 1992 Int'l Conf. on Supercomputing* (November), 188–197.

Amdahl, G. M. [1967]. "Validity of the single processor approach to achieving large scale computing capabilities," *Proc. AFIPS Spring Joint Computer Conf.* 30, Atlantic City, N.J. (April), 483–485.

Amdahl, G. M., G. A. Blaauw, and F. P. Brooks, Jr. [1964]. "Architecture of the IBM System 360," *IBM J. Research and Development* 8:2 (April), 87–101.

Amza, C., A. L. Cox, S. Dwarkadas, P. Keleher, H. Lu, R. Rajamony, W. Yu, and W. Zwaenepoel [1996]. "Treadmarks: Shared memory computing on networks of workstations," *IEEE Computer* 29:2 (February), 18–28.

Anderson, D. [2003]. "You don't know jack about disks," *Queue,* 1:4 (June), 20–30.

Anderson, D., J. Dykes, and E. Riedel [2003]. "SCSI vs. ATA—More than an interface," *Conf. on File and Storage Technology (FAST),* San Francisco, April 2003.

Anderson, D. W., F. J. Sparacio, and R. M. Tomasulo [1967]. "The IBM 360 Model 91: Processor philosophy and instruction handling," *IBM J. Research and Development* 11:1 (January), 8–24.

Anderson, M. H. [1990]. "Strength (and safety) in numbers (RAID, disk storage technology)," *Byte* 15:13 (December), 337–339.

Anderson, T. E., D. E. Culler, and D. Patterson [1995]. "A case for NOW (networks of workstations)," *IEEE Micro* 15:1 (February), 54–64.

Ang, B., D. Chiou, D. Rosenband, M. Ehrlich, L. Rudolph, and Arvind [1998]. "StarT-Voyager: A flexible platform for exploring scalable SMP issues," *Proc. of SC'98,* Orlando, Fla., November.

Anjan, K. V., and T. M. Pinkston [1995]. "An efficient, fully-adaptive deadlock recovery scheme: Disha," *Proc. 22nd Int'l Symposium on Computer Architecture* (June), Italy.

Anon. et al. [1985]. "A measure of transaction processing power," Tandem Tech. Rep. TR 85.2. Also appeared in *Datamation* 31:7 (April), 112–118.

Archibald, J., and J.-L. Baer [1986]. "Cache coherence protocols: Evaluation using a multiprocessor simulation model," *ACM Trans. on Computer Systems* 4:4 (November), 273–298.

Arpaci, R. H., D. E. Culler, A. Krishnamurthy, S. G. Steinberg, and K. Yelick [1995]. "Empirical evaluation of the CRAY-T3D: A compiler perspective," *Proc. 23rd Int'l Symposium on Computer Architecture* (June), Italy.

Asanovic, K. [1998]. *Vector microprocessors,* Ph.D. thesis, Computer Science Division, Univ. of California at Berkeley (May).

Associated Press [2005]. "Gap Inc. shuts down two internet stores for major overhaul," USATODAY.com, August 8, 2005.

Atanasoff, J. V. [1940]. "Computing machine for the solution of large systems of linear equations," Internal Report, Iowa State University, Ames.

Austin, T. M., and G. Sohi [1992]. "Dynamic dependency analysis of ordinary programs," *Proc. 19th Symposium on Computer Architecture* (May), Gold Coast, Australia, 342–351.

Babbay, F., and A. Mendelson [1998]. "Using value prediction to increase the power of speculative execution hardware," *ACM Trans. on Computer Systems* 16:3 (August), 234–270.

Baer, J.-L., and W.-H. Wang [1988]. "On the inclusion property for multi-level cache hierarchies," *Proc. 15th Annual Symposium on Computer Architecture* (May–June), Honolulu, 73–80.

Bailey, D. H., E. Barszcz, J. T. Barton, D. S. Browning, R. L. Carter, L. Dagum, R. A. Fatoohi, P. O. Frederickson, T. A. Lasinski, R. S. Schreiber, H. D. Simon, V. Venkatakrishnan, and S. K. Weeratunga [1991]. "The NAS parallel benchmarks," *Int'l. J. Supercomputing Applications* 5, 63–73.

Bakoglu, H. B., G. F. Grohoski, L. E. Thatcher, J. A. Kaeli, C. R. Moore, D. P. Tattle, W. E. Male, W. R. Hardell, D. A. Hicks, M. Nguyen Phu, R. K. Montoye, W. T. Glover, and S. Dhawan [1989]. "IBM second-generation RISC processor organization," *Proc. Int'l Conf. on Computer Design,* IEEE (October), Rye, N.Y., 138–142.

Balakrishnan, H., V. N. Padmanabhan, S. Seshan, and R. H. Katz [1997]. "A comparison of mechanisms for improving TCP performance over wireless links," *IEEE/ACM Trans. on Networking* 5:6 (December), 756–769.

Ball, T., and J. Larus [1993]. "Branch prediction for free," *Proc. SIGPLAN'93 Conference Programming Language Design and Implementation,* 300–313.

Banerjee, U. [1979]. *Speedup of ordinary programs,* Ph.D. thesis, Dept. of Computer Science, Univ. of Illinois at Urbana-Champaign (October).

Barham, P., B. Dragovic, K. Fraser, S. Hand, T. Harris, A. Ho, and R. Neugebauer [2003]. "Xen and the art of virtualization," *Proc. ACM Symposium on Operating Systems Principles.*

Barroso, L. A., K. Gharachorloo, and E. Bugnion [1998]. "Memory system characterization of commercial workloads," *Proc. 25th Int'l Symposium on Computer Architecture,* Barcelona (July), 3–14.

Barton, R. S. [1961]. "A new approach to the functional design of a computer," *Proc. Western Joint Computer Conf.,* 393–396.

Bashe, C. J., W. Buchholz, G. V. Hawkins, J. L. Ingram, and N. Rochester [1981]. "The architecture of IBM's early computers," *IBM J. Research and Development* 25:5 (September), 363–375.

Bashe, C. J., L. R. Johnson, J. H. Palmer, and E. W. Pugh [1986]. *IBM's Early Computers,* MIT Press, Cambridge, Mass.

Baskett, F., T. Jermoluk, and D. Solomon [1988]. "The 4D-MP graphics superworkstation: Computing + graphics = 40 MIPS + 40 MFLOPS and 10,000 lighted polygons per second," *Proc. COMPCON Spring,* San Francisco, 468–471.

Baskett, F., and T. W. Keller [1977]. "An evaluation of the Cray-1 processor," in *High Speed Computer and Algorithm Organization,* D. J. Kuck, D. H. Lawrie, and A. H. Sameh, eds., Academic Press, San Diego, 71–84.

BBN Laboratories [1986]. "Butterfly parallel processor overview," Tech. Rep. 6148, BBN Laboratories, Cambridge, Mass.

Bell, C. G. [1984]. "The mini and micro industries," *IEEE Computer* 17:10 (October), 14–30.

Bell, C. G. [1985]. "Multis: A new class of multiprocessor computers," *Science* 228 (April 26), 462–467.

Bell, C. G. [1989]. "The future of high performance computers in science and engineering," *Comm. ACM* 32:9 (September), 1091–1101.

Bell, C. G., and J. Gray [2002]. "What's next in high performance computing," *CACM* 45:2 (February), 91–95.

Bell, C. G., J. C. Mudge, and J. E. McNamara [1978]. *A DEC View of Computer Engineering,* Digital Press, Bedford, Mass.

Bell, C. G., and A. Newell [1971]. *Computer Structures: Readings and Examples,* McGraw-Hill, New York.

Bell, C. G., and W. D. Strecker [1976]. "Computer structures: What have we learned from the PDP-11?," *Proc. Third Annual Symposium on Computer Architecture* (January), Pittsburgh, 1–14.

Bell, G., R. Cady, H. McFarland, B. DeLagi, J. O'Laughlin, R. Noonan, and W. Wulf [1970]. "A new architecture for mini-computers: The DEC PDP-11," *Proc. AFIPS SJCC,* 657–675.

Bell, G., and J. Gray [2001]. "Crays, clusters and centers," Microsoft Research Technical Report, MSR-TR-2001-76.

Bell, G., and W. D. Strecker [1998]. "Computer structures: What have we learned from the PDP-11?" *25 Years of the International Symposia on Computer Architecture (Selected Papers),* ACM, 138–151.

Benes, V. E. [1962]. "Rearrangeable three stage connecting networks," *Bell System Technical Journal* 41, 1481–1492.

Bertozzi, D., A. Jalabert, S. Murali, R. Tamhankar, S. Stergiou, L. Benini, and G. De Micheli [2005]. "NoC synthesis flow for customized domain specific multiprocessor systems-on-chip," *IEEE Trans. on Parallel and Distributed Systems* 16:2 (February), 113–130.

Bhandarkar, D. P. [1995]. *Alpha Architecture and Implementations,* Digital Press, Newton, Mass.

Bhandarkar, D., and D. W. Clark [1991]. "Performance from architecture: Comparing a RISC and a CISC with similar hardware organizations," *Proc. Fourth Conf. on Architectural Support for Programming Languages and Operating Systems,* IEEE/ACM (April), Palo Alto, Calif., 310–319.

Bhandarkar, D., and J. Ding [1997]. "Performance characterization of the Pentium Pro processor," *Proc. Third Int'l Symposium on High Performance Computer Architecture,* IEEE (February), San Antonio, 288–297.

Bhuyan, L. N., and D. P. Agrawal [1984]. "Generalized hypercube and hyperbus structures for a computer network," *IEEE Trans. on Computers* 32:4 (April), 322–333.

Bier, J. [1997]. "The evolution of DSP processors," presentation at U.C. Berkeley, November 14.

Birman, M., A. Samuels, G. Chu, T. Chuk, L. Hu, J. McLeod, and J. Barnes [1990]. "Developing the WRL3170/3171 SPARC floating-point coprocessors," *IEEE Micro* 10:1, 55–64.

Blaum, M., J. Brady, J. Bruck, and J. Menon [1994]. "EVENODD: An optimal scheme for tolerating double disk failures in RAID architectures," *Proc. 21st Annual Symposium on Computer Architecture* (April), Chicago, Ill., 245–254.

Blaum, M., J. Brady, J. Bruck, and J. Menon [1995]. "EVENODD: An optimal scheme for tolerating double disk failures in RAID architectures," *IEEE Trans. on Computers* 44:2 (February), 192–202.

Blaum, M., J. Brady, J., Bruck, J. Menon, and A. Vardy [2001]. "The EVENODD code and its generalization," in *High Performance Mass Storage and Parallel I/O: Technologies and Applications*, edited by H. Jin, T. Cortes, and R. Buyya, IEEE & Wiley Press, New York, Chapter 14, 187–208.

Blaum, M., J. Bruck, and A. Vardy [1996]. "MDS array codes with independent parity symbols," *IEEE Trans. on Information Theory*, IT-42 (March), 529–42.

Bloch, E. [1959]. "The engineering design of the Stretch computer," *1959 Proceedings of the Eastern Joint Computer Conf.,* 48–59.

Blue Gene [2005]. *IBM J. Res. & Dev.* 49:2/3.

Boddie, J. R. [2000]. "History of DSPs," *www.lucent.com/micro/dsp/dsphist.html.*

Boggs D., A. Baktha, J. Hawkins, J. Miller, P. Roussel, R. Singhal, and B. S. Venkatraman [2004]. "The microarchitecture of the Intel Pentium 4 processor on 90nm technology," *Intel Technology Journal,* Volume 8, Issue 1.

Borg, A., R. E. Kessler, and D. W. Wall [1990]. "Generation and analysis of very long address traces," *Proc. 17th Annual Int'l Symposium on Computer Architecture*, Seattle, Wash., May 28–31, 270–279.

Bouknight, W. J., S. A. Deneberg, D. E. McIntyre, J. M. Randall, A. H. Sameh, and D. L. Slotnick [1972]. "The Illiac IV system," *Proc. IEEE* 60:4, 369–379. Also appears in D. P. Siewiorek, C. G. Bell, and A. Newell, *Computer Structures: Principles and Examples,* McGraw-Hill, New York (1982), 306–316.

Brady, J. T. [1986]. "A theory of productivity in the creative process," *IEEE CG&A* (May), 25–34.

Brain, M. [2000]. "Inside a digital cell phone," *www.howstuffworks.com/inside-cell-phone.htm.*

Brandt, M., J. Brooks, M. Cahir, T. Hewitt, E. Lopez-Pineda, and D. Sandness [2000]. *The Benchmarker's Guide for Cray SV1 Systems.* Cray Inc., Seattle, Wash.

Brent, R. P., and H. T. Kung [1982]. "A regular layout for parallel adders," *IEEE Trans. on Computers* C-31, 260–264.

Brewer, E. A., and B. C. Kuszmaul [1994]. "How to get good performance from the CM-5 data network," *Proc. Eighth Int'l Parallel Processing Symposium* (April), Cancun, Mexico.

Brin, S., and L. Page [1998]. "The anatomy of a large-scale hypertextual Web search engine," *Proc. 7th Int'l World Wide Web Conf.*, Brisbane, Qld., Australia (April 14–18), 107–117.

Brown, A., and D. A. Patterson [2000]. "Towards maintainability, availability, and growth benchmarks: A case study of software RAID systems." *Proc. 2000 USENIX Annual Technical Conf.* (June), San Diego, Calif.

Bucher, I. V., and A. H. Hayes [1980]. "I/O performance measurement on Cray-1 and CDC 7000 computers," *Proc. Computer Performance Evaluation Users Group, 16th Meeting*, NBS 500-65, 245–254.

Bucher, I. Y. [1983]. "The computational speed of supercomputers," *Proc. SIGMETRICS Conf. on Measuring and Modeling of Computer Systems*, ACM (August), 151–165.

Bucholtz, W. [1962]. *Planning a Computer System: Project Stretch,* McGraw-Hill, New York.

Burgess, N., and T. Williams [1995]. "Choices of operand truncation in the SRT division algorithm," *IEEE Trans. on Computers* 44:7.

Burkhardt, H., III, S. Frank, B. Knobe, and J. Rothnie [1992]. "Overview of the KSR1 computer system," Tech. Rep. KSR-TR-9202001, Kendall Square Research, Boston (February).

Burks, A. W., H. H. Goldstine, and J. von Neumann [1946]. "Preliminary discussion of the logical design of an electronic computing instrument," Report to the U.S. Army Ordnance Department, p. 1; also appears in *Papers of John von Neumann,* W. Aspray and A. Burks, eds., MIT Press, Cambridge, Mass., and Tomash Publishers, Los Angeles, Calif., 1987, 97–146.

Calder, B., D. Grunwald, M. Jones, D. Lindsay, J. Martin, M. Mozer, and B. Zorn [1997]. "Evidence-based static branch prediction using machine learning," *ACM Trans. Program. Lang. Syst.* 19:1, 188–222.

Calder, B., G. Reinman, and D. M. Tullsen [1999]. "Selective value prediction," *Proc. 26th Int'l Symposium on Computer Architecture (ISCA),* Atlanta, June.

Callahan, D., J. Dongarra, and D. Levine [1988]. "Vectorizing compilers: A test suite and results," *Supercomputing '88,* ACM/IEEE (November), Orlando, Fla., 98–105.

Cantin, J. F., and M. D. Hill [2001]. "Cache performance for selected SPEC CPU2000 benchmarks," *www.jfred.org/cache-data.html* (June).

Cantin, J., and M. Hill [2003]. "Cache performance for SPEC CPU2000 benchmarks, version 3.0," *www.cs.wisc.edu/multifacet/misc/spec2000cache-data/index.html.*

Case, R. P., and A. Padegs [1978]. "The architecture of the IBM System/370," *Communications of the ACM* 21:1, 73–96. Also appears in D. P. Siewiorek, C. G. Bell, and A. Newell, *Computer Structures: Principles and Examples,* McGraw-Hill, New York (1982), 830–855.

Censier, L., and P. Feautrier [1978]. "A new solution to coherence problems in multicache systems," *IEEE Trans. on Computers* C-27:12 (December), 1112–1118.

Chandra, R., S. Devine, B. Verghese, A. Gupta, and M. Rosenblum [1994]. "Scheduling and page migration for multiprocessor compute servers," *Sixth Int'l Conf. on Architectural Support for Programming Languages and Operating Systems (ASPLOS-VI),* ACM, Santa Clara, Calif., October, 12–24.

Chang, P. P., S. A. Mahlke, W. Y. Chen, N. J. Warter, and W. W. Hwu [1991]. "IMPACT: An architectural framework for multiple-instruction-issue processors," *Proc. 18th Int'l Symposium on Computer Architecture* (May), 266–275.

Charlesworth, A. E. [1981]. "An approach to scientific array processing: The architecture design of the AP-120B/FPS-164 family," *Computer* 14:9 (September), 18–27.

Charlesworth, A. [1998]. "Starfire: Extending the SMP envelope," *IEEE Micro* 18:1 (January/February), 39–49.

Chen, P. M., G. A. Gibson, R. H. Katz, and D. A. Patterson [1990]. "An evaluation of redundant arrays of inexpensive disks using an Amdahl 5890," *Proc. 1990 ACM SIG-METRICS Conf. on Measurement and Modeling of Computer Systems* (May), Boulder, Colo.

Chen, P. M., and E. K. Lee [1995]. "Striping in a RAID level 5 disk array," *Proc. 1995 ACM SIGMETRICS Conf. on Measurement and Modeling of Computer Systems* (May), 136–145.

Chen, P. M., E. K. Lee, G. A. Gibson, R. H. Katz, and D. A. Patterson [1994]. "RAID: High-performance, reliable secondary storage," *ACM Computing Surveys* 26:2 (June), 145–188.

Chen, S. [1983]. "Large-scale and high-speed multiprocessor system for scientific applications," *Proc. NATO Advanced Research Work on High Speed Computing* (June); also K. Hwang, ed., in "Superprocessors: Design and applications," *IEEE* (August), 1984.

Chen, T. C. [1980]. "Overlap and parallel processing," in H. Stone, ed., *Introduction to Computer Architecture,* Science Research Associates, Chicago, 427–486.

Chow, F. C. [1983]. *A Portable Machine-Independent Global Optimizer—Design and Measurements,* Ph.D. thesis, Stanford Univ. (December).

Chrysos, G. Z., and J. S. Emer [1998]. "Memory dependence prediction using store sets," *Proc. 25th Int'l Symposium on Computer Architecture (ISCA),* June, Barcelona, 142–153.

Clark, B., T. Deshane, E. Dow, S. Evanchik, M. Finlayson, J. Herne, and J. Neefe Matthews [2004]. "Xen and the art of repeated research," *Proc. USENIX Annual Technical Conf.,* 135–144.

Clark, D. W. [1983]. "Cache performance of the VAX-11/780," *ACM Trans. on Computer Systems* 1:1, 24–37.

Clark, D. W. [1987]. "Pipelining and performance in the VAX 8800 processor," *Proc. Second Conf. on Architectural Support for Programming Languages and Operating Systems,* IEEE/ACM (March), Palo Alto, Calif., 173–177.

Clark, D. W., and J. S. Emer [1985]. "Performance of the VAX-11/780 translation buffer: Simulation and measurement," *ACM Trans. on Computer Systems* 3:1 (February), 31–62.

Clark, D., and H. Levy [1982]. "Measurement and analysis of instruction set use in the VAX-11/780," *Proc. Ninth Symposium on Computer Architecture* (April), Austin, Tex., 9–17.

Clark, D., and W. D. Strecker [1980]. "Comments on 'the case for the reduced instruction set computer'," *Computer Architecture News* 8:6 (October), 34–38.

Clark, W. A. [1957]. "The Lincoln TX-2 computer development," *Proc. Western Joint Computer Conference* (February), Institute of Radio Engineers, Los Angeles, 143–145.

Clos, C. [1953]. "A study of non-blocking switching networks," *Bell Systems Technical Journal* 32 (March), 406–424.

Cody, W. J., J. T. Coonen, D. M. Gay, K. Hanson, D. Hough, W. Kahan, R. Karpinski, J. Palmer, F. N. Ris, and D. Stevenson [1984]. "A proposed radix- and word-length-independent standard for floating-point arithmetic," *IEEE Micro* 4:4, 86–100.

Colwell, R. P., R. P. Nix, J. J. O'Donnell, D. B. Papworth, and P. K. Rodman [1987]. "A VLIW architecture for a trace scheduling compiler," *Proc. Second Conf. on Architectural Support for Programming Languages and Operating Systems,* IEEE/ACM (March), Palo Alto, Calif., 180–192.

Colwell, R. P., and R. Steck [1995]. "A 0.6um BiCMOS processor with dynamic execution." *Proc. of Int'l Symposium on Solid State Circuits,* 176–177.

Comer, D. [1993]. *Internetworking with TCP/IP,* second edition., Prentice Hall, Englewood Cliffs, N.J.

Compaq Computer Corporation [1999]. *Compiler Writer's Guide for the Alpha 21264,* Order Number EC-RJ66A-TE, June, *www1.support.compaq.com/alpha-tools/ documentation/current/21264_EV67/ec-rj66a-te_comp_writ_gde_for_alpha21264.pdf.*

Conti, C., D. H. Gibson, and S. H. Pitkowsky [1968]. "Structural aspects of the System/ 360 Model 85, Part I: General organization," *IBM Systems J.* 7:1, 2–14.

Coonen, J. [1984]. *Contributions to a Proposed Standard for Binary Floating-Point Arithmetic,* Ph.D. thesis, Univ. of Calif., Berkeley.

Corbett, P., B. English, A. Goel, T. Grcanac, S. Kleiman, J. Leong, and S. Sankar [2004]. "Row-diagonal parity for double disk failure correction," *Proc. FAST '04.*

Crawford, J., and P. Gelsinger [1988]. *Programming the 80386,* Sybex Books, Alameda, Calif.

Culler, D. E., J. P. Singh, and A. Gupta [1999]. *Parallel Computer Architecture: A Hardware/Software Approach,* Morgan Kaufmann, San Francisco.

Curnow, H. J., and B. A. Wichmann [1976]. "A synthetic benchmark," *The Computer J.* 19:1, 43–49.

Cvetanovic, Z., and R. E. Kessler [2000]. "Performance analysis of the Alpha 21264-based Compaq ES40 system," *Proc. 27th Annual Int'l Symposium on Computer Architecture,* Vancouver, Canada, June 10–14, IEEE Computer Society Press, 192–202.

Dally, W. J. [1990]. "Performance analysis of k-ary n-cube interconnection networks," *IEEE Trans. on Computers* 39:6 (June), 775–785.

Dally, W. J. [1992]. "Virtual channel flow control," *IEEE Trans. on Parallel and Distributed Systems* 3:2 (March), 194–205.

Dally, W. J. [1999]. "Interconnect limited VLSI architecture," *Proc. of the International Interconnect Technology Conference,* San Francisco (May).

Dally, W. J., and C. I. Seitz [1986]. "The torus routing chip," *Distributed Computing* 1:4, 187–196.

Dally, W. J., and B. Towles [2001]. "Route packets, not wires: On-chip interconnection networks," *Proc. of the Design Automation Conference,* Las Vegas (June).

Dally, W. J., and B. Towles [2003]. *Principles and Practices of Interconnection Networks,* Morgan Kaufmann, San Francisco.

Darcy, J. D., and D. Gay [1996]. "FLECKmarks: Measuring floating point performance using a full IEEE compliant arithmetic benchmark," CS 252 class project, U.C. Berkeley (see *HTTP.CS.Berkeley.EDU/~darcy/Projects/cs252/*).

Darley, H. M., et al. [1989]. "Floating point/integer processor with divide and square root functions," U.S. Patent 4,878,190 (October 31).

Davidson, E. S. [1971]. "The design and control of pipelined function generators," *Proc. Conf. on Systems, Networks, and Computers,* IEEE (January), Oaxtepec, Mexico, 19–21.

Davidson, E. S., A. T. Thomas, L. E. Shar, and J. H. Patel [1975]. "Effective control for pipelined processors," *COMPCON, IEEE* (March), San Francisco, 181–184.

Davie, B. S., L. L. Peterson, and D. Clark [1999]. *Computer Networks: A Systems Approach,* second edition, Morgan Kaufmann, San Francisco.

Dehnert, J. C., P. Y.-T. Hsu, and J. P. Bratt [1989]. "Overlapped loop support on the Cydra 5," *Proc. Third Conf. on Architectural Support for Programming Languages and Operating Systems* (April), IEEE/ACM, Boston, 26–39.

Demmel, J. W., and X. Li [1994]. "Faster numerical algorithms via exception handling," *IEEE Trans. on Computers* 43:8, 983–992.

Denehy, T. E., J. Bent, F. I. Popovici, A. C. Arpaci-Dusseau, and R. H. Arpaci-Dusseau [2004]. "Deconstructing storage arrays," *Proc. 11th Int'l Conf. on Architectural Support for Programming Languages and Operating Systems (ASPLOS XI),* 59–71, Boston, Mass., October.

Desurvire, E. [1992]. "Lightwave communications: The fifth generation," *Scientific American* (International Edition) 266:1 (January), 96–103.

Diep, T. A., C. Nelson, and J. P. Shen [1995]. "Performance evaluation of the PowerPC 620 microarchitecture," *Proc. 22nd Symposium on Computer Architecture* (June), Santa Margherita, Italy.

Digital Semiconductor [1996]. *Alpha Architecture Handbook, Version 3,* Digital Press, Maynard, Mass.

Ditzel, D. R., and H. R. McLellan [1987]. "Branch folding in the CRISP microprocessor: Reducing the branch delay to zero," *Proc. 14th Symposium on Computer Architecture* (June), Pittsburgh, 2–7.

Ditzel, D. R., and D. A. Patterson [1980]. "Retrospective on high-level language computer architecture," *Proc. Seventh Annual Symposium on Computer Architecture,* La Baule, France (June), 97–104.

Doherty, W. J., and R. P. Kelisky [1979]. "Managing VM/CMS systems for user effectiveness," *IBM Systems J.* 18:1, 143–166.

Dongarra, J. J. [1986]. "A survey of high performance processors," *COMPCON,* IEEE (March), 8–11.

Dongarra, J., T. Sterling, H. Simon, and E. Strohmaier [2005]. "High-performance computing: Clusters, constellations, MPPs, and future directions," *Computing in Science and Engineering,* IEEE (March/April), 51–59.

Douceur, J. R., and W. J. Bolosky [1999]. "A large scale study of file-system contents," *Proc. 1999 ACM SIGMETRICS Conf. on Measurement and Modeling of Computer Systems (SIGMETRICS '99),* 59–69, Atlanta, Ga., May.

Douglas, J. [2005]. "Intel 8xx series and Paxville Xeon-MP Microprocessors," *Proc. Hot Chips Conference,* Stanford University, August.

Duato, J. [1993]. "A new theory of deadlock-free adaptive routing in wormhole networks," *IEEE Trans. on Parallel and Distributed Systems* 4:12 (Dec.) 1320–1331.

Duato, J., I. Johnson, J. Flich, F. Naven, P. Garcia, T. Nachiondo [2005]. "A new scalable and cost-effective congestion management strategy for lossless multistage interconnection networks," *Proc. 11th Int'l Symposium on High Performance Computer Architecture* (February), San Francisco.

Duato, J., O. Lysne, R. Pang, and T. M. Pinkston [2005]. "Part I: A theory for deadlock-free dynamic reconfiguration of interconnection networks," *IEEE Trans. on Parallel and Distributed Systems* 16:5 (May), 412–427.

Duato, J., and T. M. Pinkston [2001]. "A general theory for deadlock-free adaptive routing using a mixed set of resources," *IEEE Trans. on Parallel and Distributed Systems* 12:12 (December), 1219–1235.

Duato, J., S. Yalamanchili, and L. Ni [2003]. *Interconnection Networks: An Engineering Approach,* 2nd printing, Morgan Kaufmann, San Francisco.

Dubois, M., C. Scheurich, and F. Briggs [1988]. "Synchronization, coherence, and event ordering," *IEEE Computer* 9-21 (February).

Dunigan, W., K. Vetter, K. White, and P. Worley [2005]. "Performance evaluation of the Cray X1 distributed shared memory architecture," *IEEE Micro,* (January/February).

Eden, A., and T. Mudge [1998]. "The YAGS branch prediction scheme," *Proc. of the 31st Annual ACM/IEEE International Symposium on Microarchitecture,* 69–80.

Edmondson, J. H., P. I. Rubinfield, R. Preston, and V. Rajagopalan [1995]. "Superscalar instruction execution in the 21164 Alpha microprocessor," *IEEE Micro* 15:2, 33–43.

Eggers, S. [1989]. *Simulation Analysis of Data Sharing in Shared Memory Multiprocessors,* Ph.D. thesis, Univ. of California, Berkeley. Computer Science Division Tech. Rep. UCB/CSD 89/501 (April).

Elder, J., A. Gottlieb, C. K. Kruskal, K. P. McAuliffe, L. Randolph, M. Snir, P. Teller, and J. Wilson [1985]. "Issues related to MIMD shared-memory computers: The NYU

Ultracomputer approach," *Proc. 12th Int'l Symposium on Computer Architecture* (June), Boston, 126–135.

Ellis, J. R. [1986]. *Bulldog: A Compiler for VLIW Architectures*, MIT Press, Cambridge, Mass.

Emer, J. S., and D. W. Clark [1984]. "A characterization of processor performance in the VAX-11/780," *Proc. 11th Symposium on Computer Architecture* (June), Ann Arbor, Mich., 301–310.

Enriquez, P. [2001]. "What happened to my dial tone? A study of FCC service disruption reports," poster, *Richard Tapia Symposium on the Celebration of Diversity in Computing,* October 18–20, Houston, Tex.

Erlichson, A., N. Nuckolls, G. Chesson, and J. L. Hennessy [1996]. "SoftFLASH: Analyzing the performance of clustered distributed virtual shared memory," *Proc. 7th Symposium on Architectural Support for Programming Languages and Operating Systems (ASPLOS-VII),* October, 210–220.

Evers, M., S. J. Patel, R. S. Chappell, and Y. N. Patt [1998]. "An analysis of correlation and predictability: What makes two-level branch predictors work," *Proc. 25th Annual Intl. Sym. Comp. Arch. (ISCA),* 52–61.

Fabry, R. S. [1974]. "Capability based addressing," *Comm. ACM* 17:7 (July), 403–412.

Falsafi, B., and D. A. Wood [1997]. "Reactive NUMA: A design for unifying S-COMA and CC-NUMA," *Proc. 24th Int'l Symposium on Computer Architecture,* June, Denver, Colo., 229–240.

Farkas, K. I., P. Chow, N. P. Jouppi, and Z. Vranesic [1997]. "Memory-system design considerations for dynamically-scheduled processors," *Proc. 24th Annual Int'l Symposium on Computer Architecture,* Denver, Col., June 2–4, 133–143.

Farkas, K. I., and N. P. Jouppi [1994]. "Complexity/performance trade-offs with non-blocking loads," *Proc. 21st Annual Int'l Symposium on Computer Architecture*, Chicago (April).

Farkas, K. I., N. P. Jouppi, and P. Chow [1995]. "How useful are non-blocking loads, stream buffers and speculative execution in multiple issue processors?," *Proc. First IEEE Symposium on High-Performance Computer Architecture,* Raleigh, N.C., January 22–25, 78–89.

Fazio, D. [1987]. "It's really much more fun building a supercomputer than it is simply inventing one," *COMPCON,* IEEE (February), 102–105.

Fisher, J. A. [1981]. "Trace scheduling: A technique for global microcode compaction," *IEEE Trans. on Computers* 30:7 (July), 478–490.

Fisher, J. A. [1983]. "Very long instruction word architectures and ELI-512," *Proc. Tenth Symposium on Computer Architecture* (June), Stockholm, 140–150.

Fisher, J. A., J. R. Ellis, J. C. Ruttenberg, and A. Nicolau [1984]. "Parallel processing: A smart compiler and a dumb processor," *Proc. SIGPLAN Conf. on Compiler Construction* (June), Palo Alto, Calif., 11–16.

Fisher, J. A., and S. M. Freudenberger [1992]. "Predicting conditional branches from previous runs of a program," *Proc. Fifth Conf. on Architectural Support for Programming Languages and Operating Systems,* IEEE/ACM (October), Boston, 85–95.

Fisher, J. A., and B. R. Rau [1993]. *Journal of Supercomputing (*January*),* Kluwer.

Flemming, P. J., and J. J. Wallace [1986]. "How not to lie with statistics: The correct way to summarize benchmarks results," *Comm. ACM* 29:3 (March), 218–221.

Flynn, M. J. [1966]. "Very high-speed computing systems," *Proc. IEEE* 54:12 (December), 1901–1909.

Forgie, J. W. [1957]. "The Lincoln TX-2 input-output system," *Proc. Western Joint Computer Conference* (February), Institute of Radio Engineers, Los Angeles, 156–160.

Foster, C. C., and E. M. Riseman [1972]. "Percolation of code to enhance parallel dispatching and execution," *IEEE Trans. on Computers* C-21:12 (December), 1411–1415.

Frank, S. J. [1984]. "Tightly coupled multiprocessor systems speed memory access time," *Electronics* 57:1 (January), 164–169.

Freiman, C. V. [1961]. "Statistical analysis of certain binary division algorithms," *Proc. IRE* 49:1, 91–103.

Friesenborg, S. E., and R. J. Wicks [1985]. "DASD expectations: The 3380, 3380-23, and MVS/XA," Tech. Bulletin GG22-9363-02 (July 10), Washington Systems Center.

Fuller, S. H., and W. E. Burr [1977]. "Measurement and evaluation of alternative computer architectures," *Computer* 10:10 (October), 24–35.

Furber, S. B. [1996]. *ARM System Architecture*, Addison-Wesley, Harlow, England (see *www.cs.man.ac.uk/amulet/publications/books/ARMsysArch*).

Gagliardi, U. O. [1973]. "Report of workshop 4—software-related advances in computer hardware," *Proc. Symposium on the High Cost of Software*, Menlo Park, Calif., 99–120.

Gajski, D., D. Kuck, D. Lawrie, and A. Sameh [1983]. "CEDAR—a large scale multiprocessor," *Proc. Int'l Conf. on Parallel Processing* (August), 524–529.

Gallagher, D. M., W. Y. Chen, S. A. Mahlke, J. C. Gyllenhaal, and W.W. Hwu [1994]. "Dynamic memory disambiguation using the memory conflict buffer," *Proc. Sixth Int'l Conf. on Architectural Support for Programming Languages and Operating Systems* (October), Santa Clara, Calif., 183–193.

Galles, M. [1996]. "Scalable pipelined interconnect for distributed endpoint routing: The SGI SPIDER chip," *Proc. Hot Interconnects '96,* Stanford University, August.

Gamasutra [2005]. "Amazon Reports Record Xmas Season, Top Game Picks," *http://www.gamasutra.com/php-bin/news_index.php?story=7630.*

Game, M., and A. Booker [1999]. "CodePack code compression for PowerPC processors," *MicroNews,* 5:1, *www.chips.ibm.com/micronews/vol5_no1/codepack.html.*

Gao, Q. S. [1993]. "The Chinese remainder theorem and the prime memory system," 20th Annual Int'l Symposium on Computer Architecture ISCA '20, San Diego, Calif., May 16–19, *Computer Architecture News* 21:2 (May), 337–340.

Garner, R., A. Agarwal, F. Briggs, E. Brown, D. Hough, B. Joy, S. Kleiman, S. Muchnick, M. Namjoo, D. Patterson, J. Pendleton, and R. Tuck [1988]. "Scalable processor architecture (SPARC)," *COMPCON,* IEEE (March), San Francisco, 278–283.

Gap [2006]. "Gap Inc. Reports Fourth Quarter and Full Year Earnings," *http://gapinc.com/public/documents/Q32005PressRelease_Final22.pdff.*

Gap [2005]. "Gap Inc. Reports Third Quarter Earnings," *http://gapinc.com/public/documents/PR_Q405EarningsFeb2306.pdf.*

Gee, J. D., M. D. Hill, D. N. Pnevmatikatos, and A. J. Smith [1993]. "Cache performance of the SPEC92 benchmark suite," *IEEE Micro* 13:4 (August), 17–27.

Gehringer, E. F., D. P. Siewiorek, and Z. Segall [1987]. *Parallel Processing: The Cm* Experience*, Digital Press, Bedford, Mass.

Gharachorloo, K., A. Gupta, and J. L. Hennessy [1992]. "Hiding memory latency using dynamic scheduling in shared-memory multiprocessors," *Proc. 19th Annual Int'l Symposium on Computer Architecture,* Gold Coast, Australia, June.

Gharachorloo, K., D. Lenoski, J. Laudon, P. Gibbons, A. Gupta, and J. L. Hennessy [1990]. "Memory consistency and event ordering in scalable shared-memory multiprocessors," *Proc. 17th Int'l Symposium on Computer Architecture* (June), Seattle, Wash., 15–26.

Gibson, D. H. [1967]. "Considerations in block-oriented systems design," *AFIPS Conf. Proc.* 30, SJCC, 75–80.

Gibson, G. A. [1992]. *Redundant Disk Arrays: Reliable, Parallel Secondary Storage,* ACM Distinguished Dissertation Series, MIT Press, Cambridge, Mass.

Gibson, J. C. [1970]. "The Gibson mix," Rep. TR. 00.2043, IBM Systems Development Division, Poughkeepsie, N.Y. (Research done in 1959.)

Gibson, J., R. Kunz, D. Ofelt, M. Horowitz, J. Hennessy, and M. Heinrich [2000]. "FLASH vs. (simulated) FLASH: Closing the simulation loop," *Proc. 9th Conf. on Architectural Support for Programming Languages and Operating Systems* (November), San Jose, Calif., 49–58.

Glass, C. J., and L. M. Ni [1992]. "The Turn Model for adaptive routing," *Proc. 19th Int'l Symposium on Computer Architecture* (May), Australia.

Goldberg, D. [1991]. "What every computer scientist should know about floating-point arithmetic," *Computing Surveys* 23:1, 5–48.

Goldberg, I. B. [1967]. "27 bits are not enough for 8-digit accuracy," *Comm. ACM* 10:2, 105–106.

Goldstein, S. [1987]. "Storage performance—an eight year outlook," Tech. Rep. TR 03.308-1 (October), Santa Teresa Laboratory, IBM, San Jose, Calif.

Goldstine, H. H. [1972]. *The Computer: From Pascal to von Neumann,* Princeton University Press, Princeton, N.J.

González, J., and A. González [1998]. "Limits of instruction level parallelism with data speculation," *Proc. of the VECPAR Conf.,* 585–598.

Goodman, J. R. [1983]. "Using cache memory to reduce processor memory traffic," *Proc. 10th Int'l Symposium on Computer Architecture* (June), Stockholm, Sweden, 124–131.

Goralski, W. [1997]. *SONET: A Guide to Synchronous Optical Network,* McGraw-Hill, New York.

Gosling, J. B. [1980]. *Design of Arithmetic Units for Digital Computers,* Springer-Verlag, New York.

Gray, J. [2006]. "Sort benchmark home page." *research.microsoft.com/barc/SortBenchmark/.*

Gray, J. [1990]. "A census of Tandem system availability between 1985 and 1990," *IEEE Transactions on Reliability,* 39:4 (October), 409–418.

Gray, J. (ed.) [1993]. *The Benchmark Handbook for Database and Transaction Processing Systems,* second edition, Morgan Kaufmann, San Francisco.

Gray, J., and A. Reuter [1993]. *Transaction Processing: Concepts and Techniques,* Morgan Kaufmann, San Francisco.

Gray, J., and D. P. Siewiorek [1991]. "High-availability computer systems," *Computer* 24:9 (September), 39–48.

Gray, J., and C. van Ingen [2005]. "Empirical measurements of disk failure rates and error rates," Microsoft Research, MSR-TR-2005-166, December.

Grice, C., and M. Kanellos [2000]. "Cell phone industry at crossroads: Go high or low?," *CNET News* (August 31), *technews.netscape.com/news/0-1004-201-2518386-0.html? tag=st.ne.1002.tgif.sf.*

Groe, J. B., and L. E. Larson [2000]. *CDMA Mobile Radio Design,* Artech House, Boston.

Gunther, K. D. [1981]. "Prevention of deadlocks in packet-switched data transport systems," *IEEE Trans. on Communications* COM–29:4 (April), 512–524.

Gurumurthi, S., A. Sivasubramaniam, and V. Natarajan [2005]. Disk Drive Roadmap from the Thermal Perspective: A Case for Dynamic Thermal Management, *Proceedings of the International Symposium on Computer Architecture (ISCA),* June, 38–49.

Hagersten, E., and M. Koster [1998]. "WildFire: A scalable path for SMPs," *Proc. Fifth Int'l Symposium on High Performance Computer Architecture.*

Hagersten, E., A. Landin, and S. Haridi [1992]. "DDM—a cache-only memory architecture," *IEEE Computer* 25:9 (September), 44–54.

Hamacher, V. C., Z. G. Vranesic, and S. G. Zaky [1984]. *Computer Organization,* second edition, McGraw-Hill, New York.

Handy, J. [1993]. *The Cache Memory Book,* Academic Press, Boston.

Hauck, E. A., and B. A. Dent [1968]. "Burroughs' B6500/B7500 stack mechanism," *Proc. AFIPS SJCC*, 245–251.

Heald, R., K. Aingaran, C. Amir, M. Ang, M. Boland, A. Das, P. Dixit, G. Gouldsberry, J. Hart, T. Horel, W.-J. Hsu, J. Kaku, C. Kim, S. Kim, F. Klass, H. Kwan, R. Lo, H. McIntyre, A. Mehta, D. Murata, S. Nguyen, Y.-P. Pai, S. Patel, K. Shin, K. Tam, S. Vishwanthaiah, J. Wu, G. Yee, and H. You [2000]. "Implementation of third-generation SPARC V9 64-b microprocessor," *ISSCC Digest of Technical Papers,* 412–413 and slide supplement.

Heinrich, J. [1993]. *MIPS R4000 User's Manual,* Prentice Hall, Englewood Cliffs, N.J.

Henly, M., and B. McNutt [1989]. "DASD I/O characteristics: A comparison of MVS to VM," Tech. Rep. TR 02.1550 (May), IBM, General Products Division, San Jose, Calif.

Hennessy, J. [1984]. "VLSI processor architecture," *IEEE Trans. on Computers* C-33:11 (December), 1221–1246.

Hennessy, J. [1985]. "VLSI RISC processors," *VLSI Systems Design* 6:10 (October), 22–32.

Hennessy, J., N. Jouppi, F. Baskett, and J. Gill [1981]. "MIPS: A VLSI processor architecture," *Proc. CMU Conf. on VLSI Systems and Computations* (October), Computer Science Press, Rockville, Md.

Hewlett-Packard [1994]. *PA-RISC 2.0 Architecture Reference Manual,* 3rd ed.

Hewlett-Packard [1998]. "HP's '5NINES:5MINUTES' vision extends leadership and redefines high availability in mission-critical environments" (February 10), *www.future. enterprisecomputing.hp.com/ia64/news/5nines_vision_pr.html.*

Hill, M. D. [1987]. *Aspects of Cache Memory and Instruction Buffer Performance,* Ph.D. thesis, University of Calif. at Berkeley, Computer Science Division, Tech. Rep. UCB/CSD 87/381 (November).

Hill, M. D. [1988]. "A case for direct mapped caches," *Computer* 21:12 (December), 25–40.

Hill, M. D. [1998]. "Multiprocessors should support simple memory consistency models," *IEEE Computer* 31:8 (August), 28–34.

Hillis, W. D. [1985]. *The Connection Multiprocessor,* MIT Press, Cambridge, Mass.

Hinton, G., D. Sager, M. Upton, D. Boggs, D. Carmean, A. Kyker, and P. Roussel [2001]. "The microarchitecture of the Pentium 4 processor," *Intel Technology Journal,* February.

Hintz, R. G., and D. P. Tate [1972]. "Control data STAR-100 processor design," *COMPCON,* IEEE (September), 1–4.

Hirata, H., K. Kimura, S. Nagamine, Y. Mochizuki, A. Nishimura, Y. Nakase, and T. Nishizawa [1992]. "An elementary processor architecture with simultaneous instruction issuing from multiple threads," *Proc. 19th Annual Int'l Symposium on Computer Architecture* (May), 136–145.

Hitachi [1997]. *SuperH RISC Engine SH7700 Series Programming Manual* (see *www.halsp.hitachi.com/tech_prod/* and search for title).

Ho, R., K. W. Mai, and M. A. Horowitz [2001]. "The future of wires," *Proc. of the IEEE* 89:4 (April), 490–504.

Hoagland, A. S. [1963]. *Digital Magnetic Recording,* Wiley, New York.

Hockney, R. W., and C. R. Jesshope [1988]. *Parallel Computers-2, Architectures, Programming and Algorithms,* Adam Hilger Ltd., Bristol, England.

Holland, J. H. [1959]. "A universal computer capable of executing an arbitrary number of subprograms simultaneously," *Proc. East Joint Computer Conf.* 16, 108–113.

Holt, R. C. [1972]. "Some deadlock properties of computer systems," *ACM Computer Surveys* 4:3 (September), 179–196.

Hopkins, M. [2000]. "A critical look at IA-64: Massive resources, massive ILP, but can it deliver?" *Microprocessor Report* (February).

Hord, R. M. [1982]. *The Illiac-IV, The First Supercomputer,* Computer Science Press, Rockville, Md.

Horel, T., and G. Lauterbach [1999]. "UltraSPARC-III: Designing third-generation 64-bit performance," *IEEE Micro* 19:3 (May–June), 73–85.

Hospodor, A. D., and A. S. Hoagland [1993]. "The changing nature of disk controllers." *Proc. IEEE* 81:4 (April), 586–594.

Hristea, C., D. Lenoski, and J. Keen [1997]. "Measuring memory hierarchy performance of cache-coherent multiprocessors using micro benchmarks," *Proc. Supercomputing 97,* San Jose, Calif., November.

Hsu, P. [1994]. "Designing the TFP microprocessor," *IEEE Micro* 18:2 (April), 2333.

Huck, J., et al. [2000]. "Introducing the IA-64 Architecture" *IEEE Micro,* 20:5 (September–October), 12–23.

Hughes, C. J., P. Kaul, S. V. Adve, R. Jain, C. Park, and J. Srinivasan [2001]. "Variability in the execution of multimedia applications and implications for architecture," *Proc. 28th Annual Int'l Symposium on Computer Architecture,* Goteborg, Sweden, June 30–July 4, 254–265.

Hwang, K. [1979]. *Computer Arithmetic: Principles, Architecture, and Design,* Wiley, New York.

Hwang, K. [1993]. *Advanced Computer Architecture and Parallel Programming,* McGraw-Hill, New York.

Hwu, W.-M., and Y. Patt [1986]. "HPSm, a high performance restricted data flow architecture having minimum functionality," *Proc. 13th Symposium on Computer Architecture* (June), Tokyo, 297–307.

Hwu, W. W., S. A. Mahlke, W. Y. Chen, P. P. Chang, N. J. Warter, R. A. Bringmann, R. O. Ouellette, R. E. Hank, T. Kiyohara, G. E. Haab, J. G. Holm, and D. M. Lavery [1993]. "The superblock: An effective technique for VLIW and superscalar compilation," *J. Supercomputing* 7:1, 2 (March), 229–248.

IBM [1982]. *The Economic Value of Rapid Response Time,* GE20-0752-0, White Plains, N.Y., 11–82.

IBM [1990]. "The IBM RISC System/6000 processor" (collection of papers), *IBM J. Research and Development* 34:1 (January).

IBM [1994]. *The PowerPC Architecture,* Morgan Kaufmann, San Francisco.

IEEE [1985]. "IEEE standard for binary floating-point arithmetic," *SIGPLAN Notices* 22:2, 9–25.

IEEE [2005]. "Intel virtualization technology, computer," *IEEE Computer Society* 38:5 (May), 48–56.

Imprimis [1989]. *Imprimis Product Specification,* 97209 Sabre Disk Drive IPI-2 Interface 1.2 GB, Document No. 64402302 (May).

InfiniBand Trade Association [2001]. *InfiniBand Architecture Specifications Release 1.0.a, www.infinibandta.org.*

Intel [2001]. "Using MMX instructions to convert RGB to YUV color conversion," *cedar.intel.com/cgi-bin/ids.dll/content/content.jsp?cntKey=Legacy::irtm_AP548_9996&cntType=IDS_EDITORIAL.*

Internet Retailer [2005]. "The Gap launches a new site-after two weeks of downtime," *http://www.internetretailer.com/article.asp?id=16254.*

Jain, R. [1991]. *The Art of Computer Systems Performance Analysis: Techniques for Experimental Design, Measurement, Simulation, and Modeling,* Wiley, New York.

Jantsch, A., and H. Tenhunen (eds.) [2003]. *Networks on Chips,* Kluwer Academic Publishers, The Netherlands.

Jimenez, D. A., and C. Lin [2002]. "Neural methods for dynamic branch prediction," *ACM Trans. Computer Sys.* 20:4 (November), 369–397.

Johnson, M. [1990]. *Superscalar Microprocessor Design*, Prentice Hall, Englewood Cliffs, N.J.

Jordan, H. F. [1983]. "Performance measurements on HEP—a pipelined MIMD computer," *Proc. 10th Int'l Symposium on Computer Architecture* (June), Stockholm, 207–212.

Jordan, K. E. [1987]. "Performance comparison of large-scale scientific processors: Scalar mainframes, mainframes with vector facilities, and supercomputers," *Computer* 20:3 (March), 10–23.

Jouppi, N. P. [1990]. "Improving direct-mapped cache performance by the addition of a small fully-associative cache and prefetch buffers," *Proc. 17th Annual Int'l Symposium on Computer Architecture*, 364–73.

Jouppi, N. P. [1998]. "Retrospective: Improving direct-mapped cache performance by the addition of a small fully-associative cache and prefetch buffers," *25 Years of the Int'l Symposia on Computer Architecture (Selected Papers)*, ACM, 71–73.

Jouppi, N. P., and D. W. Wall [1989]. "Available instruction-level parallelism for super-scalar and superpipelined processors," *Proc. Third Conf. on Architectural Support for Programming Languages and Operating Systems*, IEEE/ACM (April), Boston, 272–282.

Jouppi, N. P., and S. J. E. Wilton [1994]. "Trade-offs in two-level on-chip caching," *Proc. 21st Annual Int'l Symposium on Computer Architecture*, Chicago, April 18–21, 34–45.

Kaeli, D. R., and P. G. Emma [1991]. "Branch history table prediction of moving target branches due to subroutine returns," *Proc. 18th Int'l Symposium on Computer Architecture (ISCA)*, Toronto, May, 34–42.

Kahan, J. [1990]. "On the advantage of the 8087's stack," unpublished course notes, Computer Science Division, University of California at Berkeley.

Kahan, W. [1968]. "7094-II system support for numerical analysis," *SHARE Secretarial Distribution* SSD-159.

Kahaner, D. K. [1988]. "Benchmarks for 'real' programs," *SIAM News* (November).

Kahn, R. E. [1972]. "Resource-sharing computer communication networks," *Proc. IEEE* 60:11 (November), 1397–1407.

Kane, G. [1986]. *MIPS R2000 RISC Architecture*, Prentice Hall, Englewood Cliffs, N.J.

Kane, G. [1996]. *PA-RISC 2.0 Architecture*, Prentice Hall PTR, Upper Saddle River, N.J.

Kane, G., and J. Heinrich [1992]. *MIPS RISC Architecture*, Prentice Hall, Englewood Cliffs, N.J.

Katz, R. H., D. A. Patterson, and G. A. Gibson [1989]. "Disk system architectures for high performance computing," *Proc. IEEE* 77:12 (December), 1842–1858.

Keckler, S. W., and W. J. Dally [1992]. "Processor coupling: Integrating compile time and runtime scheduling for parallelism," *Proc. 19th Annual Int'l Symposium on Computer Architecture* (May), 202–213.

Keller, R. M. [1975]. "Look-ahead processors," *ACM Computing Surveys* 7:4 (December), 177–195.

Keltcher, C. N., K. J. McGrath, A. Ahmed, and P. Conway [2003]. "The AMD Opteron processor for multiprocessor servers," *IEEE Micro* 23:2 (March–April), 66–76. dx.doi.org/10.1109.MM.2003.119116.

Kembel, R. [2000]. "Fibre Channel: A comprehensive introduction," *Internet Week* (April).

Kermani, P., and L. Kleinrock [1979]. "Virtual Cut-Through: A New Computer Communication Switching Technique," *Computer Networks* 3 (January), 267–286.

Kessler, R. [1999]. "The Alpha 21264 microprocessor," *IEEE Micro* 19:2 (March/April) 24–36.

Kilburn, T., D. B. G. Edwards, M. J. Lanigan, and F. H. Sumner [1962]. "One-level storage system," *IRE Trans. on Electronic Computers* EC-11 (April) 223–235. Also appears in D. P. Siewiorek, C. G. Bell, and A. Newell, *Computer Structures: Principles and Examples* (1982), McGraw-Hill, New York, 135–148.

Killian, E. [1991]. "MIPS R4000 technical overview–64 bits/100 MHz or bust," *Hot Chips III Symposium Record* (August), Stanford University, 1.6–1.19.

Kim, M. Y. [1986]. "Synchronized disk interleaving," *IEEE Trans. on Computers* C-35:11 (November), 978–988.

Kissell, K. D. [1997]. *MIPS16: High-Density for the Embedded Market* (see *www.sgi. com/MIPS/arch/MIPS16/MIPS16.whitepaper.pdf*).

Kitagawa, K., S. Tagaya, Y. Hagihara, and Y. Kanoh [2003]. "A hardware overview of SX-6 and SX-7 supercomputer," *NEC Research & Development J.* 44:1 (January), 2–7.

Knuth, D. [1981]. *The Art of Computer Programming,* vol. II, second edition, Addison-Wesley, Reading, Mass.

Kogge, P. M. [1981]. *The Architecture of Pipelined Computers,* McGraw-Hill, New York.

Kohn, L., and S.-W. Fu [1989]. "A 1,000,000 transistor microprocessor," *IEEE Int'l Solid-State Circuits Conf.*, 54–55.

Kontothanassis, L., G. Hunt, R. Stets, N. Hardavellas, M. Cierniak, S. Parthasarathy, W. Meira, S. Dwarkadas, and M. Scott [1997]. "VM-based shared memory on low-latency, remote-memory-access networks," *Proc. 24th Annual Int'l Symposium on Computer Architecture* (June), Denver, Colo.

Koren, I. [1989]. *Computer Arithmetic Algorithms,* Prentice Hall, Englewood Cliffs, N.J.

Kozyrakis, C. [2000]. "Vector IRAM: A media-oriented vector processor with embedded DRAM," presentation at Hot Chips 12 Conf., Palo Alto, Calif, 13–15.

Kroft, D. [1981]. "Lockup-free instruction fetch/prefetch cache organization," *Proc. Eighth Annual Symposium on Computer Architecture* (May 12–14), Minneapolis, 81–87.

Kroft, D. [1998]. "Retrospective: Lockup-free instruction fetch/prefetch cache organization," *25 Years of the Int'l Symposia on Computer Architecture (Selected Papers),* ACM, 20–21.

Kuck, D., P. P. Budnik, S.-C. Chen, D. H. Lawrie, R. A. Towle, R. E. Strebendt, E. W. Davis, Jr., J. Han, P. W. Kraska, and Y. Muraoka [1974]. "Measurements of parallelism in ordinary FORTRAN programs," *Computer* 7:1 (January), 37–46.

Kuhn, D. R. [1997]. "Sources of failure in the public switched telephone network," *IEEE Computer* 30:4 (April), 31–36.

Kumar, A. [1997]. "The HP PA-8000 RISC CPU," *IEEE Micro* 17:2 (March/April).

Kunimatsu, A., N. Ide, T. Sato, Y. Endo, H. Murakami, T. Kamei, M. Hirano, F. Ishihara, H. Tago, M. Oka, A. Ohba, T. Yutaka, T. Okada, and M. Suzuoki [2000]. "Vector unit architecture for emotion synthesis," *IEEE Micro* 20:2 (March–April), 40–47.

Kunkel, S. R., and J. E. Smith [1986]. "Optimal pipelining in supercomputers," *Proc. 13th Symposium on Computer Architecture* (June), Tokyo, 404–414.

Kurose, J. F., and K. W. Ross [2001]. *Computer Networking: A Top-Down Approach Featuring the Internet,* Addison-Wesley, Boston.

Kuskin, J., D. Ofelt, M. Heinrich, J. Heinlein, R. Simoni, K. Gharachorloo, J. Chapin, D. Nakahira, J. Baxter, M. Horowitz, A. Gupta, M. Rosenblum, and J. L. Hennessy [1994]. "The Stanford FLASH multiprocessor," *Proc. 21st Int'l Symposium on Computer Architecture,* Chicago, April.

Lam, M. [1988]. "Software pipelining: An effective scheduling technique for VLIW processors," *SIGPLAN Conf. on Programming Language Design and Implementation,* ACM (June), Atlanta, Ga., 318–328.

Lam, M. S., E. E. Rothberg, and M. E. Wolf [1991]. "The cache performance and optimizations of blocked algorithms," Fourth Int'l Conf. on Architectural Support for Programming Languages and Operating Systems, Santa Clara, Calif., April 8–11. *SIGPLAN Notices* 26:4 (April), 63–74.

Lam, M. S., and R. P. Wilson [1992]. "Limits of control flow on parallelism," *Proc. 19th Symposium on Computer Architecture* (May), Gold Coast, Australia, 46–57.

Lambright, D. [2000]. "Experiences in measuring the reliability of a cache-based storage system," *Proc. of First Workshop on Industrial Experiences with Systems Software* (WIESS 2000), collocated with the 4th Symposium on Operating Systems Design and Implementation (OSDI), San Diego, Calif. (October 22).

Lamport, L. [1979]. "How to make a multiprocessor computer that correctly executes multiprocess programs," *IEEE Trans. on Computers* C-28:9 (September), 241–248.

Laprie, J.-C. [1985]. "Dependable computing and fault tolerance: Concepts and terminology," *Fifteenth Annual Int'l Symposium on Fault-Tolerant Computing FTCS 15.* Digest of Papers. Ann Arbor, Mich. (June 19–21), 2–11.

Larson, E. R. [1973]. "Findings of fact, conclusions of law, and order for judgment," File No. 4-67, Civ. 138, *Honeywell v. Sperry-Rand and Illinois Scientific Development,* U.S. District Court for the State of Minnesota, Fourth Division (October 19).

Laudon, J., A. Gupta, and M. Horowitz [1994]. "Interleaving: A multithreading technique targeting multiprocessors and workstations," *Proc. Sixth Int'l Conf. on Architectural Support for Programming Languages and Operating Systems* (October), Boston, 308–318.

Laudon, J., and D. Lenoski [1997]. "The SGI Origin: A ccNUMA highly scalable server," *Proc. 24th Int'l Symposium on Computer Architecture* (June), Denver, Colo., 241–251.

Lauterbach, G., and T. Horel [1999]. "UltraSPARC-III: Designing third generation 64-bit performance," *IEEE Micro* 19:3 (May/June).

Lazowska, E. D., J. Zahorjan, G. S. Graham, and K. C. Sevcik [1984]. *Quantitative System Performance: Computer System Analysis Using Queueing Network models,* Prentice Hall, Englewood Cliffs, N.J. (Although out of print, it is available online at *www.cs.washington.edu/homes/lazowska/qsp/.*)

Lebeck, A. R., and D. A. Wood [1994]. "Cache profiling and the SPEC benchmarks: A case study," *Computer* 27:10 (October), 15–26.

Lee, R. [1989]. "Precision architecture," *Computer* 22:1 (January), 78–91.

Leighton, F. T. [1992]. *Introduction to Parallel Algorithms and Architectures: Arrays, Trees, Hypercubes,* Morgan Kaufmann, San Francisco.

Leiner, A. L. [1954]. "System specifications for the DYSEAC," *J. ACM* 1:2 (April), 57–81.

Leiner, A. L., and S. N. Alexander [1954]. "System organization of the DYSEAC," *IRE Trans. of Electronic Computers* EC-3:1 (March), 1–10.

Leiserson, C. E. [1985]. "Fat trees: Universal networks for hardware-efficient supercomputing," *IEEE Trans. on Computers* C–34:10 (October), 892–901.

Lenoski, D., J. Laudon, K. Gharachorloo, A. Gupta, and J. L. Hennessy [1990]. "The Stanford DASH multiprocessor," *Proc. 17th Int'l Symposium on Computer Architecture* (June), Seattle, Wash., 148–159.

Lenoski, D., J. Laudon, K. Gharachorloo, W.-D. Weber, A. Gupta, J. L. Hennessy, M. A. Horowitz, and M. Lam [1992]. "The Stanford DASH multiprocessor," *IEEE Computer* 25:3 (March).

Levy, H., and R. Eckhouse [1989]. *Computer Programming and Architecture: The VAX,* Digital Press, Boston.

Li, K. [1988]. "IVY: A shared virtual memory system for parallel computing," *Proc. 1988 Int'l Conf. on Parallel Processing,* Pennsylvania State University Press.

Lincoln, N. R. [1982]. "Technology and design trade offs in the creation of a modern supercomputer," *IEEE Trans. on Computers* C-31:5 (May), 363–376.

Lindholm, T., and F. Yellin [1999]. *The Java Virtual Machine Specification,* second edition, Addison-Wesley, Reading, Mass. Also available online at *java.sun.com/docs/ books/vmspec/.*

Lipasti, M. H., and J. P. Shen [1996]. "Exceeding the dataflow limit via value prediction," *Proc. 29th Annual ACM/IEEE Int'l Symposium on Microarchitecture* (December).

Lipasti, M. H., C. B. Wilkerson, and J. P. Shen [1996]. "Value locality and load value prediction," *Proc. Seventh Symposium on Architectural Support for Programming Languages and Operating Systems* (October), 138–147.

Liptay, J. S. [1968]. "Structural aspects of the System/360 Model 85, Part II: The cache," *IBM Systems J.* 7:1, 15–21.

Lo, J., L. Barroso, S. Eggers, K. Gharachorloo, H. Levy, and S. Parekh [1998]. "An analysis of database workload performance on simultaneous multithreaded processors," *Proc. 25th Int'l Symposium on Computer Architecture* (June), 39–50.

Lo, J., S. Eggers, J. Emer, H. Levy, R. Stamm, and D. Tullsen [1997]. "Converting thread-level parallelism into instruction-level parallelism via simultaneous multithreading," *ACM Transactions on Computer Systems* 15:2 (August), 322–354.

Lovett, T., and S. Thakkar [1988]. "The Symmetry multiprocessor system," *Proc. 1988 Int'l Conf. of Parallel Processing*, University Park, Penn., 303–310.

Lubeck, O., J. Moore, and R. Mendez [1985]. "A benchmark comparison of three supercomputers: Fujitsu VP-200, Hitachi S810/20, and Cray X-MP/2," *Computer* 18:12 (December), 10–24.

Luk, C.-K., and T. C Mowry [1999]. "Automatic compiler-inserted prefetching for pointer-based applications," *IEEE Trans. on Computers* 48:2 (February), 134–141.

Lunde, A. [1977]. "Empirical evaluation of some features of instruction set processor architecture," *Comm. ACM* 20:3 (March), 143–152.

Luszczek, P., J. J. Dongarra, D. Koester, R. Rabenseifner, B. Lucas, J. Kepner, J. McCalpin, D. Bailey, and D. Takahashi [2005]. "Introduction to the HPC challenge benchmark suite," Lawrence Berkeley National Laboratory, Paper LBNL-57493 (April 25), *repositories.cdlib.org/lbnl/LBNL-57493.*

Maberly, N. C. [1966]. *Mastering Speed Reading,* New American Library, New York.

Magenheimer, D. J., L. Peters, K. W. Pettis, and D. Zuras [1988]. "Integer multiplication and division on the HP precision architecture," *IEEE Trans. on Computers* 37:8, 980–990.

Mahlke, S. A., W. Y. Chen, W.-M. Hwu, B. R. Rau, and M. S. Schlansker [1992]. "Sentinel scheduling for VLIW and superscalar processors," *Proc. Fifth Conf. on Architectural Support for Programming Languages and Operating Systems* (October), Boston, IEEE/ACM, 238–247.

Mahlke, S. A., R. E. Hank, J. E. McCormick, D. I. August, and W. W. Hwu [1995]. "A comparison of full and partial predicated execution support for ILP processors," *Proc. 22nd Annual Int'l Symposium on Computer Architecture* (June), Santa Margherita Ligure, Italy, 138–149.

Major, J. B. [1989]. "Are queuing models within the grasp of the unwashed?," *Proc. Int'l Conf. on Management and Performance Evaluation of Computer Systems,* Reno, Nev. (December 11–15), 831–839.

Markstein, P. W. [1990]. "Computation of elementary functions on the IBM RISC System/6000 processor," *IBM J. of Research and Development* 34:1, 111–119.

Mathis, H. M., A. E. Mercias, J. D. McCalpin, R. J. Eickemeyer, and S. R. Kunkel [2005]. "Characterization of the multithreading (SMT) efficiency in Power5," *IBM J. Res. & Dev.,* 49:4/5 (July/September), 555–564.

McCalpin, J. D. [2005]. *STREAM: Sustainable Memory Bandwidth in High Performance Computers, www.cs.virginia.edu/stream/.*

McCormick, J., and A. Knies [2002]. "A brief analysis of the SPEC CPU2000 benchmarks on the Intel Itanium 2 processor," *Proc. Hot Chips Conference*, Stanford University, August.

McFarling, S. [1989]. "Program optimization for instruction caches," *Proc. Third Int'l Conf. on Architectural Support for Programming Languages and Operating Systems* (April 3–6), Boston, 183–191.

McFarling, S. [1993]. "Combining branch predictors," WRL Technical Note TN-36 (June), Digital Western Research Laboratory, Palo Alto, Calif.

McFarling, S., and J. Hennessy [1986]. "Reducing the cost of branches," *Proc. 13th Symposium on Computer Architecture* (June), Tokyo, 396–403.

McGhan, H., and M. O'Connor [1998]. "PicoJava: A direct execution engine for Java bytecode," *Computer* 31:10 (October), 22–30.

McKeeman, W. M. [1967]. "Language directed computer design," *Proc. 1967 Fall Joint Computer Conf.*, Washington, D.C., 413–417.

McMahon, F. M. [1986]. "The Livermore FORTRAN kernels: A computer test of numerical performance range," Tech. Rep. UCRL-55745, Lawrence Livermore National Laboratory, Univ. of California, Livermore (December).

McNairy, C., and D. Soltis [2003]. "Itanium 2 processor microarchitecture," *IEEE Micro* 23:2 (March–April), 44–55.

Mead, C., and L. Conway [1980]. *Introduction to VLSI Systems,* Addison-Wesley, Reading, Mass.

Mellor-Crummey, J. M., and M. L. Scott [1991]. "Algorithms for scalable synchronization on shared-memory multiprocessors," *ACM Trans. on Computer Systems* 9:1 (February), 21–65.

Menabrea, L. F. [1842]. "Sketch of the analytical engine invented by Charles Babbage," *Bibiothèque Universelle de Genève* (October).

Menon, A., A. L. Cox, and W. Zwaenepoel [2006]. "Optimizing network virtualization in xen," *USENIX Annual Technical Conf.* (June), Boston, Mass.

Menon, A., J. Renato Santos, Y. Turner, G. Janakiraman, and W. Zwaenepoel [2005]. "Diagnosing performance overheads in the xen virtual machine environment," *Proc. 1st ACM/USENIX Int'l Conference on Virtual Execution Environments,* Chicago, 13–23.

Merlin, P. M., and P. J. Schweitzer [1980]. "Deadlock avoidance in store-and-forward networks—I: Store-and-forward deadlock," *IEEE Trans. on Communications* COM–28:3 (March), 345–354.

Metcalfe, R. M. [1993]. "Computer/network interface design: Lessons from Arpanet and Ethernet," *IEEE J. on Selected Areas in Communications* 11:2 (February), 173–180.

Metcalfe, R. M., and D. R. Boggs [1976]. "Ethernet: Distributed packet switching for local computer networks," *Comm. ACM* 19:7 (July), 395–404.

Metropolis, N., J. Howlett, and G. C. Rota, eds. [1980]. *A History of Computing in the Twentieth Century,* Academic Press, New York.

Meyer, R. A., and L. H. Seawright [1970]. A virtual machine time sharing system, *IBM Systems J.* 9:3, 199–218.

Meyers, G. J. [1978]. "The evaluation of expressions in a storage-to-storage architecture," *Computer Architecture News* 7:3 (October), 20–23.

Meyers, G. J. [1982]. *Advances in Computer Architecture*, second edition, Wiley, New York.

Micron [2004]. "Calculating Memory System Power for DDR2," *http://download. micron.com/pdf/pubs/designline/dl1Q04.pdf.*

Micron [2006]. "The Micron® System-Power Calculator," *http://www.micron.com/ systemcalc.*

MIPS [1997]. *MIPS16 Application Specific Extension Product Description* (see *www.sgi. com/MIPS/arch/MIPS16/mips16.pdf*).

Miranker, G. S., J. Rubenstein, and J. Sanguinetti [1988]. "Squeezing a Cray-class super-computer into a single-user package," *COMPCON,* IEEE (March), 452–456.

Mitchell, D. [1989]. "The Transputer: The time is now," *Computer Design* (RISC supplement), 40–41.

Mitsubishi [1996]. *Mitsubishi 32-Bit Single Chip Microcomputer M32R Family Software Manual* (September).

Miura, K., and K. Uchida [1983]. "FACOM vector processing system: VP100/200," *Proc. NATO Advanced Research Work on High Speed Computing* (June); also in K. Hwang, ed., "Superprocessors: Design and applications," *IEEE* (August 1984), 59–73.

Miya, E. N. [1985]. "Multiprocessor/distributed processing bibliography," *Computer Architecture News* (ACM SIGARCH) 13:1, 27–29.

Montoye, R. K., E. Hokenek, and S. L. Runyon [1990]. "Design of the IBM RISC System/6000 floating-point execution," *IBM J. of Research and Development* 34:1, 59–70.

Moore, B., A. Padegs, R. Smith, and W. Bucholz [1987]. "Concepts of the System/370 vector architecture," *Proc. 14th Symposium on Computer Architecture* (June), ACM/IEEE, Pittsburgh, 282–292.

Morse, S., B. Ravenal, S. Mazor, and W. Pohlman [1980]. "Intel microprocessors—8080 to 8086," *Computer* 13:10 (October).

Moshovos, A., S. Breach, T. N. Vijaykumar, and G. S. Sohi [1997]. "Dynamic speculation and synchronization of data dependences," *Proc. 24th Int'l Symposium on Computer Architecture (ISCA),* June, Boulder, Colo.

Moshovos, A., and G. S. Sohi [1997]. "Streamlining inter-operation memory communication via data dependence prediction," *Proc. 30th Annual Int'l Symposium on Micro-architecture (MICRO-30),* December, 235–245.

Moussouris, J., L. Crudele, D. Freitas, C. Hansen, E. Hudson, S. Przybylski, T. Riordan, and C. Rowen [1986]. "A CMOS RISC processor with integrated system functions," *Proc. COMPCON,* IEEE (March), San Francisco, 191.

Mowry, T. C., S. Lam, and A. Gupta [1992]. "Design and evaluation of a compiler algorithm for prefetching," Fifth Int'l Conf. on Architectural Support for Programming Languages and Operating Systems (ASPLOS-V), Boston, October 12–15, *SIGPLAN Notices* 27:9 (September), 62–73.

MSN Money [2005]. "Amazon shares tumble after rally fizzles," *http://moneycentral. msn.com/content/CNBCTV/Articles/Dispatches/P133695.asp.*

Muchnick, S. S. [1988]. "Optimizing compilers for SPARC," *Sun Technology* 1:3 (Summer), 64–77.

Mueller, M., L. C. Alves, W. Fischer, M. L. Fair, and I. Modi [1999]. "RAS strategy for IBM S/390 G5 and G6," *IBM J. Research and Development* 43:5–6 (September–November), 875–888.

Mukherjee, S. S., C. Weaver, J. S. Emer, S. K. Reinhardt, and T. M. Austin [2003]. "Measuring architectural vulnerability factors," *IEEE Micro* 23:6, 70–75.

Murphy, B., and T. Gent [1995]. "Measuring system and software reliability using an automated data collection process," *Quality and Reliability Engineering International* 11:5 (September–October), 341–353.

Myer, T. H., and I. E. Sutherland [1968]. "On the design of display processors," *Communications of the ACM* 11:6 (June), 410–414.

National Research Council [1997]. *The Evolution of Untethered Communications,* Computer Science and Telecommunications Board, National Academy Press, Washington, D.C.

National Storage Industry Consortium [1998]. *Tape Roadmap* (June), *www.nsic.org.*

Nelson, V. P. [1990]. "Fault-tolerant computing: Fundamental concepts," *Computer* 23:7 (July*)*, 19–25.

Ngai, T.-F., and M. J. Irwin [1985]. "Regular, area-time efficient carry-lookahead adders," *Proc. Seventh IEEE Symposium on Computer Arithmetic,* 9–15.

Nicolau, A., and J. A. Fisher [1984]. "Measuring the parallelism available for very long instruction word architectures," *IEEE Trans. on Computers* C-33:11 (November), 968–976.

Nikhil, R. S., G. M. Papadopoulos, and Arvind [1992]. "*T: A multithreaded massively parallel architecture," *Proc. 19th Int'l Symposium on Computer Architecture,* Gold Coast, Australia, May, 156–167.

Noordergraaf, L., and R. van der Pas [1999]. "Performance experiences on Sun's WildFire prototype," *Proc. Supercomputing 99,* Portland, Ore., November.

Nyberg, C. R., T. Barclay, Z. Cvetanovic, J. Gray, and D. Lomet [1994]. "AlphaSort: A RISC machine sort," *Proc. 1994 ACM SIGMOD Int'l Conf. on Management of Data (SIGMOD '04),* Minneapolis, Minn., May.

Oka, M., and M. Suzuoki [1999]. "Designing and programming the emotion engine," *IEEE Micro* 19:6 (November–December), 20–28.

Okada, S., S. Okada, Y. Matsuda, T. Yamada, and A. Kobayashi [1999]. "System on a chip for digital still camera," *IEEE Trans. on Consumer Electronics* 45:3 (August), 584–590.

Oliker, L., A. Canning, J. Carter, J. Shalf, and S. Ethier [2004]. "Scientific computations on modern parallel vector systems," *Proc. ACM/IEEE Conference on Supercomputing,* 10.

Pabst, T. [2000]. "Performance showdown at 133 MHz FSB—the best platform for coppermine," *www6.tomshardware.com/mainboard/00q1/000302/.*

Padua, D., and M. Wolfe [1986]. "Advanced compiler optimizations for supercomputers," *Comm. ACM* 29:12 (December), 1184–1201.

Palacharla, S., and R. E. Kessler [1994]. "Evaluating stream buffers as a secondary cache replacement," *Proc. 21st Annual Int'l Symposium on Computer Architecture,* Chicago, April 18–21, 24–33.

Palmer, J., and S. Morse [1984]. *The 8087 Primer,* J. Wiley, New York, 93.

Pan, S.-T., K. So, and J. T. Rameh [1992]. "Improving the accuracy of dynamic branch prediction using branch correlation," *Proc. Fifth Conf. on Architectural Support for Programming Languages and Operating Systems,* IEEE/ACM (October), Boston, 76–84.

Partridge, C. [1994]. *Gigabit Networking,* Addison-Wesley, Reading, Mass.

Patterson, D. [1985]. "Reduced instruction set computers," *Comm. ACM* 28:1 (January), 8–21.

Patterson, D. [2004]. "Latency lags bandwidth," *CACM* 47:10 (October), 71–75.

Patterson, D. A., and D. R. Ditzel [1980]. "The case for the reduced instruction set computer," *Computer Architecture News* 8:6 (October), 25–33.

Patterson, D. A., P. Garrison, M. Hill, D. Lioupis, C. Nyberg, T. Sippel, and K. Van Dyke [1983]. "Architecture of a VLSI instruction cache for a RISC," *10th Annual Int'l Conf. on Computer Architecture Conf. Proc.,* Stockholm, Sweden, June 13–16, 108–116.

Patterson, D. A., G. A. Gibson, and R. H. Katz [1987]. "A case for redundant arrays of inexpensive disks (RAID)," Tech. Rep. UCB/CSD 87/391, Univ. of Calif. Also appeared in *ACM SIGMOD Conf. Proc.,* Chicago, June 1–3, 1988, 109–116.

Patterson, D. A., and J. L. Hennessy [2004]. *Computer Organization and Design: The Hardware/Software Interface,* third edition, Morgan Kaufmann, San Francisco.

Pavan, P., R. Bez, P. Olivo, and E. Zanoni [1997]. "Flash memory cells—an overview." *Proc. IEEE* 85:8 (August), 1248–1271.

Peh, L. S., and W. J. Dally [2001]. "A delay model and speculative architecture for pipelined routers," *Proc. 7th Int'l Symposium on High Performance Computer Architecture* (January), Monterrey.

Peng, V., S. Samudrala, and M. Gavrielov [1987]. "On the implementation of shifters, multipliers, and dividers in VLSI floating point units," *Proc. Eighth IEEE Symposium on Computer Arithmetic,* 95–102.

Pfister, G. F. [1998]. *In Search of Clusters,* second edition, Prentice Hall, Upper Saddle River, N.J.

Pfister, G. F., W. C. Brantley, D. A. George, S. L. Harvey, W. J. Kleinfekder, K. P. McAuliffe, E. A. Melton, V. A. Norton, and J. Weiss [1985]. "The IBM research parallel processor prototype (RP3): Introduction and architecture," *Proc. 12th Int'l Symposium on Computer Architecture* (June), Boston, 764–771.

Pinkston, T. M. [2004]. "Deadlock characterization and resolution in interconnection networks (Chapter 13)," *Deadlock Resolution in Computer-Integrated Systems,* edited by M. C. Zhu and M. P. Fanti, Marcel Dekkar/CRC Press, 445–492.

Pinkston, T. M., A. Benner, M. Krause, I. Robinson, and T. Sterling [2003]. "InfiniBand: The 'de facto' future standard for system and local area networks or just a scalable replacement for PCI buses?" *Cluster Computing* (Special Issue on Communication Architecture for Clusters) 6:2 (April), 95–104.

Pinkston, T. M., and J. Shin [2005]. "Trends toward on-chip networked microsystems," *International Journal of High Performance Computing and Networking* 3:1, 3–18.

Pinkston, T. M., and S. Warnakulasuriya [1997]. "On deadlocks in interconnection networks," *Proc. 24th Int'l Symposium on Computer Architecture* (June), Denver.

Postiff, M.A., D. A. Greene, G. S. Tyson, and T. N. Mudge [1999]. "The limits of instruction level parallelism in SPEC95 applications," *Computer Architecture News* 27:1 (March), 31–40.

Przybylski, S. A. [1990]. *Cache Design: A Performance-Directed Approach,* Morgan Kaufmann, San Francisco.

Przybylski, S. A., M. Horowitz, and J. L. Hennessy [1988]. "Performance trade-offs in cache design," *Proc. 15th Annual Symposium on Computer Architecture* (May–June), Honolulu, 290–298.

Puente, V., R. Beivide, J. A. Gregorio, J. M. Prellezo, J. Duato, and C. Izu [1999]. "Adaptive bubble router: A design to improve performance in torus networks," *Proc. 28th Int'l Conference on Parallel Processing* (September), Aizu-Wakamatsu, Japan.

Radin, G. [1982]. "The 801 minicomputer," *Proc. Symposium Architectural Support for Programming Languages and Operating Systems* (March), Palo Alto, Calif., 39–47.

Ramamoorthy, C. V., and H. F. Li [1977]. "Pipeline architecture," *ACM Computing Surveys* 9:1 (March), 61–102.

Rau, B. R. [1994]. "Iterative modulo scheduling: An algorithm for software pipelining loops," *Proc. 27th Annual Int'l Symposium on Microarchitecture* (November), San Jose, Calif., 63–74.

Rau, B. R., C. D. Glaeser, and R. L. Picard [1982]. "Efficient code generation for horizontal architectures: Compiler techniques and architectural support," *Proc. Ninth Symposium on Computer Architecture* (April), 131–139.

Rau, B. R., D. W. L. Yen, W. Yen, and R. A. Towle [1989]. "The Cydra 5 departmental supercomputer: Design philosophies, decisions, and trade-offs," *IEEE Computers* 22:1 (January), 12–34.

Redmond, K. C., and T. M. Smith [1980]. *Project Whirlwind—The History of a Pioneer Computer,* Digital Press, Boston.

Reinhardt, S. K., J. R. Larus, and D. A. Wood [1994]. "Tempest and Typhoon: User-level shared memory," *Proc. 21st Annual Int'l Symposium on Computer Architecture,* Chicago, April, 325–336.

Reinman, G., and N. P. Jouppi. [1999]. "Extensions to CACTI," *research.compaq.com/wrl/people/jouppi/CACTI.html.*

Rettberg, R. D., W. R. Crowther, P. P. Carvey, and R. S. Towlinson [1990]. "The Monarch parallel processor hardware design," *IEEE Computer* 23:4 (April).

Riemens, A., K. A. Vissers, R. J. Schutten, F. W. Sijstermans, G. J. Hekstra, and G. D. La Hei [1999]."Trimedia CPU64 application domain and benchmark suite," *Proc. 1999 IEEE Int'l Conf. on Computer Design: VLSI in Computers and Processors, ICCD'99,* Austin, Tex., October 10–13, 580–585.

Riseman, E. M., and C. C. Foster [1972]. "Percolation of code to enhance paralled dispatching and execution," *IEEE Trans. on Computers* C-21:12 (December), 1411–1415.

Robin, J., and C. Irvine [2000]. "Analysis of the Intel Pentium's ability to support a secure virtual machine monitor." *Proc. 9th USENIX Security Symposium,* Denver, Colo., August 14–17.

Robinson, B., and L. Blount [1986]. "The VM/HPO 3880-23 performance results," IBM Tech. Bulletin GG66-0247-00 (April), Washington Systems Center, Gaithersburg, Md.

Ropers, A., H. W. Lollman, and J. Wellhausen [1999]. "DSPstone: Texas Instruments TMS320C54x," Technical Report Nr. IB 315 1999/9-ISS-Version 0.9, Aachen University of Technology, *www.ert.rwth-aachen.de/Projekte/Tools/coal/dspstone_c54x/index.html.*

Rosenblum, M., S. A. Herrod, E. Witchel, and A. Gupta [1995]. "Complete computer simulation: The SimOS approach," in *IEEE Parallel and Distributed Technology* (now called *Concurrency*) 4:3, 34–43.

Rowen, C., M. Johnson, and P. Ries [1988]. "The MIPS R3010 floating-point coprocessor," *IEEE Micro,* 53–62 (June).

Russell, R. M. [1978]. "The Cray-1 processor system," *Comm. of the ACM* 21:1 (January), 63–72.

Rymarczyk, J. [1982]. "Coding guidelines for pipelined processors," *Proc. Symposium on Architectural Support for Programming Languages and Operating Systems,* IEEE/ACM (March), Palo Alto, Calif., 12–19.

Saavedra-Barrera, R. H. [1992]. *CPU Performance Evaluation and Execution Time Prediction Using Narrow Spectrum Benchmarking,* Ph.D. dissertation, University of Calif., Berkeley (May).

Salem, K., and H. Garcia-Molina [1986]. "Disk striping," *IEEE 1986 Int'l Conf. on Data Engineering,* February 5–7, Washington, D.C., 249–259.

Saltzer, J. H., D. P. Reed, and D. D. Clark [1984]. "End-to-end arguments in system design," *ACM Trans. on Computer Systems* 2:4 (November), 277–288.

Samples, A. D., and P. N. Hilfinger [1988]. "Code reorganization for instruction caches," Tech. Rep. UCB/CSD 88/447 (October), University of Calif., Berkeley.

Santoro, M. R., G. Bewick, and M. A. Horowitz [1989]. "Rounding algorithms for IEEE multipliers," *Proc. Ninth IEEE Symposium on Computer Arithmetic,* 176–183.

Satran, J., D. Smith, K. Meth, C. Sapuntzakis, M. Wakeley, P. Von Stamwitz, R. Haagens, E. Zeidner, L. Dalle Ore, and Y. Klein [2001]. "iSCSI," IPS working group of IETF, Internet draft *www.ietf.org/internet-drafts/draft-ietf-ips-iscsi-07.txt.*

Saulsbury, A., T. Wilkinson, J. Carter, and A. Landin [1995]. "An argument for Simple COMA," *Proc. First Conf. on High Performance Computer Architectures* (January), Raleigh, N.C., 276–285.

Schneck, P. B. [1987]. *Superprocessor Architecture,* Kluwer Academic Publishers, Norwell, Mass.

Schwartz, J. T. [1980]. "Ultracomputers," *ACM Trans. on Programming Languages and Systems* 4:2, 484–521.

Scott, N. R. [1985]. *Computer Number Systems and Arithmetic,* Prentice Hall, Englewood Cliffs, N.J.

Scott, S. L. [1996]. "Synchronization and communication in the T3E multiprocessor," *Proc. Architectural Support for Programming Languages and Operating Systems (ASPLOS-VII),* Cambridge, Mass., October, 26–36.

Scott, S. L., and J. Goodman [1994]. "The impact of pipelined channels on k-ary n-cube networks," *IEEE Trans. on Parallel and Distributed Systems* 5:1 (January), 1–16.

Scott, S. L., and G. M. Thorson [1996]. "The Cray T3E network: Adaptive routing in a high performance 3D torus," *Proc. Symposium on High Performance Interconnects (Hot Interconnects 4),* Stanford University, August, 14–156.

Scranton, R. A., D. A. Thompson, and D. W. Hunter [1983]. "The access time myth," Tech. Rep. RC 10197 (45223) (September 21), IBM, Yorktown Heights, N.Y.

Seagate [2000]. *Seagate Cheetah 73 Family: ST173404LW/LWV/LC/LCV Product Manual,* Volume 1, *www.seagate.com/support/disc/manuals/scsi/29478b.pdf.*

Seattle PI [2005}. "Amazon sees sales rise, profit fall," *http://seattlepi.nwsource.com/business/245943_techearns26.html.*

Seitz, C. L. [1985]. "The Cosmic Cube (concurrent computing)," *Communications of the ACM* 28:1 (January), 22–33.

Senior, J. M. [1993]. *Optical Fiber Commmunications: Principles and Practice,* second edition, Prentice Hall, Hertfordshire, U.K.

Sharangpani, H., and K. Arora [2000]. "Itanium Processor Microarchitecture," *IEEE Micro* 20:5 (September–October), 24–43.

Shurkin, J. [1984]. *Engines of the Mind: A History of the Computer,* W. W. Norton, New York.

Shustek, L. J. [1978]. *Analysis and Performance of Computer Instruction Sets,* Ph.D. dissertation, Stanford University (January).

Silicon Graphics [1996]. *MIPS V Instruction Set* (see *http://www.sgi.com/MIPS/arch/ISA5/#MIPSV_indx).*

Singh, J. P., J. L. Hennessy, and A. Gupta [1993]. "Scaling parallel programs for multiprocessors: Methodology and examples," *Computer* 26:7 (July), 22–33.

Singhal, R. [2004]. "Intel Pentium 4 processor on 90nm technology," presentation at Hot Chips 16 Conf., Stanford University, August.

Sinharoy, B., R. N. Koala, J. M. Tendler, R. J. Eickemeyer, and J. B. Joyner [2005]. "POWER5 system microarchitecture," *IBM J. Res. & Dev,* 49:4–5, 505–521.

Sites, R. [1979]. *Instruction Ordering for the CRAY-1 Computer,* Tech. Rep. 78-CS-023 (July), Dept. of Computer Science, Univ. of Calif., San Diego.

Sites, R. L. (ed.) [1992]. *Alpha Architecture Reference Manual,* Digital Press, Burlington, Mass.

Sites, R. L., and R. Witek, (eds.) [1995]. *Alpha Architecture Reference Manual,* second edition, Digital Press, Newton, Mass.

Skadron, K., P. S. Ahuja, M. Martonosi, and D. W. Clark [1999]. "Branch prediction, instruction-window size, and cache size: Performance tradeoffs and simulation techniques," *IEEE Trans. on Computers* 48:11 (November).

Skadron, K., and D. W. Clark [1997]. "Design issues and tradeoffs for write buffers," *Proc. Third Int'l Symposium on High-Performance Computer Architecture,* 144–155.

Slater, R. [1987]. *Portraits in Silicon,* MIT Press, Cambridge, Mass.

Slotnick, D. L., W. C. Borck, and R. C. McReynolds [1962]. "The Solomon computer," *Proc. Fall Joint Computer Conf.* (December), Philadelphia, 97–107.

Smith, A. J. [1982]. "Cache memories," *Computing Surveys* 14:3 (September), 473–530.

Smith, A., and J. Lee [1984]. "Branch prediction strategies and branch-target buffer design," *Computer* 17:1 (January), 6–22.

Smith, B. J. [1978]. "A pipelined, shared resource MIMD computer," *Proc. 1978 ICPP* (August), 6–8.

Smith, B. J. [1981]. "Architecture and applications of the HEP multiprocessor system," *Real-Time Signal Processing IV* 298 (August), 241–248.

Smith, J. E. [1981]. "A study of branch prediction strategies," *Proc. Eighth Symposium on Computer Architecture* (May), Minneapolis, 135–148.

Smith, J. E. [1984]. "Decoupled access/execute computer architectures," *ACM Trans. on Computer Systems* 2:4 (November), 289–308.

Smith, J. E. [1988]. "Characterizing computer performance with a single number," *Comm. ACM* 31:10 (October), 1202–1206.

Smith, J. E. [1989]. "Dynamic instruction scheduling and the Astronautics ZS-1," *Computer* 22:7 (July), 21–35.

Smith, J. E., G. E. Dermer, B. D. Vanderwarn, S. D. Klinger, C. M. Rozewski, D. L. Fowler, K. R. Scidmore, and J. P. Laudon [1987]. "The ZS-1 central processor," *Proc. Second Conf. on Architectural Support for Programming Languages and Operating Systems,* IEEE/ACM (March), Palo Alto, Calif., 199–204.

Smith, J. E., and J. R. Goodman [1983]. "A study of instruction cache organizations and replacement policies," *Proc. 10th Annual Symposium on Computer Architecture* (June 5–7), Stockholm, 132–137.

Smith, J. E., and A. R. Pleszkun [1988]. "Implementing precise interrupts in pipelined processors," *IEEE Trans. on Computers* 37:5 (May), 562–573. (This paper is based on an earlier paper that appeared in *Proc. 12th Symposium on Computer Architecture,* June 1988.)

Smith, M. D., M. Horowitz, and M. S. Lam [1992]. "Efficient superscalar performance through boosting," *Proc. Fifth Conf. on Architectural Support for Programming Languages and Operating Systems* (October), Boston, IEEE/ACM, 248–259.

Smith, M. D., M. Johnson, and M. A. Horowitz [1989]. "Limits on multiple instruction issue," *Proc. Third Conf. on Architectural Support for Programming Languages and Operating Systems,* IEEE/ACM (April), Boston, 290–302.

Smotherman, M. [1989]. "A sequencing-based taxonomy of I/O systems and review of historical machines," *Computer Architecture News* 17:5 (September), 5–15. Reprinted in *Computer Architecture Readings,* Morgan Kaufmann, 1999, 451–461.

Sodani, A., and G. Sohi [1997]. "Dynamic instruction reuse," *Proc. 24th Int'l Symposium on Computer Architecture* (June).

Sohi, G. S. [1990]. "Instruction issue logic for high-performance, interruptible, multiple functional unit, pipelined computers," *IEEE Trans. on Computers* 39:3 (March), 349–359.

Sohi, G. S., and S. Vajapeyam [1989]. "Tradeoffs in instruction format design for horizontal architectures," *Proc. Third Conf. on Architectural Support for Programming Languages and Operating Systems,* IEEE/ACM (April), Boston, 15–25.

Soundararajan, V., M. Heinrich, B. Verghese, K. Gharachorloo, A. Gupta, and J. L. Hennessy [1998]. "Flexible use of memory for replication/migration in cache-coherent DSM multiprocessors," *Proc. 25th Int'l Symposium on Computer Architecture* (June), Barcelona, 342–355.

SPEC [1989]. *SPEC Benchmark Suite Release 1.0* (October 2).

SPEC [1994]. *SPEC Newsletter* (June).

Sporer, M., F. H. Moss, and C. J. Mathais [1988]. "An introduction to the architecture of the Stellar Graphics supercomputer," *COMPCON,* IEEE (March), 464.

Spurgeon, C. [2001]. "Charles Spurgeon's Ethernet Web site," *wwwhost.ots.utexas.edu/ethernet/ethernet-home.html.*

Spurgeon, C. [2006]. "Charles Spurgeon's Ethernet Web Site," *www.ethermanage.com/ethernet/ethernet.html.*

Stenström, P., T. Joe, and A. Gupta [1992]. "Comparative performance evaluation of cache-coherent NUMA and COMA architectures," *Proc. 19th Annual Int'l Symposium on Computer Architecture,* May, Queensland, Australia, 80–91.

Sterling, T. [2001]. *Beowulf PC Cluster Computing with Windows and Beowulf PC Cluster Computing with Linux,* MIT Press, Cambridge, Mass.

Stern, N. [1980]. "Who invented the first electronic digital computer?" *Annals of the History of Computing* 2:4 (October), 375–376.

Stevens, W. R. [1994–1996]. *TCP/IP Illustrated* (three volumes), Addison-Wesley, Reading, Mass.

Stokes, J. [2000]. "Sound and vision: A technical overview of the emotion engine," *arstechnica.com/reviews/1q00/playstation2/ee-1.html.*

Stone, H. [1991]. *High Performance Computers,* Addison-Wesley, New York.

Strauss, W. [1998]. "DSP strategies 2002," *Forward Concepts, www.usadata.com/market_research/spr_05/spr_r127-005.htm.*

Strecker, W. D. [1976]. "Cache memories for the PDP-11?," *Proc. Third Annual Symposium on Computer Architecture* (January), Pittsburgh, 155–158.

Strecker, W. D. [1978]. "VAX-11/780: A virtual address extension of the PDP-11 family," *Proc. AFIPS National Computer Conf.* 47, 967–980.

Sugumar, R. A., and S. G. Abraham [1993]. "Efficient simulation of caches under optimal replacement with applications to miss characterization," *1993 ACM Sigmetrics Conf. on Measurement and Modeling of Computer Systems,* Santa Clara, Calif., May 17–21, 24–35.

Sun Microsystems [1989]. *The SPARC Architectural Manual,* Version 8, Part No. 800-1399-09, August 25.

Sussenguth, E. [1999]. "IBM's ACS-1 Machine," *IEEE Computer* 22:11 (November).

Swan, R. J., A. Bechtolsheim, K. W. Lai, and J. K. Ousterhout [1977]. "The implementation of the Cm* multi-microprocessor," *Proc. AFIPS National Computing Conf.,* 645–654.

Swan, R. J., S. H. Fuller, and D. P. Siewiorek [1977]. "Cm*—a modular, multi-microprocessor," *Proc. AFIPS National Computer Conf.* 46, 637–644.

Swartzlander, E. (ed.) [1990]. *Computer Arithmetic,* IEEE Computer Society Press, Los Alamitos, Calif.

Takagi, N., H. Yasuura, and S. Yajima [1985]."High-speed VLSI multiplication algorithm with a redundant binary addition tree," *IEEE Trans. on Computers* C-34:9, 789–796.

Talagala, N. [2000]. *Characterizing large storage systems: Error behavior and performance benchmarks,* Ph.D. dissertation CSD-99-1066, June 13, 1999.

Talagala, N., R. Arpaci-Dusseau, and D. Patterson [2000]. "Micro-benchmark based extraction of local and global disk characteristics," CSD-99-1063, June 13.

Talagala, N., S. Asami, D. Patterson, R. Futernick, and D. Hart [2000]. "The art of massive storage: A case study of a Web image archive," *Computer* (November).

Talagala, N., and D. Patterson [1999]. "An analysis of error behavior in a large storage system," Tech. Report UCB//CSD-99-1042, Computer Science Division, University of California at Berkeley (February).

Tamir, Y., and G. Frazier [1992]. "Dynamically-allocated multi-queue buffers for VLSI communication switches," *IEEE Trans. on Computers* 41:6 (June), 725–734.

Tanenbaum, A. S. [1978]. "Implications of structured programming for machine architecture," *Comm. ACM* 21:3 (March), 237–246.

Tanenbaum, A. S. [1988]. *Computer Networks,* second edition, Prentice Hall, Englewood Cliffs, N.J.

Tang, C. K. [1976]. "Cache design in the tightly coupled multiprocessor system," *Proc. AFIPS National Computer Conf.,* New York (June), 749–753.

Tanqueray, D. [2002]. "The Cray X1 and supercomputer road map," 13th Daresbury Machine Evaluation Workshop (December 11–12).

Tarjan, D., S. Thoziyoor, and N. Jouppi [2005]. HPL Technical report on CACTI 4.0. *www.hpl.hp.com/techeports/2006/HPL=2006+86.html.*

Taylor, G. S. [1981]. "Compatible hardware for division and square root," *Proc. Fifth IEEE Symposium on Computer Arithmetic,* 127–134.

Taylor, G. S. [1985]. "Radix 16 SRT dividers with overlapped quotient selection stages," *Proc. Seventh IEEE Symposium on Computer Arithmetic,* 64–71.

Taylor, G., P. Hilfinger, J. Larus, D. Patterson, and B. Zorn [1986]. "Evaluation of the SPUR LISP architecture," *Proc. 13th Symposium on Computer Architecture (*June), Tokyo.

Taylor, M. B., W. Lee, S. P. Amarasinghe, and A. Agarwal [2005]. "Scalar operand networks," *IEEE Trans. on Parallel and Distributed Systems* 16:2 (February), 145–162.

Tendler, J. M., J. S. Dodson, J. S. Fields, Jr., H. Le, and B. Sinharoy [2002]. "Power4 system microarchitecture," *IBM J. Res & Dev* 46:1, 5–26.

Texas Instruments [2000]. "History of innovation: 1980s," *www.ti.com/corp/docs/company/history/1980s.shtml.*

Thacker, C. P., E. M. McCreight, B. W. Lampson, R. F. Sproull, and D. R. Boggs [1982]. "Alto: A personal computer," in *Computer Structures: Principles and Examples,* D. P. Siewiorek, C. G. Bell, and A. Newell, eds., McGraw-Hill, New York, 549–572.

Thadhani, A. J. [1981]. "Interactive user productivity," *IBM Systems J.* 20:4, 407–423.

Thekkath, R., A. P. Singh, J. P. Singh, S. John, and J. L. Hennessy [1997]. "An evaluation of a commercial CC-NUMA architecture—the CONVEX Exemplar SPP1200," *Proc. 11th Int'l Parallel Processing Symposium (IPPS '97),* Geneva, Switzerland, April.

Thorlin, J. F. [1967]. "Code generation for PIE (parallel instruction execution) computers," *Proc. Spring Joint Computer Conf.,* 27.

Thornton, J. E. [1964]. "Parallel operation in Control Data 6600," *Proc. AFIPS Fall Joint Computer Conf., Part II,* 26, 33–40.

Thornton, J. E. [1970]. *Design of a Computer, the Control Data 6600,* Scott, Foresman, Glenview, Ill.

Tjaden, G. S., and M. J. Flynn [1970]. "Detection and parallel execution of independent instructions," *IEEE Trans. on Computers* C-19:10 (October), 889–895.

Tomasulo, R. M. [1967]. "An efficient algorithm for exploiting multiple arithmetic units," *IBM J. Research and Development* 11:1 (January), 25–33.

Torrellas, J., A. Gupta, and J. Hennessy [1992]. "Characterizing the caching and synchronization performance of a multiprocessor operating system," Fifth Int'l Conf. on Architectural Support for Programming Languages and Operating Systems (ASP-LOS-V), Boston, October 12–15, *SIGPLAN Notices* 27:9 (September), 162–174.

Touma, W. R. [1993]. *The Dynamics of the Computer Industry: Modeling the Supply of Workstations and Their Components,* Kluwer Academic, Boston.

Tuck, N., and D. Tullsen [2003]. "Initial observations of the simultaneous multithreading Pentium 4 processor," *Proc. 12th Int. Conf. on Parallel Architectures and Compilation Techniques (PACT'03),* 26–34.

Tullsen, D. M., S. J. Eggers, J. S. Emer, H. M. Levy, J. L. Lo, and R. L. Stamm [1996]. "Exploiting choice: Instruction fetch and issue on an implementable simultaneous multithreading processor," *Proc. 23rd Annual Int'l Symposium on Computer Architecture* (May), 191–202.

Tullsen, D. M., S. J. Eggers, and H. M. Levy [1995]. "Simultaneous multithreading: Maximizing on-chip parallelism," *Proc. 22nd Int'l Symposium on Computer Architecture* (June), 392–403.

Ungar, D., R. Blau, P. Foley, D. Samples, and D. Patterson [1984]. "Architecture of SOAR: Smalltalk on a RISC," *Proc. 11th Symposium on Computer Architecture* (June), Ann Arbor, Mich., 188–197.

Unger, S. H. [1958]. "A computer oriented towards spatial problems," *Proc. Institute of Radio Engineers* 46:10 (October), 1744–1750.

Vaidya, A. S., A Sivasubramaniam, and C. R. Das [1997]. "Performance benefits of virtual channels and adaptive routing: An application-driven study," *Proceedings of the 1997 Int'l Conference on Supercomputing* (July), Austria.

Vajapeyam, S. [1991]. *Instruction-level characterization of the Cray Y-MP processor,* Ph.D. thesis, Computer Sciences Department, University of Wisconsin-Madison.

van Eijndhoven, J. T. J., F. W. Sijstermans, K. A. Vissers, E. J. D. Pol, M. I. A. Tromp, P. Struik, R. H. J. Bloks, P. van der Wolf, A. D. Pimentel, and H. P. E. Vranken [1999]. "Trimedia CPU64 architecture," *Proc. 1999 IEEE Int'l Conf. on Computer Design: VLSI in Computers and Processors, ICCD'99,* Austin, Tex., October 10–13, 586–592.

Van Vleck, T. [2005]. "The IBM 360/67 and CP/CMS," *http://www.multicians.org/thvv/360-67.html.*

von Eicken, T., D. E. Culler, S. C. Goldstein, K. E. Schauser [1992]. "Active Messages: A mechanism for integrated communication and computation,"*Proc. 19th Int'l Symposium on Computer Architecture* (May), Australia.

Waingold, E., M. Taylor, D. Srikrishna, V. Sarkar, W. Lee, V. Lee, J. Kim, M. Frank, P. Finch, R. Barua, J. Babb, S. Amarasinghe, and A. Agarwal [1997]. "Baring it all to software: Raw Machines," *IEEE Computer* 30 (September), 86–93.

Wakerly, J. [1989]. *Microcomputer Architecture and Programming,* Wiley, New York.

Wall, D. W. [1991]. "Limits of instruction-level parallelism," *Proc. Fourth Conf. on Architectural Support for Programming Languages and Operating Systems* (April), Santa Clara, Calif., IEEE/ACM, 248–259.

Wall, D. W. [1993]. *Limits of Instruction-Level Parallelism,* Research Rep. 93/6, Western Research Laboratory, Digital Equipment Corp. (November).

Walrand, J. [1991]. *Communication Networks: A First Course,* Aksen Associates: Irwin, Homewood, Ill.

Wang, W.-H., J.-L. Baer, and H. M. Levy [1989]. "Organization and performance of a two-level virtual-real cache hierarchy," *Proc. 16th Annual Symposium on Computer Architecture* (May 28–June 1), Jerusalem, 140–148.

Watanabe, T. [1987]. "Architecture and performance of the NEC supercomputer SX system," *Parallel Computing* 5, 247–255.

Waters, F. (ed.) [1986]. *IBM RT Personal Computer Technology,* IBM, Austin, Tex., SA 23-1057.

Watson, W. J. [1972]. "The TI ASC—a highly modular and flexible super processor architecture," *Proc. AFIPS Fall Joint Computer Conf.,* 221–228.

Weaver, D. L., and T. Germond [1994]. *The SPARC Architectural Manual,* Version 9, Prentice Hall, Englewood Cliffs, N.J.

Weicker, R. P. [1984]. "Dhrystone: A synthetic systems programming benchmark," *Comm. ACM* 27:10 (October), 1013–1030.

Weiss, S., and J. E. Smith [1984]. "Instruction issue logic for pipelined supercomputers," *Proc. 11th Symposium on Computer Architecture* (June), Ann Arbor, Mich., 110–118.

Weiss, S., and J. E. Smith [1987]. "A study of scalar compilation techniques for pipelined supercomputers," *Proc. Second Conf. on Architectural Support for Programming Languages and Operating Systems* (March), IEEE/ACM, Palo Alto, Calif., 105–109.

Weiss, S., and J. E. Smith [1994]. *Power and PowerPC,* Morgan Kaufmann, San Francisco.

Weste, N., and K. Eshraghian [1993]. *Principles of CMOS VLSI Design: A Systems Perspective,* second edition, Addison-Wesley, Reading, Mass.

Wiecek, C. [1982]. "A case study of the VAX 11 instruction set usage for compiler execution," *Proc. Symposium on Architectural Support for Programming Languages and Operating Systems* (March), IEEE/ACM, Palo Alto, Calif., 177–184.

Wilkes, M. [1965]. "Slave memories and dynamic storage allocation," *IEEE Trans. Electronic Computers* EC-14:2 (April), 270–271.

Wilkes, M. V. [1982]. "Hardware support for memory protection: Capability implementations," *Proc. Symposium on Architectural Support for Programming Languages and Operating Systems* (March 1–3), Palo Alto, Calif., 107–116.

Wilkes, M. V. [1985]. *Memoirs of a Computer Pioneer,* MIT Press, Cambridge, Mass.

Wilkes, M. V. [1995]. *Computing Perspectives,* Morgan Kaufmann, San Francisco.

Wilkes, M. V., D. J. Wheeler, and S. Gill [1951]. *The Preparation of Programs for an Electronic Digital Computer,* Addison-Wesley, Cambridge, Mass.

Williams, T. E., M. Horowitz, R. L. Alverson, and T. S. Yang [1987]. "A self-timed chip for division," *Advanced Research in VLSI, Proc. 1987 Stanford Conf.,* MIT Press, Cambridge, Mass.

Wilson, A. W., Jr. [1987]. "Hierarchical cache/bus architecture for shared-memory multiprocessors," *Proc. 14th Int'l Symposium on Computer Architecture* (June), Pittsburgh, 244–252.

Wilson, R. P., and M. S. Lam [1995]. "Efficient context-sensitive pointer analysis for C programs," *Proc. ACM SIGPLAN'95 Conf. on Programming Language Design and Implementation,* La Jolla, Calif., June, 1–12.

Wolfe, A., and J. P. Shen [1991]. "A variable instruction stream extension to the VLIW architecture," *Proc. Fourth Conference on Architectural Support for Programming Languages and Operating Systems* (April), Santa Clara, Calif., 2–14.

Wood, D. A., and M. D. Hill [1995]. "Cost-effective parallel computing," *IEEE Computer* 28:2 (February).

Wulf, W. [1981]. "Compilers and computer architecture," *Computer* 14:7 (July), 41–47.

Wulf, W., and C. G. Bell [1972]. "C.mmp—A multi-mini-processor," *Proc. AFIPS Fall Joint Computing Conf.* 41, part 2, 765–777.

Wulf, W., and S. P. Harbison [1978]. "Reflections in a pool of processors—an experience report on C.mmp/Hydra," *Proc. AFIPS 1978 National Computing Conf.* 48 (June), Anaheim, Calif., 939–951.

Wulf, W. A., R. Levin, and S. P. Harbison [1981]. *Hydra/C.mmp: An Experimental Computer System,* McGraw-Hill, New York.

Yamamoto, W., M. J. Serrano, A. R. Talcott, R. C. Wood, and M. Nemirosky [1994]. "Performance estimation of multistreamed, superscalar processors," *Proc. 27th Hawaii Int'l Conf. on System Sciences* (January), I:195–204.

Yang, Y., and G. Mason [1991]. "Nonblocking broadcast switching networks," *IEEE Trans. on Computers* 40:9 (September), 1005–1015.

Yeager, K. [1996]. "The MIPS R10000 superscalar microprocessor," *IEEE Micro* 16:2 (April), 28–40.

Yeh, T., and Y. N. Patt [1992]. "Alternative implementations of two-level adaptive branch prediction," *Proc. 19th Int'l Symposium on Computer Architecture* (May), Gold Coast, Australia, 124–134.

Yeh, T., and Y. N. Patt [1993]. "A comparison of dynamic branch predictors that use two levels of branch history," *Proc. 20th Symposium on Computer Architecture* (May), San Diego, 257–266.

Index

Page references in bold represent figures and tables.

Numbers

2:1 cache rule of thumb, C-28
3ASC Purple pSeries 575, **E-20, E-44, E-56**
80x86 processors. *See* Intel 80x86
99.999% (five nines) claims, 399

A

ABC (Atanasoff Berry Computer), K-5
ABI (application binary interface), B-20
absolute addressing mode, **B-9**
absolute value function, G-24
Accelerated Strategic Computing Initiative (ASCI), **E-20, E-44, E-56**
access bits, C-50
access time, 310, F-15 to F-16
access time gap, in disks and DRAM, 359, **359**
accumulator architecture, B-3, **B-4**
acknowledgments, 217, H-39 to H-41
ACS, K-20 to K-21
Ada, integer division and remainder in, **I-12**
adaptive routing, E-47, E-53, **E-54,** E-73, E-93 to E-94
adders
    carry-lookahead, 38, I-37 to I-41, **I-38, I-40, I-41, I-42, I-44**
    carry-propagate, I-48
    carry-save, I-47 to I-48, **I-48**
    carry-select, I-43 to I-44, **I-43, I-44**
    carry-skip, I-41 to I-43, **I-42, I-44**
    faster division with one, I-54 to I-58, **I-55, I-56, I-57**
    faster multiplication with many, I-50 to I-54, **I-50 to I-54**
    faster multiplication with single, I-47 to I-50, **I-48, I-49**
    ripple-carry, I-2 to I-3, **I-3, I-42, I-44**
addition. *See also* adders
    denormalized numbers, I-26 to I-27
    floating-point, I-21 to I-27, **I-24,** I-36
    multiple-precision, I-13
    speeding up, I-25 to I-26, I-37 to I-44
address aliasing prediction, 130
address faults, C-40
address mapping
    in AMD Opteron, C-12 to C-13, C-53 to C-54, **C-54**
    in multibanked caches, 299, **299**
    page coloring, C-37
    in trace caches, 296, **309**
address size, importance of, C-56
address space, shared, 202
address specifiers, B-21, J-68
address translations (memory mapping). *See also* translation lookaside buffers
    in AMD Opteron, C-44 to C-45, **C-45**
    during cache indexing, 291–292, C-36 to C-38, **C-37, C-39**
    caches dedicated to, C-43
    illegal, C-54 to C-55
    in Intel Pentium, C-50
    memory protection and, 317

in virtual memory, C-40, C-44 to C-47, **C-45, C-47**
addressing modes
    in embedded architectures, J-5 to J-6, **J-6**
    in Intel 80x86, J-47 to J-49, **J-50,** J-59 to J-62, **J-59 to J-62**
    in MIPS data transfers, B-34 to B-35
    paged *vs.* segmented, C-3, **C-41, C-42**
    real, J-45, **J-50**
    in RISC desktop architectures, J-5 to J-6, **J-5**
    types of, B-9 to B-10, **B-9, B-11, B-12, B-13**
    in VAX, J-67, J-70 to J-71
    in vector computers, B-31 to B-32
advanced load address table (ALAT), F-27, G-40
advanced loads, G-40
advanced mobile phone service (AMPS), D-25
Advanced Research Project Agency (ARPA), E-97, E-99
Advanced RISC Machines. *See* ARM
Advanced RISC Machines Thumb. *See* ARM Thumb
Advanced Switching Interconnect (ASI), E-103
affine array indexes, G-6
age-based, E-49
aggregate bandwidth, E-13, E-17, E-24
Aiken, Howard, K-3 to K-4
ALAT table, F-27, G-40
algebraic right shift, J-33
alias analysis. *See* memory alias analysis

I-1

alias prediction. *See* address aliasing prediction
aliases, C-36
Alles, A., E-98
Alliant computers, vector processors in, F-49
Alpha
    addressing modes in, J-5 to J-6, **J-5**
    architecture overview, **J-4**
    common MIPS extensions in, J-19 to J-24, **J-21 to J-23**
    conditional branch options in, **B-19**
    instructions unique to, J-27 to J-29
    MIPS core subset in, J-6 to J-16, **J-7, J-9 to J-13, J-17**
    page size changes in, C-56 to C-57
Alpha 21064, A-43
Alpha 21164, 220
Alpha 21264, 88–89, 140
Alpha MAX, **D-11,** J-16 to J-19, **J-18**
AlphaServer 4100, 220–221, **221**
AltaVista benchmark, 221, **221, 222**
ALU instructions
    in media extensions, D-10 to D-11
    memory addressing and, **B-12**
    in MIPS architecture, B-37, **B-37**
    operand format in, B-5, **B-6**
    overview of, A-4 to A-5
    in unpipelined MIPS implementation, A-27 to A-28, A-30
AMAT. *See* average memory access time
AMD 64, J-46
AMD Athlon 64 processor
    L1 cache size in, 294
    performance of, **G-43**
    SMT performance of, 179–181, **179, 180, 181**
AMD ElanSC520, D-13, **D-13**
AMD K6, 294, D-13, **D-13**
AMD Opteron processor
    64-bit memory management, C-53 to C-55, **C-54, C-55**
    antialiasing in, C-36
    cache-coherent multiprocessors, 215

data cache organization, C-12 to C-14, **C-13, C-15**
dies, **22, 23**
    interconnection networks in, 216-217, **216**
    L1 cache size in, 294
    memory hierarchy performance, 331–335, **332, 333, 334**
    memory hierarchy structure, 326–331, **327, 328, 341**
    multibanked caches in, 299, **309**
    multilevel exclusion in, C-34
    organization of, 326, **327**
    Pentium 4 compared to, 136–138, **137, 138**
    performance on SPEC benchmarks, **35,** 37, 255–257, **255, 256, 257**
    translation lookaside buffer organization, C-44 to C-45, **C-45**
AMD Pacifica, 320, 339
Amdahl's Law
    law of diminishing returns and, 40
    limited available parallelism and, 202–203
    in multiple-issue processor performance, 184
    parallel computers and, 258–259
    pitfalls in using, 48
    resource allocation and, 40
    speedup determination, 39–40
America processor, K-21 to K-22
AMPS (advanced mobile phone service), D-25
Anderson, S. F., I-63
Andreessen, Marc, E-98
Andrew benchmark, 225
annulling, G-26
antialiasing, C-36 to C-37
antidependences, 70, G-7 to G-8, K-23
Apple Macintosh, memory addressing in, K-53
application binary interface (ABI), B-20
applied load, E-53
arbitration
    arbitration algorithm, E-49 to E-50, **E-49,** E-52
    overview of, E-21 to E-22

    in shared-media networks, E-23
    in switch microarchitecture, E-57 to E-58, E-60 to E-61, E-62
    in switched-media networks, E-24
    techniques for, E-49, **E-49**
    arbitration algorithm, E-49, E-52
areal density, 358
arithmetic. *See* computer arithmetic
arithmetic mean, 36
ARM
    addressing modes in, J-5 to J-6, **J-6**
    architecture overview, **J-4**
    common extensions in, J-19 to J-24, **J-23, J-24**
    conditional branch options in, **B-19, J-17**
    instructions unique to, J-36 to J-37
    MIPS core subset in, J-6 to J-16, **J-8, J-9, J-14 to J-17**
    multiply-accumulate in, J-19, **J-20**
ARM Thumb
    addressing modes in, J-5 to J-6, **J-6**
    architecture overview, **J-4**
    common extensions in, J-19 to J-24, **J-23, J-24**
    instructions unique to, J-37 to J-38
    MIPS core subset in, J-6 to J-16, **J-8, J-9, J-14 to J-17**
    multiply-accumulate in, J-19, **J-20**
    reduced code size in, B-23
ARPA (Advanced Research Project Agency), E-97, E-99
ARPANET, E-97 to E-98
arrays, age of access to, 304, **304**
array indexes, G-6
array multipliers, I-50 to I-54, **I-50 to I-54**
array processors, K-36
ASCI (Accelerated Strategic Computing Initiative), **E-20, E-44, E-56**
ASCI Red Paragon, **E-20, E-44, E-56**
ASCI White SP Power3, **E-20, E-44, E-56**

ASI (Advanced Switching Interconnect), E-103
associativity
    access times and, 294–295, **294**
    cache indexes and, 38, 291, C-38
    cache size and, 292
    miss rates and, 291, C-28 to C-29, **C-29, C-39**
    in multilevel caches, C-33 to C-34
    in virtual memory, C-42
Astronautics ZS-1, K-22
asynchronous events, A-40, A-41, **A-42**
asynchronous I/0, 391
asynchronous transfer mode (ATM)
    development of, E-98, E-99
    Ethernet compared with, E-89, **E-90**
    packet format for, **E-75**
    as telecommunications standard, E-79
    virtual output queues and, E-60
    as wide area network, E-4
ATA disks, 360–361, **361**, 365
Atanasoff, John, K-5
Atanasoff Berry Computer (ABC), K-5
Athlon 64 processor. *See* AMD Athlon 64 processor
Atlas computer, K-52
ATM. *See* asynchronous transfer mode
atomic exchange synchronization primitives, 238–240
atomic operations, 214
"atomic swap," J-20, **J-21**
attributes field, C-50 to C-51, **C-51**
autodecrement addressing mode, **B-9**
autoincrement addressing mode, **B-9**
availability claims, 399–400, **400**. *See also* reliability
average memory access time (AMAT)
    associativity and, C-28 to C-29, **C-29**
    block size and, C-26 to C-28, **C-26, C-27**
    cache size and, 295
    formula for, 290, C-15, **C-21**
    in multilevel caches, C-30 to C-31
    in out-of-order computers, C-19 to C-21, **C-21**
    processor performance and, C-17 to C-19

in split *vs.* unified caches, C-15 to C-17
    for two-level caches, C-30
average memory stall times, 298, C-56, **C-57**
average reception factor, E-26, E-32
average residual service time, 384

B

back substitution, G-10
backpressure, E-65
Baer, J.-L., K-54
bandwidth
    aggregate, E-13, E-17, E-24
    bisection, E-39, E-41, E-42, E-55, E-89
    communication, H-3
    defined, 15, C-2, E-13
    distributed memory and, 230
    DRAM improvements, 313
    in floating-point computations, I-62
    full bisection, E-39, E-41
    high-memory, 337–338, **339**
    improvements in, 15, **16**
    injection, E-18, E-26, E-41, E-55, E-63
    integrated instruction fetch units and, 126–127
    I/O, 371
    link injection, E-17
    link reception, E-17
    main memory, 310
    multibanked caches and, 298–299, **299, 309**
    in multiple processors, 205
    network performance and, E-16 to E-19, **E-19**, E-25 to E-29, **E-28**, E-89, **E-90**
    network switching and, E-50, E-52
    network topology and, E-41
    nonblocking caches and, 296–298, **297, 309**
    overestimating, 336, **338**
    packet discarding and, E-65
    pipelined cache access and, 296, **309**, A-7
    reception, E-18, E-26, E-41, E-55, E-63, E-89
    return address predictors and, 125, **126**

vector performance and, F-45
bandwidth gap, in disks and DRAM, 359
bandwidth matching, E-112
Banerjee, U., F-51, K-23
Banerjee tests, K-23
bank busy time, **F-15**, F-16
Barnes-Hut algorithm
    characteristics of, H-8 to H-9, **H-11**
    in distributed-memory multiprocessors, **H-28 to H-32**
    in symmetric shared-memory multiprocessors, H-21 to H-26, **H-23 to H-26**
barrier networks, H-42
barrier synchronization, H-13 to H-16, **H-14, H-15, H-16**
base fields, C-50
base registers, A-4
base station architectures, D-22
based plus scaled index mode, **J-58**
basic blocks, 67
Baskett, F., F-48
Bell, G., C-56, K-14, K-37 to K-39, K-52
benchmark suites, 30
benchmarks, 29–33. *See also* SPEC
    AltaVista, 221, **221, 222**
    Andrew, 225
    changes over time, 50
    compiler flags for, 29
    of dependability, 377–379, **378**
    desktop, 30–32
    EEMBC, 30, D-12 to D-13, **D-12, D-13, D-14**
    for embedded systems, D-12 to D-13, **D-12, D-13, D-14**
    evolution of SPEC, 30–32, **31**
    historical development of, K-6 to K-7
    Linpack, F-8 to F-9, F-37 to F-38
    NAS parallel, F-51
    Perfect Club, F-51
    reports of, 33
    reproducibility of, 33
    for servers, 32–33
    SFS, 376
    source code modifications and, 29–30
    suites, 30

benchmarks (*continued*)
  summarizing results from, 33–37,
    35
  synthetic, 29
  Transaction Processing Council,
    32, 374–375, **375**
  Web server, 32–33
Benes topology, E-33, **E-33**
Beowulf project, K-42
BER (bit error rate), D-21 to D-22
Berkeley RISC processor, K-12 to
  K-13
Berkeley's Tertiary Disk project, 368,
  369, 399, **399**
Berners-Lee, Tim, E-98
between *vs.* within instructions, A-41,
  A-42
biased exponents, I-15 to I-16
biased system, for signed numbers, I-7
bidirectional multistage, E-33
Big Endian byte order, B-7, B-34
Bigelow, Julian, K-3
BINAC, K-5
binary tree multipliers, I-53 to I-54
binary-coded decimal formats, B-14
binary-to-decimal conversion, I-34
Birman, M. A., I-58
bisection bandwidth, E-39, E-41,
  E-42, E-55, E-89
bisection traffic fraction, E-41 to E-42,
  E-55
bit error rate (BER), D-21 to D-22
bit selection, C-7
bit vectors, 232
bits
  access, C-50
  dirty, C-10, C-44
  NaT (Not a Thing), G-38 G-40
  poison, G-28, G-30 to G-32
  present, C-50
  sticky, I-18
  use, C-43 to C-44
  valid, C-8
block addressing, 299, **299,** C-8 to
  C-9, **C-8**
block multithreading, K-26
block offsets, C-8, **C-8**
block servers, 390–391
block size
  miss rates and, 252, **252,** 291,
    C-25 to C-28, **C-26, C-27,**
    C-39

multilevel inclusion and, 248–249
multiprogrammed cache misses
  and, 227–230, **228, 229**
  in shared-memory
    multiprocessors, H-27 to
    H-29, **H-29, H-31**
  SMP cache misses and, 223–224
block transfer engines (BLT), E-87,
  E-87
blocked floating point, D-6
blocking
  in centralized switched networks,
    E-32
  network topology and, E-41
  to reduce miss rate, 303–305, **304**
  in switching, E-51
blocking factors, 303
blocks
  defined, C-2
  destination, H-8
  in directory-based protocols,
    234–237, **235**
  dirty *vs.* clean, C-10
  exclusive, 210–211, **214, 215**
  invalid, 211–212, **213, 214, 215**
  modified, 211, **213,** 231
  owners of, 211, 231, **235**
  placement in main memory, C-42
  replacement, C-9, **C-10,** C-14,
    C-40, C-43 to C-44
  set-associative placement of, 38,
    289
  shared, 211, **213, 214, 215,** 231
  state transition diagrams,
    234–236, **235, 236**
  uncached, 231
  unmodified, **214**
  victim, 301
  write invalidate protocols and, 211
Blue Gene/L. *See* IBM Blue Gene/L
BOMB, K-4
Booth recoding, I-8 to I-9, **I-9,** I-48 to
  I-49, **I-49**
Bouknight, W. Jack, 195, K-36
bounds checking, C-50, **C-51**
branch costs, 80–89, **81, 84, 85, 87, 88**
branch delay, A-35 to A-37, A-60,
  A-60, A-65. *See also* delayed
    branch schemes
branch delay slot, A-23 to A-25, **A-23,**
  A-24
branch displacements, J-39

branch folding, 125
branch hazards, A-21 to A-26. *See also*
  control hazards
  instruction fetch cycle and, A-21,
    A-21
  in MIPS pipeline, A-35 to A-37,
    A-38
  in MIPS R4000 pipeline, A-64,
    A-65
  performance of branch schemes,
    A-25 to A-26, **A-26**
  reducing penalties, **A-21,** A-22 to
    A-25, **A-22, A-23, A-24**
  restarting, A-42 to A-43
branch history tables, 82–86, **83, 84,**
  85
branch prediction. *See* hardware
  branch prediction; static
    branch prediction
branch registers, J-32 to J-33
branches
  branch target distances, B-18,
    B-18
  conditional branch operations,
    B-19, **B-19, B-20**
  in control flow instructions, B-16,
    B-17, B-18, B-37 to B-38,
    B-38
  history tables, 82–86, **83, 84, 85**
  in IBM 360, J-86 to J-87, **J-86,**
    J-87
  penalties, A-36 to A-37, **A-39**
  registers, J-32 to J-33
  in RISC architecture, A-5
  straightening, 302
  vectored, J-35
branch-prediction buffers, 82–86, **83,**
  84, 85
branch-target buffers (BTB), 122–125,
  122, 124
branch-target calculations, A-35, **A-38,**
  A-39
breakpoints, **A-40, A-42**
Brent, R. P., I-63
bridges, E-78
bristling, E-38, E-92
broadcasting, E-24, H-35 to H-36
Brooks, F. P., Jr., C-49
BTB (branch-target buffers), 122–125,
  122, 124
bubble flow control, E-53, E-73

bubbles, pipeline, A-13, A-20, E-47.
See also pipeline stalls
buckets, in histograms, 382
buffered crossbars, E-62
buffered wormhole switching, E-51
buffers. *See also* translation lookaside
buffers
branch-prediction, 82–86, **83, 84,
85**
branch-target, 122–125, **122, 124**
buffered crossbars, E-62
central, E-57
development of, K-22
in disk storage, 360, **360**
instruction, A-15
limited, H-38 to H-40
load, 94, **94,** 95, 97, **101,** 102–103
reorder, 106–114, **107, 110, 111,
113,** G-31 to G-32
streaming, K-54
victim, 301, 330, C-14
write, 210, 289, 291, 300–301,
301, 309
bundles, G-34 to G-36, **G-36, G-37**
Burks, A. W., 287, I-62, K-3
buses
in barrier synchronization, H-15
to H-16, **H-16**
bottlenecks in, 216, **216**
data misses and, H-26, **H-26**
development of, K-62 to K-63
fairness in, H-13
point-to-point links replacing,
390, **390**
in scoreboarding, A-70, A-73
in shared-media networks, E-22,
E-22, E-40
single-bus systems, 217–218
in snooping coherence protocols,
211–212, **213, 214, 215**
in Tomasulo's approach, 93, 95,
96, 98, **101**
in write invalidates, 209–210, 212,
213
bypassing. *See* forwarding
byte addressing, 9, **299**
byte order, B-7 to B-8, **B-8**

C

C description language extensions,
B-9, B-36 to B-37

C language, integer division and
remainder in, **I-12**
caches
2:1 cache rule of thumb, C-28
AMD Opteron data cache
example, C-12 to C-14, **C-13,
C-15**
block addressing, 299, **299,** C-8 to
C-9, **C-8**
block placement in, C-7 to C-8,
C-7
block size, H-25 to H-26, **H-25**
data, C-9, C-13, **C-15,** F-46
defined, C-2
development of, K-53
in IBM Blue Gene/L, H-42
interprocessor communication
and, H-5
L1 (*See* L1 cache)
L2 (*See* L2 cache)
multibanked, 298–299, **299, 309**
multilevel, 291
nonblocking, 296–298, **297, 309,**
K-54
remote communication latency
and, 205
in RISC pipelines, A-7
separated, C-14
SMT challenges to, 176–177
states of, 212
in superscalar processors, 155
tags in, 210–211, 289, C-36
trace, 131, **132, 133,** 296, **309**
victim, 301, K-54
virtual, C-36 to C-38, **C-37**
virtual memory compared with,
C-40, **C-41**
writes in, C-9 to C-12, **C-10,** C-13
cache access, pipelined, 296
cache associativity. *See* associativity
cache banks, 298–299, **299**
cache blocks. *See* blocks
cache coherence problem. *See also*
cache coherence protocols
cache coherence protocols and,
207–208
I/O, 325–326
overview of, 205–207, **206**
snooping protocols, 208–209, **209**
snooping protocol example,
211–215, **213, 214, 215**

state diagrams and, **214, 215**
write invalidate protocol
implementation, 209–211
cache coherence protocols. *See also*
cache coherence problem;
directory-based cache
coherence protocols
avoiding deadlock from limiting
buffering, H-38 to H-40
directory controller
implementation, H-40 to
H-41
in distributed shared-memory
multiprocessors, H-36 to
H-37
in distributed-memory
multiprocessors, 232–233,
232, 233
in large-scale multiprocessors,
H-34 to H-41
memory consistency in, 243–246
snooping protocols and, 208–218,
H-34, H-35
spin lock scheme and, 241–242,
242
synchronization and, 240–242,
242
uniform memory access and, 217
cache CPI equation, 168
cache hierarchy. *See also* memory
hierarchy
in AlphaServer 4100, 220
cache organization overview,
288–293, **292**
multilevel inclusion, 248–249
cache hits, C-2
cache indexing
address translation during,
291–292, C-36 to C-38, **C-37,
C-39**
in AMD Opteron, 326, 329, C-12
equation for, 326, 329, **C-21**
index size and, C-38, C-46
cache misses
block replacement in, **C-10,** C-14
categories of, C-22 to C-24, **C-23,
C-24**
communication of, H-35 to H-36
defined, C-2
in in-order execution, C-2 to C-3
in invalidate protocols, 210–211
cache misses

cache misses (*continued*)
  nonblocking caches and,
    296–298, **297, 309**
  processor performance and, C-17
    to C-19
  in SMP commercial workloads,
    222–223, **222, 223**
cache optimizations, C-22 to C-38
  average memory access time
    formula, 290, C-15, **C-21**
  avoiding address translation
    during cache indexing, C-36
    to C-38, **C-37, C-39**
  categories of, C-22
  higher associativity and, C-28 to
    C-29, **C-29, C-39**
  larger block sizes and, C-25 to
    C-28, **C-26, C-27, C-39**
  larger cache sizes and, **C-23,
    C-24,** C-28, **C-39**
  miss rate components and, C-22
    to C-25, **C-23, C-24**
  multilevel caches and, C-29 to
    C-34, **C-32, C-39**
  read priorities over writes, C-34 to
    C-35, **C-39**
cache performance, C-15 to C-21
  average memory access time and,
    290, 295, C-15 to C-17
  cache size and, 293–295, **294, 309**
  compiler optimizations and,
    302–305, **304, 309**
  compiler-controlled prefetching
    and, 305–309, **309**
  critical word first and early restart,
    299–300, **309**
  hardware prefetching and, 305,
    306, 309
  high memory bandwidth and,
    337–338, **339**
  merging write buffers and,
    300–301, **301, 309**
  miss penalties and out-of-order
    processors, C-19 to C-21,
    C-21
  multibanked caches and,
    298–299, **299, 309**
  nonblocking caches and,
    296–298, **297, 309**
  optimization summary, 309, **309**
  overemphasizing DRAM
    bandwidth, 336, **338**

overview of, C-3 to C-6
pipelined cache access and, 296,
  309
predicting from other programs,
  335, **335**
sufficient simulations for, 336,
  337
trace caches and, 296, **309**
way prediction and, 295, **309**
cache prefetching, 126–127, 305–306,
  306, 309
cache replacement miss, **214**
cache size
  2:1 cache rule of thumb, C-28
  hit time and, 293–295, **294, 309**
  miss rates and, 252, **252,** 291,
    C-25 to C-28, **C-26, C-27,
    C-39**
  multiprogrammed workload
    misses and, 227–230, **228,
    229**
  performance and, H-22, H-24,
    H-24, H-27, **H-28**
  SMP workload misses and,
    223–224, **223, 224, 226**
cache-only memory architecture
  (COMA), K-41
CACTI, 294, **294**
call gates, C-52
callee saving, B-19 to B-20, B-41 to
  B-43
caller saving, B-19 to B-20
canceling branches, A-24 to A-25
canonical form, C-53
capabilities, in protection, C-48 to
  C-49, K-52
capacitive load, 18
capacity misses
  defined, 290, C-22
  relative frequency of, C-22, **C-23,
    C-24**
  in shared-memory
    multiprocessors, H-22 to
    H-26, **H-23 to H-26**
carrier sensing, E-23
carrier signals, D-21
carry-lookahead adders (CLA), 38,
  I-37 to I-41, **I-38, I-40 to
  I-42, I-44,** I-63
carry-propagate adders (CPAs), I-48
carry-save adders (CSAs), I-47 to I-48,
  I-48, I-50, I-55

carry-select adders, I-43 to I-44, **I-43,
  I-44**
carry-skip adders, I-41 to I-43, **I-42,
  I-44**
CAS (column access strobe), 311–313,
  313
case statements, register indirect
  jumps for, B-18
CCD (charged-couple device), D-19
CDB (common data bus), 93, 95, 96,
  98, **101**
CDC 6600 processor
  data trunks in, A-70
  dynamic scheduling in, 95, A-67
    to A-68, **A-68,** K-19
  multithreading in, K-26
  pipelining in, K-10
CDC STAR-100, F-44, F-47
CDC vector computers, F-4, **F-34**
CDMA (code division multiple
  access), D-25
Cell Broadband Engines (Cell BE),
  E-70 to E-72, **E-71**
cell phones, D-20 to D-25, **D-21,
  D-23, D-24**
cells, in octrees, H-9
centralized shared-memory
  architectures, 199–200, **200**.
  See also symmetric
  shared-memory
  multiprocessors
centralized switched networks, E-30 to
  E-34, **E-31, E-33,** E-48
centrally buffered, E-57
CFM (current frame pointer), G-33 to
  G-34
Chai, L., **E-77**
chaining, F-35, **F-35**
channel adapters, E-7
channels, D-24
character operands, B-13
character strings, B-14
charged-couple devices (CCD), D-19
checksum, E-8, E-12
chimes, F-10 to F-12, F-20, F-40
choke packets, E-65
Cholesky factorization method, H-8
CIFS (Common Internet File System),
  391
circuit switching, E-50, E-64
circular queues, E-56

CISC (complex instruction set computer), J-65
CLA (carry-lookahead adders), 38, I-37 to I-41, **I-38, I-40 to I-42, I-44,** I-63
clock cycles (clock rate)
    associativity and, C-28 to C-29, **C-29**
    CPI and, 140–141
    memory stall cycles and, C-4 to C-5, C-20
    processor speed and, 138–139, **139**
    SMT challenges and, 176, **179,** 181, 183
clock cycles per instruction (CPI)
    in AMD Opteron, 331–335, **332, 333, 334**
    cache, 168
    cache misses and, C-18
    computation of, 41–44, 203–204
    ideal pipeline, 66–67, **67**
    in Pentium 4, 134, 136, **136**
    pipelining and, A-3, **A-7, A-8,** A-12
    processor speed and, 138–139
    in symmetric shared-memory multiprocessors, 221, **222**
clock rate. *See* clock cycles
clock skew, A-10
Clos topology, E-33, **E-33**
clusters
    commodity *vs.* custom, 198
    development of, K-41 to K-44
    in IBM Blue Gene/L, H-41 to H-44, **H-43, H-44**
    Internet Archive, 392–397, **394**
    in large-scale multiprocessors, H-44 to H-46, **H-45**
Cm* multiprocessor, K-36
C.mmp project, K-36
CMOS chips, 18–19, 294, **294,** F-46
coarse-grained multithreading, 173–174, **174,** K-26. *See also* multithreading
Cocke, John, K-12, K-20, K-21 to K-22
code division multiple access (CDMA), D-25
code rearrangement, miss rate reduction from, 302

code scheduling. *See also* dynamic scheduling
    for control dependences, 73–74
    global, 116, G-15 to G-23, **G-16, G-20, G-22**
    local, 116
    loop unrolling and, 79–80, 117–118
    static scheduling, A-66
code size, 80, 117, D-3, D-9
CodePack, B-23
coefficient of variance, 383
coerced exceptions, A-40 to A-41, **A-42**
coherence, 206–208. *See also* cache coherence problem; cache coherence protocols
coherence misses
    defined, 218, C-22
    in multiprogramming example, **229**
    in symmetric shared-memory multiprocessors, H-21 to H-26, **H-23 to H-26**
    true *vs.* false sharing, 218–219
cold-start misses, C-22. *See also* compulsory misses
collision detection, E-23
collision misses, C-22
collocation sites, E-85
COLOSSUS, K-4
column access strobe (CAS), 311–313, **313**
column major order, 303
COMA (cache-only memory architecture), K-41
combining trees, H-18
commercial workloads
    Decision Support System, 220
    multiprogramming and OS performance, 225–230, **227, 228, 229**
    online transaction processing, 220
    SMP performance in, 220–224, **221 to 226**
committed instructions, A-45
commodities, computers as, 21
commodity clusters, 198, H-45 to H-46, **H-45**
common case, focusing on, 38
common data bus (CDB), 93, 95, 96, 98, **101**

Common Internet File System (CIFS), 391
communication
    bandwidth, H-3
    cache misses and, H-35 to H-36
    global system for mobile communication, D-25
    interprocessor, H-3 to H-6
    latency, H-3 to H-4
    message-passing *vs.* shared-memory, H-4 to H-6
    multiprocessing models, 201–202
    NEWS, E-41 to E-42
    peer-to-peer, E-81 to E-82
    remote access, 203–204
    user-level, E-8
compare, select, and store units (CSSU), D-8
compare and branch instruction, B-19, **B-19**
compare instructions, B-37
compiler optimization, 302–305
    branch straightening, 302
    compared with other techniques, **309**
    compiler structure and, B-24 to B-26, **B-25**
    examples of, B-27, **B-28**
    graph coloring, B-26 to B-27
    impact on performance, B-27, **B-29**
    instruction set guidelines for, B-29 to B-30
    loop interchange, 302–303
    phase-ordering problem in, B-26
    reducing code size and, B-43, **B-44**
    technique classification, B-26, **B-28**
    in vectorization, F-32 to F-34, **F-33, F-34**
compilers
    compiler-controlled prefetching, 305–309, **309**
    development of, K-23 to K-24
    eliminating dependent computations, G-10 to G-12
    finding dependences, G-6 to G-10
    global code scheduling, 116, G-15 to G-23, **G-16, G-20, G-22**
    Java, K-10
compilers

compilers (*continued*)
    multimedia instruction support,
        B-31 to B-32
    performance of, B-27, **B-29**
    recent structures of, B-24 to B-26,
        B-25
    register allocation in, B-26 to
        B-27
    scheduling, A-66
    software pipelining in, G-12 to
        G-15, **G-13, G-15**
    speculation, G-28 to G-32
complex instruction set computer
    (CISC), J-65
component failures, 367
compulsory misses
    defined, 290, C-22
    in multiprogramming example,
        228, **229**
    relative frequency of, C-22, **C-23,**
        C-24
    in SMT commercial workloads,
        222, **224, 225**
computation-to-communication ratios,
    H-10 to H-12, **H-11**
computer architecture
    defined, 8, 12, J-84, K-10
    designing, 12–13, **13**
    flawless design fallacy, J-81
    functional requirements in, **13**
    historical perspectives on, J-83 to
        J-84, K-10 to K-11
    instruction set architecture, 8–12,
        9, 11, 12
    organization and hardware,
        12–15, **13**
    quantitative design principles,
        37–44
    signed numbers in, I-7 to I-10
    trends in, 14–16, **15, 16**
computer arithmetic, I-1 to I-65
    carry-lookahead adders, I-37 to
        I-41, **I-38, I-40, I-41, I-42,**
        I-44
    carry-propagate adders, I-48
    carry-save adders, I-47 to I-48,
        I-48
    carry-select adders, I-43 to I-44,
        I-43, I-44
    carry-skip adders, I-41 to I-43,
        I-42, I-44

chip design and, I-58 to I-61, **I-58,**
    I-59, I-60
denormalized numbers, I-15, I-20
    to I-21, I-26 to I-27, I-36
exceptions, I-34 to I-35
faster division with one adder,
    I-54 to I-58, **I-55, I-56, I-57**
faster multiplication with many
    adders, I-50 to I-54, **I-50 to**
    I-54
faster multiplication with single
    adders, I-47 to I-50, **I-48,**
    I-49
floating-point addition, I-21 to
    I-27, **I-24,** I-36
floating-point arithmetic, I-13 to
    I-16, I-21 to I-27, **I-24**
floating-point multiplication, I-17
    to I-21, **I-18, I-19, I-20**
floating-point number
    representation, I-15 to I-16,
    I-16
floating-point remainder, I-31 to
    I-32
fused multiply-add, I-32 to I-33
historical perspectives on, I-62 to
    I-65
instructions in RISC architectures,
    J-22, **J-22, J-23, J-24**
iterative division, I-27 to I-31,
    I-28
overflow, I-8, I-10 to I-12, **I-11,**
    I-20
in PA-RISC architecture, J-34 to
    J-35, J-36
pipelining in, I-15
precision in, **I-16,** I-21, I-33 to
    I-34
radix-2 multiplication and
    division, I-4 to I-7, **I-4, I-6,**
    I-55 to I-58, **I-56, I-57**
ripple-carry adders, I-2 to I-3, **I-3,**
    I-42, I-44
shifting over zeros technique, I-45
    to I-47, **I-46**
signed numbers, I-7 to I-10, I-23,
    I-24, I-26
special values in, I-14 to I-15
subtraction, I-22 to I-23, I-45
systems issues, I-10 to I-13, **I-11,**
    I-12

underflow, I-36 to I-37, I-62
computers, classes of, 4–8
condition codes, A-5, A-46, **B-19,** J-9
    to J-16, J-71
condition registers, **B-19**
conditional branch operations
    in control flow, B-19, **B-19, B-20**
    in RISC architecture, J-11 to J-12,
        J-17, J-34, **J-34**
conditional instructions. *See*
    predicated instructions
conditional moves, G-23 to G-24
conflict misses
    defined, 290, C-22
    four divisions of, C-24 to C-25
    relative frequency of, C-22, **C-23,**
        C-24
congestion management, E-11, E-12,
    E-54, E-65
connectedness, E-29
Connection Multiprocessor 2, K-35
connectivity, E-62 to E-63
consistency. *See* cache coherence
    problem; cache coherence
    protocols; memory
    consistency models
constant extension, in RISC
    architecture, J-6, **J-9**
constellation, **H-45**
contention
    in centralized switched networks,
        E-32
    congestion from, E-89
    in network performance, E-25,
        E-53
    network topologies and, E-38
    in routing, E-45, E-47
    in shared-memory
        multiprocessors, H-29
contention delay, E-25, E-52
context switch, 316, C-48
control dependences, 72–74, 104–105,
    G-16
control flow instructions, B-16 to B-21
    addressing modes for, B-17 to
        B-18, **B-18**
    conditional branch operations,
        B-19, **B-19, B-20**
    in Intel 80x86, J-51
    in MIPS architecture, B-37 to
        B-38, **B-38**

procedure invocation options,
B-19 to B-20
types of, B-16 to B-17, **B-17**
control hazards, A-11, A-21 to A-26,
A-21 to A-26, F-3. *See also*
branch hazards; pipeline
hazards
control stalls, 74
Convex C-1, **F-7, F-34,** F-49
Convex Exemplar, K-41
convoys, F-10 to F-12, **F-13,** F-18,
F-35, F-39
Conway, L., I-63
cooling, 19
Coonen, J., I-34
copy propagation, G-10 to G-11
core plus ASIC (system on a chip),
D-3, D-19, **D-20**
correlating predictors, 83–86, **84, 85,
87, 88**
Cosmic Cube, K-40
costs, 19–25
in benchmarks, 375
of branches, 80–89, **81, 84, 85, 87,
88**
commodities and, 21
disk power and, **361**
of integrated circuits, 21–25, **22,
23**
in interconnection networks,
E-40, E-89, E-92
of Internet Archive clusters,
394–396
learning curve and, 19
linear speedups in multiprocessors
and, 259–260, **261**
prices *vs.,* 25–28
of RDRAM, 336, **338**
of transaction-processing servers,
49–50, **49**
trends in, 19–25
of various computing classes, **D-4**
volume and, 20–21
yield and, 19–20, **20,** 22–24
count registers, J-32 to J-33
CPAs (carry-propagate adders), I-48
CPI. *See* clock cycles per instruction
CPU time, 28–29, 41–45, C-17 to
C-18, **C-21**
Cray, Seymour, F-1, F-48, F-50
Cray arithmetic algorithms, I-64

Cray C90, **F-7,** F-32, F-50
Cray J90, F-50
Cray SV1, **F-7**
Cray T3D, E-86 to E-87, **E-87,** F-50,
K-40
Cray T3E, 260, K-40
Cray T90, **F-7,** F-14, F-50
Cray T932, F-14
Cray X1
characteristics of, **F-7**
memory in, F-46
multi-streaming processors in,
F-43
processor architecture in, F-40 to
F-43, **F-41, F-42,** F-51
Cray X1E, **E-20, E-44, E-56,** F-44,
F-51
Cray X-MP
characteristics of, **F-7**
innovations in, F-48
memory pipelines on, F-38
multiple processors in, F-49
peak performance in, F-44
vectorizing compilers in, **F-34**
Cray XT3, **E-20, E-44, E-56**
Cray Y-MP, **F-7,** F-32 to F-33, **F-33,**
F-49 to F-50
Cray-1
chaining in, F-23
characteristics of, **F-7**
development of, K-12
innovations in, F-48
memory bandwidth in, F-45
peak performance on, F-44
register file in, F-5
Cray-2, **F-34,** F-46, F-48
Cray-3, F-50
credit-based flow control, E-10, E-65,
E-71, E-74
critical path, G-16, G-19
critical word first strategy, 299–300,
309
crossbars, 216, E-30, **E-31,** E-60
cryptanalysis machines, K-4
CSAs (carry-save adders), I-47 to I-48,
I-48, I-50, I-55
CSSU (compare, select, and store
units), D-8
current frame pointers (CFM), G-33 to
G-34
custom clusters, 198, **H-45**

cut-through switching, E-50, E-60,
E-74
CYBER 180/990, A-55
CYBER 205, F-44, F-48
cycle time, 310–311, **313**
Cydrome Cydra 5, K-22 to K-23

D

Dally, Bill, E-1
DAMQ (dynamically allocatable
multi-queues), E-56 to E-57
Darley, H. M., I-58
DARPA (Defense Advanced Research
Projects Agency), F-51
data alignment, B-7 to B-8, **B-8**
data caches, C-9, C-13, **C-15,** F-46
data dependences, 68–70, G-16
data flow
control dependences and, 73–74
double data rate, 314–315, **314**
executions, 105
hardware-based speculation and,
105
as ILP limitation, 170
value prediction and, 170
data hazards. *See also* RAW hazards;
WAR hazards; WAW hazards
2-cycle stalls, A-59, **A-59**
minimizing stalls by forwarding,
A-17 to A-18, **A-18,** A-35,
A-36, A-37
in MIPS pipelines, A-35 to A-37,
A-38, A-39
in pipelining, A-11, A-15 to A-21,
A-16, A-18 to A-21
requiring stalls, A-19 to A-20,
A-20, A-21
in Tomasulo's approach, 96
in vector processors, F-2 to F-3,
F-10
data miss rates
on distributed-memory
multiprocessors, H-26 to
H-32, **H-28 to H-32**
hardware-controlled prefetch and,
307–309
in multiprogramming and OS
workloads, 228, **228, 229**
on symmetric shared-memory
multiprocessors, H-21 to
H-26, **H-23 to H-26**

data parallelism, K-35
data paths
    for eight-stage pipelines, A-57 to
        A-59, **A-58, A-59**
    in MIPS implementation, **A-29**
    in MIPS pipelines, A-30 to A-31,
        A-31, A-35, **A-37**
    in RISC pipelines, A-7, **A-8,** A-9
data races, 245
data rearrangement, miss rate
        reduction from, 302
data transfer time, 311–313, **313**
data trunks, A-70
datagrams, E-8, E-83
data-level parallelism, 68, 197, 199
data-race-free programs, 245, K-44
DDR (double data rate), 314–315, **314**
dead time, F-31 to F-32, **F-31**
dead values, 74
deadlock avoidance, E-45
deadlock recovery, E-46
deadlocked protocols, 214
deadlocks
    adaptive routing and, E-93
    bubble flow control and, E-53
    characteristics of, H-38
    in dynamic network
        reconfiguration, E-67
    from limited buffering, H-38 to
        H-40
    in network routing, E-45, E-47,
        E-48
DeCegama, Angel, K-37
decimal operations, J-35
decision support systems (DSS),
        220–221, **221, 222**
decoding
    forward error correction codes,
        D-6
    in RISC instruction set
        implementation, A-5 to A-6
    in unpipelined MIPS
        implementation, A-27
dedicated link networks, E-5, E-6, **E-6**
Defense Advanced Research Projects
        Agency (DARPA), F-51
delayed branch schemes
    development of, K-24
    in MIPS R4000 pipeline, A-60,
        A-60

in pipeline hazard prevention,
        A-23 to A-25, **A-23**
    in restarting execution, A-43
    in RISC architectures, J-22, **J-22**
Dell 2650, **322**
Dell PowerEdge 1600SC, **323**
Dell PowerEdge 2800, **47, 48, 49**
Dell PowerEdge 2850, **47, 48, 49**
Dell Precision Workstation 380, **45**
denormalized numbers, I-15, I-20 to
        I-21, I-26 to I-27, I-36
density-optimized processors, E-85
dependability. *See* reliability
dependence analysis, G-6 to G-10
dependence distance, G-6
dependences, 68–75. *See also* pipeline
        hazards
    control, 72–74, 104–105, G-16
    data, 68–70, G-16
    eliminating dependent
        computations, G-10 to G-12
    finding, G-6 to G-10
    greatest common divisor test, G-7
    interprocedural analysis, G-10
    loop unrolling and, G-8 to G-9
    loop-carried, G-3 to G-5
    name, 70–71
    number of registers to analyze,
        157
    recurrences, G-5, G-11 to G-12
    types of, G-7 to G-8
    unnecessary, as ILP limitations,
        169–170
depth of pipeline, A-12
descriptor privilege level (DPL), **C-51**
descriptor tables, C-50 to C-51
design faults, 367, **370**
desktop computers
    benchmarks for, 30–32
    characteristics of, **D-4**
    disk storage on, K-61 to K-62
    instruction set principles in, B-2
    memory hierarchy in, **341**
    multimedia support for, **D-11**
    operand type and size in, B-13 to
        B-14
    performance and
        price-performance of, 44–46,
        45, 46
    rise of, 4
    system characteristics, 5, **5**

Dest field, 109
destination blocks, H-8
deterministic routing, E-46, E-53,
        E-54, E-93
devices, E-2
Dhrystone performance, 30, D-12
die yield, 22–24
dies, costs of, 21–25, **22, 23**
Digital Alpha. *See* Alpha
digital cameras, D-19, **D-20**
Digital Equipment Vax, 2
Digital Linear Tape, K-59
digital signal processors (DSP), D-5 to
        D-11
    in cell phones, D-23, **D-23**
    defined, D-3
    media extensions, D-10 to D-11,
        D-11
    multiply-accumulate in, J-19,
        J-20
    overview, D-5 to D-7, **D-6**
    saturating arithmetic in, D-11
    TI 320C6x, D-8 to D-10, **D-9,
        D-10**
    TI TMS320C55, D-6 to D-8, **D-6,
        D-7**
dimension-order routing, E-46, E-53
DIMMs (dual inline memory
        modules), 312, 314, **314**
direct addressing mode, **B-9**
direct attached disks, 391
direct networks, E-34, **E-37,** E-48,
        E-67, E-92
Direct RDRAM, 336, **338**
direct-mapped caches
    block addresses in, C-8, **C-8**
    block replacement with cache
        misses, C-9, **C-10**
    defined, 289, C-7 to C-8, **C-7**
    development of, K-53
    size of, 291, **292**
directory controllers, H-40 to H-41
directory-based cache coherence
        protocols
    defined, 208, 231
    development of, K-40 to K-41
    distributed shared-memory and,
        230–237, **232, 233, 235, 236**
    example, 234–237, **235, 236**
    overview of, 231–234, **232, 233**

directory-based multiprocessors, H-29, **H-31**
dirty bits, C-10, C-44
Discrete Cosine Transform, D-5
Discrete Fourier Transform, D-5
disk arrays, 362–366, **363, 365,** K-61 to K-62. *See also* RAID
disk storage
    areal density in, 358
    buffers in, 360, **360**
    development of, K-59 to K-61
    disk arrays, 362–366, **363, 365**
    DRAM compared with, 359
    failure rate of, 50–51
    intelligent interfaces in, 360, **360, 361**
    power in, 361
    RAID, K-61 to K-62 (*See also* RAID)
    Tandem disks, 368–369, **370**
    technology growth in, 14, 358–359, **358**
    Tertiary Disk project, 368, **369,** 399, **399**
dispatch stage, 95
displacement addressing mode
    in Intel 80x86, J-47
    overview, **B-9,** B-10 to B-11, **B-11, B-12**
display lists, D-17 to D-18
distributed routing, E-48
distributed shared-memory (DSM) multiprocessors. *See also* multiprocessing
    cache coherence in, H-36 to H-37
    defined, 202
    development of, K-40
    directory-based coherence and, 230–237, **232, 233, 235, 236**
    in large-scale multiprocessors, **H-45**
    latency of memory references in, **H-32**
distributed switched networks, E-34 to E-39, **E-36, E-37, E-40,** E-46
distributed-memory multiprocessors
    advantages and disadvantages of, 201
    architecture of, 200–201, **201**
    scientific applications on, H-26 to H-32, **H-28 to H-32**

division
    faster, with one adder, I-54 to I-58, **I-55, I-56, I-57**
    floating-point remainder, I-31 to I-32
    fused multiply-add, I-32 to I-33
    iterative, I-27 to I-31, **I-28**
    radix-2 integer, I-4 to I-7, **I-4, I-6,** I-55 to I-56, **I-55**
    shifting over zeros technique, I-45 to I-47, **I-46**
    speed of, I-30 to I-31
    SRT, I-45 to I-47, **I-46,** I-55 to I-58, **I-57**
do loops, dependences in, 169
Dongarra, J. J., F-48
double data rate (DDR), 314–315, **314**
double extended precision, **I-16,** I-33
double precision, **A-64, I-16,** I-33, J-46
double words, J-50
double-precision floating-point operands, **A-64**
downtime, cost of, **6**
DPL (descriptor privilege level), **C-51**
DRAM (dynamic RAM)
    costs of, 19–20, **359**
    DRDRAM, 336, **338**
    embedded, D-16 to D-17, **D-16**
    historical performance of, 312, **313**
    memory performance improvement in, 312–315, **314**
    optimization of, 310
    organization of, 311–312, **311**
    overestimating bandwidth in, 336, **338**
    redundant memory cells in, 24
    refresh time in, 312
    synchronous, 313–314
    technology growth, 14
    in vector processors, F-46, F-48
DRDRAM (direct RDRAM), 336, **338**
driver domains, 321–322, **323**
DSM. *See* distributed shared-memory (DSM) multiprocessors
DSP. *See* digital signal processors
DSS (decision support system), 220–221, **221, 222**
dual inline memory modules (DIMMs), 312, 314, **314**

Duato's Protocol, E-47
dynamic branch frequency, 67
dynamic branch prediction, 82–86, D-4. *See also* hardware branch prediction
dynamic memory disambiguation. *See* memory alias analysis
dynamic network reconfiguration, E-67
dynamic power, 18–19
dynamic RAM. *See* DRAM
dynamic scheduling, 89–104. *See also* Tomasulo's approach
    advantages of, 89
    defined, 89
    development of, K-19, K-22
    evaluation pitfalls, A-76
    examples of, 97–99, **99, 100**
    loop-based example, 102–104
    multiple issue and speculation in, 118–121, **120, 121**
    overview, 90–92
    scoreboarding technique, A-66 to A-75, **A-68, A-71** to **A-75**
    Tomasulo's algorithm and, 92–97, 100–104, **101, 103**
dynamically allocatable multi-queues (DAMQs), E-56 to E-57
dynamically shared libraries, B-18

E
early restart strategy, 299–300
Earth Simulator, F-3 to F-4, F-51
Ecache, F-41 to F-43
Eckert, J. Presper, K-2 to K-3, K-5
e-cube routing, E-46
EDN Embedded Microprocessor Benchmark Consortium (EEMBC), 30, D-12 to D-13, **D-12, D-13, D-14**
EDSAC, K-3
EDVAC, K-2 to K-3
EEMBC benchmarks, 30, D-12 to D-13, **D-12, D-13, D-14**
effective address, A-4, B-9
effective bandwidth
    defined, E-13
    in Element Interconnect Bus, E-72
    latency and, E-25 to E-29, **E-27, E-28**

effective bandwidth (*continued*)
  network performance and, E-16 to
    E-19, **E-19**, E-25 to E-29,
    E-28, E-89, **E-90**
  network switching and, E-50,
    E-52
  network topology and, E-41
  packet size and, E-18, **E-19**
effective errors, 367
efficiency, EEMBC benchmarks for,
  D-13, **D-13, D-14**
efficiency factor, E-52, E-55
EIB (Element Interconnect Bus), E-3,
  E-70, **E-71**
eigenvalue method, H-8
eight-way conflict misses, C-24
80x86 processors. *See* Intel 80x86
ElanSC520, D-13, **D-13**
elapsed time, 28. *See also* latency
Element Interconnect Bus (EIB), E-3,
  E-70, **E-71**
embedded systems, D-1 to D-26
  benchmarks in, D-12 to D-13,
    D-12, D-13, D-14
  cell phones, D-20 to D-25, **D-21,
    D-23, D-24**
  characteristics of, **D-4**
  costs of, **5**
  data addressing modes in, J-5 to
    J-6, **J-6**
  defined, 5
  digital signal processors in, J-19
  instruction set principles in, 4, B-2
  media extensions in, D-10 to
    D-11, **D-11**
  MIPS extensions in, J-19 to J-24,
    J-23, J-24
  multiprocessors, D-3, D-14 to
    D-15
  overview, 7–8
  power consumption and efficiency
    in, D-13, **D-13**
  real-time constraints in, D-2
  real-time processing in, D-3 to
    D-5
  reduced code size in RISCs, B-23
    to B-24
  in Sanyo VPC-SX500 digital
    camera, D-19, **D-20**
  in Sony Playstation 2, D-15 to
    D-18, **D-16, D-18**

  in TI 320C6x, D-8 to D-10, **D-9,
    D-10**
  in TI TMS320C55, D-6 to D-8,
    D-6, D-7
  vector instructions in, F-47
Emer, Joel, K-7
Emotion Engine, SP2, D-15 to D-18,
  D-16, D-18
encoding, B-21 to B-24
  fixed-length, 10, B-22, **B-22**
  hybrid, **B-22,** B-23
  in packet transport, E-9
  reduced code size in RISCs, B-23
    to B-24
  variable-length, 10, B-22 to B-23,
    B-22
  in VAX, J-68 to J-70, **J-69**
end-to-end flow control, E-65, E-94 to
  E-95
energy efficiency, 182
EnergyBench, D-13, **D-13**
Engineering Research Associates
  (ERA), K-4
ENIAC (Electronic Numerical
  Integrator and Calculator),
  K-2, K-59
environmental faults, 367, 369, **370**
EPIC (Explicitly Parallel Instruction
  Computer), 114, **115,** 118,
  G-33, K-24
ERA (Engineering Research
  Associates), K-4
error latency, 366–367
errors
  bit error rate, D-21 to D-22
  effective, 367
  forward error correction codes,
    D-6
  latent, 366–367
  meaning of, 366–367
  round-off, D-6, **D-6**
escape path, E-46
escape resource set, E-47
eServer p5 595, **47, 48, 49**
Eshraghian, K., I-65
ETA-10, **F-34,** F-49
Ethernet
  as local area network, E-4
  overview of, E-77 to E-79, **E-78**
  packet format in, **E-75**
  performance, E-89, **E-90**
  as shared-media network, E-23

Ethernet switches, 368, **369**
even/odd multipliers, I-52, **I-52**
EVEN-ODD scheme, 366
EX. *See* execution/effective address
  cycle
exceptions
  coerced, A-40 to A-41, **A-42**
  in computer arithmetic, I-34 to
    I-35
  dynamic scheduling and, 91, 95
  floating-point, A-43
  inexact, I-35
  instruction set complications,
    A-45 to A-47
  invalid, I-35
  in MIPS pipelining, A-38 to A-41,
    A-40, A-42, A-43 to A-45,
    A-44
  order of instruction, A-38 to A-41,
    A-40, A-42
  precise exceptions, A-43, A-54 to
    A-56
  preserving, in compiler
    speculation, G-27 to G-31
  program order and, 73–74
  restarting execution, A-41 to A-43
  underflow, I-36 to I-37, I-62
exclusion policy, in AMD Opteron,
  329, 330
exclusive cache blocks, 210–211
execution time, 28, 257–258, C-3 to
  C-4. *See also* response time
execution trace cache, 131, **132, 133**
execution/effective address cycle (EX)
  in floating-point MIPS pipelining,
    A-47 to A-49, **A-48**
  in RISC instruction set, A-6
  in unpipelined MIPS
    implementation, A-27 to
    A-28, **A-29**
expand-down field, **C-51**
explicit parallelism, G-34 to G-37,
  G-35, G-36, G-37
Explicitly Parallel Instruction
  Computer (EPIC), 114, **115,**
  118, G-33, K-24
exponential back-off, H-17 to H-18,
  H-17
exponential distributions, 383–384,
  386. *See also* Poisson
  distribution
exponents, I-15 to I-16, **I-16**

extended accumulator architecture, B-3, J-45
extended precision, I-33 to I-34
extended stack architecture, J-45

F

failure, defined, 366–367
failure rates, 26–28, 41, 50–51
failures in time (FIT), 26–27
fairness, E-23, E-49, H-13
false sharing misses
    in SMT commercial workloads, 222, **224, 225**
    in symmetric shared-memory multiprocessors, 218–219, 224
fast page mode, 313
fat trees, **E-33**, E-34, E-36, E-38, **E-40**, E-48
fault detection, 51–52
fault tolerance, IEEE on, 366
faulting prefetches, 306
faults. *See also* exceptions
    address, C-40
    categories of, 367, **370**
    design, 367, **370**
    environmental, 367, 369, **370**
    hardware, 367, **370**
    intermittent, 367
    meaning of, 366–367
    page, C-3, C-40
    permanent, 367
    transient, 367, 378–379
fault-tolerant routing, E-66 to E-68, **E-69**, E-74, E-94
FCC (Federal Communications Commission), 371
feature size, 17
Federal Communications Commission (FCC), 371
Feng, Tse-Yun, E-1
fetch-and-increment synchronization primitive, 239–240, H-20 to H-21, **H-21**
FFT kernels
    characteristics of, H-7, **H-11**
    on distributed-memory multiprocessors, H-27 to H-29, **H-28 to H-32**
    on symmetric shared-memory multiprocessors, H-21 to H-26, **H-23 to H-26**

FIFO (first in, first out), 382, C-9, **C-10**
file server benchmarks, 32
filers, 391, 397–398
fine-grained multithreading, 173–175, **174**. *See also* multithreading
finite-state controllers, 211
first in, first out (FIFO), 382, C-9, **C-10**
first-reference misses, C-22
Fisher, J., 153, K-21
FIT (failures in time), 26–27
five nines (99.999%) claim, 399
fixed point computations, I-13
fixed-field decoding, A-6
fixed-length encoding, 10, B-22, **B-22**
fixed-point arithmetic, D-5 to D-6
flash memory, 359–360
flexible chaining, F-24 to F-25
flit, E-51, E-58, E-61
Floating Point Systems AP-120B, K-21
floating-point arithmetic. *See also* floating-point operations
    addition in, I-21 to I-27, **I-24,** I-36
    in Alpha, J-29
    chip design and, I-58 to I-61, **I-58, I-59, I-60**
    conversions to integer arithmetic, I-62
    denormalized numbers, I-15, I-20 to I-21, I-26 to I-27, I-36
    development of, K-4 to K-5
    exceptions in, A-43, I-34 to I-35
    fused multiply-add, I-32 to I-33
    historical perspectives on, I-62 to I-65
    in IBM 360, J-85 to J-86, **J-85, J-86, J-87**
    IEEE standard for, I-13 to I-14, **I-16**
    instructions in RISC architectures, **J-23**
    in Intel 80x86, J-52 to J-55, **J-54, J-61**
    iterative division, I-27 to I-31, **I-28**
    in MIPS 64, J-27
    multiplication, I-17 to I-21, **I-18, I-19, I-20**
    pipelining in, I-15
    precision in, I-21, I-33 to I-34

remainder, I-31 to I-32
representation of floating-point numbers, I-15 to I-16, **I-16**
in SPARC architecture, J-31 to J-32
special values in, I-14 to I-15
subtraction, I-22 to I-23
underflow, I-36 to I-37, I-62
floating-point operations. *See also* floating-point arithmetic
    blocked floating point, D-6
    conditional branch options, **B-20**
    instruction operators in, **B-15**
    latencies of, 75, **75**
    maintaining precise exceptions, A-54 to A-56
    in media extensions, D-10
    memory addressing in, **B-12, B-13**
    in MIPS architecture, B-38 to B-39, **B-40**
    MIPS pipelining in, A-47 to A-56, **A-48** to **A-51, A-57, A-58**
    MIPS R4000 pipeline example, A-60 to A-65, **A-61** to **A-65**
    multicore processor comparisons, 255
    nonblocking caches and, 297–298
    operand types and sizes, B-13 to B-14, **B-15**
    paired single operations and, D-10 to D-11
    parallelism and, 161–162, **162, 166,** 167
    performance growth since mid-1980s, 3
    scoreboarding, A-66 to A-75, **A-68, A-71** to **A-75**
    in Tomasulo's approach, 94, **94, 107**
    in vector processors, F-4, F-6, **F-8,** F-11
floating-point registers (FPRs), B-34, B-36
floating-point status register, B-34
floppy disks, K-60
flow control
    bubble, E-53, E-73
    in buffer overflow prevention, E-22
    in congestion management, E-65

flow control (*continued*)
  credit-based, E-10, E-65, E-71,
    E-74
  defined, E-10
  in distributed switched networks,
    E-38
  end-to-end, E-65
  link-level, E-58, E-62, E-65, E-72,
    E-74
  in lossless networks, E-11
  network performance and, E-17
  Stop & Go, E-10
  switching and, E-51
  Xon/Xoff, E-10
flow-balanced state, **379**
flush pipeline scheme, A-22, **A-25**
FM (frequency modulations), D-21
form factor, E-9
FORTRAN
  integer division and remainder in,
    I-12
  vector processors in, F-17, F-21,
    F-33, **F-34**, F-44 to F-45,
    F-45
forward error correction codes, D-6
forward path, in cell phone base
    stations, D-24
forwarding
  chaining, F-23 to F-25, **F-24**
  in longer latency pipelines, A-49
    to A-54, **A-50, A-51**
  minimizing data hazard stalls by,
    A-17 to A-18, **A-18**
  in MIPS pipelines, A-35, **A-36,
    A-37**, A-59, **A-59**
forwarding logic, 89
forwarding tables, E-48, E-57, E-60,
    E-67, E-74
Fourier-Motzkin test, K-23
four-way conflict misses, C-24
FP. *See* floating-point arithmetic;
    floating-point operations
FPRs (floating-point registers), B-34,
    B-36
fragment field, E-84
Frank, S. J., K-39
freeze pipeline scheme, A-22
Freiman, C. V., I-63
frequency modulations (FM), D-21
Fujitsu VP100/VP200, **F-7**, F-49, F-50
Fujitsu VPP5000, **F-7**
full access, E-29, E-45, E-47

full adders, I-2 to I-3, **I-3**
full bisection bandwidth, E-39, E-41
full-duplex mode, E-22
fully associative caches, 289, C-7,
    C-7, C-25
fully connected, E-34, **E-40**
function pointers, register indirect
    jumps for, B-18
fused multiply-add, I-32 to I-33
future file, A-55

G

galaxy evolution, H-8 to H-9
gallium arsenide, F-46, F-50
gateways, E-79
gather operations, F-27
gather/scatter addressing, B-31
GCD (greatest common divisor) test,
    G-7
general-purpose register (GPR)
    computers, B-3 to B-6, **B-4,
    B-6**
general-purpose registers (GPRs),
    B-34, G-38
GENI (Global Environment for
    Network Innovation), E-98
geometric mean, 34–37
geometric standard deviation, 36–37
Gibson instruction mix, K-6
Gilder, George, 357
global address space, C-50
global code motion, G-16 to G-19,
    G-17
global code scheduling, G-15 to G-23
  control and data dependences in,
    G-16
  global code motion, G-16 to G-19,
    G-17
  overview of, G-16, **G-16**
  predication with, G-24
  superblocks, G-21 to G-23, **G-22**
  trace scheduling, G-19 to G-21,
    G-20
  in VLIW, 116
global collective networks, H-42,
    H-43
global common subexpression
    elimination, B-26, **B-28**
global data area, in compilers, B-27
Global Environment for Network
    Innovation (GENI), E-98
global miss rate, C-30 to C-33, **C-32**

global optimizations, B-26, **B-28**
global scheduling, 116
global system for mobile
    communication (GSM), D-25
global/stack analysis, 164–165, **164**
Goldberg, D., I-34
Goldberg, I. B., I-64
Goldberg, Robert, 315
Goldschmidt's algorithm, I-29, **I-30,**
    I-61
Goldstine, H. H., 287, I-62, K-2 to K-3
Google, E-85
GPR (general-purpose registers),
    B-34, G-38
GPR computers, B-3 to B-6, **B-4, B-6**
gradual underflow, I-15, I-36
grain size, defined, 199
graph coloring, B-26 to B-27
greatest common divisor (GCD) test,
    G-7
grid, E-36
GSM (global system for mobile
    communication), D-25
guest domains, 321–322, **323**
guests, in virtual machines, 319–320,
    321

H

hackers, J-65
half adders, I-2 to I-3
half-duplex mode, E-22
half-words, B-13, B-34
handshaking, E-10
hard real-time systems, D-3 to D-4
hardware, defined, 12
hardware branch prediction, 80–89
  branch-prediction buffers and,
    82–86, **83, 84, 85**
  branch-target buffers, 122–125,
    122, 124
  correlating predictors, 83–86, **84,
    85, 87, 88**
  development of, K-20
  effects of branch prediction
    schemes, 160–162, **160, 162**
  in ideal processor, 155, 160–162,
    160, 162
  integrated instruction fetch units
    and, 126–127
  in Pentium 4, 132–134, **134**
  speculating through multiple
    branches, 130

tournament predictors, 86–89, **160**, 161, **162**, K-20
trace caches and, 296
hardware description notation, **J-25**
hardware faults, 367, **370**
hardware prefetching. *See* prefetching
hardware-based speculation, 104–114. *See also* speculation
  data flow value prediction, 170
  limitations of, 170–171, 182–183
  reorder buffer in, 106–114, **107, 110, 111, 113**
  Tomasulo's approach and, 105–109
Harvard architecture, K-4
hazards. *See* pipeline hazards; RAW hazards; WAR hazards; WAW hazards
head-of-line (HOL) blocking
  adaptive routing and, E-54
  buffer organizations and, E-58, **E-59**
  buffered crossbar switches and, E-62
  congestion management and, E-64
  virtual channels and, E-93
heaps, in compilers, B-27 to B-28
heat dissipation, 19
helical scan, K-59
Hennessy, J., K-12 to K-13
HEP processor, K-26
Hewlett-Packard PA-RISC. *See* PA-RISC
High Productivity Computing Systems (HPCS), F-51
higher-radix division, I-55 to I-58, **I-55, I-56, I-57**
higher-radix multiplication, I-48 to I-49, **I-49**
high-level language computer architecture (HLLCA), B-26, **B-28**, B-39 to B-43, B-45, K-11
high-level optimizations, B-26, **B-28**
high-order functions, register indirect jumps for, B-18
Hill, M. D., 247, K-54
Hillis, Danny, K-38
histograms, 382–383
historical perspectives, K-1 to K-67
  on clusters, K-41 to K-44

on computer arithmetic, I-62 to I-65
cryptanalysis machines, K-4
on DRAM, 312, **313**
early development of computers, K-2 to K-7
on floating point, K-4 to K-5
on IBM 360/370, J-83 to J-84
on instruction set architecture, B-3, B-45 to B-46, K-9 to K-15
on Intel 80x86 development, J-45 to J-46, **J-48**, J-64 to J-65
on Intel IA-64 and Itanium 2, G-44
on interconnection networks, E-97 to E-104
on magnetic storage, K-59 to K-61
on memory hierarchy and protection, K-52 to K-54
on multiprocessors and parallel processing, K-34 to K-45
on pipelining and ILP, K-18 to K-27
on quantitative performance measures, K-6 to K-7
on vector processors, F-47 to F-51
history file, A-55
hit time
  associativity and, C-28 to C-29
  average memory access time and, C-15
  during cache indexing, 291–292, C-36 to C-38, **C-37**
  cache size and, 293–295, **294**
  defined, 290
  trace caches and, 296, **309**
hit under miss optimization, 296–298, **297**
Hitachi S810/S820, **F-7, F-34**, F-49
Hitachi SuperH. *See* SuperH
HLLCA (high-level language computer architecture), B-26, **B-28**, B-39 to B-43, B-45, K-11
Hoagland, Al, 357
HOL. *See* head-of-line (HOL) blocking
home nodes, 232, **233**
Honeywell Bull, K-61
hop count, E-30, E-38, E-40, E-50

Hopkins, M., G-1
hosts, in virtual machines, 318
hot-swapping, E-67
HP Alpha Server, **339**
HP Integrity rx2620-2, **45, 46**
HP Integrity rx5670 Cluster, 47, **47, 48, 49**
HP Integrity Superdome, 47, **47, 48, 49**
HP PA-RISC MAX2, **D-11**
HP Precision Architecture, I-12
HP ProLiant BL25p, **45, 46**
HP ProLiant ML350, **45, 46, 47, 48, 49**
HPCD (High Productivity Computing Systems), F-51
HPSm, K-22
hubs, E-79
Hwu, Wen-Mei, K-24
hybrid encoding, **B-22**, B-23
hypercubes, E-36, **E-37, E-40**, E-92, K-41
HyperTransport, E-63

I

IA-32 microprocessors, A-46 to A-47
IA-64. *See* Intel IA-64
IAS computer, K-3
IBM 3ASC Purple pSeries 575, **E-20, E-44, E-56**
IBM 360, J-83 to J-89
  architecture in, J-2, **J-42**, K-10
  development of, J-83 to J-84
  dynamic scheduling in, 92
  frequency of instruction usage in programs, **J-89**
  hardware-based speculation in, 171
  instruction sets in, J-85 to J-88, **J-85, J-86, J-87, J-88**
  memory addressing in, B-8, K-9, K-53
  memory caches in, K-53
  memory protection in, K-52
  virtual memory in, K-53
IBM 360/91
  dynamic scheduling in, 92
  hardware-based speculation in, 171
  innovations in, K-20
  memory caches in, K-53

IBM 370
   development of, J-84
   floating point formats in, I-63 to I-64
   guest page tables in, 320
   memory addressing in, B-8
   vector length control in, F-18
   virtualization in, 319
IBM 701, K-3, K-5
IBM 801, K-12 to K-13
IBM 3033 cache, C-38
IBM 3090/VF, **F-34**
IBM 3480 cartridge, K-59
IBM 7030, K-18
IBM ASCI White SP Power3, **E-20, E-44, E-56**
IBM Blue Gene/L
   architecture of, **E-20,** H-41 to H-42
   computing node in, H-42 to H-44, **H-43, H-44**
   custom clusters in, 198
   development of, K-43
   interconnection networks in, E-72 to E-74
   routing, arbitration, and switching characteristics in, **E-56**
   topological characteristics of, **E-44**
IBM CodePack, B-23
IBM eServer p5 595, **47, 48, 49**
IBM eServer pSeries 690, **47, 48, 49**
IBM mainframes, virtualization in, 324–325
IBM Power2 processor, 130
IBM Power4 processor, **52,** K-27
IBM Power5 processor
   clock rate on, 139, **139**
   eServer p5 575, **178**
   instruction-level parallelism in, 156
   memory hierarchy of, **341**
   multicore, 198
   on-chip networks, **E-73**
   performance on SPEC benchmarks, 255–257, **255, 256, 257, G-43**
   simultaneous multithreading in, K-27
   SMT performance on, 176–181, **178 to 181**

tournament predictors in, 88
virtual registers in, 162
IBM PowerPC. *See* PowerPC
IBM RP3, K-40
IBM RS 6000, K-13
IBM SAGE, K-63
IBM zSeries, F-49
IBM/Motorola PowerPC. *See* PowerPC
IC (instruction count), 42–44, C-4
ID. *See* instruction decode/register fetch cycle
ideal pipeline CPI, 66, **67**
IDE/ATA disks, 368, **369**
identifier fields, E-84
Idle Control Register (ICR), D-8
IEEE Computer Society Technical Committee on Fault Tolerance, 366
IEEE standard for floating-point arithmetic
   advantages of, I-13 to I-14
   exceptions in, I-34 to I-35
   format parameters, **I-16**
   remainders, I-31 to I-32
   rounding modes, **I-20**
   standardization process, I-64
   underflow in, I-36
if conversion, G-24
Illiac IV, K-35
ILP. *See* instruction-level parallelism
immediate addressing mode, **B-9,** B-10 to B-13, **B-11, B-12, B-13**
IMPACT, K-24
implementation, in design, 8
implicit parallelism, G-34
in flight instructions, 156
inclusion property, 211
index field, C-8 to C-9, **C-8**
index vectors, F-27, F-28
indexed addressing mode, **B-9,** J-67
indexing. *See* cache indexing
indirect networks, E-31, E-48, E-67
inexact exceptions, I-35
InfiniBand, E-4, E-64, E-74 to E-77, **E-75, E-76,** E-102
infinite population model, 386
initiation intervals, A-48 to A-49, **A-49, A-62**
initiation rate, F-10

injection bandwidth, E-18, E-26, E-41, E-55, E-63
Inktomi search engine, K-42
input-buffered switch, E-57, E-59, **E-59,** E-62, E-73
input-output-buffered switch, E-57, **E-57,** E-60, **E-61,** E-62
instruction buffers, A-15
instruction cache misses, 227, **227,** 329, **C-15**
instruction commit, 105–106, 108–110, **110**
instruction count (IC), 42–44, C-4
instruction decode, 90
instruction decode/register fetch cycle (ID)
   branch hazards and, A-21
   in RISC instruction set, A-5 to A-6
   in unpipelined MIPS implementation, A-26 to A-27, **A-29**
instruction delivery, 121–127, **122, 124, 126**
instruction fetch cycle (IF)
   branch hazards and, A-21
   in RISC instruction set, A-5, **A-15**
   in unpipelined MIPS implementation, A-26 to A-27, **A-29**
instruction fetch units, 126–127
instruction formats, **J-7, J-8**
instruction groups, G-34 to G-35, **G-35**
instruction issue, A-33, A-67 to A-70, **A-68, A-71**
instruction length, J-60, **J-60.** *See also* instruction count
instruction packets, in embedded systems, D-9, **D-10**
instruction path length, 42–44, C-4
instruction set architecture (ISA), 8–12, B-1 to B-47. *See also* RISC architectures
   addressing modes and, B-9 to B-10, **B-9, B-11 to B-13**
   classification of, B-3 to B-7
   compiler role in, B-24 to B-32
   compiler technology and, B-27 to B-29

conditional branch operations, B-19, **B-19, B-20**
in Cray X1, F-41
defined, 8–9
encoding, B-21 to B-24, **B-22**
flaws in, B-44 to B-45
hardware, 9–10, **9**
high-level language structure and, B-39 to B-43, B-45
historical perspectives on, B-3, B-45 to B-46, K-9 to K-15
in IBM 360/370 mainframe, J-83 to J-89
instructions for control flow, B-16 to B-21
integer arithmetic issues in, I-10 to I-13, **I-11, I-12, I-13**
in Intel 80x86, J-45 to J-65
in Intel IA-64, G-32 to G-40, **G-35, G-36, G-37, G-39**
measurements, B-2
memory addressing in, B-7 to B-13, **B-8, B-9, B-11, B-12, B-13**
memory protection and, 324–325
multimedia instructions, B-31 to B-32
operand type and size, B-13 to B-14, **B-15**
operations in the instruction set, B-14 to B-16, **B-15, B-16**
organization of, 12
orthogonal, B-30, J-83, K-11
procedure invocation options, B-19 to B-20
reducing code size and, B-43, **B-44**
variations in, B-43, **B-44**
in VAX, J-65 to J-83
vectorized, F-3, F-4 to F-6
in virtual machines, 317, 319–320
instruction set complications, A-45 to A-47
instruction-level parallelism (ILP), 66–141. *See also* instruction-level parallelism limitations; pipelining
branch prediction buffers and, 82–86, **83, 84, 85**
compiler techniques for exposing, 74–80, **75**
data dependences and, 68–70

data hazards and, 71–72
defined, 66
development of, K-24 to K-25
in embedded systems, D-8
hardware *vs.* software approach to, 66
instruction fetch bandwidth increases in, 121–127, **122, 124, 126**
limitations in ideal processors, 154–165, **159, 160, 162, 163, 164**
limitations in realizable processors, 165–170, **166,** 181–184
loop unrolling and, 75–80, **75,** 117–118
loop-level parallelism, 67–68
multiple issue and speculation examples, 118–121, **120, 121**
overview of, 67–68
pipeline scheduling and, 75–79
processor comparisons for, 179–181, **179, 180, 181**
in RISC-based machines, 2
in simultaneous multithreading, 173, 175
SPEC92 benchmarks and, 156, **157**
switch from, to TLP and DLP, 4
thread-level parallelism *vs.*, 172
value prediction in, 130
instruction-level parallelism limitations, 154–165
data flow limit, 170
finite registers and, 162–164, **163**
hardware model, 154–156
imperfect alias analysis and, 164–165, **164**
realistic branch and jump prediction effects, 160–162
for realizable processors, 165–169, **166**
unnecessary dependences, 169–170
WAR and WAW hazards through memory, 169
on window size and maximum issue count, 156–160, 166–167, **166**
instructions per clock (IPC), 42, 253
integer arithmetic

carry-lookahead adders, I-37 to I-41, **I-38, I-40, I-41, I-42, I-44**
carry-select adders, I-43 to I-44, **I-43, I-44**
carry-skip adders, I-41 to I-43, **I-42, I-44**
conversions to floating-point, I-62
faster division with one adder, I-54 to I-58, **I-55, I-56, I-57**
faster multiplication with many adders, I-50 to I-54, **I-50 to I-54**
faster multiplication with single adders, I-47 to I-50, **I-48, I-49**
in Intel 80x86, J-50 to J-52, **J-52, J-53**
radix-2 multiplication and division, I-4 to I-7, **I-4, I-6,** I-55 to I-56, **I-55**
ripple-carry addition, I-2 to I-3, **I-3, I-42, I-44**
shifting over zeros technique, I-45 to I-47, **I-46**
signed numbers, I-7 to I-10
speeding up addition, I-37 to I-44
speeding up multiplication and division, I-44 to I-58
systems issues, I-10 to I-13, **I-11, I-12**
integer registers, B-34
integrated circuits
costs of, 21–25, **22, 23**
dependability of, 25–28
feature size in, 17
prices of, 25–29
technology growth in, 14
trends in power in, 17–19
wire delay in, 17
integrated instruction fetch units, 126–127
Intel 80x86, J-45 to J-65
comparative operation measurements, J-62 to J-64, **J-63, J-64**
conditional branch options in, **B-19**
development of, J-45 to J-46, J-64 to J-65
exceptions in, **A-40**

Intel 80x86, J-45 to J-65 (*continued*)
  floating point operations, J-52 to J-55, **J-54, J-61**
  guest OS in, 324
  instruction encoding, J-55 to J-56, **J-56, J-57, J-58**
  instruction set architecture in, 9–10, B-44 to B-45, **J-42**
  integer operations in, J-50 to J-52, **J-52, J-53**
  memory addressing in, B-8, C-56
  memory protection in, C-49, K-52
  operand addressing measurements, J-59 to J-62, **J-59 to J-62**
  Pacifica revision to, 320, 339
  registers and data addressing modes, J-47 to J-49, **J-48, J-49, J-50**
  RISC instruction sets in, B-3, J-45 to J-65
  top ten instructions in, **B-16**
  variable instruction encoding in, B-22 to B-23
  virtualization and, 320, 321, 339, **340**
Intel 387, I-33
Intel ASCI Red Paragon, **E-20, E-44, E-56**
Intel IA-32 microprocessors, A-46 to A-47, C-49 to C-51, **C-51**
Intel IA-64
  EPIC approach in, 118, G-33, K-24
  hardware-based speculation in, 171
  historical perspectives on, G-44, K-14 to K-15
  ILP performance limitations and, 184
  implicit and explicit parallelism in, G-34 to G-37, **G-35, G-36, G-37**
  instruction formats in, G-38, **G-39**
  page tables in, C-43
  register model in, G-33 to G-34
  speculation support in, G-38, G-40
Intel iPSC 860, K-40
Intel Itanium 1, G-40 to G-41, K-14
Intel Itanium 2. *See also* Intel IA-64

functional units and instruction issue in, G-41 to G-43, **G-41**
  historical perspectives on, G-44
  Itanium 1 compared to, G-40 to G-41
  peak performance in, **52**
  performance measurements of, 179–181, **179, 180, 181,** G-43, **G-43**
  SPECRatios for, **35,** 37
  Sun T1 compared with, 253
Intel MMX, B-31 to B-32, J-46
Intel Paragon, K-40
Intel Pentium
  precise exceptions in, A-56
  protection in, C-48, C-49 to C-52, **C-51,** C-55
  register renaming in, 128
Intel Pentium 4, 131–138
  AMD Opteron compared to, 136–138, **137, 138,** 334–335, **334**
  clock rate on, 139–141, **139**
  hardware prefetching in, 305, **306**
  memory hierarchy of, **341**
  microarchitecture of, 131–132, **132, 133**
  multilevel inclusion in, C-34
  performance analysis of, 133–138 **134 to 138, G-43**
  prices of, **20**
  signal propagation in, 17
  SRT division algorithm in, I-56, **I-57**
  tournament predictors in, 88
  trace caches in, 296
  way prediction in, 295
Intel Pentium 4 Extreme
  power efficiency in, 18, 183
  SMT performance in, 177, 179–181, **179, 180, 181**
Intel Pentium 4 Xeon, 215
Intel Pentium D, 198, 255–257, **255, 256, 257**
Intel Pentium III, 183
Intel Pentium M, **20**
Intel Pentium MMX, **D-11**
Intel Thunder Tiger4, **E-20, E-44, E-56**
Intel VT-x, 339–340
intelligent devices, K-62

interarrival times, 386
interconnection networks. *See also* clusters; networks
  arbitration in, E-49 to E-50, **E-49, E-56** (*See also* arbitration)
  asynchronous transfer mode (*See* asynchronous transfer mode)
  buffer organizations, E-58 to E-60
  centralized switched, E-30 to E-34, **E-31, E-33,** E-48
  characteristics of, **E-20, E-44, E-56**
  composing and processing messages, E-6 to E-9, **E-7**
  compute-optimized, E-88
  conceptual illustration of, **E-3**
  congestion management, E-64 to E-66
  connectivity in, E-62 to E-63
  density-optimized *vs.* SPEC-optimized processors, E-85
  distributed switched, E-34 to E-39, **E-36, E-37, E-40,** E-46
  in distributed-memory multiprocessors, **232**
  domains, E-3 to E-5, **E-3, E-4**
  Element Interconnect Bus, E-3, E-70, **E-71**
  Ethernet (*See* Ethernet)
  fault tolerance in, E-66 to E-68, **E-69,** E-94
  historical perspectives on, E-97 to E-104
  IBM Blue Gene/L eServer, **E-20, E-44, E-56,** E-72 to E-74
  InfiniBand, E-4, E-64, E-74 to E-77, **E-75, E-76**
  internetworking, E-2, E-80 to E-84, **E-80 to E-84**
  I/O subsystem in, E-90 to E-91
  latency and effective bandwidth in, E-12 to E-20, **E-13, E-19,** E-25 to E-29, **E-27, E-28**
  memory hierarchy interface efficiency, E-87 to E-88
  performance of, E-40 to E-44, **E-44,** E-52 to E-55, **E-54,** E-88 to E-92
  protection and user access, E-86 to E-87, **E-87**

routing in, E-45 to E-48, **E-46,**
  E-52 to E-55, **E-54, E-56**
shared-media, E-21 to E-24, **E-22,**
  E-24 to E-25, E-78
smart switches *vs.* smart interface
  cards, E-85 to E-86, **E-86**
speed of, E-88 to E-89
standardization in, E-63 to E-64
structure of, E-9 to E-12
switch microarchitecture, E-55 to
  E-58, **E-56, E-57,** E-62
switched-media, E-21, E-24, E-25
switching technique in, E-50 to
  E-52, **E-56**
in symmetric shared-memory
  multiprocessors, 216–217,
  216
topologies in, E-40 to E-44, **E-44**
zero-copy protocols, E-8, E-91
interference, **D-21,** D-22
intermittent faults, 367
internal fragmentation, C-46
International Mobile Telephony 2000
  (IMT-2000), D-25
Internet, E-81
Internet Archive, 392–397, **394**
Internet Protocol, E-81
internetworking, E-2, E-80 to E-84,
  E-80 to E-84. *See also*
  interconnection networks
interprocedural analysis, G-10
Interrupt Enable (IE) flag, 324
interrupts. *See* exceptions
invalid exceptions, I-35
invalidate protocols. *See* write
  invalidate protocols
inverted page tables, C-43
I/O, 371–379. *See also* buses; storage
  systems
  asynchronous, 391
  cache coherence problem,
    325–326
  dependability benchmarks,
    377–379, **378**
  design considerations, 392–393
  device requests, **A-40, A-42**
  disk accesses at operating
    systems, 400–401, **401**
  evaluation of, 394–396
  historical developments in, K-62
    to K-63

Internet Archive cluster, 392–397,
  394
  in multiprogramming workload,
    225–227, **227**
  NetApp FAS6000 filer, 397–398
  queuing theory, 379–382, **379,
    381**
  throughput *vs.* response time,
    372–374, **373, 374**
  transaction-processing
    benchmarks, 374–375, **375**
  virtual caches and, C-37
  virtual machines and, 320–321,
    339
  write merging and, 301
I/O per second (IOPS), 395–396
IPC (instructions per clock), 42, 253
iPSC 860, K-40
Irwin, M. J., I-65
ISA. *See* instruction set architecture
issue rates, in multiple-issue
  processors, 182
issue slots, MLT and, 174–175, **174**
Itanium 1, G-40 to G-41, K-14
Itanium 2. *See* Intel Itanium 2
iterative arbiter, E-50
iterative division, I-27 to I-31, **I-28**

J

Java bytecodes, K-10
Java Virtual Machine (JVM), K-10
JBOD, 362
JIT (just in time) Java compilers, K-10
Johnson, R. B., K-59
Jouppi, N. P., K-54
JTAG networks, H-42, **H-43**
jump prediction, 155, 160–162, **160,
  162**
jumps, in control flow instructions,
  B-16 to B-18, **B-17,** B-37 to
  B-38, **B-38**
just in time (JIT) Java compilers, K-10

K

K6, 294
Kahan, W., I-1, I-64
k-ary n-cubes, E-38
Keller, T. W., F-48
Kendall Square Research KSR-1,
  K-41
Kennedy, John F., K-1

kernel process, 316
kernels
  defined, 29
  FFT, H-21 to H-29, **H-23 to H-26,
    H-28 to H-32**
  Livermore FORTRAN, K-6
  LU, **H-11,** H-21 to H-26, **H-23 to
    H-26, H-28 to H-32**
  miss rate in multiprogramming
    example, 227–228, **229**
Kilburn, T., C-38, K-52
Kroft, D., K-54
Kuck, D., F-51, K-23
Kung, H. T., I-63

L

L1 cache. *See also* multilevel caches
  in AMD Opteron, 327, **327, 328,**
    329, **C-55**
  average memory access time and,
    291
  memory hierarchy and, **292**
  miss penalties and, 291
  multilevel inclusion and, 248
  size of, 294
  in Sun T1, 251, **251**
  in virtual memory, C-46 to C-47,
    C-47
L2 cache. *See also* multilevel caches
  in AMD Opteron, 327, **327, 334,**
    C-55
  average memory access time and,
    291
  hardware prefetching and, 305
  memory hierarchy and, **292**
  miss penalties and, 291
  multibanked caches, 299, **309**
  multilevel inclusion and, 248
  size of, 293
  speculative execution and, 325
  in Sun T1, 251–252, **251**
  in virtual machines, 323, **323**
  in virtual memory, C-46 to C-47,
    C-47
Lam, M. S., 170
lanes, F-6, **F-7,** F-29 to F-31, **F-29,
  F-30**
LANS (local area networks), E-4, **E-4,**
  E-77 to E-79, **E-78,** E-99 to
  E-100. *See also*
  interconnection networks

large-scale multiprocessors, K-40 to
    K-44
    cache coherence implementation,
        H-34 to H-41
    classification of, H-44 to H-46,
        H-45
    computation-to-communication
        ratios in, H-10 to H-12, **H-11**
    hierarchical relationships in,
        H-45, **H-46**
    IBM Blue Gene/L as, H-41 to
        H-44, **H-43, H-44**
    interprocessor communication in,
        H-3 to H-6
    limited buffering in, H-38 to H-40
    message-passing *vs.*
        shared-memory
        communication in, H-4 to
        H-6
    scientific/technical computing in,
        H-6 to H-12, **H-11**
    synchronization mechanisms in,
        H-17 to H-21, **H-19, H-21**
    synchronization performance
        challenges, H-12 to H-16,
        H-14, H-15, H-16
latency
    defined, 15, 28, C-2
    in distributed-memory
        multiprocessors, 201
    effective bandwidth and, E-25 to
        E-29, **E-27, E-28**
    in Element Interconnect Bus,
        E-72
    in floating-point MIPS pipelining,
        A-48 to A-49, **A-49, A-50,
        A-62,** A-65
    hiding, H-4
    improvements in, compared with
        bandwidth, 15, **16**
    interconnected nodes and, **E-27**
    in interconnection networks, E-12
        to E-19, **E-13,** E-25 to E-29,
        E-27
    I/O, 371
    in Itanium 2, **G-41**
    latency overlap, C-20
    main memory, 310
    packet, E-40 to E-41, E-52 to
        E-53
    in pipelining, 75–79, A-10

from remote access
        communication, 203–204
    in shared-memory
        multiprocessors, H-29
    transport, E-14
    using speculation to hide,
        247–248
    in vector processors, F-3, F-4,
        F-16, F-31 to F-32, **F-31**
latent errors, 366–367
law of diminishing returns, Amdahl's
        Law and, 40
LCD (liquid crystal displays), D-19
learning curve, costs and, 19
least common ancestor, E-48
least-recently used (LRU) blocks, C-9,
        C-10, C-14, C-43
Leighton, F. T., I-65
limit fields, C-50
line locking, D-4
linear speedups, 259–260, **260**
link injection bandwidth, E-17
link pipelining, E-16, E-92
link reception bandwidth, E-17
link registers, 240, J-32 to J-33
link-level flow control, E-58, E-62,
        E-65, E-72, E-74
Linpack benchmark, F-8 to F-9, F-37
        to F-38
Linux
    dependability benchmarks,
        377–379, **378**
    Xen VMM compared with,
        322–324, **322, 323**
liquid crystal displays (LCD), D-19
LISP, J-30
literal addressing mode, **B-9,** B-10 to
        B-13, **B-11, B-12, B-13**
Little Endian, B-7, B-34, J-49
Little's Law, 380–381, 385
livelock, E-45
liveness, 74
Livermore FORTRAN Kernels, K-6
load and store instructions
    in instruction set architecture
        classification, B-3, **B-4**
    in MIPS architecture, B-36, **B-36**
    in RISC instruction set, A-4
load buffers, 94–95, **94,** 97, **101,**
        102–103
load delays, 2-cycle, A-59, **A-59**

load interlocks, A-33 to A-35, **A-34,**
        A-63, **A-65**
load vector count and update
        (VLVCU), F-18
load-linked (load-locked) instruction,
        239–240
loads, advanced, G-40
loads, applied, E-53
load-store architecture, B-3 to B-6,
        B-4, B-6
load-store ISAs, 9, F-6, **F-7,** F-13 to
        F-14
local address space, C-50
local area networks (LANS), E-4, **E-4,**
        E-77 to E-79, **E-78,** E-99 to
        E-100. *See also*
        interconnection networks
local miss rate, C-30 to C-33, **C-32**
local nodes, 232, **233**
local optimizations, B-26, **B-28**
local scheduling, 116
locks
    queuing, H-18 to H-20
    spin lock with exponential
        back-off, H-17 to H-18, **H-17**
lockup-free (non-blocking) caches,
        296–298, **297, 309,** K-54
logical units, 390–391
logical volumes, 390–391
lognormal distribution, 36–37
loop interchange, 302–303
loop unrolling
    dependence analysis and, G-8 to
        G-9
    eliminating dependent
        computations in, G-11
    global code scheduling and, 116,
        G-15 to G-23, **G-16, G-20,
        G-22**
    hardware-controlled prefetching
        and, 306
    pipeline scheduling and, 75–80,
        75
    recurrences and, G-11 to G-12
    software pipelining as symbolic,
        G-12 to G-15, **G-13, G-15**
loop-carried dependences, G-3 to G-5
loop-level parallelism
    eliminating dependent
        computations, G-10 to G-12
    finding dependences, G-6 to G-10

greatest common divisor test, G-7
increasing ILP through, 67–68
interprocedural analysis, G-10
points-to analysis, G-9 to G-10
recurrences, G-5 to G-12
type of dependences in, G-2 to G-6
loops. *See also* loop unrolling
  barrier synchronization in, H-14
  chaining, F-35, **F-35**
  conditionals in, F-25 to F-26
  dependence distance in, G-6
  execution time of vector loop, F-35
lossless networks, E-11, E-59, E-65, E-68
lossy networks, E-11, E-65
LRU (least-recently used) blocks, C-9, **C-10,** C-14, C-43
LU kernels
  characteristics of, H-8, **H-11**
  on distributed-memory multiprocessors, **H-28 to H-32**
  on symmetric shared-memory multiprocessors, H-21 to H-26, **H-23 to H-26**

M
M32R
  addressing modes in, J-5 to J-6, **J-6**
  architecture overview, **J-4**
  common extensions in, J-19 to J-24, **J-23, J-24**
  instructions unique to, J-39 to J-40
  MIPS core subset in, J-6 to J-16, **J-8, J-9, J-14 to J-17**
  multiply-accumulate in, J-19, **J-20**
MAC (multiply-accumulate), D-5, D-8, J-18, **J-20**
machine language programmers, J-84
machine memory, defined, 320
Macintosh, memory addressing in, K-53
magnetic cores, K-4
magnetic disks. *See* disk storage; RAID

magnetic storage, history of, K-59 to K-61. *See also* storage systems
main memory, DRAM chips in, 310
Mark-I, K-3
MasPar, K-35
massively parallel processors (MPP), **H-45**
matrix operations, H-7, I-32 to I-33
Mauchly, John, K-2 to K-3, K-5
maximum transfer unit, E-7, E-76
maximum vector length (MVL), F-17, **F-17**
Mayer, Milton, E-1
McLuhan, Marshall, E-1
Mead, C., I-63
mean time between failures (MTBF), 26
mean time to failure (MTTF), 26–27, 51, 362, 396–397
mean time to repair (MTTR), 26–27, 362, 364–365
media
  extensions, D-10 to D-11, **D-11**
  physical network, E-9
  shared, E-21, E-23, E-24, E-78
  switched, E-21, E-24, E-25
memory. *See also* caches; virtual memory
  in embedded computers, 7–8, D-2 to D-3
  in interconnection networks, 216–217, **216**
  in vector processors, F-14 to F-16, **F-15,** F-22 to F-23
  virtual (*See* virtual memory)
memory access pipeline cycle, **A-44, A-51,** A-52
memory access/branch completion cycle
  in RISC implementation, A-6
  in shared-memory multiprocessors, H-29 to H-30, **H-32**
  in unpipelined MIPS implementation, A-28, **A-29**
memory accesses per instruction, C-4 to C-6
memory addressing, B-7 to B-13
  addressing modes, B-9 to B-11, **B-9, B-11, B-12,** J-47

immediate values, **B-13**
  in instruction set architectures, 9–10
  interpreting addresses, B-7 to B-8, **B-8**
memory alias analysis, 155, 164–165, **164**
memory banks, in vector processors, F-14 to F-16, **F-15**
memory consistency models, 243–248
  coherence and, 207
  compiler optimization and, 246–247
  development of, K-44
  relaxed consistency, 245–246
  sequential consistency, 243–244, 247
  synchronized programs and, 244–245
  using speculation to hide latency in, 247–248
memory hierarchy, 287–342, C-1 to C-58. *See also* cache optimizations; virtual memory
  AMD Opteron data cache example, C-12 to C-14, **C-13, C-15**
  average memory access time, 290
  block addressing, 299, **299,** C-8 to C-9, **C-8**
  block placement in caches, C-7 to C-8, **C-7**
  block replacement with cache misses, C-9, **C-10,** C-14
  cache optimization summary, 309, **309**
  cache organization overview, 288–293, **292**
  cache performance review, C-3 to C-6, C-15 to C-21, **C-21**
  cache size and hit time, 293–295, **294, 309**
  compiler optimizations and, 302–305, **304, 309**
  compiler-controlled prefetching, 305–309, **309**
  critical word first and early restart, 299–300, **309**
  hardware prefetching and, 305, **306, 309**

memory hierarchy (*continued*)
  historical perspectives on, K-52 to K-54
  in IBM Power 5, **341**
  in Intel Pentium 4, **341**
  main memory, 310
  merging write buffers and, 300–301, **301, 309**
  of microprocessors compared, **341**
  multibanked caches, 298–299, **299, 309**
  multilevel inclusion in, C-34
  nonblocking caches, 296–298, **297, 309**
  operating system impact on, C-56, **C-57**
  pipelined cache access and, 296, **309**
  projections of processor performance, 288, **289**
  sizes and access times of levels in, **C-3**
  speculative execution and, 325
  in Sun Niagara, **341**
  thrashing, C-25
  trace caches and, 296, **309**
  typical multilevel, **288**
  in virtual memory, C-40, **C-41,** C-42 to C-44, **C-43,** C-46, **C-47**
  way prediction and, 295, **309**
  writes in caches, C-9 to C-12, **C-10**
memory indirect addressing mode, **B-9, B-11**
memory mapping, C-40. *See also* address translations
memory pipelines, on VMIPS, F-38 to F-40
memory ports, pipeline stalls and, A-13, **A-14, A-15**
memory protection, 315–324, C-47 to C-55
  in 64-bit Opteron, C-53 to C-55, **C-54**
  architecture provisions for, 316
  development of, K-52
  instruction set architecture and, 324–325

safe calls from user to OS gates, C-52
  by virtual machines, 317–324, **322, 323**
  by virtual memory, 315–317, C-39, C-47 to C-52, **C-51**
memory reference speculation, G-32, G-40
memory stall cycles, C-4 to C-6, C-20 to C-21, **C-21**
memory technology, 310–315. *See also* storage systems
  DRAM, 311–315, **311, 314**
  flash memory, 359–360
  SRAM, 311, F-16
memory-constrained scaling, H-33 to H-34
memoryless processes, 384, 386
memory-memory architecture, B-3, B-5, **B-6**
memory-memory vector processors, F-4, F-44, F-48
mesh networks, E-36, **E-40,** E-46, **E-46**
MESI protocol, **213**
Message Passing Interface (MPI), H-5
message-passing communication, H-4 to H-6
message-passing multiprocessors, 202
messages, E-6 to E-8, **E-7,** E-76, **E-77**
MFLOPS ratings, F-34 to F-35, F-37, K-7
microinstruction execution, pipelining, A-46 to A-47
microprocessors
  costs of, 20, **20**
  memory hierarchy in, **341**
  performance milestones in, 15, **16**
  transistor performance improvements in, 17
migration of shared data, 207
MIIPS MDMX, J-16 to J-19, **J-18**
MIMD. *See* multiple instruction streams, multiple data streams
minicomputers, beginnings of, 3, 4
minimal paths, E-45, E-67
MIPS (Microprocessor without Interlocked Pipeline Stages), J-82, **J-82,** K-12

MIPS (million instructions per second), 169, A-4 to A-5, **B-19,** K-6 to K-7
MIPS 1, **J-1,** J-6 to J-16, **J-7, J-9 to J-13, J-17**
MIPS 16
  addressing modes in, J-5 to J-6, **J-6**
  architecture overview, **J-4**
  common extensions in, J-19 to J-24, **J-23, J-24**
  features added to, **J-44**
  instructions unique to, J-40 to J-42
  MIPS core subset in, J-6 to J-16, **J-8, J-9, J-14 to J-17**
  multiply-accumulate in, J-19, **J-20**
  reduced code size in, B-23
MIPS 32, **J-80**
MIPS 64
  addressing modes in, J-5 to J-6, **J-5**
  common MIPS extensions in, J-19 to J-24, **J-21 to J-23**
  instruction set architecture, 10, **11, 12,** A-4, B-33, B-34, **B-40**
  unique instructions in, J-24 to J-27, **J-26**
MIPS architecture, B-32 to B-39
  addressing modes for, B-34 to B-35
  ALU instructions, A-4
  common extensions in, J-19 to J-24, **J-21 to J-24**
  control flow instructions, B-37 to B-38, **B-38**
  data types for, B-34
  in embedded multiprocessors, D-14 to D-15, D-17
  floating-point operations in, B-38 to B-39, **B-40**
  instruction format, B-35, **B-35**
  instruction set usage, 9–10, B-39, **B-41, B-42**
  operations supported by, B-35 to B-37, **B-36, B-37**
  processor structure with scoreboard, A-68 to A-69, **A-68**

recommendations for, B-33
registers for, B-34
Tomasulo's approach in, **94**
unpipelined implementation of,
　A-26 to A-30, **A-29**
vector, F-4 to F-6, **F-5, F-7, F-8**
MIPS M2000, J-81, **J-82,** K-13 to
　K-14, **K-14**
MIPS pipeline
　basic, A-30 to A-33, **A-31, A-32**
　branch hazards, A-21
　branches in, A-35 to A-37, **A-38,**
　　A-39
　control implementation in, A-33
　　to A-35, **A-34**
　exceptions in, A-38 to A-41, **A-40,**
　　A-42, A-43 to A-45, **A-44**
　floating-point in, A-47 to A-56,
　　A-48 to **A-51, A-57, A-58,**
　　A-60 to A-62, **A-61** to **A-63**
　ILP limitations in, 167–169
　instruction set complications,
　　A-45 to A-47
　loop unrolling in, 76–79
　MIPS R4000 example, A-56 to
　　A-65, **A-58** to **A-65**
　out-of-order executions in, A-66
　　to A-67
　scoreboarding technique in, A-66
　　to A-75, **A-68, A-71** to **A-75**
　stopping and restarting execution
　　in, A-41 to A-43
MIPS R1000, 247
MIPS R2000/3000, A-56
MIPS R3000, I-12
MIPS R3010 chip, I-58 to I-60, **I-58,**
　I-59
MIPS R4000 pipeline, A-56 to A-65
　development of, K-19
　eight-stage structure of, A-56 to
　　A-58, **A-58, A-59,** A-60 to
　　A-62, **A-61**
　floating-point pipeline, A-60 to
　　A-62, **A-61, A-62, A-63**
　forwarding and branch delays in,
　　A-59 to A-60, **A-59, A-60**
　performance of, A-63 to A-65,
　　A-64, A-65
MIPS R8000, A-43
MIPS R10000, A-55
MIPS R12000, 128

mirroring, 362, **363,** K-61 to K-62
misalignment, address, B-7 to B-8,
　B-8
MISD (multiple instruction streams,
　single data stream), 197
misprediction rate
　in Alpha 21264, 89, 140
　from branch-prediction buffers,
　　82, **83,** 84
　for correlating predictors, 86, **87,**
　　88
　in Pentium 4, 133–134, **134**
　in static branch prediction, 81, **81**
　value prediction and, 130
miss latency, C-20
miss penalties
　block size and, C-26
　compiler-controlled prefetching,
　　305–309, **309**
　CPU time and, C-18
　critical word first and early restart,
　　299–300, **309**
　equation for, 168
　hardware prefetching and, 305,
　　306, 309
　memory stall cycles and, C-4 to
　　C-6
　multilevel caches and, 291, C-15
　　to C-16, C-29 to C-34, **C-32**
　nonblocking caches and,
　　296–298, **297, 309**
　in out-of-order processors, C-19
　　to C-21, **C-21**
　read misses and, 291, C-34 to
　　C-35
　in virtual memory, C-40, C-42
miss rates
　associativity and, 291, C-28 to
　　C-29, **C-29**
　average memory access time and,
　　C-15 to C-16
　block size and, 291, C-25 to C-28,
　　C-26, C-27
　cache size and, 291, C-28
　compiler optimizations and,
　　302–305, **304, 309**
　compiler-controlled prefetching,
　　305–309, **309**
　CPU time and, C-18
　defined, C-4
　hardware prefetching and, 305,
　　306, 309

in instruction *vs.* data caches,
　C-14, **C-15**
local *vs.* global, C-30 to C-31
main categories of, 290
measurement of, C-4 to C-5
in multilevel caches, C-30 to
　C-33, **C-32**
process-identifier tags and, C-36,
　C-37
misses per instruction, 290, C-5 to
　C-6, C-30 to C-31. *See also*
　miss rates
Mitchell, David, K-37
Mitsubishi M32R. *See* M32R
mixed caches, C-14
M/M/I queues, 386
M/M/m multiple-server model,
　388–389, **388**
MMX, B-31 to B-32, J-46
Modula-3, **I-12**
module availability, 26
module reliability, 26, 49
modulo scheduling, K-23
MOESI protocol, **213**
Moore's Law, 312
Mosaic, E-98
Motorola 680x0, **A-40, J-42,** K-53
Motorola 68882, I-33
MPI (Message Passing Interface), H-5
MPP (massively parallel processors),
　H-45
MSP (Multi-Streaming Processors),
　F-40 to F-41, **F-41,** F-43
MTBF (mean time between failures),
　26
MTTF (mean time to failure), 26–27,
　51, 362, 396–397
MTTR (mean time to repair), 26–27,
　362, 364–365
multibanked caches, 298–299, **299,**
　309
multicasting, E-24
multicomputers, defined, K-39
multicore processors
　Element Interconnect Bus, E-70
　　to E-72, **E-71**
　MINS compared with, E-92
　origin of name, 198
　performance on SPEC
　　benchmarks, 255–257, **255,**
　　256, 257

Multiflow processor, K-22 to K-23
multigrid methods, H-9 to H-10
multilevel caches, 291, **C-21,** C-29 to
    C-34, **C-32, C-39.** *See also*
    caches; L1 cache; L2 cache
multilevel exclusion, C-34
multilevel inclusion, 248–249, C-34,
    K-54
multilevel page tables, C-53, **C-54**
multimedia support, J-16 to J-19, **J-18,**
    J-46
multipath fading, **D-21**
multiple instruction streams, multiple
    data streams (MIMD)
    advantages of, 198
    Amdahl's Law and, 258–259
    centralized shared-memory
        architectures, 199–200, **200**
    clusters in, 198
    distributed-memory architectures,
        200–201, **201**
    historical perspectives on, K-36
    multicore, 198, 199
multiple instruction streams, single
    data stream (MISD), 197
multiple-issue processors,
    development of, K-20 to
    K-23. *See also* superscalar
    processors; VLIW processors
multiple-precision addition, I-13
multiplexers
    in floating-point pipelining, A-54
    in MIPS pipelining, **A-31,** A-33,
        A-35, **A-37**
    in set-associative caches, C-18
multiplication
    faster multiplication with many
        adders, I-50 to I-54, **I-50 to
        I-54**
    faster multiplication with single
        adders, I-47 to I-50, **I-48,
        I-49**
    floating-point, I-17 to I-21, **I-18,
        I-19, I-20**
    higher-radix, I-48 to I-49, **I-49**
    operands of zero, I-21
    precision of, I-21
    radix-2 integer, I-4 to I-7, **I-4, I-6**
    shifting over zeros technique, I-45
    with single adders, I-47 to I-50,
        I-48

speeding up, I-47 to I-50, **I-48,
    I-49**
system issues in, I-11
of two's complement numbers, I-8
multiply trees, I-52 to I-53, **I-53**
multiply-accumulate (MAC), D-5,
    D-8, J-18, **J-20**
multiply-step instruction, I-11 to I-12
multiprocessing. *See also* distributed
    shared-memory
    multiprocessors; large-scale
    multiprocessors; symmetric
    shared-memory
    multiprocessors
    advantages of, 196
    bus-based coherent, K-38 to K-40
    cache coherence protocols,
        205–208, **206,** 211–215, **213,
        214**
    centralized shared-memory
        architectures, 199–200, **200**
    challenges of, 202–204
    classes of, K-43
    data stream numbers in, K-38
    defined, K-39
    directory-based coherence in,
        234–237, **235, 236**
    distributed shared memory in,
        230–234, **232, 233**
    in embedded systems, D-3, D-14
        to D-15
    historical perspectives on, K-34 to
        K-45
    invalidate protocol
        implementation, 209–211
    large-scale, K-40 to K-44 (*See
        also* large-scale
        multiprocessors)
    limitations in, 216–217
    memory consistency models in,
        243–248
    message-passing, 202
    models for communication and
        memory architecture,
        201–202
    multilevel inclusion, 248–249
    multiprogramming and OS
        workload performance,
        227–230, **228, 229**
    nonuniform memory access in,
        202

optimizing software for, 261–262
reasons for rise of, 262–264
references on, K-44 to K-45
SMP performance, 218–227, **222
    to 226**
snooping protocols, 208–209,
    209, 216–218
SPEC benchmark performance,
    255–257, **255, 256, 257**
synchronization in, 237–242, **242**
T1 processor performance,
    249–254, **250 to 254**
taxonomy of, 197–201, **201**
in vector processors, F-43
multiprogrammed workloads,
    225–230, **227, 228, 229**
multiprogramming, C-47 to C-48
multistage interconnection networks,
    E-30, E-92
Multi-Streaming Processors (MSP),
    F-40 to F-41, **F-41,** F-43
multithreading, 172–179. *See also*
    thread-level parallelism
    coarse-grained, 173–174, **174,**
        K-26
    development of, K-26 to K-27
    in the directory controller, H-40
    fine-grained, 173–175, **174**
    overview, 172–173, 199
    parallel processing and, 253, **254**
    processor comparison for,
        179–181, **179, 180, 181**
    processor limitations in, 181–183
    simultaneous, 173–179, **174, 178**
    in Sun T1 processor, 250–252,
        251, 252
MVL (maximum vector length), F-17,
    F-17
MXP processor, D-14 to D-15
Myrinet switches, K-42
Myrinet-2000, **E-76**

N

NAK (negative acknowledgment),
    H-37, H-39 to H-41
name, defined, 70
name dependences, 70–71. *See also*
    antidependences; output
    dependences
NaN (Not a Number), I-14, I-16
NAS parallel benchmarks, F-51

NaT (Not a Thing), G-38, G-40
natural parallelism, 172, D-15
n-body algorithms, H-8 to H-9
n-cube, E-36
NEC SX/2, **F-7**, **F-34**, F-49
NEC SX/6, **F-7**, F-51
NEC SX/5, **F-7**, F-50
NEC SX/7, 338, **339**
NEC SX/8, **F-7**, F-51
NEC VR 4122, D-13, **D-13**
NEC VR 5432, D-13, **D-13**
negative acknowledgment (NAK), H-37, H-39 to H-41
negative numbers, I-12, **I-12**, I-14
nest page tables, 340
NetApp FAS6000 filer, 397–398
Netburst design, 131, 137
Network Appliance, 365, 391, 397–398
network attached storage (NAS) devices, 391
network bandwidth
    congestion management and, E-65
    performance and, E-18, E-26 to E-27, E-52 to E-55, E-89, **E-90**
    switching and, E-50 to E-52
    topologies and, E-40 to E-41
network file service (NFS), 376, **376**
Network File System (NFS), 391
network interface, E-6, E-62, E-67, E-76, E-90
network interface cards (NIC), 322, **322**, E-87, **E-88**
Network of Workstations, K-42
network reconfiguration, E-66
network-on-chip, E-3
networks. *See also* interconnection networks
    centralized switched, E-30 to E-34, **E-31**, **E-33**, E-48
    dedicated link, E-5, E-6, **E-6**
    direct, E-34, **E-37**, E-48, E-67, E-92
    distributed switched, E-34 to E-39, **E-36**, **E-37**, **E-40**, E-46
    dynamic reconfiguration, E-67
    indirect, E-31, E-48, E-67
    local area, E-4, **E-4**, E-77 to E-79, **E-78**, E-99 to E-100
    lossless, E-11, E-59, E-65, E-68

lossy, E-11, E-65
mesh, E-36, **E-40**, E-46, **E-46**
multistage interconnection, E-30, E-92
on-chip, E-3, **E-4**, E-70, **E-73**, E-103 to E-104
performance and cost of, **E-40**
shared link, E-5
shared-media, E-21 to E-24, **E-22**, E-78
storage areas, E-3, E-102 to E-103
switched point-to-point, E-5
system areas, E-3, E-72 to E-77, **E-75 to E-77**, E-100 to E-102
wide area, E-4, **E-4**, **E-75**, E-79, E-97
wireless, D-21 to D-22, **D-21**
NEWS communication, E-41 to E-42
Newton's iteration, I-27 to I-29, **I-28**
NFS (Network File System), 32
NFS (network file service), 376, **376**
Ngai, T.-F., I-65
Niagara, K-26
NIC (network interface cards), 322, **322**, E-87, **E-88**
Nicely, Thomas, I-64
Nintendo-64, F-47
nodes
    home, 232, **233**
    in IBM Blue Gene/L, H-42 to H-44, **H-43**, **H-44**
    interconnected, **E-27**
    local, 232, **233**
    remote, 233, **233**
    X1, F-42, **F-42**
nonaffine array indexes, G-6
nonaligned data transfers, J-24 to J-26, **J-26**
nonatomic operations, 214
nonbinding prefetches, 306
nonblocking caches, 296–298, **297**, **309**, K-54
non-blocking networks, E-32, E-35, E-41, E-56
nonfaulting prefetches, 306
non-minimal paths, E-45
nonrestoring division algorithm, I-5 to I-7, **I-6**, I-45 to I-47, **I-46**
nonuniform memory access (NUMA) multiprocessors, 202. *See also* distributed

shared-memory (DSM) multiprocessors
nonunit strides, F-21 to F-22, F-46, F-48
normal distribution, 36
no-write allocate, C-11 to C-12
nullification, A-24 to A-25, J-33 to J-34
n-way set associative cache placement, 289, **C-7**, C-8

O
occupancy, message, H-3 to H-4
Ocean application
    characteristics of, H-9 to H-12, **H-11**
    on distributed-memory multiprocessors, H-28, **H-28 to H-32**, H-30
    on symmetric shared-memory multiprocessors, H-21 to H-26, **H-23 to H-26**
OCN (on-chip networks), E-3, **E-4**, E-70, **E-73**, E-103 to E-104
octrees, H-9
off-load engines, E-8, E-77, E-92
offset, in RISC architectures, A-4 to A-5
OLTP. *See* online transaction processing
Omega, E-30, **E-31**
on-chip multiprocessing, 198, 205. *See also* multicore processors
on-chip networks (OCN), E-3, **E-4**, E-70, **E-73**, E-103 to E-104
one's complement system, I-7
one-third-distance rule of thumb, 401–403, **403**
one-way conflict misses, C-25
online transaction processing (OLTP)
    benchmarks for, 374–375, **375**
    performance evaluation for, 46, **47, 48**
    in shared-memory multiprocessors, 220–224, **221, 222**
OOO (out-of-order) processors, miss penalty and, C-19 to C-21, **C-21**
opcode field
    encoding instruction sets, B-21 to B-24, **B-22**

opcode field (*continued*)
    in MIPS instruction, B-35, **B-35**
    operand type and, B-13
Open Systems Interconnect (OSI),
    E-81, **E-82**
OpenMP consortium, H-5
operands
    address specifiers for, B-21
    decimal, B-14
    in instruction encoding, **B-22**
    instruction set architecture
        classification and, B-3, **B-4,**
        B-5, **B-6**
    in Intel 80x86, J-59 to J-62, **J-59**
        to J-62
    in MIPS, 10
    shifting, J-36
    type and size of, B-13 to B-14,
        B-15
    in VAX, J-67 to J-68, **J-68**
operating systems
    asynchronous I/O and, 391
    disk accesses in, 400–401, **401**
    memory hierarchy performance
        and, C-56, **C-57**
    multiprogrammed workload
        performance, 225–230, **227,**
        228, 229
    page size changes and, C-56 to
        C-57
    Ultrix, **C-37**
    user access to, C-52
    in virtual machines, 318, 319, 320
operation faults, 367, **370**
operations, in instruction sets, B-14 to
    B-16, **B-15, B-16**
operator dependability, 369–371
Opteron processor. *See* AMD Opteron
    processor
order of instruction exceptions, A-38
    to A-41, **A-40, A-42**
organization, defined, 12
orthogonal architectures, B-30, J-83,
    K-11
OS. *See* operating systems
OSI (Open Systems Interconnect),
    E-81, **E-82**
Otellini, Paul, 195
out-of-order completion, 90–91, A-54,
    A-66

out-of-order execution, 90–91, A-66 to
    A-67, A-75 to A-76, C-3. *See*
    also scoreboarding
out-of-order (OOO) processors, miss
    penalties and, C-19 to C-21,
    C-21
output dependences, 71, K-23
output-buffered switches, E-57, E-59
overflow, I-8, I-10 to I-12, **I-11**, I-20
overhead
    occupancy and, H-4
    packet switching and, E-51
    receiving, E-14, E-17, E-63, E-76,
        E-88, E-92
    routing algorithms and, E-48
    sending, E-14, E-16, E-63, E-76,
        E-92
overlapping triplets, I-49, **I-49**
overlays, C-39
owner of a cache block, 211, 231, **235**

P
Pacifica, 320, 339
packets
    in asynchronous transfer mode,
        E-79
    discarding, E-65
    in Element Interconnect Bus,
        E-71 to E-72
    headers, E-6, E-48, E-52, E-57 to
        E-58, E-60, E-72
    in IBM Blue Gene/L 3D Torus,
        E-72
    in InfiniBand, E-76
    latency, E-12, **E-13**
    size of, E-18, **E-19**
    switching, E-50, E-77
    trailers, E-6, **E-7**, E-61
    transport, E-8 to E-9, E-94
packing operations, B-14
Padua, D., F-51
page allocation, 262
page coloring, C-37
page faults, C-3, C-40
page offsets, 291, C-38, C-42
page remapping, in virtual machines,
    324
page sizes, C-45 to C-46, C-56 to C-57
page tables
    inverted, C-43

memory protection and, 316–317
    multilevel, C-53 to C-54, **C-54**
    nested, 340
    page sizes and, C-45, C-53
    paging of, C-44
    process protection and, C-48
    shadow, 320
    in virtual memory mapping, **C-43**
page table entries (PTEs)
    in AMD Opteron, 326–327, C-54
    in Intel Pentium, C-50
    in virtual memory, C-43, **C-43**
paged segments, C-41, **C-42**
page-level protection, C-36
pages
    in 64-bit Opteron memory
        management, C-53 to C-55,
        C-54
    in virtual memory, C-30, C-41 to
        C-42, **C-41, C-42**
paired single operations, B-39, D-10 to
    D-11
PAL code, J-28
Panda, D. K., **E-77**
Paragon, K-40
parallel, defined, 68
parallel processing
    historical perspectives on, K-34 to
        K-36
    in large-scale multiprocessors,
        H-2
    performance with scientific
        applications, H-33 to H-34
parallelism. *See also* instruction-level
    parallelism; thread-level
    parallelism
    Amdahl's Law and, 258–259
    challenges of, 202–204
    data dependences and, 68–70
    data-level, 68, 197, 199
    at the detailed digital design level,
        38
    explicit, G-34 to G-37, **G-35,**
        G-36, G-37
    hardware *vs.* software approach
        to, 66
    historical perspectives on, K-24 to
        K-25, K-34 to K-36
    implicit, G-34
    at the individual processor level,
        37

multithreading and, 253, **254**
natural, 172, D-15
in scoreboarding, A-74
at the system level, 37
taxonomy of, 197–201, **200, 201**
in vector processing, F-29 to F-31,
    F-29, F-30
paravirtualization, 321–324
PA-RISC
    common MIPS extensions in, J-19
        to J-24, **J-21 to J-23**
    conditional branch options in,
        B-19
    extended precision in, I-33
    features added to, **J-44**
    instructions unique to, J-33 to
        J-36, **J-34**
    MIPS core subset in, J-6 to J-16,
        J-7, J-9 to J-13, J-17
PA-RISC 1.1, **J-4**
PA-RISC 2.0, J-5 to J-6, **J-5**
PA-RISC MAX2, J-16 to J-19, **J-18**
partial store order, 246
partitioned add operations, D-10
Pascal, integer division and remainder
    in, **I-12**
passes, optimizing, B-25, **B-25**
path loss, **D-21**
Patterson, D. A., K-12 to K-13
payload, E-6, E-61
PCI-Express (PCIe), E-29, E-63
PC-relative addressing, B-10, B-18
PC-relative control flow instructions,
    B-17
PDP-11
    address size in, C-56
    memory caches in, K-53
    memory hierarchy in, K-52
    Unibus, K-63
peak performance, 51, **52**
peer-to-peer architectures, D-22
peer-to-peer communication, E-81 to
    E-82
Pegasus, K-9
Pentium. *See* Intel Pentium; Intel
    Pentium 4; Intel Pentium 4
    Extreme
Pentium chip, division bug in, I-2, I-64
    to I-65
Pentium D, 198
Pentium III, 183
Pentium M, **20**

Pentium MMX, **D-11**
Perfect Club benchmarks, F-51
perfect-shuffle permutation, E-30
performance. *See also* benchmarks;
    cache performance; processor
    performance
Amdahl's Law and, 184
average memory access time and,
    C-17 to C-19
bandwidth and, E-16 to E-19,
    E-19, E-25 to E-29, **E-28,**
    E-89, **E-90**
of branch schemes, A-25 to A-26,
    A-26
cache misses and, C-17 to C-19
cache size and, H-22, H-24, **H-24,**
    H-27, **H-28**
of commercial workload,
    220–230, **221 to 229**
of compilers, B-27, **B-29**
contention and, E-25, E-53
of desktop computers, 44–46, **45,**
    46
development of measures of, K-6
    to K-7
of DRAM, 312–315, **313, 314**
effective bandwidth and, E-16 to
    E-19, **E-19,** E-25 to E-29,
    E-28, E-89, **E-90**
Ethernet, E-89, **E-90**
of floating-point operations, **3**
flow control and, E-17
I/O, 371–379, **372 to 376, 378**
of multicore processors, 255–257,
    255, 256, 257
of multiprocessors, 218–230,
    249–257
of online transaction processing,
    46, **47, 48**
peak, 51, **52**
pipeline stalls and, A-11 to A-13
real-time, 7, D-3
of scientific applications, H-21 to
    H-26, **H-23 to H-26**
of servers, 46–48, **47, 48**
simultaneous multithreading and,
    177–179, **178**
of superscalar processors, **16,**
    179–181, **179, 180, 181**
topology and, E-40 to E-44, **E-44,**
    E-52
transistors and, 17–19

of vector processors, F-34 to F-38,
    F-35, F-40, F-44 to F-45,
    F-45
virtual channels and, E-93
in VMIPS, F-36 to F-38
periodic functions, I-32
permanent failures, E-66
permanent faults, 367
PetaBox GB2000, 393, **394**
phase-ordering problem, B-26
phases (passes), optimizing, B-25,
    B-25
phits, E-60, E-62, E-71
physical caches, defined, C-36
physical channels, E-47
physical memory, in virtual machines,
    320
physical volumes, 390–391
pi (p) computation, I-32
PID (process-identifier tags), C-36,
    C-37
piggyback acknowledgment field,
    E-84
Pinkston, T. M., E-104
pin-out constraint, E-39, E-71, E-89
pipe stages, A-3, A-7
pipeline bubbles, A-13, A-20. *See also*
    pipeline stalls
pipeline depths, F-12 to F-13
pipeline hazards, A-11 to A-26. *See*
    also dependences
    control hazards, A-11, A-21 to
        A-26, **A-21 to A-26**
    data hazards, A-11, A-15 to A-21,
        A-16 to A-21
    detection of, A-33 to A-35, **A-34**
    in floating-point pipelining, A-49
        to A-54, **A-51, A-57, A-58,**
        A-61 to A-65, **A-61 to A-63**
    load interlocks, A-33 to A-35,
        A-34
    in longer latency pipelines, A-49
        to A-54, **A-50, A-51**
    multicycle operations and, A-46 to
        A-47
    performance of pipelines with
        stalls, A-11 to A-13
    structural hazards, A-11, A-13 to
        A-15, A-64, **A-65**
pipeline latches, A-30, **A-36**
pipeline registers, A-8 to A-10, **A-9,**
    A-30, A-35

pipeline reservation tables, K-19
pipeline scheduling, loop unrolling
     and, 75–80, **75,** 117–118
pipeline stalls
     bubbles, A-13, A-20
     data hazards requiring stalls, A-19
          to A-20, **A-20, A-21**
     diagrams of, A-13, **A-15**
     in floating-point pipelines, A-51,
          A-51
     minimizing by forwarding, A-17
          to A-18, **A-18,** A-35, **A-36,**
          A-37
     in MIPS pipelines, A-33 to A-35,
          A-34
     in MIPS R4000 pipeline, A-63 to
          A-65, **A-63, A-64**
     performance and, A-11 to A-13
     in SMPs, **222**
     in vector processors, F-9 to F-10
pipelined cache access, 296, **309**
pipelined circuit switching, E-50, E-71
pipelines, self-draining, K-21
pipelining, A-2 to A-77
     in addition, I-25
     basic MIPS, A-30 to A-33, **A-31,**
          A-32
     condition codes in, A-5, A-46
     data dependences and, 69–70
     depth of, A-12
     dynamic scheduling in, A-66 to
          A-75, **A-68, A-71, A-73 to**
          A-75
     in embedded systems, D-7 to
          D-10, **D-7**
     encoding instruction sets and,
          B-21 to B-22
     exceptions in, A-38 to A-41, **A-40,**
          A-42
     five-stage pipeline for RISC
          processors, A-6 to A-10, **A-7,**
          A-8, A-9, A-21
     floating-point, A-47 to A-56, **A-48**
          to **A-51, A-57, A-58,** A-60 to
          A-62, **A-61 to A-63**
     freezing/flushing, A-22
     historical perspectives on, K-10,
          K-18 to K-27
     increasing instruction fetch
          bandwidth in, 121–127, **122,**
          124, 126

in interconnection networks,
     E-12, E-25, E-51 to E-52,
     E-60, E-65, E-70
interlocks, A-20, A-33 to A-35,
     A-34, A-52, F-9 to F-10
in Itanium 2 processor, G-42
link, E-16, E-92
microinstruction execution, A-46
     to A-47
MIPS branches in, A-35 to A-37,
     A-38, A-39
multicycle operations and, A-46 to
     A-47
in multiplication, I-51
overview of, 37, A-2 to A-3
in Pentium 4, 131–132, **132, 133**
performing issues in, A-10 to
     A-11
SMP stalls in, **222**
software, D-10, G-12 to G-15,
     G-13, G-15
stopping and restarting execution,
     A-41 to A-43
superpipelining, A-57
in switch microarchitecture, E-60
     to E-61, **E-60**
in vector processors, F-31 to F-32,
     F-31
Pleszkun, A. R., A-55, K-22
pointers
     current frame, G-33 to G-34
     dependences and, G-9
     function, B-18
     urgent pointer field, E-84
     in VAX, J-71
points-to analysis, G-9 to G-10
point-to-point links, 390, E-24, E-29,
     E-79
poison bits, G-28, G-30 to G-32
Poisson distribution, 384–390, **388**
Poisson processes, 384
polycyclic scheduling, K-23
Popek, Gerald, 315
POPF, 338
position independence, B-17
postbytes, J-57, **J-57**
POWER, **J-44**
power
     in cell phones, D-22, D-24
     dynamic, 18–19
     EEMBC benchmarks for
          consumption of, D-13, **D-13**

in multiple-issue processors, 182
redundancy of supplies, 27–28
reliability of, 49
static, 19
transistor and wire scaling and,
     17–19
Power processors, 128
Power2 processor, 130, A-43
Power4 processor, **52**
Power5 processor. *See* IBM Power5
     processor
PowerEdge 1600SC, **323**
PowerEdge 2800, **47, 48, 49**
PowerEdge 2850, **47, 48, 49**
PowerPC
     addressing modes in, J-5 to J-6,
          J-5
     AltiVec in, F-47
     common extensions in, J-19 to
          J-24, **J-21 to J-23**
     conditional branch options in,
          B-19
     features added to, **J-44**
     instructions unique to, J-32 to
          J-33
     MIPS core subset in, J-6 to J-16,
          J-7, J-9 to J-13, J-17
     multimedia support in, J-16 to
          J-19, **J-18**
     performance per watt in, D-13,
          D-13
     reduced code size in, B-23
PowerPC 620, A-55
PowerPC AltiVec, B-31, **D-11**
precise exceptions, A-43, A-54 to A-56
Precision Workstation 380, **45**
predicated instructions, G-23 to G-27
     annulling instructions, G-26
     in ARM, J-36
     concept behind, G-23
     conditional moves in, G-23 to
          G-24
     exceptions in, G-25 to G-26
     in Intel IA-64, G-38, **G-39**
     limitations of, G-26 to G-27
     moving time-critical, G-24 to
          G-25
predication, D-10
predicted-not-taken scheme, A-22,
     A-22, A-25, A-26, **A-26**
predicted-taken scheme, A-23, **A-25,**
     A-26, **A-26**

prefetching
  in AMD Opteron, 330
  compiler-controlled, 305–309, **309**
  development of, K-54
  hardware, 305, **306, 309**
  instruction set architecture and, B-46
  integrated instruction fetch units and, 126
  in RISC desktop architectures, **J-21**
prefixes, in instructions, J-51, J-55
present bits, C-50
price-performance, in desktop computers, 5, **5**
prices *vs.* costs, 25–28
primitives, 239–240, H-18 to H-21, **H-21**
principle of locality, 38, 288, C-2
private data, 205
probability mass function, 384
procedure invocation options, B-19 to B-20
process switch, 316, C-48
processes
  defined, 199, 316, C-47 to C-48
  protection of, C-48 to C-49
process-identifier tags (PID), C-36, **C-37**
processor consistency, 245
processor cycle, A-3
processor performance, 28–44. *See also* benchmarks
  Amdahl's Law and, 39–42, 184
  average memory access time and, C-17 to C-19
  benchmarks in, 29–33, **31, 35**
  of desktop systems, 45–46, **45, 46**
  equation for, 41–44
  execution time in, 28–29
  focusing on the common case, 38
  parallelism and, 37–38
  peak performance, 51, **52**
  price and, 45–46, **45, 46**
  principle of locality in, 38
  real-time, D-3 to D-5
  summarizing benchmark results, 33–37, **35**
  using benchmarks to measure, 29–33, **31**

using parallelism to improve, 37–38
processor-dependent optimizations, B-26, **B-28**
processors. *See also* digital signal processors; multiprocessing; superscalar processors; vector processors; VLIW processors; *names of specific processors*
  array, K-36
  directory-based multiprocessors, H-29, **H-31**
  in embedded computers, 7–8
  importance of cost of, 49–50
  massively parallel, **H-45**
  microprocessors, **5**, 15, **16**, 17, 20, **20, 341**
  multicore, 255–257, **255, 256, 257**, E-70 to E-72, E-92
  out-of-order, C-19 to C-21, **C-21**
  performance growth since mid-1980s, 2–4, **3**
  Single-Streaming, F-40 to F-41, **F-41**, F-43
  VPU, D-17 to D-18
producer-server model, 371, **372**
profile-based predictors, 161, **162**
program counter (PC), B-17. *See also* PC-relative addressing
program order. *See also* out-of-order completion; out-of-order execution
  control dependences and, 72–74
  data hazards and, 71
  memory consistency and, 243–246
  in shared-memory multiprocessors, 206
propagation delay, E-10, E-13, E-14, E-25, E-40
protection. *See also* memory protection
  in 64-bit Opteron memory management, C-53 to C-55, **C-54, C-55**
  call gates, C-52
  capabilities in, C-48 to C-49
  in Intel Pentium, C-48 to C-52, **C-51**
  rings in, C-48

protocol families, E-81
protocol fields, E-84
protocol stacks, E-83, **E-83**
protocols, E-8, E-62, E-77, E-91, E-93. *See also names of specific protocols*
PS2. *See* Sony Playstation 2
PTE. *See* page table entries

Q
QR factorization method, H-8
QsNet, **E-76**
quad precision, I-33
queue, 380
queue depth, 360, **360**
queue discipline, 382
queuing locks, H-18 to H-20
queuing theory, 379–390
  examples of, 387
  overview, 379–382, **379, 381**
  Poisson distribution of random variables in, 382–390, **388**

R
races, 218, 245
radio waves, D-21 to D-22, **D-23**
RAID (redundant arrays of inexpensive disks). *See also* disk arrays
  availability benchmark, 377, **378**
  development of, K-61 to K-62
  levels of, 362–366, **363, 365**
  logical units in, 391
  reliability, 400
RAID-DP (row-diagonal parity), 365–366, **365**
RAMAC-350, K-59 to K-60, K-62 to K-63
RAMBUS, 336
random block replacement, C-9, **C-10**
random variables, distributions of, 382–390, **388**
RAS (row access strobe), 311–312, **313**
Rau, B. R., K-23
RAW (read after write) hazards
  in floating-point MIPS pipelines, **A-50**, A-51 to A-53, **A-51**
  hardware-based speculation and, 112, 113
  as ILP limitations, 71

RAW (read after write) hazards
  (*continued*)
  load interlocks and, A-33
  in scoreboarding, A-69 to A-70,
    A-72
  Tomasulo's approach and, 92
read miss
  directory protocols and, 231, **233**,
    234–237, **236**
  miss penalty reduction and, 291,
    C-34 to C-35, **C-39**
  in Opteron data cache, C-13 to
    C-14
  in snooping protocols, 212, **213**,
    214
real addressing mode, J-45, **J-50**
real memory, in virtual machines, 320
real-time constraints, D-2
real-time performance, 7, D-3
rearrangeably non-blocking networks,
  E-32
receiving overhead, E-14, E-17, E-63,
  E-76, E-92
reception bandwidth, E-18, E-26,
  E-41, E-55, E-63, E-89
RECN (regional explicit congestion
  notification), E-66
reconfiguration, E-45
recovery time, F-31, **F-31**
recurrences, G-5, G-11 to G-12
red-black Gauss-Seidel multigrid
  technique, H-9 to H-10
Reduced Instruction Set Computer
  architectures. *See* RISC
  (Reduced Instruction Set
  Computer) architectures
redundant arrays of inexpensive disks.
  See RAID
redundant quotient representation,
  I-47, I-54 to I-55, **I-55**
regional explicit congestion
  notification (RECN), E-66
register addressing mode, **B-9**
register fetch cycle, A-5 to A-6, A-26
  to A-27, **A-29**
register indirect addressing mode
  jumps, B-17 to B-18, **B-18**
  in MIPS data transfers, B-34
  overview of, **B-9**, B-11, **B-11**
register prefetch, 306
register pressure, 80

register renaming
  finite registers and, 162–164, **163**
  in ideal processor, 155, 157
  name dependences and, 71
  reorder buffers *vs.*, 127–128
  in Tomasulo's approach, 92–93,
    96–97
register rotation, G-34
register stack engine, G-34
register windows, J-29 to J-30
register-memory ISAs, 9, B-3, **B-4**,
  B-5, **B-6**
register-register architecture, B-3 to
  B-6, **B-4, B-6**
registers
  base, A-4
  branch, J-32 to J-33
  count, J-32 to J-33
  current frame pointer, G-33 to
    G-34
  finite, effect on ILP, 162–164, **163**
  floating-point, A-53, B-34, B-36
  general-purpose, B-34
  history and future files, A-55
  in IBM Power5, 162
  instruction encoding and, B-21
  in instruction set architectures, 9,
    9
  integer, B-34
  in Intel 80x86, J-47 to J-49, **J-48,**
    J-49
  in Intel IA-64, G-33 to G-34
  link, 240, J-32 to J-33
  loop unrolling and, 80
  in MIPS architecture, B-34
  in MIPS pipeline, A-30 to A-31,
    A-31
  number required, B-5
  pipeline, A-8 to A-10, **A-9**
  predicate, G-38, **G-39**
  in RISC architectures, A-4, A-6,
    A-7 to A-8, **A-8**
  in scoreboarding, **A-71**, A-72
  in software pipelining, G-14
  in Tomasulo's approach, 93, **99**
  in VAX procedure, J-72 to J-76,
    J-75, J-79
  vector-length, F-16 to F-18
  vector-mask, F-26
  in VMIPS, F-6, **F-7**
  VS, F-6

regularity, E-33, E-38
relative speedup, 258
relaxed consistency models, 245–246
release consistency, 246, K-44
reliability
  Amdahl's Law and, 49
  benchmarks of, 377–379, **378**
  defined, 366–367
  "five nines" claims of availability,
    399–400, **400**
  implementation location and, 400
  in interconnection networks, E-66
  module, 26
  operator, 369–371
relocation, C-39
remote memory access time, H-29
remote nodes, 233, **233**
renaming. *See* register renaming
renaming maps, 127–128
reorder buffers (ROB)
  development of, K-22
  in hardware-based speculation,
    106–114, **107, 110, 111, 113,**
    G-31 to G-32
  renaming *vs.*, 127–128
  in simultaneous multithreading,
    175
repeat (initiation) intervals, A-48 to
  A-49, **A-49, A-62**
repeaters, E-13
replication of shared data, 207–208
requested protection level, C-52
request-reply, E-45
reservation stations, 93, **94**, 95–97, **99,**
  101, 104
resource sparing, E-66, E-72
response time. *See also* execution
  time; latency
  defined, 15, 28, 372
  throughput *vs.*, 372–374, **373, 374**
restarting execution, A-41 to A-43
restoring division algorithm, I-5 to I-7,
  I-6
restricted alignment, B-7 to B-8, **B-8**
resuming events, A-41, A-42
return address predictors, 125, **126,**
  K-20
returns, procedure, B-17 to B-19, **B-17**
reverse path, in cell phone base
  stations, D-24
rings, C-48, E-35 to E-36, **E-36, E-40,**
  E-70

ripple-carry addition, I-2 to I-3, **I-3, I-42, I-44**
RISC (Reduced Instruction Set Computer) architectures, J-1 to J-90
 ALU instructions in, A-4
 classes of instructions in, A-4 to A-5
 digital signal processors in embedded, J-19
 five-stage pipeline for, A-6 to A-10, **A-7, A-8, A-9, A-21**
 historical perspectives on, 2, K-12 to K-15, **K-14**
 lineage of, **J-43**
 MIPS core extensions in, J-19 to J-24, **J-21 to J-24**
 MIPS core subsets in, J-6 to J-16, **J-7 to J-16**
 multimedia extensions in, J-16 to J-19, **J-18**
 overview of, A-4 to A-5, **J-42**
 pipelining efficiency in, A-65 to A-66
 reduced code size in, B-23 to B-24
 simple implementation without pipelining, A-5 to A-6
 unique instructions in, J-24 to J-42, **J-26, J-31, J-34**
 virtualization of, 320
RISC-I/RISC-II, K-12 to K-13
ROB. *See* reorder buffers
rotate with mask instructions, J-33
rounding
 double, I-34, I-37
 in floating-point addition, I-22
 in floating-point division, I-27, I-30
 in floating-point multiplication, I-17 to I-18, **I-18, I-19, I-20**
 floating-point remainders, I-31
 fused multiply-add, I-32 to I-33
 in IEEE floating-point standard, I-13 to I-14, **I-20**
 precision and, I-34
 underflow and, I-36
round-off errors, D-6, **D-6**
round-robin, E-49, E-50, E-71, E-74
routing
 adaptive, E-47, E-53 to E-54, **E-54**, E-73, E-93 to E-94

 algorithm for, E-45, E-52, E-57, E-67
 deterministic, E-46, E-53 to E-54, **E-54**, E-93
 packet header information, **E-7**, E-21
 in shared-media networks, E-22 to E-24, **E-22**
 switch microarchitecture and, **E-57**, E-60 to E-61, **E-61**
 in switched-media networks, E-24
routing algorithm, E-45, E-52, E-57, E-67
row access strobes (RAS), 311–312, **313**
row major order, 303
row-diagonal parity (RAID-DP), 365–366, **365**
Rowen, C., I-58
RP3, K-40
RS 6000, K-13

S

SAGE, K-63
Saltzer, J. H., E-94
SAN (system area networks), E-3, E-72 to E-77, **E-75 to E-77**, E-100 to E-102. *See also* interconnection networks
Santayana, George, K-1
Santoro, M. R., I-26
Sanyo VPC-SX500 digital camera, D-19, **D-20**
SAS (Serial Attach SCSI), 361, **361**
SATA disks, 361, **361**
saturating arithmetic, D-11, J-18 to J-19
scalability, 37, 260–261, K-40 to K-41
scaled addressing mode, **B-9, B-11,** J-67
scaled speedup, 258–259, H-33 to H-34
scaling, 17–19, 259, H-33 to H-34
Scarott, G., K-53
scatter-gather operations, F-27 to F-28, F-48
scheduling, historical perspectives on, K-23 to K-24
Schneck, P. B., F-48
scientific/technical computing, H-6 to H-12

 Barnes application, H-8 to H-9, **H-11**
 computation-to-communication ratio in, H-10 to H-12, **H-11**
 on distributed-memory multiprocessors, H-26 to H-32, **H-28 to H-32**
 FFT kernels, H-7, **H-11**, H-21 to H-29, **H-23 to H-26, H-28 to H-32**
 LU kernels, H-8, **H-11**, H-21 to H-26, **H-23 to H-26, H-28 to H-32**
 need for more computation in, 262
 Ocean application, H-9 to H-12, **H-11**
 parallel processor performance in, H-33 to H-34
 on symmetric shared-memory multiprocessors, H-21 to H-26, **H-23 to H-26**
scoreboarding, A-66 to A-75
 basic steps in, A-69 to A-70, A-72, **A-73, A-74**
 costs and benefits of, A-72 to A-75, **A-75**
 data structure in, A-70 to A-72, **A-71**
 development of, 91, K-19
 goal of, A-67
 in Intel Itanium 2, G-42, G-43
 structure of, A-67 to A-68, **A-68, A-71**
scratch pad memory (SPRAM), D-17, **D-18**
SCSI (small computer systems interface), 360–361, **361**, K-62 to K-63
SDRAM (synchronous DRAM), 313–314, 338, **338**
SDRWAVE, I-62
sector-track cylinder model, 360–361
security. *See* memory protection
seek distances and times, 401–403, **402, 403**
segments
 segment descriptors, C-50 to C-51, **C-51**
 in virtual memory, C-40 to C-42, **C-41, C-42,** C-49
self-draining pipelines, K-21

self-routing property, E-48
semantic clash, B-41
semantic gap, B-39, B-41, K-11
sending overhead, E-14, E-16, E-63, E-76, E-92
sense-reversing barriers, H-14 to H-15, **H-15**, H-21, **H-21**
sentinels, G-31, K-23
sequential consistency, 243–244, K-44
sequential interleaving, 299, **299**
serial advanced technology attachment (SATA), 361, **361**, E-103
Serial Attach SCSI (SAS), 361, **361**
serialization, 206–207, H-16, H-37
serpentine recording, K-59
serve-longest-queue, E-49
server benchmarks, 32–33
servers
    characteristics of, **D-4**
    defined, 380, **381**
    downtime costs, **6**
    instruction set principles in, B-2
    memory hierarchy in, **341**
    operand type and size in, B-13 to B-14
    performance and price-performance of, 46–48, **47, 48**
    price range of, **5**, 6–7
    requirements of, 6–7
    transaction-processing, 46–48, **47, 48**
    utilization, 381, 384–385, 387
Service Level Agreements (SLA), 25–26
Service Level Objectives (SLO), 25–26
service specification, 366
set-associative caches
    defined, 289
    miss rate and, C-28 to C-29, **C-29**
    n-way cache placement, 289, **C-7, C-8**
    parallelism in, 38
    structure of, C-7 to C-8, **C-7, C-8**
sets, defined, C-7
settle time, 402
SFS benchmark, 376
SGI Altix 3000, **339**
SGI Challenge, K-39
SGI Origin, H-28 to H-29, **H-31**, K-41
shadow fading, **D-21**

shadow page tables, 320
shadowing (mirroring), 362, **363**, K-61 to K-62
shared data, 205
shared link networks, E-5
shared memory. *See also* distributed shared-memory multiprocessors; symmetric shared-memory multiprocessors
    communication, H-4 to H-6
    defined, 202
    multiprocessor development, K-40
    synchronization, J-21
shared-media networks, E-21 to E-25, **E-22**, E-78
shared-memory communication, H-4 to H-6
shifting over zeros technique, I-45 to I-47, **I-46**
shortest path, E-45, E-53
sign magnitude system, I-7
signal processing, digital, D-5 to D-7, **D-6**
signals, in embedded systems, D-2
signal-to-noise ratio (SNR), D-21, **D-21**
signed numbers, I-7 to I-10, I-23, **I-24**, I-26
signed-digit trees, I-53 to I-54
sign-extended offsets, A-4 to A-5
significands, I-15
Silicon Graphics MIPS 1. *See* MIPS 1
Silicon Graphics MIPS 16. *See* MIPS 16
SIMD (single instruction stream, multiple data streams)
    compiler support for, B-31 to B-32
    defined, 197
    in desktop processors, D-11, **D-11**
    in embedded systems, D-10, **D-16**
    historical perspectives on, K-34 to K-36
    Streaming SIMD Extension, B-31
simultaneous multithreading (SMT), 173–179
    approaches to superscalar issue slots, 174–175, **174**
    design challenges in, 175–177
    development of, K-26 to K-27

potential performance advantages from, 177–179, **178**
    preferred-thread approach, 175–176
single extended precision, **I-16**, I-33
single instruction stream, multiple data streams (SIMD). *See* SIMD
single instruction stream, single data streams (SISD), 197, K-35
single-chip multiprocessing, 198. *See also* multicore processors
single-precision numbers
    IEEE standard on, **I-16**, I-33
    multiplication of, I-17
    representation of, I-15 to I-16
    rounding of, I-34
Single-Streaming Processors (SSP), F-40 to F-41, **F-41**, F-43
SISD (single instruction stream, single data streams), 197, K-35
Sketchpad, K-26
SLA (Service Level Agreements), 25–26
sliding window protocol, E-84
SLO (Service Level Objectives), 25–26
Slotnick, D. L., K-35
small computer systems interface (SCSI), 360–361, **361**, K-62 to K-63
Smalltalk, J-30
smart switches, E-85 to E-86, **E-86**
Smith, A. J., K-53 to K-54
Smith, Burton, K-26
Smith, J. E., A-55, K-22
SMP. *See* symmetric shared-memory multiprocessors
SMT. *See* simultaneous multithreading
snooping protocols, 208–218
    cache coherence implementation and, H-34
    development of, K-39 to K-40, **K-39**
    examples of, 211–215, **213, 214, 215, K-39**
    implementation of, 209–211, 217–218
    limitations of, 216–217, **216**
    overview, 208–209, **209**
SNR (signal-to-noise ratio), D-21, **D-21**

SoC (system-on-chip), D-3, D-19, **D-20,** E-23, E-64
soft real-time systems, 7, D-3
software
optimization, 261–262, 302–305, **304, 309**
pipelining, D-10, G-12 to G-15, **G-13, G-15**
speculation, control dependences and, 74
Solaris, 377–379, **378**
Sony Playstation 2 (PS2)
block diagram of, **D-16**
embedded microprocessors in, D-14
Emotion Engine in, D-15 to D-18, **D-16, D-18**
Graphics Synthesizer, **D-16,** D-17 to D-18
vector instructions in, F-47
source routing, E-48
SPARC
addressing modes in, J-5 to J-6, **J-5**
architecture overview, **J-4**
common extensions in, J-19 to J-24, **J-21 to J-23**
conditional branch options in, **B-19**
exceptions and, A-56
extended precision in, I-33
features added to, **J-44**
instructions unique to, J-29 to J-32, **J-31**
MIPS core subset in, J-6 to J-16, **J-7, J-9 to J-13, J-17**
multiply-step instruction in, I-12
register windows in, J-29 to J-30
SPARC VIS, **D-11,** J-16 to J-19, **J-18**
SPARCLE processor, K-26
sparse array accesses, G-6
sparse matrices, in vector mode, F-26 to F-29
spatial locality, 38, 288, C-2, C-25
SPEC (Standard Performance Evaluation Corporation)
evolution of, 29–32, **31,** K-7
Perfect Club and, F-51
reproducibility of, 33
SPEBWeb, 32, 249
SPEC CPU2000, 31, **35**
SPEC CPU2006, 30, **31**

SPEC89, 30
SPEC92, **157**
SPEC2000, 331–335, **332, 333, 334**
SPECfp, E-87
SPEChpc96, F-51
SPECint, E-87
SPECMail, 376
SPEC-optimized processors, E-85
SPECrate, 32
SPECRatio, 34–37, **35**
SPECSFS, 32, 376
Web site for, 30
special-purpose register computers, B-3
spectral methods, computing for, H-7
speculation. *See also* hardware-based speculation
compiler, G-28 to G-32
development of, K-22
dynamic scheduling in, 104
memory latency hiding by, 247–248
misspeculation rates in the Pentium 4, 134–136, **135**
multiple instructions and, 118–121, **120, 121**
optimizing amount of, 129
register renaming *vs.* reorder buffers, 127–128
software, 74
through multiple branches, 129
value prediction and, 130
speculative code scheduling, K-23
speculative execution, 325
speed of light, E-11
speedups
Amdahl's law and, 39–41, 202–203
in buffer organizations, E-58 to E-60
cost-effectiveness and, 259, **260**
execution time and, 257–258
linear, 259–260, **260**
as performance measure in parallel processors, H-33 to H-34
from pipelining, A-3, A-10 to A-13
relative *vs.* true, 258
scaled, 258–259, H-33 to H-34
from SMT, 177–178, **178**

superlinear, 258
switch microarchitecture and, E-62
spin locks
coherence in implementation of, 240–242, **242**
with exponential back-off, H-17 to H-18, **H-17**
spin waiting, 241, **242**
SPRAM (scratch pad memory), D-17, **D-18**
spread spectrum, D-25
square root computations, I-14, I-31, I-64, J-27
squared coefficient of variance, 383
SRAM (static RAM), 311, F-16
SRC-6 system, F-50
SRT division, I-45 to I-47, **I-46,** I-55 to I-58, **I-57**
SSE (Streaming SIMD Extension), B-31
SSE/SSE2, J-46
stack architecture
extended, J-45
high-level languages and, B-45
historical perspectives on, B-45, K-9 to K-10
in Intel 80x86, J-52
operands in, B-3 to B-5, **B-4**
stalls. *See also* dependences; pipeline stalls
bubbles, A-13, A-20, E-47, E-53
control, 74
data hazard, A-19 to A-20, **A-20, A-21,** A-59, **A-59**
forwarding and, A-17 to A-18, **A-18**
reservation stations and, 93, **94,** 95–97, **99, 101,** 104
write, C-11
standard deviation, 36
Stanford DASH multiprocessor, K-41
Stanford MIPS computer, K-12 to K-13, K-21
start-up time, in vector processors, F-11 to F-12, **F-13,** F-14, **F-20,** F-36
starvation, E-49
state transition diagrams, 234–236, **235, 236**
static branch prediction, 80–81, **81,** D-4

static scheduling, A-66
steady state, **379,** 380
sticky bits, I-18, **I-19**
Stop & Go flow control, E-10
storage area networks, E-3, E-102 to
        E-103
storage systems, 357–404. *See also*
        disk storage; I/O
    asynchronous I/0, 391
    block servers *vs.* filers, 390–391
    dependability benchmarks,
        377–379, **378**
    disk arrays, 362–366, **363, 365**
    disk storage improvements,
        358–361, **359, 360, 361**
    faults and failures in, 366–371,
        369, 370
    filers, 391, 397–398
    flash memory, 359–360
    Internet Archive, 392–397, **394**
    I/O performance, 371–379, **372 to
        376, 378**
    point-to-point links and switches
        in, 390, **390**
    queuing theory, 379–382, **379,
        381**
    sector-track cylinder model,
        360–361
    Tandem disks, 368–369, **370**
    Tertiary Disk project, 368, **369,**
        399, **399**
    throughput *vs.* response time,
        372–374, **373, 374**
    transaction-processing
        benchmarks, 374–375, **375**
StorageTek 9840, K-59
store buffers, 94–95, **94,** 97, **101,**
        102–104
store conditional instruction, 239–240
store-and-forward switching, E-50,
        E-79
streaming buffers, K-54
Streaming SIMD Extension (SSE),
        B-31
Strecker, W. D., C-56, J-65, J-81,
        K-11, K-12, K-14, K-52
Stretch (IBM 7030), K-18
stride, F-21 to F-23
strided addressing, B-31
strip mining, F-17 to F-18, **F-17,** F-39
striping, 362–364, **363**

strong typing, G-10
structural hazards, A-11, A-13 to A-15,
        A-70. *See also* pipeline
        hazards
subset property, 248
subtraction, I-22 to I-23, I-45
subword parallelism, J-17
Sun Java Workstation W1100z, 46–47,
        46
Sun Microsystems, fault detection in,
        51–52
Sun Microsystems SPARC. *See*
        SPARC
Sun Microsystems UNIX, C-36 to
        C-37
Sun Niagara processor, 300, **341**
Sun T1
    directories in, 208, 231
    multicore, 198, 205
    multithreading in, 250–252, **251**
    organization of, 249, **250, 251**
    overall performance of, 253–257,
        253 to 257
Sun Ultra 5, 35
Sun UltraSPARC, E-73
Super Advanced IC, **D-20**
superblocks, G-21 to G-23, **G-22**
supercomputers, 7
SuperH
    addressing modes in, J-5 to J-6,
        J-6
    architecture overview, **J-4**
    common extensions in, J-19 to
        J-24, **J-23, J-24**
    conditional branch options in,
        B-19
    instructions unique to, J-38 to
        J-39
    MIPS core subset in, J-6 to J-16,
        J-8, J-9, J-14 to J-17
    multiply-accumulate in, J-19,
        J-20
    reduced code size in, B-23 to
        B-24
superlinear speedup, 258
"superpages," C-57
superpipelining, A-57
superscalar (multiple-issue) processors
    characteristics of, **115**
    development of, **16,** K-21 to K-22,
        K-25 to K-26

    in embedded systems, D-8
    goals of, 114
    ideal, 155–156, **157**
    increasing instruction fetch
        bandwidth in, 121–127, **122,
        124, 126**
    issue slots in, 174–175, **174**
    limitations of, 181–183
    SMT performance comparison on,
        179–181, **179, 180, 181**
    speculation in, 118–121, **120, 121**
    types of, 114
    vectorization of, F-46 to F-47
supervisor process, 316
Sur, S., **E-77**
Sutherland, Ivan, K-26
SV1ex, **F-7**
Swartzlander, E., I-63
switch degree, E-38
switch microarchitecture, E-55, E-60
switch statements, register indirect
        jumps for, B-18
switched point-to-point networks, E-5
switched-media networks, E-21, E-24,
        E-25
switches
    context, 316
    input-buffered, E-57, E-59, E-62,
        E-73
    input-output-buffered, E-57,
        E-57, E-60, **E-61,** E-62
    microarchitecture, E-55 to E-58,
        E-56, E-57, E-62
    output-buffered, E-57, E-59
    pipelining, E-60 to E-61, **E-61**
    point-to-point, 390, **390**
    process, 316, C-48
    smart, E-85 to E-86, **E-86**
switching
    buffered wormhole, E-51
    circuit, E-50, E-64
    cut-through, E-50, E-60, E-74
    defined, E-22
    network performance and, E-52
    packet, E-50, E-77
    pipelined circuit, E-50, E-71
    in shared-media networks, E-23
    store-and-forward, E-50, E-79
    in switched-media networks, E-24
    technique of, E-50, E-52

virtual cut-through, E-51, E-73, E-92
wormhole, E-51, E-58, E-92
syllables, G-35
symmetric shared-memory multiprocessors (SMPs), 205–218
    architecture of, 200, **200**
    cache coherence protocols in, 205–208, **206**
    coherence in, 205–208
    commercial workload performance in, 220–224, **221 to 226**
    in large-scale multiprocessors, **H-45**
    limitations of, 216–217, **216**
    scientific application performance on, H-21 to H-26, **H-23 to H-26**
    shared *vs.* private data in, 205
    snooping protocol example, 211–215, **213, 214, 215**
    snooping protocol implementation in, 208–211, 217–218
symmetry, E-33, E-38
Synapse N + 1, K-39, **K-39**
synchronization, 237–242
    barrier, H-13 to H-16, **H-14, H-15, H-16**
    development of, K-40, K-44
    hardware primitives, 238–240, H-18 to H-21, **H-21**
    implementing locks using coherence, 240–242, **242**
    memory consistency and, 244–245
    performance challenges in large-scale multiprocessors, H-12 to H-16, **H-14, H-15, H-16**
    sense-reversing barriers, H-14 to H-15, **H-15**
    serialization in, H-16
    software implementations, H-17 to H-18, **H-17**
synchronous DRAM (SDRAM), 313–314, 338, **338**
synchronous events, A-40, A-41, **A-42**
synchronous I/O, 391
synonyms, 329, C-36
synthetic benchmarks, 29

system area networks (SAN), E-3, **E-4,** E-72 to E-77, **E-75 to E-77,** E-100 to E-102. *See also* interconnection networks
system calls, 316
system-on-chip (SoC), D-3, D-19, **D-20,** E-23, E-64

T

tag field, C-8, **C-8**
tags
    function of, 289, C-8
    in Opteron data cache, C-12 to C-13
    process-identifier, C-36, **C-37**
    in snooping protocols, 210–211
    in SPARC architecture, J-30, **J-31**
tail duplication, G-21
tailgating, F-39 to F-40
Takagi, N., I-65
Tandem disks, 368–369, **370**
Tanenbaum, A. S., K-11
TB-80 cluster, **394,** 396–397
TCP/IP, E-81, E-83, **E-84,** E-95
TDMA (time division multiple access), D-25
telephone company failures, 371
temporal locality, 38, 288, C-2
Tera processor, K-26
terminating events, A-41, **A-42**
Tertiary Disk project, 368, **369,** 399, **399**
test-and-set synchronization primitive, 239
TFLOPS multiprocessor, K-37 to K-38
Thinking Machines, K-35, K-61
Thinking Multiprocessor CM-5, K-40
Thornton, J. E., K-10
thread-level parallelism (TLP), 172–179. *See also* multiprocessing; multithreading
    defined, 172
    instruction-level parallelism *vs.*, 172
    in MIIMD computers, 197
    processor comparison for, 179–181, **179, 180, 181**
    processor limitations in, 181–183
    reasons for rise of, 262–264

simultaneous multithreading in, 173–179, **174, 178**
threads, 172, 199
three-hop miss, **H-31**
three-phased arbitration, E-49
throttling, E-10, E-53
throughput. *See also* bandwidth; effective bandwidth
    congestion management and, E-54, E-65
    defined, 15, 28, 372, E-13
    deterministic *vs.* adaptive routing and, E-53 to E-54, **E-54**
    I/O, 371
Thumb. *See* ARM Thumb
Thunder Tiger4, **E-20, E-44, E-56**
TI 320C6x, D-8 to D-10, **D-9, D-10**
TI 8847 chip, I-58, **I-58, I-59,** I-61
TI ASC, F-44, F-47
TI TMS320C55, D-6 to D-8, **D-6, D-7**
time division multiple access (TDMA), D-25
time of flight, E-13, E-25
time per instruction, in pipelining, A-3
time-constrained scaling, 259, H-33 to H-34
time-domain filtering, D-5
time-sharing, C-48
time-to-live field, E-84
TLB. *See* translation lookaside buffers
TLP. *See* thread-level parallelism
Tomasulo's approach to dynamic scheduling, 92–104
    advantages of, 98, 104
    algorithm details, 100–101, **101**
    basic processor structure in, 94, **94**
    dynamic scheduling using, 92–97
    hardware-based speculation in, 105–114
    instruction steps in, 95
    loop-based example, 102–104
    multiple issue and speculation example, 118–121, **120, 121**
    register renaming in, 127–128
    reorder buffer in, 106–114, **107, 110, 111, 113**
    reservation stations in, 93, **94,** 95–97, **99, 101,** 104
    software pipelining compared to, G-12

topology, E-29 to E-44
  in centralized switched networks, E-30 to E-34, **E-31, E-33**
  defined, E-21
  in distributed switched networks, E-34 to E-39, **E-36, E-37, E-40**
  network performance and, E-40 to E-44, **E-44**, E-52
torus
  in IBM Blue Gene/L, E-53 to E-55, **E-54**, E-63, E-72 to E-74
  overview of, E-36 to E-38
  performance and cost of, **E-40**
  total ordering in, E-47
total store ordering, 245
tournament predictors, 86–89, **160, 161, 162**, K-20
toy programs, 29
TP (transaction-processing) benchmarks, 32–33, 374–375, **375**
TPC (Transaction Processing Council), 32, 374–375, **375**
TPC-A, 32
TPC-App, 32
TPC-C, 32, 46–47
TPC-H, 32
TPC-W, 32
trace caches, 131, **132, 133**, 296, **309**
trace compaction, G-19
trace scheduling, G-19 to G-21, **G-20**
trace selection, G-19
traffic intensity, 381
Transaction Processing Council (TPC), 32, 374–375, **375**
transaction time, 372
transaction-processing benchmarks, 32–33, 374–375, **375**
transaction-processing servers, 46–48, **47, 48**
transactions, steps in, 372, **373**
transcendental functions, I-34, **J-54**
transfers, instructions as, B-16
transient failures, E-66
transient faults, 367, 378–379
transistors, performance scaling in, 17–19

translation buffers (TB). *See* translation lookaside buffers
translation lookaside buffers (TLB)
  in AMD Opteron, 326–327, **327, 328**, C-55, **C-55**
  cache hierarchy and, 291, **292**
  development of, K-52
  in MIPS 64, K-52
  misses and, C-45
  speculation and, 129
  virtual memory and, 317, 320, **323**, C-36, C-43 to C-45, **C-45**
Transmission Control Protocol, E-81
transmission speed, E-13
transmission time, E-13 to E-14
transport latency, E-14
trap handlers, I-34 to I-35, I-36, J-30
trap instructions, A-42
tree height reduction, G-11
tree-based barriers, H-18, **H-19**
trees
  binary tree multipliers, I-53 to I-54
  combining, H-18
  fat, **E-33**, E-34, E-36, E-38, **E-40**, E-48
  multiply, I-52 to I-53, **I-53**
  octrees, H-9
  signed-digit, I-53 to I-54
  tree height reduction, G-11
  tree-based barriers, H-18, **H-19**
  Wallace, I-53 to I-54, **I-53**, I-63
Trellis codes, D-7
trigonometric functions, I-31 to I-32
TRIPS Edge processor, E-63
Trojan horses, C-49, C-52
true sharing misses, 218–219, 222, **224, 225**
true speedup, 258
tunnel diode memory, K-53
Turing, Alan, K-4
Turn Model, E-47
two-level predictors, 85
two-phased arbitration, E-49
two's complement system, I-7 to I-10
two-way conflict misses, C-25
two-way set associative blocks, **C-7**, C-8

TX-2, K-26
type fields, E-84

U

Ultracomputer, K-40
Ultra-SPARC desktop computers, K-42
Ultrix operating system, **C-37, E-69**
UMA (uniform memory access), 200, **200, 216**, 217
unbiased exponents, I-15
uncertainty, code, D-4
underflow, I-15, I-36 to I-37, I-62
unicasting, E-24
Unicode, B-14, B-34
unified caches, C-14, **C-15**
uniform memory access (UMA), 200, **200, 216**, 217. *See also* symmetric shared-memory multiprocessors
unit stride addressing, B-31
UNIVAC I, K-5
unpacked numbers, I-16
unpacking operations, B-14
up*/down* routing, E-48, E-67
upgrade misses, H-35
upgrade requests, 219
urgent pointer fields, E-84
use bits, C-43 to C-44
user maskable events, A-41, **A-42**
user miss rates, 228, **228, 229**
user nonmaskable events, A-41, **A-42**
user productivity, transaction time and, 372–374, **373, 374**
user-level communication, E-8
user-requested events, A-40 to A-41, **A-42**

V

valid bits, C-8
value prediction, 130, 154–155, 170, K-25
variable-length encoding, 10, B-22 to B-23, **B-22**
variables, register types and, B-5
variance, 383
VAX, J-65 to J-83
  addressing modes in, J-67, J-70 to J-71

architecture summary, **J-42,** J-66
    to J-68, **J-66**
CALLS instruction in, B-41 to
    B-43
code size overemphasis in, B-45
condition codes in, J-71
conditional branch options in,
    B-19
data types in, **J-66**
encoding instructions in, J-68 to
    J-70, **J-69**
exceptions in, **A-40,** A-45 to A-46
frequency of instruction
    distribution, J-82, **J-82**
goals of, J-65 to J-66
high-level language architecture
    in, K-11
historical floating point formats
    in, I-63
memory addressing in, B-8, B-10
operand specifiers in, J-67 to J-68,
    J-68
operations, J-70 to J-72, **J-71,**
    J-73
pipelining microinstruction
    execution in, A-46
sort procedure in, J-76 to J-79,
    J-76, J-80
swap procedure in, J-72 to J-76,
    J-74, J-75, J-79
VAX 11/780, 2, **3,** K-6 to K-7, K-11
VAX 8600, A-76
VAX 8700
    architecture of, K-13 to K-14,
        K-14
    MIPS M2000 compared with,
        J-81, **J-82**
    pipelining cost-performance in,
        A-76
VAX 8800, A-46
vector architectures
    advantages of, B-31 to B-32, F-47
    compiler effectiveness in, F-32 to
        F-34, **F-33, F-34**
    in Cray X1, F-40 to F-41, **F-41**
    in embedded systems, D-10
vector instructions, 68
vector length
    average, F-37
    control, F-16 to F-21, **F-17, F-19,**
        F-35
    optimization, F-37

registers, F-16 to F-18
vector loops, execution time of, F-35.
    See also loop unrolling
vector processors, F-1 to F-51
    advantages of, F-2 to F-4
    basic architecture of, F-4 to F-6,
        F-5, F-7, F-8
    chaining in, F-23 to F-25, **F-24,**
        F-35
    characteristics of various, **F-7**
    conditionally executed statements
        in, F-25 to F-26
    Cray X1, F-40 to F-44, **F41, F-42**
    Earth Simulator, F-3 to F-4
    historical perspectives on, F-47 to
        F-51
    instructions in, **F-8**
    load-store units in, F-6, **F-7,** F-13
        to F-14
    memory systems in, F-14 to F-16,
        F-15, F-22 to F-23, F-45
    multiple lanes in, F-29 to F-31,
        F-29, F-30
    multi-streaming, F-43
    operation example, F-8 to F-10
    peak performance in, F-36, F-40
    performance measures in, F-34 to
        F-35, **F-35**
    pipelined instruction start-up in,
        F-31 to F-32, **F-31**
    scalar performance and, F-44 to
        F-45, **F-45**
    sparse matrices in, F-26 to F-29
    sustained performance in, F-37 to
        F-38
    vector execution time, F-10 to
        F-13, **F-13**
    vector stride in, F-21 to F-23
    vector-length control, F-16 to
        F-21, **F-17, F-19,** F-35
vector-mask control, F-25 to F-26,
    F-28
vector-mask registers, F-26
vector-register processors
    characteristics of various, **F-7**
    components of, F-4 to F-6, **F-5,**
        F-7, F-8
    defined, F-4
    vector-length control in, F-16 to
        F-21, **F-17, F-19**
VelociTI 320C6x processors, D-8 to
    D-10, **D-9, D-10**

versions, E-84
very long instruction word processors.
    See VLIW processors
victim blocks, 301, 330
victim buffers, 301, 330, C-14
victim caches, 301, K-54
virtual addresses, C-36, **C-54**
virtual caches, C-36 to C-38, **C-37**
virtual channels
    head-of-line blocking and, E-59,
        E-59
    in IBM Blue Gene/L ED Torus,
        E-73
    in InfiniBand, E-74
    performance and, E-93
    routing and, E-47, E-53 to E-55,
        E-54
    switching and, E-51, E-58, E-61,
        E-73
virtual cut-through switching, E-51,
    E-73, E-92
virtual functions, register indirect
    jumps for, B-18
Virtual Machine Control State
    (VMCS), 340
virtual machine monitors (VMMs)
    instruction set architectures and,
        319–320, 338–340, **340**
    Intel 80x86, 320, 321, 339, **340**
    overview of, 315, 318
    page tables in, 320–321
    requirements of, 318–319
    Xen VMM example, 321–324,
        322, 323
virtual machines (VM), 317–324
    defined, 317
    impact on virtual memory and
        I/O, 320–321
    instruction set architectures and,
        319–320
    overview of, 317–318
    Xen VMM example, 321–324,
        322, 323
virtual memory, C-38 to C-55
    in 64-bit Opteron, C-53 to C-55,
        C-54, C-55
    address translations in, C-40,
        C-44 to C-47, **C-45, C-47**
    block replacement in, C-43 to
        C-44
    caches compared with, C-40,
        C-41

virtual memory (*continued*)
   defined, C-3
   development of, K-53
   function of, C-39
   in IBM 370, J-84
   impact of virtual machines on,
      320–321
   in Intel Pentium, C-48, C-49 to
      C-52, **C-51**
   mapping to physical memory,
      C-39, **C-40**
   in memory hierarchy, C-40, **C-41,**
      C-42 to C-44, **C-43**
   miss penalties in, C-40, C-42
   in Opteron, C-53 to C-55, **C-54,**
      C-55
   page sizes in, C-45 to C-46
   paged *vs.* segmented, C-40 to
      C-42, **C-41, C-42**
   protection and, 315–317,
      324–325, C-39
   relocation in, C-39, **C-40**
   size of, C-40
   translation lookaside buffers and,
      317, 320, **323,** C-36, C-43 to
      C-45, **C-45**
virtual output queues (VOQ), E-60,
      E-66
virtually indexed, physically tagged
      optimization, 291–292, C-38,
      C-46
VLIW Multiflow compiler, **297**
VLIW processors, 114–118. *See also*
      Intel IA-64
   characteristics of, 114–115, **115**
   in embedded systems, D-8 to
      D-10, **D-9, D-10**
   EPIC approach in, G-33
   historical perspectives on, K-21
   overview of, 115–118, **117**
VLVCU (load vector count and
      update), F-18
VM. *See* virtual machines
VME racks, 393, **394**
VMIPS
   architecture of, F-4 to F-6, **F-5,**
      F-7, F-8
   memory pipelines on, F-38 to
      F-40
   multiple lanes in, F-29 to F-31,
      F-29, F-30
   operation example, F-8 to F-10

   peak performance in, F-36
   processor characteristics in, **F-7**
   sustained performance in, F-37 to
      F-38
   vector length control in, F-19 to
      F-20
   vector stride in, F-22
VMM. *See* virtual machine monitors
voltage, adjustable, 18
von Neumann, J., 287, I-62, K-2 to
      K-3
von Neumann computers, K-3
VPU processors, D-17 to D-18
VS registers, F-6
VT-x, 339–340

W
wafer yield, 23–24
wafers, costs of, 21–22, **23**
waiting line, 380. *See also* queuing
      theory
Wall, D. W., 154, 169–170, K-25
Wallace trees, I-53 to I-54, **I-53,** I-63
wall-clock time, 28
WAN (wide area networks), E-4, **E-4,**
      E-75, E-79, E-97 to E-99. *See*
      also interconnection
      networks
Wang, W.-H., K-54
WAR (write after read) hazards
   hardware-based speculation and,
      112
   as ILP limitations, 72, 169
   in pipelines, 90
   in scoreboarding, A-67, A-69 to
      A-70, A-72, **A-75**
   Tomasulo's approach and, 92, 98
wavelength division multiplexing
      (WDM), E-98
WAW (write after write) hazards
   in floating-point pipelines, A-50,
      A-52 to A-53
   hardware-based speculation and,
      112
   as ILP limitations, 71, 169
   in pipelines, 90
   in scoreboarding, A-67, A-69,
      A-75 to A-76
   Tomasulo's approach and, 92,
      98–99
way prediction, 295, **309**
Wayback Machine, 393

WB. *See* write-back cycles
WCET (worst case execution time),
      D-4
weak ordering, 246, K-44
Web server benchmarks, 32–33, 377
Web sites
   availability of, 400
   on multiple-issue processor
      development, K-21
   for OpenMP consortium, H-5
   for SPEC benchmarks, 30
   for Transaction Processing
      Council, 32
weighted arithmetic mean time, 383
Weitek 3364 chip, I-58, **I-58, I-60,**
      I-61
West, N., I-65
Whetstone synthetic program, K-6
Whirlwind project, K-4
wide area networks (WAN), E-4, **E-4,**
      E-75, E-79, E-97 to E-99. *See*
      also interconnection
      networks
Wilkes, Maurice, 310, B-1, K-3, K-52,
      K-53
Williams, T. E., I-52
Wilson, R. P., 170
Winchester disk design, K-60
window (instructions)
   effects of limited size of,
      158–159, **159,** 166–167, **166**
   defined, 158
   limitations on size of, 158
   in scoreboarding, A-74
   in TCP, **E-84**
windowing, E-65
wireless networks, D-21 to D-22, **D-21**
within *vs.* between instructions, A-41,
      A-42
Wolfe, M., F-51
word count field, **C-51,** C-52
word operands, B-13
working set effect, H-24
workloads, execution time of, 29
World Wide Web, 6, E-98
wormhole switching, E-51, E-58,
      E-88, E-92 to E-93
worst case execution time (WCET),
      D-4
write allocate, C-11 to C-12
write back, in virtual memory, C-44
write buffers

defined, C-11
function of, 289, 291
merging, 300–301, **301, 309**
read misses and, 291, C-34 to
    C-35
in snooping protocols, 210
write invalidate protocols
    in directory-based cache
        coherence protocols, **233,** 234
    example of, 212, **213, 214**
    implementation of, 209–211
    overview, 208–209, **209**
write merging, 300–301, **301, 309**
write miss
    directory protocols and, 231, **233,**
        234–237, **235, 236**
    in large-scale multiprocessors,
        H-35, H-39 to H-40
    sequential consistency and, 244
    in snooping protocols, 212–214,
        213, 214
    in spinning, 241, **242**
    write allocate *vs.* no-write
        allocate, C-11 to C-12
write result stage of pipeline, 96,
    100–101, **103,** 108, 112
write serialization, 206–207
write speed, C-9 to C-10
write stalls, C-11
write update (broadcast) protocol, 209,
    217
write-back caches
    advantages and disadvantages of,
        C-10 to C-12
    cache coherence and, H-36
    consistency in, 289
    defined, C-10
    directory protocols and, 235, **236,**
        237
    invalidate protocols and, 210,
        211–212, **213, 214**
    in Opteron microprocessor, C-14
    reducing cost of writes in, C-35
write-back cycles (WB)
    in floating-point pipelining, **A-51,**
        A-52
    in RISC instruction set, A-6
    in unpipelined MIPS
        implementation, A-28, **A-29**
writes, to disks, 364

write-through caches
    advantages and disadvantages of,
        C-11 to C-12
    defined, C-10
    invalidate protocols and, 210, 211,
        212
    I/O coherency and, 326
    write buffers and, C-35
Wu, Chuan-Lin, E-1

X
X1 nodes, F-42, **F-42**
Xen VMM, 321–324, **322, 323**
Xeon-MP, 198
XIE, **F-7**
XIMD architecture, K-27
Xon/Xoff flow control, E-10

Y
Yajima, S., I-65
Yamamoto, W., K-27
Yasuura, H., I-65
yields, 19–20, **20,** 22–24

Z
zero
    finding zero iteration, I-27 to I-29,
        I-28
    in floating-point multiplication,
        I-21
    shifting over, I-45 to I-47, **I-46**
    signed, I-62
zero-copy protocols, E-8, E-91
zero-load, E-14, E-25, E-52, E-53,
    E-92
zSeries, F-49
Zuse, Konrad, K-4

About the CD

The CD that accompanies this book includes:

- *Reference appendices.* These appendices—some guest authored by subject experts—cover a range of topics, including specific architectures, embedded systems, and application-specific processors.

- *Historical Perspectives and References.* Appendix K includes several sections exploring the key ideas presented in each of the chapters in this text. References for further reading are also provided.

- *Search engine.* A search engine is included, making it possible to search for content in both the printed text and the CD-based appendices.

Appendices on the CD

- **Appendix D:** Embedded Systems
- **Appendix E:** Interconnection Networks
- **Appendix F:** Vector Processors
- **Appendix G:** Hardware and Software for VLIW and EPIC
- **Appendix H:** Large-Scale Multiprocessors and Scientific Applications
- **Appendix I:** Computer Arithmetic
- **Appendix J:** Survey of Instruction Set Architectures
- **Appendix K:** Historical Perspectives and References

§

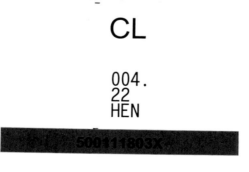